Content Area Reading and Writing

Content Area Reading and Writing

Fostering Literacies in Middle and High School Cultures

SECOND EDITION

NORMAN UNRAU

CALIFORNIA STATE UNIVERSITY, LOS ANGELES

PEARSON

Merrill
Prentice Hall

Upper Saddle River, New Jersey
Columbus, OH

Library of Congress Cataloging in Publication Data

Unrau, Norman.
  Content area reading and writing : fostering literacies in middle and high school cultures / Norman Unrau.—2nd ed.
   p. cm.
  Includes bibliographical references and index.
  ISBN-13: 978-0-13-229854-4
  ISBN-10: 0-13-229854-6
  1. Language arts (Secondary)—United States.   2. Language arts—Correlation with content subjects—United States.
  I. Title.
  LB1631.U57 2007
  428.0071'2—dc22
                                                    2007017550

Vice President and Executive Publisher: Jeffery W. Johnston
Senior Editor: Linda Ashe Bishop
Senior Development Editor: Hope Madden
Senior Production Editor: Mary M. Irvin
Senior Editorial Assistant: Laura Weaver
Design Coordinator: Diane C. Lorenzo
Cover Designer: Kellyn E. Donnelley
Cover Image: Jupiter Images
Production Manager: Pamela D. Bennett
Director of Marketing: David Gesell
Marketing Manager: Darcy Betts Prybella
Marketing Coordinator: Brian Mounts

This book was set in Galliard by Aptara, Inc. It was printed and bound by Edwards Brothers. The cover was printed by Phoenix Color Corp.

Photo Credits: p. 2: Getty Images—Photodisc; p. 32: Prentice Hall School Division; p. 62: Terry Fincher/Getty Images Inc.—Hulton Archive Photos; p. 98: Scott Cunningham/Merrill; p. 148: Norman Unrau; pp. 178, 210: Anthony Magnacca/Merrill; p. 242: GeoStock /Getty Images—Photodisc; p. 278: Anne Vega/Merrill; p. 320: Lynn Saville/Prentice Hall School Division; p. 358: Vicky Kasala/Getty Images, Inc.—Photodisc

Pearson Education Ltd.
Pearson Education Singapore Pte. Ltd.
Pearson Education Canada, Ltd.
Pearson Education—Japan

Pearson Education Australia Pty. Limited
Pearson Education North Asia Ltd.
Pearson Educación de Mexico, S.A. de C.V.
Pearson Education Malaysia Pte. Ltd.

10 9 8 7 6 5 4 3 2

ISBN 13:   978-0-13-229854-4
ISBN 10:   0-13-229854-6

Preface

Middle and secondary teachers' primary concern is whether their students can comprehend course content. But there is more to it than that. Can students comprehend the text itself? Are they motivated to learn? If they are reluctant to learn, what is the reason and how can it be addressed successfully? How are the students' cultures—whether peer group, ethnicity, family, or other culture—affecting their learning?

Knowing your students—what cultures affect them, how they construct meaning, and what affects their motivation—is the first step in teaching them. The next step is to determine students' needs for literacy development and to address those needs by helping students acquire literacy strategies that make text materials accessible and promote learning in content areas. When more teachers in our middle and high schools engage their students in learning with literacy's tools, more students will gain content knowledge and skills while acquiring strategies for lifelong learning.

Purposes for This Book

Understanding culture's effects. Helping teachers understand how cultures shape language, literacy, and learning is one main purpose of this book. Every community, whether family, ethnic group, school, or peer group has a culture. This culture, which shares traditions, rules, ethics, values, and a social order, shapes minds. When teachers understand how cultures merge and emerge in school settings, they can better understand how cultures contribute to students' literacy development.

Exploring student engagement and motivation. Disengaged, unmotivated students who rarely complete reading or any other homework assignments often puzzle and dismay beginning teachers in every content area. Thus, another purpose for this book is to help you understand what factors affect literacy engagement and what you can do to increase it.

Understanding the reading process. Reading is fundamental to every student's learning in the content areas, and helping teachers understand the reading process forms a fundamental purpose for this book. The model of reading presented in this text shows teachers how their students read, what contributes to good reading, and how reading for learning may falter. Knowing where reading may break down and how to detect those breakdowns enables teachers to see what steps they can take to improve reading and learning for all students.

Developing literacy strategies. To develop student reading, writing, and learning skills, content area teachers can apply research-based strategies. These strategies promote literacy and learning when teachers work with an entire class, provide opportunities for cooperative learning in small groups, or arrange for pairs of students to collaborate. Critical reading strategies explained in this book develop students' reasoning and thinking skills; writing strategies help teachers observe, evaluate, and promote their students' learning.

Fitting it all into subject-specific instruction. New teachers often wonder how they can possibly fit all they have learned about teaching, including strategies to enhance literacy, into their instructional day. Addressing state standards has contributed to many beginning teachers' bewilderment. This book is designed to help you plan for the alignment of standards and objectives with instruction and assessment practices.

Reorganization and Changes In the Second Edition

Many important changes have been made in the second edition of this book in response to newer research, several years of experience gained from teaching with the first edition, and a desire to make the book's content more accessible to readers. For example, the book's content has been completely reorganized into three major parts:

Part I: Knowing Your Students and Their Literacies
Part II: Enhancing Your Students' Literacies through Strategic Instruction
Part III: Designing Literacy Into Academically Diverse Content Area Classes

Part I: Knowing Your Students and Their Literacies.

Part I focuses on the information that will serve as your foundation for developing students' literacy skills to encourage content learning. Middle and secondary students bring years of background knowledge, personal culture, struggles and talents with them to the classroom. Part I seeks to guide you through understanding your students, preparing you to focus your instruction in the most effective ways.

Chapter 1, Engaging Cultures and Literacies for Learning, shows how cultures shape the minds of middle and high school students and explores the influence of culture on students' school, community, and personal literacies. It goes on to review research-based practices and resources for teachers to meet these challenges, especially in schools and classrooms with struggling readers and disengaged learners.

Chapter 2, Motivation to Read Content Area Texts, focuses on student engagement with reading and learning, examining the ways motivation affects engagement and providing you with suggestions for deepening student engagement in your classrooms.

Chapter 3, Inside the Meaning Construction Zone: Readers Reading looks inside a readers' meaning construction zone to gain a better understanding of how a student reads and negotiates meanings.

- This completely revised chapter reflects a renewed focus on the critical contributions that word recognition and fluency make to comprehension.
- The function of components in the model of reading have been more precisely described and further clarified. The instructional recommendations in subsequent chapters are rooted in that model of reading.

Chapter 4, Assessing Readers and Their Texts, provides a step-by-step approach to diagnostic teaching. Building on the model of reading presented in Chapter 3, this chapter introduces you to a range of formal and informal methods to assess your students' reading, especially their reading of your content area texts, and provides methods for evaluating texts used in your instructional program.

Special Features to Help You Know Your Students

- *Motivating Reluctant Readers* features provide classroom-tested guidance for encouraging uninterested and disengaged learners.
- *Diagnostic Windows* provide tips that will help you gather information on your students' abilities and needs.
- *Double Entry Journal* activities at the beginning and end of every chapter help you understand yourself as a learner, and model the kind of strategies you'll use to help your students grapple with texts.

Part II: Enhancing Your Students' Literacies through Strategic Instruction

In Part II you'll be given tools to build successful literacy. This is achieved through creative strategies and supportive scaffolding to motivate students and to develop their literacy skills while fostering their understanding and learning in all content areas. Here you will find a wide range of specific classroom strategies, applicable and useful across all content areas.

Chapter 5, Developing Vocabulary, Concepts, and Fluency for Content Area Literacy, focuses on vocabulary development and strategies you can use to help your students learn unfamiliar words and build fluency, which is essential to comprehend content area texts.

- Chapter 5 examines classroom-tested approaches to vocabulary instruction especially useful to struggling readers.

Chapter 6, Strategies to Enhance Comprehension, offers strategies to develop students' reading comprehension skills. Many of these strategies will also deepen your understanding of your students' reading processes so you can promote their growth.

Chapter 7, Writing to Assess, Promote, and Observe Learning, provides a model of the writing process and explores how you can use writing to evaluate and accelerate your students' learning.

Chapter 8, Critical Reading of Print and Nonprint Texts, presents procedures to enhance your students' critical reading of print as well as nonprint texts.

- The chapter's focus has been expanded to help teachers develop their students' critical reading of multiple media, including Internet and Web-based information, in a concerted effort to develop academic literacy.

Special Features to Help You Enhance Your Students' Literacies

- *Strategy in Practice* provides tools to take directly into the content area classroom.
- *Step by Step* features provide targeted guidance for implementing strategies to facilitate learning effectively.

Part III: Designing Literacy into Academically Diverse Content Area Classes. Part III presents perspectives and practices that will help you address the diverse learning and literacy needs your students bring to your classroom.

Chapter 9, Collaborating for Literacy and Learning: Group Strategies, provides methods to link whole-class, collaborative, and cooperative classroom learning activities with literacy growth.

Chapter 10, Struggling Readers and English Learners: Addressing Their Cognitive and Cultural Needs, addresses instructional programs and strategies for struggling readers and English learners, focusing on the best ways to address their cognitive and cultural needs across the curriculum.

- Chapter 10 presents a new research-based model of reading intervention, looking closely at essential features that assist struggling readers and promote literacy development.

Chapter 11, Designing Literacy into Academically Diverse Content Area Classes to Promote Understanding, shows you how literacy-enhancing strategies presented in earlier chapters can be integrated into lessons, units, and year-long planning for differentiated instruction.

- This completely revised chapter shows how standards-based instruction with integrated literacy strategies can be designed into science, math, history, English, and physical science classes.
- This chapter also provides a new method, a planning pyramid, to help teachers design effective standards-based lessons and units that integrate literacy instruction and promote inquiry.

Supplements

Instructor Resource Center.
The Instructor Resource Center at www.prenhall.com has a variety of print and media resources available in downloadable, digital format—all in one location. As a registered faculty member, you can access and download pass-code protected resource files, course management content, and other helpful online content directly to your computer.

Digital resources available for *Content Area Reading and Writing: Fostering Literacies in Middle and High School Cultures, 2e* include:

- A test bank including multiple choice and essay tests.
- PowerPoints specifically designed for each chapter.
- Teacher Prep correlation guide to help you make the best use of the Teacher Prep website in your classes.

To access these items online, go to *www.prenhall.com* and click on the Instructor Support button and then go to the Download Supplements section. Here you will be able to log in or complete a one-time registration for a user name and password. If you have any questions regarding this process or the materials available online, please contact your local Prentice Hall sales representative.

Acknowledgments

Many people have contributed to the emergence of the second edition of this book. First, I taught high school for 25 years and discovered enormous ranges in my students' capacities to read, write, think, and learn. Those discoveries have driven me to provide support and invent tools that would help students at all levels. Those high school students also deepened my appreciation for the meaning and pleasure of a vital classroom and for the tools of literacy in building vibrant classroom communities. Second, I've taught hundreds of credential candidates in a literacy and learning course at California State University, Los Angeles. Those candidates also taught me. From them I was repeatedly reminded of the magnitude of the challenge of addressing literacy while covering content and of how much new teachers need tools to meet that challenge. Third, I worked for four years as a university coach at Nightingale Middle School in the Los Angeles Unified School District. I focused my coaching on literacy. Classrooms of energetic, inquisitive students, too many of whom struggled to understand texts of any kind, focused my attention on their literacy development. Fourth, I served as editor of the *Journal of Adolescent and Adult Literacy* and saw how hundreds of teachers and researchers world-wide worked to help people young and old acquire literacy and a better life. Fifth, I had the good fortune of serving on a Single Subject Reading Task Force organized by California State University's Center for the Advancement of Reading and composed of professors and instructors who taught at state universities throughout California. Our work together clarified the importance of integrating reading and writing strategies into all content areas and the kind of instruction likely to result in the growth of both learning and literacy. Special thanks go to Nancy Brynelson, Denise Fleming, Dana Grisham, Nancy Farnan, Cindi Harris, Laura Young, and Marcy Merrill. From all these sources, I absorbed and guided energy into the creation on this book's second edition. To all these students, teachers, and colleagues my thanks.

I've also continued to have the good fortune of working with Dr. Robert Ruddell, now Professor Emeritus from the University of California, Berkeley. In co-editing with him *Theoretical Models and Processes of Reading* (5th edition), I was able to extend my knowledge of literacy research, deepen my understanding of literacy processes, and see more clearly how strategic instruction contributes to their improvement. In addition, my work with colleagues at California State University, Los Angeles who seek to improve teaching and learning for students in urban schools has provided ideas, resources, and encouragement. I'd especially like to thank Bob Land, Andrea Maxie, John Eichinger, Judy Washburn, Nancy Hunt, Ann Snow, Jonah Schlackman, and Carole Srole.

As for the publication of the second edition of this book, I want to extend my appreciation to Linda Bishop and Hope Madden at Merrill/Prentice Hall for helping in the reconfiguration of this second edition. Their suggestions and encouragement stimulated the book's further development. The thoughtful and constructive recommendations of reviewers also contributed deeply to my rethinking of both organization and content. For what they saw and envisioned, many thanks to Kathy Bussert-Webb, The University of Texas at Brownsville; Janet C. Richards, University of South Florida; Sheila M. Flihan, The College of Saint Rose; Cynthia R. Shanahan, University of Illinois at Chicago; Deanna Birdyshaw, University of Michigan; and Francis Sullivan, Temple University. Many others provided guidance and support during production, including Mary Irvin, Becky Savage, Maria Vonada, Linda Thompson, and Shelley Creager.

Finally, I want to dedicate this book once again to my wife Cherene and my daughter Amy. Cherene listened to months of progress reports on my writing and rewriting. If I am the ink, she is still the paper.

Brief Contents

Contents

Part II
ENHANCING YOUR STUDENTS' LITERACIES THROUGH STRATEGIC INSTRUCTION   147

5 Developing Vocabulary, Concepts, and Fluency for Content Area Literacy   148

Part III

DESIGNING LITERACY INTO ACADEMICALLY DIVERSE CONTENT AREA CLASSES 277

9 Collaborating for Literacy and Learning: Group Strategies 278

10 Struggling Readers and English Learners: Addressing Their Cognitive and Cultural Needs 320

Note: Every effort has been made to provide accurate and current Internet information in this book. However, the Internet and information posted on it are constantly changing, so it is inevitable that some of the Internet addresses listed in this textbook will change.

About the Author

Norman Unrau is a Professor Emeritus at California State University, Los Angeles, in the Division of Curriculum and Instruction. He continues to teach courses to beginning teachers that address literacy and learning in content classrooms and to serve as Coordinator of the MA in Education with a focus on middle and high school curriculum and instruction. He served as editor of the *Journal of Adolescent and Adult Literacy*, a publication of the International Reading Association for educators interested in the development of students' reading and writing. He also co-edited the fifth edition of *Theoretical Models and Processes of Reading*, a text widely used to help educators understand the scope and depth of research on reading. For several years he served as a university coach to develop literacy and learning in a large urban middle school in the Los Angeles Unified School District. He has also served as a member of the Single Subject Reading Task Force convened by the California State University through the Center for the Advancement of Reading to review and recommend improvements in content area literacy courses required of secondary credential candidates.

Dr. Unrau completed his master's degree at Columbia University's Teachers College. After teaching in Brooklyn and Vermont, he taught English and psychology in a San Francisco Bay area high school district. His teaching engagement in that district continued fruitfully for about 25 years, toward the end of which he began a doctoral program in education at the University of California, Berkeley. His work at Berkeley focused on cognition in reading and writing, an area that has long fascinated him. Dr. Unrau previously wrote *Thoughtful Teachers, Thoughtful Learners: A Guide to Helping Adolescents Think Critically* (1997). That book, also translated into Russian, has been used by teachers in countries formerly part of the Soviet Union. He has also published several articles on reading, writing, critical thinking, assessment, motivation, and models of literacy processes that have appeared in the *Journal of Adolescent and Adult Literacy, Journal of Educational Research, Teacher Education Quarterly*, and other professional journals.

Part I

KNOWING YOUR STUDENTS AND THEIR LITERACIES

Although knowledge of subject matter is at the heart of teaching, so is an abiding commitment to students and their learning. Each of the following four chapters is dedicated to a common quest: to know your students and their literacies. That quest informs and invigorates teaching in all content areas.

The first chapter, "Engaging Cultures and Literacies for Learning," explores the role of culture in shaping individual minds and literacies. It urges teachers to deepen their students' engagement in inquiry and learning with the resources of our cultures and literacies.

The second chapter, "Motivation to Read Content Area Texts," targets students' motivation for literacy, especially the factors that contribute to students' engagement with reading and learning and how teachers can deepen both. If we can deepen students' engagement in literacy and learning, we can strengthen the bridge we provide for them to master knowledge in our subject areas.

The third chapter, "Inside the Meaning Construction Zone: Readers Reading," provides a tour of our meaning construction zone when we read. Knowing more about the cognitive and social processes used when students read becomes a resource for understanding how we can improve students' reading to learn in our content areas. The model also serves as a paradigm for understanding cognition and learning in multiple literacies.

The fourth chapter, "Assessing Readers and Their Texts," focuses on assessment-based instruction. Diagnostic teaching increases the likelihood that we can know our students' literacy strengths and build upon them. The chapter demonstrates methods to discover our students' literacy skills and the strategies they use to read and learn from their texts. It also provides methods to evaluate the accessibility of the texts we use to teach students in our content areas.

Chapter 1

ENGAGING CULTURES AND LITERACIES FOR LEARNING

After reading chapter 1, you should be able to answer the following questions:

1. How do cultures shape minds?
2. What cultures affect middle and high school students?
3. What literacies influence students' thinking and behavior in and out of school?
4. Where is our adolescent literacy crisis rooted?
5. How can teachers respond to literacy and learning challenges in their content area classrooms?

Double-Entry Journal: Before Reading

Before beginning to read this chapter, I would like you to try a comprehension strategy. You can complete the first phase of a strategy called the Double-Entry Journal (DEJ) by writing about 200 words in response to the "Before Reading" prompt just below. After reading the chapter, I'll ask you to complete a second journal entry to complement your first entry.

To what cultures did you belong while in high school? For cultures, you could consider but not limit yourself to these: family, community, ethnic, school, classroom, teen, and any other subcultures. Looking back, which culture(s) seemed to influence you most? Why do you think that was the case? Create headings for each culture of which you were a part and list the kinds of influences it had on you and your behavior. Put a star next to those cultures that had the strongest effects. After creating this matrix of cultures and their effects, write about the effects those cultures had on your use of language both in school and out.

Beginning Teachers Remember Their High School Cultures and Literacies

To help beginning teachers connect with the power and complexity of cultures and literacies that shape our schools, communities, and selves, I ask teachers in my credential program course to reflect on their high school days and to write a brief memoir about those days. I ask them to describe the cultures to which they belonged and the literacies they practiced during high school. Through these memoirs I get to know my students, and they get in touch with aspects of their past that may influence their future as teachers. The range of responses varies dramatically. I've selected three of these very brief memoirs to give you an idea of how beginning middle or high school teachers remember the cultures and literacies that affected them. The first, Yvette Bess, was a head cheerleader while attending a public high school. The second, Eva Padilla, was bilingual as an adolescent and spoke Spanglish with her friends outside the classroom. The third, Cindy Thai, came to America from China as a young girl but was fluent in English when she began high school. As you have guessed, I selected them because they each had very different cultural and literacy experiences.

Looking Back (*by Yvette Bess*)

Looking back to my high school days seems almost like another life now, a life where finding out where the parties were going to be that weekend, who was dating who, and what I should wear tomorrow seemed to be my biggest dilemmas. Don't get me wrong. Academics were important, especially since I was head of the cheerleading squad and, if you did not maintain a certain GPA, you would be expelled from the squad. High school was a time in my life when I did not think for myself. My friends told me what to do, when to do it, and how. I was always trying to fit in with them. The problem was that I was not the real me. . . . I did my own homework, unlike my friends who would just ask others wishing to be popular to do their homework for them. They would tease me and call me "bookworm," but I took it as a compliment. . . . There was a lot of pressure to fit in and be popular. We reigned for almost two and a half years as the "in crowd," and I can say it was pretty cool!

All of my friends were Hispanic, but none of us knew how to speak Spanish. Most of our language context consisted of: "Like I totally hate him" or "Oh–My–God! Did you see what she is wearing?" The words "like" and "totally" were essential in every other sentence. Since all my friends were in regular education classes and I was in college prep classes, I was able to escape in the classroom and be someone different than I was on campus. I loved speech and debate class, chemistry, and literature. Teachers never seem to expect much from cheerleaders and jocks, so it was easy to just use my friend the thesaurus and a few deep thoughts to impress my teachers. I definitely was not challenged in high school nor did I ask to be. I did "A" and "B" work knowing that I could do better. . . . I look back at the few teachers who challenged me, and I really thank them now. I was a total bookworm in junior high, but during high school, I no longer had time to read for fun. I limited myself to the required reading and would skim through it at best.

High school was filled with good memories. I really enjoyed the social aspect. . . . It made me more outgoing and companionable. As for my academic endeavors, well, high school did not prepare me for college.

My High School Cultures and Literacies (*by Eva Padilla*)

Looking back, I have many great memories of my high school and of the people that were part of my life at that time. My friends in particular were the most influential in my decision making and in my self-development. I believed this was so because we were constantly together in and outside of the classroom. Most of us had the same honor or AP classes, and some of us participated in the same sports: Cross Country and Track and Field. Personally, sports played a huge role in my academic and personal life. For one, in order to be eligible for sports, I had to maintain a certain GPA or be dropped from the team. Second, sports gave me the opportunity to spend more time with friends and less time at home.

Overall, our group was considered "different" because as a group we did not fit into one category. Our group had members that were viewed or labeled by the school as smart, artistic, athletic, or social butterflies. Other noticeable differences were that we all dressed differently, and we all had friends outside our social group. Of course, we had many similarities, and one of them was our use of language.

The school literacy I practiced inside the classroom was English. And though English is considered my second language, I was fluent in it and Spanish by the time I arrived in high school. However, outside of the classroom my friends and I spoke in Spanglish (a mixture of English and Spanish). Here are some examples: "Sí, I heard you cuando kijiste that you were going to el cine." "No, pienso that el maestro saw you passing la nota to Jose." "Quient dijo that Manuel asked me a comer this Viernes?" We chose to speak this way mainly because we were fluent in both languages and felt trapped between the Mexican and American culture and cliques within the school. Also, we spoke this way to make it difficult for people to understand our conversations.

As for the community literacy that existed outside of Mountain View High School, the community was predominately influenced by the Mexican culture. It seemed everywhere I walked I could hear tunes of norteño music, I could smell homemade tortillas, or see pictures of the Virgen de Guadalupe on cars or T-shirts. These images gave me a sense of being "at home" and "belonging" to the city. Also, these sounds, smells, and visuals helped me to appreciate my Mexican culture.

In terms of personal literacy, I was aware of my ethnic/cultural background at a young age. My family was the kind of family that took great pride in our family history and encouraged us to be proud as well. However, in school my ethnic/cultural identity was hardly ever mentioned in schoolbooks. I recall only a few instances when my ethnic/cultural identity was addressed and described as "backwards" or "inferior." At times, I felt angry and confused by these mixed messages that I found in school and in my community. This might explain why my friends and I chose to speak Spanglish, why we chose to be our own persons, and why we chose to go to college.

Finally, I do think that my cultures and my literacies from high school have shaped my self-development. Today, . . . I have a great interest in learning about different cultures and languages . . . . As for my perspectives as an adult, I feel that my community and personal literacies have been the most profound in shaping my perspectives. For one, I perceive all communities (such as school, culture, sub-cultures, etc.) as valuable assets to each individual. Therefore, as a future educator it is my responsibility to incorporate different types of literacies in my classroom and to encourage respect for all types of communities in and outside of the classroom.

Moving Between Two Cultures (*by Cindy Thai*)

High school was an interesting four-year experience. . . . As first generation Americans in our family, my brother and I adapted fairly well in high school. My family and I immigrated to the United States from China. I was two years old then. I attended public school and assimilated into an American. However, our family dinners did not consist of discussions about current affairs in the newspaper or how my day was at school. My parents talked mostly about their business. Looking back now, I wish I were more involved with the events of the nation at the time. I was, however, very Americanized and thus made it through high school without experiencing any culture shock. I was an average student in high school. But, thinking back now, I feel I was an underachiever with regards to my grades. My parents did not have the time or the capabilities to assist me with my schoolwork. My mother stressed the importance of continuing on to college but did not demand it of me. My father wanted my brother and me to skip college altogether. My father never saw the importance of an education. He wished for us to learn his trade and take over the family business after high school. My family culture was most influential during my high school years.

The school literacy I practiced in high school was English. I was already fluent in English by the time I reached high school. My social skills were fairly good, and I had my share of friends. When I was in high school, computers were not as abundant as they are now. Therefore, my computer literacy was not very good. As for my community literacy, I spoke English at school as well as to my friends. However, I spoke both English and Cantonese when I was at home. I saw myself as an American during my high school years. The Chinese culture that my parents practiced was overwhelmed by the powers of our assimilation into this country. In hindsight, I have come to realize that it was somewhat of a struggle for me to accommodate both cultures.

My perspectives on life now are quite different than they were then. And besides the age factor, I do acknowledge that I was fighting the two different cultures that were thrust upon me. The cultures and literacies of my high school years are a big part of who I am today. I have grown and matured as a result of my experiences during high school.

Cindy's being caught between cultures demonstrates struggles that almost all American teenagers experience as they progress through middle and high school on their way to adulthood. Although her struggle may have been more intense because of the differences between her family's culture and that of her new country, teenagers are frequently pulled and pushed in different cultural directions as they struggle to define themselves, their values, and their purposes. Because cultures and languages are intimately related, Cindy's shifting from Chinese to English as her dominant language was significant in her assimilation and emerging identity. But in their memories of high school, both Yvette in her persona as cheerleader and Eva as an emerging educator display many of the cultural tensions that all students experience in our classrooms, school corridors, and communities. In this chapter, we explore further the nature of culture and especially its connections with literacy.

How Do Cultures Shape Minds?

Cultures thrive everywhere. In concentration camps and battlefields, in equatorial jungles and arctic villages, cultures sustain. Get a group of people together, and they're going to start a culture. We have mass culture, pop culture, youth culture, and culture wars. In his conception of culture, the renowned journalist Walter Lippmann (1913/1962) included "what people are interested in, . . . the books they read and the speeches they hear, their table-talk, gossip, controversies, . . . the quality of life they admire. All communities have a culture. It is the climate of their civilization." In schools and classrooms, the lives of teachers are inevitably immersed in cultures. But how well do we read and comprehend them?

What Is Culture?

When we enter a culture, primitive or complex, we face a system, a "vast apparatus," as noted anthropologist Bronislaw Malinowski (1944) called it, that is part material, part human, and part spiritual. That culture allows people to cope with the many problems they must face to survive in an environment that is sometimes friendly, sometimes dangerous.

We might also view culture as a system of symbols and meanings that a group of people share. Through these shared meanings, people communicate and convey their knowledge of life, as well as the attitudes they hold toward life (Geertz, 1973). People holding these shared meanings and symbol systems interpret life experience through their own subjectivity. They use their own cultural lens to understand their experiences. This notion of a cultural lens shaping experience is not trivial for teachers. Both our students' definition of themselves and how they make meaning from their experiences are shaped by culture. As teachers we, too, try to interpret and make sense of experiences through our own cultural subjectivity.

How Cultures Shape Minds

The influence of cultures on minds is by no means a new area of investigation. In the golden age of Greek civilization, Plato in his *Republic* expressed deep concern about how society shaped minds. But few people have paid as close attention to the ways in which culture becomes a part of each person's mind as did Lev Vygotsky, a Russian psychologist and author of *Mind in Society* (1978).

Vygotsky's ideas on culture.   Among Vygotsky's (1978, 1986) many ideas, three are of particular importance for understanding the connections between culture and the development of minds. First, Vygotsky embraced the idea that we must understand the historical and cultural contexts of each child's experiences to truly understand that person's intellectual or cognitive development. For example, through Yvette's memoirs we can begin to appreciate her mind's evolution by discovering the context of her life, the communities in which she grew up, and the schools she attended. She developed in a specific historical and cultural context that shaped her mind in unique ways.

Second, Vygotsky believed that our individual development depends on language that allows each of us to interact with others in our culture and to strive for self-mastery. Language and our writing system enable us to develop skills and higher mental functions. As children, Yvette, Eva, and Cindy all learned to speak English and applied their growing knowledge of language to the challenge of learning to read.

Third, Vygotsky believed that every step in a child's cultural development appeared twice: first, as a process between people, and second, as an individual process within each child. Interpersonal processes, such as our use of language to communicate with each other, are transformed into intrapersonal ones, such as our use of inner speech when we talk our way through to the solution of a complex problem. For example, I am explaining some of Vygotsky's key ideas to you (interpersonal process between you and me). You will internalize the language I've used and transform it into your own understanding of the ideas I've explained here. You could then carry on your own internal dialogue about Vygotsky's ideas, question them, look for evidence to confirm or challenge them, and perhaps even teach them to your students in language they would grasp. If you read about this two-stage concept of development but experience only the first stage and do not internalize it for your individual use, then it has not and cannot contribute to your development as a teacher.

What should be apparent to us is the great importance these notions of culture, language, and development have upon us as teachers attempting to understand the influence of culture. In sum, Vygotsky (1978, 1986) expressed the belief that we internalize our culture's sign systems. As we internalize these sign systems, such as our culture's language, they function as a bridge that enables us to transform our behavior and our mental life. We become, as Elinor Ochs and Bambi Schieffelin (1984) have pointed out, competent members of our society largely through language and its acquisition.

The zone of proximal development.   On our way toward competence, we interact with and learn from others. To understand how that learning progresses, we should explore another of Vygotsky's ideas, the zone of proximal development (ZPD), which emphasizes the importance of the interactive, socially based nature of learning. The ZPD is the difference between what one can achieve alone and what one can achieve with the help of a more knowledgeable or capable person. Interactions between more able and less able learners in the ZPD can enable less knowledgeable partners, to acquire information or skills to solve problems on their own that they could have solved before only with the help of their more able partners. As a result of educationally successful interactions between children and more able adults in the ZPD, children internalize culturally appropriate knowledge and behaviors that they can eventually demonstrate independent of their teachers. Cindy, who arrived in America from China, could not have learned English independently. She had to interact with those knowing more English than she knew.

In Vygotsky's words, "An essential feature of learning is that it creates the zone of proximal development" (1978, p. 90). If we, as teachers, are not within that zone, our students are not learning those things that will awaken them to further development. If we are below that zone, students are likely to be bored because we are trying to teach what they already know. If we are above that zone, students are apt to be so frustrated they can't learn. We, as teachers, must be in the ZPD for optimum learning to progress.

Besides helping us understand culture's influence on learning, Vygotsky's ideas have extensively influenced educators; this influence is reflected in many recommendations for literacy development throughout this textbook. Examples are everywhere, from effective student assessment practices to appropriate strategy instruction that enhances comprehension and understanding.

School Cultures Shaping Students' Minds

Although many cultural forces (a "dominant" American culture; a "pop" culture of film, television, and music; gender culture; and peer culture) shape our students' minds, school cultures are among the most powerful and problematic: powerful because of their effect on both students' knowledge base and their attitudes; problematic because they present students with many conflicts, including those between a growing personal identity and the pressures of conformity to a school's standards for conduct and learning.

School Cultures

Teachers create an organizational culture in their schools after responding to their school environment in similar patterns over many years (Gruenert, 2000). The culture creates expectations for teachers' behaviors and problem solving. While this culture doesn't affect student performance directly, it does so indirectly—somewhat as a parent's personality affects a child's achievement—by providing a context for learning and a foundation for growth.

As first-year teachers reflect on their schools' cultures, we can learn a great deal about what they and other beginning teachers may experience. During their first year of teaching, five teachers who graduated from Harvard's Graduate School of Education met, discussed, and wrote about their experiences (Van der Bogert, Donaldson, & Poon, 1999). They responded to two questions: (a) How have you affected your school? (b) How has your school affected you? The following section summarizes their perceptions of the school cultures they found and tried to affect.

Beginning Teachers Discovering School Cultures

Kelly Klinefelter-Lee taught at a middle school in Chelsea, Massachusetts, about a mile or two north of downtown Boston. The student population was diverse, with about a third of her students speaking English as a second language. Social issues of poverty surrounded her, but most difficult for her to digest was the school's response to its students. The school sought to standardize students with rules and test scores. Although she believed in the importance of rules, she perceived "a culture of unwritten rules" that forced teachers to demand obedience through control. Her conflict with the school's philosophy of control was aggravated because she advocated student-centered instruction, such as cooperative learning, discussion, and student-led projects. Accustomed to authoritarian rule in the classroom, her students could not behave appropriately and took advantage of her methods. Because her students didn't obey her commands, she felt that she had failed as a teacher and became isolated from her colleagues. In sum, the culture at the school exhausted her spirit.

Brian Poon taught at Brookline High School in a middle-class neighborhood a couple miles east of Boston. He approached his first year of teaching excited but scared. He strove to create classroom communities but found himself feeling that students took advantage of him at times. Although exhausted physically and mentally by November, he decided to bring change to the school community. His first target was the school cafeteria. Chunks of food and debris that littered the cafeteria after lunch, and failed efforts to get students to patrol their own mess disgusted him. He started a Change the Culture of the School Club to get students interested in improving their environment. His plans for change were dashed by too many no-shows at every meeting. He, too, succumbed to the culture of apathy at the school.

Following episodes of disrespect for teachers when they attempted to control the bullying of others at a basketball game or criticized inappropriate drinking on a bus bringing students to a prom, Brian retreated to territory he could control: his classroom. There, as he put it, "the abstractions of book learning were steeped in the reality of everyday life." His ideal of teaching was "diverse folk learning from one another and taking a vested interest in their vital role in a community," but he never expected anything to touch that ideal. However, his ideal was touched when he pulled together a mock trial team that competed effectively. He discovered that, although he couldn't change the big picture at the high school, he could carve out a piece and work with it. He modeled care where he could to change the institution.

While teaching at a suburban high school in Wayland, Massachusetts, Allyson Mizoguchi discovered that her students were obsessed with documented achievements that would pave the way to elite colleges. Grade-grubbing talk drowned out questioning and learning. What she witnessed in her students she had herself pursued while a student in a suburban high school. Voiceless in high school, she found that her first year of teaching was her opportunity to find her voice. Being the teacher gave her a perspective of education she had missed before, the determination to drop multiple-choice tests in favor of rubrics and portfolios, and the opportunity to discover that she didn't know how to teach her students to learn. While she was learning to learn, she was discovering how to teach her students to do the same. She found that questioning was at the center of learning. Driven from her comfort zone of right answers, she mustered the courage to move gradually into the zone of questioning. She began to take on a new self-image, that of advocate, debater, negotiator, and mediator, all labels she would have never used earlier to describe herself as a teacher. Still seeing her students shackled to SAT scores, GPAs, and multiple-choice exams, she strove to help them find a voice. Although she wondered if her emerging voice for change would ever be heard beyond her classroom walls, she found that teaching was about change from within and change driven through self-discovery. While finding her own voice, she hoped to reach silent students and give them speech.

These first-year teachers made major discoveries about the school cultures they entered and about the effects they could have on those cultures. All experienced some degree of isolation. However, reflecting on their teaching with other teachers and writing about their dilemmas enabled them—and us—to see more clearly their challenges and responses to them. For these beginning teachers, collaboration held out hope for change. Collaborative school cultures that enable effective student and teacher learning can be nurtured through the study of a school's culture, the creation of structures for collaboration, the collection of data to assess school progress, and incentives for teacher cooperation (Gruenert, 2000).

Links Between Cultures and Literacies

Our minds construct symbolic forms, such as the words you are reading on this page. We communicate with them, and we build and maintain our cultures through them. These symbols—words, music, language, and art—contain both meaning and feeling, but neither the meanings they express nor the feelings they transmit are always obvious (S. Langer, 1942). The meaning and feelings of Beethoven's *Fifth Symphony* are ours to interpret, as is a Picasso painting, a Martha Graham dance, or a novel by Henry James.

Every day we and our students read all kinds of texts, signs, and symbols. They include not only the words you are now reading but all the signs and symbols that our minds interpret and generate. Whether words on a page, images on a screen, music in the air, or gestures on a stage, symbolic expression is everywhere. One symbolic form, such as a movie or singer's CD, may lead to understanding of another symbolic form, such as a printed story in a student's anthology, an explanation of DNA replication, or a pattern in human history. As teachers, we can draw upon and apply these symbolic representations of our cultures and literacies to promote our students' understanding and growth.

What Is Literacy?

Words gain meanings through the ways we use them. When we ask ourselves what literacy means, we can turn to the ways we usually use the word. The primary meaning of literacy used to be *the ability to read*. Today the word literacy is used in other ways to mean other things. It may be time to move beyond the false dichotomy of a person being literate or illiterate in terms of reading and writing. Maybe it's time to think in terms of a student's "literacy profile," composed of many literacies used in a variety of social contexts, including our classrooms. Students may then be computer literate and technologically fluent and introduce their teachers to the language of an electronic medium to which the teachers were deaf. Or, moving to a different symbolic universe, a clarinetist fluent in the jazz idiom can enter and create music in a domain of music from which other, less fluent musicians would be locked out because they lacked musical literacy.

Acknowledging that literacy and culture are inseparable, Judith Langer (1987) suggested broadening our conception of literacy to include ways of thinking and doing in cultural contexts. Literacies, such as computer literacy or math literacy, are then seen as tool sets for getting things done in various cultures and contexts. When viewing literacy as a way of thinking, reasoning, and doing, math literacy becomes a special symbol system that enables a teacher and students to communicate in math classrooms, to address math problems, and to discover ways to solve them.

Teachers may not always be experts in all school-used literacies. For instance, with years of exposure to the culture of the Internet, some students may be far more computer literate than their teachers. By viewing literacies as culturally based ways of thinking and acting, we transcend the limitations of seeing literacy as just reading and writing. It opens our view of literacy to include how students think and function in their classrooms, schools, and communities where they live. Moreover, it opens our view of literacy to include who they are as individuals.

Three main literacies: School, community, and personal. Some of the literacies we have mentioned, such as reading and writing, play a larger role in middle and high schools than do others. Having thought through what counts as literacy in and out of school, Margaret Gallego and Sandra Hollingsworth (2000) created three categories of literacies:

- school literacies,
- community literacies, and
- personal literacies.

School Literacies. **School literacies** encompass not only cognitive processes, such as reading, but also social, cultural, and political processes. But standard English is the prime literacy, probably the most valued cultural capital in content classrooms (unless students are speaking French, German, or Spanish). Getting students to read, write, speak, and listen to standard, school-based English consumes an enormous amount of our time and energy as teachers. However, students also acquire content area literacies in math, science, and history. They often work toward mastering whole bodies of culture-based knowledge to gain, at least to some degree, what Hirsch (1987) referred to as cultural literacy. In some classrooms, students develop visual literacy through studying film, photographs, and paintings or diagrams, graphs, time lines, and maps (Moline, 1995). By building computer literacy, teachers help students become more conversant with Internet resources, our growing Web world, and Netspeak, the new language of blogs, chat rooms, and e-mail (Crystal, 2001). With teachers promoting critical literacy (Freire, 1993/1970), students develop a "critical consciousness," a form of awareness enabling them to examine the power structure operating within their community and how that structure influences their behavior. Critical literacy and its application in classrooms to enable students to gain a deeper understanding of how cultures define them are addressed in a later chapter on critical reading.

Community Literacies. **Community literacies** include out-of-school cultures and literacies, such as that of a student fluent in Russian who speaks the language with his newly immigrated family. Sometimes these out-of-school literacies are accommodated in school; sometimes they are not. Knowing how children learn to communicate in their culture helps us understand the potential for mismatches between students' communication styles and those in the classroom. Among the Warm Springs Native Americans living on their reservation in Oregon and carefully described in Philips' (1983) classic study, regulation of turn taking during conversations differed from the Anglo rules that governed talk in classrooms. Whereas Native American organization of interaction focused upon maximizing each individual's control over taking turns, Anglo interaction, which dominated school discourse, involved significantly greater control over turn-taking opportunities. Philips found three mechanisms contributing to the regulation of social interaction among the Native Americans:

1. Rather than focusing on a particular person during conversation in a group, speakers addressed the group in general.
2. A speaker's talk didn't always necessitate a response, certainly not an immediate one. Long pauses between turn taking were common.
3. Speakers were not interrupted. They stopped talking when they wanted.

Although we might think that a system of that kind could be exploited by a speaker who wouldn't stop talking, Philips observed that talk was usually equally distributed among participants who wished to take part in a conversation.

In school classrooms, however, a different set of guidelines prevailed because a teacher regulated turn taking and interaction. Getting or giving up the floor was under a teacher's control. Native American children were not accustomed to these conditions of social interaction. Furthermore, they were not accustomed to a single adult being in authority because, in their community, many people affected the socialization of children. Although Philips observed that Anglo children sought attention, Native American children did not compete for parental attention. These cultural factors within the Native American community contributed to Native American children withdrawing from classroom interaction, avoiding teacher-controlled responses, and failing to participate in show-and-tell opportunities. Teachers unaware of cultural differences between their own cultural styles and those of children from the Warm Springs Reservation might not see how culture contributes to conflicts or breakdowns in classroom communication.

Personal Literacies. **Personal literacies** involve students' critical awareness of themselves. This personal awareness arises from their examination of their backgrounds and histories in their schools and communities. From reading the brief memories that Yvette, Eva, and Cindy wrote, we gain significant insights into their personal literacies.

Personal literacies influence students' interpretations of texts. How much students know about their own inner lives or about the impact of their community on their thinking influences the ways they respond to and understand texts. The richness of that capacity is particularly apparent when a student with an acute awareness of her cultural identity, such as Eva, recognizes how that personal literacy may guide self-development, just as it guided her interest in learning about different cultures and languages in college.

Tension can arise between school literacies and personal literacies. Evidence of these conflicts appears in the development of girls as well as that of African Americans. Although researchers (Morse, 1998) have no compelling evidence that single-sex education enables girls to gain more school literacies than coeducation, single–sex programs for girls have made it easier for them to take risks in academic settings and to gain confidence, especially in relation to academic performance. Perhaps some girls' personal literacies are less likely to flourish in some coeducational schools. In addition, by embracing standard English, African Americans risk abandoning their community literacy and a dialect that enables them to connect with their culture (Fecho, 1999).

If, like Cottle (2001), you believe adolescents are growing up in a "culture of distraction" that diverts them from reflection on their personal and social selves, then you may find that personal literacies will not be much of a factor in your classroom. But perhaps your classroom could provide a haven from the "mind fields" of popular culture, allowing students the time and space to reflect on themselves as learners and individuals.

Reenvisioning literacies and their consequences.   Traditionally educators have viewed school literacies, such as the acquisition of standard English, as a pathway to social success in the world outside the school. However, the assumption that the literacy acquired in today's classroom will contribute substantially to success in tomorrow's world merits careful scrutiny (Carrington & Luke, 1997; New London Group, 1996).

As we have seen, students use multiple literacies, including those of school, community, and self, to construct visions of who they are, the worlds they inhabit, what they will be like in the future, and how they could be that person. Stories students tell themselves and others about who they are, their realities, their futures, and the paths to be taken to those futures are often composed in our schools' classrooms, corridors, and playing fields.

We have already looked at how school, community, and personal literacies can contribute to the development of identities. Some literacy educators envision "New Literacy Studies" for "New Times" (J. P. Gee, 1996, 2000; Street, 1995). In these studies, J. P. Gee sees students acquiring social languages that they use "to enact, recognize, and negotiate different socially situated identitites and to carry out different socially situated activities." These social languages become integrated with other nonlanguage information, like objects, settings, and tools, to create discourses. In these "new times," discourses and literacies are viewed as cultural capital that contribute to students' social success in contexts beyond the school and the classroom.

To discover more about school culture and literacies, you can engage in some descriptive anthropology (or ethnography) by arranging to shadow a student at school. The ethnographic procedure is explained in Figure 1.1.

Is There an Adolescent Literacy Crisis?

We would not find it difficult to build a pretty strong case for the existence of an adolescent literacy crisis. We could point out that, during the transition to middle and high school, students at risk become increasingly more likely to leave school, either psychologically or by actually dropping out. We could add that the numbers of students leaving school physically or through disengagement are most staggering in our urban centers, where learning and literacy in school are often valued less as children approach adulthood and their identities coalesce on the streets rather than in the classrooms. Teachers in inner-city schools all too often report that few of their students complete—or even start—homework assignments that involve reading and writing. This lack of connection to literacy and learning has contributed to problems not only in our schools but also in our communities and in the workplace. Lacking literacy skills, young people are more subject to unemployment, crime, and gang affiliations.

The fact is, though, that adolescent literacy, according to national test reports, is no more of a problem today than it was 35 years ago. The National Assessment of Educational Progress (NAEP) reading scores for 17- and 13-year-old students tell a story of little change over 35 years (Perie, Moran, & Lutkus, 2005). In 1971, the average reading proficiency of 17-year-old students was 285 (on a 500-point scale). Seventeen-year-olds achieved the same score, 285, in 2004. Meanwhile, the reading scores of 13-year-old students are significantly higher, even though the total point gain is small, moving from 255 in 1971 to 259 in 2004. (See Figure 1.2.) With these

Figure 1.1   Shadowing a Student: Engaging in Ethnography.

"ONLY THE SHADOW KNOWS"

Learning how students utilize and make sense of school is critical to every beginning teacher's understanding of students' engagement and the development of students' literacies. While new teachers sometimes assume that they know what "doing school" means because they did it, shadowing a student can lead to assumption-shedding discoveries that allow more accurate readings of students' lives and learning experiences in school classrooms.

The purpose of shadowing a student is to provide opportunities to witness schooling and school culture through students' eyes. As you glide through a student's schedule of classes like a silent shadow, you learn how a student responds to teachers, peers, and classroom instruction. Playing the shadow, you'll get to know the degree to which a student flows with teacher expectations and improvises on the themes of daily classroom and school life.

THE ASSIGNMENT

I have adapted the work of Bullough and Gitlin (1995) for this walking shadow assignment:

For this activity, you are to "shadow" a student for a full school day (or as much of the day as possible). You can arrange for shadowing by talking with your cooperating or master teacher or school site administrator. You should select a student whom you find intriguing and who comes from a background different from yours. It's important that you explain to the student what you are going to be doing and that you have the student's consent to shadow. Otherwise shadowing may look more like stalking. Like any ethnographer, take "field notes" based on your observations. Describe what you witness in as much detail as you can capture. Save interpretation for later, but note insights as they come to mind so they aren't lost.

You want to learn as much as possible about this student's way of life in classrooms and school cultures. These questions may guide your note taking and later analysis:

- How is the student's time structured? How does he/she fit into those structures? How does the student "wiggle" within the boundaries set for him/her?
- What engages the student during the day? When is he/she most "alive"? What topics or activities does he/she engage or avoid engaging?
- What are the characteristics that describe relationships with teachers and peers? What are sources of excitement, satisfaction, or irritation?
- How does the student's language and literacy skills influence, reflect, or enable participation in classrooms and groups?
- What roles do teachers play and how does your student respond to teachers?

In writing your shadow paper, describe summarily your observations class by class, analyze and interpret your observations (with particular attention to how your student experiences school and how teachers shape that experience), and finally reflect on the significance of what you've discovered about your role as an emerging teacher and observer of students' cultural lives.

small changes in scores, we would have a difficult time arguing that a crisis had arisen over the past 35 years.

However, we could argue that these average reading proficiency scores are not sufficient for a nation whose economy is as large as that of the United States and whose political influence is as extensive worldwide. Students scoring at the 250 level

Figure 1.2 Trends in Average Scale Scores for the Nation in Reading. *Significantly different from 2004.

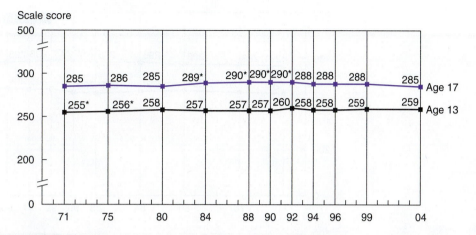

Source: M. Perie, R. Moran, & A. D. Lutkus. *NAEP 2004 Trends in Academic Progress: Three Decades of Student Performance in Reading and Mathematics* (NCES 2005–464). U.S. Department of Education, Institute of Education Sciences, National Center for Education Statistics. Washington, DC: Government Printing Office, 2005.

use intermediate skills and strategies to locate and organize information from relatively long passages. They can recognize a paraphrase of what they've read and make inferences as well as generalizations about the main ideas in passages related to social studies, science, or literature. However, NAEP data (Perie et al., 2005) show that only 6% of students at age 17 can learn from specialized reading materials, including historical documents, scientific texts, and literary essays. Students at this level can synthesize, extend, and restructure complex texts. At age 13 only 13% of students can understand complicated literary and informational passages, such as those encountered in content area classrooms. Thirteen-year-olds at this level can analyze and integrate less familiar texts and provide reactions to and explanations of those texts. If we believe that we must have far more than 1 out of 20 high school juniors or 1 out of 10 eighth-graders functioning at advanced literacy levels, then we could argue that these findings confirm a staggering adolescent literacy crisis.

Groups Struggling with School Literacy

It is important to keep in mind that reading proficiency among students in the United States is not evenly distributed. Segments of our student population struggle with reading and writing. A close look at reading data categorized by social, economic, racial, and ethnic groups or by parents' level of education shows quite clearly that some students are at a distinct disadvantage in terms of literacy.

Trends in average NAEP reading scale scores by race and ethnicity reveal just such a pattern (Perie et al., 2005). While the average reading scale score for whites age 17 in 2004 was 293, the average score for both black and Hispanic students age 17 was 264. These are dramatically significant differences. The good news is that the average for 17-year-old Hispanics has risen from 252 in 1975, whereas the average for African Americans has risen from 239 in 1971. A similar pattern of average reading scores for white, Hispanic, and African American students appears among 13-year-olds. In short, the gaps are shrinking but are still large. (See Figure 1.3.)

Figure 1.3 Trends in Average Reading Scale Scores by Race/Ethnicity. *Significantly different from 2004.

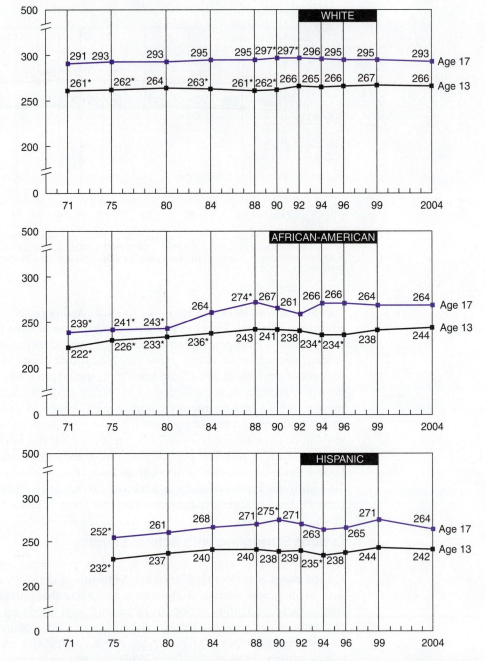

Source: M. Perie, R. Moran, & A. D. Lutkus. *NAEP 2004 Trends in Academic Progress: Three Decades of Student Performance in Reading and Mathematics* (NCES 2005–464). U.S. Department of Education, Institute of Education Sciences, National Center for Education Statistics. Washington, DC: Government Printing Office, 2005.

Although some improvement in reading has occurred over the past few years in some groups, our efforts to increase the literacy levels of all students have not met with uniform success. From this point of view, we could argue solidly that our country has pockets of adolescent literacy crises. Many of those pockets are in our large cities, where continuing disadvantages lead to students not being able to progress success-fully through middle and high school and on into the workforce or into college.

Is There a Crisis of Engagement With Learning at the Core of Middle and High School Cultures?

Perhaps the "literacy crisis" is a symptom of a more troubling trend in many of our schools. Some educators have observed and documented that many students engage less with learning in many communities as they progress from elementary to middle and on to high schools (Gottfried, Fleming, & Gottfried, 2001; Lepper, Corpus, & Iyengar, 2005; National Research Council, 2004; Otis, Grouzet, & Pelletier, 2005). In her study entitled *Literacies Lost,* Cyrene Wells (1996) describes what happened to students as they moved from a progressive middle school to a traditional high school. She makes four assumptions about schooling that will help us understand her discoveries.

- First, she believes that schools are "agents of cultural transmission," and that what is transmitted is a reflection of those having the power to run the school, in-cluding community members and school faculty. Students attending different schools will have different experiences because each school has its own unique culture.
- Second, she believes that culture is learned, that students acquire a set of customs from their cultural environment.
- Third, she feels, students, as they become enculturated, come to know what skills and knowledge are valued and how to gain both.
- Fourth, she thinks that students also acquire attitudes toward learning that per-sist as an aspect of their sense of self even as they move from one learning envi-ronment or school to another.

In summary, the entire school culture, with its structure, organization, values, and traditions, affects student learning.

In Meadowbrook, the progressive middle school that Wells studied, students val-ued caring teachers, multiple approaches to learning content, choice in activities, and a welcoming classroom. They also felt that community was integral to learning and that they learned from each other as well as from the teacher. Talking was part of enjoyable learning. Grades were only one form of evaluation; students sometimes evaluated their own work. Importantly for us, they saw reading and writing as integral to learning.

Disconnects Between Students, Their Teachers, and the Curriculum

Students found a different set of traditions, expectations, and beliefs about learning in high school. According to Wells (1996), order predominated, even in meetings of the school's faculty. Little time was given to articulating a shared vision, in part because teachers were not encouraged to voice their educational philosophy or encouraged to innovate. Control dominated creativity in classrooms and curricula. Grades and the punitive consequences of poor ones were more important than students understand-ing course content.

A short time after beginning their acculturation at the high school, students were disappointed that teachers showed much less care than their middle school teachers, with some of their new teachers not even making an effort to learn their names. With some assignments amounting to no more than filling in worksheets or writing seemingly senseless essays—to which teachers responded by commenting about grammar problems—these freshmen reoriented themselves. Some did what was demanded in order to get good grades. Some began to manifest behavior problems, such as showing up late for class, not completing worksheets, or talking back to teachers. Others, who felt the work meaningless, "psyched out the system" and did only what was essential to get by.

Source: CALVIN AND HOBBES © 1987 Watterson. Dist. By UNIVERSAL PRESS SYNDICATE. Reprinted with permission. All rights reserved.

As for literacy and its development, the position of writing and reading at the high school was quite different. At the middle school, writing had been integral to learning, but at the high school, instruction was driven by textbooks, with very few opportunities to write about what was studied. Memorization replaced understanding. Reading became a search for answers to worksheet questions or questions at the end of a textbook chapter. Showing mastery of vocabulary words on tests was paramount for good grades. Wells, pointing out how boredom oppressed students, cites one student, who said, "I have so much to learn, and I'm stuck here in this class." Few students felt any sense of connection with their teachers or sense of enthusiasm about learning. What sustained students was their social life and the pleasures of talking with friends.

Focusing on her theme of literacies lost, Wells noted that the middle school students at Meadowbrook wrote in many genres. They composed many types of fiction and nonfiction, including journals of many types, reflections, summaries, reports, self-evaluations, interpretations, and arguments. Teachers treated writing as a process over which students could confer as they composed. Students also did independent research using multiple methods of inquiry, from library searches to personal interviews. Students at Meadowbrook read a wide variety of texts, both fiction and nonfiction. They learned to read for different purposes (scanning versus reading for detail), and they were encouraged to demonstrate their understanding of the texts they read in many modes, from written and oral reports to debates, skits, and group discussions. Integrating—not segmenting—subject areas was encouraged.

In high school, students were frequently told to read text chapters and respond by preparing for quizzes, writing outlines, completing textbook publisher's worksheets, and answering questions at the end of chapters. Little was asked of students by way of inquiry, exploration, integration, or reflection. Unfortunately, students are not as interested without authentic, meaningful, or significant work. Although few former Meadowbrook students complained about learning with textbooks, they did complain about not doing more. Although the students adapted to the high school teachers' expectations, their range of literacy development became more routine and controlled.

Can We Generalize?

Wells (1996) looked carefully at one middle school and one high school. Each was unique—all schools are unique in terms of culture, leadership, community, and individual students and teachers. Can we use her specific findings about these two schools to say anything worthwhile about middle and high schools in general?

Although not many measures of engagement among high school students exist, the results of several studies echo findings that Wells (1996) reported. According to one researcher (Steinberg, 1996), about 40% of the students in schools he studied were "just going through the motions" of high school. These findings were based on student self-reports regarding their levels of effort in four main subject areas (English, math, social science, and science), time spent on homework, academic expectation levels, and class attendance. Well over a third of the students said that when they were in class, they were either not paying attention to instruction or not trying very hard. According to Steinberg, more than one out of three students were disengaged because they did not feel challenged or held accountable.

In another study of a well-regarded, academically competitive high school seen through the eyes of five students, Pope (2002) discovered that these students experienced rare moments of genuine engagement. Most of their time was spent working the system, "doing school," as one of them put it. They did their work because they had to—not out of interest or curiosity. For some, getting engaged with the work would only slow them down and possibly reduce their shot at a top-notch university and a high-paying job.

If Wells' study were among the few finding that school conditions limit engagement with learning and literacy growth, we could dismiss it more swiftly. However, several studies of high schools (Boyer, 1983; Goodlad, 1984; H. M. Marks, 2000; McNeil, 1988; Newmann, 1992; Sizer, 1992; Steinberg, 1996; Wagner, 1994) have drawn rather similar pictures. Levels of engagement with the content area curriculum or with the minds of teachers tend to be low, whereas levels of boredom and peer socializing tend to be high.

Researchers show time and time again that schools are demonstrating what Eisner (1988) terms *structured fragmentation*. The traditional middle and high schools typically break the day into six or seven periods, with a break for nutrition after two periods and a break for lunch after four periods. At the ringing of a computerized bell system, students move through the day from classroom to classroom, where teachers present lessons in English, math, social studies, science, and a range of other electives, which include art, music, and foreign languages. Connections between the subject areas are rare, and teachers do not usually discuss curriculum development or its integration with other teachers.

In most large middle and high schools, there are few opportunities for caring relationships to develop between teachers and students. Students move through their scheduled day, often spending about 50 minutes in a classroom with 25 to 30 other students. They are controlled by the teachers' need to get through a required curriculum so that students will be prepared for their next instructional level—a higher course in an academic subject or possibly college.

Perhaps Wells (1996, p. 174) is correct when she concludes that "the system is not set up for caring teachers" who might use a multitude of means, including those that integrate and promote literacy in the content areas, to develop relationships and rapport with their students. While this story of transition into the freshman year in high school may be repeated in communities all too often, there are schools that continue to engage students in their efforts to understand, to acquire a range of literacies, and to grow as learners.

We know, too, that students are deeply affected by their school and classroom cultures (Newmann, 1992a). An important part of what we do as teachers is to foster communities and classroom cultures that will engage students in what they perceive to be meaningful learning. That is far from a trivial challenge. But, it is one that teachers must undertake to make a genuine difference in students' lives.

Beyond the crisis of engagement.   Among the many issues that underlie students' crisis of engagement are two we should examine closely. One of those issues is determining which literacies should be central in the school curriculum. Currently, most states describe their expectations for literacies using content standards that guide state accountability programs. However, researchers have challenged the content of such a curriculum and have asked if it actually serves the students who are expected to master it (J. P. Gee, 1996, 2000; National Council of Teachers of Mathematics [NCTM], 2006; Symcox, 2002). Meanwhile, students disengaged from the curriculum and leaving school may be indicating that this curriculum is far from central to their concerns or interests. Perhaps more attention needs to be given to determining which literacies would entice students into engaged learning.

Source: CALVIN AND HOBBES © 1992 Watterson. Dist. By UNIVERSAL PRESS SYNDICATE. Reprinted with permission. All rights reserved.

The second issue arises from the kinds of instruction that would best support the literacies chosen. Years of research have moved us forward in identifying what contributes to good instruction (Good & Brophy, 2003), but we are far from deciding how specifically to teach a wide range of literacies, including mathematics, science, and the social studies.

Cultures and Literacies as Resources for Engagement

Students bring cultures and literacies with them to our classrooms; these are priceless resources with which we can and must build the knowledge and skills that accompany our content area specialization. We can weave these threads of cultures and literacies into the fabric of our instruction.

First, we can use these threads to help us know and understand our students. We can draw upon these threads to discover how students' cultures have shaped them and what personal literacies compel each student to speak with a unique voice. In describing how her school experience affected her, Eva wrote that her friends had the most influence in shaping who she was becoming and what decisions she made along the way. Although the school literacy she practiced in the classroom was English, she and her friends spoke in Spanglish, a free-flowing mixture of English and Spanish, outside the classroom. Asking questions of each other, such as "¿Quien dijo that Manuel asked me a comer this Viernes?" made it difficult for outsiders to understand their conversation. She said their use of Spanglish also reflected their sense of being trapped between the Mexican and American culture and cliques in the school. However, even though her cultural knowledge and interest could have been used as a resource to deepen her engagement with school, her "ethnic/cultural identity was hardly ever mentioned in schoolbooks." Her only recall of her cultural background being mentioned was pejorative, an experience that made her angry and confused. By being attuned to the cultures and literacies that were shaping Eva's identity, her teachers might have deepened their understanding of her and her interests.

Second, we can use the cultural resources and literacies of our students and their community to design and enrich the content of our curriculum. We can draw upon the funds of knowledge that are embedded in a school's surrounding community and that our students have acquired from interacting with various cultures to build our own instructional programs. For example, William Brozo, Paul Valerio, and Minerva Salazar (1996) integrated reading and writing strategies into a unit on Hispanic American culture that engaged eighth graders, made them more aware of their heritage, and improved their literacy. In Corpus Christi, Texas, these educators enabled students to walk through a Mexican American faith healer's garden and learn from her about the healing properties of plants. Students read Anaya's (1972) *Bless Me, Ultima*, a novel rich in curanderismo (traditional Mexican American faith healing), and discovered how they could work cooperatively to construct meanings for the book. By using their community as a cultural resource, these students and their teachers enriched their understanding of the novel and the heritage that surrounded them.

Third, if we so desire, we can use the cultures and literacies students bring with them as cornerstones for building a curriculum that enables students to explore and grasp the influence their cultures and literacies have had upon them. We can examine students' cultures to help them discover ways to understand the structure and power base that formed and perpetuated the culture's practices and principles. For example, Cindy Thai might have read Amy Tan's *Joy Luck Club* to explore aspects of Chinese culture and their influence on families and relationships.

Finally, all the cultural experiences and literacies that students bring to class with them can be used to help interpret and understand the texts they read. Those texts include not only their current classroom textbooks, but also the multiple texts that make up our cultural lives. The background knowledge that students carry with them provides between-text resources to make sense of new texts. That occurs when knowledge of a Biblical story or a Disney movie enables a student to interpret a new poem or when knowledge of the American revolution helps a student understand revolutions elsewhere.

Addressing Teachers' Nightmares

Even with these cultural and literacy resources at hand, some teachers find the literacy challenges overwhelming. William Bintz (1997), a middle and high school teacher for many years, didn't know how to deal with students who rarely read his assignments or who wanted to read them but struggled and asked for assistance he didn't know how to give. Although he wanted to help his students, his teacher-education program did not include any courses in reading. Having instructional nightmares of his own, Bintz spent several years collecting the reading nightmares of middle and high school teachers. He asked them to describe the nightmare in their reading closet, questions they had about reading they couldn't answer, and a wish that would help them get rid of their nightmare once and for all if it came true. He collected more than a hundred nightmares of teachers in all the content areas, including science, math, social studies, English, home economics, and art.

Questions these teachers asked frequently related to their classroom teaching dilemmas: How do I make factual reading more interesting? How do I get more involved in reading when I don't read much myself? How am I able to help students comprehend what they are reading when no one else has? How do I have time to work on reading when I don't have time to present the subject matter I teach? How do I make sure that students grasp the important concepts in reading?

The hopes these teachers had for a reading solution are reflected in their wishes: I wish I knew how to teach reading and math together. I wish that every teacher regardless of the content area would recognize the importance of reading. I wish I could stop time so I could catch all kids up in reading.

Bintz proposes a number of solutions, which include making sure new and apprenticing teachers gain a deeper understanding of reading and experience teaching it than he did during his university training. He also acknowledges that perceptions of the value and importance of reading need to be changed. Rather than viewing reading as a nagging problem, teachers could establish a climate that says, We value reading in our school. Schools could focus on reading in their professional development programs that include asking teachers from across the curriculum to share reading strategies and the effects of those strategies on their students' reading and learning. Rather than viewing reading as a fanged ghoul dragging its reluctant victim beneath the black river, Bintz would like to see all schools, teachers, and students experience reading as a "tool for learning and thinking."

Content Literacy: A Rationale and a Story

One of the math teachers whose nightmare Bintz collected said, "So many students struggle in math because of not being able to read and understand the problem, and I don't have time to go back and teach them how to comprehend what they are reading." A science teacher told him, "My nightmare is reading comprehension. Students don't comprehend well because many are very behind with reading abilities to begin with, plus a majority of science textbooks are written on a level well above most high school students." Content area literacy has evolved to help content teachers like those whose nightmares are reported here to increase their capacity to help students who struggle with literacy. We have a very long tradition in our middle and high schools of teaching in specific departments, such as math, science, or social studies, and along with those traditions have come expectations about what to teach, why to teach it, and how to teach it. Many new teachers have never taken a course in their discipline that integrated literacy development with content knowledge. The focus was content. However, as our nation moved toward the 21st century, teacher-education programs across the country began to include courses in literacy so that all teachers would know how to use reading and writing to facilitate the growth and mastery of knowledge in all disciplines.

Literacy instruction in middle and high schools has a relatively short history. Although reading instruction has been at the heart of our educational systems since Colonial days, attention to reading in middle and high schools came in the form of remedial instruction. From the 1930s through the early 1970s, remediation for reading problems took center stage, with attention given only to students having distinct problems in reading. In the later 1970s and 1980s, attention turned toward reading development, including programs aimed at middle schools, as well as the spread of writing across the curriculum. During the early and mid-1990s, educators focused on early reading instruction as they argued over alternative approaches to the teaching of reading. In some states, the advent of content and performance standards during the late 1990s contributed to growing concern about adolescent literacy, a concern that national organizations such as the International Reading Association and the National Council of Teachers of English began to address.

In 1999, the International Reading Association's Commission on Adolescent Literacy developed a "Position Statement" and explored some of the reasons behind the lack of appropriate literacy instruction for adolescents in our country as we entered the 21st century. The Commission (Moore, Bean, Birdyshaw, & Rycik, 1999) identified a set of seven principles that could guide and support literacy growth for middle and high school students.

1. Adolescents deserve access to a wide variety of reading material that they can and want to read.
2. Adolescents deserve instruction that builds both the skill and desire to read increasingly complex materials.
3. Adolescents deserve assessment that shows them their strengths as well as their needs and that guides their teachers to design instruction that will best help them grow as readers.
4. Adolescents deserve expert teachers who model and provide explicit instruction in reading comprehension and study strategies across the curriculum.
5. Adolescents deserve reading specialists who assist individual students having difficulty learning how to read.
6. Adolescents deserve teachers who understand the complexities of individual adolescent readers, respect their differences, and respond to their characteristics.
7. Adolescents deserve homes, communities, and a nation that will support their efforts to achieve advanced levels of literacy and provide the support necessary for them to succeed.

If rigorously acknowledged and applied, these principles could radically alter the literacy support that adolescents receive in schools across the county. Without doubt, many states, districts, schools, and individual teachers have responded, especially with the parallel development of state content standards and the implementation of the No Child Left Behind Act.

Literacies as cultural capital.   The expanding influence of advocates for social justice and equality through literacy has paralleled the growth in awareness that literacy development needs to be nurtured far beyond the elementary years. These advocates believe that literacy could open doors to understanding how social, political, and economic factors could define students, provide opportunity, or limit freedom (Fecho, 1999; Freire, 1993/1970; J. P. Gee, 1996, 2001). It has often been observed that the acquisition and use of a particular literacy, such as standard English, has radically different values in different cultural contexts (Heath, 1983; Ogbu & Simon, 1998). A student of mine who was preparing to become a teacher clearly showed me how the cultural capital he acquired through gaining literacies could both open and close doors. During his years in middle and high school, he faced a culturally related literacy dilemma daily. His mother, who worked in a private school outside their immediate community, received tuition-free education for her children. All the children had to do was travel out of the community in which they lived to attend the private school. Having done so throughout his middle school years and into high school, this student acquired an exceptional education. However, whenever he entered the community where he lived, he had to be ready to adopt a mode of communication, including the current slang of the street, that resonated with kids living in his community. Numerous painful experiences revealed to him the price he would have to pay if he insisted on using the manner of speaking he acquired at the private school. On the other hand, as he gained literacies from his schooling, he became aware of the doors those literacies could open for him that otherwise would be closed.

New Literacies

The concept of "new literacies" has been evolving with the 21st century. More traditional conceptions of print are being replaced with broader conceptions of literacy shaped by information and communication technologies (Leu, Kinzer, Coiro, & Cammack, 2004). These developments in technology include computer games, Internet communication, search engines, and Web pages. Students now spend hours of out-of-school time online creating and consuming blogs or participating in virtual reality role-playing games. These innovations have begun to profoundly affect our conception of literacy and what it means to be literate. The exact effects these newly emerging literacies will have on school literacies, the curriculum, and teaching strategies are in flux. However, there is no doubt that many of these out-of-school literacies will have a growing influence over in-school literate practices and provide resources for adolescent literacy growth.

An entire field of investigation in education, called New Literacy Studies (NLS), has developed. Educators working in this field are developing new perspectives of literacy that embrace not only new technology's impact on literacy but also the effects of a global economy frequently leveled by instantaneous electronic communication worldwide (J. P. Gee, 2000; Leu et al., 2004). Answers to questions such as the following are of fundamental concern to NLS researchers and all content area teachers working with adolescents:

- What forms does literacy take?
- How does technology inform and reform literacy?
- What roles do cultures play in becoming literate?
- What kinds of cultural capital, such as language skills, do working-class students versus middle-class students acquire?

- How does literacy define and position its users?
- Who gains or loses power through literate activity?
- How can students become wiser, more critical users of technology and media?

In Chapter 8, we explore possible answers to these questions in more detail and discover how their deeper exploration can bring inquiry into the classroom.

Lessons from "Beating the Odds" Classrooms

How can teachers promote meaningful learning while developing literacy? Because literacy coupled with learning is our focus, I have drawn on the work of Judith Langer (2001), who found teachers using practices that led to their school's students "beating the odds" when it came to performance on standards-based state assessments. Langer identified educational practices that enabled students, mostly from schools in culturally diverse and poorer communities, to perform significantly better than students in comparable schools. Although her study focused on teachers of English in middle and high schools, her findings directly address literacy development across the curriculum, while providing direction for meaningful learning. Active and meaningful engagement marked and facilitated the superior performance of students in "beating the odds" classrooms. Students were on task most of the time in academically rich instructional environments that promoted learning. Characteristics of literacy instruction that set these higher performing middle and high school classrooms and teachers apart from comparable but lower performing schools can aid in decisions about what needs to be done in classrooms to address literacy growth while promoting meaningful learning across the content areas.

Langer (2001) focused on six issues at the center of the current education debate in literacy: (a) enabling strategies, (b) approaches to skills instruction, (c) connected instruction, (d) conceptions of learning, (e) classroom organization, and (f) test preparation. Each of these six issues was reflected in differences observed in typical classrooms and practices in "beating the odds" classrooms that are summarized in Figure 1.4.

Meaningful and successful learning in "beating the odds" classrooms and schools arose from (or was associated with) teachers whose instructional practice was based upon the following:

1. *The overt teaching of enabling strategies to carry out reading, writing, and thinking tasks.* "Beating the odds" teachers taught their students strategic procedures, such as the use of graphic organizers, techniques of reciprocal teaching, or a process approach to writing, that they could use to address learning tasks and that resulted in enhanced performance. These strategies (all of which are covered in later chapters in this book) helped students plan, organize, complete, and reflect upon their work. "Beating the odds" teachers often modeled and discussed procedures that would guide students toward successful task completion by breaking down complex tasks into parts and providing rubrics for the evaluation of their performance.

2. *The systematic use of separated, simulated, and integrated skill instruction.* "Beating the odds" teachers did not allow their teaching of skills to be dominated by any one approach, such as the direct instruction of an isolated skill. Most used all three methods to introduce and teach literacy skills. For example, in teaching vocabulary, one "beating the odds" teacher selected unfamiliar words from a text her students were reading, showed them how they could apply the new words to

Figure 1.4 Practices in "Beating the Odds" Classrooms.

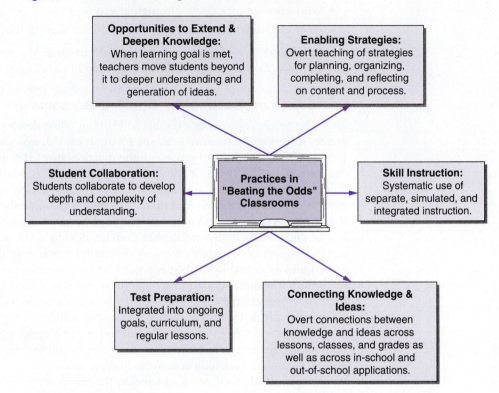

classroom discussions, and found ways for them to incorporate those words in their writing assignments. She was using separated instruction when she presented vocabulary she believed to be challenging, simulated instruction when she asked students to apply their knowledge of these words to texts they were reading, and integrated instruction when she urged her students to use the newly acquired words in their class discussions and essay writing.

3. *The creation of overt connections between new knowledge across lessons, classes, grades, and even communities.* Ample research (Bransford, Brown, & Cocking, 1999) demonstrates that students are more likely to learn and remember concepts if they are connected to prior knowledge acquired both in and outside of school. "Beating the odds" teachers overtly made webs of inter-connections among multiple forms of student learning: within lessons; across lessons, classes, and grades; and between in- and out-of-school knowledge. For example, during self-study at one "beating the odds" high school, teachers sought ways to foster connected learning both within the school and between the school and the community it served. They focused on ways students could become more effective communicators in all grades across the curriculum.

4. *The belief that achieving a learning goal is not an end point but an opportunity to extend and deepen understanding.* What is it to know something, to understand it? With only about 1 in 20 high school students able to deal analytically with challenging reading material, a high priority should be to examine, extend, and elaborate on the meanings of either literary or informative texts (Perie et al., 2005), going beyond a command of facts to engage in thoughtful learning. In

"beating the odds" classrooms, teachers encourage their students to think and use knowledge—not acquire and bury facts or concepts in memory's cemetery. One "beating the odds" middle school teacher moved her students from learning to use the World Wide Web as a tool for research to discovering information about their surnames and genealogies to engaging in research on African Americans, their history, and their lives in present-day America. In these classrooms, learning a concept or skill isn't an end in itself but a signal to begin to use the skill for thinking critically and for gaining deeper understanding.

5. *The notion that students collaborate in classrooms to gain depth and complexity of understanding.* In "beating the odds" classrooms, students collaborate in a community of interactive learners to develop deep levels of understanding. Students bring their cultural histories and the voices of multiple literacies into the classroom conversation. Learning is interactive. Literacy is a socially grounded activity. Classroom cultures thrive on sharing knowledge, interpretations, and discoveries. Students share ideas, respond to each other's interpretations, test out the soundness of their reasoning, and—through cognitive collaboration—build unique learning cultures. A "beating the odds" teacher, Myra LeBendig, favors discussions and fosters classroom collaboration for discovery. One of the first National Board Certified teachers in America, she said to her students at the beginning of the school year, "Fight to teach me." She wanted them to challenge her and their classmates, to engage in vigorous thinking, to ask the probing questions, and to explore her and their understanding of meanings they formed from books they read.

6. *Integrating test preparation into current learning goals, regular lessons, and units.* With the spread of standards-based instruction and accountability programs to assess progress toward the achievement of standards, some schools across the nation, hoping to improve their performance, have adopted stand-alone test-preparation modules. In short, they teach to the test. In efforts to get students test-ready, teachers have been asked to teach test-taking skills. In "beating the odds" schools, teachers work on the assumption that integrating literacy skills into the year-round curriculum will improve both learning and student performance on state and local tests. After learning what they could about assessment programs and examining the structure and content of the accountability system, teachers in higher performing schools revised and restructured their literacy curriculum. Teachers and administrators in some "beating the odds" schools analyzed samples of items usually included in test batteries; discovered what specific literacy skills, strategies, and knowledge would benefit their students; and revised the instructional program to promote mastery of those skills, strategies, and knowledge domains. Instruction related to the testing program was infused and integrated. It was not set up as a separate intervention to address students' testing program needs.

These "beating the odds" teachers, many serving in high-poverty communities, appear to operate on a common principle: We learn best while engaged in activities that are personally and socially meaningful. Although more typical teaching may share that principle, teachers in higher achieving classrooms integrate the practices reviewed and weave them together into a tapestry of instruction.

Meeting the Challenges of Literacy and Learning

Features found in "beating the odds" classrooms point to knowledge, skills, and strategies that teachers can integrate into their classroom instruction. Also essential to

Figure 1.5   Eight Steps to Meeting Literacy and Learning Challenges.

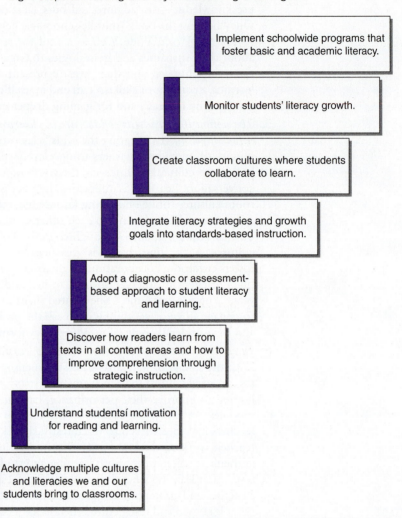

Implement schoolwide programs that foster basic and academic literacy.

Monitor students' literacy growth.

Create classroom cultures where students collaborate to learn.

Integrate literacy strategies and growth goals into standards-based instruction.

Adopt a diagnostic or assessment-based approach to student literacy and learning.

Discover how readers learn from texts in all content areas and how to improve comprehension through strategic instruction.

Understand studentsí motivation for reading and learning.

Acknowledge multiple cultures and literacies we and our students bring to classrooms.

meaningful learning are your desire and disposition to know students, to discover how they learn, to understand what they need to progress, to formulate and achieve literacy and learning goals, and to reflect on what's working and what needs reworking. Acknowledging that there is no formula, no magic potion of procedures for creating engaged instruction in every classroom, there are several steps based on research and best practices and summarized in Figure 1.5 that new and growing teachers can take to address the literacy and learning challenges they will meet in today's classrooms:

1. *Acknowledge the multiple cultures and literacies we and our students bring to classrooms.* As we have seen in this chapter, cultures play big parts in the drama of classroom instruction. In a sense, cultures are the settings for instructional episodes in which we and our students participate. Knowing what values, assumptions, beliefs, background knowledge, and expectations students bring into our classrooms enables us to make better judgments about what will engage them, what resources to use, and what tools we need to put into their hands so they will be successful learners.

Closely related to the cultures brought to our classrooms are the participants' literacies. What literacies affect their thinking and acting in our classroom? How do our students express knowledge of literacies in the way they think and act?

2. *Understand students' motivation for reading and learning.* Teachers, especially those new to classrooms, are sometimes baffled by their students' disengagement with learning, which is often revealed because they do not read assigned texts. There are reasons for the disconnect, and there are ways to heighten motivation, both internal and external. If teachers discover and appropriately apply these motivational methods, they can enhance their students' engagement in classrooms, school cultures, and in lifelong literacy growth.

3. *Discover how readers learn from texts in all content areas and how to improve comprehension through strategic instruction.* In the past 35 years, we have learned what good readers do when they read, what may not be working well in weak readers, and what might be done to help struggling readers overcome frustrating obstacles to learning. To appreciate what can be done to help readers improve performance, we need first to know in more detail what happens in the mind of a reader. This textbook presents a model of the reading process based on extensive reading process research and implications of that model both for day-to-day instruction in classrooms and for struggling readers.

   When apprenticing teachers master literacy strategies that influence both thinking and problem solving, they can help their own students overcome obstacles to productive learning, acquire vocabulary, improve comprehension, and deepen understandings across the disciplines. Many of these strategies enable teachers to activate their students' background knowledge, help them engage texts with purpose-guiding questions, and teach them tools to represent, organize, and reflect upon knowledge constructed from interacting with texts.

4. *Adopt a diagnostic or assessment-based approach to student literacy and learning.* We can acquire assessment skills and strategies to look more closely at our students' work, appreciate their strengths, and discover their frustrations so that we can envision instruction to improve reading and learning in all content areas. These tools for assessment enable teachers to make informed decisions about how best to approach students in academic trouble and improve the learning of those who are already successful in our classrooms.

5. *Integrate literacy strategies and growth goals into standards-based instruction.* As we saw in the classrooms of "beating the odds" teachers, thinking and strategy instruction are among their highest priorities. Once content is acquired, deeper understandings can be pursued. They integrate literacy-enhancing strategies throughout their instructional programs and help students internalize those strategies for use in other learning contexts. Through step-by-step explanations, apprenticing teachers can discover how they can accomplish these learning goals and design instruction so that standards, strategies, and assessment practices align.

6. *Create classroom cultures where students collaborate.* Classrooms in "beating the odds" schools were usually organized to encourage collaboration between students and the interactive exploration of concepts and ideas through discussion or the completion of projects. Apprentice teachers can learn techniques to pursue literacy development through whole class discussions, cooperative learning teams, or tutorials arranged within a class or across age groups. These forms of group interaction can help students, especially English learners, acquire content knowledge and skills while becoming proficient with literacy and learning strategies.

7. *Monitor students' literacy growth.* With periodic progress measurements, teachers can determine the effectiveness of intervention programs they have put in place. The feedback from students provides teachers with information about students' reading, writing, and learning that guide decisions about future instructional improvements. Some schools collect periodic curriculum-based measurements (or CBMs) to discover students' progress in reading and use that information to supplement measurement of student performance from state testing programs. Instruction may require modifications to show more growth in academic literacy as students prepare for postsecondary education and the workplace.

8. *Implement schoolwide programs that foster basic and academic literacy.* Entire schools can create literacy programs that improve reading for all students at all grade levels or provide courses to strengthen gains in academic literacy. Some of these programs, such as sustained silent reading, engage students and faculty in several minutes of daily reading. Other programs that are focused on teaching all students vocabulary and comprehension techniques may require a full period or more every day. Still others begin with extensive literacy training for teachers, who then integrate techniques such as reciprocal teaching or analytical approaches to expository texts into their curriculum and daily lesson plans to promote content learning and academic literacy growth.

You may wonder how you can learn to integrate these literacy and learning techniques into your content area teaching. As you may have guessed, this series of steps echoes the content and structure of the textbook you are now reading.

In short, this textbook will explore and discover ways to work with students that will:

- enhance our capacity to understand how they read and learn,
- identify sources of trouble in struggling readers,
- decide what steps we can take to strengthen comprehension and learning of all our students,
- evaluate students' progress in literacy growth, and
- build richer, more caring teacher-student relationships and cultures.

By empowering ourselves with knowledge, strategies, and skills, we can provide more meaningful and productive schooling for all our students.

Double-Entry Journal: After Reading

Now that you have read Chapter 1, you are ready to complete the postreading Double-Entry Journal (DEJ). To do that, write about 150 words in response to the following directions. Your instructor may collect and respond to your DEJs or ask you to submit them over the Internet.

Having read this chapter, review what you wrote about the cultures that influenced you during high school. Which literacies did you practice while a student in high school? You could address these three: school, community, and personal. Do you think cultures and literacies from your high school years shaped or influenced your development and your perspectives as an adult? If not, why not? If they did, how did they? How would you draw upon your own students' cultures and literacies to enhance teaching and learning in your content area?

Chapter 2

MOTIVATION TO READ CONTENT AREA TEXTS*

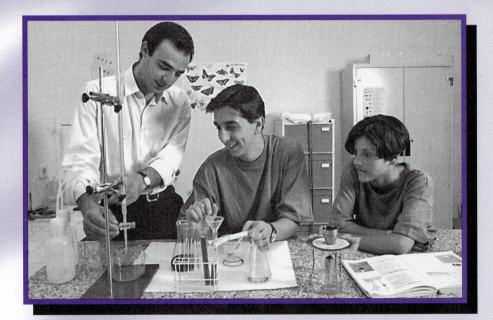

After reading chapter 2, you should be able to answer the following questions:

1. How does motivation for reading change as students move through their school years?

2. How does self-determination theory explain student engagement in reading and changes in engagement through the school years?

3. What student factors contribute to a student's motivation to read texts in the content areas?

4. What teacher factors contribute to a student's motivation to read texts in the content areas?

---

*This chapter took its inspiration from a chapter that Robert Ruddell and I wrote (Ruddell & Unrau, 1997). That chapter was published in Reading Engagement, a volume edited by John Guthrie and Allan Wigfield. Ruddell, Guthrie, and Wigfield's ideas contributed to this chapter's structure and content.

Motivation to Read

At one low point during her first year at Jefferson Middle School, Ms. Hawthorne asked her eighth-grade social studies students how many of them completed their homework assignment to read eight pages about the origins of the American Civil War for that day's lesson. The day's lesson activity depended upon students' having done their reading. In her class of 29, 13 students raised their hands. Ms. Hawthorne faced a dilemma, perhaps a civil war of her own. How could she go ahead with her lesson activity knowing that more than half the students had not read the section of the book they needed to know to engage productively in the activity?

Thinking she was going to have to delay an investigation of the Civil War's causes to investigate the causes of her own students' lack of responsibility, Ms. Hawthorne asked them why they hadn't done their reading.

"It was soooooo boring," one student groaned.

"I couldn't understand it," said another. "There were too many words I didn't know, so I just stopped."

"I just couldn't get around to it," another coolly stated.

Clearly, Ms. Hawthorne saw signs of disengagement and frustration.

Ms. Hawthorne's Challenge

Ms. Hawthorne's battle is repeated thousands of times every day in classrooms all over the United States. Some teachers faced with this frustration respond to their students' resistance, malaise, or laziness by trying to find activities that will get them engaged. They try games, which sometimes help. They resort to videos, which can augment instruction. They do a round-robin reading in class that takes the whole period and that few students follow. So teachers summarize and review the reading's content. Or they lecture. In one way or another, they retreat from requiring that students read the assigned work on their own. But none of these methods directly helps students learn to read texts effectively or learn from them.

When Ms. Hawthorne asked her colleagues what they did, several said the sensible thing to do was just to lecture and have students take notes. Or, they suggested, have students do their reading in class. Other teachers believed that a more sensible approach is to tell students that all texts are not equally exciting. Reading *Seventeen, Road and Track,* an article on Kanye West, or Harry Potter's latest adventure is likely to be more immediately interesting than reading a history, science, or English text. However, learning to read important texts directly relates to students' future welfare. So, some argue (Jago, 2000), teachers must insist that students have a responsibility to read about the history of the American Civil War, the functions of DNA, and the adventures of Huckleberry Finn.

Placing these demands on students sounds entirely reasonable. Unfortunately, we cannot always predict whether or not students will join our side in the struggle to read and learn more effectively when given these demands. However, we can go beyond clarifying that students have obligations to learn and demanding that they do so.

As teachers, we all learn quite early that a substantial canyon too often lies between students' mastering skills and applying them to learn. Inertly sitting on one side of the canyon with disengaged skills and knowledge, students may have little disposition to get to the other side to use what they know and can do to discover new knowledge. Far too often middle and high school teachers tell me that in some of their classes they can't get more than one out of four students to read assignments they give for homework. These assignments are given to disengaged students who can read but are not motivated to do so.

As teachers, we also learn that not being motivated to read is most often part of a larger motivational quandary. It's not just reading—often, it's learning in general or doing any schoolwork. In fact, we have evidence that levels of motivation decline as students progress from elementary to middle school and on to high school, a pattern of change in motivation that we explore in a moment.

Motivation lies at the heart of classroom instruction (Good & Brophy, 2003). When we look at what's happening in a classroom, motivation is one factor we never want to overlook. Some classrooms buzz with learning. In others, some students are only a heartbeat or two from brain death. The clock's countdown is their sole life support.

When asking questions about students' motivation, we are asking about what got them fired up in the first place, in which direction they are headed, how hard they will work to get there, and how long they are likely to go at it. What moves students like Ms. Hawthorne's to read? How might their skills as readers grow? What kinds of activities might be used in her social studies classes to promote literacy engagement?

Changes in Motivation to Read Through the School Years

Because our knowledge base for understanding the reading motivation of middle and high school students is relatively thin, some educators refer to it as "the dark hole" in research on reading. Yet knowing as much as we can about factors that contribute to middle and high school students' development of academic literacy as they prepare for the challenges of high school and subsequent education is vitally important to our daily teaching. Fortunately, researchers have made some significant discoveries that help us understand the trajectory of students' reading motivation through the school years.

In general, researchers have repeatedly found that students' motivation declines as they progress from elementary school through high school. Researchers have focused their attention in particular on intrinsic and extrinsic motivational trends. **Intrinsic motivation** describes internal tendencies to seek challenges, explore interests, satisfy curiosity, expand personal capacities, and enjoy the process of learning. **Extrinsic motivation** describes performance that is externally regulated through rewards or punishments (Ryan & Deci, 2000). In the early 1980s, Harter (1981) found that students in grades 3 through 9 reported gradual declines in intrinsic motivation. Declining intrinsic motivation from grades four through the high school years was also documented by Gottfried, Fleming, & Gottfried (2001); however, they found that some content areas showed more precipitous declines than others, with math and science having the largest declines, reading having more modest deterioration, and social studies revealing no significant drop. In a 3-year longitudinal study of students progressing from middle to high school, researchers (Otis et al., 2005) found that both students' intrinsic and extrinsic motivation decreased gradually as they moved from grades 8 to 9 and 10. Many educators have speculated about the reasons for the weakening of school-related motivation, including the notion that efforts to motivate students through various reward systems may undermine their own interests and natural curiosity (Kohn, 1993). Although the reasons for a general decline in motivation are sure to be complex, we should explore further our interest in motivation for reading in particular.

We know that students' attitudes toward reading in elementary school worsen as they move through the grades (McKenna, Kear, & Ellsworth, 1995). Attitudes began at a relatively positive level in the first grade and ended in "relative indifference" by the sixth grade. Unfortunately, an increasingly negative attitude toward academic reading grew regardless of readers' ability. Girls had more positive attitudes than boys at every grade level; however, these differences between boys and girls were unrelated to ability.

We might expect that further gradual declines in reading motivation would occur as children enter middle school because of the general decline in motivation for school that has been repeatedly documented. In fact, a colleague and I (Unrau & Schlackman, 2005, 2006) conducted research on motivation for reading that revealed a decline in motivation as our sample of urban students moved through the middle school grades. As the sixth graders moved on to the seventh grade, their motivation declined significantly, as did the motivation of seventh graders moving into the eighth grade. Of course, our findings may not be typical of every middle school; however, we suspect that the population we sampled may not be too different from other middle school populations across the country.

We (Unrau & Schlackman, 2006) confirmed the findings of researchers who looked at connections between intrinsic motivation and performance by finding that students who were intrinsically motivated tended to score significantly higher on measures of reading comprehension and that their motivation for reading deteriorated less from grades six to seven and seven to eight. These results from intrinsically motivated students are likely to reflect their greater reading proficiency.

For those of us teaching middle and high school students, one implication of the research done on motivation, especially that for reading, is that we will be facing many challenges. Among them will be discovering what motivates our students to read and learn, understanding how we can reach more students, and knowing what steps we can take to develop our students' interests and desire to learn, especially in each of our content areas.

Toward a Unifying Vision of Motivation to Read: Self-Determination Theory

We can use self-determination theory to better understand and address the promise and challenges of literacy development, especially that of struggling or at-risk students (Deci & Ryan, 1985; Ryan & Deci, 2000). **Self-determination theory (SDT)** provides us with a research-based perspective of motivation, especially motivation related to school and literacy growth in particular. SDT emphasizes the central importance of each individual's need for personal development and self-regulation. More self-directed motivation can serve as an antidote to students' passivity and alienation, which often comes from too much outside regulation.

Educators who developed SDT (Deci & Ryan, 1985; Ryan & Deci, 2000) make distinctions between intrinsic and extrinsic motivation based on extensive investigations. Intrinsic motivation arises from an individual's personal interest in a topic or activity and is satisfied through pursuit of that interest or activity. Intrinsic motivation, central to self-regulated learning and self-determination, embodies a student's desire for mastery, spontaneous curiosity, and inquiry. An intrinsically motivated middle school reader who was enthralled by the Harry Potter series would find internal satisfaction in reading a book in the series, entering Harry's world, and participating in his magical adventures. On the other hand, extrinsic motivation arises from participation in some activity, not for its own sake, but for rewards or the release from some external social demand. An extrinsically motivated middle school reader facing a quiz on a chapter in *The Giver* and wanting to get a high grade would read to perform well on the test and perhaps to avoid a teacher's or parent's rebuke. However, students whose initial interest in some topic, such as cell division, is extrinsically motivated because of an important test may internalize that interest, extend it to the study of cancer, and become intrinsically motivated to pursue scientific knowledge.

According to self-determination theory, there are three needs essential for driving internally motivated personal growth: competence, autonomy, and relatedness. Children strive to develop a sense of competence, a sense that they can tackle a task and accomplish it successfully. We will see that sense of competence reflected in our discussion of self-efficacy. We will also see how, as content area teachers, we can detect it and foster its growth. To gain a sense of competence, students require an internal **locus of control**, which is a belief that they and not some other agent are at the center of their decisions and actions. When students' locus of control is seen to be within them, they experience an increase in **autonomy**, the sense that their decisions and actions are coming from them and are theirs to own. That autonomy is essential to enhance students' feelings of competence—and their desire to engage in learning activities that lead to feelings of satisfaction, gratification, or personal fulfillment. The third element essential for intrinsic motivation's growth—namely, relatedness—can be addressed through the behavior of caring teachers. By providing opportunities for students to experience autonomy during inquiry, caring teachers encourage the development of self-determination. If students are to become intrinsically motivated to learn, activities, problems, and challenges must have an intrinsic interest to them or an interest that can become internalized, as in the case of the student who became interested in cell division in order to understand more about cancer.

We are far more likely to understand why our students want to read or decide not to read if we look upon their motivation as a system or network of interacting factors, not any single cause (Alderman, 1999). Many factors contribute to a student's engagement in reading and learning. Some are more directly and more immediately controlled or influenced by a teacher, but other factors, mostly under student control, may be only indirectly affected by our decisions and behavior. And, although we might like the situation to be otherwise, some student factors are probably completely independent of our classroom decisions.

The Focus of Motivation

Using an image to help us understand motivational factors, we can picture the eye as a metaphor for focusing motivation. At the center of Figure 2.1 lies the *focus of motivation*. It may be compared to the eye's pupil focusing motivation not in response to light but to the convergence of many motivational factors that influence readers. This

Figure 2.1 Student and Teacher Factors Contributing to Student's Motivation to Read.

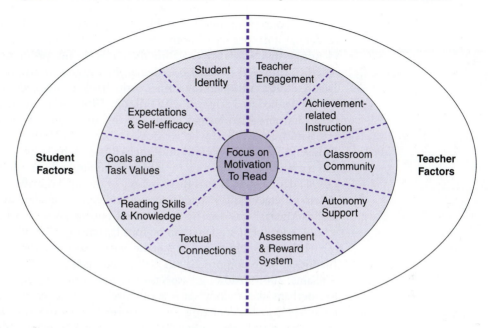

focus is the center point of the mind's intent, of its direction, purpose, and intensity when interacting with a learning environment. In describing the factors that influence the focus of motivation, we are on the way to helping our students become more self-regulated in their reading and learning.

Student Factors Contributing to a Student's Motivation to Read

Student Identity

Since Melody was three and played school with her brothers and sisters, she knew she wanted to be a teacher when she grew up. Her mother was a teacher. Her father had been a school principal. From age 2, Penelope had a backpack filled with her "schoolbooks" and pencils, just like her older sisters. Throughout middle and high school, she believed her future work would be in a classroom as a teacher.

Michael, on the other hand, was born an athlete. His dad and he played ball whenever they could. Michael was miserable when his admired older brother excluded him from any team. By 6, Michael's bedroom closet was a sports locker. His mom drove him to Little League daily during the season. In high school, he went out for football, basketball, and baseball all 4 years. School seemed in the way, but his parents always told him that, if he wanted to play ball, he had to keep up his grades. Even then, getting him to study took a lot of effort. Although he loved sports, Michael went through high school totally confused about what he would do when he got his diploma.

Opportunities to read, write, and talk about books helped Melody form her identity in school. All her teachers, including her mother and father, admired her work and encouraged her. But Michael's identity as a student formed in opposition to those same opportunities. Teachers and his parents had to corral him to get school work done. He rarely found that reading or writing gave him much satisfaction.

The concept of identity enables us to understand the motivation of students as readers at a deeper level. Both Melody and Michael had distinct identities, and the identities that students enact in their classrooms promote or limit engagement, whether those classrooms be science, math, art, or any other subject (Moje and Dillon, 2006). Although the term identity has been defined many ways, for us **identity** will be defined as a sense of self (Erikson, 1968). That sense of self includes remembered and imagined images of the self and stories about the self that tell us who we are, who we were, and who we hope to become (Markus & Nurius, 1986; Sfard & Prusak, 2005). Both Melody and Michael had such a sense of self based in self-images and narratives confirmed by their friends, family, and community. Garcia and Pintrich (1994) demonstrated that these images of the self contribute to a student's desire to develop literacy skills (Melody) or to a diligent avoidance of that project (Michael). Just as Michael was sure he loved sports but unsure of what he would do after high school, adolescent students can be torn by tension over who they are becoming.

However, identity is not a static state, especially for most adolescent students. Identities, once composed, can be revised (Erikson, 1968; Gee, 2006; Rex, 2001; Williams, 2006). Although aspects of a student's core identity may be formed early in life, perhaps like Melody's image of herself as a teacher, many individuals revise their identities. Movies depicting the transformation of students whose identity is rooted in resistance to literacy and schooling, such as *Dangerous Minds*, *Dead Poets Society*, and *Educating Rita*, have a mythic appeal. Stepping out of the theater, we realize that such Hollywood transformations minimize or cloak the deep work and personal struggle that change in student identity actually requires. For students disidentified and disengaged from school literacies, the fight for identity arouses troubling anxiety and confusion (Williams, 2006).

Researchers (Rex, 2001) studying tracked schools have described the changing identity of readers as they evolved from "general" students, who read to construct "correct" meanings, to "inquirers," who responded critically and creatively to texts. As general students underwent identity revision, teachers also changed by directing emergent inquirers to converse with the more proficient inquirers and by sharing teacher authority with the class. Engaged and responsive teachers are likely to recognize that their students' identities, and thus their students' motives for learning, are shaped by crises of identity before and during schooling. They are also shaped as students identify with family, community, and cultural figures.

Identity and the home.   Parents play a key role in the development of an adolescent's identity (Erikson, 1968). They provide the foundation for basic trust in the world and the cradle in which children develop their sense of autonomy and the capacity to act independently. That base provides the springboard into schooling and the acquisition of skills and knowledge that enable them to function with confidence in both their social and learning worlds. Identity consolidates with childhood's end and the beginning of youth. Thoughout those early years, the home shapes literacy's development (Baker, 2003; Heath, 1983), including the motivation to read.

Researchers (Baker, Scher, & Mackler, 1997) have confirmed the correlation between parents' education and income levels with children's home literacy exposure. As we will see in the chapter on vocabulary and its development (chapter 5), children from working-class or welfare families have far fewer opportunities to hear and use words than children from professional families (Hart & Risley, 1995, 2003). By early adolescence and middle school, students who have more encouragement to read in the home, because of available reading materials and parents who read to them, read more on their own (Greaney & Hegarty, 1987; Shapiro & Whitney, 1997). They also score higher on measures of attitude toward reading and reading achievement (Baker, 2003).

From studies focused on how parents experience literacy, Baker (2003) found three different parental perspectives that boiled down to literacy as (a) a set of skills, (b) a useful tool in daily routines, such as shopping, or (c) a source of entertainment. Children in homes dominated by the view that reading is a source of entertainment excelled in reading performance compared to children raised in homes which saw reading as skill development. Children raised in a reading-as-entertainment climate appear to be more likely to share in their parents' enjoyment of reading and pursue that enjoyment. This transfer occurs, in part, because parents who view reading as entertainment give their children more opportunities to identify with and adopt that perspective as part of their identity.

Identity and gender. Boys and girls are different, even in their attitudes toward reading. Culture undoubtedly contributes to the shaping of their self-schema as male or female. Studies consistently show that girls have more positive attitudes about reading (McKenna et al., 1995). Furthermore, the Nation's Report Card indicates that girls have outperformed boys on reading proficiency for three decades (Perie et al., 2005). That performance undoubtedly increases girls' sense of competence as readers, which contributes to their comfort and success in reading. More boys don't feel competent to succeed as readers. It's not that boys don't value reading. They do. But boys tend to pursue more out-of-school literacies, such as video games, comics, and magazines. Boys tend to reject school literacies because they lack relevance, immediacy, functionality, fun, and humor (Smith & Wilhelm, 2002). Boys tend to see novels as a "girls' thing."

An example will illustrate the motivational strength of both self-image and gender. Jimmy Santiago Baca is a poet and a teacher who discovered the power of literacy in prison. He went on to win an American Book Award and found Black Mesa Enterprises, an organization that provides young people with alternatives to violence through a language-centered community. However, he struggled with his self-image: He profoundly rejected literacy before becoming a writer. While he was in jail, Jimmy confronted a self-image that announced:

> Sissies read books. You couldn't do *anything* with a book. You couldn't fix a '57 Chevy with a book. You couldn't take money from some hustler with a book. You couldn't convince or persuade anybody with a book. Books were in the way. And not only that, they were the great enemy. Books were where you found the pain. Books were where you found the shame, and books were where you found the lies that my grandparents had been lazy Mexicans and that I was no good, that I couldn't be as good as the next person. *That's* what was in books. So why should I go open a book and give myself all this pain? I didn't *need* that. I would rather go numb with a good bottle of tequila.

However, literacy, the power of words, and another possible self pulled him into what he calls "the fiercest typhoon I have ever been in and from which I have never escaped. I have continually swirled like a leaf" (Moyer, 1995, pp. 35–36).

Identity and culture. An anthropologist who focused on minority group education, Ogbu (1983, 1991; Ogbu & Simons, 1998) explained differences in the performance of students from minority groups with a culturally based theory. Ogbu classified minorities into voluntary and involuntary groups. **Voluntary minorities** willingly immigrated to America, usually to improve their opportunities and those of their children. Examples of voluntary minorities include Korean, Japanese, and Mexican immigrants. **Involuntary minorities** have been enslaved, colonized, or conquered. They became part of American society unwillingly. They usually view their being in America as a condition forced upon them. Examples of involuntary minorities include black Americans who came in chains and early Mexican Americans who were conquered.

Although individual differences exist, Ogbu (1991; Ogbu & Simon, 1998) proposes that voluntary minorities see the United States as a "land of promise," whereas involuntary minorities see their social and economic situation as far less promising than that of most white Americans. Crossing cultural and language barriers means different things to voluntary and involuntary minorities. Both voluntary and involuntary minorities see culture and language differences as barriers or challenges that can be met and overcome through learning. Whereas American culture and language skills add to the identity of voluntary minorities, they detract from or threaten the identity of involuntary minorities. To varying degrees, the identities of involuntary minorities are defined by distinctions from or opposition to American identity.

These observations about voluntary and involuntary minorities contribute to our understanding of differences in school performance, including reading achievement. Voluntary minorities perceive American society, its culture, and its schools in ways that align far more closely with a vision of self-determination than do the perceptions of involuntary minorities. Voluntary minorities frame their situation in America as one that promotes their self-realization through the pursuit of opportunity in a new land. They believe that the new culture and language they are learning will expand their identity rather than subvert the culture and language of their heritage.

For involuntary minorities, on the other hand, the path to adopting America's culture and language is likely to be filled with far more conflict, ambivalence, and hesitation. Many features in their cultural model of America contribute to the belief that control of their destinies lies not in themselves but in the hands of others. Involuntary minorities may feel their situation in America is not promising in social and economic terms. Hard work and education may not enable them to achieve their vision of a self-determined future. Moreover, the new culture and language they are expected to absorb may threaten their heritage and identity. Thus, in-school literacies, including the acquisition of English, may not always be perceived as an achievement that will let them pursue their vision of a self-determined future.

Students with little hope that academic success will yield vocational or professional success are unlikely to invest energy in a school's vision of their future. Others, who believe that working hard in school will allow them to realize personal and

Motivating Reluctant Readers: Student Identity

1. Discover how your students experience reading by reading through their eyes. Appreciate the diverse personal, family, and cultural backgrounds that may contribute to each student's identity as a reader.

2. Adolescents may have defined tastes that influence the reading they savor. Knowing their tastes could help us feed and even expand their palates.

3. Provide students with opportunities to reflect on their learning and learning processes by asking them to respond to questions such as, What am I learning? How does it relate to me?

4. Encourage students, when feasible, to relate stories from their own life experiences that connect to content you're presenting.

5. Encourage home literacy support by communicating with parents about their child's literacy development and providing suggestions for ways parents might help, such as increasing access to books and magazines, pleasurable reading in the home, talking about books read in and out of school, reading to make something together (such as a cake or a model car), and sharing with parents school resources for developing literacy.

professional dreams, are far more likely to participate in a school's cultural and curricular programs (Newmann, 1992b).

Knowing the connection between identity and school performance, teachers understand that many young people, especially those attending inner-city schools, may feel excluded from the school's culture and seek identity affirmation and affiliation elsewhere, such as in gangs or on the streets (Heath & McLaughlin, 1993). While a sense of school membership is the basis for educational engagement (Wehlage, Rutter, Smith, Lesko, & Fernandez, 1989), some students may dis-identify with student roles and academic expectations as early as the middle school years. Gang life may be their source of socialization and identity (Vigil, 1993). A "negative" identity, in comparison to community norms, could assure these adolescents more than a sense of having no identity at all. Even a culture of violence and drugs provides meaning to those who have not found it elsewhere. However, some more fortunate at-risk students may discover programs that build a positive identity in the schools, such as community service programs, or a teacher who builds bridges to a more promising vision of life.

On occasion, a student alienated from both home and school finds solace in reading. Such was the case for Robin, a high school dropout who became one of my credential students striving to become a teacher.

> By the time that I dropped out of school in the tenth grade, I had attended 6 high schools in 3 states. With the exception of one teacher, who had a profound impact on my life, virtually nothing that occurred within the walls of these schools influenced me in a significant manner. Throughout my formal education, I got to experience several different types of being "the Other." . . . Because we moved around so much, we put little effort into making a connection with our peers after the second or third grade. Then, in a classic case of being in the wrong place at the wrong time, my sibling and I got to enjoy the experience of being bused out of Boston (to school) in the mid-to-late 1970s.
>
> Ironically, I believe that riding buses may have had the most significant impact on the development of my personal literacies and my identity. I didn't realize it at the time, but those hours spent traveling to and from my dysfunctional, overcrowded home and the hostile environment of my school were the only real moments of peace and solitude that I had. How did I ever find peace and solitude on a crowded bus? I read.

Although attracted and attached to being a "nihilistic punk rocker," Robin read her way into "testing out new identities to replace the identity with which I was no longer comfortable." Her discovery of characters struggling with alienation and entrapment in stifling identities helped her find a voice to articulate her own dilemmas.

Self-Expectations and Self-Efficacy

Perceptions of ability and the expectations they trigger constitute major factors in current views of motivation. Expectations that shape students' behavior come in two main categories: self-expectations and teacher expectations. However, the expectations of teachers may become self-expectations, as Good and Brophy (2003) suggest.

Self-expectation. What a student expects of his or her own behavior or **self-expectation**, is often shaped by the expectations of others, especially teachers. Covington (1992) noted that students' personal expectations influence what they expect to achieve. That expectation, in turn, may be affected by the expectations of others, especially teachers in school settings.

It is critical for teachers to communicate positive beliefs and attributions to young learners. We know that children achieve at a higher level in classrooms where teachers expect all children to learn (Stipek, 2002). From studies of teachers and their students, we know a strong relationship exists between a teacher's beliefs about his or her own ability to teach students and the students' beliefs about their own abilities and chances for success (Midgley, Feldlaufer, & Eccles, 1989). Students who had high-efficacy teachers—teachers who were task oriented and believed their efforts would result in incremental student growth—became significantly more positive (or demonstrated less negative change) compared to students who had low-efficacy teachers and who developed more negative beliefs during the school year.

What we believe we are capable of doing or learning constitutes our **self-efficacy**. A student's self-efficacy predicts his or her motivation for engaging in reading (Schunk & Zimmermann, 1997). Accordingly, a student with high self-efficacy will work harder, longer, and more willingly than one with low self-efficacy. Bandura (1986) found that self-efficacy judgments influence not only what activities students will undertake or avoid but also the amount of effort and time that students will expend in the pursuit of the activity.

Source: CALVIN AND HOBBES © 1988 Watterson. Dist. By UNIVERSAL PRESS SYNDICATE. Reprinted with permission. All rights reserved.

Studies of self-efficacy are frequently linked to the attribution theory, which had its origins in the study of what people think causes behavior to occur (Schunk, 1994). A teacher like Ms. Hawthorne, who believes that continued effort will lead to student success, is more likely to design lessons that provide her students with knowledge of strategies and opportunities to apply and evaluate. Likewise, students who believe that effort applied over time will lead to incremental improvements in such things as reading and writing are likely to persist in mastering challenges.

Alderman (1999) suggests several methods for acknowledging students' competency and developing self-efficacy:

- When students do think-alouds, you can direct attention to effective strategies they use to comprehend texts.
- As a teacher, you can use think-alouds to model how you make sense of difficult passages in your textbook.
- After identifying peer models who use strategies effectively and persist in learning, you can ask these students how they figured out the meaning of a difficult

passage so that their problem-solving strategies become visible and, perhaps, can be emulated.

- You could also tell a story about how you solved or overcame a difficult reading and learning problem.

Motivating Reluctant Readers: Self- Expectations & Self-Efficacy

1. Ask students to describe what they believe they are good at in relation to your area of specialization.

2. Ask students to describe what kind of reader/writer they are.

3. Ask students to explain how they have learned best in the past.

4. Ask students to describe goals they have set for themselves in relation to the course you're teaching, including grades they would like to attain and content they would like to master.

5. Students could write letters to you sometime near the beginning of a course and periodically throughout the course to cover the first four points.

Self-efficacy can also be developed through goal setting and strategy instruction, both of which are discussed in this chapter.

Teacher expectations can become self-fulfilling. If a teacher expects certain behaviors from a student, his or her behavior is likely to influence how the student behaves. Good and Brophy (2003) created a model to describe the process whereby a teacher's expectation brings about the expected student behavior:

1. At the start of the school year, a teacher develops expectations for each child's behavior and achievement.

2. Based on expectations for each student, the teacher behaves differently with each.

3. The teacher's behavior communicates expectations about how each student is to behave and perform.

4. This treatment is likely to affect students' self-concept, achievement motivation, and goal setting.

5. The teacher's expectations will be reinforced when students begin to conform to the teacher's expectations.

6. Eventually, this process influences student motivation and performance. High expectations for students will motivate them to perform at or near their potential; low expectations for students will result in students not performing as well as they might have if they were expected to do better.

According to Good and Brophy, self-fulfilling prophecies created through a teacher's expectations occur if and only if each aspect of their model is present. If, for example, a student rejects or resists the teacher's expectations, then the model's predictions would fail. When teaching, Ms. Hawthorne tries to monitor the expectations she develops for her students. She notes how those expectations influence her behavior toward them and pays special attention to negative expectations that crop up, because they could adversely affect a student's motivation to achieve.

Goals and Task Values

Goals. Goals have both direction and intensity. The **direction of a goal** refers to its location in an instructional setting and the sequence of actions that need to take place to reach that goal. If Ms. Hawthorne's goal were to have all her students complete a reading assignment for homework, her students could take a number of different actions, such as taking the book home for study, that would help them reach the goal. If students resist Ms. Hawthorne's goal direction because they refuse to adopt the goal or because they have other goals that are more important to them, she is going to have a very long day.

Besides students' accepting the direction of the goal, they also need to be willing to work hard enough to attain the goal. A reader's **goal intensity**, the energy allocated for specific goal achievement, varies. Many factors affect goal intensity: the value placed on the goal, the difficulty of reaching the goal, the resources that can be activated to achieve the goal, the goal-seeker's level of self-confidence, and quite a few other factors that we'll look at later in this chapter. If students adopt the goal and are willing to make the effort needed to achieve it, Ms. Hawthorne is more likely to find significant satisfaction in her day's work.

If you value reading this text and understanding it, if you perceive the goal as within your reach, if you think you have the resources (such as background knowledge and reading skills) to achieve the goal, if you're feeling confident about your abilities in relation to the goal's attainment, then you are likely to be a motivated reader.

Do different goal orientations make a difference in student achievement? To answer that question, we'll first need to explore achievement goals and the difference between what motivational psychologists call mastery goals and performance goals. If a student asks himself or herself whether or not reading a book is leading toward becoming a more competent student or merely toward the demonstration of superior skills in comparison to his or her classmates, the student is, according to Nicholls (1984), questioning **achievement goals**. Achievement goal theory stresses the engagement of the learner in selecting, structuring, and making sense of achievement experience.

Meece (1994) points out that research has focused on two kinds of achievement goals: **mastery, learning, or task-oriented goals** and **performance or ego-oriented goals**. Those seeking learning goals are intrinsically motivated to acquire knowledge and skills that lead to their becoming more competent. Students seeking to master an understanding of DNA to satisfy their curiosity exemplifies learning goals. Those pursuing performance goals are eager to seek opportunities to demonstrate their skills or knowledge in a competitive, public arena. Students would show performance or ego-oriented goals if they were motivated to read their stories to their classmates primarily to show others their skills as storytellers.

Many researchers (Ames, 1992; Dweck & Leggett, 1988) believe that a learning or mastery goal orientation yields multiple benefits, including higher levels of interest, self-efficacy, persistence, and performance. They also believe that performance goal orientations, in contrast, generate fewer benefits in terms of motivation, strategy use, and outcome. This would be the case especially if students were concerned with performing only to outdo their classmates and had little concern for mastery.

But couldn't a student avoid performance opportunities as well as seek them? And couldn't that make a difference with regard to the impact of performance goals on behavior and learning? Several researchers (Elliot, 1997; Pintrich, 2000a, 2000b) have found evidence for different directions and intensities of motivation arising from what they call **approach performance goals** and **avoidance performance goals**. If students were focused on approach performance goals, they would want to perform in class to show others their skills, perhaps to show them off in order to impress their classmates with their accomplishments. If, however, students were focused on avoidance performance goals, they would attempt to avoid appearing incompetent, ignorant, or foolish. That avoidance orientation would most likely result in their avoiding opportunities to read their stories to classmates because they would fear their classmates' disapproval or disdain.

If students seek to do well in comparison to others and also embrace mastery goals, argues Pintrich (2000b), they would be adopting an orientation at least as healthy and productive as those students adopting only mastery goals. Researchers (Hidi & Harackiewicz, 2000) have found that students influenced by both perform-ance *and* mastery goals achieved at higher levels than students influenced by only one or the other goal orientation. These findings suggest that students' motivation to read and learn could be heightened through the positive interaction between mastery and performance goals. Learning about something that will help readers to master a valued task, such as designing an electric car, while demonstrating to friends how well they read can occur simultaneously among teenagers.

What might move a student toward one or the other orientation? Perceptions of personal ability constitute one critical factor influencing patterns of achievement (Meece, 1994). If students believe they can become better readers by making an ef-fort, they are more likely to embrace a mastery goal orientation. They see themselves as able to improve by degrees over time through making an effort to master chal-lenging tasks. Students who, over time, acquire knowledge and skills that lead to per-ceptions of incremental growth in competency illustrate a mastery orientation. Through making that effort to acquire knowledge and skills, the students' feelings of self-worth and competence are likely to increase.

Learners who adopt an ego or performance orientation see their abilities as more or less stable or fixed, and they judge them in comparison to others, such as their colleagues, peers, or classmates. If, for example, a student must make more of an effort, ego or performance-oriented learners judge that classmate as having less ability, given similar outcomes. Performance-oriented learners become preoccupied with ability and see it as basic to success in school performance. As an illustration, in a Calvin and Hobbes cartoon, Calvin (who appears to embrace performance goals) sees that Susie is hitting the books and asks her, "What are you doing? Homework?" To that question, a studious-looking Susie, who seeks to master knowledge, replies, "I wasn't sure I understood this chapter, so I reviewed my notes from the last chapter and now I'm rereading this." In response to Susie's mastery-oriented explanation, Calvin exclaims, "You do all that **work**?!" He then walks out of the cartoon box saying, "Huh! I used to think you were smart."

Among children, these goal orientations appear to arise, at least in part, because they internalize parental perspectives, especially the mother's view, of effort and ability in learning (Ames & Archer, 1987). But school learning environments have also been found to shape students' goal orientations. Teachers can encourage students to embrace mastery goals by creating environments that accentuate self-improvement, discovery, practicality, and engagement in meaningful tasks while diminishing the importance of competition, demonstration of intellectual skills, outperforming others, and public comparisons with others (Ames, 1992; Hagen & Weinstein, 1995). Influential teachers not only build task-oriented environments in their classrooms but also serve as models of learning to whom students can relate as they build their identities as students. Like beating the odds teachers we met in the first chapter of this book (J. A. Langer, 2001), these teachers provide challenging and meaningful learning goals that engage their students until they understand core concepts and are ready to apply them. Once their students master core concepts, these teachers extend understanding by showing students how newly conquered concepts are interconnected with other domains of knowledge, even across disciplines.

Here we again consider how teacher's expectations influence students, especially in relation to the teacher's degree of emphasis on task/mastery goals. When looking at the differences in students' strategy-use patterns in high- and low-mastery classes, Meece (1994) found significant differences between teachers' expectations for students. High- and low-mastery classes were identified by a questionnaire that determined students' degree of task/mastery goal orientation. In the high-mastery classes, where students wanted to master tasks and improve competence, teachers expected students to understand, apply, and make sense of their learning. However, in low-mastery classes students spent more time memorizing information and had few opportunities to actively construct meaning or apply their learning in new situations. Such examples illustrate how teachers' expectations can potentially shape students' literacy performance. Teachers can promote engagement in literacy by emphasizing a mastery orientation that stresses conceptual understanding, provides for collaborative learning, minimizes social competition, and allows students to participate in curricular decision making.

For example, at Foshay High School in Los Angeles, Myra LeBendig pushed for conceptual understanding through whole-class discussion (J. A. Langer, 2001). She taught her students how to work and learn in a community that depended upon discussion to exchange, explore, clarify, and shape ideas. She challenged students to understand works like Ellison's *Invisible Man* from multiple perspectives and to connect those perspectives with their own ethnicity and identity. As she taught for understanding, she urged her students to make sense of literary works they read and apply what they learned to their own lives.

Such examples illustrate how teachers' expectations can potentially shape students' literacy performance. However, as Hidi and Harackiewicz (2000) point out, teachers seeking to motivate the academically unmotivated need to recognize that mastery and performance goals interact and develop hand-in-hand over time. Students who lack mastery goals for academic success may need some forms of external intervention and reward on the road to developing sustained interests and task-directed goals.

Motivating Reluctant Readers: Goals & Task-Values

1. Anne Reeves (2004), in her exploration of adolescents' resistance to engagement with texts, found that students wanted to enter and engage in a character's world if they could identify with that character. Less experienced readers need help in seeing how a character's challenges connect to their own or how new knowledge contributes to their betterment. Prereading activities, such as presenting a puzzle or problem the reading will help solve, can tantalize readers. (See also Anticipation Guides, p. 182.)

2. Discover what your students like to learn, study, investigate, or even read about when no one is teaching them.

3. What is a profession or vocation your students believe is important to them or to our society? Why do they so believe?

4. In a position paper (see p. 231), ask your students early in the course to explain to you if they are more interested in earning a specific grade in your course or learning content of some kind. Ask for an explanation of their position.

Task Values.   Wigfield and his associates (Wigfield, 1994; Wigfield & Eccles, 1992) have identified and investigated a number of interacting components that make up an individual's perception of task values. These components include:

- attainment value (or the importance a learner attributes to a task),
- intrinsic interest value (or the task's subjective interest to a learner),
- utility value (or the usefulness of a task in light of a learner's future goals), and
- the cost of success (or the "downside" of accomplishing a task, such as anxiety arousal).

Meece, Wigfield, and Eccles (1990) investigated the connections between the subjective value adolescents place on various activities and the choices they make with regard to the activities. They found that students' task values predicted their actual decisions to take certain courses. This discovery suggests, he believes, that if students claim to value reading, there is a greater likelihood that they would engage in that activity. Most students usually weigh the value of a task, such as a reading assignment, before undertaking it. Their appraisal of its worth helps them answer the question, What will I get out of doing this specific reading task? When asked what they valued most in their reading and language arts classes, middle school students preferred free reading time the most (Ivey & Broaddus, 2001).

Motivating Reluctant Readers: Reading Skills & Knowledge

1. Using a Group Reading Inventory or Curriculum-Based Measurement and retellings that are described in chapter 4, "Assessing Students and Their Texts," measure your students' fluency and comprehension in relation to texts you plan to use in your course. Using these informal tools, you can discover which students are likely to struggle with texts you ask them to read and how you might provide support so that their chances of success improve.

2. Engage students in think-alouds to discover their reading strengths, challenges, and strategies. (See chapter 4.)

3. Ask students to complete the Metacognitive Awareness of Reading Strategies Inventory (MARSI). (See chapter 4.)

Reading Skills and Knowledge

Reading skills and knowledge refer to cognitive processes and resources that enable readers to undertake a reading task. These resources provide tools to accomplish the tasks for which readers are motivated. However, the equipment readers bring to bear on a reading task will affect motivation as well. How well the resources and tools work to enable readers to make sense of the texts they read influences their motivation to continue reading—and to enjoy it—or to stop.

In the next two chapters, we explore in depth the reader's text-processing resources and how to assess a student's reading skills and knowledge.

Textual Connections

Interesting Texts.   Guthrie and Wigfield (2000) define interesting texts as "single-authored works in which the text matches the topic interest and cognitive competency of the reader." As bees with flowers, so are students with interesting books: there's more buzz. Students spend more time reading interesting texts than uninteresting ones. Furthermore, in a study of high school students, topic interest was positively related to quality of experience during reading and to quality of text learning (Schiefele, 1996). One of the hallmarks of successful Sustained Silent Reading programs is access to an abundance of high-interest books in classrooms (Pilgreen, 2000). By surveying students about their reading interests, more books with appeal can join classroom and school libraries. Matching texts to both students' interests and reading levels, as is done with programs like Reading Counts!, also promotes their motivation to read.

However, there are different kinds of interest. Patricia Alexander (2003) points out that, when readers' needs or desires are energized, heightened energy may be *individual* or *situational*. If the interest is individual, as is mine with respect to the topic of content literacy, then the reader's long-term investment and involvement in the target field is engaged (Hidi, 1990). If, however, the interest is situational, as when a student in a biology class becomes fascinated by metamorphosis, then the reader's interest is momentary and attention is temporary. Something in the context of the text has trigged that situational interest, but it's not likely to last. Over time, as readers develop greater proficiency, situational interest plays a smaller role and individual interest takes on a much larger one. That's usually because readers engaged by individual interests are far more intrinsically motivated and bring internal enthusiasm, even passion, to reading tasks. Alexander believes that those readers who become more competent and move toward proficiency must connect with written language.

Intrinsic "Flow" State.   If you have ever been completely absorbed or consumed by a sporting activity, such as tennis, or by playing a musical instrument, you have experienced the *flow* of intrinsic motivation. According to Csikszentmihalyi (1990a, 1990b), motivation is closely related to **autotelic experiences** that are self-contained and self-rewarding. Autotelic experiences are pursued for their intrinsic worth or enjoyment, not for any future purpose or goal.

When readers experience a sense of flow while reading, they are enjoying the reading process as a self-justifying event. To experience this intrinsically rewarding flow while reading, readers must attain a balance between reading challenge and reading ability. Many students have experienced frustration when trying to read books that were too difficult for them to enjoy on their own. Many have been very bored when trying to read texts that were too simplistic for them or of no interest. If students can discover an optimal balance between challenge and ability, they are likely to enter and enjoy more fully the flow of reading (Csikszentmihalyi, 1990b).

Ms. Hawthorne knows that reading she assigns in her course does not always evoke flow experience for her students. However, she mixes into her curriculum opportunities to read engaging historical narratives, biographies, or other informative texts more likely to consume students' attention and heighten their enthusiasm. She watches for moments in the present when she can bring to her students' awareness the intrinsic pleasure of reading and reliving moments in the past.

Stance.   In literacy studies, **stance** pertains to the perspective and orientation that a reader adopts toward a particular text. By guiding the reader's perspective and purpose, instructional stance influences a reader's motivation to read. Rosenblatt (1978) strongly influenced the field with her identification and elaboration of two stances: efferent and aesthetic. When adopting the **efferent stance**, the reader concentrates on ideas and concepts to be taken away from a text. When taking an **aesthetic stance**, the reader enters the text world through imagination and feeling so that attention is on what the reader is living through while engaged in reading rather than on gathering information. When reading stories about people in times past, students can adopt an aesthetic stance and enter the "old-fashioned" world created in their imaginations. Readers are more likely to experience the intrinsic enjoyment of flow and a deeper engagement with a text during aesthetic readings that draw readers into narrative and imagery.

These are not either-or stances; rather, they are on a continuum along which the degree of emphasis may change. To varying degrees, the reader can control stance. While progressing through a text, the teacher may encourage an instructional stance

Motivating Reluctant Readers: Textual Connections

1. Ask students to report (in writing or orally) their three most important books and why they are important.

2. Ask students to describe a flow-state experience they have had when reading.

3. Design reading assignments as opportunites for inquiry and discovery that connect with students' interests.

4. Students want quick connections. They've become used to pressing buttons to instantly change channels, phone lines, Web sites, and tunes. They don't want to wait for a plot to develop or an idea to eventually have value for them. Whatever we can do to show connections early on will contribute to their interest in reading.

5. Ask students to describe an efferent and aesthetic stance experience related to a book or story they have read.

6. Be alert for opportunites to stimulate and build on students' interests by providing interest-related readings.

that guides readers toward an aesthetic or efferent engagement or an integration of both. For example, Ms. Hawthorne could ask her students to read *The Red Badge of Courage,* a novel by Stephen Crane about the American Civil War. When reading about the young soldier's first tastes of war, she could encourage students to take an aesthetic stance by focusing on the sound and sense of bullets and smoke, the images of wide-eyed soldiers slumbering in death, and the horror aroused against Nature's serene backdrop. Later, when shifting to an efferent stance and analyzing what the author did to create the panorama of battle, Ms. Hawthorne could focus her students' attention on the writer's techniques and the imagery he painted into the battlefield to convey a vivid sense of war's destruction and devastation. According to Rosenblatt (1985), teachers favor that more efferent, analytic stance at the expense of aesthetic readings. Such teachers expect students to analyze texts rather than urging students to live through the experiences depicted in the literature they read. That overemphasis on efferent readings may, in some instances, reduce the value and enjoyment that students have when reading. However, an emphasis on efferent responses may help students develop analytical skills that build critical thinking.

Teacher Factors Contributing to Students' Motivation to Read

As we've already seen, you can do several things to influence your students' motivation to read and engage in learning. Perhaps you can't transform all the traits and habits forming your students' identities so that they identify with school, see value in all its aspects, and align their goals with your daily curriculum. But you can discover what those identities are, what values your students hold, what aspiration they hold, and what reading skills they have to pursue their studies. Over time, you can affect their expectations and their self-efficacy. In many instances, you can exercise control over the texts your students read or even choose to read. These factors that you might influence are very important.

We turn next to motivational factors over which you usually have more control. These factors include teacher engagement, your achievement-related instructional program, the classroom community, the autonomy support you can provide for your students, and your assessment and reward system.

Teacher Engagement

Your students have an identity that affects their learning; so too do you have an identity that influences your motivation to teach. How you see yourself functioning as a teacher, what commitments you hold, and what beliefs guide your practice will strongly affect how engaged you are as a teacher and the kinds of interactions you have with your students. You may not enjoy complete control over all the elements of your identity, but you probably have control over some.

We know that teachers can be influential. How they influence their students depends upon who they are and how they engage in their work as teachers. Because responsive, reflective teaching of literacy does not occur without a responsive, reflective teacher, we'll explore the characteristics that such teachers bring to teaching. From the study of influential teachers, their behavior in the classroom, and their impact on students (R. B. Ruddell, 1994, 1995; R. B. Ruddell, Draheim, & Barnes, 1990; R. B. Ruddell & Haggard, 1982), we can garner insights into responsive teachers as well as ways they promote literacy engagement.

Influential teachers are teachers who have a significant impact on a student's academic or personal success in school. From studies of influential teachers, we know that they share characteristics in several areas that include the following:

- They show that they care about their students.
- They manifest excitement and enthusiasm about what they teach.
- They adapt instruction to the individual needs, motives, interests, and aptitudes of their students while having high expectations for them.
- They use motivating and effective strategies when they teach, including clarity in stating problems, use of concrete examples, analysis of abstract concepts, and application of concepts to new contexts.
- They engage students in a process of intellectual discovery.
- They help their students understand and solve their personal and academic problems.

High-achieving students, those more motivated for learning, can identify at least twice as many influential teachers as their lower achieving counterparts. When I ask my students who are seeking their teaching credentials to talk about their influential teachers, I frequently discover they have had at least one or more, sometimes within their own families. Whether high or low achieving, students see their influential teachers as having clear instructional goals, plans, and strategies that contribute to a learning environment closely monitored by the teacher (R. B. Ruddell, 1994, 1995). Furthermore, these influential teachers elicit students' internal motivation by stimulating intellectual curiosity, exploring their students' self-understanding, and focusing on problem solving.

The pattern of engagement demonstrated by the influential teachers that Ruddell studied also appears in a study of secondary science teachers. John Eichinger (1997) found that, as successful college science students looked back on their middle and high school science teachers, those students identified many features in the characteristics and methods of their teachers that reflected the "influential teacher" pattern. Successful science students perceived their influential teachers to be knowledgeable, enthusiastic, and effective communicators who were committed, friendly, competent, and creative. By the way, nonscience majors looking back on their secondary school science instruction were especially appreciative of their more patient and caring science teachers.

A study of the effects of teacher engagement on the achievement and motivation of 10th graders generated findings important to our discussion. Knowles (1999) outlines four important elements of teacher engagement:

1. pedagogical knowledge in the content area,
2. pedagogical knowledge about student motivation,
3. teachers' intrinsic motivation toward teaching, and
4. teachers' self-efficacy toward teaching.

She found that teachers' engagement predicted tenth-grade student achievement and motivation. Her finding suggests that, if we want to positively influence our students' achievement and motivation, we might give serious thought to building our knowledge of student motivation, increasing knowledge of our subject, and cultivating our own motivation to teach.

Evidence indicates that problems with student learning are tied to teacher detachment and alienation from their work. These are teachers who, at the end of a school year, hardly know their students' names. Most students find learning in these teachers' classrooms an uphill grind. Fortunately, communities with lower social and economic status often have schools with involved and caring teachers. When looking into schools with engaged teachers serving disadvantaged students, Louis and Smith (1992) found four types of teacher engagement:

1. engagement with the whole school as a social unit,
2. engagement with students as unique individuals,
3. engagement in the academic achievement of students and colleagues, and
4. engagement with the teacher's own subject.

Motivating Reluctant Readers: Teacher Engagement

1. Strive to realize the first proposition of the National Board for Professional Teaching Standards: commitment to students and their learning.
2. Reflect on your practice as a teacher to identify moments or episodes of teaching in which you manifested characteristics found among influential teachers, such as excitement and enthusiasm about your teaching, caring for students, and adapting instruction in response to students' individual needs, interests, and aptitudes.

They focused their inquiry on how these forms of teacher engagement can be reinforced. With respect to teacher culture, they found several elements that positively affected teacher engagement: a strong sense of participating in a school with a common mission, an emphasis on closeness and helpfulness among colleagues, and a demand for active problem solving among fellow teachers. With respect to school leadership, they found a style that promoted engagement: Principals delegated to and empowered teachers, spent time on daily routines, buffered teachers to reduce distractions from teaching, and confronted unengaged teachers. Louis and Smith (1992) found that teachers in schools promoting teacher engagement worked to realize their instructional goals and student achievement; however, they had access to supportive social structures within their schools to carry them through episodes of frustration and disenchantment. Many of these features also occurred in "beating the odds" classrooms that J. A. Langer (2000, 2001) investigated and that I explore in the first chapter of this book.

Evidence for the reciprocal effects of teacher behavior and student engagement have also been found (Skinner & Belmont, 1993). Researchers discovered that, while students who showed higher initial engagement got more engaged responses from their teachers, those students who were less engaged or disengaged received fewer such responses, perhaps undermining their motivation further. Perhaps the rich do get richer, at least as far as support for motivation in classrooms goes.

Achievement-Related Instruction

Learning Over Performance. As we saw when looking at the kinds of goals that drive student achievement, a learning or mastery goal orientation has a number of distinct advantages over a performance orientation. This includes the fostering of long-term achievement through belief in incremental improvement through effort (Ames, 1992; Meece, 1994). So, in designing lessons, a learning goal orientation might guide

Figure 2.2 Strategies to Enhance Students' Self-Efficacy.

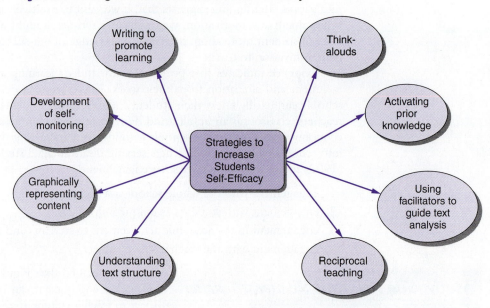

your curricular and instructional decisions. Even though your students may themselves prefer performance (or ego-oriented) goals and glorify ability, you can set up instruction to emphasize effortful mastery of knowledge and skills rather than their public display for personal status gains. All the instructional elements, including strategy instruction, authentic instruction, and an emphasis on higher-order thinking, that we are about to review have been shown to augment students' engagement. Furthermore, they can all enhance a learning goal orientation.

Strategy Instruction.   Integrating strategic instruction with content area reading can positively influence your students' motivation (Guthrie, Wigfield, & VonSecker, 2000; Shuell, 1996). As Guthrie and Wigfield (2000) point out, **strategy instruction** includes a teacher's direct instruction, scaffolding, and guided practice when students are reading to learn. Because success in reading assignments encourages engagement and strategies promote success, strategy instruction is both empowering and motivating. However, because many reading strategies are not easily internalized, they take time and perseverance to acquire. Students must also learn when specific strategies are best applied. Several strategies shown in Figure 2.2 and others described in this text (chapters 5 through 11) are designed to increase students' self-efficacy.

Authentic Work.   **Authentic work** has been defined as "tasks that are considered meaningful, valuable, significant, and worthy of one's effort" (Newmann, Wehlage, & Lamborn, 1992). That is in contrast to "busy work," as students call tasks they consider trivial, meaningless, or useless. Authentic work is more likely to engage students and promote achievement because it leads to "socially valued outcomes," such as a brochure informing community residents of public health resources or 10th graders tutoring struggling readers in the third grade (Wehlage et al., 1989). In part, authentic work engages students because of its connection with the real world. In undertaking authentic tasks, students often work with others, both in school and out, to accomplish learning goals. They get quick, clear evidence of success or the need to revise what they're doing, and they believe that the tasks they are undertaking have value beyond the immediate classroom.

Classroom instruction that consists of real-life cognitive activities rather than artificial activities will challenge even the most creative and resourceful of teachers. The challenge may be overwhelming in communities feeling the pressure of accountability through standardized testing. However, secondary teachers use hands-on activities to motivate their students. Science students in Eichinger's study (1997) preferred active, participatory, and student-centered instruction, such as labs and projects, over more traditional methods, such as textbooks, lectures, memorization, and worksheets. A middle school science teacher I observed creatively engaged his students in a moon explorer simulation program using robotic rovers to map the moon's surface. Such hands-on science curriculum with embedded literacy strategy instruction could increase reading comprehension, strategy use, and problem solving (Guthrie, Van Meter, McCann, Anderson, & Alao, 1998). History teachers, like Ms. Hawthorne, can also use role-playing of historical characters and events, projects creating useful products, current events that connect with their students' lives, and artifacts from historical sites to make inferences about a community's agriculture and culture (Hootstein, 1995).

Higher-Order Thinking. Throughout her middle and high school years, I periodically asked my daughter about the best question she heard in school on a particular day. Most of the time she reported that no one asked a question, and teachers neither asked for questions nor provided time to hear them. On some occasions, she said her teachers told students to "listen up" and hold down their questions. Answers, presumably, would come through the day's lecture. In "Taking Students Seriously," Gamoran and Nystrand (1992) report that, in most of the 54 English classrooms they studied, teachers delivered information, defined learning as information recall, and played the role of examiner. There were few occasions of high-quality discourse in which teachers helped students explore their ideas and thoughts, interpret literature, or argue for their point of view—just the kinds of things these authors believe teachers must do if they are to take students seriously as thinkers.

But what evidence do we have that challenging students to think will lead to deeper levels of student engagement? Newmann (1992b) and his associates watched about 500 social studies classes and interviewed teachers, department chairs, and principals in 16 high schools. He found significant correlations between the level of engagement and both the levels of student thoughtfulness and students' sense of being challenged. The results convinced him that students are "more likely to try, to concentrate, and to be interested in academic study when they are challenged to think." If you wanted to imitate teachers in the most thoughtful classrooms in his study, you would identify student thinking as your highest priority and view the development of your students' thinking as more important than delivering subject area content, because that is what Newmann found that teachers in those classrooms did. All the social studies teachers in one school that emphasized the development of thinking began classes by posing a

Motivating Reluctant Readers: Achievement-Related Instruction

1. Explore, practice, and reflect upon mastery-oriented instruction.

2. Teach strategies, such as reciprocal teaching, that students can internalize for deeper processing of texts.

3. Facilitate real-world connections, such as activities in which students see how the content of their learning applies to problems in their own lives and the life of their community.

4. Encourage and challenge students to engage in higher-order thinking, such as analysis of issues and problems, synthesizing information from multiple sources, and evaluating solutions to significant problems.

central question to focus student inquiry and structured class discussion to answer that question. Strategies useful for promoting higher order and critical thinking in content area classrooms are presented in several chapters of this book, especially chapter 8.

In spite of our knowledge that challenging students to understand concepts yields higher levels of engagement, there are barriers to conducting content area classrooms where promotion of thinking takes a high priority. Teachers may need support to pursue thoughtful classrooms in schools (Tishman, Perkins, & Jay, 1995; Unrau, 1997).

Classroom Community

The power of the classroom social climate to engage or disengage students should not be underestimated. A classroom community that nurtures inclusion, invites inquiry, and supports challenging learning can heighten students' motivation, perhaps even keep them in school. When Wehlage et al. (1989) studied schools that had a successful track record with at-risk students, they found one common factor among all the schools: social bonds connecting students to their school. When a student's sense of identity is affirmed in schools and classrooms, the student will feel more of a member of the group (Alderman, 1999). But social identification with a group does not mean the student will automatically work hard to achieve your learning goals. In fact, like Ms. Hawthorne, you may face just the opposite, a culture of antiachievement or nonachievement. However, Brown (1993) urges teachers to cultivate a positive peer culture to enhance academic motivation by:

1. becoming aware of peer group structures and value systems, including the risks to students of "acting White" or becoming a "home boy," without stereotyping students. Students may be concerned about the loss of their cultural and social identity if they adapt to the school's performance expectation;
2. avoiding a grading or tracking system that labels winners and loser; and
3. enhancing the value of academic achievement.

There are other steps you can take to promote literacy engagement by building on students' need for social interaction and bonding in classrooms. These include developing variety in instructional methods, using cooperative learning, engaging students in meaningful negotiation, and adopting the practices of culturally responsive teachers.

Variety in Instructional Methods.   Paris, Wasik, and Turner (1991) advocate *multidimensional* classrooms, in which teachers provide students with meaningful literacy tasks, use a variety of instructional approaches, and make opportunities for success available to all. A variety of tasks motivated students in classrooms, offered students different forms of cognitive engagement, and required them to apply different strategies for completion. Different methods of instruction also afforded more students opportunities to participate, achieve, and gain recognition.

Cooperative Groups.   Many cooperative learning techniques build classroom communities. These cooperative learning methods promote social bonding, improve intergroup relations, enhance motivation, and heighten achievement (Slavin, 1995). Specific strategies covered in chapter 9 include Numbered Heads Together, Think-Pair-Share, Group Investigation, Group Reading Activity, and Jigsaw. When designing group activities, remember to build in both some form of group recognition or reward and individual accountability. Reciprocal teaching, though not originally designed as a cooperative learning activity, also promotes team building, while at the same time helping students develop reading strategies such as summarizing, predicting, and questioning.

Reader Response Groups.   Some teachers use the principles of cooperative learning (Slavin, 1995; Slavin, Madden, Karweit, Dolan, & Wasik, 1994) to design **reader response groups** in English classes. The teacher delegates authority to each group that in turn has to delegate authority to each group member. In mixed-ability groups, members share responsibilities for learning, get a group grade, and are individually accountable for their learning and contributions. Reader response groups can be structured so that each team reads a different book that the teacher selects based on each team's interests. If a teacher knew that several of his or her students were interested in history, the teacher could put them in a cooperative team to read historical novels focused on a specific event, such as the American Civil War.

> ## Motivating Reluctant Readers: Classroom Community
>
> 1. Focus on choices that further the development of a positive peer culture.
> 2. Vary strategies, tempo, and climate in the classroom.
> 3. Explore cooperative learning techniques and their effects on your students and your students' learning.
> 4. Discuss meanings of texts and problem-solving strategies and procedures within a classroom context.

Collaborative Meaning Making.   The factors, involving both the student and the teacher, that influence a reader's focus on motivation and achievement also affect the making of meaning during discussion of texts in classroom contexts. Those factors form the foundation not only for the meanings that individual readers construct, but also for meanings developed and discussed between individuals during reader-based instruction in classroom contexts. In addition, the design and function of the classroom learning environment further affect motivation to engage in literacy events and learning (Marshall, 1992; Unrau & Ruddell, 1995). (I explain this classroom negotiation process in chapter 3.) We can expect readers to engage with reading, interact in the classroom community, and participate in discussions to construct meanings if they are motivated to read and to learn, if prior knowledge is activated, if tasks are personally relevant, and if they are encouraged to actively make meanings. As mentioned, the teacher who incorporates features like these is considered to be mastery-goal oriented and is more likely to witness productive learning among students (Ames, 1992; Covington, 1992).

Negotiating meanings of texts through interaction in classrooms will help your students deepen their engagement and motivation. You can provide activities, such as reader response logs, reading or dialogue journals, and whole-class discussions of text interpretations, that enable your students to shape and share meanings. Sharing those meanings enables them to participate in the evolution of an interpretive community.

Culture Pluralism and Inclusion.   When building communities in multicultural classrooms, Ginsberg and Wlodkowski (2000) cite four interacting motivational elements that culturally responsive teachers and their students continually re-create:

1. *Establishing inclusion.* Teachers exercise principles and practices that create a climate in which teacher and students feel respected and connected.
2. *Developing a positive attitude.* Teachers apply principles and practices that contribute to a "favorable disposition toward learning."
3. *Enhancing meaning.* Teachers design instruction that results in both challenging and engaging learning.
4. *Engendering competence.* Teachers employ principles and practices that engage students in learning what they value.

Autonomy Support

Autonomy is our capacity to make independent decisions, have our actions arise from within ourselves, and feel that those actions are our own rather than arising from some external source (Deci & Ryan, 1985). When students are autonomously motivated, they report that the cause for their actions comes from within themselves and sense they have a choice over those actions (Reeve, Jang, Carrell, Jeon, & Barch, 2004). They feel free during the self-chosen activities and are able to make decisions about when, how, and whether to pursue them. Inflexible, externally controlled assignments exemplify the flip side of autonomy.

Autonomy support occurs when a teacher nurtures a student's internally centered, freely chosen actions. That nurturing may take many forms in school settings. It occurs when teachers ask students what or how they want to learn. Whenever teachers find ways to identify and increase their students' internally initiated acts of learning, whether those acts entail a choice over curriculum or the independence to ask and answer their own questions, they are engaged in autonomy support (Reeve & Jang, 2006; Stefanou, Perenceivich, DiCintio, & Turner, 2004).

Researchers (Reeve et al., 2004) interested in the effects of autonomy support trained high school teachers across content areas to nurture student interest, provide rationales for assignments, and use noncontrolling language. The more teachers used autonomy support during instruction, the more their students were engaged (Reeve & Jang, 2006). Evidence suggests that literacy programs emphasizing autonomy support, including a wide range of choices in learning opportunities, can promote intrinsic motivation, conceptual understanding, and perceived confidence, all of which enable students to engage more deeply in the development of their literacies (Stefanou et al., 2004).

While providing choice may be motivating, teachers have a curriculum to teach that's probably based on state standards. As Alderman (1999) points out, you can give students opportunities to exercise control over certain domains, but you need not give them unlimited control. You can set boundaries, expectations, and responsibilities. But, depending on your students' degree of maturity, you can support their autonomy as they pursue learning goals. For those with low levels of maturity, you may need to use more structure, including goals, directions, frequent monitoring, and feedback with corrections. For these students, you may need to develop an in-class library of books and resources for students rather than opening their choices to a local or regional library. For students with high maturity levels, you may not need to provide much guidance because students will come to you when they need help. These students are more likely to visit a large regional library to select books and resources but ask you if they are good choices for them and their projects. Teachers can exercise autonomy support by using projects in social studies classes or inquiry-oriented science labs. In these settings, students are freer to set their own goals and work toward their achievement independently (Ames & Ames, 1996).

Motivating Reluctant Readers: Autonomy Support

1. Design an environment that intentionally builds student autonomy by providing choices in content and methods of learning, both of which are quite possible within a standards-driven curriculum. Self-selections are often incentives for self-determined, self-regulating growth.

2. Develop an atmosphere in which students see the acquisition of knowledge, skills, and strategies as incremental and issuing from effort that becomes increasingly self-regulated.

3. Provide explanations to students so they know why they have been asked to read particular books or learn strategies to master content in those books.

4. Offer hints to students rather than giving them explicit answers to questions they ask about their reading and course content.

5. Encourage students to generate their own questions about their reading rather than answering only your questions.

6. Acknowledge your students' perspectives even though they may differ from your own.

7. Strive to develop a classroom climate in which students can safely explain their own thinking to each other.

Although the curriculum may not always allow teachers to let students select what they want to read, engage in science inquiry, or investigate topics in history as their interests dictate, Atwell (1998) found in her reading workshop approach that her students read more if they were given ample choices of interesting books. Opportunities for self-selection are incentives for literacy growth (Gambrell & Marinak, 1997). In a survey of what makes students want to read in middle school classrooms, Ivey and Broaddus (2001) found that students were motivated by discovering good reading materials and having freedom of choice over which they could read. However, just more choice over what is read may not be enough to ignite internal, self-driven motivation. A more powerful form of autonomy support would encourage independent thinking. When students read texts, develop their own interpretations about what they've read, and engage in discussions that challenge those interpretations so that they explore and explain their thinking in supportive climates, then we have provided a more vital arena for the growth of cognitive autonomy (Stefanou et al., 2004).

Assessment and Reward Systems

Assessment and reward systems, depending on how they are designed and implemented, can have a wide range of effects on students' motivation for reading and engagement in learning. An assessment system that is diagnostically oriented, such as one measuring students' fluency, comprehension skills, and metacognitive knowledge, can provide teachers with useful information about their students' reading abilities. That information can then be used to design instruction that strengthens students' skills, builds their knowledge, and improves their motivation. A diagnostically oriented assessment program could lead to instruction that increases students' beliefs in their ability to take on reading tasks and complete them successfully. With growth in self-efficacy for reading tasks, students are more likely to engage in reading. For struggling readers, that growth in self-efficacy is especially important.

Unfortunately, some reading assessment programs do not produce information that teachers can use directly to evaluate their students' immediate literacy needs for instruction. Norm-referenced tests that give information about a student's percentile or grade-level reading score can help teachers make gross evaluations of students' reading abilities but tell little about how to address development. However, many states place students into categories based on their reading performance, such as proficient, basic, and below basic, and provide recommendations for the kinds of books that could foster growth in reading.

To implement an assessment program based on motivation principles, Mac Iver (1993) designed a system that encouraged a mastery-focused orientation emphasizing learning goals, that gave equal opportunities for students of differing abilities to succeed, and that required strategic efforts for success. The system consisted of setting a base score and then giving students the goal of increasing their base scores by several points. If the students met their specific goals, they would get improvement points. Students who raised their performance level received official recognition. Slavin (1980, 1995) developed a similar system called Individual Learning Expectations (ILE), which recognized students for their improvement. Slavin found that, in comparison to traditional grading, ILE significantly increased student achievement.

Just as assessment programs can impact students' motivation in a variety of ways, rewards can also affect students' motivation differently. Rewards for reading come in many forms, even get-out-of-homework-free cards. Teachers have an armory of techniques to reward student's reading performance, including fast-food meals, pizza, money, and books (Gambrell & Marinak, 1997). However, teachers usually view grades as one of their most potent incentives to induce student reading and learning.

When reading for school courses carries little inherent interest or value for students, extrinsic incentives become important as motives for learning. Based on the weight middle school students give to grades on the Motivation for Reading Questionnaire (Baker & Wigfield, 1999), they are very powerful motivators. Of 10 clusters influencing motivation to read, including curiosity, challenge, recognition, and compliance, no cluster contributing to reading motivation was given more weight than grades.

To evaluate the impact of a Sustained Silent Reading program on students in a Los Angeles middle school, I surveyed more than 1,600 students and found that slightly more than 75% thought that getting a letter grade for SSR time would make them work harder at it. Ironically, SSR is intended to build intrinsic motivation by providing students with choice and time to read whatever they might enjoy, so teachers were quite reluctant to provide students with the grade incentives that students apparently thought would get them to read more.

Although teachers frequently use extrinsic incentives, some educators have voiced concerns that students may be adversely affected by reward systems. They argue that students may be "punished by rewards" that undermine their inherent or intrinsic motivation to learn (Kohn, 1993). Some researchers have expressed the concern that, if students who simply enjoy reading are given pizza or money for doing it, their intrinsic motivation will diminish, especially when the rewards are withdrawn (Deci, Vallerand, Pelletier, & Ryan, 1991).

While some studies indicate that tangible incentives can undermine intrinsic motivation (Deci, 1971), other studies show that tangible incentives can enhance it (Lepper, Greene, & Nisbett, 1973). Incentives appear to be particularly potent when participants' levels of interest are initially low and the activity does not become attractive until some time has been put into it or some degree of mastery is attained. Gambrell and Marinak (1997) emphasize that, in general, findings point to the key roles played by the kind of incentive provided and the kind of reader to whom it is given. Giving rewards for a task that students are already intrinsically motivated to undertake, such as fast-food coupons to good readers, may undermine inherent interest in the task. But important and relevant rewards given to weakly motivated readers may heighten their motivation to read. In time, these incentives can be withdrawn as students become more interested and competent in the activity (Stipek, 2002).

Extrinsic incentives in the form of direct praise or feedback to students about their reading have been found to enhance student performance. Upon review of 96 experimental studies, Cameron and Pierce (1994) found evidence that would support the following principles related to intrinsic motivation:

- Intrinsic motivation increases through verbal praise and positive feedback because they communicate useful information to the reader.
- Intrinsic motivation is not undermined through tangible incentives if they are given when students complete a task according to set standards.

Gambrell (1996; Gambrell & Marinak, 1997) points out the importance of a close link between the incentive and the behavior. Her "reward proximity hypothesis" states that, when incentives are linked to desired behavior, intrinsic motivation is enhanced. According to the hypothesis, if you want to build your students' intrinsic motivation to read, you would provide incentives clearly linked to reading behavior, such as books or more reading time.

Consistent with self-determination theory (SDT), student academic reading is probably driven by a blending of intrinsic and extrinsic motivation (Deci & Ryan, 1985; Lepper & Henderlong, 2000; Ryan & Deci, 2000). Although extrinsic motives or reward systems, such as grades, may heighten students' perceptions that their actions are controlled externally, not all forms of extrinsic motivation lead inevitably to the undermining of intrinsic motivation. Some forms of extrinsic motivation may become internalized and "owned" by the student. According to SDT, extrinsic motivation can take four different forms, ranging from motivation in people who are less self-determined to motivation in those who are potentially high in self-determination. The perceived centers motivating an action include (a) external regulation (least autonomous), (b) introjected regulation (motive and associated behavior not fully embraced as one's own), (c) identified regulation (valuing of a goal or regulation and associated behavior as personally important), and (d) integrated regulation (most autonomous extrinsic motivation that is fully assimilated into the self and one's own values but not inherently enjoyed). The last two forms of extrinsic motivation, identified and integrated regulation, are most likely to become adopted by young readers as inherently meaningful or valuable. Many students internalize getting good grades as a personally meaningful and valuable pursuit.

The magnitude of extrinsic and intrinsic motivation may also differ, as when students' curiosity about the roots of our Civil War is more important than their getting a good grade on an essay that describes the evolution of the war. Not only does the magnitude of different kinds of motivation vary at any given time, magnitudes of motivation change over time. Students' motivation to get a passing grade on today's unit exam covering World War II may be overshadowed tomorrow by their desire for an A on a paper they wrote about the sacrifices and suffering that families endured during the conflict.

Summary

In summary, we can see clearly the centrality of motivation to our work with students, of our understanding motivation's many dimensions, and of our capacity to use that understanding to deepen student engagement with reading and learning. As we strive to create engaging communities in classrooms, we benefit from knowledge of motivational factors that students bring with them and from heightened awareness of factors we as teachers contribute and control. In this chapter, we also discovered an array of strategies both to understand and to intensify our students' motivation to read and their engagement with learning in our classrooms and beyond.

Double-Entry Journal: After Reading

Having read this chapter, review the goals and reasons you initially wrote down for reading it. What goals and reasons in your prereading DEJ fit the motivational factors identified and explained in this chapter? Are there additional motivational factors that were brought to mind by reading this chapter that you would now add to your prereading list? Were any factors on your initial list not mentioned in the chapter? When designing instruction to promote literacy in your content area, what three or four motivational factors would you consider most important? Why do you think those factors are more important than others reviewed in the chapter?

Activity Box: Ms. Hawthorne's Dilemma

Ms. Hawthorne was discontented with the social studies program she found when she came to Jefferson Middle School 2 years ago. During her first year, she discovered that some of her eighth-grade students did read and complete tasks she assigned, but too many did so halfheartedly, infrequently, or not at all. The curriculum seemed unresponsive, impersonal, and unengaging. She knew that she and they could do better. With the encouragement of a couple of colleagues, a new principal, and faculty at a local university, she decided to investigate what she might do to redesign her program so that more students would become engaged.

She began her action research by collecting as much information as she could about her students to discover what made them tick—not only as readers but also as people. To get to know individual students better, to understand their motivation and their reading strategies, Ms. Hawthorne decided to conduct a few tutorials once a week after school.

On the day she made her announcement about the possibility of a tutorial with her, several students responded. One student, Cynthia, jumped at the opportunity.

At the beginning of the school year, Ms. Hawthorne got the impression that Cynthia was a slightly hyperactive "social butterfly." But, as she got to know Cynthia during the tutorial meetings, she discovered far more complexity. The enthusiasm that Cynthia expressed when Ms. Hawthorne offered tutorial help demonstrated some aspects of Cynthia's sense of self and her complex motivation to learn. At her initial tutoring session, Cynthia told Ms. Hawthorne that she had good memories about school. She said she liked it because she had lots of opportunities to socialize with her friends. Both her parents helped her with schoolwork, her mother in reading and writing and her father in math. In earlier elementary grades, Cynthia was often on the honor role. Like her mother, Cynthia was thinking about becoming a nurse, but she also imagined herself being a story writer, a travel agent, a model, and a fashion designer. She was obviously exploring possibilities for herself.

Cynthia said her favorite subject was history, and she had a passion for books about "old-fashion" family life and orphans. She told Ms. Hawthorne that she had lots of these stories in her head and would much rather write them than complete assignments. During their first meeting together, Cynthia told Ms. Hawthorne that two of her goals for the year were to improve her reading and to reduce the number of mistakes she made in her writing.

To get an idea of Cynthia's reading achievement, Ms. Hawthorne administered an Informal Reading Inventory. She found that Cynthia had an independent reading level of fourth grade, an instructional level of fifth grade, and a frustration level of sixth grade. She also discovered that Cynthia, who said that she understood the text that she had read, was unable to answer many literal and interpretive-level questions about that text. After the assessment, Cynthia complained to Ms. Hawthorne that the last paragraph on the test, one at the eighth-grade level, was unfair because there were words in it that she didn't recognize. During the assessment and later in the tutorial, Ms. Hawthorne found that Cynthia had difficulty comprehending what she read and connecting concepts to make meaning. Ms. Hawthorne also observed that Cynthia would give up easily with text she had difficulty understanding and would express boredom or self-defeat rather than increased effort.

Ms. Hawthorne was impressed with Cynthia's "zest for writing." She could construct concept maps or outlines and finish a five-paragraph essay in one period. However, Ms. Hawthorne discovered that Cynthia would often misplace her essays before turning them in. Furthermore, Ms. Hawthorne thought that Cynthia's writing was rudimentary in content and structure. In an essay containing paragraphs with four or five simple sentences, she would just restate the assignment and discuss only the most obvious points, making for what Ms. Hawthorne described as "conceptually dull" writing. Furthermore, her essays contained many grammar and spelling errors, an aspect of her writing that Cynthia wanted to improve.

As the special tutoring progressed, Ms. Hawthorne discovered that Cynthia's self-projected image of an enthusiastic learner wasn't always consistent with Cynthia's behavior. While Cynthia first appeared earnest in seeking help for her literacy needs, Ms. Hawthorne began to think that she was seeking attention and trying to evade standard class work. Ms. Hawthorne also noticed that, while Cynthia wrote enthusiastically, she often did not complete reading assignments, and her written work rarely got turned in when it was due. Inconsistency and "irresponsibility" marked her performance. In short, even though Cynthia showed enthusiasm for improvement, she appeared to have problems with self-regulation in addressing schoolwork.

Cynthia's portrait is similar to that of many middle and high school students who reveal a mosaic of selves, including images of the enthusiastic learner, the engaged reader, the fast problem solver, the school socialite, the irresponsible kid, and the budding historian. Cynthia has had opportunities that others in her school have missed, such as a mother and father she views as supportive, but she is beset with motivational problems that keep her from making the kinds of effort that would result in more positive success.

Responding to Ms. Hawthorne's Dilemma

If Cynthia were in your class, what steps would you take to help her progress in her academic development? Describe what you would do to enhance Cynthia's motivation and/or help her improve some aspect(s) of her school work. Explain what you would do, along with your reasons for doing it.

INSIDE THE MEANING CONSTRUCTION ZONE: READERS READING

After reading chapter 3, you should be able to answer the following questions:

1. What are some myths about how good readers read?

2. What do good readers do when they read?

3. How would a model of the reading process help me to teach?

4. What does a peek into the meaning construction zone during reading reveal?

5. What are the implications of the sociocognitve model of reading for my teaching?

Read the following paragraph about Tony and observe what goes on in your mind as you read it. Watch closely what your mind does with the text you read. Detach yourself a little from the meaning you construct and focus on the *processes* that lead to that meaning's construction. After reading the paragraph, record your observations in a page or two. Draw a picture, diagram, or map of the process you observed in your mind as you made sense of the passage (Please do not draw a picture of the event described in the passage itself.)

Tony slowly got up from the mat, planning his escape. He hesitated a moment and thought. Things were not going well. What bothered him most was being held, especially since the charge against him had been weak. He considered his present situation. The lock that held him was strong, but he thought he could break it. He knew, however, that his timing would have to be perfect. Tony was aware that it was because of his early roughness that he had been penalized so severely—much too severely from his point of view. The situation was becoming frustrating; the pressure had been grinding on him for too long. He was being ridden unmercifully. Tony was getting angry now. He felt he was ready to make his move. He knew that his success or failure would depend on what he did in the next few seconds. (From R. C. Anderson, R. E. Reynolds, D. L. Schallert, & E. T. Goetz. Frameworks for comprehending discourse. *American Educational Research Journal, 14* (1977), 367–382.)

How Students Construct and Negotiate Meanings

When I was teaching American literature to eleventh graders, I enjoyed engaging them in discussions of J. D. Salinger's short stories. While grappling with the meaning of these stories, students contributed to the building of an interpretive classroom community in which they made significant discoveries about both the stories and themselves as readers. Here's a glimpse of that process.

After my students read Salinger's "The Laughing Man" and wrote their summaries or interpretations of it in their logs, they gathered in groups of three to read and discuss each others' summaries and interpretations. Each team selected a recorder to write down ideas and a reporter to communicate those ideas to the entire class after the small-group discussions. The remaining group member was asked to be a prompter, to keep the group on task, and to ask questions that would keep the conversation moving toward the goal of collecting ideas about the meaning of the story.

During the talk between students in small groups, meanings for the story often changed significantly as a result of reading—and then discussing—what others had written. For example, Kirk, whose initial response in his log was, "I cannot figure out what the story means, and its significance, so I will summarize it," commented that Susan "brought all my thoughts and understanding together" during small-group discussion. In her journal, Susan had written, "I think the story is about a broken heart. The story inside the story was parallel. . . . When the Chief and Mary broke up, the Laughing Man died over the death of his wolf. He died of a broken heart, at the same time of the death of the love of Mary and the Chief." Several students said that reading such commentary and discussing various interpretations made them think in new ways about the story's significance.

After students in small groups read and discussed their reactions, the reporters presented ideas to the whole class. As groups reported, I encouraged the expression and elaboration of group and individual meanings—not only meanings for the entire story, but also meanings for specific events or objects in the story. For example, during the discussion, several students expressed different interpretations of the vial of eagle's blood that the Laughing Man crushes before he dies.

"We thought it represented his love for Mary Hudson," said Erica.

"How would that work out?" I asked.

"When their relationship was going well, the Laughing Man survived by drinking the blood," said Erica. "But, when Mary and the Chief broke up, the Laughing Man crushed the vial, and he died along with his love for Mary."

"Sort of his life blood being crushed?" I echoed in a question.

"Yeah," said Erica. "Something like that."

"What other explanations for the crushed vial came up in your small group discussions?" I asked the class.

"I thought it stood for the children in the Comanche Club," said Mark.

"How does that work?" I asked.

"I don't know. Just seems that way," answered Mark.

"But we need to tie the meaning to something. Events in the story. Ideas you had when reading it. Something so it makes sense," I said.

"Seemed to me that the children of the Comanche tribe were keeping the Laughing Man alive," Mark said.

"I thought it was the baseball game," said Alison.

"Someone in our group said it stood for a false lifestyle," said Katie.

"Does anyone want to explain how those meanings would make sense in the context of the story?" I asked.

"I don't know about baseball," added Katie, "but I thought there was something false about how the Chief was living or about his relationship with Mary and that when the truth was out, the relationship died."

"I'm not absolutely sure what the vial is," said John, "but, if it has a deep meaning, I'm sure it isn't baseball or the kids because they are not really deep issues. I can see the false lifestyle but there are inconsistencies in the story because the Chief doesn't have a false life but a different life than the kids see. The mask would be more appropriate."

"So what do you think the vial represents?" I asked John.

"I'd have to agree with Erica," he said. "The vial would be Mary and the Chief's love."

I explored these and other meanings with students. I frequently asked them to explain how an interpretation could be grounded in the text and how it made sense in relation to the whole story. But I tried not to impose my own "reading" of the story on the students—favoring interaction among them and with the text. Although I mentioned that the story might be saying some important things about the creative process and the unconscious mind, no students picked up or expanded upon that idea, even though I pointed out the relationship between real-life experience and its transformation into our dream life.

Nevertheless, the whole-class discussion gave students an opportunity to create a class meaning for the story or parts of it. One student wrote, "The discussion changed my view of the story completely. I never saw any link between the Coach's life and his bizarre stories. I didn't understand that the Laughing Man's death meant anything."

This classroom discussion of Salinger's short story provides us with a glimpse of readers reading. It serves as a view into the meaning construction zone, where readers make meaning for texts through several cognitive and social processes that are examined in the rest of this chapter.

"By God, for a minute there it suddenly all made sense!"

Source: © The New Yorker Collection 1986 Gahan Wilson from cartoonbank.com. All Rights Reserved.

Although we will be focusing on meaning construction during reading in this chapter, we need to keep in mind that meaning construction when writing has similar features. Perhaps the most obvious will be that, when we write, we must read our own composition, construct meaning for it, compare what we've written with what we intended to say, and revise as needed. In a later chapter, we examine the meaning construction process when writers write, and you'll discover other similarities between reading and writing processes. In fact, similarities exist between all language functions that reveal themselves in an analogy: Listening is to speaking as reading is to writing. When we listen, we construct meaning as we do when we speak.

Myths of the Good Reader

Several allegations about the qualities of good readers need to be presented and examined. We can look at these statements, which are summarized in Figure 3.1, and ask ourselves how much evidence supports them. Some educators (Whimbey & Lochhead, 1999) view these as myths of reading proficiency. After we examine these myths, we'll look at a second set of research-based characteristics of good readers.

Figure 3.1   Myths of the Good Reader.

1. Good readers can read at 1,000 words a minute or more with improved comprehension.
2. Good readers don't subvocalize.
3. Good readers read only the key words.
4. Good readers recognize words as wholes.
5. Good readers read groups of words as a unit of thought.
6. Good readers never look back.

First Good Reader Myth: *They Can Read at 1,000 Words a Minute or More with Improved Comprehension*

Many speed-reading courses proclaim that students can accelerate their reading rate and get more homework done more efficiently. In our time-driven lives, such accelerated reading sounds quite appealing. But, have you ever tried to read a college or high school physics text at 1,000 words a minute? How about a chemistry text? Or consider reading Shakespeare, Emily Dickinson, or Wallace Stevens at that rate. How about *The Federalist Papers* or Wittgenstein's *Philosophical Investigations*?

After taking a speed-reading course and reading Tolstoy's voluminous Russian novel *War and Peace* in 20 minutes, Woody Allen summarized the book: "It's about Russia." When we look more carefully at the rate of eye fixations as able readers read, we'll see why average reading rates of 1,000 words per minute or more are mythic. Speed reading enables readers to cover more words per minute, but they pay a price: Comprehension drops (Just & Carpenter, 1987).

Obviously, we need to think of reading at different rates for different purposes. Although studies have shown repeatedly that readers sacrifice comprehension if they read more than about 300 words a minute, some texts require even a more plodding speed—with several rereadings! Perhaps we could think about having various reading gears: a skim gear, a pleasure reading gear, a newspaper gear, a cognitive challenge gear, and a low-speed, frustration management gear. And, by the way, remember that some readers really enjoy savoring the sounds of words and phrases, the images words may evoke, and the pleasures of reflecting on an insight about life's meanings or its ironic twists.

A reviewer of books for *The New York Times* (Volk, 1999) wrote that she read *Faster: The Acceleration of Just About Everything* by James Gleick in 412 minutes. I did a little calculation. The book runs 324 pages; the approximate number of words per page came to about 400. That means the book has about 130,000 words. At 412 minutes, that means the book reviewer, who is also a novelist and essayist, was cruising along at about 315 words per minute. In a book critical of our accelerating just about everything, including reading, this reviewer was maintaining a pretty sensible—and predictable—speed.

Second Good Reader Myth: *They Don't Subvocalize*

Subvocalization occurs when you hear the words you read in your mind or when your lips or tongue muscles move as you read. Some "experts" advise visual reading only, without subvocalization of any kind. However, subvocalization appears to be a very important part of learning to read, and the inner echo in our mind of words on the page may enable us to improve our comprehension—especially of more difficult texts. Suppressing subvocalization is also likely to suppress comprehension (Waters, Caplan, & Hildebrandt, 1987). We will discover more about subvocalization and its connection with the role of phonological processing later in this chapter.

Third Good Reader Myth: *They Read Only the Key Words*

As Whimbey and Lochhead (1999) point out, how will we know in advance of reading a text what key words we must make sure we read to comprehend a passage? Trying to read only key words frequently results in readers' misinterpreting the text. Marilyn Adams (1990) points out that readers probably process every word they come upon in a text to gain an understanding of a text's meaning. Skipping even one word, such as a word that negates a statement, in the hunt for only the key words may result in a complete misreading of the text. Good readers are frequently word-by-word readers, a phenomenon that will make more sense when we see later how the mind processes print.

Fourth Good Reader Myth: *They Recognize Words as Wholes*

While good readers appear to recognize words as wholes, they also process virtually every letter of each word they read (Adams, 2004). Undoubtedly, good readers recognize many words at a glance. However, less frequently read words, words that may bear an enormous amount of importance for the meaning of a passage, are far more likely to be processed letter by letter (Ehri, 1991).

Fifth Good Reader Myth: *They Read Groups of Words as a Unit of Thought*

We may form units of thought, what we will call *propositions*, as we read. However, trying to take in a group of three or four words in one fixation and transform the words into a proposition or part of a main point is unlikely to work. A cluster of words may not form a coherent or useful thought. Texts are more complex in the arrangement of their units of meaning, especially as we begin to construct an internal text representation in our minds. As mentioned before, Adams (1990, 2004) found evidence that we usually read each word, one at a time. Nevertheless, some words may appear so frequently that we take them in as "sight words"—words such as *the,* or, *and*—that could be tied to other less frequently sighted words in a text. We might, on occasion, combine these words so rapidly that it appears as if we were taking in units of thought. However, pushing a reader to read in word groups, as is often done with a device called a *tachistiscope,* which briefly flashes words or phrases on a screen, may increase the overall reading rate for certain kinds of texts but add nothing noteworthy to comprehension.

Sixth Good Reader Myth: *They Never Look Back*

Speed-reading experts may urge readers to push their eyes forward, to grasp groups of words as units of thought, or to practice by increasing the speed at which a tachistiscope or computer program flashes words or groups of words from a text. In forcing themselves to push forward, readers may miss important monitoring messages their minds are sending, messages such as, "I don't follow what's going on here. I need to reread this to understand." The reread strategy is one of the most basic solutions to the problem of misunderstanding or losing the thread of a text. As you'll soon discover, good readers summarize and ask themselves questions about their levels of understanding. If good readers don't understand a text, they have strategies like looking back to help them comprehend successfully.

Characteristics of Good Readers

In the first part of this chapter, we explore what goes on in the minds of good readers. A number of researchers (A. L. Brown, Palincsar, & Armbruster, 1984; Duke & Pearson, 2002; Pearson, Roehler, Dole, & Duffy, 1992; Pressley, El-Kinary, & Brown, 1992) have investigated the way good readers read and have identified several skills that contribute to their fluent reading. Although highly skilled readers may not engage in all these comprehension-fostering activities all the time, they are likely to use several of them, especially if they begin to have problems with comprehension.

1. Good readers activate and connect with the knowledge base related to the subject of the reading. We see later in this chapter how this mental activity that fosters comprehension is connected with schema theory and the function of our long-term memory.

2. Good readers monitor their comprehension process while reading and recognize those moments of mental blackout and misunderstandings that lead us into confusion. Later, we will see how this activity is related to metacognition.

3. Good readers pay attention to the spectrum of information they are reading and categorize it from important to unimportant, giving priority to major content and secondary attention to trivia.

4. Good readers both make inferences and test them while reading. These inferences include hypotheses, interpretations, predictions, and conclusions.

5. Good readers periodically review what they have read and ask themselves questions about the reading. As we will discover, summarizing and questioning are powerful comprehension-fostering processes.

6. Good readers do not ignore comprehension breakdowns or lapses. They take steps to correct comprehension problems once they are recognized.

7. Good readers also clarify for themselves why they are reading and try to understand what is expected of them as readers and learners.

8. Good readers make sure the meanings they are constructing while reading are internally consistent and compatible with what they know and what makes sense. This constitutes part of their internalized standards of text evaluation.

9. Good readers identify key concepts or major propositions (also known as macropropositions) when reading expository texts and use them as knowledge organizers.

10. Good readers also make good use of their working memory so they can hold alternative interpretations of a text in mind, compare them, and evaluate them to determine which interpretation should be granted greater credibility.

Of course, good readers do not engage in all these praiseworthy mental activities whenever they read, but many good readers have access to these skills and use them automatically or selectively to help themselves comprehend text. As we build a mental model of the reading process, we want to be able to take into account all of these activities and their contributions to the construction of meaning during the reading process.

The Benefits of a Reading Process Model

Like most teachers, you probably have an implicit "model" of the reading process, even though that model may not be explicitly described—unless you're asked to picture and explain your understanding of the process, as you were at the beginning of this chapter. Nevertheless, your implicit understanding of reading may influence your instructional strategies in the classroom. Understanding the reading process more fully and explicitly contributes to deeper knowledge of your students' learning and improvements in instructional practice for your students (Beck, 1989). The benefits of a reading model are summarized in Figure 3.2 and described in the following paragraphs.

First, a model integrates research findings, makes theory graphic, and provides us with an explanation of how reading takes place in accord with what we currently know (Tierney, 1994). Taking a car's engine apart helps us see how it works and how to repair it. But dismantling the reading process presents us with a very different problem. Reading is a highly complex and hidden process with no pistons, valves, or crankshafts to pull out for observation. However, we do have a substantial amount of research and theoretical knowledge about reading. Millions learn how to read, even though we may not know all the details about how reading happens. What we do know from research and theory enables us to construct a model to visualize this mysterious, invisible, and very complex process.

Second, knowing something about how the reading process works and having a model to render that knowledge enables us to make predictions about the reading process. For example, the model can help you to understand how the activities of good readers contribute to their high levels of comprehension.

Third, a model of reading will help you detect where points of breakdown in comprehension occur. Glitches happen. Perplexities arise. Things don't make sense. A model can help you visualize what components are vulnerable or fail to contribute to smooth meaning made while reading. In short, a model will help you understand what's going on when diagnosing a student's struggle with reading.

Fourth, a model can give you clues about intervention strategies that may help struggling readers at different points in the reading process. While viewing the model as a sure resource for formulating prescriptions that we can administer to the ailing reader may be dangerous, we can use it as a resource for good hints. There may be no clear, direct path from the model to classroom curriculum or tutoring strategies, but a model creates more opportunity for instructional interventions.

Figure 3.2 Benefits of a Reading Model.

- Explains how reading takes place in accord with current research.
- Makes theory graphic and easier to understand.
- Enables teachers to make predictions about the reading process.
- Helps teachers detect breakdown points in comprehension.
- Provides clues about strategies to improve reading fluency and comprehension.
- Reveals how students construct meanings and understanding in many content areas.

Lastly, a model of reading can reveal how we go about constructing meaning and gaining understanding in almost every content area. Walter Kintsch (1998) argues that what happens in our minds during reading comprehension provides us with a pattern for cognition in general. Comprehension occurs when we construct meaning using information from texts and knowledge stored in our minds as resources for building (Samuels, 2002). The comprehension processes captured in the model of reading to be presented can also describe the cognitive process of understanding that occurs in constructing an answer for a math problem or constructing a hypothesis about a chemical interaction, testing that hypothesis in a lab, and discussing one's findings with others.

How Personal Theories of Reading Affect Reading Processes and Outcomes

Teachers should be aware that personal theories about reading can strongly shape how texts are read and how learning proceeds (Simpson & Nist, 2002). Middle and high school students have most likely developed personal theories about reading that affect their approach to texts and learning from them. For example, if students in an English class believe that, when reading a poem, they must discover the one meaning the poet intended the poem to transmit, their experience of reading poetry will be driven solely by the need to discover the poet's unique message. As Billy Collins (2001), America's former Poet Laureate put it, some readers facing a new poem want to "tie the poem to a chair with rope/and torture a confession out of it." On the other hand, students who have adopted a reader response model of reading, such as that developed by Louise Rosenblatt (2004), would more likely approach the reading of a poem as an opportunity to enter into the poem's world, to respond to its imagery, to construct a meaning for themselves based on the poem's language, and to discuss their meanings with others in classroom contexts. For the first student, poetry may become inaccessible. For the other, poetry opens doors to the creative imagination. And what of teachers' personal theories about reading and learning from reading? Should we expect that those beliefs could shape not only how teachers read texts, but also how they teach them?

A Peek Into The Reader's Construction Zone

What we are going to go through in order to appreciate reading's complexity is a type of reading program or cognitive flowchart that replicates the reading process of a good reader. We cannot possibly replicate or even describe our mind's many parallel activities while we read. However, we can begin to see how the reading process works by breaking it down into components, subprocesses, and outcomes. In that way, we can begin to appreciate the knowledge, skills, and processing speed of good readers. Like almost any tour guide, I'll insert commentary about important landmarks as we pass them. Along the way, I'll point out factors that contribute to the trouble that some readers—both expert and struggling—may have when they read texts that are challenging for them. I'll also provide Diagnostic Windows, points at which teachers can view the meaning construction zone to assess readers and gain information about their reading processes that could guide their instruction.

An Overview of the Reading Model

The reading model that I will present consists of several components and processes that contribute to our making sense of print as we read. In a more generalized form, the model also describes or parallels cognition, solving problems, and making meaning

Figure 3.3 Overview of Sociocognitive Reading Model.

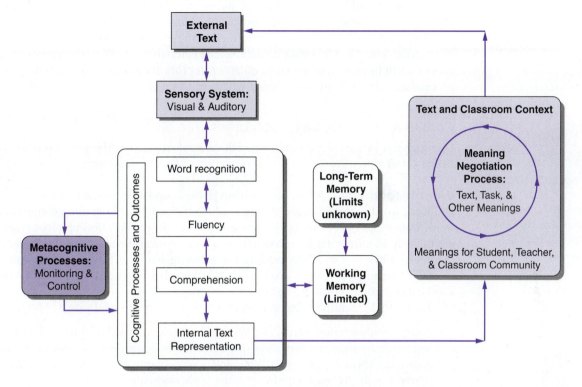

in many symbolic domains, including solving math problems or even making sense of chemical formulas and reactions. To understand the components and processes of reading, however, we are going to begin with an overview of the whole system. (See Figure 3.3.) After the overview, we'll examine its parts in more detail to help you gain a deeper understanding of reading in school contexts.

The model consists of four major components, as shown in Figure 3.3:

1. our *sensory system,* which is stimulated by an external text we see or hear,
2. our *cognitive processes and their outcomes,* which include word recognition, fluency, comprehension, internal text representations, and long-term and working memory,
3. our *metacognitive processes,* which include both monitoring and control of our cognitive processes and outcomes, and
4. a *text and classroom context* in which we read, interpret, comprehend, discuss, analyze, and evaluate texts.

As I present the major components of the model, I will magnify and elaborate on the sensory system, the cognitive and metacognitive processes, and the classroom context so that you can look much more closely at how each component contributes to the process of reading.

The Sensory System

For the purposes of reading, we use two primary modes of sensation: visual and auditory. Visually, we perceive images of letters and words from the external text. Text can be printed on a page or electronically transmitted. These visual images initiate the processing of letters and words as symbols, also called *orthographic processing*. When a reader reads aloud, we hear sounds as speech symbols that we process as syllables, phonemes, and words, also called *phonological processing*.

Both print and sounds that communicate language are symbolic systems that we learn to decode. That decoding process begins when print stimulates receptors in our eyes or when the sound of words stimulates receptors in our ears. However, these two processing systems frequently interact when readers read.

Cognitive Processes and Outcomes

Our cognitive processes and outcomes include *word recognition, fluency, comprehension, internal text representations, working memory and long-term memory.*

Word recognition.

Word recognition is the foundation of the reading process, and weak word recognition is a strong predictor of problems in reading comprehension (Stanovich, 1991). Without sufficient practice in reading, less efficient readers are unlikely to automatically recognize words or develop speed in word recognition (Samuels, 2002, 2004). With reading for meaning hampered by word-recognition problems, struggling readers rarely enjoy reading, become engaged in it, or build knowledge and skills from it.

Ehri (1994) identified several ways in which a reader can read words:

- *Sight.*   Only familiar words, like *the, dog,* and *ran,* are read by sight. When reading words by sight, readers access their mental dictionary and identify the word's meaning, spelling, pronunciation, and even grammatical roles in sentences. These words are read rapidly as units with no analysis of or breaks between phonemes (or letter sounds). What's an example of a word you read by sight?

- *Analogizing.*   When analogizing, readers search their memory for known words that have the same parts or spellings as an unfamiliar word. When reading the word *Armorica* as a geographical location mentioned in James Joyce's *Finnegans Wake,* a reader could figure out the meanings of that word by analogizing to America, armor, and amor (love)—all of which lend meaning to Joyce's neologism (or new word making) as he begins his never-ending story. Beginning readers use analogies in far less esoteric reading tasks than deciphering Joyce.

- *Spelling patterns (or orthographic patterns).*   For readers to use spelling patterns to figure out a word's meaning, they need to have the spellings of many words stored in their memories to take advantage of pattern recognition. When letter clusters are identified, words with the same patterns are activated. That leads to the word's pronunciation and on to the discovery of its meaning.

- *Context.*   As readers read, they set up expectations about what is coming next, just as we do when we listen to a friend's conversation and anticipate what will next be said. The text that readers have comprehended creates a context in which they can guess the meaning of unfamiliar words. Unfortunately, unfamiliar content words in an informational text often carry an abundance of meaning, and guessing from context may not provide accurate information for understanding of the unfamiliar word.

- *Decoding (or phonological recoding).*   Decoding is slower than reading sight words because, when decoding, readers transform the sight of a word into its component sounds by applying their knowledge of the relationship between letters and their sounds (grapheme-phoneme correspondences). Decoding is the

Diagnostic Window

Is the student's vision sufficiently acute for reading without any eyestrain? If vision is questionable, arrange for the student to have an eye examination.

Diagnostic Window

Evaluation of your students' word recognition skills can be accomplished through a list of familiar words, Miscue Analysis, or an Informal Reading Inventory. These informal methods are described in the next chapter. A more formal test, the Wide Range Achievement Test—Revised (WRAT-R) for word recognition (Jastak & Wilkinson, 1984), can also be used.

process of phonologically recoding letters and words seen in print. After decoding a word, readers search their mental dictionaries for meanings that are associated with that word's pronunciation. Although you can hear beginning readers decode when they process words orally, more experienced readers do it mentally, even though you may detect some subvocalizing as they experiment with possible sounds for an unknown word. Word recognition in skilled readers most commonly occurs through decoding.

Orthographic processing.   You read in tiny moments of eye fixations on a word or a small group of words. Each fixation usually lasts about a quarter to a half a second. These fixations take up about 90% to 95% of your reading time. After a fixation, your eyes jump to the next fixation. Reading psychologists call the jumps **saccades**, and each saccade takes about 20 milliseconds, or 2% of 1 second (Just & Carpenter, 1987). Bauer (1994) compared reading to a slide show in which our eyes are exposed to about four slides per second. Each slide provides graphic information about the words that we rapidly process into a meaningful mental movie. If we assume that at each fixation skilled readers take in about one word, that means they read at about 240 words per minute (4×60 seconds). Knowing, as we do, that good readers occasionally take in two words or more at some fixations (and occasionally reread), we could easily justify an average silent reading rate of about 300 words per minute for a skilled reader.

But do the whole words always translate into meanings or do good readers perceive individual letters and letter patterns before processing the word? Although on the surface good readers appear to grasp words as units, we have evidence that they actually process individual letters of words in the texts they read (Adams, 1990, 2004; McConkie & Zola, 1981). However, good readers link letters into patterns that they have seen over and over again so that they do not always experience the letters as independent units (Ehri, 1991).

Among the operations that occur during **orthographic processing** are the encoding of letter order and the division of long words into parts, or syllables. For a struggling reader, grasping the letter order for the words *inspire, conspire, perspire, suspire,* and *transpire* would itself be daunting, but then each word needs to be divided into its meaning-revealing syllables, that is, its prefix and root. While poor readers have trouble reporting letter order in the words they read, good readers rarely make errors of that kind. Good readers have gained sufficient knowledge of letter patterns and their more common associations. Weak readers, who lack sufficient knowledge of letter associations, are less able to use their memory of letter patterns to help with word recognition and the reporting of letter order. While a good eighth-grade reader is unlikely to have trouble identifying the pattern of letters that make up *frequent* in the word *frequently,* a weak eighth-grade reader who infrequently reads the word would. Frequent errors in reporting letter order have been interpreted as a manifestation of dyslexia. However, researchers have shown that the root cause of frequent errors in letter order probably arises from insufficient opportunities to develop knowledge of letter patterns (Stanovich, 2000).

The other function of the orthographic process is its capacity to break down polysyllabic words, such as *antidisestablishmentarianism.* As you read such words, you may notice that you attack the word by breaking it into syllables (12 in this case) rather than seeing it letter by letter. Researchers (Adams, 1990; Wilkinson & Silliman, 2000) have shown that good readers use their knowledge of letter strings and associations to break longer words into parts or syllables. Because they have over-learned word patterns and common associations, good readers segment longer words at such a rapid pace that it appears automatic. Less skilled readers, however, may take an uncomfortably long time to pronounce a word such as *reverence,* yet not identify its meaning.

As a knowledgeable reader, you know the word *cat* at a glance. You see *c* in the word, but, because the whole word lies in your visual span at one fixation, you also see *a* and *t*. Each letter contributes to greater awareness of the associated network of the word *cat*. If you were just beginning to read, your recognition of the word *cat* would not have been as automatic. However, because you have read, heard, spoken, and written the word hundreds of times, you recognize its pattern instantaneously. Adams (1990) has pointed out that if beginning readers cannot recognize individual letters and letter patterns automatically and transform those letters into words that have meaning for them, then their frustration will probably keep them from reading at all.

Catalogue: There's that *cat* again. But this is no word at a glance for early or weak readers. For this word, the reader has to have a pretty good knowledge of its spelling pattern and be able to break it down into its parts (Just & Carpenter, 1987). A good reader, skilled in parsing words and nearly automatic when faced with finding information from a catalogue of words, will have little trouble with the associated letter patterns and meaning stored in long-term memory.

A basic question about the processing of letters and words is this: Do readers sound them out? To answer this question, we must look at the role of phonological processing in reading.

Phonological processing. **Phonological processing** occurs as letters, associated patterns of letters, or words activate (usually automatically in good readers) their corresponding sounds. But must these sounds always be activated for a reader to become aware of a word's meaning? Or is there a more direct route to meaning? Earlier in the history of reading research, educators widely accepted a "dual-route" model (Stanovich, 1991). According to that model, two pathways following visual stimulation could be taken. One path bypassed letter-sound correspondence and led directly to word meanings. A second route, more indirect, went through phonological processing, wherein stored spelling-to-sound correspondences were activated.

Many other researchers (Adams, 1990, 2004) have confirmed that good readers automatically produce letter-to-sound translations. Rather than being an obstacle to readers, the phonological loop that echoes in sound what is seen can support reading in a couple of ways. First, it can function as a backup system to orthographic processing. Second, it facilitates readers' working memory by heightening word activation and thereby enhances comprehension, especially for more challenging texts.

The "feedback" sound of the word may help us process the printed letters more carefully, especially if we are having trouble recognizing an unfamiliar word. We are more likely to pay more attention to letters that could be skipped and to see how letters, when sounded, form recognizable strings.

Because many of the words we read are often repeated and over-learned, we do not always have to translate letters and words into sounds to grasp their meaning. But these overlearned words, such as *dog,* constitute only a small portion of the words we read. Most words, such as *canine,* are encountered infrequently. These infrequently used words often carry much of a text's meaning. And readers processing content area texts, such as those in math or science, frequently encounter large numbers of unfamiliar or new words.

Good eleventh grade readers can use their phonological backup system to help them understand less familiar words, such as *tangential,* and attack those that are entirely new, such as *inculcate.* Less visually familiar words may, when sounded, trigger stronger associations with word meanings held in long-term memory, as might occur when *tangential* triggers *tangent.* And longer words, such as tangential, may have syllables that, when sounded, can help readers dissect and combine word elements to discover meaning. Orthographic knowledge, of course, also helps in these attacks on unknown words, because readers visually associate strings of letters and recall common syllable break points.

Readers may also pronounce words because they look like others they know. Knowledge of letter-phoneme correspondence isn't the sole mechanism readers use to recode phonologically. Researchers (Goswami, 2000; Moustafa, 1997) have found that children use analogies in reading and that their use increases as vocabularies enlarge. If we know how to say the word *light* and come across the word *fight,* we may be able to analogize from the known pronunciation of *-ight* to the unknown word.

What is the relationship between word recognition and fluency? Timothy Radsinski (1990) investigated this relationship and found that word recognition accuracy could predict reading rate, an important dimension of fluency. Lloyd Eldridge (2005) found that word recognition had causal effects on both accuracy and reading speed and that word recognition was a necessary condition for fluency. If readers must expend more attention and consume more working memory on decoding or word recognition, then both fluency and comprehension will decline (Kuhn & Stall, 2004).

Of course, pronouncing a word doesn't magically release its meaning. Word recognition should be viewed as a means to an end, that of increasing fluency and comprehension, and not as an end in itself (Baker, 2005).

Fluency.   Defining **fluency** has been a challenge to educators and researchers. That challenge has arisen because researchers have not consistently agreed on a global meaning for fluency or on the components that make it up (Koponen & Riggenbach, 2003). However, while fluency has multiple meanings, they are closely related. The *Literacy Dictionary* defines it as "freedom from word recognition problems that might hinder comprehension" (Harris & Hodges, 1995). The National Reading Panel (2000) defined fluency as "the ability to read a text quickly, accurately, and with proper expression." A useful definition would reveal the key function of fluency in reading comprehension, as does that suggested by Pikulski and Chard (2005): "Reading fluency refers to efficient, effective word recognition skills that permit a reader to construct the meaning of text. Fluency is manifested in accurate, rapid, expressive oral reading and is applied during, and makes possible, silent reading comprehension." When listening to a fluent reader, we would expect a text to be read accurately, quickly, effortlessly, and expressively. When fluent readers read silently, they automatically recognize words and group them in patterns that enable the reader to construct meaning.

Fluency is a bridge between word recognition and comprehension, as illustrated in Figure 3.3. Fluent readers identify words automatically and accurately, thus allowing the readers to use their working memory for comprehension (Samuels, 2004). Less fluent readers who do not automatically recognize letter patterns struggle with word recognition. They cannot construct meanings for a text or create knowledge networks from it because much of their memory and attention must be directed to decoding and understanding individual words.

Diagnostic Window

You can evaluate your students' fluency through a Curriculum-Based Measurement, Running Record, or an Informal Reading Inventory, each of which is described in the next chapter.

However, fluency fluctuates with text density and difficulty. If a reader is familiar with words and their meanings in a text as well as the text's content, silent reading is likely to be efficient, and reading aloud sounds smooth and expressive. Nevertheless, even a good, experienced reader may struggle with reading efficiently or expressively if a text on an unfamiliar topic contains many infrequently encountered words.

Although oral reading fluency averages for high school students at different grade levels have not yet been well documented, we do have a spring fluency average for eighth-grade students, which is 171 correct words per minute at the 50th percentile (Johns & Berlund, 2002). As a touchstone for oral fluency rates, most students in middle and high school usually read between 135 and 185 correct words per minute. Students reading content area texts at less than 80 correctly read words per minute are more likely to encounter comprehension problems. Of course, just reading words, even at 150 words per minute, does not mean that readers understand what they are reading. Once again, comprehension—not speed of reading—should be the aspiration we share with our students.

What is the relationship between fluent reading and comprehension? Put another way, does fluency predict comprehension? Studies of oral reading fluency have provided research-based support for viewing fluency as a valid and reliable indicator of reading skill and comprehension (Breznitz, 2006; Fuchs, Fuchs, & Maxwell, 1988; Reutzel & Hollingsworth, 1993; White, 1995). Reachers (Fuchs, Fuchs, Hosp, & Jenkins, 2001) have found the relationship between oral reading fluency and comprehension to be quite strong with correlations as high as .80 or .90. This research-based connection will be of value to us in assessing our students' readiness to read the content area texts we expect them to understand, a topic we take up in the next chapter.

Without a memory system, word recognition and fluency would be impossible—as would the essence of reading: comprehension. So before we explore how comprehension occurs, we will first discover what we know about the kinds and functions of memory that enable us to read.

Working memory.   Without memory you simply could not read this. The letters and words would go through your sensory system and brain as though it were a sieve with no meaningful residue whatsoever. There are brain-damaged individuals who can't remember any new experiences, including what they read. Fortunately, most of us have several forms of memory; explaining these forms will help you understand how they help—and limit—reading. What have psychologists learned about memory that would help us understand how it works when we read?

Let's begin with **working memory**, one of two major memory components depicted in Figure 3.3. Working memory is where we represent the immediate world, actively compute solutions, such as making sense out of this text, and remember the results for short periods of time. (Do you remember the first word of the last sentence you read?) Working memory also creates mental and learning bottlenecks. That's because its capacity to hold information is very limited, and the limited amount of information it can hold deteriorates rather fast. So what we have is a limited memory bank or cognitive resource to proceed with reading and to keep short-term track of our progress through symbolic representations. Fortunately, mental functions, such as recognizing the meaning of a word, can become automatic and reduce the demands on working memory so that it can work harder on tougher tasks, such as comprehending more complex passages.

While reading, working memory keeps essential meaning construction data and skills active, including letters and words from the text on the page and knowledge from long-term memory that transfers into working memory. From the text being read, working memory holds orthographic information in the form of letters and phonological responses in the form of sounds that correspond to the text observed and internalized. Dog, as a pattern of letters, and //dŏg/ as corresponding sounds, interact to reinforce and maintain meaning in memory. Knowledge and skills transferred into working memory from long-term memory include word meanings, text-structure knowledge, and other knowledge networks. All these forms of knowledge and skills enable us to make sense of texts. Working memory also maintains access to the result of our text-building efforts: an active mental text representation that is continually updated as we read.

Some educators (Ericsson & Kintsch, 1995; Kintsch, 1998) believe that two different kinds of working memory interact to access deeper wells of long-term memories, enabling us to read and perform other kinds of cognitive tasks. These two forms are short-term working memory (ST-WM) and long-term working memory (LT-WM). Short-term working memory is insufficient as a resource for meaning construction during reading. We know that the capacity of short-term memory is limited, perhaps to as few as four chunks of information (Broadbent, 1975) although earlier estimates put it at seven plus or minus two (Miller, 1956). To comprehend a text, readers must access more information than short-term memory can contain. To achieve higher levels of memory usage while reading, forms of long-term memory link to forms of ST-WM so that chunks of information readily come into consciousness. When a student is reading about Picasso in an art class, her ST-WM, which may be her conscious processing of information about Picasso's "blue period," links with her LT-WM of specific paintings from Picasso's blue period, such as *The Old Guitarist*, *The Tragedy*, or *Blue Room*. Through this arrangement, ST-WM information (a sentence just read about Picasso's blue period) is linked by retrieval structures to long-term memory (examples of Picasso's paintings). Information and imagery flow instantaneously into consciousness as LT-WM that can quickly be accessed while reading further. Thus, readers can use LT-WM to expand working memory.

Long-term memory. What comes into working memory from past learning and experience arrives there only because of its access to long-term memory. **Long-term memory (LTM)** is like the hard drive on a computer that stores large amounts of information until we erase it—or until our hard drive crashes and we lose it. It holds abundant information for long periods of time—unlike working memory, where smaller amounts of information dissolve rather quickly. We draw on information stored in LTM to help us deal with issues or problems that are currently alive in working memory.

How does long-term memory serve readers? Readers hold many forms of information in LTM that have a number of different functions. Forms of LTM that are critically important to reading include declarative, procedural, and conditional knowledge, knowledge of language, word analysis skills, encoding productions, text-structure knowledge, comprehension strategies, and metacognitive knowledge and strategies. The activation and application of nearly all these forms of knowledge held in LTM is best understood through schema theory (Ruddell & Unrau, 2004).

Schema Theory. Schema theory helps to explain how knowledge is stored in memory, how that knowledge is activated, and how a schema influences meaning construction while reading. A **schema** is a knowledge network that guides our behavior, including what we do with information gathered from reading. We can compare it to files of knowledge with associated "slots" that a reader fills with related information gained from a text (Rumelhart, 1980). If readers have activated a schema for knowledge about what they are reading, the schema can provide slots for incoming data. According to schema theory, what we know about grocery stores, restaurants, football, animals, World War II, ecology, and even reading is organized into associated networks, or schemas.

Although I've used a computer metaphor to describe long-term memory and schemas, we need to keep in mind that long-term memory and the schemas are created from social interaction. Schemas are not isolated, decontextualized knowledge networks removed from human interaction; rather, they are information that is very much a part of interpersonal, social, and cultural experience (McVee, Dunsmore, & Gavelek, 2005). Memory and culture nourish each other.

A schema can represent a network of social events that commonly occurs when a specific situation arises, such as going to a restaurant. As researchers on scripts in memory have observed (Bower, Black, & Turner, 1994; Schank & Abelson, 1977), going to a restaurant triggers a series of events: entering, ordering, eating, and exiting. A series of events occurs within each of these scenes. When entering a restaurant, customers look for a table, decide where to sit, go to the table, and sit down. When reading a narrative text, readers presented with characters entering a restaurant are likely to activate the slots that compose the restaurant script and arouse expectations that may be met by the text or that may distort events that actually are described in the text. In short, activated schemas raise readers' expectations that content already known may arise in the text.

However, schemas also serve as knowledge resources that enable us to build new knowledge structures (Spiro, 1988/2004, 2000/2004). According to Cognitive Flexibility Theory, readers do not always mechanistically fill slots but take chunks of knowledge from many different, yet related, knowledge structures and assemble new knowledge structures and new meanings. Newly constructed schemas allow for more organic, interdependent links than linear, rigidly conceived schemas. For example, if students in a biology class have, as an assignment, the challenge of diagnosing a cat's illness based on a range of symptoms, including a high temperature, muscle weakness, dehydration, and no appetite, the students would need to activate and apply knowledge from various schemas, assemble new knowledge, and formulate a diagnosis. When working with patients, doctors frequently engage in that form of cognitive flexibility.

With respect to how schemas affect learning and remembering from text, Anderson (2004) identified several of their functions:

1. *Schemas provide scaffolding that enables us to create meanings out of new information we read and organize that new knowledge in relation to prior knowledge.* When reading about strategies to motivate your students to learn, your schemas related to motivation and motivational strategies would become activated and guide your comprehension of the text you're reading. How you have organized information about motivation would then influence how you process, use, or transform new information you acquire from the text. Existing schemas may also be modified if new learning compels readers to alter their existing schemas in the direction of new information. If newly read information does not fit into the slots of readers' existing schemas, readers will often extend more effort attempting to comprehend the text.

2. *Schemas influence attention allocation.* If readers have schemas for a topic, such as Dublin, Ireland, those knowledge structures will influence the amount of attention that readers would give to aspects of the text being read, such as James

Joyce's *Dubliners*. Knowing something about the topic, readers will focus on those features of the text they deem most important.

3. *Schemas stimulate readers to go beyond the literal to make inferences and to draw less obvious implications and conclusions from text content.* If readers have no pre-existing knowledge about a topic being read, they cannot activate a schema that will help them comprehend either the explicit text or its implications. I encounter this problem when I try to read articles in the journal *Science* about research on genetics or neurotransmitters. However, if readers have a schema for the text, they can use it to make inferences that enable readers to go beyond what is stated in the text itself. They can also use the schema to fill in knowledge gaps when information may be left out or forgotten. That inferential elaboration and reconstruction can strengthen readers' overall text comprehension.

4. *Schemas facilitate summarizing.* As we discovered earlier, summarizing is an important activity in which good readers engage. If readers have a schema for a topic being read, say motivation, that old network of knowledge about motivation can make summarizing newly acquired knowledge about motivational strategies much less effortful and more comprehensive.

Schemas hold the key to understanding the bottom-up and top-down interactive nature of the reading process. While readers process individual letters and words from the page, or bottom, activated and abstract schemas from the top interact with that letter and word, which are bottom-up data, and influence the construction of meaning from the top down. This construction-integration process occurs after each reading cycle that runs from the moment a word starts to be processed until we're ready for the next word (Just & Carpenter, 1987; Kintsch, 2004). As we will see at a later point in the model's description, readers can activate and apply schemas to build web-like representations of the text rather than rigid, slot-filled representations.

Declarative, Procedural, and Conditional Knowledge.   Background knowledge stored as schemas in LTM has been divided into information about what's in the world, how it works, and when to use it. Cognitive psychologists refer to these as declarative, procedural, and conditional knowledge, respectively (Paris, Lipson, & Wixson, 1983). **Declarative knowledge** is knowledge of facts, objects, events, language, concepts, and theories that contributes to our personal construction and understanding of reality. **Procedural knowledge** consists of strategies and skills for using and applying knowledge, from knowing how to replace an electrical wall outlet to starting a barbecue. We may not even be able to describe some of this procedural knowledge, such as riding a bicycle or reading the last sentence you read. Finally, **conditional knowledge** refers to the when and why of using information, such as when and why to apply a known classroom-management procedure such as assertive discipline. When we read, we usually use all three of these forms of knowledge because we must access our memory of facts and words, engage our reading skills, and decide when and why to use our knowledge to facilitate comprehension.

Language Knowledge.   To construct meaning, readers must engage various forms of knowledge about language. Readers' language knowledge includes schemas that represent orthographic, phonological, lexical, and syntactical knowledge. Although most of these knowledge forms are well developed before a child even enters school (Heath, 1983), word and sentence structure knowledge continues to grow throughout the school years.

Phonological knowledge is well established in the memories of most children by the time they are 4 years of age (Gibson & Levin, 1985). They can identify words that conform to English phonology, in contrast to sound clusters that make no sense, such as *click* versus *dlek* (Morehead, 1971). Some children, however, enter school with English as a second language or with phonological problems that emerge as they learn to read (Stanovich, 2000).

Orthographic knowledge accumulates over time as readers decode words that have similar patterns and as they store similarly spelled sight words in LTM (Ehri, 1994). Readers may also acquire orthographic knowledge as they learn to spell words with similar patterns. Many spelling patterns, including word roots (in*tend*ed, ex*tend*ing, *tend*ency) and word endings (-ed, -ing, -ency) may be observed by readers and remembered.

Lexical knowledge, also known as semantic memory, refers to knowledge of words and their meanings. If, for example, you know the meaning of cathedral, you have lexical knowledge for that word. Knowledge of words is closely connected with a reader's background knowledge in the forms of declarative, procedural, and conditional knowledge as well as knowledge of the world in general because it is through words that these forms of knowledge find expression. Furthermore, some researchers (D. D. Johnson, Toms-Bronowski, & Pittelman, 1981) have found that words representing concepts are clustered into categories that are arranged in hierachically structured schemas. In turn, these categories are connected with other conceptual structures.

Extensive research on vocabulary (Beck & McKeown, 1991) also indicates that lexical knowledge is directly related to comprehension and meaning construction. To efficiently connect meaning to words, readers must have knowledge of concepts. Readers depend upon their internal lexicon of remembered words as their route to those concepts. How would I ever explain the process of reading to you without having the vocabulary to do so? How would you ever understand it without having the vocabulary I use? The larger a reader's lexicon, the larger is the reader's capacity to understand texts.

The size of a reader's lexicon is important, but so is speed of access to it. Research on lexical access reveals that the meaning of more frequently used words, such as *when*, are more rapidly activated than less frequently used ones (Just & Carpenter, 1987). Fluent readers usually have faster lexical access speeds than dysfluent readers, who may have to activate phonological information about a word before gaining lexical access (Stanovich, 2000). Because of the importance of vocabulary to concept development, chapter 5 focuses on techniques for building word knowledge in content areas.

Syntactical knowledge, like phonological knowledge, is well developed before children begin reading. The basic ability to understand and generate language is inborn (Chomsky, 1959, 1965). According to Bruner (1986), we are born with a Language Acquisition Device (LAD), or an ability to acquire and manipulate language. This ability requires a Language Acquisition Support System (LASS), or an environment that encourages language acquisition. The LASS is embedded in our culture, as we saw in an earlier chapter, and emerges in various social settings (Vygotsky, 1986). A child's innate capacity to understand and generate syntactical structures will not develop normally if it is not sufficiently stimulated and supported through social interaction.

Word Analysis Skills.   Word analysis enables readers to recognize words, to transform visual symbols in print to mental representations for meaning construction. Word-analyzing skills are grounded in each reader's early experiences with print and

Diagnostic Window

You can assess the correspondence between a text's grade level and a reader's reading level by using a standardized reading test that yields grade-level equivalents. You can also use surveys, questionnaires, and interviews to get information about a student's knowledge base related to a text's main topic. Cloze tests also provide information about the level of challenge that a specific text is likely to present to a student. Each of these procedures is described in subsequent chapters.

invented spellings and grow through the school years into the automatic processing of known words (Samuels, 2004) and the conscious analysis of new words (Ehri, 1994).

Encoding Productions.   Numerous encoding productions are also stored in LTM. Encoding refers to the change or transformation of symbols, whether visual or auditory, into memory patterns. You encoded these words in order to understand them. For encoding to occur, we have to learn many productions. A *production* is similar to a computer's program because, just like a production, a program states an action that is to be carried out and the conditions that need to be met for that action to take place.

In LTM we have many production rules or statements consisting of IF-THEN connections that are activated under the right conditions, such as when we're multiplying numbers or reading—for example, IF 7×7, THEN 49. Together, these production rules make up a production system that is just like the computer program I'm using to type this sentence on my monitor. This program has a rule like this: IF I spell *their* as *thier*, THEN it will underline *thier* in red. Encoding productions and word analysis skills contribute to readers' recognition of words, a process we examined earlier.

Text Structure Knowledge.   As readers respond to texts and construct meanings for them, they often try to figure out if the text is narrative (fiction) or expository (nonfiction). These text structures and strategies for figuring out in what form a text is likely to fit are stored as schemas in LTM. These schemas, if appropriately activated, can help readers discover how a writer organized a text and how to organize a mental representation of that text. Narrative text structures follow a "story grammar" that includes setting, initiating event, characters' responses to that event, characters' behaviors, consequences of the behaviors, and a resolution. Although often mixed, expository texts typically take one of six forms: description, sequence, causation, problem solution, comparison, and persuasion. These text structures are more fully described with examples in chapter 6.

Comprehension Strategies.   **Comprehension strategies** are techniques or activities that facilitate a reader's understanding of a text. Readers apply these strategies to promote meaning construction and learning from texts under certain conditions—for example, when faced with an unfamiliar text structure, when comprehension breaks down, or when engaged in critical reading. I would also add word identification strategies that may be triggered when less familiar words, such as *approbation*, appear in texts and readers may need to analyze the word or use context cues in order to increase the likelihood of its being recognized.

As we saw from our review of characteristics of good readers, they usually have many comprehension strategies stored in LTM that they can activate when they get into trouble reading a challenging text. However, less skilled and struggling readers have far fewer strategies to activate and apply. That is why a major portion of this text presents strategies that you can teach growing readers so that they have more resources to use in attacking challenging texts in the content areas.

Comprehension.   Before readers can experience **comprehension**, several prior conditions are necessary. For comprehension to occur, a reader must interact with a text. Readers must have adequate decoding and word recognition skills. Words and even strings of associated words need to be read with sufficient fluency to leave readers enough working memory to comprehend what is read. Without sufficient fluency, the process of comprehension cannot take place efficiently. We also assume that readers need certain other cognitive conditions, such as adequate forms of memory, that are essential for comprehension and adequate motivation to pursue a reading task.

With these conditions met, comprehension becomes attainable. But what constitutes comprehension, this essence of reading? Comprehension, as Walter Kintsch (2004) has pointed out, is a useful but imprecise term. We know from our everyday use of the word what it means; however, defining it can be a challenge. What would satisfy us as a criterion for stating that we or our students have comprehended a text? That we can state its gist? That we can state what it means without missing essential points? That we can critically evaluate the information we have constructed? That we can pass a test composed of questions we are asked about the text? Or are there other measures of comprehension that would give teachers even more precise indications of students' understanding of what they've read? There are undoubtedly many outcomes of comprehension, each of which ought to be assessed to capture comprehension's multidimensional richness (RAND Reading Study Group, 2002). After reviewing research on comprehension, the RAND Study Group (p. 11) defined comprehension as "the process of simultaneously extracting and constructing meaning through interaction and involvement with written language."

In the most general sense, text comprehension can be seen as the interaction of many cognitive elements and processes, such as word recognition, schema activation, imagery, and mental models, until those elements form a stable and interacting relationship in the mind of the reader. That stable relationship constitutes comprehension (Kintsch, 1998; 2004). But it comes about only after several interactive processes take place. We know quite a bit about some of those processes. Others are more mysterious, with features that are still to be discovered and explained.

Forming and Integrating Propositions.   As readers recognize word meanings, these individual meanings combine into longer units of meaning. Effective readers quickly construct phrases and clauses that make sense, just as you are doing now. To make phrase and sentence sense, readers encode symbols into usable forms, building propositions and integrating meanings.

Proposition construction occurs when readers, often automatically, combine individually recognized words and other cues into basic meaning structures. A proposition is the smallest unit of knowledge that we can put to a test of being true or false (Bauer, 1994). For example, the sentence "Sam took the right fork" contains several propositions or meaning structures, some contributing to ambiguity.

1. Sam exists. (Noun function/Subject)
2. A fork exists. (Noun function/Object)

    2.1. Fork may mean eating utensil.

    2.2. Fork may mean farm tool.

    2.3. Fork may mean branch in road.

3. Sam "take" fork. (Past/Verb function)

    3.1. Take may mean grasp with the hand(s).

    3.2. Take may mean to go in a specific direction.

4. Forks can be right or wrong, in terms of correctness.
5. Forks can be right or left, in terms of direction.

To clarify this statement and to construct an appropriate meaning based on these propositions, readers refer to the context of the statement.

Part of constructing phrases, clauses, and sentences that make sense depends upon readers' grammatical or syntactical knowledge. Much of this sentence-generation knowledge is innate (Chomsky, 1959, 1965; Bruner, 1986) and realized through interaction in social settings. Because of this, readers are able to construct a sensible grammatical structure, such as a phrase, clause, or sentence, from individual words, their endings or inflections, and often their placement in a sentence pattern, such as subject + verb + object. If readers have trouble recognizing how words fit together into a clause or sentence pattern, then reading slows until readers recognize patterns that make sense (Just & Carpenter, 1987, Kintsch, 1998, 2004; van Dijk & Kintsch, 1983). Young children learning English eventually generate syntactically appropriate statements because of their interaction with parents who speak the language and scaffold its development in their children's minds.

Proposition integration occurs when readers combine simple propositions into more complex units of meaning: grammatical sentences that make sense (Kintsch, 1994, 2004). Returning to "Sam took the right fork," we can see that once readers are able to connect which meaning of *fork* goes with which meaning of *right*, they are able to integrate the propositions embedded in the words and construct an unambiguous, meaningful sentence.

As readers integrate propositions into meaningful sentences, the schema related to the topic becomes activated (Kintsch, 1998, 2004). If the meaning for *fork* is that of eating utensil, then, according to schema theory, we would expect knowledge about eating utensils and perhaps dining to become activated and moved from long-term memory to long-term working memory. Schema for what dinnerware is (declarative knowledge), how it is used (procedural knowledge), and when it is used (conditional knowledge) are likely to influence text comprehension. If the meaning for fork is that of a split in a road, then we would expect a very different kind of schema to be reconstructed from memory and to influence comprehension. Activated but irrelevant schemas would decay, while relevant schemas would be energized.

To develop a coherent representation of a text, the reader has to connect constructed clauses and sentences. Each new clause and sentence has to be integrated with prior information that has been constructed from the text or brought into awareness from past learning that is held in long-term memory. When integration occurs, knowledge structures are made or modified to represent information that the reader revises or acquires. The combination into compressed units or chunking of knowledge constructed earlier with new knowledge structures enables limited working memory to have access to more information than it could otherwise hold.

Imagery in Comprehension.   According to the Dual Coding Theory (Sadoski & Paivio, 2001), our minds operate with two different but connected mental systems that derive from our verbal and nonverbal experiences. While one of these systems is specialized for processing verbal information, the other processes nonverbal information, such as imagery. These two systems can function independently or in parallel through a network of interconnections. The Dual Coding Theory complements schema theory because it accounts for both the verbal dimensions of comprehension that schema theory does explain and the mental imagery that schema theory does not adequately explain.

Nonverbal mental imagery makes several contributions to reading (Sadoski & Paivio, 2001). First, mental imagery helps readers comprehend texts, both narrative and expository, without any special instruction or training. This corresponding nonverbal activity is especially likely with narrative texts eliciting imagery. Often, when we read fiction, our minds are vibrant with the images conveyed through a riveting text. However, the storage of imagery occurs in response to reading expository as well as narrative texts. Mental imagery appears as a natural and spontaneous process, one that we might extend or expand to facilitate comprehension of all kinds of texts. Teachers can encourage imagery that can foster comprehension and recall of expository content area texts that are unlikely to promote much imagery naturally.

Second, imagery enhances long-term recall for texts. Concrete sentences and paragraphs, those laden with imagery, are much more likely to be recalled than abstract texts. Imagery, perhaps as mental "pegs" on which to hang related information, appears to facilitate both storage and recall of printed information. Third, while verbal cognition plays a significant part in readers' aesthetic response or emotional reaction to texts, imagery is essential for a "lived" experience of literature. Imagery also contributes to the lived experience of other kinds of texts, such as those based on science and history. Some secondary school texts, such as *Biology: Visualizing Life* (G. Johnson, 1998), have been designed to make use of students' nonverbal systems to increase understanding, comprehension, and recall.

Intratextual and Intertextual Connections.   As we can see, reading is much more than activating schemas and filling in the slots they contain. **Intratextual** links occur when readers make connections between ideas that appear at different phases of a single text, such as in different parts of a magazine article (Hartmann, 1994). When a student makes a connection between one sentence and another in the same passage or between Puritanism mentioned early in a chapter of her U.S. history text and the Protestant ethic mentioned later in the same chapter, she is making an intratextual link. During the reading of that chapter, she does not activate any connections with texts outside the chapter; however, she might do so after reading the chapter and thinking about its content in relation to texts outside it, such as Arthur Miller's *The Crucible*.

Intertextuality also shapes text building (Hartman, 1991, 1994), but it differs from intratextuality. **Intertextuality** is the process of connecting developing texts with past texts to construct meanings. Those past texts can include not only printed texts, but also the texts of movies, television, and other forms of art or cultural communication (Bloome & Bailey, 1992). You can think of intertexuality as the interaction between the text being read and the many "texts" internalized from our cultural experiences. If, for example, your "muggle" (nonmagic) students have read the earlier books in J. K. Rowling's *Harry Potter* series, their reading of the later books in the series will be affected by intertextuality, providing a richer, fuller understanding of Harry's growth and development as a wizard. And if you read the Potter books along with the books of the psychologist Carl Jung, you'll discover troves of intertextuality.

Furthermore, as elements of a text begin to form a recognizable text pattern, such as that of an adventure story, a satire, an autobiography, or an argument, the schema for that particular genre may be activated. If so, the text may arouse readers' expectations for the upcoming structure and content of the text and affect their interpretation of the text (Anderson, 2004; Ruddell & Unrau, 2004). Let's take for our example Mark Twain's *The Adventures of Huckleberry Finn*. If, upon beginning to read the novel, readers activate an adventure story schema, they may expect to fill the slots of that genre with a series of Huck's adventures. With those expectations activated, readers may find it difficult, if not impossible, to experience the novel as a satire about parenthood, religion, education, morality, and human gullibility. However, readers anticipating a satirical novel or attuned to the potential for ironic slots are more likely to discover and enjoy Twain's humor.

Internal text representations.

We construct internal text representations as we form, link, and integrate propositions, engage background knowledge, and generate general meanings. An internal text representation is a reader's personal interpretation of a text created through background knowledge, intertextual connections, and personal experience activated from long-term memory and integrated with the text's surface code (Kintsch, 1998, 2004; van den Broek, Young, Tzeng, & Linderholm, 2004).

Because of the enormous variation in readers, internal text representations for the same text can take an infinite variety of forms. Some representations include relatively few inferences, especially if the text read is short and quite simple, as in "The newspaper landed on the porch with a smack." Other internal representations may contain an elaborate array of inferences, especially if the text is extensive, activates a wide range of schemas, has rich intertextual (between texts) and intratextual (within a text) connections, and arouses a variety of emotional responses, as could a reading of *The Adventures of Huckleberry Finn* or *Crime and Punishment*. Research (Long, Seely, Oppy, & Golding, 1996) suggests that weaker readers appear to make fewer inferences and do not expand beyond the text-on-the-page representation, while stronger readers make more inferences and construct richer interpretations of the text.

Key propositions that we construct as we make our way through a text often control the development of an internal text representation. These key propositions may be compared to high hills or even mountains in a textual landscape. They help orient us with respect to a text's central meanings. In expository prose, key propositions may be contained in a paragraph's topic sentence, as Just and Carpenter (1987) have found. These *macropropositions*, as van Dijk and Kintsch (1983) call them, become organizing principles that influence subsequent text interpretation. They often serve as landmarks that help us keep our bearings as we travel through a dense novel or a complicated chapter in a biology text.

Although the internal text representation appears as a separate entity in the model, we store it in long-term memory, and it is accessible to consciousness through links between short-term working memory and long-term working memory. We can also activate text representations for passages we have processed earlier and stored in long-term memory. That text representation may often be brought into working memory when we look back to summarize a text or to interpret newly processed text.

Metacognitive Processes

Following years of research and investigation, educators (Hacker, 1998a; Baker, 2005) widely agree that the concept of metacognition includes (a) knowledge of one's own knowledge and cognitive processes and (b) the ability to monitor and regulate one's knowledge and cognitive processes.

Metacognitive knowledge, which is stored in LTM, usually accumulates over years of experience with learning and problem solving. We learn how we think about ourselves as thinkers, about tasks, and about strategies that help us accomplish tasks (Garner, 1992). Metacognitive self-knowledge is exemplified by students knowing that they are better at solving word problems in math than at reading Shakespeare. As a teacher, we would see metacognitive knowledge about tasks in a student who recognizes that he remembers reading about colonial American history more than the New Deal era in our history because he knows more about early America and is more interested in it. Metacognitive knowledge about strategies appears when a student decides to make a knowledge map to represent information she has just learned about different types of cell division.

Monitoring and control. Metacognitive monitoring and control include various kinds of self-assessment and self-management, both of which are of keen interest to educators seeking methods to develop self-regulating learners. Self-assessment and self-management can focus on various processes when reading, including word recognition and comprehension. When applying metacognition to word recognition, you can ask yourself what strategies you can use to decode a word. You might ask if the word can be broken into smaller recognizable parts, as would occur in segmenting the word *recognition* into *re-* and *cognition*. In doing that, you might discover recognizable words inside a larger word. Whereas proficient readers activate these strategies automatically, teachers can help struggling readers assess their word attack strategies and thereby heighten metacognitive awareness and strategic knowledge (Paris & Flukes, 2005).

As for comprehension, proficient readers also activate metacognitive knowledge and strategies when constructing meaning for challenging texts. When you get bogged down in reading something you're having trouble understanding, such as a Shakespearean sonnet or a description of DNA replication, what do you usually do to help yourself understand? The answer you give exemplifies metacognitive knowledge in the form of self-assessment. Acts of reflection on your thinking include discovering knowledge not only about what you know and how you think, but also about when and how you use your knowledge and strategies. Do you have a purpose in mind whenever you read? Do you make mental summaries? Do you go back and forth in a text to make connections between ideas? Do you make guesses about a passage's meaning and then check to see if your guess was right?

As the diagram of the model shows (Figure 3.3), **metacognitive processes** entail both the monitoring and controlling of cognition while reading. To control the construction of texts during reading, we might engage several different metacognitive processes: standards of evaluation, metacognitive strategies, and planning. In some ways, these metacognitive processes function like an executive observing, evaluating,

Figure 3.4 Standards of Evaluation.

Standard	Question to Ask
External Consistency	Do my knowledge of the topic and my understanding of this text harmonize?
Internal Consistency	Does anything I comprehend from the text contradict other parts of it?
Syntactical	Are individual words or word groups correct grammatically?
Structural Cohesiveness	Does each proposition or sentence hold together within itself?
Propositional Cohesiveness	Do propositions or sentences fit together with each other?
Clarity and Completeness	Is the information I understand in this text clear and complete?
Lexical	Do I understand all the individual words in the text?

Source: Figure from Linda Baker. Differences in the standards used by college students to evaluate their comprehension of expository prose. *Reading Research Quarterly, 20*(3), 297–313. (Spring 1985). Copyright by the International Reading Association. All rights reserved.

and improving the quality of our reading. Together, our metacognitive capacity to monitor and control text building enables us to engage in what Hacker (1998b) calls self-regulated comprehension.

Skilled readers monitor the representational products of the reading process to watch for various kinds of miscues, word-recognition problems, incongruities within an evolving text, and incongruities between an evolving text and existing world knowledge or current schemas. Perhaps as you have been reading about this model, parts of it support your existing knowledge of reading, while other parts don't fit so well and require your further examination to see if you can accept them.

Among the strategies that good readers may use to enhance their comprehension of a text is the application of **standards of evaluation**. Baker (1985) identified a number of comprehension-monitoring standards that influence the quality of the internal text representation. These standards are presented in Figure 3.4 as questions you might ask yourself, consciously or unconsciously, about your evolving internal text representations. Baker states that good readers, those with high verbal ability, use these standards more frequently than readers with less ability.

Metacognitive strategies. Strategic readers also have an assortment of *metacognitive strategies* that they can activate and apply if and when they find that something has gone amiss during the construction of a text representation. Metacognitive strategies are routines or procedures designed to help readers promote the meaning construction process. Garner (1992, p. 245) defines strategies as "sequences of activities undertaken to reach goals efficiently."

Metacognitive planning. When skilled readers encounter comprehension problems while forming a text representation, *metacognitive planning* can enable them to decide on an appropriate course of action to solve the problems, including the selection of strategies that best address the problems posed. Readers may develop plans,

Diagnostic Window

You can discover to what degree your students engage in metacognitive activities through an Informal Reading Inventory or a Metacognition Interview (Unrau, 1997) or by using the Metacognitive Awareness of Reading Strategies Inventory (MARSI) (Mokhtari & Reichard, 2002), which is described in the next chapter. After you discover how aware students are of their metacognitive processes, you may want to teach them reading strategies they could use to improve their monitoring and control of comprehension.

review them, and select the plan and strategies that appear to have the most problem-solving promise (Davidson & Sternberg, 1998). For example, when readers face a challenging reading task, they may design a plan with subgoals and multifaceted, but related, strategies, including using different reading rates, graphic organizers, and textual, technological, and human resources.

If teachers and students learn more about metacognition in reading and learning, will they read and learn more effectively? Much research on developing metacognitive knowledge and applying metacognitive strategies indicates that it does help (Hacker, 1998a). Many of the strategies you will find later in this textbook can be classified as metacognitive, and they have been shown to improve reading and to help students become more self-regulating.

Text and Classroom Context

Up to now, we have been looking into the *meaning construction zone* within a reader's mind. Sometimes comparing the mind to a computer, I have tried to break apart an organic, instantaneous process that occurs on many levels, frequently at the same time, into its many components. As we have seen, social contexts also play a key role in the construction of meaning while reading, and it's to that social context that we now return.

According to Rosenblatt's (1978) transactional theory of reading, every act of reading is a transaction between a particular reader and a particular text at a particular time in a particular context. The reader and the text compose a transactional moment. The meaning doesn't preexist in the text or in the reader but results from the transaction between reader and text.

Furthermore, readers adopt a "stance," or a perspective and orientation toward the text with which they are transacting. Rosenblatt (1978) believes that readers experience texts through two stances on a continuum: efferent to aesthetic. With efferent reading, the reader focuses on information to be taken from the text. With aesthetic reading, the reader becomes absorbed in the imaginative world of character, plot, and setting evoked by the text. Efferent and aesthetic stances may be mixed to different degrees, or the reader may elect to emphasize one stance over the other. This occurs, for example, when readers adopt the efferent stance when reading Dicken's *Great Expectations* to find out what traits to include in an essay about Pip's growth as a character in the novel.

Some educators and literacy specialists have taken the position that an objective meaning can be found in a text. However, others with a view more similar to Rosenblatt (Bleich, 1980; Culler, 1980; Fish, 1980) have argued that the meaning of a text is a more personal response to be found in the reader's mind. Meaning is the result of the reader's meaning construction that engages his or her unique background knowledge and cognitive processing. That meaning is not entirely in either the text or the reader but evolves from interactions among reader, text, teacher, classroom community, and context.

With these interacting features in mind, Robert Ruddell and I (Unrau & Ruddell, 1995) designed a model (see Figure 3.5) that represents text interpretation in classroom contexts.

The model was induced from numerous studies, both theoretical and empirical (Ruddell & Unrau, 1994, 2004), as well as my own classroom teaching experience. The text and classroom context includes the text, task, sources of authority, and sociocultural meanings. The design and features of that environment have a strong influence

Figure 3.5   Text and Classroom Context.

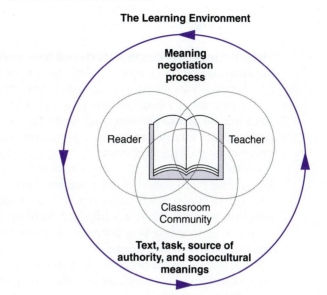

not only on a student's decision to read but also on the ways in which the reading progresses. Our students are more likely to engage in reading if they are motivated, if their prior knowledge is activated, if they feel a personal connection with the tasks they undertake, and if they play a central role in constructing knowledge. In school environments with these features, our students are more likely to read and learn productively.

The meaning negotiation process.   You and your students will negotiate meanings in your classroom for much more than just the printed text. Your students also need to read and construct meanings for the tasks, the authority structure of the classroom, your intentions and expectations, and the sociocultural setting of your classroom.

However, whose meaning will be viewed as valid or correct in your classroom of 25 to 30 students? Will your interpretation alone dominate? Will your students have a say in what texts mean? Will you suppress your personal beliefs about the meaning of texts while enabling your students to express theirs?

While many interpretations by different readers and us should be brought into the learning environment, I believe that the work of both students and ourselves is to confirm that interpretations are well grounded in both the actual text and in our students' unique responses to the text. Interpretations should be reasonably supported with reference to events, statements, or claims made in the text.

Although classroom negotiation over the meanings of a text may not be the final authority, negotiation has many benefits. You and your students share meanings in the classroom community so that, through dialogue, a community of readers comes to hold a range of possible meanings. In Figure 3.5, the three overlapping circles represent the interactive nature of meaning negotiation. Notice, however, that the interactive process overlaps a real text upon which the dialogue is founded. The diagram demonstrates symbolically that the text itself is not the sole object carrying meaning; meanings also arise from transactions between individuals and the text.

During negotiation, your students bring meanings to the interaction, you bring your understandings, and all members of the class interact with the text and each other to clarify meaning.

The hermeneutic circle.   Texts and their interpretations exist in what is called a **hermeneutic circle** (Dilthey, 1976). In that circle, meanings we evoke as readers can perpetually reemerge in modified or new forms. As you and your students voice your views about a text's meaning, a cycle of hypothesis and confirmation or disconfirmation spins. Furthermore, while the meanings we construct for an entire text influence interpretations of its parts, our understanding of the parts shapes our interpretation of the entire text. Why the ghost of Hamlet's father haunts Hamlet becomes increasingly clear as scene after scene exposes treachery in Elsinore Castle. But will we ever know if Hamlet was truly mad? The cycle of interpretation is represented in Figure 3.5 by the circle with arrowheads surrounding the meaning negotiation process. While reading and forming meanings, you and your students should keep in mind that interpretations are forever reinvented as dialogue, disagreement, and debate deem.

The notion of meanings subject to constant reinvention may be unsettling for some domains of knowledge, such as the physical sciences. In fact, fresh meanings are more likely to spring from literature, poetry, or history than from scientific texts. When reading biology or math texts, the emergence of multiple meanings is likely to be more restricted than it would be when reading history or literature. In part, that condition arises from scientific or mathematical texts having a foundation in meanings that are widely agreed upon within their respective communities. In addition, science and math texts are less likely to contain ambiguities that contribute to alternative interpretations. Nevertheless, the history of science tells us that even those meanings that are widely adopted and agreed upon in a scientific community, such as Newtonian physics, can be put under such pressure from new research and theory that scientists must renegotiate the old meaning of texts (T. S. Kuhn, 1962).

Readers reading different kinds of "texts."   We should keep in mind that all learners negotiate several different kinds of meaning: text, task, sources of authority, and aspects of the sociocultural setting. We will examine these separately to understand them more deeply.

Text Meanings.   We know from our understanding of the reading process that different readers construct different meanings for texts because of variables such as their knowledge base, processing skills, and emotional states. In some subjects, such as English, different readings may be more likely than similar ones. However, all teachers in all content areas should understand that legitimate divergent meanings may arise in any subject. More importantly, we should have some clear ideas about how to cope with multiple interpretations of the same text. Our classrooms can, for example, become forums for the articulation and negotiation of multiple meanings in the hermeneutic circle. While shared meanings become part of the classroom's understanding of a text, those meanings are never fixed forever. They may be reinterpreted as the classroom's conversation continues.

Task Meanings.   Tasks are structured activities that are related to the text and that are designed or selected by either us or our students. Students who are capable and effective may interpret these tasks in different ways. As teachers, we may think we have clearly described an activity or exercise we expect students to complete in a particular way. But we are sometimes surprised, as I have often been, to discover that students have constructed divergent interpretations for the task that, upon inspection, I see are quite feasible.

Linda Flower (1987) found that students interpreted assignments differently from each other and from the teachers she observed. A teacher may clearly see in her own mind what she wants her students to do when she asks the students to analyze their response to a problem they had to solve, such as figuring out the causes of the American Revolution. She wants students to step back a little from their problem-solving processes and to reflect on them. However, some students may not have been asked to engage in that form of self-reflection in the past and so find the assignment perplexing, even if fully explained and modeled. Because they lack a clear schema for engaging in self-reflection on their problem-solving processes, students may come up with answers that reveal their representation of the assignment is different from others.

Discussing the multiple interpretations our students may have in response to an assignment is often helpful. Such discussions may help our students to see how others in the class have understood the task and to hear us explain our expectations. In any event, we and our students both need to monitor and assess our decisions about the meanings that have been assigned to tasks.

Source of Authority Meanings.   In classrooms, we and our students inevitably arrive at an understanding of who is the authority. That authority could reside in the text, our student readers, ourselves, or the classroom community. It could also arise from the interactions among these potential sources of authority as we negotiate meanings.

In traditional classrooms, students commonly identify the teacher as the source for authority. When questions about the meaning or interpretation of a text arise during students' learning or classroom discussions, the teacher's understanding of the text is the meaning students usually accept, perhaps as truth. In these classrooms, students have interpreted the learning environment in such a way that teachers are the source of authority. Some students may question the "truths" that teachers transmit in those classrooms, but most students continue to perceive teachers as the final arbiters of accuracy. After all, who gives and grades the tests?

In some classrooms, the text may appear to have the ultimate position as authority. When texts have such power, they are frequently consulted to determine their author's possible intentions. If the text holds the position as ultimate source for authority in the classroom, a reader's interpretation could easily be invalidated because it fails to correspond with the teacher's interpretation in the author's meaning. These invalidations of meaning may occur even though we know that readers construct unique meanings because of their personal background knowledge.

At the opposite extreme are those rather rare classrooms in which the only recognized source for the authority of meaning is the reader's mind. In these classes, rare though they are, only the reader's personal interpretations of a text count.

Each of us in our classrooms decides how much time and thought we want to give to negotiation over the source of authority for text meanings. To a significant degree, the content area in which we teach will influence our decisions about appropriate sources of authority. Some of us may find that the text speaks loudest; some may decide our understandings should have most significant authority; some will encourage their students to exercise textual authority; and some will continually negotiate the proper source of authority on different occasions. Just as the meanings of a printed text need not be fixed forever in a specific meaning, the source of authority for a text's meaning is always negotiable.

Sociocultural Meanings.   Sociocultural meanings are shaped by values and attitudes held in our classrooms, schools, and the larger community within which we and our students live and learn. While we and our students bring our own sociocultural values into the classroom, we also interpret the social life and culture we discover there. In addition, we are likely to interpret aspects of the sociocultural life of the classroom in different ways. For example, in the same classroom, some of our students may believe that their school is a rich ground of resources for learning at the same moment that other students perceive the school as a blackboard jungle of obstruction and frustration. We also construct very different interpretations of our school's sociocultural life. Meanwhile, many of us and our students are likely to share sociocultural interpretations.

To sum up, we and our students read many texts in classrooms. The interpretations we construct of these texts often go unexamined. However, if we are aware of the multiple interpretations that our students create, we have distinct advantages during meaning negotiation. We can help our students discover each other's meanings and explore the evidence that contributes to those meanings. In so doing, we can help our students think through their interpretations and modify them in the light of reasoned discussion. Engaging in the process of reflecting rationally on the meanings they have constructed for texts provides us with opportunities to exercise and develop their tools of critical thinking.

Negotiating meanings in a classroom context: An example.
Now that I've explained the model of meaning negotiation in classrooms, I'd like to tell you a story about a story about a story—but you'll see what that's all about before we're done. The story I want to tell is about a series of instructional episodes that took place in my eleventh-grade classroom.

My class of 27 eleventh graders had read Salinger's *Catcher in the Rye* and was about to begin reading his short story entitled "The Laughing Man" (Salinger, 1981). We were late in the second month of the fall semester, so my students were still acclimating to the reader-based environment that I was encouraging with response logs, sharing of responses in small teams, and ample, whole-class discussions about meanings. As an initial task to activate background knowledge and heighten motivation, I asked my students to predict the story's content based on its title. "Knowing what you know about Salinger's writing," I asked them, "What do you think a story entitled 'The Laughing Man' is going to be about?" Several students responded.

Eric: I think it'll be about a crazy person in a mental hospital. He thinks everything's hysterical.

Sally: Maybe it's about the death of a comedian or a clown.

Margaret: I'd expect it to be ironic. Maybe about someone who's depressed and unhappy with their life but puts on a facade by laughing all the time to make people think he is happy.

The predictions often seemed to reflect what students had learned about Salinger's characters and to show that my students' prior knowledge shaped their thinking. Actually, Margaret was not too far off.

Synopsis of "The Laughing Man."   A brief summary of "The Laughing Man" is essential for your understanding of the meaning-negotiation that occurred in our classroom:

John Gedsudski, the story's almost hero, was a shy, rather short law student who went to New York University and who chaperoned and coached the Comanches, a group of young, energetic boys—mostly about 9 or 10 years old. One of the Comanches, who is now about 35, tells the story as he remembers John, whom the boys considered just short of heroic. It was baseball season, and the Chief (that's what the boys called John) took them in his bus to parks where they could play ball. As they traveled to and from parks in the bus, the boys were frequently entranced by the Chief's exciting stories about a mysterious character called the Laughing Man.

The Laughing Man was disfigured as a boy when Chinese bandits put his head in a vice because his missionary parents wouldn't pay a ransom. He grew up among the bandits but was so ugly he would be tolerated only if he wore a mask over his face. Though shunned by people, he befriended animals in the forest. He imitated the bandits' style, soon surpassed them in crime, and aroused their jealousy to such an extent that they longed to kill him. In a short time, the Laughing Man accumulated a fortune and gave most of it to a monastery but was pursued by an internationally famous detective, Dufarge. He evaded Dufarge with his four friends: a wolf, a dwarf, a Mongolian giant, and a beautiful Eurasian girl. He was never seen without his mask.

Each time the Chief drove the boys to their baseball game, he told them another installment of the story. One unusual day, the Chief stopped his bus on the way to a game to pick up a girl, Mary Hudson. She was, in the boys' eyes, a beauty, but, when she asked to play baseball with them, she got a big 'this-isn't-a-girl's-thing' response. She insisted and eventually took center field. Her fielding of the ball was terrible, but she got a hit every time at bat. The team forgave her fielding, and, for more than a month, she would join the team a couple of days each week.

One day on the bus while the Comanches waited for Mary Hudson to arrive, John told another episode about the Laughing Man. Through detective Dufarge's cheap trickery, the Laughing Man was captured. He removed his mask, stunning his captors. But Dufarge, who had a coughing fit at the moment of the unveiling, didn't look at the horrid face. Covering his eyes, he emptied his gun at the sound of the Laughing Man's heavy breathing. There the episode ended, even though Mary Hudson hadn't arrived.

Without Mary, the Chief drove the bus to the park where the boys were to play baseball. During the middle of the game, she arrived but refused to play ball. The narrator of the story, who was nine at the time, explains that he couldn't figure out what was going on between the Chief and Mary, but he knew she wouldn't play again. She was crying on a distant bench. When the game was called because of darkness, the Chief went over and held the sleeve of Mary's coat. She broke from him and began running away. He didn't follow.

Back on the bus, the Comanches learned that four of detective Dufarge's bullets hit the Laughing Man. As Dufarge approached, however, the Laughing Man spit out the bullets, a feat that burst Dufarge's heart. But the Laughing Man continued to bleed day after day. The animals in the forest soon summoned the Laughing Man's friend, the dwarf, who came with a fresh supply of eagle's blood, a vital food for the Laughing Man. But when the Laughing Man heard that Dufarge had killed the wolf, Black Wing, he crushed the vial of eagle's blood in his hand. As he died, Laughing Man removed his mask.

At the end of the story, one of the Comanches was crying and the narrator's knees were shaking with emotion.

Conventional Interpretation.   A conventional interpretation of "The Laughing Man" posits a parallel between events in the Chief's relationship with Mary Hudson and episodes in the story the Chief tells to his Comanches. Often, the Chief is viewed as a mask for the Laughing Man. As the Chief's relationship with Mary dies, so does the famous and beloved masked bandit. The end of the Chief's affair with Mary is transformed through a creative process into the Laughing Man's demise. Although no one in the class predicted that "The Laughing Man" would be a love story or a story about the creative process, in several ways—under its mask—it is both. However, I was careful not to impose or even to reveal this conventional reading to my students. Instead, I tried to remain open to their discoveries.

Students' Initial Interpretations.   When my students finished reading the story, I asked them to write in their learning logs about the story's meaning—or, if they were totally clueless, as some students said, then to write a summary of it.

Mira and Emily's responses to the story and the classroom context in which we discussed the story exemplify what happens in many classrooms as meanings are negotiated.

Mira, a student who said she "didn't really have an understanding when I first read the story," wrote the following summary of it in her log:

> The story is about a young boy who is reflecting back on his childhood when he was in a boys' group called the Comanches. He is telling us how their "Chief" was adored and loved by all. Even though he wasn't very handsome, the boys still thought of him as gorgeous, and he was their hero. He would take them to the park on weekends to play ball. Then, after the game on the way home, he would tell them an installment of the Laughing Man. The Laughing Man was a disfigured man who stole and murdered, but he did it for good. The boys all looked up to him. Once the Chief had a girlfriend whom the boys adored, but she left suddenly one day. That day the boys saw the fall of two of their favorite heroes, for that was the day the Chief also killed the Laughing Man.

The summaries that students such as Mira wrote represented their understanding of "The Laughing Man" prior to interacting with other readers.

However, even before small-group discussion began, other students wrote their initial interpretations of the story instead of summaries. Emily was one of those students. In her log, she wrote:

> Don't judge a book by its cover. The Laughing Man is a made up creative character. He is hideously ugly so he keeps his face hidden. However, the Laughing Man has a beautiful inside. He means well and has a loving soul. . . . When humans saw Laughing Man's face, they were frightened. However, the animals didn't know Laughing Man was ugly. They didn't know the difference between it, so the animals loved Laughing Man. They reached further down than just skin to realize how wonderful Laughing Man was. J. D. Salinger I believe wants us to be mature enough not to judge people by their outside appearance.

Emily's interpretation is one of many different meanings that students initially attributed to the story.

After reading the story and writing summaries or interpretations of it in their logs, students met in small groups to share their journal entries. I introduced this chapter with a description of my students' working in small groups. Their discussions led to significant changes or shifts in meanings for both the smaller parts of the story and the story as a whole.

During whole-class discussions, I urged my students to explore these alternative meanings and asked them to explain how they arrived at them. The process contributed to our creating a classroom community meaning for both the story and its parts.

Interpretations Negotiated and Reformed.   A few days after the small-group and class discussions, I asked my students to write their current understanding of the story and to describe how and why their interpretation changed—if it had. Most students reported that they had formed or reformed the meanings they had given to the story during or after the small-group and class discussions. Mira, whose initial summary was presented earlier, arrived at a meaning that went significantly beyond that initial response. She wrote:

> I think that the story of the Laughing Man that the chief would tell the Comanches was in a sense the way he saw himself. The Laughing Man was an alter ego of John Gedsudski, the Chief. Both were not handsome and shunned by their society and peers. Both had a band of loyal followers who looked up to them. For the Chief, it was the kids; for the Laughing Man, it was a dwarf, a Mongolian, and a beautiful Eurasian girl. At around the time that the Laughing Man is held captive by Dufarge, the Chief is having problems with Mary Hudson. When the Laughing Man gets shot, it is at the same time the Chief and Mary break up. This just enforces my theory that the Chief and the Laughing Man are one in the same. The Chief takes the installments from his own day to day life, but he enhances them and makes them more exciting.

Many students like Mira contributed to what became a classroom community meaning for the relationship between the Chief and Laughing Man, that is, that the two paralleled each other in many ways. As for the vial of eagle's blood that could have saved the Laughing Man, Mira wrote that it "represents the Chief's love for Mary."

Emily, whose initial, rather stock response to the story was "You can't judge a book by its cover," later wrote that the story was "tragic." She thought that the Chief was so hurt and depressed by the breakup of his relationship with Mary that he "took it out on the players."

> That night, driving home on the bus, John began telling the story of the Laughing Man once again. In this final story, John killed the Laughing Man because Mary left him, and because his love was taken away from him, he did the same to the Comanches. They loved the Laughing Man so John took him away from them.

Although Emily interprets the meaning of the Laughing Man's death quite differently from Mira, Emily wrote that the vial of eagle's blood that might have saved Laughing Man represented John's love for Mary, which was crushed.

Benefits of meaning negotiation.   Responding to texts in an environment that encouraged the formation and expression of individual interpretations and their negotiation in a classroom community appeared to benefit many of my students. One of them, Sarah, wrote the following:

> Too many teachers think that their understanding is the only correct one. Now I understand that a story can mean so many things, and as long as you can back it with at least some good thought, it's right—for yourself. Now I feel I can just put more of my thoughts out there even if other people don't agree. I basically think that's why my interpretation of "The Laughing Man" has changed. I think I have a little more freedom to say what I think.

What is important about "The Laughing Man" example for our discussion is not only the divergent interpretations of the story by different students, but also the dialogue, the meaning negotiation process, that occurred among students and between students and teacher.

The more you know about meaning construction and negotiation in your classrooms, the more reflective you and your students may become. Teachers who encourage their students' active engagement in meaning negotiation directly contribute to their students' capacity to think more critically about what to believe about texts and what actions to take based upon those beliefs. In short, with greater understanding of classroom discourse over texts, you can help students become more critical readers.

Implications of the Model for Teaching

Before launching upon this journey into a model of reading, I stated that one of the benefits of having a model could be the hints and clues it gives about intervention strategies that may help struggling readers improve at different points in the reading process. What are these hints and clues to make us better teachers of literacy and content knowledge?

- Background knowledge stored in memory serves as an essential and valuable resource for all readers. We can assess that background knowledge, discover methods to activate it, work with students to extend or expand it, and apply procedures to assess its growth.

- Without solid and automatic decoding skills, such as rapid processing of letter-sound correspondences and the application of effective word attack skills, readers will not have enough working memory to construct meaning for texts they struggle to read. We should assess our students' decoding skills to help decide if assigned texts are manageable.

- Knowledge of word meanings, including immediate access to the meanings of high-frequency words, is critical to the reader's meaning construction process. Building vocabulary knowledge removes obstacles to comprehension.

- Ready knowledge of sentence patterns and structures contributes to more automatic processing when reading. With speedy construction of propositions in the form of phrases and sentences, less working memory must be devoted to basic elements in the meaning making process, and more memory can be devoted to questioning, analyzing, comparing interpretations, and evaluating.

- Readers should be trained and encouraged to monitor continuously the meaning construction process. Readers can be taught to watch for breakdowns in comprehension and for inconsistencies in their internal text representation.

- Comprehension-fostering strategies serve readers well. The more effective strategies readers learn and use, the better the chances of high-quality comprehension. Strategies to encourage monitoring and detection of confusion can be taught to students at all reading levels.

- Readers build mental text representation in both verbal and visual forms. Readers can be encouraged to attend to both coding modes to enhance comprehension.

- An examination of the meaning negotiation process in classroom contexts yields several practical suggestions for growing interpretive, thoughtful classroom communities:

  a. Encourage readers in their construction and exploration of meanings.
  b. Use teams to share and shape reader responses to texts.

    c. Encourage and orchestrate more student-to-student interaction patterns rather than student-to-teacher patterns.

    d. Design team activities so that stores of knowledge and interpretations shared will be brought to the whole class for discussion.

    e. Engage in whole-class conversations that build upon reader's individual responses, explanations of their derivation, and comparisons between them.

    f. Discuss standards for the validity of interpretations to enable the interpretive community to acknowledge and understand its assumptions.

    g. Cultivate in readers an evolutionary perspective of texts (a hermeneutic perspective) rather than seeking final, absolute interpretations of texts.

    h. Prompt readers to explain or support their interpretations with reference to reasons, such as evidence from the text interpreted.

    i. Encourage students through instruction and climate control to request explanations from each other for the grounds of text interpretations.

    j. Through classroom activities and interactions, show the importance of dialogue in shaping meanings not only for the printed texts read in class, but also for tasks that are assigned, for sources of classroom authority, and for sociocultural features, such as students' perceptions of their own role and function in classrooms.

    k. Encourage a welcoming, open, inquisitive, questioning, and skeptical spirit with respect to the meaning formation process and the meanings formed.

- With this reading model as a foundation and reference point, we can identify a range of reading abilities and define several categories of readers that are likely to appear in our classrooms. We can also see what problems plague struggling readers and what skills enhance the performance of highly proficient ones.

Double-Entry Journal: After Reading

Review the description of the reading process you reported after reading the passage about Tony but before reading this chapter. What features, if any, would you add to capture what researchers have found goes on when a reader reads? How could your understanding of reading influence the way you could help students master content knowledge/skills and develop literacy?

Chapter 4

ASSESSING READERS AND THEIR TEXTS

After reading chapter 4, you should be able to answer the following questions:

1. What is diagnostic teaching?

2. How will diagnostic decision making help in setting sound learning goals and developing appropriate instruction for students?

3. What are major differences between formal and informal assessment and what are some examples of each related to reading?

4. How can informal assessments, such as retellings, think-alouds, and portfolios, help provide a closer look at students' comprehension processes and ways to improve them?

5. How can I discover what comprehension strategies my students use and how much metacognitive awareness they have?

6. What categories of adolescent readers am I likely to find in my classroom?

7. How can I determine the readability and accessibility of texts for my students?

If, at the beginning of a class, you wanted to evaluate your students to discover how well they read and what problems they had with reading, what steps would you take?

Diagnostic Teaching

History is littered with examples of solutions that failed because the problems they were to solve were inaccurately described and explained. An 18th-century Scottish physician, John Brown, treated diseases by administering large doses of either stimulants or sedatives to his patients. Based on his observations, he concluded that diseases were caused by too much or too little stimulation. As you might guess, his solution caused considerable harm to many people because the basis of the treatment method was wrong.

Describing and explaining how a process works when it works correctly enables us to understand what changes need to be made when a procedure is flawed. We all have witnessed successful problem-solving moments when we have discovered the right fit between a problem's description and the solution we have selected for it.

Some of these solutions are quite simple. After we flip a light switch in the hallway, a lightbulb fails to come on. We examine the bulb, discover the filament is broken, replace the bulb, flip the switch, and illuminate the hallway.

Some problems are far more difficult to solve. Without clear descriptions and explanations of learning processes, we are going to have trouble bringing light to the problems our students encounter when trying to learn. Why struggling students cannot create meanings from a text they are trying to read is many a teacher's dark puzzle. Gaining clearer descriptions and explanations of how our students read and why their lights too often fail to go on is the purpose of this chapter.

Teachers, like physicians, can view themselves as diagnosticians. But the illnesses teachers treat are those caused by improper conceptualization, lack of appropriate skills, misconceived strategies, and ineffective thinking. They engage in what Solomon and Morocco (1999) describe as *critical scrutiny* of student output to discover ways to improve performance. Diagnostic teachers carefully examine student work for signs of healthy, productive thinking that leads to correct understanding and good solutions, but they also look for signs of conceptualizations and problem-solving procedures that are unproductive and ineffective. And, like physicians, diagnostic teachers find ways they can carefully administer new conceptions to students, new procedures, and new strategies that lead to productive thinking and learning.

Throughout our professional careers, we should embrace the endless opportunities to observe how students' minds are working to solve the learning problems that we and the world present to them. The more we learn over years of careful observation and the more strategies we can bring to bear in helping students solve the problems they face, the better we can be at diagnosing and correcting our students' problems with learning.

Although we will be reviewing standardized, norm-referenced tests as well as other assessment tools, our goal should not be simply the ranking of our students by level of skill or knowledge. Instead, the diagnostic teacher's focus should be on understanding the features, gross and subtle, of each student's thinking, that is, of each student's mental operations when reading and learning. That knowledge gained from critical scrutiny should then guide teaching practice. The diagnostic teacher emphasizes building students' capacity to learn rather than simply depositing information.

When diagnostic teachers view reading (as well as writing) as meaning-making processes, as we've seen in the previous chapter, these teachers are far more likely to make efforts to understand how their students make meaning from texts. They look for each student's particular way of comprehending texts, and they try to discover how to improve the quality of that comprehension rather than delivering generic, one-size-fits-all solutions.

Content Teachers' Diagnostic Decision Making About Reading

A diagnostic decision-making approach to instruction calls for a thoughtful diagnostic assessment of students before, during, and after instruction. The purpose for engaging in that assessment is to develop diagnostic teaching sessions and appropriate reading instruction. Although time away from content coverage is the bane of many a teacher, assessing students and their texts will help you design instruction that accounts for your student's reading level and its further development. That diagnostic approach should be applied to instructional programs that use literacy skills and strategies, such as reading, to master knowledge in content courses.

A diagnostic approach to reading assessment for content area teachers answers several questions, some of which Kibby (1995) poses:

1. What is the student's current level of reading ability, and is it satisfactory for the reading expected in the course?
2. Which reading strategies and skills strengthen or limit the student's reading?
3. What factors are associated with the student's reading ability?
4. What instructional conditions most favor the student's learning?
5. What recommendations or referrals will further the student's reading development?

Going through the steps of the diagnostic decision-making process with students enables you to answer each of these questions and provide optimum reading instruction and growth for students in your classes.

In adapting Kibby's (1995) diagnostic decision-making process to middle and high school teaching, I identified seven steps to guide the assessment of students in content classrooms:

Step 1. Begin learning about each student's identity, history, goals, values, and interests.

Step 2. Determine the expected level of reading at which students will need to perform satisfactorily in the course.

Step 3. Assess each student's reading capacity using a standardized reading test, Group Reading Inventory, or Curriculum-Based Measurement. For students reading below grade level or observed to have significant problems comprehending course texts, administer an Informal Reading Inventory (IRI) to clarify instructional needs.

Step 4. Develop an overall literacy profile for the whole class of students, including strengths and weaknesses of the entire group.

Step 5. Inventory and review available teaching strategies and resources.

Step 6. Engage in diagnostic teaching to maximize compatibility between content texts and readers' capacity.

Step 7. Continue instructional monitoring, modifications, and recommendations, including referrals for remedial reading instruction.

In the following discussion, I'll describe each step in more detail, explaining procedures to apply in your classrooms. Figure 4.1, the Content Teachers Diagnostic Decision-Making Model, provides a graphic summary of the process.

Step 1. Student's Identity, History, Goals, Values, and Interests

Recall that often-heard educator's quip, "I teach students—not (fill in the subject)"? Of course, there's much to commend the view that what comes first is the student's mind and not the content knowledge teachers may want to deposit there. There's plenty of evidence on influential teachers (Ruddell, 1995; Ruddell, Draheim, & Barnes, 1990) to assert that students favor and respond favorably to some teachers more than others. Students tend to prefer teachers who take a personal interest in their learning, who ask questions about how they are responding to instruction, and who want to engage their students by discovering what interests them and how they can become more interested in a course's content.

None of this is meant to demean the importance of teachers' knowledge of their subjects. As the National Board for Professional Teaching Standards (2007) puts it: "Teachers know the subjects they teach and how to teach those subjects to students." Both knowledge of your subject *and* of the procedures to teach it must enlighten your classrooms.

For diagnostic teaching, the student must come first. Diagnostic teachers want and need to discover as much as they can learn about their students' identities, their educational histories, their aspirations, their values, and their interests. Although we investigate these antecedents of instructional engagement much more carefully in chapter 2 on motivation, diagnostic teachers should be committed to discovering what they can about their students in order to put each student's reading into perspective.

Early in the school year, you can discover a lot about your students' reading and attitudes toward reading through surveys and questionnaires. Nancy Atwell (1998), the author of *In the Middle,* has designed a reading survey she gives to her middle school students so she can learn about each student's reading experiences and attitudes at the beginning of the school year. She asks about how they learned to read, why they read, what they think it takes to be a good reader, what kinds of books they like to read, how often they read at home on their own, and how they feel about reading in general. During the first week of school, students complete her surveys, and she reads them over, makes notes about who her students are, and puts the surveys into individual folders for each student.

Jeff Waid, a teacher at Los Angeles High School, keeps a "student chronicle," a continuous and evolving record of each of his students throughout the school year. He starts the chronicle with a Student Information Sheet, which provides background

Figure 4.1 Content Teacher's Diagnostic Decision-Making Model.

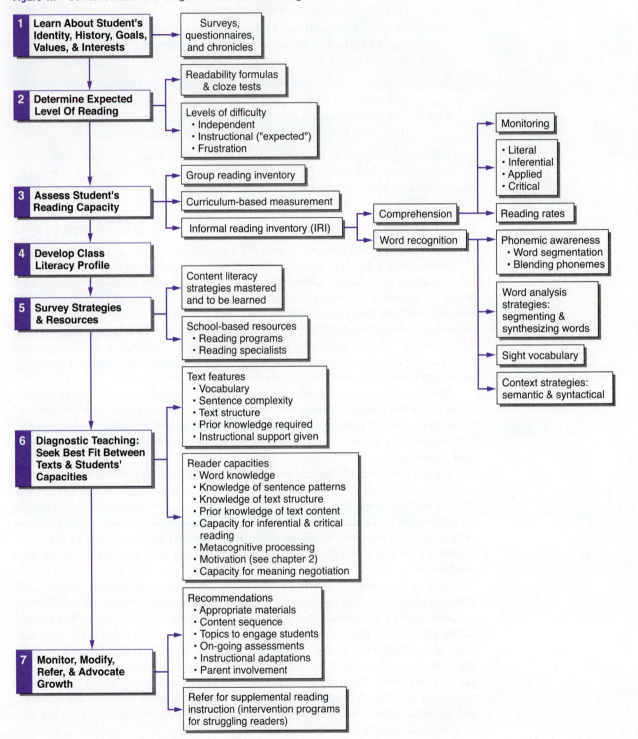

data about each student's home language, after-school jobs, responsibility for siblings, and personal information about favorite movies and music. (See Figure 4.2.) Early in the school year, Jeff asks students to write an autobiography that includes information gathered through interviews of family members—information about each student's language history, learning goals, and home life. Jeff believes that, by maintaining chronicles for his students, they recognize that their history and home life are valued and "feel confident in bringing their entire experience to bear as readers and writers" in his classroom (Waid, 2002). The evolving chronicles deepen the ways in which he interacts with his students and they interact with him.

Step 2. Expected Level of Reading

Expected level of reading is the level of difficulty that a text presents to a reader. It's the level of reading at which a reader is expected to perform. But at what level *is* the student expected to perform? Usually, the readability of a text is measured with a readability formula or a cloze test. Readability formulas yield a grade level, so a readability level of 9 means that, to successfully construct meaning for that text, a student should be able to read at the ninth-grade level or better. Cloze tests yield categories of text difficulty. These categories span the independent, instructional, or frustration levels. More details about measures of readability are given later in this chapter.

The expected level for satisfactory reading performance in a class is usually the *instructional*, which means the reader is reading at grade level. Unlike the independent level, the instructional level assumes that you will provide support for reading texts. However, while some of your students will find the text to be at their frustration level, other students may need more challenging texts in order to grow.

Step 3. Assessment of Students' Reading Capacity

The next step entails your assessing each student's current reading capacity to decide if the student has the capacity to satisfactorily engage and learn from your content area texts. Your student's silent-reading comprehension may be measured with any of several reading comprehension tests, such as the Gates-MacGinitie Reading Comprehension Test. Many states annually administer their own standardized tests of reading. The results of a standardized reading comprehension test may be a percentile rank, a stanine score, a normal curve equivalent (NCE), or a grade-equivalent score. I'll explain these scores when we discuss test interpretation later in this chapter. Often scores from standardized reading tests are available in a student's cumulative file. However, if scores are more than a year old, I recommend testing to obtain a more current score.

You can also give your students a Group Reading Inventory (GRI) and/or a Curriculum-Based Measurement (CBM) to assess their capacity to read texts normally used in your content area. The procedures for constructing and giving GRIs and CBMs are also provided later in this chapter.

If a student is more than a year below grade level or is manifesting significant frustration in comprehending the course's reading material, I recommend administration of an Informal Reading Inventory.

An Informal Reading Inventory, or IRI, generates more-detailed information about a student's reading process than standardized reading tests, GRIs, or CBMs. An IRI yields estimates for a student's independent, instructional, and frustration levels and information about performance on different kinds of comprehension and aspects

Figure 4.2 Student Information Sheet.

STUDENT INFORMATION SHEET

Please take your time and fill out this sheet as completely and honestly as possible. And hey, please write neatly.

Name _____
                    First   Middle   Last

The name you go by _____ Birthday _____ Grade _____

Parent(s)/Guardian _____ Relationship _____
                              First   Last

Parent(s)/Guardian _____ Relationship _____
                              First   Last

Address _____ City _____ Zip _____

Telephone Number _____

                                          Not at all ⟵——————⟶ Very Well
I speak and understand English (circle one):   1   2   3   4   5
My parents speak and understand English: 1   2   3   4   5

If you speak another language besides English, please answer the following questions:

What other languages do you speak? _____

                    Not Fluently ⟵——————⟶ Very Fluently
How fluently?   1   2   3   4   5

In what other countries have you lived? _____

How long have you lived in the United States? _____

Please describe any special limitations about you that I should be aware of so I can best help you in this class (For instance, do you need to sit close to the front to see?)

_____

Is there anything that prevents you from studying or doing your homework? Please explain (e.g., "I have to share a bedroom with my sister who talks too much and bugs me every time I try to do my work.") _____

_____

_____

If you have a job, where is it? _____

How many hours a week do you work? _____

What are your responsibilities around the house (e.g., chores, caring for brothers and sisters)? _____

_____

_____

Source: Originally designed by Keri Lew and Nick M. Deligencia and modified by Jeff Waid.

Figure 4.2   *Continued*

Please do your best to answer the following:

What is your favorite:

Television Show? _____

    Why? _____

Radio Station? _____

    Why? _____

Music Group? _____

    Why? _____

Individual Singer? _____

    Why? _____

Song? _____

    Why? _____

Latest Movie? _____

    Why? _____

All-time Movie? _____

    Why? _____

Actor/Actress? _____

    Why? _____

What hobbies, clubs, sports, or outside activities have you enjoyed? _____

_____

_____

What are your plans for the future? _____

_____

What are your plans for now? _____

_____

What college would you like to attend? _____

Please complete the following sentences:

The greatest things about me are: _____

_____

_____

The greatest problems confronting me now are:

_____

_____

In the space below, write down three questions that you would like to ask me.

THE REAL-LIFE READING AND COMPREHENSION TEST...

CAUTION DRY PAINT

Source: NON SEQUITUR © 2001 Wiley Miller. Dist. by UNIVERSAL PRESS SYNDICATE. Reprinted with permission. All rights reserved.

of word recognition. You may not have the time to administer IRIs to all your students because they take between 30 and 45 minutes. However, other specialists in your school could give the inventory and provide you with information about the results.

Step 4. Class Literacy Profile

After your students have been given tests to measure their reading capacities, you can create a profile for the entire class. That profile should reveal the reading levels for each student as indicated by standardized reading tests, GRIs, and CBMs. Students who are likely to be struggling readers in your course should be given further diagnostic testing, such as the IRI recommended in Step 3. Their strengths and weaknesses should be taken into account as you design lessons that entail reading. Some of these struggling readers may need additional reading instruction beyond what you could possibly offer. We discuss the importance of appropriate referral of such students in Step 7.

You do not need to gather information about all students before instruction begins. As we've seen, diagnostic teaching entails ongoing observation. Group surveys, questionnaires, and standardized group tests can be administered at the beginning of the course or school year.

Step 5. Teaching Strategies and Resources

At this stage, diagnostic teachers survey the strategies and resources available for their use in helping students read and learn from reading. Resources may include reading specialists or literacy coaches in your school or district and reading intervention programs. Throughout this text, I'll introduce you to strategies to enhance comprehension. So even if you are a beginning teacher feeling limited by the number of instructional strategies you currently know, in a few days or weeks you'll be introduced to many more. All can be tried in the diagnostic teacher's classroom to discover how they enable your students to read and learn more effectively.

Step 6. Diagnostic Teaching

Diagnostic teachers strive for compatibility between their students' reading capacities and course texts. When selecting content textbooks and supplementary reading materials, you should weigh and balance readers' capacities with features of the texts. At the diagnostic teaching stage in the decision-making process, you should have gathered enough information to discover the kinds of instructional conditions generally favorable to your students.

If text comprehension requirements are too great, even readers with good monitoring and control skills, high motivation, and considerable capacity for meaning negotiation over texts in the classroom will need lots of teacher support—or they will be overwhelmed.

Text features.   When evaluating texts that your students will encounter, you need to consider several text features that determine a text's accessibility to your students. You should survey the text's vocabulary to discover what types of problems with word recognition and word meanings your students are likely to encounter. You should also examine and evaluate sentence length and complexity, including the number of embedded phrases and clauses. Fry's Readability Formula, described later in this chapter, will help you evaluate the challenge of both vocabulary and sentences because those features are built into that formula. The kinds of text structures that an author uses to convey content are important to assess, as are the forms and depth of prior knowledge expected of readers and the kinds of instructional support, such as graphic organizers, definitions of terms, summaries, and questions, provided in the text.

Reader capacities.   To estimate a text's accessibility to your students, you will need to evaluate several of their capacities as readers. These include their knowledge of words, sentence patterns, and text structure; their prior knowledge related to a text; their ability for inferential and critical thinking; their metacognitive skill; their motivation; and their capacity for meaning negotiation. An assortment of instruments, formal and informal, are described in this chapter and other chapters to help you determine your students' compatibility with the texts they will read.

Finding, adapting, and supporting texts for instruction.   Finding reading materials that fit a specific profile of needs for just *one* struggling reader is challenging. Finding the best fit between available content texts and the composite literacy profile for an entire class is a greater challenge. However, I have come to believe that good diagnostic teaching requires us to make serious and genuine efforts to attain that best fit. Too often the mismatch between students' reading capacities and a course's text-reading requirements results in massive frustration for both students and teachers.

We should remember, however, that texts at students' instructional levels could be made accessible with teacher support. Even texts that are at your students' frustration levels can often be adapted or presented so those students can gain access to the information in them. Many reading comprehension strategies described in the next chapter help readers construct meaning through directed or guided interaction with challenging texts. At the other end of the spectrum from readers who find content texts frustrating are those who find the texts to be at an easy independent-reading level. You'll need to take into account more knowledgeable and skilled readers who may not be sufficiently challenged by the course reading materials.

Through diagnostic discovery and teaching, you can plan your lessons to provide your students greater opportunity to master the material you present to your classes. While teaching, observe and collect information to guide your instructional decision making. With that knowledge, you can more effectively choose teaching strategies and resources to provide your students additional opportunities to learn strategies and skills that will help them grow as readers and learners.

Step 7. Instructional Monitoring, Modification, and Recommendations

Diagnostic teachers who follow Solomon and Morocco's (1999) suggestions monitor and observe their students' reading and learning in detail and continue to make judgments about (a) students' strategies and comprehension, (b) their acquisition of subject-matter knowledge, and (c) the effectiveness of teaching strategies and practices used in the classroom. You can observe a wide range of factors affecting learning from texts:

- your students' levels of interest and motivation,
- their responses to success as well as failure,
- their attention span,
- the effects of pace on their learning, and
- the amount of additional support and review of content required for their success.

Using these observations, you can modify your teaching, note the impact of those modifications, and make recommendations. Those recommendations include the assignment of appropriate materials, the selection of topics to engage students, instructional adaptation, and ongoing assessment.

While parental involvement in children's literacy development tends to taper off as children progress through the middle and high school years, I believe parents' continued engagement has many benefits. Keeping parents informed of students' progress in reading development, while sometimes overlooked, is especially important for struggling readers. Parents can offer at-home support for literacy growth as well as encouragement for school-related literacy tasks. In some families, middle and high school students discuss school and independent reading with parents. These discussions can provide students with opportunities to explore aspects of their reading they may otherwise miss. Some teachers promote communication with parents by developing and sending home newsletters that give parents information about the curriculum, including books, their children are covering in school.

Recommendations for individual reading remediation. Serious reading problems are too often ignored or denied because no program has been established to address the literacy needs of struggling readers. As Kibby (1985, p. 53) points out, individual reading remediation should be recommended "even if there are no individual instructional facilities available or funds for such facilities." His rationale for these recommendations make complete sense because parents may not seek alternative reading remediation resources if they are not informed of their children's reading difficulties. Urging students and their families to seek help may prompt school personnel and other educational agencies to provide essential programs for struggling readers who may be at risk of failing and of eventually dropping out of school.

Assessment Instruments for Diagnostic Teaching

You are the best assessment instrument your students have. Your observational and interpretive powers comprise the most powerful set of reading and learning assessment tools that your students could ever face. What you observe, how deeply you observe, and how you interpret those observations are the basis for critical dimensions of teaching, such as your understanding of your students' comprehension levels, skills, and needs. Your observations of your students' behavior in classrooms—how they interact with texts and how they participate in text-based discussions—often yield information and insights far more useful than data from a standardized test. However, both formal and informal reading assessment tools can focus and magnify your observational powers to help you discern what's going on in the minds of your students as they read and learn.

To effectively implement a diagnostic decision-making process, you should understand what instruments can aid diagnostic work and how to use them. Some of these instruments are formal tests; others are informal assessment instruments.

Formal Assessment

Several features define the difference between formal and informal assessment. (See Table 4.1 for a summary.) Formal tests are standardized. All test-takers complete similar tasks and follow similar procedures; this allows comparisons between individuals or groups taking the test. Given directions must be followed, and time limits, if provided, must be observed. Formal testing includes international-, national-, state-, and district-level assessment. The instruments used for these large-scale evaluations are usually designed by testing experts. Some formal tests, such as the National Assessment of Educational Progress (NAEP) or the Scholastic Achievement Test (SAT), include test items that are usually used once and retired, to be replaced by similar but unique items. Other formal tests, such as the Gates-MacGinitie Reading Test or the Stanford Achievement Test, include passages and items that are used repeatedly. Reading-comprehension tests often have two or more different forms at the same grade levels to measure growth over time.

Formal testing in middle and high schools is extensive. Middle school testing programs often include the Stanford Achievement Tests, the Iowa Test of Basic Skills, or a state's accountability test aligned with content standards, such as the Texas

Table 4.1 Two Methods of Assessment Compared

	FORMAL ASSESSMENT (AKA: "HIGH-STAKES")	INFORMAL ASSESSMENT (AKA: "AUTHENTIC" OR "NATURALISTIC")
Purposes, Uses for Data	• Measurement of student performance, usually in groups, to compare reading levels or determine growth following intervention. • Measure change for state accountability and reward programs. • Determine reading levels to select texts. • Measure reading ranges in a class. • Categorize students, e.g., to identify struggling or delayed readers for further diagnosis or placement.	• Identify qualities of students' reading performance, such as fluency and miscues. • Discover strategy use while reading. • Monitor and detect problems in comprehension. • Resources for teacher team meetings. • Data for benchmarks to monitor development (e.g., CBMs). • Feedback to evaluate effectiveness of teaching.
Designers	Testing companies and committees of experts.	Teachers, reading experts.
Student Interaction with Tasks	All subjects complete similar tasks, follow similar procedures, observe same time limits. Students usually complete test in groups according to schedule.	May complete similar or different tasks; procedures usually similar but may vary; time limits less likely. Usually given in small groups or one-on-one. May be repeatedly given to measure progress or monitor development.
Teacher's Role	Administer test, monitor, interpret results. May do some test preparation.	Observe reading behavior, interact with students, record reading behavior, analyze data.
Method of Measurement	Multiple choice, other forms of closed-ended questions, quantitative.	Observations, more open-ended questions, qualitative.
Examples	IEA, NAEP, State Testing Programs (STAR in California, TAKS in Texas), test batteries (Stanford Achievement Test, Iowa Test of Basic Skills), Gates-MacGinitie, Scholastic Aptitude Test (SAT).	Informal Reading Inventory (IRI), Group Reading Inventory, Curriculum-Based Measures, Running Records, cloze, portfolios, teacher-made tests, classroom observations, student self-reports.

Assessment of Knowledge and Skills (TAKS). Teachers may also administer some form of reading test, such as the Nelson-Denny or the Gates-MacGinitie. While all these tests may also appear in high school testing programs, other kinds of "high-stakes" formal testing for college admission, such as the Scholastic Achievement Tests (SAT) or the American College Test (ACT), absorb the attention of thousands of students. Many other state-, district-, or school-sponsored testing programs have flourished in recent years, adding to a test-heavy schedule.

Your role in these testing programs will usually be that of monitor. However, because some of these tests may be aligned to teaching standards and reflect instruction, you and your school's administrators may have some significant stake in their outcome. The extent of that stake varies from state to state, district to district, and school to school. While some school cultures are sensitive to test performance, others are far less so.

Norm-Referenced Tests

A norm-referenced test is a standardized test that can be used to compare one student's reading performance with that of a reference group. The reference groups are often composed of thousands of students who are drawn from a wide sampling of schools in different communities. Norms are ranges of scores representing an average and are used to compare a student's performance with others who have taken the test.

Norm-referenced survey reading tests yield several different kinds of scores: raw score, percentile rank, stanine, normal curve equivalent, and grade-equivalent score.

The **raw score** is nothing other than the total number of items a student got correct on the test or its subparts. The subparts of a norm-referenced reading test usually consist of separate comprehension and vocabulary tests. You can refer to appropriate tables and transform raw scores into more meaningful scores, such as those described next.

The **percentile rank** reveals where a student's raw score lies, in percentage categories from 0% to 99%, within a range of scores. It tells the percentage of students in the same grade with lower raw scores. For a percentile score of 37, a student has done better than 37% of the students in the norm-referenced group who took the test. A percentile score of 50 shows that the test taker has done better than half the students in the norm-referenced group.

Similar to percentile ranks, **normal curve equivalents (NCEs)** present a student's reading level relative to other students at the same grade level. NCEs are based on percentile ranks, but those percentiles have been changed into a scale of equal reading achievement units. Because each NCE unit is equal throughout the scale, NCEs can be used for computing averages and making comparisons between scores.

Stanines divide the spectrum of reading achievement into nine score bands, or categories. Because each stanine measures reading in a relatively broad band of achievement, stanines do not encourage focusing on what may be meaningless, small score differences.

Grade-equivalent scores (GEs) rank students' reading performance within groups that include students from all grades. They characterize performance in terms equal to that of other readers in a particular grade. A grade equivalent of 8.5 indicates that the reader performed as well as the average eighth grader in the sixth month (February) of the eighth grade because the first month (September) would be scored as 8.0. GEs are not standards or criteria to be reached. They are simply measures of performance.

Criterion-Referenced Tests

Although a norm-referenced test yields results that enable comparisons between test takers—and, thereby, may foster competition—criterion-referenced tests are designed to measure a student's performance against a set standard or criterion. Teachers in some states must score at or above a set standard on tests of basic skills, such as reading comprehension, essay writing, and mathematics, in order to be eligible to receive a teaching credential.

As a teacher, you may also establish standards of performance that your students must attain before they can progress to the next unit. Some districts establish literacy criteria, such as a certain level of performance on reading and writing tasks that must be reached before a student can progress to the third grade, transition from middle to high school, or receive a diploma.

Currently, many states use norm-referenced testing programs that may not be closely tied to a school's, a district's, or even a state's curriculum. Because criterion-referenced tests provide information about students' mastery of specific curriculum content, many educators (Calkins, Montgomery, & Santman, 1998) are urging their use rather than norm-referenced testing. With criterion-referenced tests, teachers, students, and their parents can determine what kind and degree of mastery in reading or any other subject has been established by assessment policy. Furthermore, standards, frameworks, teacher preparation programs, and mission statements of discipline-based professional organization can be aligned with content criteria. Knowing those expectations, you and your students can work together toward their attainment.

Assessing the Assessment Instruments

Validity.
To evaluate the quality of assessment instruments, we need to take into account a test's validity and its reliability. For a test to be valid, it must measure what its designers claim it will measure. If test designers say that a test is made to measure reading comprehension but provide no evidence that it actually does, we cannot view the test as a valid instrument.

Several concepts of validity are commonly applied, including construct and content validity. **Construct validity** refers to the degree to which some theory (or construct) is reflected in a test. Thus, if your students were able to rapidly identify the meaning of words on a test of vocabulary, they would, in theory, have enough automaticity and semantic knowledge to read well. So a test measuring a student's memory for the meaning of a list of vocabulary words has construct validity as a test of reading. **Content validity** refers to the match between the content of a test and the reading or tasks that are taught in the curriculum. A valid test of reading strategy instruction must reflect the strategies taught as part of the curriculum. If you teach your students how to activate background knowledge related to a topic about which they were to read and you give them a test to see if they used that approach when reading, your test has content validity.

Reliability.
A test may measure what it purports to measure at one time. But does it do so consistently? A **reliable test** is one that consistently measures what it is designed to measure. So, if one of your students retakes a reliable test, you would expect that student to receive approximately the same result.

Standard error of measurement.
A single resulting score on a test should be viewed as a more or less narrow range or spectrum of scores rather than an absolute point on a scale. That's because no test is perfect, and scores are likely to have errors built into them. Statisticians refer to these errors as the *standard error of measurement*, or SEM. An SEM is an estimate of the variance between the score actually received and the score that would result from a "perfect" test.

Reading Processes That Cannot Be Adequately Assessed

We can learn quite a lot about our students' reading processes through formal procedures that now exist. With commercial reading comprehension tests, we can measure vocabulary and comprehension of several kinds, such as literal, inferential, applied, and critical comprehension. However, several aspects of the reading process are difficult, if not impossible, for us to adequately quantify or measure with formal, norm-referenced tests. Among those are our students'

- background knowledge relevant to specific texts encoded in long-term memory (LTM);
- range of genre knowledge, including poetic language and argumentation, held in LTM;
- depth of engagement experienced with texts;
- range of reading strategies (stored in LTM) activated when reading, especially when the going gets tough;
- capacity to summarize, ask questions, and make predictions while reading (metacognitive strategies);
- degree of automaticity in word identification; and
- application of learning to near and far transfer tasks.

Some of these features can be measured or examined more closely with informal assessment instruments.

Informal Assessment

While informal tests may be made to measure any population of students on just about any skill and provide more flexibility in administration, they lack a standard scale (norms) for categorizing or ranking student performance. However, with informal instruments, you can often discover more about students' background knowledge, range of genre knowledge, depth of engagement, strategy use, metacognitive skills, word recognition processes, and comprehension. Informal assessments, such as miscue analysis or informal reading inventories, often provide detailed information that helps with decision making. Without detailed information about how your students respond to texts often used in your classroom instruction, you will have less information with which to make informed decisions about what kinds of texts are best used for content instruction. Furthermore, informal assessments can provide insights about how your students think and construct meaning while they read.

Informal assessments of reading are often called *authentic* reading assessments. Usually, authentic assessments engage students in the reading of actual texts used in classroom instruction or in tasks undertaken in a natural environment, such as a classroom, rather than tasks completed in a clinical or test-structured environment. Authentic assessments are often based on reading materials and tasks normally a part of daily classroom teaching.

Informal, or authentic, reading assessment will also allow you to see more clearly your students' thinking and meaning construction processes. By looking closely at those thinking processes, you can better understand what is working and what is breaking down as your students construct meaning through interaction with content area texts.

Among the informal reading assessments we will review are the Group Reading Inventory (GRI), miscue analysis, running records, Curriculum-Based Measurement (CBM), retellings, comprehension think-alouds, and interviews.

Group Reading Inventory (GRI)

To discover how your students are likely to comprehend texts used in your class, you can administer a **Group Reading Inventory (GRI)**. Its purpose is to discover which students will probably find a particular textbook frustrating to read and will, therefore, need additional support and guidance to comprehend it. For normal teaching purposes, students should be reading texts at an instructional level if teachers are to work with the text in class or at an independent level if students are to read the texts on their own. With a GRI, you can time students to get a reading rate and test comprehension with a set of questions assessing vocabulary and various forms of comprehension. Because of wide differences in interests and background knowledge, students should be given GRIs for each content area text they are expected to read.

Step-By-Step: Group Reading Inventory

Step 1. From the textbook or other material that students will be reading, select a passage of about 500 words that students have not yet read.

Step 2. Prepare 10 or 20 questions to assess vocabulary, literal comprehension, such as main ideas, details, or sequence, and inferential comprehension. The questions may be either multiple choice or open ended. A sample GRI reading with questions (Rakes & Smith, 1992) appears in the Strategy in Practice.

Step 3. Develop an answer key with original questions and appropriate answers. Identify the type of skill each question requires to answer correctly, such as identifying main ideas or comprehending details. A sample GRI answer key (Rakes & Smith, 1992) also appears in the Strategy in Practice.

Step 4. Distribute the passage to students or tell them which pages from their text they are to read and explain that you will be asking them to time themselves. To help in this regard, secure a timing clock that all students can see. Otherwise, write down the time on the board in 10-second intervals. (Later, students will compute a words-per-minute score by dividing the total number of words in the passages they read by the time taken to read them.)

Step 5. When finished reading the passage, students should either close their books or flip their papers over and answer questions you've provided.

Step 6. Review results of the GRI to determine how many students scored at an independent (90% or higher), instructional (60% to 90%), or frustration level (50% or less). Students who comprehend 70% to 75% of well-designed questions based on the passage should be able to understand the text with some instructional support in class. That support should include key vocabulary, study methods, and strategy instruction to promote comprehension.

Strategy in Practice

GROUP READING INVENTORY (GRI): ASSESSING STUDENTS' COMPREHENSION

Directions: Read the selection beginning on page _____ through page _____ to find out how the early novel developed and the various forms it took. When you have finished reading the selection, raise your hand and you will be given a short questionnaire over the material.

The Novel

One of the nicest pleasures in life for many people is to curl up in a comfortable place and read a good novel. Novels have been in existence for a relatively short time, compared to other forms of literature. For example, the drama has existed for centuries, whereas the novel came into being only about 300 years ago. Basically, a novel can be defined as a long story, written in prose, and having many characters and more than one plot.

Prior to the development of the novel in its present form, stories were often written in verse. These verse stories were known as "romances" during the Middle Ages. Usually the stories revolved around characters, such as kings, queens, knights in armor, and other heroes. Rarely were ordinary people and their problems ever subjects for romances—they were considered unfit subject matter for literature.

During the Renaissance, dating between the 14th and 16th centuries, people began to see that ordinary people and their lives could be interesting and meaningful subjects for stories, often changing their point of view about life and literature.

Among these important changes were the geographical expansions of many countries. . . .

Comprehension Questions

1. What is a novel?
2. What was the picaresque novel?
3. Approximately when did the novel come into being?
4. What is a plot novel?
5. How did the invention of the printing press affect literature?
6. What are romances?
7. How does the plot novel differ from the adventure novel?
8. If our society were composed of only the very rich and the very poor, with no middle class, what type(s) of novel(s) might we have today?
9. How did exploration affect the merchants?
10. What type of modern literature do you think may have been an outgrowth of space exploration?
11. What are two examples of adventure or journey novels in English or American literature?
12. How might the mass media (television, newspapers, etc.) negatively affect the novel today?
13. Why did the novel develop the way it did?
14. What social topics might be found in modern novels today?

Source: Rakes, T. A., & Smith, T. L. (1992). Assessing reading skills in the content areas. In E. K. Dishner, T. W. Bean, J. E. Readence, & D. W. Moore (Eds.), *Reading in the content areas: Improving classroom instruction* (3rd ed., pp. 399–426). Dubuque, IA: Kendall/Hunt.

Group Reading Inventory: Sample Answer Key

SKILL	QUESTION AND POSSIBLE ANSWER
Main Idea	1. What is a novel? (long prose story with many characters and more than one plot; paragraph 1)
Context	2. What was the picaresque novel? (stories of adventures of rogues or rascals who traveled about the country; from the Spanish word *picaro*, meaning rascal; paragraph 5)
Detail	3. Approximately when did the novel come into being? (during the Renaissance; between 14th and 16th centuries; paragraph 3)
Context	4. What is a plot novel? (stories of love between people, set in only one place and having few characters)
Detail	5. How did the invention of the printing press affect literature? (large quantities of books available at reasonable cost)
Context	6. What are romances? (stories written in verse, usually about kings, queens, knights, or other heroes; paragraph 2)
Detail	7. How does the plot novel differ from the adventure novel? (plot novels are usually set in one place and have fewer characters)
Inference	8. If our society were composed of only the very rich and the very poor, with no middle class, what types(s) of novel(s) might we have today? (answers will vary)
Detail	9. How did exploration affect the merchants? (gave them more markets in which to sell products)
Inference	10. What type of modern literature do you think may have been an outgrowth of space exploration? (science fiction)
Detail	11. What are two examples of adventure or journey novels in English or American literature? (*David Copperfield, Oliver Twist, Huckleberry Finn, Robinson Crusoe,* or *Joseph Andrews*)
Inference	12. How might the mass media (television, newspapers, etc.) negatively affect the novel today? (answers will vary)
Main Idea	13. Why did the novel develop the way it did? (people were becoming more practical and realistic; discovered that the "ordinary" could make good stories; other varied answers)
Inference	14. What social topics might be found in modern novels today? (answers will vary)

Performance Levels

Independent: 0–2 questions missed
Instructional: 3–6 questions missed
Frustration: 7 or more questions missed

Reading Rate

Words-per-minute rate = Total number of words read/Time = _____.

Miscue Analysis

Miscues are oral reading responses that vary from those expected. Kenneth Goodman (1969, 1994) observed that mistakes in oral reading should be viewed as miscues in a "psycholinguistic guessing game" rather than errors because these mistakes are actually attempts to construct meaning. Examining miscues can help you understand how a reader decodes texts and tries to make sense of them.

Table 4.2 Word Recognition Miscues: Scored and Unscored

MISCUE TYPE	EXAMPLE	COMMENTS
Use of Nonsense Word or Mispronunciation	(regmint) The ~~regiment~~ went on to defeat the enemy.	Reader attempts pronunciation but produces a nonsense word.
Substitution	when ~~want~~	An incorrect real word gets spoken in place of one on the page.
Omission	For the first time, Fanny ran behind the tall ~~Blue~~ Spruce. (Reader leaves out Blue.)	Reader does not appear to notice that any word was skipped.
Reversal	He stood on the pad. (The word *pad* is pronounced "dap.")	Reader reverses words or letters.
Insertion	The (puffy) blue cloud floated all the way to Toledo. ("Puffy" is inserted.)	Word or series of words that are not in the text are inserted.
No attempt to pronounce a word	Jamie looked into the ~~sarcophagus~~ and fainted. (Reader does not say word.)	Reader refuses to say a word that the teacher says so assessment can go on.

Word Recognition Miscues That Are NOT Scored

MISCUE	EXAMPLE	COMMENTS
Self-Corrections	Jaime went to the store (door). (Reader says "door" first, then corrects without prompting.)	After making an error, reader recognizes the mistake and corrects it.
Repetition	Alex listened to the ("the" repeated) hit album six times.	Reader repeats word or phrase at least once.
Pause	(. . .) Take my (purse) and throw it into the lake.	Reader makes long pause before pronouncing a word correctly.
Missing the Point	Two independent sentences separated by a period are read as if they were one sentence. No stopping point is intoned.	Reader pays no attention to periods, commas, or other points of punctuation.

Miscue analysis is often done as part of a larger informal reading inventory (IRI), but a miscue analysis can be done independently. Certain kinds of miscues that are judged "mistakes" and should be scored as word-recognition miscues are described in Table 4.2, along with miscues that should not be scored as mistakes. Although procedures for scoring miscues during an oral reading analysis or an IRI vary among authors, the rationale for including items to be scored or not scored on a miscue analysis are based on recommended procedures in Burns and Roe (1999), McCormick (2007), and Wilde (2000).

Running Records

A **running record** is an informal oral reading assessment that you can use to discover if the material you present to your students is at a manageable reading level

Table 4.3   Running Record Guidelines

DEGREE OF DIFFICULTY	PERCENTAGE OF CORRECT RESPONSES
Easy	95%–100%
Instructional	90%–94%
Hard	80%–89%

Source: From Thomas G. Gunning. *Assessing and Correcting Reading and Writing Difficulties* (3rd ed.). Boston, MA: Allyn & Bacon. Copyright © 2006 by Pearson Education. Reprinted by permission of the publisher.

and what strategies your students use to decode difficult words. It's relatively quick and easy. As your student reads, you record his performance using predetermined miscue guidelines. For miscues, you can use a system like that provided in Table 4.2.

Running records can be used with any text your students read. Mark miscues in a copy of the text while each of your students is reading. When miscues occur, circle the word or mark the text and note the kinds of errors the student made.

To calculate the percentage of correct responses, you can simply divide the number of words correctly read by the total number of words in the reading. Although running record standards for determining degree of text difficulty vary somewhat, Gunning (2006) offers guidelines in Table 4.3 that you could apply.

If one of your students has less than a 90% correct response rate and manifests other behaviors that indicate problems in comprehension, such as the inability to answer basic comprehension-check questions, the text you are asking him or her to read may simply be too difficult.

While similarities between running records and both IRIs and miscue analysis are apparent, the merit of the running record is that it can be done on the spur of the moment with little advanced preparation. However, planned running records with preselected texts of 200 words or so can also be used with each of your students to obtain benchmarks of individual student and even whole-class progress.

Curriculum-Based Measurement (CBM)

The oral reading fluency of students and their improvement can be quickly and efficiently assessed with **Curriculum-Based Measurement (CBM)**. Fluency can be measured by counting the number of words a student reads correctly in 1 minute. Researchers (Fuchs, Fuchs, Hosp, & Jenkins, 2001) have gathered evidence to demonstrate that oral reading fluency serves as an indicator of reading competence.

CBMs provide useful information to both teachers and students. Measuring and monitoring changes in a student's fluency while reading curriculum-based texts provides indications of your students' reading development in your content area classroom. Data from CBMs can help you decide what kinds of texts your students can read at an instructional level, their responsiveness to content area instruction, and their need for reading intervention programs. Meanwhile, CBM data can help students monitor their own growth in reading and serve as the basis for graphs of reading progress in their portfolios.

An initial CBM provides a baseline for students' reading fluency, an opportunity to observe miscues, and a method of determining the degree of difficulty that a particular text is likely to present to individuals and, collectively, to a class. The miscues will provide you with data to use as the basis for developing helpful instructional programs tailored to individual students or small groups of students sharing similar reading problems.

As explained in the previous chapter, low fluency rates may significantly impede comprehension. Studies of high school students indicate that fluency appears to be a significant indicator of success in reading and in students' overall academic development (Rasinski et al., 2005). Several studies (Prescott-Griffin & Witherell, 2004) of oral reading revealed that sixth-graders average about 160 words per minutes, plus or minus about 20. Rasinski et al. suggest that middle and high school students are likely to encounter problems in comprehension if, when reading texts at their grade level, their CBM scores are significantly below 100 correct words per minute. When preservice or in-service teachers in my classes have given CBMs to their middle or high school students individually with content area texts at grade level and found that their CBM scores were 80 correct words per minute or below, that reading rate usually correlated with weak comprehension and problems with learning from texts in the content area.

Although you can conduct CBM data for oral reading fluency by determining the number of words a student reads correctly in 1 minute (Fuchs et al., 2001), I suggest using a 2-minute reading to increase the accuracy of the measurement. During a 1-minute reading, a student may encounter unfamiliar words that significantly reduce their fluency rate. More time reading improves the chances that you will get a more accurate picture of your students' general fluency. It takes a little more time and a little more math, but it yields a more reliable measurement.

Step-By-Step: Curriculum-Based Measurement (CBM)

Step 1. Select a passage of about 600 words from a language arts, history, or science text designed for the grade level the students are currently in or are about to enter. Make sure the passage has a reasonable starting point with respect to content and does not include a large number of specialized words infrequently encountered in students' reading at their grade level.

Step 2. For the student copy, type the text in approximately the same font and size as the original.

Step 3. For the teacher's copy, produce the same text as you did for the student copy; however, on the right-hand side of the page, make a column for line-by-line cumulative word counts. At the top of the page, create space for the student's name, grade, date, and assessing teacher. On the bottom of the page, create a rate box with space for the following information: words read in 2 minutes, total number of scored miscues, total number of words correctly read in 2 minutes, and average number of words correctly read in 1 minute (or words correctly read in 2 minutes ÷ 2).

Step 4. Using the student copy of the text, the student reads aloud for 2 minutes. Assure students that they should read for understanding and not just for speed. When exactly 2 minutes are up, put a slash mark after the last word read. (Alternatively, you can tape-record the student reading for 2 minutes and carry out the following assessment steps soon after the recorded reading.)

Step 5. As the student reads, the assessing teacher marks miscues on the teacher's copy by putting a line through miscued words or writing in an inserted word. Miscues are responses to texts that differ from expected responses. They occur when the reader reads words that are different from those on the assessor's copy. Miscues include use of nonsense words, substitutions (e.g., ran for rain), omissions, reversals (words not read in the correct order are miscues), inserted words, and no attempt to say a word. However, self-corrected words, repeated words, hesitations, words read with an accent or dialect, and improper intonation resulting from ignored punctuation marks are all scored as correct. (See Table 4.2 and the earlier section, "Miscue Analysis," for further explanation and examples.)

Step 6. Observing readers' problem-solving strategies while they are reading a text is quite instructive. Teachers should observe carefully what readers do when they encounter a difficult word. Do they try to sound it out, use context cues, ask for help, or give up? Do some of the mistakes make sense? For example, Gunning (2006) emphasizes the importance of observing semantic (was for were) or graphic (letter for leather) similarities between miscues and the actual text. How well does the reader monitor the reading process? How are errors corrected? Answers to questions such as these provide insights into students' reading strengths and clues about ways struggling readers can be helped. In the Teacher Observation Notes, write answers to any of these questions or other observations made during the assessment.

Step 7. After a student reads the text for 2 minutes, the assessing teacher calculates the student's oral fluency rate or number of words correctly read in 1 minute. This is done by dividing the total number of words read correctly in 2 minutes by 2. For example, in the first minute of reading a selection from her world history textbook, Maria read 73 words and in the second minute she read 66, for a total of 139. However, she made 5 miscues, which reduced the total number of correctly read words to 134. After dividing by 2, Maria's average number of words read correctly was 67. (See the Strategy in Practice.)

Step 8. Oral-fluency rates should be kept for each struggling reader and, if possible, for each student. The same text can be used at three points over the traditional academic year to measure oral-fluency development: September, January, and May. Minor variations in this schedule should not affect results. However, frequent use of the same text is likely to result in learning that could influence the CBM's validity. CBM data for an entire class or grade level can also be calculated and graphically displayed to show development over time.

Step 9. Teachers can also calculate CBM rates for any other text they wish by following the guidelines provided here. Such information will help teachers decide on the appropriateness of a text for a given student or even for a whole class and the amount of instructional scaffolding that students may need to read the text successfully.

CURRICULUM-BASED MEASUREMENT: SAMPLE DATA-COLLECTION FORMAT

CBM Data Sheet (SAMPLE FORMAT)

Student's Name Maria Russell   Grade: 6   Date: 9/15/2002

Teacher's Name Joseph Knell

Text: *Ancient World: Adventures in Time and Place*	Word Count
(Banks, et al., 2000) *omitted -ed* Pericles became Athens' leader in 462 B.C. He quickly acted to boost the role of poor or working citizens in government. Pericles said that citizens *help* should be paid when they held a government job or *as omitted -d* served on a jury. A jury is a group of citizens chosen to hear evidence and make decisions in a court of law. This money would allow farmers and other working citizens to take time off / from work so they could serve in government.	73 wpm
Democracy Grows Pericles won enough votes in the citizen assembly for his bill to become law. As a result, many citizens were able to become involved in government during Athens' Golden Age. Even the poor citizens could *would* accept important jobs in government. Look at the diagram on page 356. What kinds of jobs did citizens do / to keep Athens running smoothly?	66 wpm
All citizens were now able to take part in votes that affected their own lives. When they voted for Athens to go to war, for example, it meant that they themselves would fight. Unlike many other city-states, citizens made up the bulk of the Athenian army and navy, not a group of hired soldiers.	

RATE CALCULATION

Total Number of Words Read in Two Minutes: 139

Total Number of Scored Miscues: 5

Total Number of Words Correctly Read: 134

Average Number of Words Correctly Read in 1 Minute
   (words correctly read in 2 minutes ÷2)   67

Teacher Observation Notes:

Maria read haltingly but at a consistent pace. At a couple of points, she did not read as though she knew a sentence came to an ending. That suggests that she may not be paying attention to units of meaning while she reads. Her comprehension of informational text should be monitored. Her average number of words read correctly per minute (67) also suggests that she is having trouble with decoding and recognizing words. She clearly did not automatically recognize several words in the passage, such as *held, served,* and *allow*, which she initially pronounced as also but corrected. The passage, according to a readability formula, is written at a 5.8 grade level. However, she clearly has difficulty with the passage and will need significant scaffolding to help her comprehend this text.

Informal Assessments for a Closer Look at Comprehension Processes

Neither a standardized reading test nor a miscue analysis provides detailed information about a reader's comprehension process. Whereas an oral reading and miscue analysis provide valuable information about a reader's decoding skills and processes, they do not tell the whole story about what meanings that reader constructed. Nor do standardized reading tests, such as the Gates-MacGinitie, which often depend upon a student's recognition rather than recall to answer multiple-choice items. Other procedures, including retellings, think-alouds, and interviews, magnify a student's thinking while reading and furnish more detailed information about comprehension. That information can help you understand how thoroughly your students comprehend narrative or expository texts, how they organize knowledge, and what they do when meaning making breaks down.

Retellings

A **retelling** is just what its label indicates. After a student reads a narrative or expository text, she tells you what meanings she constructed. Rather than mere recognition, retellings require recalling knowledge from a reading selection.

Step-By-Step: Retelling

Step 1. Select a text, narrative or expository, that is difficult enough to engage a student in using strategies to make sense out of challenging reading materials. If possible, choose a text that is not at the reader's frustration level.

Step 2. Create an outline of the selected text that includes the main points and supporting details. The outline will serve as your guide and as a source for generating probing questions to prompt the recall of information the student omitted from the retelling.

Step 3. Explain to your student that you will request a retelling after reading and then have him read the text silently. Observe your student's behavior while reading the selection to identify any strategies used to aid comprehension, such as previewing the selection, rereading sections, and so forth.

Step 4. Ask students to retell everything that they can remember about the passage they read without referring to the text. It's important to ask for all the reader can recall. Otherwise, a superficial summary may be recited.

Step 5. You can use the outline you created in Step 2 to get an estimate of the percentage of the text that your student recalls.

Step 6. If a reader missed important elements in the text that are noted in the outline, you should ask follow-up questions, or probes (McCormick, 2007). These probes can also elicit levels of comprehension beyond the literal level, such as understandings about a story's themes or generalizations that might be drawn from an expository text.

Some teachers prefer to tape-record retelling sessions so that they can compare the retelling with the text's outline. You, too, may find this an efficient method. McCormick (2007) points out that some students may provide a disorganized retelling that suggests poor comprehension. However, that may not be an accurate impression. The student may comprehend successfully but structure the retelling poorly. Practice in retelling usually remedies disorganized responses.

If time for retellings is limited or you are working with large groups, students could write out summaries of the texts they read. Although some things may be lost using this method, such as opportunites to probe for details, other things are gained, such as time and a written record that can be scored and kept on file.

Comprehension Think-Alouds

An effective way to discover how your students think when they read is to do a Comprehension **Think-Aloud** with them. During think-alouds, readers describe their thoughts as they form meanings through interaction with the text. The think-aloud provides a view of cognitive processes that readers use to make sense of what they are reading. Struggling readers often have trouble carrying out processes that good readers engage in automatically, processes we saw when we reviewed their qualities in chapter 3. You'll recall that, among other things, good readers activate background knowledge, make predictions, form mental images as they read, monitor their comprehension progress, and fix up problems as they go along. While doing think-alouds with your students, you can watch for examples of these processes.

To show students how to do a think-aloud, you should demonstrate the process first. You may activate background knowledge and associate a story's or article's title to concepts held in long-term memory. You may admit moments of confusion, use fix-up strategies, and discuss multiple meanings as you work through ambiguities. However, you should try to keep your associations close to the text and limited in length. Your demonstration then serves as a model that your students can use to understand what they will do when engaged in a think-aloud.

To investigate how different readers in a Los Angeles middle school culture construct meaning for John Masefield's "Sea Fever," I videotaped think-alouds by a teacher and sixth-grade students. The videos were intended not only to demonstrate the think-aloud technique, but also to observe meaning construction in process and to study differences between expert and novice readers. To help you hear what the middle school teacher, Remi Silva, said in response to the poem, I present the poem on the left and her comments on the right in Strategy in Practice.

This think-aloud shows students how a teacher constructs meaning for a complex reading task. Mrs. Silva pauses to say she wants to reread the poem to get into it before explaining what she's gotten out of it. As she explains her understanding of the poem's meaning, she makes an important intertextual connection with *The True Confessions of Charlotte Doyle* by Avi. That "young adult" novel is about a 13-year-old girl who makes a life-changing voyage to America from England in 1832. She's the only passenger on a ship with a tyrannical, cruel captain and a mutinous crew, with whom she eventually unites but not before winning their trust. After Charlotte arrives safely in America and rejoins her family, she decides to abandon the comforts of home for the adventures of the sea. This intertextual link helps Mrs. Silva put "Sea Fever" in context, make sense of its language, and compare the sea-enchanted Charlotte to the poem's sailor, who also becomes feverish for the sea.

Strategy in Practice

TEACHER THINK-ALOUD

"SEA FEVER" BY JOHN MASEFIELD	R. SILVA'S "THINKING ALOUD"

I must go down to the sea again,
    to the lonely sea and the sky,
And all I ask is a tall ship
    and a star to steer her by,
And the wheel's kick and the wind's song
    and the white sail's shaking
And a gray mist on the sea's face
    and a gray dawn breaking. (pause)
	After reading the first section of the poem aloud, Mrs. Silva said, "First of all, I would go back and reread it silently." After doing so, she said, "I think it's a sailor or somebody who's working on a ship who needs to be back on the ocean again, to feel what it's like to be out there again. He needs a tall ship to guide him through the seas and a star to let him know where he's going. He hears wind and sees gray mist, and that's how he sees the sea, feels it."

I must go down to the seas again,
    for the call of the running tide
Is a wild call and a clear call
    that may not be denied; (pause)
	"Something is calling him (or her) there. He (or she) has a need to be there. The running tide and the wild call are things asking him to come."

And all I ask is a windy day
    with the white clouds flying,
And the flung spray and the blown spume,
    and the sea-gulls crying. (pause)
	"To make this day complete, it would be a nice windy day with the white clouds flying above spraying ocean water, and sea gulls crying above."

I must go down to the seas again
    to the vagrant gypsy life,
To the gull's way and the whale's way
    where the wind's like a whetted knife;
    (pause)
	"This and the previous passage actually remind me of *Charlotte Doyle* by Avi and the men who were on that ship. . . . They just loved the sea. It was their way of life. At the end (of the novel), she feels called back to the boat."

And all I ask is a merry yarn from a laughing fellow rover,	"She missed the camaraderie she had there. That's what he misses besides the sea. Having peace within himself."
And a quiet sleep and a sweet dream when the long trick's over.	I next asked Mrs. Silva if she had any other comments about what the author was conveying to the reader or how she would express the poem's main idea. She said, "Everyone has a place where they want to be, and his place is on the sea."

Source: Courtesy of The Society of Authors as the Literary Representative of the Estate of John Masefield.

One of the sixth graders, Liliana, who also completed a think-aloud for "Sea Fever," had a remarkably different intertextual link. The connection she made reveals both her struggle to make sense of the poem and her use of background knowledge to do so. She made an intertextual connection between "Sea Fever" and a movie entitled *Free Willy.* In that film, a young boy and his family conspire to free a whale from captivity. To this young reader, the poem was not about a man yearning for the sea and the sailor's life but about people and animals interacting—about people wanting to protect and help animals so they won't lose their friendships or families. The seagulls were crying because they wanted men to stop trying to get the whales, and the wind wanted a knife to free the whales. Comparing the two think-alouds reveals how differently two readers can interpret the same text and activate background knowledge that sustains or elaborates upon the meanings they construct. Comparing the think-alouds also reveals the potential power they hold in helping teachers see and understand their students' meaning construction processes.

Step-By-Step: Doing a Comprehension Think-Aloud

Step 1. If you have not demonstrated the think-aloud process with your students, you can introduce this strategy to them with a challenging text for you, perhaps one in your discipline. Use a selection that is semantically and syntactically demanding in your field but that is also one with which you are comfortable. Give a copy of the text to your students. As you are doing the think-aloud, have your students take notes on the process. When you've finished, conduct a class discussion focused on what you did and said during the think-aloud. The demonstration should prepare students to try the strategy themselves.

Step 2. Select a passage of about 200 words for a student that is new to him or her and is at the instructional level. It should challenge but not overwhelm the reader. You should preread the passage and identify one or more sentence chunks of text with stop-points.

Step 3. Explain to the reader that the passage will be read in segments marked with stop-points and that at those points he or she will explain what meaning has been gained from the text. Warn the reader that you may ask a few questions, such as "What do you think this is about?" to encourage the development of text-based hypotheses.

Step 4. Prepare to record the session so that you can make a transcription of it, along with your observations of the student's meaning construction processes.

Step 5. After the think-aloud is complete, talk with the student about what he or she observed and learned from doing a think-aloud.

Step 6. Analyze the results to determine if the reader

- formulates hypotheses,
- provides information to support the hypotheses generated,
- draws upon background knowledge and makes intertextual connections, such as those Mrs. Silva and Liliana made,
- uses strategies, such as rereading, to cope with breakdowns in comprehension,
- uses strategies to figure out the meaning of unfamiliar words,
- notices inconsistencies between interpretations and the textbase, and
- understands the gist of the passage.

Interviews and Interactions

You can learn much about your students' reading habits, preferences, and processes simply by talking with them, asking questions, and being observant during instructional interactions.

Discovering how your students decode texts provides diagnostic information that can influence your decisions about promising interventions to improve struggling readers' word identification abilities. Interviews, careful observation, and questions all can help. Gunning (2006) suggests a "word identification interview" based on questions that, when answered, lead to insights about how a student thinks and creates meaning while reading. He suggests word identification questions such as these:

- How do you feel about reading?
- What is the hardest thing for you to do when you read?
- Why do you think it's hard for you to recognize words when reading?
- Why do you think it's hard to learn words?
- What would make it easier?
- What makes it hard to figure out some words?
- What kinds of words are hardest to learn?

Answers to questions like these may amplify and clarify clues and hints about reading problems that trouble struggling readers in your classes. You may have made some diagnostic discoveries through standardized tests or informal assessments, but talking with your students about how they read can release information that sharpens your diagnosis and points to sensible ways to intervene.

Comprehension processes can also be made clearer through several informal assessment procedures. You can include questions like these during interviews with students about comprehension:

- How do you know you understand something you are reading?
- Do you ever notice when you're reading that you can't make any sense out of it? What do you do when that happens?
- When, if ever, do you ask yourself questions about what you're reading?
- Do you ever ask yourself questions about the book you're reading and then try to answer them as you read along?
- Do you ever find yourself guessing what's going to happen next in a story?
- When you're having trouble understanding a book, do you let your teacher know?
- What are some things you do to help yourself when you're having trouble understanding what you're expected to read?
- What are some things teachers do that help you understand your reading assignments?

Obtaining answers to these questions and others like them will help you see what strategies students use to construct meanings for text and to discover what kinds of strategic instruction would benefit your struggling readers.

Portfolio Assessment in Content Area Classrooms

What are portfolios?   For diagnostic teaching, portfolios provide an extraordinary means of discovering how each of your students reads, writes, thinks, and grows. Furthermore, portfolio assessment encourages your students to look more carefully at their own work and reflect upon it. Basically, a **portfolio** is a collection of work. But that collection of work can be selected, organized, analyzed, and reviewed so that it provides a kaleidoscopic as well as microscopic view of each student's engagement in content area learning. The portfolio can reveal how much work your students are doing, how well they are doing it, what kinds of help they need to progress, and how they conceptualize their own progress. Moreover, thoughtful observation of students' portfolios can guide productive classroom instruction because, as you perceive your students' learning needs, you can formulate plans to address them. Those diagnostically responsive plans could include individual instruction, cooperative learning teams, minilessons, or whole-class teaching.

Benefits and limitations of portfolios.

In comparison with standardized, formal testing, portfolios have several distinctive advantages. While standardized tests are one-shot, often high-stakes performances, portfolios allow ongoing assessment. Standardized tests often communicate a formal judgment about one-time outcomes rather than a developmental perspective over time. With standardized tests, goals for improving performance are more removed from immediate classroom achievement. With portfolios, your goals for improvement are formed on the basis of immediate prior classroom accomplishments. While standardized test results rarely provide direct information to you or your students about what could be done to improve performance, portfolios provide avenues for clear and direct intervention. After taking a standardized test, students are given a score, perhaps one that is machine generated and printed out. With portfolios, your students can assess their own achievement and progress. They must be accountable to their own sources of evidence. When formal, standardized tests are used to assess students' learning and achievements, the tests may not be directly aligned with your classroom teaching. However, the content of your students' portfolios reflects directly on your standards and your classroom teaching practices.

However, portfolios have their drawbacks in comparison with formal testing. To gain validity and increase reliability, portfolio scoring requires the development of rubrics or scoring guides. Reading the content of the portfolio and scoring that content, usually with rubrics, takes patience and time. Even by using rubrics and exercising patience, standardized tests usually have greater statistical validity and reliability. Furthermore, standardized tests are often easier to administer and definitely easier to score.

Using portfolios in the content area to examine student work.

What goes into a student's portfolio? Although portfolios can function as showcases for your students' best works, their value as an assessment tool resides in their allowing both you and your students to examine a variety of student work emerging from classroom assignments. To fulfill their function as mirrors of students' reading, writing, and thinking in a content area, you must decide what materials will reflect your students' learning achievements, progress, and problems. The choices are many: homework assignments, quizzes, tests, a graph of grades received, reading logs, learning logs, responses to readings, lab reports, questionnaires, notes on lectures, responses to discussions, drafts of papers from first to last revision showing progression of thought and organization, or letters to you from your students and from you to your students.

You and your students can examine individual items, such as an essay, to identify strengths, areas of growth, and specific needs for further development. When you have a writing conference with a student, both of you can look over the student's work to identify those specific aspects of writing that need to be addressed for the student writer to progress. If a problem in writing, such as pronoun-antecedent agreement, troubles only one of your students, you can reach out to that particular student and help her address it in her writing. If the problem troubles many of your students, you can design a minilesson for the whole class that addresses that weakness. (See chapter 9.) Portfolios can be used to diagnose and design instruction for students in math, science, social studies, or other content area classes.

Linnea Dahl, an English teacher in an arts magnet high school (Los Angeles County High School for the Arts), asked her seniors near the end of their high school careers to reflect on portfolios of work that they kept all year. She designed a series of three lessons that included a reflective essay on their portfolios and their evaluation.

For the first assignment, Linnea asked her students to complete a planning sheet that included several tasks. She asked students to select the best six assignments in their portfolios and rank them. Any written assignments they turned in during the year that had more than five mistakes had to be revised. She also asked them to reflect on any other written work they had done throughout high school, including any pieces they had published. She then said, "Look at what you have to work with. What is your initial reaction?" Students were to compose a "freewrite" focused on what their portfolio said to them about who they were as seen through their written work in high school.

For the second assignment, Linnea's seniors had to examine and write about all the writing in their class portfolios. She explained that the portfolio essay should "delve into the person that the writing has come from" and be a comparison between early and more recent efforts. Explicit prompts called out for students to

- describe how they saw themselves as writers earlier in high school and "what kind of writer you are now,"
- target areas of specific improvement and areas where they still lacked confidence,
- examine ways their personalities influenced their writing,
- define future writing challenges and how they will be met,
- identify what they would like someone to "really see or understand" about their writing.

The third assignment was an independent evaluation of their essays. Earlier Linnea and her students developed a criteria chart that she used to prepare a rubric or scoring guide. Using that rubric, students had to assess their work, give themselves a grade, and (with reference to the rubric) explain how they arrived at that grade. Linnea, using the same rubric, also evaluated their portfolios and met with them when differences in ratings arose. She added her perceptions of their writing and its development that they may have overlooked. Linnea decided to use this portfolio evaluation process in lieu of a final examination grade.

In response to this assignment, one of her seniors wrote the following:

Throughout most of high school I wrote papers in the standard, simple format for the sole purpose of getting a grade. There was no personal flair to them and they did not reflect my personality, but I found this acceptable since I had little attachment to the assignment. I told myself that if the paper was only for class and therefore was of no particular significance to me, then it was alright (sic) for me to do a mediocre job. I never felt satisfied with these papers. I was timid and embarrassed to turn them in because I knew that, despite there (sic) adequate outward appearance, they were not work I could honestly be proud of.

My analytical/academic writing is the most obvious example of how my uncommitted feelings influence my work. I have always wanted to write well, but I was not willing to put my heart into the writing. The essay I wrote on *Slaughterhouse Five* is a good example of my writing, not at its worst, but far from its most stimulating. It is not always clear what I am talking about and although there are sections of inspired thought when it seems that there is a real connection or realization taking place, such as in the last paragraph, those tidbits are few and far between. Writing analysis of books is not difficult for me since I am generally perceptive to themes and subtleties in writing, but I am still searching for a way to make the process of writing, and the subsequent paper, more interesting and alive.

My more inspired writing comes when I am involved in a more creative pursuit, such as playwriting. The new morning elective playwriting class has been such an inspirational experience for me and has allowed me to discover a wonderful new way with which to express myself. . . .

This activity not only allowed Linnea's students to explore the development of their writing, it also gave them an opportunity to explore aspects of their identities, who they are, and who they are becoming in terms of evolving literacies.

Portfolios and the student-led conference.

Portfolios can also be the engines that power student-led conferences. A **student-led conference** is a meeting at school between a student and parent or other adult over course work kept in a portfolio (Austin, 1994). Student-led conferences have many benefits:

- Students must be responsible and accountable to themselves, their teachers, and their parents.
- Students communicate course curriculum and expectations to their parents.
- Students must keep track of their work and its progress.
- Students have to organize and maintain a portfolio of their work.
- Students review the portfolio's documents and write periodic self-evaluations.
- Students conduct conversations with their parents about their school work.
- Students must be ready to refer to evidence in their portfolio that supports claims they make about their academic progress as well as problems in learning.
- Students construct learning goals that are based on their portfolio and conference and that are shared with the student's parent(s) and the teacher.

In summary, these benefits contribute to your students' becoming more self-regulated and motivated learners in all content area classrooms. Although student-led conferences have been more widely used in middle schools, their value in high school instruction has, I believe, often been overlooked. They can vitalize and deepen students' engagement.

But how can you build student-led conferences into your instructional plans? At the beginning of the school year, you should notify parents that their students will be maintaining portfolios of work in your course and that parents will be invited to school so that their children can discuss the portfolios. You can notify parents at an open house or have students write a letter home describing student-led conferences and explaining what their parents' role in them will be. In one way or another, parents learn that they will be meeting with their children at least twice during the school year to talk about the portfolio, its contents, and their children's progress.

What goes into portfolios for student-led conferences? One answer is *everything*. Another is to let the student decide. Yet another is what makes the student's work in the course look good. Still another is to include documents that show learning. None of these answers is ideal. Some teachers believe it is best to analyze their state or local standards, curriculum goals, instructional strategies, and assignments to determine which documents and data are to be included and the rationale for their inclusion. I believe that last solution, though requiring some decision making on your part, holds considerable promise for the success of student-led conference portfolios.

At the beginning of the course, you should let your students—as well as their parents—know what will be kept in the portfolio and how to maintain it. Knowing that the contents of their portfolios will be presented to parents often serves as a significant motivator for students and as a focus of interest to parents. A list of standards and portfolio items related to the standards can be affixed to the file's inside front cover. Graphs of grades to track test and quiz performance could also be displayed. If desired, the portfolio could also include learning logs, letters (to teachers or other students about course material), attendance records, lecture notes, and more.

In preparation for a student-led conference, each of your students should

1. review the work in the portfolio,
2. write a report that covers the period under review, and
3. state a learning goal that will be evaluated as part of the next student-led conference and reasons for choosing it.

You can give your students specific questions to answer as part of their report. These questions can focus on specific kinds of work, such as essays, logs, lab reports, chapter tests, projects, cooperative team presentations, and the like. Documents in the portfolio then serve as evidence for claims about learning and performance that your students make in their reflections.

Teachers using student-led conferences usually write letters to parents letting them know when the conference will be held and what aspirations the teacher and student have for the meeting. You can explain that you'll be available in the conference room for consultation should the need arise. In the letter, you can also provide some guidelines to parents that will help them understand how their responses to their student's work can have a positive, motivating effect. In addition, you may wish to have your students write a welcoming invitation to their parents to attend the student-led conference. Also, it's not a bad idea to include an RSVP with the student's invitation, which will enable you to plan for refreshments or surrogate parents, if required.

As an orchestrator of student-led conferences, you will have to schedule times for parents to come to school. Most teachers schedule no more than 10 student-led conferences to be held in the same room simultaneously. The length of the conference depends on the amount of material to be reviewed. However, conferences usually run about 45 minutes or so. During the conference, you'll roam, troubleshoot, and (most importantly) shadow presentations to get a sense of how they are progressing.

Part of the preparation for student-led conference day is practice. Students, even those having done conferences in the past, may need rehearsal time. Some teachers recommend using education students from a nearby college as rehearsal parents (Austin, 1994). In some classes where cooperative learning groups have been established and the climate is supportive, students could practice presenting their portfolio to another member of their co-op team. For the rehearsal, a list of procedures will help your students know and remember what steps they should take—from introducing parents to the teacher at the beginning to thanking parents for attending at the end. These directions can even be tailored to the specific content of key documents in the portfolio to make sure they are covered during the student-led conferences.

You are likely to have some students whose parent cannot attend the conferences, and, of course, you'll wonder to whom the student can present their portfolio. Usually, teachers find other teachers or administrators to serve as parent surrogates during the student-led conferences. Ideally, teachers serving as parent surrogates have the student in their own classes. That way your colleagues will learn much about how students they are teaching are performing in other classrooms with other teachers. Such interactions can be quite enlightening for teachers.

After the student-led conference, you should plan to give your students an opportunity to debrief and discuss the event. Following the discussion, students benefit from writing a report. The discussion and report can include the following:

- what went well,
- what needs some improvement,
- what the student got from the experience, and
- what the student thought the parents got from it.

The report can help you make decisions about modifications to the student-led conference process and lead students to consider how they might improve their next conference presentation. Of course, this concluding report is filed in their portfolios.

Stephanie Pearson, a middle school teacher in Los Angeles, engages her students in after-conference reflections. One of her students, Grace, had a range of comments about how things went during the conference, what could have gone better, what she gained from the experience, and what she thought her dad gained. Grace felt the conference went well "because I felt that I was speaking a littler clearer to my father. Also, I explained about what I was doing in class. I felt I did an okay job explaining what it was we do in class." She felt things might have gone better "if maybe he wasn't in a rush to go home and work. Then I probably could of talked a little more." She wrote that she would have told him more about the process her class went through when writing essays. As for what she gained, Grace wrote that she thought she could have spoken "a little louder and clearer to my dad 'cause I don't talk a lot. Also it showed how much I knew about the class and what the goals and points of it were." She felt that the conference helped her dad get a "better understanding of what I'm doing in class and if I was doing good."

Inventories of Reading Strategies

Two informal instruments reviewed in this section include a diagnostic reading series to gauge a student's comprehension skills and an inventory to measure metacognitive awareness of a student's reading strategies. *Milestones in Reading* (Curriculum Associates, 2003) gives students opportunities to assess and practice their own comprehension skills. The Metacognitive Awareness of Reading Strategies Inventory, or MARSI (Mokhtari & Reichard, 2002), is designed to evaluate students' awareness and use of reading strategies while reading content area texts.

Comprehensive assessment of reading strategies. The *Milestones in Reading* diagnostic series (Curriculum Associates, 2003) provides feedback for students on their reading skills and feedback to teachers about student skill levels, information that can inform further instruction in reading. The series assesses middle and high school students' mastery of comprehension objectives, especially students who are delayed or struggling readers. The reading comprehension skills or objectives, as they are called in some standardized test programs, include summarizing, finding a word's meaning from its context, drawing conclusions, making inferences, recalling facts and details, understanding sequence, making predictions, comparing and contrasting, recognizing cause and effect, identifying an author's purpose, finding the main idea, and distinguishing between fact and opinion. Some of these objectives, such as finding the main idea, entail basic understanding of a text, while others, such as comparing and contrasting, require analysis and evaluation, which are forms of critical reading. The assessment consists of 10 reading selections accompanied by 12 questions, one for each comprehension skill measured. This diagnostic series can also help you design instruction to improve student performance by identifying strengths and weaknesses in student skills usually assessed on standardized reading tests.

Metacognitive awareness of reading strategies inventory.   The MARSI assesses the reading metacognition of students in grades 6 through 12. While making students more aware of what they do when coping with content area reading, MARSI helps teachers understand the instructional needs of their students. Mokhtari and Reichard (2002) identified three categories (or factors) into which their inventory items fell: Global Reading Strategies, Problem-Solving Strategies, and Support Reading Strategies. Global Reading Strategies include setting a purpose for reading, activating prior knowledge, and skimming to note text structure. Problem-Solving Strategies include adjusting reading rates, rereading, and visualizing information presented. Support Reading Strategies include taking notes while reading, underlining, and asking self-questions. The inventory itself, including information about the category to which each strategy belongs and a scoring rubric, is a Strategy in Practice.

Strategy in Practice

METACOGNITIVE AWARENESS OF READING STRATEGIES INVENTORY (MARSI)

Directions: Listed below are statements about what people do when they read *academic* or *school-related materials* such as textbooks or library books. Five numbers follow each statement (1, 2, 3, 4, 5), and each number means the following:

- **1** means "I **never or almost never** do this."
- **2** means "I do this **only occasionally**."
- **3** means "I sometimes do this" (about **50%** of the time).
- **4** means "I **usually** do this."
- **5** means "I **always or almost always** do this."

After reading each statement, **circle the number** (1, 2, 3, 4, or 5) that applies to you using the scale provided. Please note that there are **no right or wrong answers** to the statements in this inventory.

TYPE	STRATEGY	SCALE
GLOB	1. I have a purpose in mind when I read.	1 2 3 4 5
SUP	2. I take notes while reading to help me understand what I read.	1 2 3 4 5
GLOB	3. I think about what I know to help me understand what I read	1 2 3 4 5
GLOB	4. I preview the text to see what it's about before reading it.	1 2 3 4 5
SUP	5. When text becomes difficult, I read aloud to help me understand what I read.	1 2 3 4 5
SUP	6. I summarize what I read to reflect on important information in the text.	1 2 3 4 5
GLOB	7. I think about whether the content of the text fits my reading purpose.	1 2 3 4 5
PROB	8. I read slowly but carefully to be sure I understand what I'm reading.	1 2 3 4 5
SUP	9. I discuss what I read with others to check my understanding.	1 2 3 4 5
GLOB	10. I skim the text first by noting characteristics like length and organization.	1 2 3 4 5
PROB	11. I try to get back on track when I lose concentration.	1 2 3 4 5
SUP	12. I underline or circle information in the text to help me remember it.	1 2 3 4 5
PROB	13. I adjust my reading speed according to what I'm reading.	1 2 3 4 5
GLOB	14. I decide what to read closely and what to ignore.	1 2 3 4 5
SUP	15. I use reference materials such as dictionaries to help me understand what I read.	1 2 3 4 5
PROB	16. When text becomes difficult, I pay closer attention to what I'm reading.	1 2 3 4 5
GLOB	17. I use tables, figures, and pictures in text to increase my understanding.	1 2 3 4 5
PROB	18. I stop from time to time and think about what I'm reading.	1 2 3 4 5
GLOB	19. I use context clues to help me better understand what I'm reading.	1 2 3 4 5
SUP	20. I paraphrase (restate ideas in my own words) to better understand what I read.	1 2 3 4 5
PROB	21. I try to picture or visualize information to help remember what I read.	1 2 3 4 5
GLOB	22. I use typographical aids like boldface and italics to identify key information.	1 2 3 4 5
GLOB	23. I critically analyze and evaluate the information presented in the text.	1 2 3 4 5
SUP	24. I go back and forth in the text to find relationships among ideas in it.	1 2 3 4 5
GLOB	25. I check my understanding when I come across conflicting information.	1 2 3 4 5
GLOB	26. I try to guess what the material is about when I read.	1 2 3 4 5
PROB	27. When text becomes difficult, I reread to increase my understanding.	1 2 3 4 5
SUP	28. I ask myself questions I like to have answered in the text.	1 2 3 4 5
GLOB	29. I check to see if my guesses about the text are right or wrong.	1 2 3 4 5
PROB	30. I try to guess the meaning of unknown words or phrases.	1 2 3 4 5

Scoring Rubric

Student name: _____   Age: _____   Date: _____

Grade in school: ❏ 6th   ❏ 7th   ❏ 8th   ❏ 9th   ❏ 10th   ❏ 11th   ❏ 12th   ❏ College   ❏ Other

1. Write your response to each statement (i.e., 1, 2, 3, 4, or 5) in each of the blanks.
2. Add up the scores under each column. Place the result on the line under each column.
3. Divide the subscale score by the number of statements in each column to get the average for each subscale.
4. Calculate the average for the whole inventory by adding up the subscale scores and dividing by 30.
5. Compare your results to those shown below.
6. Discuss your results with your teacher or tutor.

GLOBAL READING STRATEGIES (GLOB SUBSCALE)	PROBLEM-SOLVING STRATEGIES (PROB SUBSCALE)	SUPPORT READING STRATEGIES (SUP SUBSCALE)	OVERALL READING STRATEGIES
1. _____	8. _____	2. _____	GLOB
3. _____	11. _____	5. _____	PROB
4. _____	13. _____	6. _____	SUP
7. _____	16. _____	9. _____	
10. _____	18. _____	12. _____	
14. _____	21. _____	15. _____	
17. _____	27. _____	20. _____	
19. _____	30. _____	24. _____	
22. _____		28. _____	
23. _____			
25. _____			
26. _____			
29. _____			

_____ GLOB score   _____ PROB score   _____ SUP score   _____ Overall score

_____ GLOB mean   _____ PROB mean   _____ SUP mean   _____ Overall mean

Key to averages: 3.5 or higher = high   2.5–3.4 = medium   2.4 or lower = low

Interpreting your scores:

The overall average indicates how often you use reading strategies when reading academic materials. The average for each subscale of the inventory shows which group of strategies (i.e., global, problem-solving, and support strategies) you use most when reading. With this information, you can tell if you score very high or very low in any of these strategy groups. Note, however, that the best possible use of these strategies depends on your reading ability in English, the type of material read, and your purpose for reading it. A low score on any of the subscales or parts of the inventory indicates that there may be some strategies in these parts that you might want to learn about and consider using when reading.

Source: Metacognitive Awareness of Reading Strategies Inventory (Version 1.0) by Mokhtari and Reichard, from "Assessing students metacognitive awareness of reading strategies" in *Journal of Educational Psychology, 94* (2), 249–259. Copyright © 2002 by the American Psychological Association. Reprinted with permission.

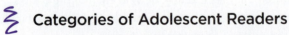

Categories of Adolescent Readers

With our cognitive model, a battery of reading assessment tools, and ample research on struggling as well as skilled readers (Beers, 1998, 2003; Hacker, 1998b; Spear-Swerling & Sternberg, 1996), we can now identify several categories of readers you are likely to find in many of your classrooms. (See Table 4.4.) These categories range from nondecoders, who have little, if any, alphabetic knowledge and little, if any, knowledge of letter-sound correspondences, to highly proficient readers, who can

Table 4.4 Categories of Adolescent Readers

READER TYPE	CHARACTERISTICS
1. *Nondecoders or Weak Decoders*	• Nonalphabetic readers who have not grasped the alphabetic principle that each speech sound has a graphic representation; • Have very impaired reading comprehension and word recognition; • Have little letter–sound or phonological knowledge; • Have profound spelling difficulty.
2. *Compensatory Readers*	• Grasp alphabetic principle; • Have impaired word recognition and reading comprehension; • Have limited orthographic and phonological knowledge; • Use sight-words and sentence context to compensate for lack of phonological knowledge; • Have significant spelling difficulty.
3. *Slow Comprehenders, or Nonautomatic Readers*	• Have accurate but nonautomatic, effortful word recognition; • Have naming-speed correlated with slowness in word recognition; • Lack of practice reading also contributes; • Use sentence context to help with word recognition; • Have impaired reading comprehension; • Have significant spelling difficulty.
4. *Delayed Readers*	• Have slow acquisition of automatic word recognition skills; • Have few comprehension strategies, lack awareness of text organization; • Have impaired reading comprehension; • Lag behind others of similar age; • Exhibit some difficulty with spelling; • Attribute problems with reading to ability ("stupid") rather than to lack of effort; • Thus, use fewer strategies; • Questions arise about cause of strategy deficits.

5. *Readers with Monitoring Difficulties*	• Fail to monitor comprehension;
	• Experience "illusions of knowing";
	• Root of monitoring difficulty may lie in one or more of the following areas (Hacker, 1998b):
	  • Lack linguistic or topic knowledge to detect dissonance,
	  • Have linguistic and topic knowledge but lack monitoring strategies,
	  • Have knowledge and strategies but lack conditional knowledge about when and where to apply them,
	  • Comprehension and/or monitoring demand too much of readers' memory and other resources, and
	  • Lack motivation to engage in monitoring.

6. *Readers with Control Difficulties*	• Fail to execute control over perceived breakdowns in reading process;

	• Root of control difficulty may lie in one or more of the following areas (Hacker, 1998b):
	  • Lack knowledge needed to control problems monitored,
	  • Have knowledge needed to control problems but lack strategies to apply their knowledge,
	  • Have strategies for application but lack conditional knowledge about when and where to apply them,
	  • Comprehension and/or control demand too much of readers' memory and other resources, and
	  • Lack motivation to engage control resources.

7. *Readers Lacking Specific Topic Knowledge*	• Decode but have trouble making meaning because of weak topic knowledge in a particular domain, including vocabulary, specifically in relation to subject of current reading; • May attain proficiency in some topic domains.
8. *Sub-Optimal Readers*	• Have no problems with word recognition; • Have limited repertoire of basic comprehension strategies; • Have few higher-level language skills/strategies, such as knowledge of different genre, syntax sophistication, grammar mastery; • Exhibit adequate spelling skills.
9. *Disengaged or Inactive Readers*	• Have adequate to advanced knowledge base, skills, and strategies but lack motivation or sufficient degree of connection with schooling to read; • Don't make time in their schedules for reading; • May also be seen as disaffiliated or disidentified readers.
10. *English Learner*	• Includes students in "immersion" programs, English as a Second Language programs, and Bilingual programs; • Students in programs using specially designed academic instruction in English techniques.
11. *Advanced, Highly Proficient Readers*	• See qualities of good readers (chapter 3).

integrate ideas and information from many genres, make meaning from texts with challenging syntax and rhetorical devices, and comprehend specialized content.

I did not design this system of categories to serve as a classification system that identifies the underlying cause of a student's reading problem. We often can't diagnose specifically what has caused the condition we encounter in struggling readers. Causes are frequently so complex and interactive that attributing the problem to a specific cause is an impossible dream. So these categories are based on symptoms that struggling readers present. However, discovering your struggling readers' symptoms is likely to give you some hints about possible causes. Having some idea of the possible causes provides the potential to apply sensible interventions.

When categorizing readers, we also need to keep in mind a developmental perspective of reading. Alexander (2003) identified three stages in a lifespan model of reading development: (a) acclimation, (b) competence, and (c) proficiency/ expertise. A reader's age or grade may have little to do with that reader's stage of reading development. In the acclimation stage, readers are getting acquainted with reading as a complex process that requires a lot of knowledge and strategic effort. Although their knowledge base for reading is limited and fragmented, they may know about specific topics, such as video games or the Harry Potter series, that they can access. Because of their limited knowledge base, acclimating readers are likely to find it difficult to distinguish between relevant or irrelevant or correct or incorrect content. Furthermore, acclimating readers are not likely to have strong personal interests that focus their minds and engage their attention when reading. Compared to acclimating readers, competent readers manifest more knowledge and apply more deep-processing strategies when reading. They are likely to depend less on momentary interests aroused by reading because they have discovered individual, long-term interests that enliven their purposes for reading so that it becomes an intrinsically motivated pursuit. Proficient/expert readers have a richly developed knowledge base, use strategies efficiently, and usually have a personal investment in some subject matter about which they are knowledgeable, such as methods of teaching geometry or problems in explaining evolution. They have often acquired technical vocabularies and reading strategies specific to their field of interest, allowing them to generate inferences, raise questions, and identify problems they are inclined to investigate. As teachers, you may already see in yourself many of these attributes.

Who Can Be Helped and How?

Most struggling readers who fit in the categories described in Table 4.4 can be helped with appropriate interventions, such as programs that build phonological processing, word recognition, and strategic knowledge and skills. Slow comprehenders may benefit from activities that increase automaticity, such as learning sight-words, and abundant practice in reading. Students lacking topic knowledge can be provided with information that facilitates comprehension. However, some struggling readers who also fit these categories are less likely to respond to appropriate instruction because of underlying limits, such as deficits in working memory and phonological processing problems that may be biologically based (Stanovich, 1990; Stanovich & Siegel, 1994).

Students with monitoring and control problems can be helped with activities that build metacognitive skills and strategies. Lacking the ability to detect comprehension problems, struggling under an illusion of knowing, or failing to activate strategies to repair reading problems can sometimes be improved through strategies such as reciprocal teaching or collaborative reading.

Students in the "Disengaged" category who are unmotivated or uncommitted to reading, who do not see themselves as readers, and who even have negative attitudes toward those who do read may be disconnected because they had few enjoyable experiences with reading as young children. Beers (1998) found that children with negative attitudes toward reading had parents who read to them infrequently and for short periods of time. They remembered few, if any, enjoyable reading experiences. Students with positive attitudes toward reading could remember many enjoyable and worthwhile reading episodes with their parents. Beers also found that even reluctant readers with quite negative attitudes can become more engaged in reading if they can

- choose their own books,
- select books with lots of illustrations,
- see a movie based on the book and then read it,

- have books read aloud to them, and
- respond to reading books by creating art works.

Additional strategies to engage struggling readers are found in chapter 2, which focused on motivation to read in content area classes.

In any case, you need to carefully evaluate your students to determine the full range of their reading strengths and problems. In some instances, you will be able to evaluate your students with activities and instruments described and explained in this chapter. Other students with profound reading problems may require a thorough evaluation by trained reading specialists, special education teachers, or school psychologists to discover the strengths, weaknesses, and appropriate educational programs for those students.

Assessing Texts: Readability and Accessibility

No matter how much you learn about your students' reading skills and attitudes, you'll still need to evaluate the books you are going to ask your students to read. If you don't evaluate the books you expect them to read, you may be presenting your students with reading that is far too difficult, too easy, too "inconsiderate," too inaccessible, or simply too unfriendly. Our purpose is to work toward a good fit between students and the texts to be read. Instruments available to help us engage in that evaluation include readability formulas, cloze tests, and text evaluation scales.

Readability Formulas

What features would help us to determine a text's level of reading difficulty? Should we depend on how engaging the text is, its predictability, its decodability, its text structure, the number of unfamiliar words in it, its content or ideas or themes, or perhaps its literary elements? The determination of text difficulty presents teachers, text makers, standards writers, and curriculum developers with significant challenges.

Readability formulas, which were used throughout most of the 20th century to determine grade-level difficulty, usually depend upon two primary variables to determine a grade-level score: sentence length and word difficulty. The grade-level score tells us what level of reading achievement a student should have to successfully comprehend the text. If the calculation for a specified text yields a score of 10, students should supposedly be able to read at the 10th-grade level in order to understand the text. However, several important variables that predict reading difficulty or ease are not included in readability formulas.

Readability formulas spit out narrow, specific numbers. However, you'll be wise to think of those grade-level numbers as elastic measures, loosely calibrated to establish text difficulty (Hiebert, 2002). Among the variables questionably represented in readability formulas are sentence length and word difficulty, their two main components. The reason that sentence length is not always a good predictor of grade-level complexity is that short sentences may be difficult to understand if their structure and content are complex: "To be or not to be, that is the question." However, long sentences could be quite easy to follow if their structure and meaning are quite simple. Furthermore, word length does not always correspond to level of difficulty. Take the short words *epic, protist,* and *value.* Each is two syllables, but each is quite complex in meaning. Longer words, however, might not be so challenging, even to younger readers: *Disneyland, gymnasium, Mississippi.*

Among the variables not represented at all are background knowledge, paragraph structure, level of abstraction, and reader interest in a topic. Whether or not a reader has background knowledge to consider in response to a text can strongly influence level of comprehension. For example, readers having lots of background knowledge about biology may have no problem whatsoever with the word *protist,* while a student with little biology background would be left guessing.

Paragraphs that have clear topic sentences and that are clearly developed are usually far easier to comprehend than paragraphs with implied topic sentences and ambiguous development. E. M. Forster, the English author of *Aspects of the Novel* and *A Passage to India,* struggled to make his sentences and paragraphs models of clarity. Other authors, such as the English romantic poet Coleridge, believed that readers should have to be willing to work to get an author's meaning.

Highly abstract texts with few vivid examples or illustrations are often far more difficult to comprehend than texts with examples that excite visual imagery. Some philosophical texts, for example, can be difficult to read because they cover abstract ideas and may have few examples that make their content graphically clear.

Lastly, reader motivation can significantly affect comprehension. At the risk of gender stereotyping, I would suggest that an adolescent girl faced with a magazine or text in which she may have little or no interest, such as *Car and Driver* or *A Military History of the Napoleonic Wars,* could find reading the text to be an uphill march, whereas *Seventeen* or Alcott's *Little Women* might be more engrossing.

The Fry Readability Graph. Keeping these limitations in mind, let's take a look at one of the most popular readability formulas, namely, the Fry Readability Graph (Fry, 1977). Designed to measure the grade level of a text from grade 1 through college, the Fry depends upon only sentence length and word length in 100-word passages. Instead of using only one passage of 100 words to determine grade level, Fry suggests using three passages and calculating an average. Fry claims that his readability graph predicts text difficulty within one grade level.

Step-By-Step: Calculating Readability with Fry's Formula

Fry (Fry, Kress, & Fountoukidis, 2000) provides the following directions for calculating the difficulty level of a text:

Step 1. Randomly select three sample passages and count out exactly 100 words, beginning with the beginning of a sentence. Count proper nouns, initializations, and numerals.

Step 2. Count the number of sentences in the hundred words estimating length of the fraction of the last sentence to the nearest one-tenth.

Step 3. Count the total number of syllables in the 100-word passage. If you don't have a hand counter available, an easy way is to put a mark above every syllable over one in each word, and then when you get to the end of the passage, count the number of marks and add 100. Small calculators also can be

Figure 4.3 Graph for Estimating Readability—Extended.

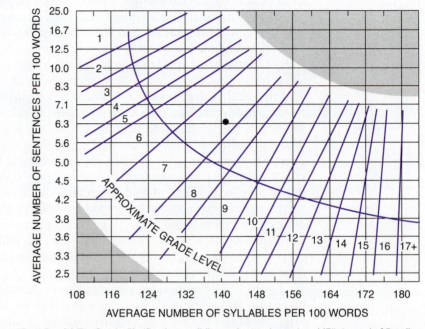

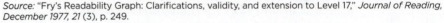

Source: "Fry's Readability Graph: Clarifications, validity, and extension to Level 17," *Journal of Reading, December 1977, 21* (3), p. 249.

used as counters by pushing numeral "1," then push the "+" sign for each word or syllable when counting.

Step 4. Enter on a graph the *average* sentence length and *average* number of syllables; plot a dot where the two lines intersect. The areas where a dot is plotted will give you the approximate grade level. (See Figure 4.3.)

Step 5. If a great deal of variability is found in syllable count or sentence count, it is a good idea to put more samples into the average.

Step 6. A word is defined as a group of symbols with a space on either side; thus, "Joe," "IRA," "1945," and "&" are each one word.

Step 7. A *syllable* is defined as a phonetic syllable. Generally, there are as many syllables as vowel sounds. For example, *stopped* is one syllable and *wanted* is two syllables. When counting syllables for numerals and initializations, count one syllable for each symbol. For example, "1945" is four syllables, "IRA" is three syllables, and "&" is one syllable.

The worksheet in Table 4.5 outlines the procedure for calculating the score based on the number of sentences and the number of syllables in each of three 100-word passages.

Table 4.5 Fry Readability Graph Worksheet

		NUMBER OF SYLLABLES	NUMBER OF SENTENCES
Passage 1	(page:)	_____	_____
Passage 2	(page:)	_____	_____
Passage 3	(page:)	_____	_____
	Totals	_____	_____
		(Divide totals by 3.)	
	Average	_____	_____
	(Enter averages on graph to plot intersection.)		
	Grade Level (+ or − 1)		_____

Cloze Tests

Cloze procedures have several uses: (a) to determine the readability of a passage, (b) to test a student's reading ability for placement, (c) to teach comprehension strategies, or (d) to review content knowledge. Our primary purpose here is to understand how the cloze test can be used to determine the readability of a text or an estimate of how competently a student can read a given text.

Cloze tests, originally conceived by Taylor (1953), work because of our mind's tendency to create closure. In verbal contexts, we want to close in blank gaps with meaningful words. How well we close in those gaps depends on our background knowledge and facility with language. As readers interact with a text that has words missing, those readers often think of words that fit the author's meaning exactly. In fact, authors who fill in blanks systematically in their own writing do so at a statistically higher rate than competent readers, a discovery that has been used to detect plagiarism.

Step-By-Step: How to Administer a Cloze Readability Test

When using the cloze procedure to determine text readability, you can take the following steps to prepare, administer, score, and interpret it.

Step 1. Preparation

- Select two passages of about 300 words from a text that your students have not yet read but will be assigned. Two passages are chosen to increase the accuracy of the procedure.
- For each passage, leave the first sentence as written. However, starting with the second sentence, you should delete each fifth word and put in a blank space about 10 to 15 spaces in length. Delete exactly 50 words, but retain the last sentence as written. A sample cloze passage appears in Figure 4.4.

Step 2. Administration

    2.1. Begin by asking students to read over the entire passage first.

    2.2. Then, ask them to go back and fill in each blank with the word they believe was deleted.

Figure 4.4 Sample Cloze Passage.

Your dermis also has tiny muscles that are attached to the hairs in your skin. When you are cold _1_ afraid, the muscles contract, _2_ the hairs upright. This _3_ process happens in the _4_ of other mammals. The _5_ of a cat, for _6_ , will stand up when _7_ cat is threatened by _8_ dog, making the cat _9_ larger and more dangerous. _10_ the cat is cold, _11_ fur fluffs up and _12_ more air near its _13_ . Because trapped air is _14_ good insulator, this _15_ the cat stay warm. _16_ muscles in your skin _17_ just like those of _18_ cat. However, because you _19_ have fur, you just _20_ goose bumps—a leftover _21_ our evolutionary past.

_22_ skin, like all other _23_ parts of your body, _24_ nourishment to live. This _25_ is supplied by blood _26_ courses through tiny blood _27_ in the dermis. In _28_ to carrying nutrients, the _29_ in these vessels carries _30_ waste products and helps _31_ body temperature. Blood radiates _32_ into the air as _33_ passes near the surface _34_ the skin. If your _35_ becomes too hot, the _36_ blood vessels enlarge, allowing _37_ blood to flow through _38_ dermis near the body _39_ . This increased flow of _40_ is easy to see _41_ light-skinned people as their _42_ becomes reddish during strenuous _43_ .

Sweat is another way _44_ your body removes excess _45_ . Your skin contains _46_ 100 sweat glands per _47_ centimeter. The evaporation of _48_ from the surface of _49_ skin removes heat much _50_ efficiently than simply radiating heat from the blood into the air. Without sweat, you would have great difficulty cooling your body on a hot day or after exercising.

Source: Excerpt from *Holt Biology: Visualizing Life,* by G. B. Johnson. Copyright © 1994 by Holt, Rinehart and Winston. Reprinted by permission of the publisher.

2.3. If students have problems filling in a word, tell them to skip it, complete the rest of the passage, and return to the blank for another try.

2.4. The test is not timed.

2.5. A short practice test helps to prepare students for the actual testing.

2.6. While some students experience cloze testing as an entertaining and challenging puzzle, others may find it quite frustrating and may require some encouragement.

Step 3. Scoring

3.1. When scoring the cloze test, only exact words replaced are correct.

3.2. Correct spelling of replaced words is not required.

3.3. To calculate percent of correct words, divide 50 into the total number of correctly replaced words. If Cynthia replaced 30 words correctly, her score would be 60%.

3.4. When using two passages to increase accuracy, the percentages of correctly replaced words for each passage are averaged. If Cynthia got 60% on the first passage and 68% on the second, her average would be 64%.

Step 4. Interpretation

4.1. Criteria for determining reading levels were developed by Bormuth (1968):

Percentage Correct	Reading Level
57% or more	Independent level
44%–57%	Instructional level
Below 44%	Frustration level

4.2. Students scoring over 57% can probably read and understand most of the tested text on their own.

4.3. Students scoring between 44% and 57% can probably read the material tested with supportive teaching of vocabulary, comprehension strategies, and study guidelines.

4.4. Students scoring below 44% will probably have so much difficulty with the tested text that you will have to find alternative texts or methods of teaching the content knowledge you want those students to learn.

Benefits and limitations of cloze testing.   The benefits of cloze tests are that they are relatively easy to prepare, administer, and score. They can help you get a rather quick fix on how each of your students is likely to engage and comprehend specific content texts. That's more than you'll get after calculating a readability formula for a textbook. Although the cloze procedure remains controversial, researchers (Shanahan & Kamil, 1984) have found fairly high correlations (0.6 to 0.8) between cloze tests and standardized reading comprehension tests using multiple-choice items. For determining students' reading levels, Cziko (1983) demonstrated that these tests are valid and reliable measures.

However, cloze tests tell us very little, if anything, about our students' capacity for higher-order thinking in the form of interpretive or inferential comprehension. Many standardized reading tests assess that form of comprehension, as do most IRIs.

In addition, many students get quite frustrated when taking a cloze test. I've even heard many teachers in credential programs complain of their frustration when I've asked them to complete a cloze test on a text that's being used in a teacher preparation program. Middle and high school students may need substantial encouragement and a clear message that their performance on the "test" will not be averaged into their course grade!

Friendly Text Evaluation Scale

There are dimensions of texts that none of the more traditional instruments we've covered manage to measure. For example, how accessible is the text to its readers? Henry Singer (1992) developed a scale to help educators determine the "friendliness" of a text. His Friendly Text Evaluation Scale can help you focus on a text's organization, consistency, and cohesiveness, as well as on its capacity to explain concepts clearly. This Friendly Scale also includes several items focusing on a text's instructional devices, their variety, and their effectiveness. Information of this kind provides a different view of texts from those generated by readability formulas and cloze tests. The entire Friendly Text Evaluation Scale is given in Table 4.6.

After reading this textbook, I invite you to apply the Friendly Text Evaluation Scale to these pages. And I hope you and your instructor will let me know what needs to be done to improve the book's accessibility.

Table 4.6 Friendly Text Evaluation Scale

Directions: Read each criterion and judge the degree of agreement or disagreement between it and the text. Then circle the number to the right of the criterion that indicates your judgment.

1. SA = Strongly Agree
2. A = Agree
3. U = Uncertain
4. D = Disagree
5. SD = Strongly Disagree

I. ORGANIZATION	SA	A	U	D	SD
1. The introductions to the book and each chapter explain their purposes.	1	2	3	4	5
2. The introduction provides information on the sequence of the text's contents.	1	2	3	4	5
3. The introduction communicates how the reader should learn from the text.	1	2	3	4	5
4. The ideas presented in the text follow a unidirectional sequence. One idea leads to the next.	1	2	3	4	5
5. The type of paragraph structure organizes information to facilitate memory. For example, objects and their properties are grouped together in order to emphasize relationships.	1	2	3	4	5
6. Ideas are hierarchically structured either verbally or graphically.	1	2	3	4	5
7. The author provides cues to the way information will be presented. For example, the author states, "There are five points to consider."	1	2	3	4	5
8. Signal words (conjunctions, adverbs) and rhetorical devices (problem-solution, question-answer, cause-effect, comparison and contrast, argument-proof) interrelate sentences, paragraphs, and larger units of discourse.	1	2	3	4	5
Discourse consistency					
9. The style of writing is consistent and coherent. For example, paragraphs, sections, and chapters build to a conclusion. Or, they begin with a general statement and then present supporting ideas. Or, the text has a combination of these patterns. Any one of these patterns would fit this consistency criterion.	1	2	3	4	5
Cohesiveness					
10. The text is cohesive. That is, the author ties ideas together from sentence to sentence, paragraph to paragraph, and chapter to chapter.	1	2	3	4	5
II. EXPLICATION	**SA**	**A**	**U**	**D**	**SD**
11. Some texts may be read at more than one level, (e.g., descriptive vs. theoretical). The text orients students to a level that is appropriate for the students.	1	2	3	4	5
12. The text provides reasons for functions or events. For example, the text, if it is a biology text, not only lists the differences between arteries and veins but also explains why they are different.	1	2	3	4	5
13. The text highlights or italicizes and defines new terms as they are introduced at a level that is familiar to the student.	1	2	3	4	5
14. The text provides necessary background knowledge. For example, the text introduces new ideas by reviewing or reminding readers of previously acquired knowledge or concepts.	1	2	3	4	5
15. The author uses examples, analogies, metaphors, similes, personifications, or allusions that clarify new ideas and make them vivid.	1	2	3	4	5
16. The author explains ideas in relatively short, active sentences.	1	2	3	4	5
17. The explanations or theories that underlie the text are made explicit.	1	2	3	4	5

III. CONCEPTUAL DENSITY	SA	A	U	D	SD
18. Ideas are introduced, defined, clarified, and integrated with semantically related ideas previously presented in the text, and examples are given before additional ideas are presented.	1	2	3	4	5
19. The vocabulary load is appropriate. For example, usually only one new vocabulary item per paragraph occurs throughout the text.	1	2	3	4	5
20. Content is accurate, up-to-date, and not biased.	1	2	3	4	5

IV. METADISCOURSE	SA	A	U	D	SD
21. The author talks directly to the reader to explain how to learn from the text. For example, the author states that some information in the text is more important than other information.	1	2	3	4	5
22. The author establishes a purpose or goal for the text.	1	2	3	4	5
23. The text supplies collateral information for putting events into context.	1	2	3	4	5
24. The text points out relationships to ideas previously presented in the text or to the reader's prior knowledge.	1	2	3	4	5

V. INSTRUCTIONAL DEVICES	SA	A	U	D	SD
25. The text contains a logically organized table of contents.	1	2	3	4	5
26. The text has a glossary that defines technical terms in understandable language.	1	2	3	4	5
27. The index integrates concepts dispersed throughout the text.	1	2	3	4	5
28. There are overviews, proposed questions, or graphic devices such as diagrams, tables, and graphs throughout the text that emphasize what is to be learned in the chapters or sections.	1	2	3	4	5
29. The text includes marginal annotations or footnotes that instruct the reader.	1	2	3	4	5
30. The text contains chapter summaries that reflect its main points.	1	2	3	4	5
31. The text has problems or questions at the literal, interpretive, applied, and evaluative levels at the end of each chapter that help the reader understand knowledge presented in the text.	1	2	3	4	5
32. The text contains headings and subheadings that divide the text into categories that enable readers to perceive the major ideas.	1	2	3	4	5
33. The author provides information in the text or at the end of the chapters or of the text that enables the reader to apply the knowledge in the text to new situations.	1	2	3	4	5
34. The author uses personal pronouns to make the text more interesting to the reader.	1	2	3	4	5

SCORE TOTALS _____
   Add the numbers circled.
   Score range: 34 to 170.
INTERPRETATION OF SCORES
   A score closer to 34 implies the text is friendly; scores closer to 170 suggest the text is unfriendly.

Source: H. Singer, Friendly texts: Description and criteria. In E. K. Dishner, T. W. Bean, J. E. Readence, & D. W. Moore (Eds.), *Reading in the content areas* (3rd ed., pp. 155–168). Dubuque, IA: Kendall/Hunt, 1992.

Summary

In this chapter, we explored the principles and benefits of diagnostic teaching with specific application to literacy, its assessment, and its development. A model of diagnostic decision making presented seven steps to guide teachers through the diagnostic teaching process. Formal assessments, including norm-reference tests, and informal assessments, such as Group Reading Inventories, Curriculum-Based Measurements, and think-alouds, were demonstrated and compared. Methods of assessing students' comprehension strategies and metacognitive awareness were provided, as were methods of assessing texts to determine their accessibility and readability levels.

Double-Entry Journal: After Reading

Having read this chapter, how would you modify your plan (if at all) to evaluate the reading performance of students at the beginning of a new class? Besides evaluating your students' reading levels, how would you approach teaching "diagnostically" in your content area? What benefits would you expect to gain from that approach?

Part II

ENHANCING YOUR STUDENTS' LITERACIES THROUGH STRATEGIC INSTRUCTION

When students gain strategic knowledge, they acquire powerful tools to build multiple literacies for learning across the curriculum. Each of the following four chapters focuses on the development of strategic knowledge that will enable your students to use the tools of literacy to become more self-determined and self-regulated learners.

Chapter 5, "Developing Vocabulary, Concepts, and Fluency for Content Area Literacy," reviews what research has taught us about vocabulary development and effective practices that promote the growth of word knowledge. It reveals the pivotal role vocabulary plays in reading fluency and presents strategies to build word and concept knowledge that teachers can integrate with content instruction.

Chapter 6, "Strategies to Enhance Comprehension," provides step-by-step procedures for the application of comprehension strategies. The strategies facilitate students' interactions with text and the growth of self-directed learning. The chapter also includes approaches to teach students text structures and to visually organize and display concepts being discovered.

Chapter 7, "Writing to Assess, Promote, and Observe Learning," describes fundamental developments in education that give support to the use of writing across the curriculum. Methods for promoting learning and academic literacy through a variety of writing-to-learn activities are described, as is the window that student writing provides to observe learning.

Chapter 8, "Critical Reading of Print and Nonprint Texts," begins with a rationale for the development, in students, of proficiency in reading more complex texts. It explains how students can learn to evaluate claims and assumptions in all the disciplines. Recognizing the power of media in the lives of today's "screenagers," we explore how texts define their readers and how teachers can help their students gain a more critical consciousness to understand the enormous power of texts.

Chapter 5

DEVELOPING VOCABULARY, CONCEPTS, AND FLUENCY FOR CONTENT AREA LITERACY

After reading chapter 5, you should be able to answer the following questions:

1. How do we transform printed words into meanings?
2. Why is knowing a word so complicated?
3. What have researchers learned about teaching vocabulary?
4. How could you help students learn and use strategies to discover the meanings of unknown words?
5. How can you help students learn new words through "just reading"?
6. How can technology foster vocabulary growth?

Double-Entry Journal: Before Reading

How do you feel about encountering and learning new words? What methods have you used to learn them? How could you increase your students' knowledge and appreciation of words?

Words are small wonders. When spoken, they're puffs of air. When written, they're jiggles on paper. These puffs and jiggles enable us to communicate, to convey our love, to pursue justice, to contain our histories, and to carry on our culture. As a teacher, your words serve as a bridge for your students to enter new worlds of knowledge and new fields of understanding. As your students acquire subject matter vocabulary, they acquire the tools to work and to communicate in that field. Vocabulary, the repertoire of words people use to understand their world and to express their perceptions of it, is the best single indicator we have of intelligence (R. J. Sternberg, 1988). The purpose of this chapter is to provide you with the knowledge and strategies to help your students gain the vocabulary they need to grow and to succeed.

Transforming Words Into Meanings

If you focus on the role of words in the model of reading presented in chapter 3, you will soon see that neither word knowledge nor its acquisition is simple. Being able to read a word, either a basic word such as *cat* or a complex one such as *catalogue*, requires considerable background knowledge and skill—not to mention intricate cognitive processes we are still discovering. To recognize a word when reading, a reader must have command of knowledge and skills that take years to develop. If you consider how much word knowledge students need to approach proficient comprehension in a content area such as history, math, biology, or physics, you can begin to appreciate the complexity of vocabulary development.

Decoding

Without the ability to decode a word or recognize it, a reader is lost. To help you envision the reading process as presented in chapter 3, especially the cognitive and metacognitive processes related to vocabulary, I've included in Figure 5.1 those components of the model that depict word recognition, word knowledge, and metacognition. From this return visit to the model, you will recall that without being able to transform letters and words into their corresponding sounds—that is, to decode—your students will struggle when trying to read. If the texts you give them contain many unfamiliar words, they will experience varying degrees of frustration. One way or the other, you will have to cope with their vocabulary needs and strengths.

Many educators believe that word-level decoding is a bottleneck in readers' meaning construction efforts. If readers can't decode a word, they simply can't understand it. And, if large portions of working memory are tied up in decoding, comprehension will falter (Samuels, 2004, 2006). For better understanding and fluency, readers need to acquire **automaticity**, that is, they need to process letters and words accurately with little attention to them when decoding. Efficiency in reading depends upon rapid word recognition that can't occur without fluid decoding.

Figure 5.1 Key Vocabulary Processing Components of the Sociocognitive Reading Model.

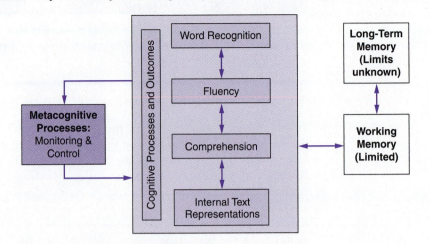

The Lexicon in Long-Term Memory

As depicted in Figure 5.1 and the complete reading model, readers' knowledge of words and their meanings is stored in long-term memory. As readers recognize words and activate their meanings, they construct a mental representation for the text being read. With a lexicon of recallable words, readers access their knowledge of concepts. The more words a reader has stored for activation, the greater the reader's chances of understanding content area texts. As we learned, speed of access to word meanings also contributes to fluent reading. Every reader's working memory functions better when it is not burdened with a struggle to decode a word or access its meaning.

Researchers (Levy, 2001; Tan & Nicholson, 1997) have found that weak readers who practiced recognizing "target words" visually until they could do so automatically benefited significantly from the training in comparison to a control group. In the control condition, subjects engaged in discussion about the meaning of target words but never saw them. Visual word recognition appeared to be a key to better comprehension. Other research (Breznitz, 1997; Torgesen & Hudson, 2006) also confirmed that comprehension improved when subjects could decode words rapidly. As we have seen, this probably occurs as struggling readers gain more working-memory capacity and use it to construct extended meaning.

From Word Recognition to Fluency

When looking into the meaning construction zone while reading, we confirmed that fluency was a critical bridge between word recognition and comprehension. To read texts with fluency, students need to process words efficiently and accurately. When word recognition is labored, comprehension often becomes impeded. To gain comprehension in reading content area texts, readers should rapidly grasp the meanings of words, string them together into understandable statements, and form internal networks of meaning. When facing unfamiliar words within relatively new conceptual contexts, students benefit from opportunities to learn important conceptual words deeply and to practice using them so they become more familiar.

We know from studies of fluency-oriented instruction which has been done mostly with elementary school students, including studies conducted by the National Reading

Panel (NPR), that guided oral reading has significant positive effects on both fluency and comprehension (National Reading Panel 2000). Because the range of fluency problems is wide, we should adopt a try-and-see approach in using fluency-building strategies with struggling readers. A single, narrow approach may not address the underlying difficulties that are troubling dysfluent students.

With the help of a closer look at fluency-oriented activities by Kuhn and Stahl (2004), we can add practices that are likely to affect students' fluent reading performance. They found that several strategies were effective: assisted reading, repeated reading, and paired reading. These fluency-oriented strategies are presented in detail in this chapter and in the chapter that focuses on group strategies teachers can use to help struggling readers comprehend content area texts. (See chapter 9.) But remember that reading speed is no guarantee of comprehension. When the meanings of words evade readers, proposition formation and integration will be disrupted. Knowing what important content area words mean—not just how they are pronounced—should become each student's primary objective, an objective that we can help students achieve by supporting their growth in vocabulary knowledge.

Metacognition and Making Meaning from Words

Looking at the vocabulary-related components of the model of reading in Figure 5.1, we can see the critical role that metacognition plays in the monitoring and control of text processing. Monitoring and control are essential for word recognition and the contribution of individual words to the landscape we construct to represent a text internally. Metalinguistic ability is made up of monitoring and controlling the processing of words (Nagy & Scott, 2000). Metalinguistic awareness includes knowledge of word parts and their contritutions to a word's meanings, use of a word's surrounding textual context, and understanding how definitions of words function in the construction of meaning.

Knowledge of the parts of a word is usually referred to as *morphological awareness*. A **morpheme** is a distinct unit of meaning in a word. Morphemes can be added to a root word to create inflected or compound words based on that root. The word *unfounded*, for example, is composed of three distinct morphemes that contribute meaning to the word: *un-*, meaning not, the root word *found*, meaning based, and *-ed*, which, in this case, is used to form the past participle of the verb so it functions as an adjective. The contribution of morphological knowledge and awareness to vocabulary growth is enormous and usually underestimated (Nagy & Anderson, 1984). Researchers (Nagy & Scott, 2000) believe that the application of morphological knowledge to word learning depends on metalinguistic awareness that expands throughout high school. That research-based belief might guide our decisions about what to teach our middle and high school students about word parts as they progress.

Context constitutes a second domain of metalinguistic awareness that contributes to word learning. However, students will need to know a very large percentage of the words around an unknown word if they hope to figure it out from its context. As we've all experienced at one time or another, even knowing all the words that surround an unknown word will not open the door to the unknown word's meaning. Furthermore, every word is embedded in some syntactical structure, and we've known for some time that students with higher levels of syntactic awareness comprehend texts better (Weaver, 1979). Knowing how to monitor and use context clues, such as words surrounding an unknown word or syntax, increase the likelihood that a reader can create meaning for the larger text.

Metalinguistic awareness of definitions, a third metacognitive domain related to word recognition, can enable readers to maximize the benefits and limit misunderstandings that accompany a word's definitions. Young readers, in particular, have trouble getting hold of a word's meaning and use from its definition. In part, this may occur when students take a portion of a word's meaning to represent the whole meaning of the word and when they simultaneously are unable to identify the correct part of speech of the word. Given a definition of maintenance as the upkeep of a building, a student might focus on the *building* aspect of the definition, fail to see that *-ance* at the word's end signals its noun function, and think that the word means the same thing as the verb to build, as in, He maintenanced the store.

The Complexities of Simply Knowing a Word

Knowing a word appears to be a fairly simple form of knowledge; however, beneath that appearance of simplicity, we quickly discover how complicated knowing a word really is. Nagy and Scott (2000) identified five aspects of word knowledge complexity:

1. Knowing a word is not a yes-no dichotomy but a matter of degrees. Students know words on a continuum from complete ignorance of a word to proficiency in crafting sentences with that word.

2. Knowing a word entails many dimensions of knowledge. These dimensions include knowledge of a word's spoken form, written form, grammatical form, conceptual meaning, synonyms, antonyms, frequency of use, and responsiveness to contexts.

3. Words frequently have many meanings. To know a word well implies knowing much more than a single memorized definition. Many words, such as *rose* or *fork,* have multiple meanings and nuances within individual meanings.

4. Knowledge of a single word isolated from all others is impossible. Words live and acquire meanings in interconnected networks. That is especially true of words relevant to academic disciplines, such as words used by geologists or physicists.

5. What it means to know a word depends on the kind of word you are talking about knowing. For example, knowledge of an article, such as *the,* or of a conjunction, like *and,* is quite different from knowledge of nouns such as *conjugation, polynomial,* or *catalyst.*

Although most researchers and teachers have recognized the complexity of word knowledge for many years, traditional vocabulary instruction, such as memorizing definitions for a weekly quiz, often fails to take that complexity into account. Because of the complexity behind word knowledge, explicit instruction in word definitions must be reinforced with multiple and varied exposure to target words. Knowing a word well entails knowing how that word works in our language system, how it is used in multiple contexts, and what you can do with it, not simply what it means in isolation. As Nagy and Scott (2000, p. 273) insightfully observe, "In most cases, knowing a word is more like knowing how to use a tool than it is like being able to state a fact."

Word Counts

How many words do students know? How many do they usually learn each year? Answers to these questions depend upon several prior questions: What counts as a word?

What does it mean to know a word? What dictionary or list of words will be used to measure totals and rates of growth? How will that body of words be sampled? What populations will be sampled to determine size and growth rates? Because different researchers (Beck & McKeown, 1991) have answered these questions differently, the answers to our questions about total words known and rates of growth vary.

As for vocabulary size, estimates for college students vary from 19,000 to 200,000 known words. For first graders, estimates range from 2,500 to 25,000. As part of an extensive study of vocabulary development, Biemiller and Slonim (2001) estimated the number of words at each **Living Word Vocabulary (LWV)** grade level and the proportion of those that were root words. The LWV is a comprehensive assessment of 44,000 word meanings known by children through high school and into adulthood (Dale & O'Rourke, 1981). A root word was defined as a morpheme, and, as we've seen, morphemes can be added to a root word. If readers understand *plan* as a root word, or morpheme, they would also understand *planned, planning,* and *unplanned,* each of which have added morphemes, such as -ed, -ing, and un-, to the root word. Biemiller and Slonim estimated that 67% to 80% of 8th graders knew about 22,000 LWV meanings and about 11,000 root words, whereas 67% to 80% of 12th graders knew about 30,500 LWV meanings and about 15,000 root words. After their review of relevant research, Beck and McKeown (1991, p. 794) concluded that "absolute statements about vocabulary size of various populations cannot be made." However, we know that huge individual differences in word knowledge among students exist. For example, in M. K. Smith's (1941) study, high-performing seniors in high school knew about four times the number of words that low-performing seniors knew. Furthermore, high-performing third-graders knew as many words as low-performing seniors in high school.

Differences in word knowledge.

Differences in word knowledge are evident in students with different social and economic backgrounds. By age 4, children raised in professional families have experienced about 45 million words, whereas children raised in working-class families experienced about 26 million (Hart & Risley, 1995, 2003). Moreover, children from welfare families have experienced only 13 million words, 32 million fewer than children in professional families. Instances of encouraged or affirmative feedback also differ widely between the three groups, with children in professional families experiencing almost six instances of encouraging feedback for each single instance of encouraging feedback in working-class environments. Meanwhile, children in welfare families experienced far more discouragements than encouragements. These gaps in early life experiences with words foretell the struggles with reading and learning that many students from families in poverty have in middle and high school classrooms.

We know from extensive research that a limited vocabulary contributes to the achievement gap between social groups. Furthermore, as students with limited vocabularies progress through the grades, they tend to fall farther behind in word knowledge (Chall, Jacobs, & Baldwin, 1990). That development reflects what Stanovich (1986) dubbed the "Matthew effect," whereby those rich in word knowledge become richer, whereas the poor become poorer. "For unto every one that hath shall be given, and he shall have abundance; but from him that hath not shall be taken away even that which he hath." That line from the Gospel according to Matthew provides the allusion for the Matthew effect. Students who have already acquired reading skills and extensive word knowledge have a strong base on which to build. Students with few skills and less word knowledge must try to learn with what they have in spite of their overall tendency to fall farther behind. It's a rich-get-richer, poor-get-poorer scenario, and Stanovich provides ample evidence to support the claim for the Matthew effect. These findings underscore how much words count and how vital our attention to vocabulary development is.

As for rates of growth in vocabulary, children learn about 2,000 or more words each year (Nagy & Scott, 2000). While some children from grades 1 through 5 learn at higher rates per year, students whose background has not provided a substantial language base need to gain knowledge of words at twice the pace (at least) of their more fortunate peers. Fortunately, Biemiller and Slonim (2001) present evidence that schooling does help to close the gap in the early grades.

High- and Low-Frequency Words

Readers are exposed to words at different rates, or frequencies. Although exposure to words varies along a continuum, reading specialists tend to think of words as belonging in two extreme categories: high- and low-frequency words. **High-frequency words** are the shortest, most frequently occurring ones and, oddly enough, are a source of difficulty for many struggling readers. Quite a few of these high-frequency words, such as *the, of,* or *would,* don't carry a heavy load of meaning. They are usually abstract function words. Even though students may process and reprocess some of these high-frequency words, such as *where* or *were,* hundreds of times, some students still have trouble with them. For fluent readers, however, most of these high-frequency words are *sight words,* words that are instantly recognized and processed orthographically without analysis.

Educators (Fry et al., 2000; Zeno, Ivens, Millard, & Duvvuri, 1995) have compiled lists of the words that appear most often in text materials that school children read. Fry et al. observed that the first 25 words on their "instant-word" list make up about one third of everything in print, while the whole list of 100 words makes up about half of all written material (see Table 5.1). Kucera and Francis (1967) discovered that, in a sample of 1,000,000 words of adult text, 50% of the text was composed of only 133 words.

Most students learn these high-frequency, or "instant" words, early in their reading career, many by about the third or fourth grade, if not earlier. However, some students continue to struggle with them, in part because of limited practice or lack of ability to process the words or sounds (Gunning, 2006). Some of these students can gain greater automaticity through reading a wide range of easy books, through reading more frequently, or through repeated reading (Samuels, 2004). When doing repeated readings, students choose a passage that is difficult to read fluently and make a record of word-recognition errors and speed for the passage. The students, like a pianist learning to play a score, then practice rereading the passage independently, working as needed with particularly challenging words, until they are ready to be tested again for time and errors. When students read the passage with fluency, it's time to move on to a new selection. If you have students who have problems with high-frequency words, their difficulty may signal a need for attention to delayed reading development. Chapter 10 includes strategies for assisting struggling readers and presents information to help you and your colleagues address these problems.

For our students, **low-frequency words** usually carry more content area knowledge. Unfortunately, readers encounter these low-frequency words far less often. Carroll, Davies, and Richman (1971) discovered that 90% of kindergarten through eighth-grade texts they analyzed were constructed of 5,000 common words. But

Table 5.1 Instant Words or High-Frequency Words

First Hundred			
WORDS 1–25	**WORDS 26–50**	**WORDS 51–75**	**WORDS 75–100**
the	or	will	number
of	one	up	no
and	had	other	way
a	by	about	could
to	word	out	people
in	but	many	my
is	not	then	than
you	what	them	first
it	were	so	been
he	we	some	call
was	when	her	who
for	your	would	oil
on	can	make	its
are	said	like	now
as	there	him	find
with	use	into	long
his	an	time	down
they	each	has	day
I	which	look	did
at	she	two	get
be	do	more	come
this	how	write	made
have	their	go	may
from	if	see	part

Source: From *The Reading Teacher's Book of Lists* (p. 47), by E. B. Fry, J. E. Kress, and D. L. Fountoukidis, 2000. Copyright © 2000 by John Wiley & Sons, Inc. Reprinted with permission of John Wiley & Sons, Inc.

many less common words also appear in those texts. The remaining 10% of the words (about 80,000) accounted for the vast majority of words readers had to understand to grasp the text's full meaning.

Of course, a word may be low frequency for one reader but not for another. Because one of your students may spend a lot of time reading about car engines and tinkering with the car's engine, the word *torque* may be a relatively high-frequency word, although that same word could easily fall on another student's low-frequency list. A word's degree of frequency depends on the reading experience of the reader. Consequently, the speed with which weaker readers recognize low-frequency words is likely to be slower, especially for words with an irregular letter-sound pattern.

Greater knowledge of lower frequency words contributes directly to higher scores on tests of word knowledge. It follows that bigger banks of lower frequency words will translate into better reading comprehension for a wide variety of texts. Most standardized reading tests are composed of a vocabulary section and a reading comprehension section that are highly correlated and combined to yield a total reading score. The more word knowledge a reader has, the higher the score on the reading test.

Knowing what we do about high- and low-frequency words, we can see what our word knowledge instructional challenge will be: discover ways to enable our students to acquire the low-frequency words that permeate our content area teaching.

Word tiers.   To help us think through which words are important for us to teach to students, Beck, McKeown, and Kucan (2002) categorized words into three levels they call *tiers*. They consider Tier I words to be the most basic, words such as *door, drum,* or *deep,* which are learned at home or in the student's community. Words in the Tier III category are words of low frequency that are often important content- or domain-specific words, such as *phenotype, cosign,* or *metonymy.* Between these two levels of words lies Tier II, a large group of relatively high-frequency words, at least for mature speakers of a language. These include words such as *require, maintain,* or *benevolent.* Tier II words can be identified by their importance and utility (they appear often in many different contexts), their instructional potential (students can build rich representations of these words and connect them to other words or concepts), and their contribution to conceptual understanding (they add precision and specificity to concept descriptions). Teaching vocabulary explicitly with these Tier II words as primary targets can, according to Beck et al., extend our students' facility with language.

Student-Led Vocabulary Growth: A Strategy-Integrated Model

Many middle and high school teachers face daunting literacy challenges. The challenges are magnified in schools serving students from communities with large numbers of low-income, minority families who speak languages other than English in the home. Those challenges could be met, in part, through an aggressive, coordinated vocabulary development program across the content areas. We could call it VAC, Vocabulary Across the Curriculum, with teachers in all the disciplines committed to word-knowledge growth. Teachers would design and coordinate the vocabulary program, but students would play a key role in energizing it. Their engagement would be critical.

Fortunately, the blueprint for such a program exists at Lincoln High School in Los Angeles. One of their seasoned English teachers, Dennis De Pauw, has taken on the challenge of vocabulary development in a highly productive way with his 9th and 11th-grade English classes. The program might be described as "vocabulary triage." Knowing the importance, utility, and instructional potential of Tier II words that we met earlier in this chapter (Beck et al., 2002), Dennis bases his vocabulary acquisition program on them.

He gives his students, most of whom are from lower income families and minority backgrounds, an idea of what a Tier I, II, and III word is. Then he focuses his program on the Tier II words. He requires his students to develop, maintain, and be instructionally responsible for a specific number of words, usually 10 to 15, over a defined time period, such as a week. His students, who know and value the power of words, are in the driver's seat as far as which words they select from their reading. He does not require responsibility for any specific words, but as "Word King," he might advocate an occasional "gift word." Furthermore, the words accumulate week by week, and students become responsible for an expanding deck of words as the semester progresses. After the deck grows to 50 or more cards, he sometimes asks students to cluster their words in some creative network of meanings.

Students give the words a specific treatment, learn the words, and are evaluated on their knowledge of the words. For each word selected, students complete a 3 × 5 card with the word on one side and information about the word on the other, such as the word's definition, its part of speech, and the sentence from the text from which it came. Once a week, usually on Friday, students come up to Dennis's desk during class so that he can interview them and assess their word learning based on their own word deck. He selects about five words, more or less at random, from the deck and asks his students to define the words, checks to see if they can use the words correctly in a sentence, and/or explain their significance to the content domain from which it came. The scene is often a dialogue of convivial word play. Dennis gives each student a score based on how many of the selected words he or she knew and used accurately. He then records the vocabulary scores and, at the end of each semester, uses those scores as his vocabulary grade factor. The student with her deck of vocabulary cards pictured on the first page of this chapter is preparing for her weekly interview.

The kind of vocabulary development program that Dennis orchestrates in his classroom could be conducted in every discipline, including math and physical education. With such schoolwide participation, more students would stand a chance of being better prepared for the academic challenges of college and the practical demands of the workplace.

Step-By-Step: Student-Led Vocabulary Development

1. Explain to your students what Tier I, II, and III words are. Provide examples of each tier and engage them in a few word-level identification exercises so that they can practice detecting Tier II words.

2. Explain that each week they are going to be responsible for identifying 10 to 20 words (you can decide on the exact number) that come from their readings in the class and that they believe meet the criteria for Tier II words.

3. Show them how to complete 3 × 5 cards with definitions, synonyms, parts of speech, a word map of some kind, and a sentence using the word. These cards form their vocabulary deck.

4. Explain they are responsible for learning all the words in their deck, plus their spellings, over a specified time, say a week or two. (Holding students responsible for a growing word bank that accumulates during a semester is also a productive practice.)

5. When time to demonstrate vocabulary learning comes, ask students to approach your desk one at a time with their deck of cards. Select about five, more or less randomly, and check for understanding.

6. Put the score for words known correctly in your record book and use those scores at the end of the grading period to calculate the vocabulary factor that contributes to students' grade.

Flashbacks: The Return of the Vocabulary Card

How many millions of students have used flashcards to learn words? Long ago, before television and maybe even before radio, students helped themselves learn vocabulary by putting unknown words on one side of a card and, on the opposite side, by putting the meaning, part of speech, and a sentence using the word correctly. Recent research (Tan & Nicholson, 1997) suggests that this ancient technique, still alive in some word-building classrooms, could be effective in helping readers become more fluent.

Although most of your students, just like those in Dennis's high school English classes, will have gained automatic recognition of sight words, some may not. Although you probably will not have to take your entire class through sight-word training, some students may require that kind of instruction. If so, you may have a specialist or assistant who could help these delayed readers increase word-recognition speed through drilling students on those "instant" words. (See Table 5.1.) Practice with flashcards should continue until students immediately recognize targeted high-frequency words. Some computer-based reading programs can also help struggling readers recognize high-frequency words more automatically.

Source: CALVIN AND HOBBES © 1986 Watterson. Dist. By UNIVERSAL PRESS SYNDICATE. Reprinted with permission. All rights reserved.

What We Know About Teaching Vocabulary

As long ago as the mid-1970s, researchers (Becker, 1977) claimed that one of the major contributing factors to the failure of disadvantaged children in our schools was inadequate knowledge of vocabulary, implying that students received inadequate vocabulary instruction.

When I began to teach English in the 1960s, I taught my students vocabulary from lists of words students were expected to know. I usually took words from novels or essays we were reading as a class. In one school where I taught, lists were compiled by the English department for specific grade levels, and English teachers were expected to cover all the vocabulary for the grade level they taught. When my students and I disagreed over a word's meaning or when a word (such as fray) had multiple meanings, we'd agree on a specific dictionary definition that students would have to know for their Friday vocabulary quiz. It seemed like a sensible approach. It had its merits. Parents approved. It worked like a current SAT word list. All of us, to the best of my knowledge, used an approach that emphasized students' looking up a word's definition and composing a sentence using it "appropriately." At the time I had some misgivings about the process, but I hung with it. Years later, research began to emerge that confirmed my misgivings about the definitional approach we used.

Principles to Guide Vocabulary Learning

When pulling together research on vocabulary instruction throughout the grades, the National Reading Panel (NICHD, 2000) made several discoveries that bear on our needs as content area teachers in middle and high school classrooms. Knowing as we do that word knowledge is complex and multidimensional, we should not be surprised with their finding that a single vocabulary instruction method does not yield optimum learning. Multifaceted approaches are far more likely to provide students with opportunities to expand and deepen their knowledge of words.

Fortunately, teachers can guide their decisions about vocabulary instruction with research-based conclusions that the National Reading Panel (NICHD, 2000) was able to make. Among their relevant findings are the following:

- For specific texts, which would include those in all content areas, direct instruction of vocabulary words is beneficial.
- Multiple exposures to and repetition of vocabulary are critical to gaining word knowledge.
- Words of the kind that appear in Tier II are most beneficial because those words are encountered in multiple contexts.
- Active engagement in a variety of learning tasks facilitates vocabulary growth.
- Incidental word learning is a critical path to vocabulary development. Students cannot possibly learn by direct instruction all the words that represent their expanding vocabularies.
- Instructional technologies, including computer-assisted programs and access to Web worlds, enrich vocabulary instruction.

Follow-up studies of vocabulary instruction completed since the publication of the NRP report have provided no new discoveries (Kamil & Hiebert, 2005).

Creating Word-Rich Environments

Students, especially those who have had fewer opportunities for language development and may be losing ground, need an environment of exposure to print that fosters word knowledge. According to the *environmental opportunity* hypothesis (Stanovich, Cunningham, & West, 1998), vocabulary differences that we see in our students result from their varying opportunities to learn words. In accord with this hypothesis, some students with opulent vocabularies have thrived in language-rich environments, while others with impoverished vocabularies eked out their word knowledge from desertlike conditions. But there is an argument that counters this environmental opportunity hypothesis. Called the *cognitive efficiency* hypothesis, it suggests that differences in students' word knowledge stem from differences in readers' cognitive abilities and the contribution those abilities make to the efficient construction of meanings for words, even unfamiliar words, in a context.

Without engaging in extended debate over the nurture vs. nature issue, perhaps we could go directly to what should be done to promote word learning in our classrooms, assuming that both arguments have merit. If we accepted both hypotheses, we'd want to provide our students with every opportunity for word growth in a word-rich environment while giving them strategies to harvest the word crop of that environment. If we knew what nurtured word-knowledge growth for our students, we could manipulate the environment to provide nurturing for word knowledge to thrive.

As noted, exposure to a word-enriched environment alone may not lead to its efficient uptake and use. Internalized strategies can have a strong effect on word learning and knowledge acquisition (Sternberg, 1987, 1988). Researchers (Pressley, 2000) have shown that teaching literacy-enhancing strategies can improve student reading and learning from texts. We know that learning individual target words does improve comprehension when those words are related to the material that students are reading (Beck, McKeown, & Omanson, 1987).

Fostering Word Consciousness

To Anderson and Nagy (1992), consciousness of words includes both awareness of them and interest in learning them. Word consciousness motivates word learning. To foster word consciousness, Graves and Watts-Taffe (2002) make several specific recommendations that can be integrated into daily instruction.

- *Model, recognize, and encourage attention to word usage.*   You are a model of the importance of words and how they are used whenever you communicate with your students. You can acknowledge the challenge of new words in reading assignments and in students' use of words in their speaking and writing. You can also encourage your students to become more aware of how they use words to convey their perceptions and understanding of concepts in your content area. Implementing "The Daily Word" by highlighting and weaving it throughout the day's lesson demonstrates your attention to the importance of words and their proficient use. Words speak volumes.

- *Promote word play.*   Your enjoyment of words, their sounds, and their uses contribute to a word-aware environment in your classroom. No matter what discipline you teach, words are actors. They strut and struggle across the stage of every classroom. Awareness of the verbal tricks those actors play in puns, cliches, metaphors, and inappropriate applications adds significant dimensions of understanding and humor to teaching. Encouraging your students to play with words provides opportunities for them to discover the character of words and the myriad roles they play.

- *Involve students in investigations.*   When students embark on an original investigation or research an aspect of the discipline you teach, they can be encouraged to pay special attention to vocabulary. Students can watch for ways different authors writing about the same topic use words differently to convey meaning. For example, students could pay attention to less familiar words encountered during their discovery. If investigating a current event, students could discover how writers published in two or three different newspapers or magazines use different words to describe and to analyze it. A student might tally the number of unfamiliar words in each article and reflect on the significance of those differences. *The American Heritage Word Frequency Book* (Carroll et al., 1971) would facilitate their tallying of less frequently used words.

Gaining Word Knowledge Through Strategy Instruction

Knowing, as we do, the importance of vocabulary growth and instruction to the development of students' knowledge base and content area, what can we do to enhance their opportunities to gain word knowledge, both in school and out of school?

Since the mid-1970s, several hundred studies focused on vocabulary instruction have been published (Blachowicz & Fisher, 2000). Educators (Baumann & Kaméenui, 1991; Irvin, 1990; M. R. Ruddell, 1994) have distilled much of what has been learned from about 25 years of research into a set of insights that teachers could apply to their classroom instruction. After reviewing the research, Blachowicz and Fisher identified four main principles to guide vocabulary instruction:

1. Students should be active learners as they acquire specific vocabulary and strategies to enlarge their vocabulary base.
2. Students benefit from personalizing the learning of words.
3. Students gain from immersion in words.
4. Students augment their vocabulary through repeated exposure to words.

These principles for learning words can be applied in many different contexts, including struggling readers and English language learners. From these principles, we can conclude that to teach new words, we need to immerse our students in active and repeated opportunities to integrate word instruction with knowledge students have already acquired in our discipline.

Julian Roberts integrated several word-learning strategies into his 9th-grade world history class to help his students understand ancient Greek history and its contributions to today's culture. His class of 30 students ranged in reading ability from 4th to 11th grade. They came from many cultural backgrounds, including African American, Hispanic, and Asian. Their motivation was, so to speak, all over the map. A few of his students were academic achievers, several were pleasant but quietly passive, and some were completely disidentified with school.

The text for world history was chronologically organized. The social studies department had selected it 3 years before. It was written at about the ninth-grade level and was well designed by a staff of specialists and teachers, providing clearly written prose accompanied by colorful supporting pictures, end-of-chapter questions, and a glossary. From past years of teaching, Julian knew that if he just assigned a section of the text to read, very few students would read the assignment. Many students found the text inaccessible, "boring," or both, in spite of its lively writing style. Julian discovered in the first year he used the new history textbook that one of the major problems many students had with reading it was their own limited vocabularies. The text was at a frustration level for more than a third of his students, some of whom were English language learners. Many others needed instructional support to comprehend it. Very few could read it independently with reasonable comprehension.

Some of his teaching colleagues had more or less given up on using the text. Instead, they lectured. They required students to take notes. Some had students read out loud to each other and paraphrase the text. Others used videos that paralleled the text's content and discussed the videos with students. But these approaches did little to build weaker students' reading capacity or vocabulary.

In his first year, he was stunned to discover that most of his ninth graders were reading on the fifth-grade level, some on third- or fourth-grade levels. Reading the social studies text was frustrating for them because they simply didn't have the reading tools to understand what they read. But he learned that he could help many of them if he gave them lots of support, "scaffolding," and some prereading vocabulary instruction.

To make the text more accessible, Julian began by working out a vocabulary instruction program for the first two or three months of the school year. He reviewed his teaching goals and standards and the material students would be reading. Based on a review of that material, he made decisions about which vocabulary he thought his ninth-graders would find unfamiliar. Then he created two categories of words: those he thought would be essential to the students' understanding of the texts to be assigned and those he considered less essential. He also provided students with the opportunity to let him know which words they knew and wanted to know by using a Word Knowledge Check and a Vocabulary Self-Collection Strategy (VSS). These strategies are described later in this chapter.

Addressing Vocabulary

The chapter in the text covering ancient Greece included a section on Greek art, culture, and philosophy, with many words Julian knew would be unfamiliar to most of his students. He had to make choices about which words he would target for intensive instruction. To help make those choices, he kept in mind Allen's (1999) 10 decision-making questions:

1. Which words are most important to understanding the text?
2. How much prior knowledge will students have about this word or related concept?
3. Is the word encountered frequently?
4. Does the word have multiple meanings?
5. Is the concept significant and does it therefore require preteaching?
6. Which words can students figure out from context?
7. Can some words be grouped together to enhance understanding of a concept?
8. What strategies could I use to help students integrate the concept (and related words) into their lives?
9. How can I make repeated exposures to the word/concept possible, productive, and even pleasant?
10. How can I help students use the word/concept in meaningful ways in multiple contexts?

Keeping those guidelines in mind, he went through the section they were to read on arts and philosophy to identify essential and less essential words. Essential words he defined as those required to grasp the central ideas and concepts presented in the reading. So he got his essential list together:

Acropolis, polis, politics, culture, philosophy, systems of thought, adhere, tragedy, and *comedy.*

Under less essential words he grouped those that he thought most students would recognize or that were not needed in order for them to comprehend the basic information given. His less essential list of words (and concepts) that he could teach while discussing the reading or afterward included:

Architecture, Parthenon, Athena, cutting-edge, philosopher, Socrates, Pericles, government, prefer, mask, and *scholar.*

After a first reading of the text, students could add unfamiliar words to the list through the Vocabulary Self-Collection Strategy, or VSS (Haggard, 1982, 1986). He suspected that some words he selected for the less essential list would appear on students' VSS lists.

After deciding on the vocabulary he thought was essential for his students to understand an upcoming reading on Greek culture, he reviewed the reservoir of strategies he could draw upon: a Word Knowledge Check, the keyword method, word maps, word parts, interconnected concepts, and crossword puzzles.

Table 5.2 A Word Knowledge Check

	I NEVER SAW IT BEFORE	I HEARD IT BUT DON'T KNOW WHAT IT MEANS	I RECOGNIZE IT IN CONTEXT AS RELATED TO SOMETHING I KNOW	I KNOW IT WELL	I CAN USE IT IN A SENTENCE
Polis					
Politics					
Culture					
Philosophy					
Systems of thought					
Adhere					
Tragedy					
Comedy					

Word Knowledge Check

A **Word Knowledge Check** is a technique to let you know how well your students know certain words. Researchers (Dale, 1965; Paribakht & Wesche, 1997) have hypothesized several stages of word knowledge that are reflected in a Word Knowledge Check's five levels of word awareness. (See Table 5.2.) Because Julian selected words and concepts that he suspected his students would not know, using a Word-Knowledge Check would confirm or correct his hunches. He would ask students to look over the words and tell him their level of familiarity with each word.

Keyword Method

Pressley and his associates (Pressley, Levin, & Delaney, 1983; Pressley, Levin, & McDaniel, 1987) have developed and empirically verified the effectiveness of the mnemonic keyword method. A **mnemonic** is a systematic procedure designed to improve memory use. Although the method was first designed to help second-language learners acquire vocabulary (Atkinson, 1975), the **keyword method** works well in helping native speakers learn new words in their mother tongue.

The process can be broken down into three steps: recoding, relating, and retrieving.

1. When *recoding,* you select part of the unknown word that looks or sounds like a word you know. For example, I would like to learn the vocabulary word *adhere* and notice that the word sounds like "add here."

2. When *relating,* you relate the recoded word to the unknown word's definition using some image. I imagine adding Post-its that say "here" on them to an ad for glue.

3. When *retrieving,* you need to think of the keyword for the newly learned word. When I see the word *adhere,* I would picture the image of those Post-its being added to the glob, reminding me that adhere means to stick to something or to obey.

Word Maps

Julian used three kinds of word maps with his ninth-grade students: Question Map, Structured Overview, and Concept Mastery Map.

A **Question Map** allows students, perhaps working in small groups, to generate questions about important words and concepts. Students can list any and all questions they have about an unknown or unfamiliar word or concept and have no concern about being wrong. Julian elected to work with the word *philosophy,* a word so full of juice for him that he had to pick it. So his Question Map (Figure 5.2) presented the kinds of questions he suspected his students would generate, along with several that he wanted to add.

A **Structured Overview** is for concepts that have subordinate and superordinate relationships, such as the concept *phylum* used to exemplify this kind of map in Figure 5.3. To practice this method of organizing the relationships between concepts, you could create a structured overview for this chapter. It would show how concepts are organized and presented. Some writers and readers find that graphically organizing material in this way after reading about it or before writing about it serves them well.

Figure 5.2   A Question Map.

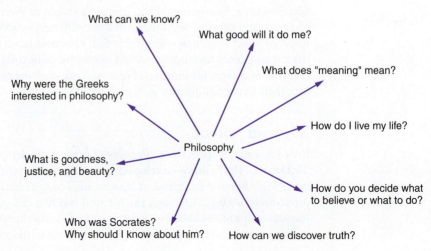

Figure 5.3 Structured Overview.

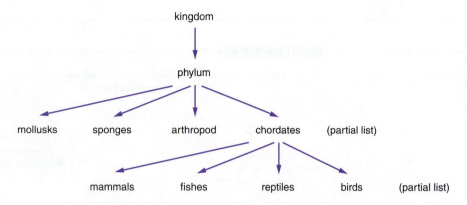

A **Concept-Mastery Map** graphically presents information about a word or concept, how it interrelates with other knowledge, and how you might integrate it with memory-enhancing features. Its oval or circular format suggests how concept mastery is interrelated with many forms of knowledge. The rectangles to be filled in around the oval or circle, going clockwise from high noon, include

- concept (or word) and its dictionary definition,
- example from reading or real life,
- original sentence using the word,
- antonym,
- word origin,
- synonym,
- a situation in which you'd use the concept or word, and
- something you'd like to know about the concept or word.

The format and an example using the concept of *comedy* are in the Strategy in Practice.

Word Parts

Knowing roots, prefixes, and suffixes helps readers learn unfamiliar words (Baumann et al., 2002; Nagy & Anderson, 1984). Researchers (Nagy & Scott, 2000) have also found that it contributes to reading ability through the high school level. To help students understand how words are created, you can focus on word parts (prefixes, suffixes, and roots) when studying new words and show them how parts of one word may appear in many other words.

Although the effects of teaching word parts appears to degrade over time (Baumann et al., 2002), we know that knowledge of morphemes is important to vocabulary growth. I took Latin in high school, and, while I was far from a fluid translator of Caesar's *Gallic Wars*, I did learn enough Latin vocabulary to help me understand several English word roots and prefixes. Thompson (1958) combined 14 roots and 20 prefixes into 14 "master words," which—if mastered—provide readers with a useful set of roots and prefixes that apply to more than 14,000 words in *Webster's Collegiate Dictionary*. (See Table 5.3.)

CONCEPT MASTERY MAP

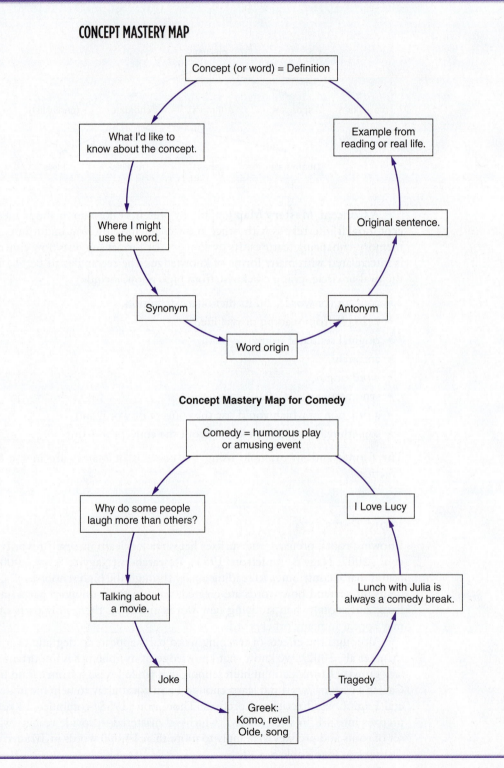

Concept Mastery Map for Comedy

Table 5.3 Fourteen Words: Keys to the Meaning of 14,000 Words

WORD	PREFIX	COMMON MEANING	ROOT	COMMON MEANING
1. aspect	Ad-/As-	(to, toward)	Specere	(see)
2. detain	De-	(away, down)	Tenere	(hold, have)
3. epilogue	Epi-	(upon)	Legein	(say, study of)
4. indisposed	In- Dis-	(into) (apart, not)	Ponere (pos)	(put, place)
5. insist	In-	(into)	Stare	(stand)
6. intermittent	Inter-	(between, among)	Mittere	(sent)
7. mis-transcribe	Mis- Trans-	(wrong) (across, beyond)	Scribere	(write)
8. monograph	Mono-	(alone, one)	Graphein	(write)
9. nonextended	Non- Ex-	(not) (out, beyond)	Tendere	(stretch)
10. offer	Ob-	(against)	Ferre	(bear, carry)
11. oversufficient	Over- Sub-	(above) (under)	Facere	(make, do)
12. precept	Pre-	(before)	Capere	(take, seize)
13. reproduction	Re- Pro-	(back, again) (forward, for)	Ducere	(lead)
14. uncomplicated	Un- Com-	(not) (with)	Plicare	(fold)

Source: Adapted from E. Thompson, The "Master Word" Approach to Vocabulary Training. *Journal of Developmental Reading, 2* (1958), 62–66.

You can also teach word parts on an ad hoc basis in your content area. If you have texts with words that are unknown to your students and that have Latin or Greek roots or word parts, it could be a good time for you to teach those word parts to your students. For example, in the text on Greek history that Julian taught to his ninth-graders, he focused on the roots of several important words: *philosophy, polis, politics, acropolis, comedy,* and *tragedy.*

Lots of words in Julian's lesson were based in Greek, so going to their roots seemed a natural instructional step. Philosophy comes directly from the Greek words *philos,* meaning friendly, dear, or loving, and *sophia,* meaning wisdom, which together mean a lover of wisdom. Polis means a Greek city-state, and politics (the art of government) has its root in polis. Acropolis also has its root in polis with *acr-,* meaning topmost or beginning, in front of it, just like *acr*ophobia, or fear of heights. Comedy finds its root in the Greek words for revel, *komo,* and song, *oide.* Tragedy comes from two Greek words: *tragos,* meaning goat, and *oide,* which you now know means song; put together, they mean goat song. Some scholars believe that tragedy had its roots in Dionysian rituals that involved the hero's becoming a "scapegoat," a sacrifice to cleanse or purify the community of evil.

Vocabulary Self-Collection Strategy (VSS)

The main purpose of the **Vocabulary Self-Collection Strategy (VSS)** is to enable students to integrate new content words into their vocabularies (Haggard, 1982). Students identify and select words they want to know because those words are important for understanding a passage or because of their curiosity. Students also feel they have some control over what they will learn.

Step-By-Step: Vocabulary Self-Collection Strategy (VSS)

Step 1. Begin VSS instruction after any learning event, especially after your students have read a text for the first time. Ask students to note the words they want to learn as they read. Explain that they will nominate a certain number of those words to appear on the vocabulary list related to their reading. You will also nominate a certain number of words.

Step 2. Students answer several questions (M. R. Ruddell, 2004):

- Where did you find the word? (Please provide page number and sentence.)
- What do you think the word means in the context?
- Why do you think the class should learn this word? (or) What is the importance of this word to the topic we are reading about?

Step 3. If working in teams, students can answer these three questions for words the team selects and report to the whole class about those words.

Step 4. Review all the submissions and select a reasonable and representative number of words for your class list.

Activities for Mastering VSS and Other Important Words

You can use some of the activities I have already described, such as the keyword method, word maps, and word parts, to help students learn more about the vocabulary words obtained from the VSS exercise. Knowing that a variety of techniques and repeated exposures in learning new words show benefits (Beck & McKeown, 1991), you can incorporate other activities into your lessons that have research support. Researchers (Blachowicz & Fisher, 2000) have confirmed the benefits of semantic relatedness techniques, including semantic maps, synonym webs, and semantic feature analysis.

Semantic maps.   Although the term **semantic map** often refers to any graphic organizer showing a relationship between words, I am using the term for a specific format that includes a theme or concept at the map's heart, important ideas or terms highlighted with boxes or circles, and lines connecting related ideas or concepts that are not hierarchically organized. When using semantic maps for vocabulary instruction, you control the terms and concepts for which your students will contribute related concepts and specific examples.

Step-By-Step: Semantic Maps

Step 1. Before or after a first reading of a text, you write the word you want your students to explore in the center of a board. If you want your students to integrate related words, write them on an adjacent board.

Step 2. Talk with your students about the target word, its meanings, and its use in the text from which it came. Ask students what they know about the concept or word.

Step 3. As your students generate related words, concepts, ideas, and examples, jot these down on the board. Add your own related ideas as your discussion with the class proceeds.

Step 4. Ask your students to copy the semantic map into their notebooks or journals so they can add to it as their knowledge of the target word expands.

Once you have modeled semantic maps with your class, such as the example using the vocabulary word *architecture* (see Figure 5.4), you can ask students to try completing them on their own. You can start them on their way with a partially completed map they will use as a base for elaboration, and you can provide related words you would like them to integrate. As they become more adept at completing semantic maps, you can give them a target word and ask them to complete the map on their own.

Synonym webs. While a semantic map includes all types of concepts related to the target word, a **synonym web** limits the exploration of semantic relationships only to

Figure 5.4 Semantic Map: Architecture.

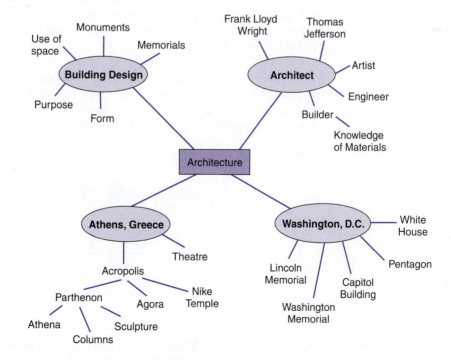

words similar in meaning. When students are trying to learn words with multiple meanings, words on our list such as *adhere* or *systems,* synonym webs are particularly helpful.

Step-By-Step: Synonym Webs

To have small groups construct synonym webs, I have adapted Blachowicz and Fisher's (1996) suggestions into the following steps:

Step 1. Ask students working in teams of three or four to generate all the synonyms they can for the target word. Then have each team use a thesaurus to add to their team's list of synonyms.

Step 2. Ask the team to categorize the words they listed. Each team should discover which words seem to cluster or fit together in some way. You can work with teams needing help with building categories. Students should be ready to explain how the meanings connect.

Step 3. Each team makes a web to demonstrate patterns of relationship.

Step 4. The teams present their webs to the class.

Step 5. Students, using their team's web as a base, extend that web with ideas presented by other teams. They copy their webs and extensions into their journals.

Figure 5.5 shows a possible synonym web for the word *system.*

Semantic feature analysis.   As we saw in chapter 3, readers use knowledge networks and structures (schemas) to help them make sense of their reading. These networks, if externalized, can show us how students organize knowledge about their world into categories. If we can get our students to activate and compare some of their existing categories with new or unfamiliar words and concepts they encounter, it will help them to learn new words. However, there are many instructional variations of **semantic feature analysis**. What they all have in common is a grid with shared semantic features plotted against a list of related words. For example, features that can be attributed to Greek gods are listed down the left-hand column and the names of several gods are listed across the top. Notations in the columns indicate students' awareness of connections between features listed and the Greek gods.

Figure 5.5   Synonym Web: System.

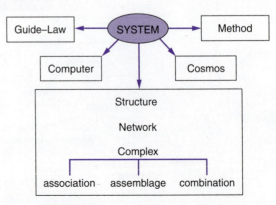

Step-By-Step: Semantic Feature Analysis

Step 1. Select a category. A likely candidate for a unit on ancient Greek civilization is a category such as mythology.

Step 2. You then generate names of concepts or objects related to the category. Eventually, students should help in this step. In the case of mythology, I might suggest words like *Aphrodite*, *Athena*, *Eros*, *Hades*, *Hermes*, *Poseidon*, *Prometheus*, and *Zeus*. These names are placed at the top of each column.

Step 3. In lines to the left of the columns, you next list features that can be attributed to the concepts or objects identified in the previous step. For our example, one or more of the gods are: immortal, married, one of the 12 Olympians, of no mother born, and so on.

Step 4. Students put "+" signs where connections occur, "−" signs where they don't, and "?" where students are uncertain.

The Strategy in Practice shows an example of a semantic feature analysis on the identity of Greek gods.

Strategy in Practice

SEMANTIC FEATURE ANALYSIS: GENERATING WORDS AND CONCEPTS

Names of Greek Gods

FEATURES	APHRO-DITE	ATHENA	EROS	HADES	HERMES	POSEI-DON	PROME-THEUS	ZEUS
Titan (elder gods)	−	−	−	−	−	−	+	−
One of the 12 Olympians	+	+	−	+	−	+	−	+
One of the "lesser" Olympian gods	−	−	+	−	−	−	−	−
Supreme ruler	−	−	−	−	−	−	−	+
Of no mother born	−	+	−	−	−	−	−	−
Immortal	+	+	+	+	+	+	+	+
Brought fire to earth	−	−	−	−	−	−	+	−
Married	−	−	−	+	?	?	?	+
Messenger of the gods	−	−	−	−	+	−	−	−
Ruler of the underworld	−	−	−	+	−	−	−	−
Guide of the dead to the underworld	−	−	−	−	+	−	−	−

Growing Word Knowledge: Just Reading

I'd like to begin this discussion about promoting vocabulary growth by focusing on general word knowledge development through wide reading and the impediments of struggling readers. From the 5th grade on, avid readers process millions of words each year. The California Department of Education's *English–Language Arts Content Standards* (1998) call for students in the 8th grade to read 1 million words on their own in addition to books they read for their English class. By the 12th grade, the *Standards* call for students to read 2 million words on their own besides class assignments. According to Stanovich (1993), reading volume is an "explanatory variable" that predicts cognitive outcomes and trends.

Why does reading build vocabulary knowledge? Exposure to moderate- and low-frequency words occurs in reading material more often than in speech, including TV and radio talk (D. P. Hayes, 1988). And that reading is a source for lower-frequency words that contribute to better performance on vocabulary tests. In school or out, talking is "no substitute for reading" (Stanovich, 1993).

To appreciate the potential value of reading to develop vocabulary over watching a film adaptation of the same novel, let's look at what Baines (1996) discovered when he compared the language of three novels with their film versions. The novels he selected have been required reading over the past 40 years in the secondary English curriculum, and the film versions of those novels have been widely acclaimed. Baines found that what is reduced when a novel moves from page to screen is the number of polysyllabic words, the complexity of sentence structure, the amount of lexical diversity, and the complexity of dialogue, plot, character, and theme.

Although all these reductions should be of concern, we are especially interested in lost vocabulary. To illustrate the kinds of loss in lexical diversity and polysyllabic words, we're going to focus on *To Kill a Mockingbird* by Harper Lee. The information in Table 5.4 provides a measure of the total number of different words found in a 2,500-word sample from the novel and from the film script and the number of one-, two-, and three-or-more-syllable words from novel and script. A similar pattern appeared for samples of both *Wuthering Heights* and *Of Mice and Men*.

Table 5.4 Lexical Diversity and Polysyllabic Words in *To Kill a Mockingbird*

TITLE	LEXICAL DIVERSITY*	ONE SYLLABLE	TWO SYLLABLE	THREE OR MORE SYLLABLES
To Kill a Mockingbird (novel)	870	148	568	154
To Kill a Mockingbird (film script)	642	259	316	67

*Number of different words in a 2,500-word sample.

Another indicator of lexical diversity can be found in the number of different words beginning with different letters. Table 5.5 shows the number of words beginning with the letter *U* in the samples of 2,500 words from the script and from the novel.

With film's reliance on visual image and condensed dialogue to convey information, the language of novels is condensed, simplified, or eliminated. With reduced lexical diversity and more familiar one-syllable words, viewers of the film who didn't read the book would have had few, if any, chances to gain word knowledge.

Print exposure is associated with vocabulary knowledge and the growth of general knowledge (Stanovich, 1993). Reading appears to be a "uniquely efficacious way of acquiring vocabulary" and serves as an "unparalled" tool for building content-knowledge structures. As readers acquire content area knowledge, that knowledge contributes to their efficiency when processing information. Electronic sources (TV, radio) commonly lack both depth and conceptual richness provided by print. "Only print provides opportunities for acquiring broad and deep knowledge of the world," writes Stanovich.

According to Stanovich (1993), most of the enormous differences in vocabulary knowledge between high- and low-performing students can be attributed to what students do outside of school—not in it. Nonschool reading can account for most of the differences between successful and struggling readers, including differences in word knowledge. Summer-break reading has accounted for more of the gap between high- and low-achieving students than in-school reading (D. P. Hayes & Grether, 1983).

As teachers, we have the challenge of reversing the downward spiral of struggling readers who frequently find themselves enmeshed in reading materials that are too difficult for them to use as a source for learning in our classes. Much of that difficulty arises from low-frequency, content area vocabulary that impedes their efforts to comprehend.

However, immersion in literature and reading may not be the best pathway to gaining extensive word knowledge. Some students can read avidly but make only minor gains in vocabulary if they have little inclination to understand words they don't know. Many bright and avid readers with good comprehension show only mild

Table 5.5 Words Beginning with the Letter U in *To Kill a Mockingbird*

SCRIPT		NOVEL	
ugly	upstairs	unceiled	unique	upon
under	us	uncontrollable	unless	upstairs
until	used	uncrossed	unlighted	us
up		under	unpainted	use
		undress	until	used
		unhitched	up	

interest in independently pursuing the meanings of unfamiliar words in novels they read, including those required for their honors and Advanced Placement English courses. Context doesn't seem to provide sufficient cueing for these students to discover a word's meaning. They may also lack strategies to take words apart or resources for discovering their meanings. So, given that immersion itself doesn't lead directly to word-knowledge growth, we need to look for ways to help students acquire strategies that could increase their vocabulary acquisition while pursuing independent reading.

Fortunately, we have strategies to help students acquire vocabulary through independent reading. Some are rather basic, others are more complex. We'll review both. You can decide which approaches you can offer for your students' use.

Word Play: Language Games in Context

More than half a century ago, W. S. Gray (1946) had a superb moment of synthesis. He pulled together several strategies that he believed could help a reader figure out the meaning of a word when the reader encountered it in a text. Gray labeled the four-step method simply *CSSD: Context, Structure, Sound, and Dictionary.* What Gray encouraged was an early form of metalinguistic awareness or word consciousness, including the ability to reflect on and manipulate language structures (Nagy & Scott, 2000). To figure out the meaning of an unknown word, Gray recommended that readers first look for cues in the context of the text that would contribute to figuring out the word's meaning. Second, readers should consider the word's structure, looking for roots, prefixes, or suffixes that could provide clues to meaning. Third, readers should sound out the word in hopes of triggering like-sounding, known words. And, lastly, readers can use a dictionary to discover meaning. But do good readers use a system like this to detect the meanings of unknown words when reading?

Looking Closely at Students Constructing Word Meanings

When Harmon (2000) listened carefully to think-alouds that revealed how avid middle school readers figured out the meaning of unfamiliar words encountered in independent novel reading, she discovered they did not use the same problem-solving pattern each time they encountered an unknown word. Each approach was unique and engaged various strategies in nonlinear order.

- Students she listened to drew more upon a text's immediate context and events rather than upon more global background knowledge to figure out words.
- When students used content connections, which they did in nearly every unknown word instance, they focused on immediate events and on language structures much more often than they applied ideas beyond the text.
- Students used word-level analysis, that is, looking at word parts, while attending to context determiners of meaning.
- Syntax proved to be an essential cueing element to help these students discover unknown word meanings.
- Students frequently used synonyms as substitutions for unknown words and often found that strategy enhanced their incidental word learning.
- As a last resort, these young readers used a dictionary when they were baffled or, in a couple of instances, to confirm their guesses.
- Most importantly for Harmon was her observation that these readers did not follow a sequential use of strategies, as Gray's CSSD sequence seemed to urge.

Harmon (2000) found that these students used a variety of strategies on a highly personal or idiosyncratic basis. They did not repeatedly use the same approach to unknown words but approached each unknown word uniquely. Although one of these students did use orthographic clues to help her figure out by analogy what a word might mean, the sound of unknown words seemed to be of little importance to most students. The implication for instruction is that we would be wiser to help students build a repertoire of strategies that they can evoke on a case-by-case basis.

Using Context to Learn Words with PASSION

To move in the direction of helping students learn an assortment of strategies to discover word meanings, I'm going to focus on context for two reasons: First, students apparently learn more words from context than we could ever teach them explicitly; second, we have learned more about how readers' minds work when extracting meaning from context (Sternberg, 1985, 1987, 1988; Sternberg & Powell, 1983). If we can teach our students how to improve their use of context to gain word knowledge, they can become more effective independent word learners for life. In the next section, I'll introduce you to an integrated method to help your students focus on unfamiliar words they encounter in their reading in order to discover their meanings.

Unfortunately, too many students breeze past unfamiliar or unknown words when they are reading in their pursuit of the final sentence (Beck et al., 2002). If students are to learn any words independently, they need a set of integrated strategies likely to help them focus more intently on the unknown words and on how to make them known. Looking back at the vocabulary-related components of the model of reading presented earlier in this chapter (Figure 5.1), we are reminded of the critical role that metacognition and metalinguisitic awareness play in word recognition and comprehension.

To take advantage of metacognitive and metalinguistic knowledge that students may have and to encourage its further development, students can approach unknown words with PASSION. **PASSION** is an acronymn for a sequence of activities that students should engage when they meet an unfamiliar or unknown word. Students should get a list of these steps and some training in their application.

- **Pause.** Stop when you meet a word you don't know.
- **Access long-term memory.** Use it and your inner dictionary to check for possible meanings: Have you seen or heard this word before? Can you recall its meaning?
- **Survey the word's structure.** Check its root, its prefix, and its suffix for clues to its meaning.
- **Synonym play.** Try to find a word that means the same thing, especially in the unknown word's context, including synonyms that have the same part of speech.
- **Investigate the context.** What clues do the word's neighbors give you about the unfamiliar word's meaning? Is its meaning restated in some way? Does the word appear again with different neighbors that you know?
- **Outsource.** If your internal mental work doesn't yield the word's meaning, try resources outside your self, such as a dictionary or a friend.
- **Note it down.** Write the word on a 3 × 5 card. On the opposite side, write its meaning, part of speech, perhaps a drawing to represent the word's meaning, and a sentence using it for later reference.

PASSION is a strategy that can help students increase their vocabulary and content area knowledge. A similar procedural facilitator with an extensive set of instructional modules helped fifth-graders in a Title I school learn self-selected words and make statistically significant gains in reading comprehension, vocabulary achievement, and metacognitive skills (Lubliner & Smetana, 2004). As has been found with other vocabulary instruction programs (R. J. Sternberg, 1985), students would gain significantly from teachers' breaking PASSION into its steps and teaching each step to students so they can learn the procedure through modeling and practice. Teaching students about using context efficiently will heighten the impact of the strategy. With PASSION, students can develop their metacognitive or metalinguistic awareness while reading and so learn far more words.

Using Technology to Foster Vocabulary Growth

Several years ago, the National Reading Panel (NICHD, 2000) recognized the potential contribution to reading development inherent in computer technology. Today, information and computer technology provides a rapidly growing and rich array of resources to promote vocabulary growth in all readers, from those excited by the esoteric word to those learning vocabulary in a new language. That array of resources includes programs or devices that make the discovery of a word's meaning quite simple and fun.

- Word-processing programs commonly include a dictionary and a thesaurus, which help readers and writers not only check on a word's spelling but also on its meaning and a parade of synonyms.
- CD Rom encyclopedias provide extensive information about concepts and words related to those concepts across every content area.
- Portable optical character-recognition (OCR) devices, such as the Quicktionary Reading Pen II, can display an unknown word's meaning on a liquid crystal display and even pronounce it. A reader can scan a printed word, obtain a dictionary definition, and access the syllabication feature. We know such technologies help students, including those with learning disabilities, improve their reading comprehension (Higgins & Raskind, 2005).

Students can also access numerous Internet resources that facilitate word learning. These include the following:

- Online dictionaries, such as www.m-w.com, provide a dictionary and thesaurus along with a "Word of the Day" selection.
- Sites such as www.dictionary.net use multiple sources to provide definitions of words.
- Some sites, such as www.wordexplorations.com, provide Latin and Greek roots for words and a dictionary of Latin and Greek words used in English.
- Ask an Expert, at www.askanexpert.com, connects users with experts from astronauts to zookeepers. If a student wants to know what a word means in a particular field, this could be the site that filled him or her in.
- Wikipedia, the online, communal encyclopedia that anyone can edit at www.wikipedia.org, has had more than a million entries since its inception in 2001. It also provides hypertext so that readers can click on unfamiliar words and concepts so that definitions or background information will appear.
- Teachers and students can use crossword puzzle makers, such as EclipseCrossword or Crossword Weaver, to radically simplify the challenges of weaving newly learned words into puzzles that provide students with game-based exposure to new and less familiar words. (Some programs require small fees.)

Entire books are available free online as e-books, which can be downloaded into a computer, electronic reader, or personal digital assistant (PDA). That's not the big news relevant to vocabulary learning, even though more reading would foster word growth. The more important aspect of e-book reading is immediate, instantaneous access to a dictionary. Dictionary software, often built in, enables readers puzzled by a word's meaning to click on a word or tap it with the PDA stylus and get the word's definition. Researchers (Boone & Higgins, 2003) acknowledge that e-book hypertext links to a dictionary or reference material helps students learn new vocabulary.

A Summary of Research Guiding Instruction in Vocabulary Development

In condensing what we know about word learning so that knowledge can guide classroom instruction, I would have to include the following:

1. Word recognition and word knowledge are essential for a reader to construct meaning from texts.
2. Students acquire between 2,000 and 4,000 words per year during middle and high school.
3. Research has shown that several instructional techniques, such as keyword, semantic relatedness strategies, and computer technologies, have significant effects on vocabulary learning.
4. Teachers cannot possibly teach as many words as students learn during their secondary school years.
5. Students learn many words incidentally by inferring meaning from context. To learn more than 3,000 words per year, students need to read between 500,000 and 1,000,000 words.
6. Some research has shown that instruction in using context to improve word learning has significant effects.
7. Motivation, as well as cognition, is important to learning words. Word consciousness promotes motivation.
8. Educators are not sure about best practices for teaching word knowledge in middle and high school classrooms. Tension exists between those advocating just more reading and those advocating instructional intervention to build vocabulary directly.

From this digest of research information, what's a teacher in the content areas to do? Three general, overlapping teaching purposes emerge: (a) Foster word consciousness among your students, (b) find and apply vocabulary-building techniques that help students comprehend content area texts, and (c) encourage more independent reading while providing strategy instruction in gaining vocabulary.

Double-Entry Journal: After Reading

What are three concrete steps you could take to increase your students' awareness of words, especially in your content area? What strategies for heightening word awareness and word learning would you build into your instructional program? Explain why you think these strategies would work with your students in your subject.

Chapter 6

STRATEGIES TO ENHANCE COMPREHENSION

After reading chapter 6, you should be able to answer the following questions:

1. How do comprehension-enhancing strategies help students activate background knowledge, set purposes, and promote deeper engagement while reading?

2. Which comprehension strategies help students activate and integrate knowledge?

3. How do reading strategies, such as SQ3R and PLAN, facilitate independent student study?

4. Why does knowledge of text structures enhance comprehension?

5. How would you use outlines, graphic organizers, and concept maps to help your students organize information acquired through reading?

Double-Entry Journal: Before Reading

Have you ever thought about the strategies you use to comprehend what you read? What strategies were you taught in school to improve your reading comprehension? Have you discovered any on your own? Which of these strategies do you use when you read? Why are they useful to you? What strategies would you teach to your students and how would you convince them that these strategies help comprehension?

The most popular strategy that students use to help their comprehension when reading is underlining. Or should we call it painting the text? Researchers have found that, among college students, underlining, or highlighting, was vastly more popular than any other study strategy (Annis & Annis, 1982; Peterson, 1992). However, those who benefit most from this strategy seem to be manufacturers of marking pens. Simply reading a passage would do these students just as much good as underlining, or highlighting, at least when it comes to preparing for a test (Marxen, 1996). The conclusion from underlining research (McAndrew, 1983; Marxen, 1996) appears to be that, when reading material for a test, no underlining is best. Having underlined, or highlighted, what must be hundreds of miles of text myself, I rather doubt that informing students about underlining research will alter their habits much. For those of us addicted, underlining provides us with a sense of purpose, even relaxation.

Underlining, or highlighting, does have useful applications, other than studying for tests. It may be used to keep track of ideas a reader may use in writing papers. (At least some of my underlined, or highlighted, text was intended to help me keep track of ideas I thought I'd use in my writing, including ideas that wound up in this chapter.) Underlining could also be useful to students whose teachers have identified parts of a text for special study. Marking that text could facilitate its more careful examination. Fortunately, other strategies exist that may help our students effectively comprehend texts.

In this chapter, I'll present numerous strategies more likely to improve comprehension and learning in content areas than underlining. We know that good readers are strategic and that struggling readers can become better if they learn to use strategies appropriately (Gersten, Fuchs, Williams, & Baker, 2001). Looking back at the model of reading presented in chapter 3 should clarify why strategies enable readers to comprehend better. When readers build a text representation, they draw upon their long-term memory for background knowledge. Without strategies that enable readers to make connections between their own background knowledge and a new text, readers are less likely to activate information that will help them organize and comprehend new knowledge. As readers link sentences into more complex networks, they can apply graphic organizers to help them represent ideas expressed in a passage. During text building, readers with summarizing strategies construct gist of each passage. With knowledge of text structures, readers can see how an author has organized information into a plan to convey the passage's main ideas. Without knowledge of text structures, readers may simply accumulate random pieces of information rather than build a coherent pattern to represent a text's meanings. But these strategies to connect with background knowledge, summarize, and construct internal text landscapes must be stored in a reader's long-term memory and accessible for application at appropriate times.

Readers who lack reading strategies, such as those that will be presented in this chapter, can acquire and apply them in their content area courses. We know from extensive research (Hattie, Biggs, & Purdie, 1996) that strategies to improve learning are best taught in specific contexts and through tasks that are in the same subject as the target content. So, if you wanted to teach your biology students to use a reading strategy to improve their comprehension of the biology text, you would increase your likelihood of success if you taught students the strategy using biology readings. Embedding teaching strategies in our course content is the underlying reason for teachers in all content areas to learn and apply literacy enhancing strategies such as the ones we are about to discover in this chapter.

Comprehension-Enhancing Strategies to Activate and Integrate Knowledge

Researchers have conducted many studies to discover the effects of activating background knowledge before learning new information related to that knowledge. In general, these studies confirm that activating relevant background knowledge heightens both understanding and retention of new knowledge (Corkill, 1992; Mayer, 1984; Pressley, Woloshyn, et al., 1990; Pressley, Wood, et al., 1992). However, if prior knowledge is lacking or weak, strategies to activate background knowledge before acquiring new, related knowledge may be counterproductive (Alvermann et al., 1985). On balance, engaging students in activities that heighten their awareness of prior knowledge is a sensible and productive instructional approach. We'll explore several of these knowledge-activation strategies that students can use not only to increase their understanding and recall of texts, but also to motivate them to engage in reading.

Double-Entry Journal (DEJ)

For this and every other chapter, you are asked to create two journal entries. This activity was designed to activate your own prior knowledge. You can also ask your students to participate in the **Double-Entry Journal (DEJ)**. Readers should be encouraged to write responses using 150 to 250 words to answer the questions before the reading and approximately the same number of words to answer questions that follow the chapter. As you might have guessed, this particular form of DEJ is so called because the reader writes before reading and after reading the text (Vaughan, 1990).

The before-reading questions are intended to get readers thinking about the topics to be explained and explored in the text, as well as to have readers activate relevant background knowledge. The post-reading questions are designed to help readers integrate new knowledge into existing knowledge networks or modify them to accommodate the new information.

Although some teachers like to have students use a notebook dedicated to DEJs, I have found it more effective to have students write and label the entries as "Prereading" and "Postreading." In part, I've adopted that format because increasing numbers of students e-mail assignments to me rather than turning in notebooks for evaluation. Which method you elect will depend upon your own preferences and the benefits you think will come to your students from a particular format.

When I assign DEJs, I ask students to be sure they have completed them before class because I use the DEJs to begin a class discussion. For example, I would use students' DEJ responses for this chapter by asking students at the start of class to get together in teams of three or four to share their pre- and postreading entries.

The classroom scenario might work like this: I would ask the teams to discuss among themselves the reading comprehension strategies each of them had used or been taught and to compile a list of them. Then I would have one team member report to the class on strategies his or her team members mentioned. I would list these strategies on the board so that I would know which strategies were already familiar to some class members and which were unfamiliar. I would then know which teams or students I might call upon to talk about their experiences with a particular comprehension-fostering strategy. I would also know which strategies, if new to all, might require more time to explain and practice.

Step-By-Step: How to Design and Implement DEJs

Step 1. Before designing DEJs, read carefully the targeted text.

Step 2. Identify some of the key topics or concepts from the reading selection that readers are likely to have encountered in the past.

Step 3. Formulate questions or request responses that will activate information about those topics or concepts. Keep in mind that you want to activate relevant knowledge during this prereading activity.

Step 4. Formulate postreading questions or response prompts that will require readers to review the reading selection in order to reflect productively. Identify aspects of the reading that are likely to lead either to growth in knowledge or understanding or to applications of knowledge for problem solving. Using those, I generate postreading prompts.

Step 5. Ask students to write about 150 to 250 words in response to both pre- and postreading prompts. The appropriate length of written response will vary from class to class and from text to text.

Step 6. Provide opportunities for students to meet in pairs or small groups to read and share their DEJs during class time, perhaps in preparation for a class discussion.

Step 7. After each student reads his or her partner's DEJ, ask students to comment on them by finding a sentence they like, underlining it, and writing a brief marginal statement explaining why it was selected. As weeks go by, ask partners to write more extensive commentary in response to a DEJ.

For the DEJ I developed for this chapter (to which I hope you responded before you began reading the chapter), I wanted my readers to focus on comprehension strategies and activate knowledge about those they use when reading. I also wanted readers to think about how those strategies worked for them, which strategies they would consider teaching to their own students, and how they would get their students engaged in learning them. But that's not the end of the DEJ story. You will come upon another DEJ at the end of this chapter. At that point you'll be asked to write more about strategies I've covered. I don't want to give away the surprise ending, but I'm likely to ask you once again to reflect on strategies presented here, ask you to tie them to what you knew about strategies before, and maybe ask you to reconsider how and why these strategies are likely to help your students.

Anticipation Guide

An **Anticipation Guide** is a list of statements you generate about a subject to which your students react before they read about it. After your students complete the Anticipation Guide, you conduct a conversation with them to identify their preconceived ideas and attitudes about the topic. As you talk about their knowledge and beliefs, you can encourage your students to connect what they will learn with what they already claim to know. By getting them to connect what they know with what they may learn, you can deepen their engagement and purpose for reading.

Step-By-Step: How to Prepare and Present Anticipation Guides

Step 1. Read the text you are going to assign and identify key concepts you would like your students to understand, challenge, or both.

Step 2. Compose six to eight statements that are likely to challenge your students' beliefs about the topic or express an opinion about it.

Step 3. Arrange the statements in a true-false or you-author format (see the Strategy in Practice).

Step 4. Ask students to complete the Anticipation Guide individually before reading the text to which it relates.

Step 5. Discuss their responses, making efforts to highlight possible conflicts between their beliefs and the content of the text they are to read.

Step 6. After the discussion, ask students to read the material.

Step 7. Ask students to review their responses to the Anticipation Guide when they complete their reading of the text material. Students should put a check in the AUTHOR column if the statement is consistent with the author's belief. Students should also identify any changes in their own beliefs about the topic.

Strategy in Practice

ANTICIPATION GUIDE EXAMPLE: READERS READING INSIDE THE MEANING CONSTRUCTION ZONE

If I were to have designed an Anticipation Guide for chapter 3, "Readers Reading: Inside the Meaning Construction Zone," I could have done so as follows.

Directions: Following are several statements about reading. If you agree with the statement, put a plus sign next to the sentence under YOU. If you disagree, put a zero there. After you have read the related selection, put a plus sign in the AUTHOR column if the statement is consistent with the author's beliefs. You may also indicate in your column any change in beliefs you had as a result of your reading the selection.

YOU	AUTHOR	STATEMENT ABOUT READING
		1. Good readers can read at 1,000 words a minute or more while maintaining good comprehension.
		2. Good readers both make inferences and test them while reading.
		3. Good readers don't subvocalize.
		4. Good readers clarify for themselves why they are reading.
		5. Good readers read only the key words.
		6. Good readers always recognize words as wholes.
		7. Good readers never look back.
		8. Good readers make sure the meanings they are constructing while reading are internally consistent and compatible with what they know and what makes sense.

Directed Reading-Thinking Activity (DR-TA)

Before you read further, what do you think a Directed Reading-Thinking Activity is, given its title? What do you think a teacher would do to conduct one? What would a student do who was engaged in one? Remember to pause for a moment to tell yourself what you think.

Designed by Russell Stauffer (1969), the **Directed Reading-Thinking Activity (DR-TA)** engages students in making predictions about a text, reading the text, and discovering the accuracy of those predictions. Although developed in the 1960s, the DR-TA is still recognized as an effective tactic to advance comprehension and develop metacognitive skills. When making a prediction about a text, students activate background knowledge. After prereading the text and marking stop points, I begin by explaining that there really are no right or wrong responses because everyone will be guessing. Some may be more lucky at guessing than others, but I encourage all responses—warm or cold. I urge students to remember their predictions because they will get a chance to test, verify, or modify them. When reading the text, students find out if the text confirms their hypotheses or if they need to change them.

For example, I asked you to make a prediction about what a DR-TA was before you read the description. You activated knowledge about these associated words to see if you could predict what the essence of the activity was. Now that you've gotten a brief description of the activity, you should be able to confirm your prediction or modify it to conform to what you have learned.

Step-By-Step: How to Do a DR-TA

Step 1. Decide what text you are going to use to conduct the DR-TA. The text could be part of a chapter in a content textbook, the first section of a novel or story, a poem, or an article.

Step 2. Read the text and mark promising stop points, where you will ask students to make predictions about what will happen next or what will be examined next. Start by asking something like, Looking at the title, what do you think this chapter (or article or story) is going to be about? After the title, break the text at sensible points, such as at headings or after a couple of meaty paragraphs if the text is extensive and complex.

Step 3. To reduce students' temptation to read ahead, provide them with a sheet of paper to cover the text and ask them to slip it down the text only as far as your next stop point. (You can also later use the same sheet of paper to have students make a graphic organizer or map of the information given in what they've read.) Or you can put the text on a transparency or into a PowerPoint presentation and expose the text section by section.

Step 4. Get your questions ready so that at stop points you will be prepared to guide student responses. As students respond, you might ask some students to explain why they thought what they did. Ask questions such as, Given what the author has already written, what do you think will happen next? Why do you think so? or What topic do you think the writer will explain next? Why?

There are a few points to keep in mind when doing DR-TAs. First, you have to be flexible about the choice of text. Some texts are much more amenable to DR-TAs than others. I had excellent experience with texts that are more figurative or narrative. Highly literal texts may work less well; however, you should experiment with your students to see what works with them.

Second, you need to be patient when first trying DR-TAs. Students may not respond enthusiastically the first time you try it. Students may need to warm up to the technique and to build some trust in your accepting their guesses. Some students hate making any kind of mistake in class because they don't want to look foolish. So it may take a few times before the DR-TA begins to look like a vehicle students will accept. In a class I observed, a new teacher tried to get his sometimes disengaged, sometimes sleepy students to respond to a DR-TA. The first day only three or four students got engaged, and a couple of students had their heads on desks. The second day no heads were down, and there was a sense of modest excitement in the air. After he had tried the activity three or four more times, most students had gained enough interest and trust in the process that they were contributing to a lively discussion about their reading. It became safe to be wrong and fun to discover whether or not guesses were on target.

Third, as students warm up to DR-TAs, their motivation to read a text rises. That's actually one reason I usually ask students to cover the text we're reading with a sheet of blank paper. Covering the texts reduces the temptation to read ahead, a temptation that seems to grow on some students as their motivation to read heightens.

Lastly, DR-TAs should not be used too frequently. Although they are relatively easy to prepare compared to other reading activities, their interest to students can be kept alive if their welcome isn't worn out by too much use.

As an example of a DR-TA in action, I'm going to walk you through how I've used it to teach poetry to high school students, some of whom are less than ecstatic when I present them with a poem to discuss. Often, I find that the roots of their distaste are grounded in their feelings of inadequacy and confusion as they face lines of words lying like mysteries they must solve without looking too stupid. However, DR-TA spreads poetic kindness. Why? Because students don't have to have the right answers to the meaning of each mysterious line. A DR-TA promotes speculation, or guessing about interpretations, which is just what students need to do when faced with new, unfamiliar language.

Strategy in Practice

DIRECTED READING-THINKING ACTIVITY (DRTA): MAKING PREDICTIONS
"My Last Duchess," by Robert Browning

My Last Duchess **(SP1)**	
That's my last duchess painted on the wall, Looking as if she were alive. I call That piece a wonder, now; Fra Pandolf's hands Worked busily a day, and there she stands. Will 't please you sit and look at her? **(SP2)** I said "Fra Pandolf" by design, for never read Strangers like you that pictured countenance, The depth and passion of its earnest glance, But to myself they turned (since none puts by The curtain I have drawn for you, but I) And seemed as they would ask me, if they durst, How such a glance came there; so, not the first Are you to turn and ask thus. **(SP3)** Sir, 'twas not Her husband's presence only, called that spot Of joy into the Duchess' cheek; perhaps Fra' Pandolf chanced to say, "Her mantle laps Over my lady's wrist too much," or, "Paint Must never hope to reproduce the faint Half-flush that dies along her throat." Such stuff Was courtesy, she thought, and cause enough For calling up that spot of joy. She had A heart—how shall I say?—too soon made glad, Too easily impressed; she liked whate'er She looked on, and her looks went everywhere. **(SP4)** Sir, 'twas all one! My favor at her breast, The dropping of the daylight in the west, The bough of cherries some officious fool Broke in the orchard for her, the white mule She rode with round the terrace—all and each Would draw from her alike the approving speech, Or blush, at least. She thanked men—good! but thanked Somehow—I know not how—as if she ranked My gift of a nine-hundred-years-old name With anybody's gift. **(SP5)** Who'd stoop to blame This sort of trifling? Even had you skill In speech—(which I have not)—to make your will Quite clear to such a one, and say, "Just this Or that in you disgusts me; here you miss, Or there exceed the mark"—and if she let Herself be lessoned so, nor plainly set Her wits to yours, forsooth, and made excuse, —E'en then would be some stooping; and I choose Never to stoop. **(SP6)** Oh, sir, she smiled, no doubt, Whene'er I passed her; but who passed without Much the same smile? This grew; I gave commands;	**(SP1)** Given this title, what do you think this poem will be about? **(SP2)** What do you think is happening in the poem? Why? Who is present? Where are they? **(SP3)** What do you think now about who's talking to whom and where? What do you predict will happen? **(SP4)** What has happened? Which of our hunches about what is going on are being confirmed in the poem? What do you think of the duke? Why do you think that? What impression of the duchess do you have? **(SP5)** Which of our impressions of the duke are being confirmed? Do you have more thoughts about his character? What do you predict he'll do about the duchess? **(SP6)** What other qualities of the duke emerge?

Then all smiles stopped together. **(SP7)** There she stands
As if alive. Will 't please you rise? We'll meet
The company below, then. I repeat,
The Count your master's know munificence
Is ample warrant that no just pretense
Of mine for dowry will be disallowed;
Though his fair daughter's self, as I avowed
At starting, is my object. **(SP8)** Nay, we'll go
Together down, sir. Notice Neptune, though,
Taming a sea horse, thought a rarity,
Which Claus of Innsbruck cast in bronze for me! **(SP9)**

Note: Fra Pandolf and Claus of Innsbruck are imaginary artists
from the Renaissance.

(SP7) What do you think he has done?

(SP8) What are the duke's plans? How do you think they fit with our impression of his character?
(SP9) Do these last lines confirm anything we said about the duke earlier or add anything new?

The Strategy in Practice shows you where I'd put stop-points for a DR-TA using Robert Browning's "My Last Duchess." When I presented this poem, I put it on a transparency, covered all the text before projecting it, and then revealed only those lines before my next stop-point question. For this Strategy in Practice, I've signaled stop-points (SP) I think work well with the poem and questions I'd ask students to speculate upon. Remember, I'm trying to encourage them to speculate, to make guesses, and to hypothesize about the meaning of words as I guide them through the poem.

Know-Want to Know-Learned (K-W-L) Strategy

Before setting out to teach about a topic, teachers frequently want to discover what their students already know about it and what more they would like to learn. To gather that information and more, Ogle (1986) developed the **K-W-L strategy** by which teachers can find out what their students already know (K), what they would like to learn (W), and (following reading and instruction) what they learned (L).

Step-By-Step: How to Do a K-W-L

Step 1. Ask students to fold a sheet of paper into three columns and to label the first column with a *K*, the second with a *W*, and the third with an *L*.

Step 2. Explain to students that the first column (K) is for them to write all they know about the topic for the activity. This part of the exercise activates students' background knowledge. Before filling in the column, students could get together in small groups of three or four to talk about what they know.

Step 3. Working alone or in their small groups, students generate questions that they place in the "want to know" (W) column.

Step 4. Help students organize the information on their K-W-L sheets. This can be done by asking students to report what they know and want to know while someone writes the information on the board. As an alternative, one student in each group can be responsible for writing up the information.

Step 5. The students read the text that you divide into reasonable sections. After students read a portion of the text, they should refer to their questions to see if they have been answered or if they have additional questions to write on their lists.

Step 6. After completing their reading, students write down what they have learned in the L column. Students can then share that information with others in their group and class.

Step 7. Students acknowledge not only what they have learned, but they also take note of what questions remain unanswered and what new questions have arisen.

As a follow-up, many educators combine K-W-Ls with maps so that the knowledge they gain can be consolidated. We cover graphic organizers in the next section of this chapter.

I often use K-W-Ls in my own teaching. In one case, I was preparing to teach credential candidates about cooperative learning, a topic we take up in a later chapter, and I wanted to know what my students knew and what they wanted to learn about it. After we studied cooperative learning, I returned the K-W-L charts to my students for them to complete, enabling me to discover what they had learned—or wanted to learn more about. One of my students—a musician named Nadia, who was preparing to teach music in secondary schools—completed her K-W-L chart as shown in the Strategy in Practice.

Strategy in Practice

K-W-L CHART COOPERATIVE LEARNING

KNOW	WANT TO KNOW	LEARNED
1. Works in groups 2. Groups are often made up of different levels of students 3. Some believe it enables students to build social & learning skills necessary to integrate with colleagues in the "real" world 4. Can be problematic if some students do all the work and others "freeload" 5. Some believe it helps all students to function at a higher level 6. Can support a classroom goal/atmosphere of creativity & encouragement	1. What *really* are the benefits of co-op learning? 2. What are the best ways to engage students through cooperation? 3. Are some methods of engaging students better than others? 4. Does co-op learning benefit all students? 5. How do I assess students who have worked cooperatively? 6. How would co-op learning work in a creative arts setting?	1. More specific ways to implement co-op learning 2. The parameters for implementation, including delegating authority, roles, individual accountability, shared responsibility, mixing of levels, complex tasks 3. More about how to arrange groups in a sensitive manner to ensure the success of the group 4. Some examples of what *not* to do (e.g., limiting the student by *always* working in groups or placing them in difficult situations) 5. Assessment can take various forms based on assignment

The Prereading Plan (PreP)

Judith Langer (1981, 1982) developed a strategy to encourage students to think about ideas associated with topics or concepts about to be encountered in a reading assignment. Through the **Prereading Plan (PreP)**, you can prepare your students to read by having them recollect prior knowledge and reflect on the sources of that knowledge. After class discussion but before jumping into the actual reading, you should prompt your students to think about the effects the discussion had on their thinking about the topic and to articulate any changes in their knowledge and understanding.

Step-By-Step: How to Do a PreP

Langer (1981) described the three phases of the process.

Step 1. *Create initial associations with the concept.* In this first phase, say, "Tell anything that comes to mind when (for example) you hear the word *Congress*." When this activity was carried out in a middle school class, one student, Bill, said, "important people." Another student, Danette, said, "Washington, D.C." As your students tell what ideas initially come to their minds, jot each response on the board. During this phase, your students have their first opportunity to find associations between the key concept and their prior knowledge.

Step 2. *Reflect on initial associations.* During the second phase of PreP, ask, "What made you think of . . . (the response given by a student)?" This phase helps your students develop awareness of their network of associations. They also have an opportunity to listen to each other's explanations, to interact, and to become aware of their changing ideas. Through this procedure, they may weigh, reject, accept, revise, and integrate some of the ideas that came to mind. When Bill was asked what made him think of important people, he said, "I saw them in the newspaper." When Danette was asked what made her think of Washington, D.C., she said, "Congress takes place there."

Step 3. *Reformulate knowledge.* In this phase, ask your students the following: "Based on our discussion and before we read the text, have you any new ideas about (for example) Congress?" This phase allows students to verbalize associations that have been elaborated or changed through the discussion. Because they have had a chance to probe their memories to elaborate on their prior knowledge, the responses elicited during the third phase are often more refined than those from the first. This time, Bill said, "lawmakers of America." And Danette said, "U.S. government part that makes the laws."

Once you have used PreP with your class, you will have a clearer idea of the knowledge base that students will bring to the readings. Students whose network of associated ideas may not be as rich as others are likely to need additional support and guidance when trying to comprehend the reading. If only a few students have much knowledge to share, that may indicate that some further preliminary teaching, midway discussion, or postreading comprehension activities are warranted for the entire class.

Directed Inquiry Activity (DIA)

A strategy that activates students' topic knowledge while providing both purpose for reading and some degree of teacher control over concepts students must master is the **Directed Inquiry Activity (DIA)**. Keith Thomas (1986) developed DIAs to enable teachers to guide their students' inquiry and discovery.

Teachers frame inquiry questions based upon the texts their students will be reading. These questions answer any or all of the questions about who, what, when, where, why, and how. After students are given the questions, they survey and skim their text for information. This overview is intended to give students information to predict answers to the teachers' inquiry questions. As students make predictions, the teacher puts them on the board or records them for later use.

Step-By-Step: How to Do a DIA

Step 1. Review or write the content mastery goals for the body of material about to be taught.

Step 2. Compose several inquiry questions based on the goals and the text to be read. (See the Strategy in Practice.)

Step 3. Distribute questions to students.

Step 4. Have students skim the text to discover the information that will help them answer the questions. Discuss with students how they think the questions will be answered.

Step 5. As students make their predicted answers, ask students to explain why they think the answers they predict will be accurate. How does their prereading guess connect to their background knowledge and their brief review of the text?

Step 6. Have students read the text carefully.

Step 7. After students have read the text, return to a discussion about the correct answers to your inquiry questions. This discussion, together with their reading of the text, should provide students with knowledge to clarify, modify, or extend their predicted answers.

Strategy in Practice

DIRECTED-INQUIRY ACTIVITY : GIVING A PURPOSE FOR READING

These DIA Questions are based on a chapter entitled "The Heritage of Ancient Greece" from a secondary-level textbook, *World History:* Patterns of Civilization, by B. F. Beers (1993).

1. Looking at a map of ancient Greece, how do you think geography influenced its economy and society?
2. What historical events laid the groundwork for the rise of the Greek city-states?
3. What form of government guided the city-state and society of Athens?
4. How did society in the city-state of Sparta differ from that in Athens?
5. How did the Persian and Peloponnesian Wars shape Athens' history and government?
6. What contributions did the Greeks make to drama, philosophy, and the arts?
7. What were Alexander the Great's ambitions and achievements?

SQ3R

Like the Directed Inquiry Activity, **SQ3R** (Robinson, 1946) is designed to help students set purposes for reading and engage them in reading for answers to significant questions. Furthermore, the method urges readers to survey what is to be read, generate self-posed questions, and review what has been covered in the text. SQ3R stands for *Survey, Question, Read, Recite,* and *Review.*

When I use SQ3R, I begin by looking over the reading material to get an impression of its scope and depth (Survey). Then, I use headings in the text to pose questions to myself (Question). These questions then contribute to my purpose for reading (Read). While reading, I watch for textual information that will contribute to my answering the questions I've posed for myself (Recite). And, after reading the passage and answering my questions, I go back over the material I've covered (Review).

While more than half a century old and the most often taught independent reading strategy, SQ3R as a system appears to improve comprehension only about as well as just rereading (Caverly, Orlando, & Mullen, 2000). To gain effectiveness, students must learn each step in the strategy and how to apply it. Even more important, students must believe in the procedure to make the effort needed to complete its steps.

PLAN

David Caverly and his associates (1995) developed a variant of SQ3R that was found to have significant effects on the reading performance of secondary students. The strategy is called **PLAN**, an acronym for four separate tactics: Predict, Locate, Add, and Note. The separate tactics are integrated to facilitate comprehension before, during, and after independent reading.

When *Predicting* a text's content before a careful reading, students draw a likely representation of a text after previewing it. A student's map or diagram represents the author's key ideas taken from the title, headings and subheadings, and graphs or charts. The map, or diagram, reveals the student's predictions about the text's meaning

Figure 6.1 Predicting Phase of PLAN.

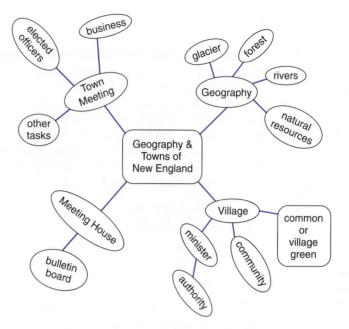

and its importance to the reader. A sample of the Predicting phase of PLAN appears in Figure 6.1. After previewing a chapter on the geography and towns of New England in their social studies textbook, *The United States Yesterday and Today* (Helmus, Toppin, Pounds, & Arnsdorf, 1988), middle school students collaborated on creating the map with teacher guidance. They predicted that the chapter would cover villages, town meetings, meeting houses, and the geography of typical towns.

When *Locating*, students use a check mark (✔) on the map to indicate those concepts they find familiar and use a question mark (?) to show those that are unfamiliar to them. In doing this before reading, students are assessing their schemas (or lack thereof) related to the text's content. Determining what is known and unknown helps students assess the depth of their prereading concept mastery, focus attention, and select appropriate reading rates.

During reading, students engage in *Adding* words and phrases to capture the meaning of unfamiliar concepts labeled with question marks while elaborating on familiar ones that they checked. If a student reads a text and finds no content addressing concepts indicated with question marks, it may mean that the student overlooked important text content. Selective rereading may be the next tactic to use.

After reading, students *Note* new understandings of concepts on their maps or reconstruct a new map, integrating the newly learned concepts with those formerly known. Predictions made early may need to be modified in the light on a closer reading of the text. Follow-up *Noting* may also include writing a summary of the text, a log entry, or notes and questions for a discussion.

Making Reading Meaningful

A few years after Ellen Langer, a professor of psychology at Harvard University, wrote *Mindfulness* (1989), she turned her attention to writing *The Power of Mindful Learning* (1997). In the earlier book, Langer shows what she means by mindfulness and how we can become more mindful in many dimensions of our daily lives. She explains that a mindful person demonstrates several key characteristics when approaching an activity: (a) the creation of new categories, (b) openness to new information, and (c) an implicit awareness of multiple perspectives. She contrasts this mindful state with mindlessness (which I've enumerated with negative numbers to emphasize how they subtract from learning): (−1) entrapment in old categories, (−2) automatic behavior that blocks attention to new signals, and (−3) vision limited to a single perspective.

In *The Power of Mindful Learning,* Langer presents a creative alternative to two prevalent methods of teaching. The first of these two methods, exemplified by lecturing, is top-down. We listen and learn. The second, exemplified by direct experience, structured practice, and memorization, is bottom-up. We repeat and learn. The third alternative she suggests is "sideways" learning, the goal of which is to maintain a mindful state. When engaged in sideways learning we manifest these characteristics:

- openness to novelty,
- alertness to distinction,
- sensitivity to different contexts,
- implicit, if not explicit, awareness of multiple perspectives, and
- orientation in the present.

From Langer's research with Matt Lieberman (Lieberman & Langer, 1995) on mindful learning, we can discover approaches that hold out the promise of improved reading comprehension. She asked two groups of ninth graders to read two different essays from their literature anthology. One group was instructed to simply learn the material. The second group was told, as described next, *to make the material meaningful to themselves:*

> This may entail thinking about how certain parts of the information remind you of past, present, or future experiences, deciding how the information could be important to yourself or someone else, or simply finding some significance of the story in relation to anyone and/or anything. Remember, what is meaningful to one person is not necessarily meaningful to another.

After a 20-minute reading period, all students were tested. Students in the second group, the make-it-meaningful-to-yourself group, who did not resort to memorization in order to perform well on the test outperformed all others by recalling more information from the reading. They also wrote essays judged better by a group of evaluators; however, we are looking most closely at reading comprehension and performance.

In a related experiment, Lieberman and Langer (1995) investigated the effects of mindful reading with tenth graders. To make an episode about the enactment of the Kansas–Nebraska Act from a high school history text meaningful, students were asked to read it from the perspective of the United States senator who presented the legislation. Students were to think about how they would feel and what they would think if they were in the senator's situation or how they would see things from the perspective of the senator's grandchild. The control group was asked only to learn the passage.

Students in both the experimental and control groups were tested on the chapter at the end of the class period and one week later. As in the earlier experiment, students reading mindfully scored better on recall of information on both tests. Their essays were also judged to be more creative and insightful.

In sum, these investigations reveal that, if students can make material more meaningful by adopting different perspectives and discovering that information depends on context, they can improve the quality of their comprehension and understanding of texts.

The studies also validate an alternative to the technique of finding ways to make the content of reading selections relevant to students' interests and values. In Langer's experiments, the attitudes of students in relationship to the reading material were changed. The researchers guided students into discovering approaches to texts that made them more personally meaningful. Teachers can replicate these mindful, "sideways" learning practices by encouraging students to read from multiple perspectives, become more sensitive to different contexts, be alert to drawing distinctions, and create new categories.

Step-By-Step: How to Help Students Make Reading Meaningful

Step 1. Explain to your students what a mindful learning orientation is and that you want to encourage them to approach all their reading more mindfully.

Step 2. One way to approach reading more mindfully is to entertain and adopt multiple perspectives. Rather than simply reading text from the perspective of a student who just wants to get through the reading and, it is hoped, to learn it, ask students to create a perspective that would make the text especially important to them or to someone they know. For example, if they were to read a chapter about the history of World War I, how would the content of that chapter be perceived by a cadet at West Point who was in training to be a military leader? As an alternative, students could try to discover how information they are to read reminds them of past, present, or future experiences or events. Explain to students that what is meaningful to one reader will not necessarily be meaningful to another reader.

Step 3. Ask students to write down what they found as a way to make the reading meaningful to them and take a few minutes to share those perspectives in class.

Text Structure

What do the "Three Little Pigs," "Cinderella," and the Biblical story of Job have in common? All share a pattern of narrative development called story grammar (Stein & Glenn, 1979; Trabasso & Stein, 1997). A narrative's structure, or its story grammar, typically consists of (a) a setting, (b) an initiating event signaling change, (c) characters' goal-defining responses to the initiating event, (d) characters' goal-directed behaviors, (e) the consequences of those behaviors, and (f) a resolution. Teachers of young readers in the elementary grades have recognized that children who have a sense of story structure seem to ask good questions about stories and to comprehend them better. Furthermore, many studies show the effectiveness of using story-grammar elements to help students, including struggling readers, comprehend narrative texts (Gersten et al., 2001). Although knowledge of story structure clearly helps readers understand narratives, does knowledge of expository text structure help readers comprehend expository passages, such as those found in history, science, or math textbooks?

To answer this question, we can draw two conclusions from research connecting knowledge of expository text structure to its comprehension: (a) The ability to identify and use expository text structure contributes to comprehension, and (b) readers comprehend some expository text structures more easily than others (Gersten et al., 2001). One of the factors complicating comprehension of expository passages is that they may contain not one text structure but several mixed together. Beside that, a reading of today's front-page newspaper stories will quickly convince you that expository texts frequently include story-grammar elements, such as settings and characters who get themselves into trouble even worse than the Three Little Pigs.

Nevertheless, with knowledge of text structures, readers can approach texts with expectations and a plan of attack (Englert, 1990). If readers recognize that a text has a particular structure, they can expect elements of the text to contribute to that known structure. With knowledge of text structures, readers can organize the text mentally as they read it. Without that knowledge, readers cannot approach texts with such expectations or plans. Instead, these readers pick and choose information more randomly (Meyer, Brandt, & Bluth, 1980).

Types of Text Structures

In work spanning more than 30 years, Bonnie Meyer and her colleagues (Meyer et al., 1980; Meyer & Freedle, 1984; Meyer & Poon, 2001) have focused on the impact that text structure has on the amount and kind of information readers remember. Text structures arise from the way their authors organize information. Meyer and her colleagues identified five ways to organize discourse: description, sequence (including ordering by time or events), causation, problem-solution (including effect or evaluation of the solution), and comparison. A sixth text structure, persuasion, or argument, is presented in chapter 8.

Effects of Text-Structure Knowledge

From studies of text-structure knowledge effects that Meyer and her associates (Bartlett, 1978; Meyer et al., 1980; Meyer & Freedle, 1984) conducted with high school and college students, she distilled several major findings:

- Ideas at the top of a text's structure are remembered better than those lower in a text's hierarchy. For example, in a magazine article about supertankers, readers are far more likely to remember the top level of the problem presented (oil spills) and its solution (training, ground control stations, improved tanker design) than they are lower-level descriptions of specific tanker accidents and the number of birds destroyed.

- A text's overall plan and major relationships between its paragraphs have a more powerful effect on its recall than the organization of details. For example, if readers see that a text's overall structure is problem-solution, as was the case in the oil spill article, they will remember it better.

- Some top-level text structures, such as causation and comparison, facilitate readers' recall of a text's content more than others. For example, students are less likely to remember descriptions of a specific tanker accident in England's North Sea than a cause-effect relationship (oil spills causing thousands of birds to die).

- Strategic instruction in the recognition and use of top-level structures improves students' capacities to remember the content of texts. For example, after students were given direct instruction in text structures over five 1-hour sessions during their English classes, they demonstrated statistically superior recall of texts in comparison to their pretraining scores and in comparison to a control group. Students who received the training also demonstrated performance advantages across the curriculum (Bartlett, 1978).

Five Basic Text Structures

The five discourse patterns Meyers identified (description, sequence, causation, problem-solution, and comparison) appear in newspapers, scientific writing, political speeches, and (of course) school texts. In order to know when an author is organizing information into one of these five text structures, students will benefit from definitions, identifying cues, likely contexts, and examples of each type.

Description. Descriptive texts provide information about the specific attributes of a topic and, perhaps, its setting.

Cues. The organization of text structure is based on a listing of attributes or features. This text structure may include explicit language to draw a reader's attention to several attributes of a topic and enumerate them as first, second, third, and so forth. Signaling words or phrases include the following: for instance, for example, such as, includes, consists of.

Contexts. Description of a painting, a living room, a person's face, a garden, an event reported in a newspaper or magazine, a battle scene, a product for sale, or the features that make up story grammar.

> *Example:* From *The Great Gatsby* by F. Scott Fitzgerald (1925), p. 8. New York: Charles Scribner's Sons.*
>
> We walked through a high hallway into a bright rosy-colored space, fragilely bound into the house by French windows at either end. The windows were ajar and gleaming white against the fresh grass outside that seemed to grow a little way into the house. A breeze blew through the room, blew curtains in at one end and out the other like pale flags, twisting them up toward the frosted wedding-cake of the ceiling, and then rippled over the wine-colored rug, making a shadow on it as wind does on the sea.
>
> The only completely stationary object in the room was an enormous couch on which two young women were buoyed up as though upon an anchored balloon. They were both in white and their dresses were rippling and fluttering as if they had just been blown back after a short flight around the house. I must have stood for a few moments listening to the whip and snap of the curtains and the groan of a picture on the wall. Then there was a boom as Tom Buchanan shut the rear windows and the caught wind died out about the room, and the curtains and the rugs and the two young women ballooned slowly to the floor.

Sequence. Texts using sequence as their organizing principle group ideas on the basis of time or order.

Cues. Texts using sequence present items serially and progress orderly or chronologically. Signaling words or phrases include the following: at the beginning, next, then, later, over time, and at last.

Contexts. Directions for assembling a bookcase from packed parts, oatmeal cookie recipe, history of battles in the American Civil War, stages of cognitive development from infancy to adulthood, procedures for a chemistry experiment.

*Reprinted with the permission of Scribner, an imprint of Simon & Schuster Adult Publishing Group, from THE GREAT GATSBY by F. Scott Fitzgerald. Copyright 1925 by Charles Scribner's Sons. Copyright renewed 1953 by Frances Scott Fitzgerald Lanahan.

Example: From A. Cayton, E. I. Perry, L. Reed, & A. M. Winkler. *America: Pathways to the Present.* Boston, MA: Pearson/Prentice Hall, 2007, p. 389.

The Battle of Antietam

With Richmond no longer threatened, Lee decided that the time had come to invade the North. He hoped that a victory on Union soil would arouse European support for the South and turn Northern public opinion against the war. So, in early September 1862, Lee's army bypassed the Union troops guarding Washington and slipped into western Maryland. McClellan had no idea where the Confederates were. Then one of his soldiers found a copy of Lee's orders wrapped around some cigars near an abandoned Confederate camp. Now that he knew the enemy's strategy, McClellan crowed, "If I cannot whip Bobbie Lee, I will be willing to go home."

True to his nature, however, McClellan delayed some 16 hours before ordering his troops after Lee. This gave the Confederate general, who had learned that his plans were in enemy hands, time to prepare for the Union attack. The two armies met at Antietam Creek near Sharpsburg, Maryland, on September 17. Lee had about 40,000 troops, McClellan over 75,000, with nearly 25,000 more in reserve.

Union troops attacked throughout the day, suffering heavy losses. In the first three hours of fighting, some 12,000 soldiers from both sides were killed or wounded. By day's end Union casualties had grown to over 12,000. Lee's nearly 14,000 casualties amounted to more than a third of his army. The next day the battered Confederates retreated back into Virginia, Lincoln telegraphed McClellan, "Destroy the rebel army if possible." But the ever-cautious general did not take advantage of his opportunity to destroy Lee's army.

Causation.   Using causation text structure, writers present cause-and-effect relationships between ideas or concepts. Usually, effects appear in texts before their causes. To enhance comprehension, readers should look for causes when effects begin to appear in texts.

Cues.   Texts organized with a cause-effect structure include phrases or words that signal causal analysis, including the following: reasons for this, because, was caused by, so.

Contexts.   A medical manual explaining causes of illnesses, historical factors contributing to outbreak of war, reasons why animal species are becoming extinct, compilation of computer glitches and their possible causes, why a president's administration flourished, or features leading to a nation's economic expansion.

Example: From K. R. Miller & J. Levine. *Biology.* Boston, MA: Pearson/Prentice Hall, 2006, p. 435.

Until recently, most researchers looked for a single, major cause for each mass extinction. For example, one hypothesis suggests that at the end of the Cretaceous Period, the impact of a huge asteroid . . . wiped out the dinosaurs and many other organisms. Scientific evidence confirms that an asteroid did strike Earth at that time. The impact threw huge amounts of dust and water vapor into the atmosphere and probably caused global climate change. It is reasonable to assume that this kind of event played a role in the end of the dinosaurs.

Many paleontologists, however, think that most mass extinctions were caused by several factors. During several mass extinctions, many large volcanoes were erupting, continents were moving, and sea levels were changing. Researchers have not yet determined the precise causes of mass extinctions.

What effects have mass extinctions had on the history of life? Each disappearance of so many species left habitats open and provided ecological opportunities for those organisms that survived. The result was often a burst of evolution that produced many new species. The extinction of the dinosaurs, for example, cleared the way for the evolution of modern mammals and birds.

Problem-solution. In problem-solution text structures, ideas are presented in two sections: a problem section and a solution section. Sometimes this text plan appears in a question-answer form. The question presents a problem and the answer provides its solution. Some problem-solution plans also include an evaluation or consequences of solutions provided.

Cues. Problem, solution, question, answer, reasons are many.

Contexts. Papers published in scientific journals, newspaper editorials, history texts, political and policy documents, advertisements.

Example: Rat Allergy

Psychologists who work with rats and mice in experiments often become allergic to these creatures. This is a real hazard for investigators who spend hours a week running rats in experiments. These allergies are a reaction to the protein in urine excreted by rats when they get upset.

At a meeting sponsored by the National Institutes of Health, Dr. Andrew Slovak, a British physician, recommended that experimenters be kind to rats and mice. Psychologists who pet and talk softly to their rats are less often splattered with urine and the protein that causes the allergic reaction. (Adapted from Meyer, Young, & Bartlett, 1989, p. 137.)

Comparison. Texts organized under the comparison principle relate ideas in terms of their differences and similarities. Different points of view may be expressed about the same issue, as occurs in political debates or pro and con statements in newspapers and magazines.

Cues. On the other hand, in contrast, from another perspective, however.

Contexts. Debatelike material or political speeches comparing the value of different solutions, perspectives, purposes, or policies.

Example: From W. A. McClenaghan. *Magruder's American Government.* Boston, MA: Pearson/Prentice Hall, 2006, pp. 123–124.

Membership in a party is purely voluntary. A person is a Republican or a Democrat, or belongs to a minor party, or is an independent—belonging to no organized party—because that is what he or she chooses to be.

Remember, the two major parties are broadly based. In order to gain more votes than their opponents, they must attract as much support as they possibly can. Each party has always been composed, in greater or lesser degree, of a cross section of the nation's population. Each is made up of Protestants, Catholics, and Jews; whites, African Americans, Lationos, and other minorities; professionals, farmers, and union members. Each party includes the young, the middle-aged, and the elderly; city-dwellers, suburbanites, and rural residents among its members.

It is true that the members of certain segments of the electorate tend to be aligned more solidly with one or the other of the major parties, at least for a time. Thus, in recent decades, African Americans, Catholics and Jews, and union members have voted more often for Democrats. In the same way, white males, Protestants, and the business community have been inclined to back the GOP. Yet, never have all members of any group tied themselves permanently to either party . . . .

Economic status also influences party choice, although generalizations are quite risky. Historically though, those in higher income groups are more likely to be Republicans, while those with lower incomes tend to be Democrats.

Levels of Text Structure

Texts in the content areas have multiple text structures. Main ideas expressed in text structures at the top of the hierarchy will be fleshed out with details expressed in other text structures at lower levels. For example, the top-level structure for an article on oil tankers could be problem-solution: We can prevent oil spills from supertankers by training personnel who operate the ships, designing better tankers, and installing control stations. Meanwhile, lower-level text structures, including causation, description, and sequence, provide information to support and explain the text's main problem-solution plan of organization in detail (Meyer et al., 1989).

We know from research that a good predictor of readers' recall of passages is whether or not they recognize and use a passage's top-level structure to organize their recall of the passage (Meyer et al., 1980). When information high in the hierarchical structure of a passage is remembered better than lower level information, that phenomenon is called levels effect. If readers attend to and recall higher-level text structure and the information expressed in it, that reveals the readers' responsiveness to the relative significance of ideas represented in a passage. The reason for the effect of different levels may be attributed to more attention being given to high-level content or to the repeated processing of the main idea while reading a lower-level text (Meyer, 1984).

What's the Structure?

Recognizing that students who are unaware of text patterns have trouble both comprehending and writing content materials, Janet Richards and Joan Gipe (1995) created a game to help students recognize common text structures. Before introducing the game, Richards and Gipe teach their students major content writing patterns using passages from the students' textbooks covering various subject areas. With text passages on a transparency, they show the text structure to students and point out the kinds of connective words and phrases typically used with a particular text pattern.

Step-By-Step: **What's the Structure?**

Step 1. Put your students into groups of six or eight.

Step 2. Give each group a game board modified from one that Richards and Gipe designed (see Figure 6.2) and five packets of color-coded cards that contain text from content area books. Packets of red cards will contain identical

Figure 6.2 Game Board for What's the Structure?

1.	2.	3.
What are the connective words and phrases in the passage? How is information in the passage organized?	How do the connective words and phrases provide clues to the writing pattern or combination of patterns in the passage? What is the top-level text structure?	Why do you think the author of this passage used this particular text structure?
8.		**4.**
Write a short summary of the information in the passage and share it with others in your group.	**What's the Structure?**	What other text structures at lower levels, if any, does the author use in this passage?
7.	**6.**	**5.**
What are the most important ideas in the passage?	Create a map showing how the facts and concepts in the passage are connected to each other. Share your map with other group members.	Share some connections between the facts and concepts in the passage and your own experiences and background knowledge.

Source: Richards, Janet Clarke, & Gipe, Joan P. (1995, May). Open to Suggestion: What's the Structure? A game to help middle school students recognize common writing patterns. *Journal of Reading, 38* (8), 667–669. Copyright by the International Reading Association. All rights reserved.

copies of a description passage; green cards will contain copies of a sequence passage; blue will contain causation; yellow will have problem-solution; and orange will have a comparison passage.

Step 3. A student in each group begins the game by selecting a packet of cards and giving one card in the packet to each group member. After players read the passage on the card, circulate among the groups giving suggestions and encouragement while students respond to the numbered activities (1 through 8) on the game board (Figure 6.2) and collaborate toward solutions.

Step 4. The game goes on until cards with passages illustrating all five writing patterns have been distributed and discussed, using the game board to guide discussion.

To continue practice with text-structure passages of different kinds, students can bring passages they find to class for inclusion in future episodes of What's the Structure? Students can also be encouraged to use these text plans to help them organize and write their own content passages, which can also be included among the passages when the game is played.

Text Structures and Genres in Different Disciplines

Reading and writing in different disciplines often means encountering very different genres and text structures. English teachers are more likely to engage their students in reading narrative texts than teachers in other disciplines. That means knowledge of story grammar is likely to help students anticipate and comprehend what might happen to a character in works from E. B. White's *Stuart Little* to Steinbeck's *Grapes of Wrath*. That doesn't mean that the five text structures we've just reviewed won't make an appearance in these works. Narratives often contain descriptive, sequence, causation, problem-solution, or comparison structures that move the story forward by describing characters or their dilemmas, presenting a sequence of events, explaining what caused a spider to spin a message, providing a problem with its solution, or comparing events or characters.

Whereas narrative texts certainly do appear in history or government reading materials, other kinds of texts are more likely to appear, such as expository writing in a history book, noteworthy speeches, or newspaper articles. Expository text may contain all the text structures we've reviewed in a mix that moves the events of history forward. When reading books and articles for a research paper in a history class, students are sure to encounter most of them. That research report is likely to describe a historical topic to investigate, such as the events and factors contributing to the outcome of the election between Abraham Lincoln and Stephen Douglas. The purpose of the paper may be to clarify what events or decisions made by the candidates and their supporters were critical to the candidate's success—or loss—in the election of 1860. Political speeches often contain arguments intended to persuade their listeners to adopt the speaker's perspective or support his or her policy, and arguments often contain all the text forms we've reviewed.

In the science classroom, however, reading and writing lab reports with an introduction, procedure, results, and discussion sections are inevitable. These reports also contain description, sequence, causation, problem-solution, and comparison text structures. However, in lab reports, they appear in forms quite different from those in which they appear in novels, short stories, or history papers. In lab reports, these text structures enable a student to depict the scientific method in action. Students carefully observe and describe a situation, construct a hypothesis, test that hypothesis, and report their findings—tasks that may require a mixture of the text structures we've explored. The purpose of the lab report is usually to convey, in careful language, an empirical, experimental process intended to test a well-crafted proposition.

In magazine articles, just as in newspaper articles, all forms of the text structures we've identified occur. Whether the article appears in *Sports' Illustrated*, *Science*, *Harpers*, *Vogue*, *Fortune*, *Teen*, or *Foreign Affairs*, knowledge of text structures can help students understand what purpose an author has adopted and how the author plans to realize that purpose through the design of the article, including the pattern of text structures invoked.

Strategies for Organizing Knowledge (Knowledge Organizers)

After reading, students frequently benefit from constructing a representation of what they discovered and learned. These representations help students remember information needed to study for examinations or to use in research projects. Four general methods or categories of knowledge representation from which students benefit are outlines, Cornell notes, graphic organizers, and concept maps.

Outlines

For many years, teachers have encouraged students to write a formal outline after they have read a selection in order to see the structure and sequence of information presented in the reading. That more traditional, linear approach to organizing knowledge sequentially works well for many students. Main points and supporting details can be built into an outline that reflects the author's knowledge structure as depicted in the reading. Of course, readers who are expected to create outlines should have the reading skills necessary for identifying main ideas and supporting evidence or detail. Many comprehension-fostering strategies already presented or to come contribute to students' identifying key ideas and their supporting claims.

There are two kinds of outlines in general use: topic outlines and sentence outlines. **Topic outlines**, as their name implies, are outlines that organize information by key concepts or key words. Readers must be able to capture the gist, or essence, of passages and paragraphs as well as subordinate ideas and to be able to state those gists and subordinate ideas in their own concise words. Readers compose **sentence outlines** by stating key and subordinate concepts as complete sentences.

There are several formats currently in use to identify levels of subordination in an outline. The more traditional pattern begins with Roman numerals identifying superordinate or main ideas. The next level of importance is represented by capital letters. Below that come Arabic numerals, followed by lowercase letters. Traditionally and logically, outlines are balanced in that at least two numbers or letters make up each lesser section of an outline. An outline sequence and its balanced structure are shown in Figure 6.3.

To guide students' development of formal outlines, you can point out that numbers and letters used in the overall structure signal the importance of terms and concepts

Figure 6.3　Structuring Outlines.

I. The Greek City-States
  A. Early City-States
    1. Greek Colonies
      a. Colonies put Greeks in touch with other Mediterranean societies.
      b. Contact with others led to sharing of ideas.
    2. Rise of tyranny
      a. Military service was every citizen's duty.
      b. Citizen-soldiers demanded greater voice in government.
      c. Discontent led to rise of tyrannies.
      d. In some city-states, democracy replaced tyranny as a form of government.
  B. Foundation of Democracy in Athens
    1. Beginnings of reform
      a. Solon and his reforms in Athens.
      b. Unrest persisted.
      c. Tyrannical government of Pisistratus emerged.
    2. Cleisthenes and movement toward democratic government
      a. Made the Athenian Assembly into a lawmaking body.
      b. Granted citizenship to some immigrants and slaves.
      c. Extended power of citizens through use of ostracism or temporary exile of citizen from city-state.

Source: Adapted from "The Heritage of Ancient Greece," a chapter in *World History: Patterns of Civilization,* by B. F. Beers, 1993.

in an outline. Similar numbers and letters mark points of more or less equal importance in the outline. Information of relatively little importance to the knowledge contained in the reading is excluded from the outline. When reading a text, students can use its headings to help them identify main points, subordinate points, and the text's overall organization. The topic sentences of paragraphs also signal information of significant importance in the text.

Note Taking (from Lectures and Readings)

The **Cornell Note Taking System** was developed at Cornell University's Reading Research Center over many years (Pauk, 1989). Although useful for taking lecture notes, the Cornell method adapts readily to taking notes while reading to gather main and supporting concepts for study. When using the Cornell system for taking lecture notes, students use ordinary ruled paper, draw a 2-inch-wide left margin, and take notes only to the right of that margin. After class, students reorganize and rephrase their notes for clarity and accuracy. In the left margin, they insert questions, headings, and cues to facilitate learning and mastery of content. When review time arrives, students cover notes in the right column and use cues in the left margins to trigger content recall. Not surprisingly, the quality and quantity of a student's notes correlates highly with his or her achievement (Armbruster, 2000).

Adapting and extending the Cornell method to reading is quite simple. I've added a feature or two from research on note taking from textbooks (Caverly et al., 2000), such as the importance of recognizing text structure to find "big ideas" and the need to explicitly teach note-taking strategies.

The format for taking notes from texts that I've adapted from the Cornell method is illustrated in the Strategy in Practice. It includes the following:

1. reference to the assignment read at the top of the note page,
2. right-column space for notes from the reading (especially key, or "big," ideas and supporting concepts), types of text structure recognized or imposed when the text structure is not clear to a reader, and key terms, and
3. left-column space for questions generated during or after reading that relate directly to notes in the right-column and unanswered questions generated from the reading; the questions in the left column should be crafted to guide review of the reading material for class discussion and tests.

Graphic Organizers

Graphic organizers help students organize knowledge and see more clearly how elements in a text are related to each other. In addition to an all-purpose cluster organizer, the graphic organizers presented here will enable students to represent visually the variety of text structures we just explored. These organizers graphically capture description, sequence, causation, problem-solution, and comparison.

Clusters.   **Clusters** are visual arrangements of terms, events, people, or ideas. They have a couple of purposes, including an alternative form of outlining, a strategy for studying, and a method of brainstorming. They help us see how things relate or connect, and they may confirm the adage that a picture is worth a thousand words.

As an alternative to a linear outline designed to represent information presented in a lecture or a reading, clusters enable listeners to more freely and visually arrange ideas, events, dates, and people. As students read, they can draw clusters of ideas that

Strategy in Practice

THE NOTE TAKER

Reading Assignment Text: *Call to Freedom* (Stuckey & Salvcci, 2000)	Chapter: 5	Date: 10/11/XX Pages: 136–138
Questions (after Reading)	**Key and Supporting Concepts (while reading)**	
What are revivals?	Revivals: public church meeting where large groups of people gathered to hear sermons given by preachers. People sometimes renewed their religious commitment during an emotional ceremony.	
What was the Great Awakening?	Great Awakening: unorganized, widespread movement of evangelical Christian church meetings where emotional sermons were delivered.	
	Important leaders: Jonathan Edwards. Gave dramatic sermons like "Sinners in the Hands of an Angry God."	
	George Whitefield: Began giving revivals in the south and later in New England that drew thousands.	
Effects of G.A. on Churches?	Divided some churches into traditionalists and members following evangelical preachers.	
	Old Lights = traditionalists	
	New Lights = followers of G.A.	
	Some Old Light ministers opposed G.A. because they doubted that it could actually awaken one's inner spiritual life (Charles Chauncy, minister of Boston's First Church).	
Unanswered Questions	**Types of Text Structure Recognized**	
Why was the Great Awakening so appealing to some colonists?	Description (Revival, Great Awakening) Comparison (Old & New Lights)	

may in turn be connected to other concept networks to produce a mental map of interrelated ideas.

Clustering is also known as mind-mapping, semantic mapping, mindscaping, and webbing. Hyerle (1996) refers to clusters as brainstorming webs. They are a little like sand play or sketching because the process is loose—certainly less structured than graphic organizers, to come later.

To make a cluster, students write a key word in the center of a page, circle the word, and place associated words or ideas around the key word and connect them with a line. The example in Figure 6.4 began with the key word *clusters*.

Students can effectively use clusters for taking notes from lectures or from reading content textbooks, developing presentations, and initially organizing ideas for

Figure 6.4   Clustering/Mind-Mapping/Webbing.

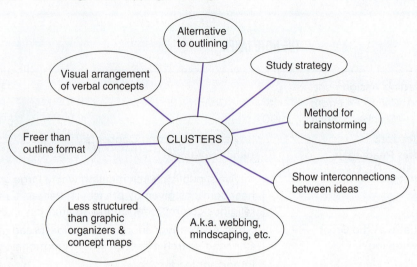

essays or research reports. While clusters are helpful visual representations of ideas, they are rudimentary forms of visual thinking. Organizers and content maps are more structured ways to represent knowledge and its branches.

Graphic organizers to represent text structures.   Organizers are useful ways for readers to present their understanding of what they have read in visual terms. Once learned, these organizers can be used across the disciplines as the need arises. For example, the process organizer could be used to show how to run an experiment, take a photograph, or write a research paper in English. The sequence of graphic organizers presented here can be used to represent the sequence of text structures presented earlier. For example, descriptive text structures can be represented using a characteristics organizer, as the next described.

Characteristics Organizer.   Textbooks in all content areas, including math, history, and science, describe the characteristics of many concepts they present. Readers can better comprehend, understand, and perhaps remember these characteristics when using a **characteristic organizer**. To create this form of organizer, your students should first draw a circle or ellipse and put the target term in it. They then encircle the target term with characteristics and draw lines or arrows between the term and each characteristic.

If you return to the example of descriptive text structure from *The Great Gatsby* (p. 195), you can see that "room by the sea" is the target term, and characteristics of the room would be placed in bubbles around the target and connected to it. Characteristics organizers can also display much larger bodies of text. A whole chapter entitled "The Behavior of Gases" from a high school chemistry text (Wilbraham, Staley, Matta, & Waterman, 2000) could be visually summarized in a characteristics organizer as in Figure 6.5.

Process Organizer (Flowchart).   A **process organizer** does what it says it does: It organizes a process. If students read about a process, such as making a cake, a federal law, or a Frankenstein monster, they can use the process organizer to visualize and describe the steps in the process. Process organizers display sequence text structures that present

Figure 6.5 Characteristics Organizer.

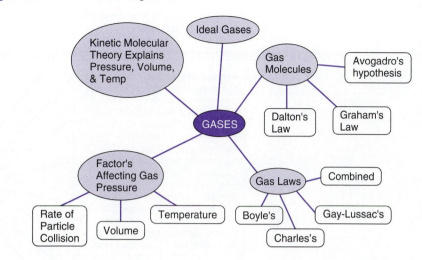

ideas in terms of time or order. You could use one to display the sequence of events during the civil war battle of Antietam given earlier as an example of sequence text structure. Revealing its applicability to other sequences, the process organizer in Figure 6.6 depicts the steps needed to solve the following geometry problem: Two angles of an isosceles triangle (*A* and *B*) each have a measure of 30°. Find the measure of the third angle (*C*).

Cause-Effect Organizer.   **Cause-effect organizers** are designed to graphically represent an array of causes that contributed to some specific event. They depict causation text structures, such as the passage from a biology text explaining the causes for mass extinction. In Figure 6.7, the information constituting the cause-effect organizer for the outbreak of World War II came from two chapters, "The Rise of Totalitarian States" and "The World at War," in a high school–level world history text (B. F. Beers, 1993).

Problem-Solution-Evaluation Organizer.   Organizers can provide a visual method to represent texts that are problem oriented, as is the case with problem-solution text structures. The passage on rat allergy that illustrated problem-solution text structures could easily be depicted in a **problem-solution-evaluation organizer**. In Figure 6.8, I've diagrammed an article from the *New York Times* presenting the problem of water flow in the Florida Everglades and the threat of reduced water to animal and plant habitats (Stevens, 1999). I've also presented the proposed solution and an evaluation of its results.

Figure 6.6 Process Organizer.

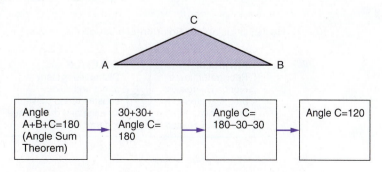

Figure 6.7 Cause-Effect Organizer.

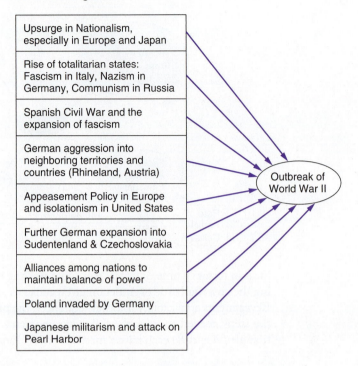

Upsurge in Nationalism, especially in Europe and Japan

Rise of totalitarian states: Fascism in Italy, Nazism in Germany, Communism in Russia

Spanish Civil War and the expansion of fascism

German aggression into neighboring territories and countries (Rhineland, Austria)

Appeasement Policy in Europe and isolationism in United States

Further German expansion into Sudentenland & Czechoslovakia

Alliances among nations to maintain balance of power

Poland invaded by Germany

Japanese militarism and attack on Pearl Harbor

Outbreak of World War II

Compare/Contrast Organizer. **Compare/contrast organizers** can take many graphic forms, including the one shown in Figure 6.9. In this case, the theatrical concepts of comedy and tragedy are compared and contrasted. With an organizer of this kind, readers can summarize similar features of two concepts and their unique characteristics. The example used to illustrate a comparison text structure (pp. 197–198) focused on traits of American citizens who are members of the Republican or Democratic party. The similarities and differences between members of the two parties could be shown in a graphic organizer similar to the one used to represent similarities and differences between comedy and tragedy.

There is an infinite variety of methods of representing texts. With the graphic organizers shown in this chapter as a base, you can encourage your students to explore new approaches to depicting the texts they read graphically. In chapter 8 on critical reading, we explore a method to take apart written arguments, organize them in a chart, and discover how their elements work together.

Figure 6.8 Problem-Solution-Evaluation Organizer.

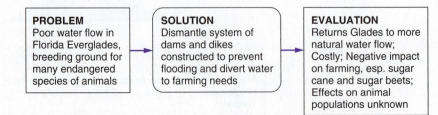

PROBLEM
Poor water flow in Florida Everglades, breeding ground for many endangered species of animals

SOLUTION
Dismantle system of dams and dikes constructed to prevent flooding and divert water to farming needs

EVALUATION
Returns Glades to more natural water flow; Costly; Negative impact on farming, esp. sugar cane and sugar beets; Effects on animal populations unknown

Figure 6.9 A Compare/Contrast Organizer.

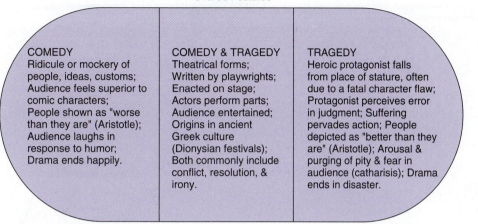

Dramatic Comedy and Tragedy

Shared Features

COMEDY
Ridicule or mockery of people, ideas, customs; Audience feels superior to comic characters; People shown as "worse than they are" (Aristotle); Audience laughs in response to humor; Drama ends happily.

COMEDY & TRAGEDY
Theatrical forms; Written by playwrights; Enacted on stage; Actors perform parts; Audience entertained; Origins in ancient Greek culture (Dionysian festivals); Both commonly include conflict, resolution, & irony.

TRAGEDY
Heroic protagonist falls from place of stature, often due to a fatal character flaw; Protagonist perceives error in judgment; Suffering pervades action; People depicted as "better than they are" (Aristotle); Arousal & purging of pity & fear in audience (catharisis); Drama ends in disaster.

Concept Mapping

Concept mapping pushes graphic organizing into even more meaningful realms of student learning. Although they may demand more time, analysis, and creativity than the organizers I have already presented, Concept Maps are much more likely to show how concepts are linked to each other and to a learner's prior knowledge.

While looking for a sound method of capturing what students know about a topic before and after instruction, Novak and his colleagues (1991, 1998) came upon Concept Maps as a means of representing students' knowledge structures. A **concept map** is a method of showing key concepts and their relationships in graphic form. Novak examined students' reports of learning concept words and propositions. These indicators of a student's understanding could be configured into a constellation of concepts and propositions to represent the knowledge that the student constructed. Given a set of concepts, students can arrange them to show how they relate to the students' current knowledge structure and how connections between the concepts can be described. Figure 6.10 contains an example of a Concept Map showing key ideas and principles of good Concept Maps that Novak himself created.

Novak attributes the inspiration for his Concept Maps to Ausubel's (1968) theory of meaningful learning. In contrast to rote learning, meaningful learning relates to relevant aspects of a learner's existing knowledge structure. For example, simply asking students to memorize by rote the definition of a Concept Map is less meaningful than asking students to construct a Concept Map showing how it is related to their prior knowledge about ways to organize information. One of Ausubel's contingent principles is that learners must be free to choose meaningful learning as a means of constructing new knowledge representations in long-term memory.

Simply teaching students to do Concept Maps and providing them with opportunities to practice mapping skills may enhance their recall of texts they read but do not explicitly map. Researchers (Chmielewski & Dansereau, 1998) conducted studies using a concept-mapping strategy. In comparison to a control group, students who were taught how to construct Concept Maps demonstrated better recall of both macro- and microlevel concepts in articles they read but never mapped. It is quite possible that training and practice in mapping texts enable readers to attend to the

Figure 6.10 A Concept Map of Concept Mapping.

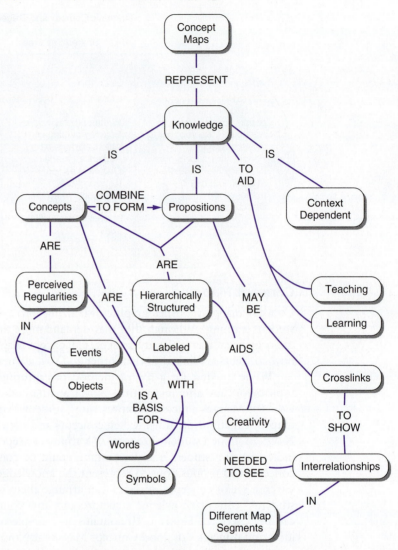

structure of passages and to watch for key concepts along with their relationships to other concepts and subconcepts.

Step-By-Step: How to Design a Concept Map

Step 1. Formulate a question that relates to the knowledge domain or problem to be mapped. Identify 10 to 20 concepts pertaining to that question and list them separately on Post-its™ or 3 × 5 cards, limiting each concept to one or two words. Maps may also be constructed electronically using an appropriate computer program to make, move, and connect labeled concepts.

Step 2. Place the most inclusive or most general concept(s) at the top of the map.

Step 3. Choose two to four subconcepts to put under each of the most general concepts. If more than four subconcepts cluster around a single superordinate concept, try to find a concept of intermediate inclusivity to build into your hierarchy.

Step 4. Define the relationships between concepts, draw a line between them, and use a few linking words to clarify the relationship. The hierarchical relationships constructed allow a structure of meaning for the knowledge domain to emerge.

Step 5. Revise the map's structure. Add, remove, and rearrange concepts and their relationships. This process of revision may occur several times.

Step 6. Try to identify cross-links between concepts located in different regions of the map and connect these with descriptive linking words.

Tech Tip

You can download Concept Map software developed at the Institute for Human and Machine Cognition at the University of West Florida. This software can be used to create simple and highly complex multimedia Concept Maps. Information about concept maps, a Cmaps Tools program to construct them, several samples of Concept Maps, and a tutorial can be found at http://cmap.ihmc.us.

You can also use Inspiration, a software program from Inspiration Software (www.inspiration.com) that enables users to electronically design knowledge organizers, including webs, idea maps, and Concept Maps. This software transforms hierarchical outlines into graphic forms and diagrams into outlines. By inserting a web address into either a diagram or outline, Inspiration automatically creates a hyperlink.

Summary

This chapter presented an armory of strategies that should improve your students' comprehension of content area texts significantly more than the famous underlining tactic. Several of the strategies presented, such as Anticipation Guides, Directed Reading-Thinking Activity (DR-TA), Know-Want to Know-Learned (KWL), and PLAN, activate readers' background knowledge and provide multiple opportunities to integrate new information with prior knowledge. Other strategies to enhance comprehension included a review of text structures and of knowledge organizers, several of which can be used to show graphically the content of the text structures we reviewed.

Double-Entry Journal: After Reading

What new comprehension-fostering strategies did you discover, and which of the strategies in this chapter would you teach to your students? Why do you think these strategies would help your students? More specifically, how does knowledge of text structure make sense as a comprehension-fostering strategy in the context of the model of reading presented in the early part of this text?

Chapter 7

WRITING TO ASSESS, PROMOTE, AND OBSERVE LEARNING

After reading chapter 7, you should be able to answer the following questions:

1. What happens in the minds of writers who are writing?
2. What is the process approach to writing, and how do you engage students in it?
3. What do we know about the effects of writing on learning?
4. How can you use writing to assess, promote, and observe learning?
5. What factors should you consider in deciding what kind of writing assignments to give to your students?
6. How do content area teachers respond to student writing?

Double-Entry Journal: Before Reading

Recall three or four specific examples of how your high school or college instructors used writing to promote your learning. What were you learning and how did writing help you learn? How would you use writing to help your students learn?

Changes and Challenges in Writing to Learn

Do students write better or more in school today than they did in the past? Our major source of data on American students writing performance comes from the National Assessment of Educational Progress (NAEP). Every few years, student writing is scored by trained raters using a 6-point scale with standards for evaluation varying by grade levels. Students have been evaluated at grades 4, 8, and 12 at three achievement levels: basic, proficient, and advanced. From 1998 to 2002, the percentage of students scoring at a proficient or higher level increased from 27% to 31% for 8th graders and from 22% to 24% for 12th graders. Twelfth graders performing at a proficient level "produce an effectively organized and fully developed response within the time allowed that uses analytical, evaluative, or creative thinking." Furthermore, that writing includes "details that support and develop the main idea of the piece, and it should show that these students are able to use precise language and variety in sentence structure to engage the audience they are expected to address" (National Assessment of Educational Process, 2003, p. 11). While there are signs of improvement in the NAEP data over the short term in the percentages of students writing at the proficient level, approximately three out of four students perform below that level of competency.

With regard to the amount of writing students do, evidence indicates significant increases in writing. In the early 1980s, Arthur Applebee (1981, 1984) completed an extensive study of writing in secondary classrooms across subject areas. He found that students spent about 3% of in-class or homework time on writing of a paragraph or more in length. Twenty years later, George Hillocks (2002; 2006) found that nearly all teachers he interviewed spoke only about asking students to write multiparagraph essays. Typically, the focus was on the five-paragraph essay. Hillocks believes that with many states including writing in their standards-based assessment programs, students are writing significantly more than they did two decades ago, when such statewide testing programs did not exist.

Four major educational developments—besides the standards movement—during the past 30 years should have supported and encouraged the expanded use of writing in content area courses. First, researchers and teachers have learned more about the writing process, how to engage students in it, and how to adapt it to the needs of urban classrooms. Second, many teachers across the curriculum have become intent upon engaging their students in the construction of knowledge through exploration and discovery rather than through memorization. Third, researchers and teachers have been drawn to the promise of writing to learn. And fourth, the National Writing Project was born and expanded to serve teachers across the disciplines. These four broad developments, together with state testing programs that include the assessment of student writing, have contributed to major changes in teaching and learning in many classrooms.

A Peek into the Writer's Construction Zone

Having given you a guided tour inside the reader's construction zone, I plan to take you on a literacy-related tour of the writer's construction zone. We'll find several similar sites because reading and writing share many components and processes (Kucer, 1985; 2001). Even though reading and writing have much in common, most people believe that writing is usually a more demanding task than reading. That impression makes sense because writing entails creating new texts, not just reading those constructed.

The writing model we're going to visit was designed primarily by John Hayes (1996/2004). It's a revision of an earlier model of writing that he and Linda Flower (Flower & Hayes, 1981) developed and that was based on a substantial body of writing research (Emig, 1971; Flower, 1979; Flower & Hayes, 1977, 1980; J. R. Hayes & Flower, 1980; Perl, 1979). Hayes calls his depiction an individual-environment writing model that contains two major components, namely, the task environment and the individual. (See Figure 7.1.) The description of the writing model has been compressed, but you'll see several parallels with the reading model and some differences.

The **task environment** consists of both social and physical dimensions. The social dimensions include the audience for whom the writer is writing and any cowriters, such as partners in a team, with whom a writer must cooperate and co-create. The

Figure 7.1 Individual-Environmental Writing Model.

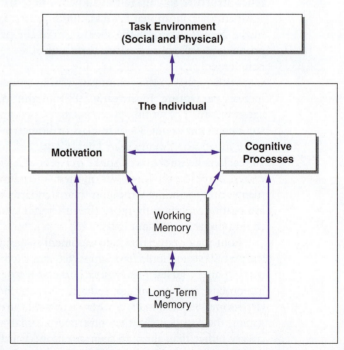

Source: Adapted from Hayes, J. R. (1996/2004). A new framework for understanding cognition and affect in writing. In R. B. Ruddell & N. Unrau (Eds.), *Theoretical models and processes of reading* (5th ed., pp. 1399–1430). Newark, DE: International Reading Association. (Originally published in Levy C. M. & Ransdell. S. (Eds.) (1996), *The Science of Writing: Theories, Methods, Individual Differences, and Applications* (pp. 1–27). Hillsdale, NJ: Erlbaum.

physical dimensions include the text that has so far been created, including the space in which it is being written, and the medium (pencil, tape recorder, or computer) through which it is composed.

The individual, as a major component in the writing model, has several dimensions: working memory, long-term memory, cognitive processes, and motivation/affect.

Working memory, just as in reading, plays a central role in constructing text while writing. As in reading, working memory has a limited capacity and can be a bottleneck. For Hayes, working memory consists of a central executive that carries out key control functions, such as retrieving information from long-term memory. It also includes two forms of memory that support writing: a phonological loop and a visual sketchpad. The phonological loop acts as an inner voice echoing information that needs to be accessed during composition. The sketchpad keeps relevant visual and spatial images active.

Long-term memory houses resources for writing that are similar to the kinds of knowledge essential to the reading process. The writing resources include task schemas and knowledge of topics, audience, language, and genre. Task schemas contain procedural knowledge that enables writers to carry out a variety of writing tasks, such as schemas for textbook reading, for revising texts, and for drafting an argumentative essay or writing a lab report. Knowledge of a writer's audience is of critical importance to a writer. Writing to a class friend evokes a style and strategies quite different from writing a report on the Reformation for a history teacher. As in reading, knowledge of language and genre is fundamental to writing. If you're going to write an expository essay, you need schemas to guide the process.

Cognitive processes include text interpretation, reflection, and text production. Text interpretation, as in the reading model, ranges from word recognition through meaning negotiation. For writers, text interpretation also includes a mental representation of their writing task, such as a teacher's writing assignment. Writers internalize and reflect on those task representations, activate resources, such as background knowledge, and review information and strategies that could contribute to completing a writing task. During text production, writers plan, generate propositions, organize them, and produce written outcomes, such as a summary of a short story or a description of a chemical process for a lab assignment (Flower & Hayes, 1981). These externalize written outcomes are then reviewed.

John Hayes (1996/2004) provides a detailed description of the revision process that includes comprehending a writer's written text, evaluating that text, detecting problems, and finding remedies for them that appear in the revised text. Reading, as you can see, plays a central part in writing. That reading includes source texts, writing assignments, and one's own writing for the purpose of revision.

The **motivation/affect** component of Hayes's model includes goals, predispositions, beliefs and attitudes, and cost-benefit estimates. Writers, perhaps even more so than readers, have complex and interacting goals, such as covering appropriate content, conveying a good impression, and fitting the written text to a teacher's length requirements. However, writers and readers share many identical motivating factors, including textual connections, reading (and writing) skills and knowledge, goals and task values, self-efficacy, and—especially—their sense of identity as students and writers. As with readers, writers can be significantly affected by teacher-controlled dimensions of motivation, such as the teacher's expectations of student writing, the autonomy or choices given to students with respect to writing tasks, and the classroom community to which a student's written work will contribute.

How Process Upstaged Product

Much of the research contributing to the model of writing just presented also contributed to the development of a process approach to the teaching of writing. Prior to the 1970s, writing in classrooms was product centered. Teachers and researchers focused on instructional strategies that got students to write and on evaluating their written products. Since the 1970s, writing as a process in a context has struggled to upstage and replace the formerly dominant product perspective. However, product-oriented writing has not been pushed into the wings. As our national educational drama plays year after year, writing as a product strolls back to center stage periodically to deliver its pleas for grades.

Decades of research on writing have led to several significant generalizations about what happens when writers write. To define what was known about writing and what needs to be learned, several researchers at the Center for the Study of Writing (Freedman, Dyson, Flower, & Chafe, 1987) pulled together a set of generalizations about the nature of the writing process:

- Writing consists of several main processes—planning, transcribing text, and reviewing. They do not occur in any fixed order; rather, thought in writing is not linear but jumps from process to process in an organized way, which is largely determined by the individual writer's goals (Emig, 1971; Flower, Schriver, Carey, Haas, & Hayes, 1989; Flower & Hayes, 1981).
- The writing process is a hierarchically organized, goal-directed, problem-solving process (Bereiter & Scardamalia, 1980; Flower & Hayes, 1981).
- Experts and novices solve the problems posed by the task of writing differently (Flower, 1979; Flower & Hayes, 1977; Perl, 1979).
- The nature of the writing task changes the writer's strategies (Applebee, 1984; Carey, Flower, Hayes, Schriver, & Haas, 1989; Emig, 1971).

If you reflect on your own writing experiences, you are likely to find personal evidence for these observations and insights.

Some of these discoveries about the nature of writing contributed to what was and is widely called the *process approach* to teaching writing. Usually, "writing as a process" gets broken down into several steps or stages: prewriting, drafting, revising, proofreading, and publishing (Michigan State Board of Education, 1994). In each stage, the writer engages in different activities, such as those described in Figure 7.2.

However, these stages are not linear. Researchers have repeatedly confirmed that the writing process is recursive in nature and encourage teachers to create environments where students can rethink ideas and ways to express them at all stages of composition.

How Writing Furthers Constructivism

We've seen that, like reading, writing is a meaning construction process. While writing itself often involves writers in the construction of meaning, writing can also be used to promote constructivism in the form of knowledge-building classrooms in which students use writing to learn through inquiry.

When I, as an English teacher, first engaged my high school juniors in inquiry projects that required extensive research, I don't think I knew how important writing would be to help me and my students achieve our goals. I used writing to discover what they wanted to do and to monitor where students were going, how they were getting there, and how well the journey was going for each of them. Writing helped

Figure 7.2   The Process of Writing.

Writing Stage	Writing Activities
Prewriting	Plan by brainstorming, researching, note taking, listing, clustering, organizing.
Drafting	Construct a preliminary form by selecting a format, writing drafts, deciding on an audience.
Revising	Review or reflect on earlier drafts by rethinking, adding, dropping, rearranging, rewriting.
Proofreading	Prepare for publication by polishing, correcting spelling, punctuation, and grammatical problems.
Publishing	Share with a target audience by reading, displaying, anthologizing, submitting for publication.

them ride out the bumps and find productive roadways. Without constantly writing back and forth, in logs and letters, I would have been lost.

I enjoyed designing units that opened opportunities for students to explore topics, usually of their own choice, and to build on their knowledge base. Using inquiry to raise questions and stimulate investigation, I engaged students in projects and problem solving. I used writing to facilitate their growth of understanding. Students, meanwhile, constructed knowledge as they made connections between what they knew and new information they discovered. I asked them to write lots of summaries. Sometimes, although not always, my classroom became a community of learners who used writing to become both more knowledgeable and more thoughtful.

Similarly, in history classes using a constructivist perspective, students are not simply told about the events of World War I through lectures, even though teachers may use lectures at some times. Instead, students read and discuss textbook chapters about World War I, along with original documents describing historical events leading up to U.S. engagement in the war, the war's battles, and its aftermath. They might be presented with topics for inquiry:

- What economic and political relationships prevailed among European countries in 1914 before the outbreak of war?
- At what points and in what ways could the series of events that led to the outbreak of war in Europe have been broken?
- Which battles best typified battlefield tactics and the kind of suffering soldiers endured during the war?
- Looking back, was the U.S. decision to enter the war a good decision? Should the United States have entered the war or should it have maintained an isolationist policy?
- Looking forward, what can we learn from the events of World War I that could guide our foreign policy and decision making in the 21st century?

Students, perhaps working in cooperative learning teams, engage in gathering and interpreting information that help them to answer these questions. They prepare documents for the teacher and the class that reveal their discoveries and their answers to these questions. But how could a teacher move these students forward, observe their work, and offer productive suggestions? What better tool than writing?

Through writing, students record their discoveries in the form of notes and summaries, guided by the teacher's questions and recommendations. After discussing their discoveries in their teams, they write about their discussions in journals. As they move toward answering their team's major questions, they draft and share their analyses and arguments. Finally, they compile a final copy of their documents for the teacher and use their writing as a basis for their presentation to their classmates, who engaged in similar inquiries and writing in their own teams. In this way, classrooms become communities to promote learning and scholarship through inquiry and the construction of knowledge.

Teachers across the land and across the disciplines realized the potential of writing to learn and to construct knowledge. The use of writing in content area courses gathered so much attention that it became a movement called Writing Across the Curriculum (or WAC).

Classroom instruction across the United States now reflects the process approach to writing. In *The NAEP 1998 Writing Report Card for the Nation and the States* (Greenwald, Persky, Campbell, & Mazzeo, 1999), about 9 out of 10 students in grades 8 and 12 report that their teachers always or sometimes ask them to write more than one draft of a paper. Furthermore, students in the 8th and 12th grades who were always asked in their classes to write more than one draft performed better on measures of writing achievement than their peers, who were only sometimes or never asked to write multiple drafts. As for prewriting activities, the majority of students at both grades 8 and 12 report that their English teachers asked them to plan their writing at least once a week. Students who planned their writing also demonstrated higher levels of writing achievement.

Effects of Social Contexts on the Writing Process

Many of the generalizations about writing that researchers and educators induced, such as the *process approach*, were derived from laboratory-like conditions rather than the natural context of classrooms. Freedman and her colleagues (1987) foresaw a need for educators to become more aware of other dimensions that influence writing, including the effects of social contexts on the writing process. Out of these purposes grew studies that investigated many aspects of writing, including **situated learning**, or learning embedded in a certain environment(Freedman, Flower, Hull, & Hayes, 1995). Their purpose was to discover what goes on when students learn in specific situations, such as multicultural urban classrooms.

In one such study, Sarah Freedman and her collaborators (Freedman, Simons, Kalnin, Casareno, & the M-CLASS teams, 1999) investigated literacy processes in urban classrooms. They engaged 24 Boston, Chicago, New Orleans, and San Francisco–area teachers of English and social studies in university-supported teacher-research projects. The teachers in the network they established examined their classroom literacy and learning practices and described what they did and saw in order to serve as models for other teachers facing multicultural classrooms across the United States. Teachers formulated their own research questions, and their search for answers guided their investigation. They met in groups from time to time to share their findings and to find encouragement and direction from collaborating teachers.

Writing played an important role in many of these teachers' classrooms (Freedman et al., 1999). With teacher guidance, students used writing for a multitude of purposes: to record connections between personal experiences and reading experience, to promote learning in geography, to shape the stories of their lives, to confront racism, to expand their ethnic identity, and to understand their feelings of marginality.

These teachers did not all embrace a process approach to teaching writing. Some, agreeing with Lisa Delpit's (1986, 1988) critique of process writing and advocacy of explicit instruction in literacy skills, believed that their students needed a much more structured approach than the process pedagogy provided. One of these network teachers argued that the process approach held students responsible for what they haven't been taught and haven't learned. Their nonstandard English, while expressive of their own lives, would not empower them in the wider world. Her teacher-research question was, "How can I help students internalize correctness so it becomes a part of their repertoire?" Although she used a red pen to mark errors, gave grammar mini-lessons daily, and varied in other ways from a process-writing pedagogy, she had very mixed feelings about doing so. However, her teacher-research confirmed for her that she was on the right track with her multicultural students (Freedman et al., 1999).

These teacher–researchers learned some important lessons about how their work could benefit the educational community at large. One of the general findings that emerged from these inquiries was that, if teachers wanted to achieve high standards for writing while empowering their students, they would need to teach explicitly the conventions of standard edited English. That guideline applied to both nonnative speakers of English and those speaking a nonstandard dialect. Teachers should also provide explicit instruction in other writing skills and knowledge, including composition structures and writing styles. The script for the process approach to teaching writing, as some teachers saw it, was modified in urban classrooms to meet the specific learning needs of diverse students.

These new discoveries about the writing process and its use in the social context of school were not the only elements drawing teachers' attention to writing. Teachers were also lured by the value of writing to learn.

The Promise of Writing to Learn

Writing can work as a cultural tool to build and examine knowledge (Vygotsky, 1978). But before writers externalize knowledge as written text, they engage in what Vygotsky called "inner speech," a form of self-talk in which talkers (and writers) try to make sense of their thoughts. Unfortunately, inner speech does not always enter consciousness in standard English. Especially for struggling writers, it emerges in fragments with words and details left out. Coherence and structure may also be left out (Everson, 1991). Nevertheless, if we can provide an instructional environment in which students can externalize their inner speech, writing can serve as a medium for learning.

Plenty of research supports the claim that writing promotes learning (Durst, 1987; Hillocks, 2006; J. A. Langer & Applebee, 1987; Newell, 1998). Newell and Winograd (1995) found that, in comparison to studying without writing, studying with writing yields a considerable advantage. Writing then presents itself to teachers as a promising learning tool. In fact, Newell believes writing offers at least three promises:

- Writing provides a means to explore and make sense of ideas and experiences.
- Writing can alter both the role of teachers (by transforming them from evaluators to collaborators) and students (by transforming them from memorizers to meaning makers) while changing the value of knowledge in the content areas (by transforming it from facts to ways of understanding their culture, their traditions, and their selves).
- Writing across the disciplines can help students learn about the wide range of genres and formats used in various content areas.

These are functions of critical importance for writing to perform in our classrooms. It's a tool for discovery, for changing the way students learn, and for guiding students into the forms of writing that are common in each content area.

Types of Writing

Not all kinds of writing produce the same results. Different types of writing foster different kinds of learning and reasoning (Newell, 1998).

Restricted writing.   **Restricted writing**, exemplified by answering study questions focused on comprehension of a text, usually engages students' minds in a basic search and transcription process. For example, after reading passages about Andrew Jackson's presidency, students are asked to explain in writing the doctrine of nullification and Jackson's response to it. Little or no composing or transformation of knowledge occurs when students engage in this form of writing. Teachers can use it for a couple of instructional purposes: (a) to review content of a text before a test or class discussion and (b) to prepare students for a more complex instructional task, such as comparing alternative theories or explanations once individual explanations have been comprehended (Newell & Winograd, 1995).

Summary writing.   **Summary writing** focuses on ideas at a deeper level than a mental review but at a more superficial level than analytic writing. Summaries do require students to compress and integrate information to capture the gist of a text while representing the original text's structure. So, knowledge is transformed to some degree. But students emerge with a distillation of the original text rather than an analysis or evaluation of it. Like restricted writing, summary writing can prepare students for more complex tasks.

Analytical writing.   **Analytical writing** engages students in reformulating and extending the text. In science, a student could analyze and compare two different explanations of a laboratory event. In history, students could analyze multiple text sources to answer complex inquiry questions, such as those about the origins of World War I, its consequences, and how the war might have been avoided. In English, a student could analyze a character, such as Hester Prynn or Willy Loman; state a theme and justify it; or inspect the effects of setting in a novel. These manipulations of ideas to organize an argument or to persuade a reader of a student's position are likely to create a more enduring representation of content through reformulation and integration (Langer & Applebee, 1987; Newell, 1998; Newell & Winograd, 1995).

Effects of Writing on Learning

Certain forms of writing would seem to support certain kinds of learning. This looks like important pedagogical knowledge for us to have. If we want students to learn a lot of general information about a chapter in a history text, we'd better think through what kind of writing (if any) they should do. Would asking students to "write a report" on the chapter lead to the kind of knowledge we'd like our students to gain for an examination testing their comprehension of the whole chapter? Probably not.

Studies have clearly shown that different kinds of writing (analytical or summary) activate very different kinds of cognitive processes, which results in students' learning different things, perhaps even important things. However, they may not be things we're planning to include on an exam.

Penrose (1989) found that whether or not writing promotes learning depends on what kind of writing and learning we're talking about. In her study, students read two academic articles during two different sessions. During one session, students were assigned a written "report" on the text. During the second session, students were instructed to "study for a test" using whatever strategies they thought would work. After completing the assigned tasks, students took a test that included four different types of comprehension questions: simple recall of facts, complex recall of two or more related facts, main idea, and application.

The results overall showed that, when students studied rather than wrote, they scored higher on the comprehension test. Furthermore, students spent about 35% more time on the writing task.

But what would have happened to students' comprehension scores if Penrose had asked them to write a *summary* rather than a report and had included specific expectations with respect to the summary's content and structure? As we saw earlier, summary writing has some rather specific effects on knowledge construction. Students writing summaries are more likely to condense the original text rather than reflect upon or evaluate some aspect of it. That condensation in memory might prove to be helpful in answering comprehension questions of various kinds.

In a follow-up analysis of her study, Penrose (1992) looked more carefully at the various ways that students interpreted the writing task, noting that other studies (Flower et al., 1990) have confirmed that students often interpret writing assignments in ways that differ from their teacher's and from other students' interpretations. How a writer interprets an assignment influences what kind of learning will occur. Penrose observed that students, while focusing on the analysis of a single aspect of the text they read, may not have taken in the broader picture. In so doing, students may not have attended to individual facts, knowledge of which was tested through comprehension questions. Penrose concluded that what students learned depended more on their interpretation of the writing tasks than on the tasks as she intended them.

What, then, can be said about the promise of writing to learn? Writing holds a lot of promise for you as a tool for learning; however, you will need to put significant thought into the selection and presentation of writing assignments for that promise to be realized in learning. You need to give students clear specifications for the kind of writing you want and clear statements about the purposes you want the writing to serve. Sharing rubrics with students before writing assignments are due will clarify what kind of writing you want and what purposes it will serve.

The National Writing Project (NWP)

In the early 1970s, several teachers, teacher educators, and professors in the San Francisco Bay area became interested in finding a format in which teachers using writing in the schools could meet with other teachers to improve student writing. In 1974, James Gray (2000) and his colleagues at the University of California, Berkeley, broke new educational ground with the first Summer Institute of the Bay Area Writing Project (BAWP).

During the school year, BAWP held monthly meetings, to which teachers from the Bay area came to give and get ideas about writing in their classrooms. All teachers of all grades and all content areas were encouraged to attend. Also during the school year, BAWP ran workshops for schools and districts. Workshops consisted of several sessions, usually about 10, focused on one Writing Project teacher's 2- to 3-hour presentation. Teachers, whose workshop attendance was voluntary, wrote and shared their writing in response to the presenter's demonstration of a teaching method.

BAWP caught on. Soon teachers and teacher educators representing campuses in California and other states heard about BAWP's successes and wanted to model a teacher development program along similar lines. By the late 1970s, the stage was set for the emergence of the National Writing Project (NWP). During the 1980s and 1990s, NWP sites sprang up at about 150 universities. These sites housed writing project centers to which teachers of all disciplines were invited to do essentially what was done at the first BAWP meetings: share ideas with other teachers to improve student writing. NWP sites have trained and served well more than a million teachers.

Among the basic assumptions that continue to guide the NWP work are the following:

- Teachers learn well from other teachers because of their credibility.
- Writing is a tool that facilitates learning in science, math, history, and other disciplines as well as in English.
- Teachers who teach writing also write.
- To be effective, professional development programs must be on-going so that teachers come together throughout their careers to exchange ideas about writing.
- Teachers must be free to participate voluntarily in NWP programs.
- Knowledge about teaching writing comes from both research and classroom practice.
- The NWP encourages the critical examination of a variety of approaches to the teaching of writing and promotes no single writing pedagogy.
- Working together, teachers and universities can guide and support school reform (National Writing Project, 2001).

In general, the National Writing Project has a progressive and constructivist theory guiding its practices. Students learned to write by writing, as did teachers, and learning wasn't something teachers deposited in their students' minds. Students used writing to explore ideas and construct knowledge. Meanwhile, teachers reflected on their practice, shared ideas with other teachers, and built communities of learners.

Across the country, teachers at all grade levels attend NWP Summer Institutes, participate in NWP-supported in-service workshops, and share in monthly meetings where teacher-to-teacher contacts foster effective writing practices in the schools. In these various settings, teachers present the problems and successes they have in teaching their students to learn and to write.

In summary, these four developments in education had significant effects on the uses of writing in content area classrooms. First, new discoveries about the writing process provided incentive to displace earlier product-centered views of writing and to engage students in the development of more process-oriented writing skills, such as planning and editing. Second, constructivism encouraged teachers to focus more intently on helping their students to build knowledge, and writing served as a flexible but durable tool to do that building. Third, writing held out an appealing promise to teachers: Students could learn through using the tool of writing. And, fourth, with the development of the National Writing Project, teachers could find universities and sites where their efforts to infuse and to improve writing across the disciplines would find strong support and guidance.

Categories of Writing

When it comes to deciding on the kind of writing assignment to give to your students, knowing what kinds of writing tasks exist and knowing something about the effects of those tasks on learning will help guide your decision making. We now turn to a review of that knowledge.

Animals often slip neatly into a biological category like a bear into its cave or a hermit crab into its shell. But different types of writing don't always fit easily into a category. Some types of writing creep around looking for the appropriate category to slip into. Not only do these types of writing look for a category in which to be housed, they change. Some specialists in rhetoric and new genre studies (Herrington & Moran, 2005) believe that it's difficult to define, classify, and teach forms of writing because they are unstable. From this perspective, a genre is a living organism; it evolves. New forms may come into the world, often born and nursed on the Internet or some other electronic medium. Regardless of our recognition that genres may be unstable creatures, categories of discourse go all the way back to Aristotle's *Rhetoric* and *Poetics,* and some teachers still use his system of classification.

In spite of the dynamic nature of genres, educators have created several other category systems (or typologies) to describe the uses for writing in school (Applebee, 1981; Britton, 1970; Moffett, 1989). Currently, the National Assessment of Education Progress (Greenwald et al., 1998) evaluates three categories of writing in the schools: narrative, informational, and persuasive writing. A textbook that is based on genre theory and that has been through many editions (Axelrod & Cooper, 2006) names eight specific genres, models of which students read and imitate in their own writing: autobiography, observation, reflection, explaining concepts, evaluation, speculation about causes and effects, proposal to solve a problem, and position papers that present arguments. All these genres are germane to academic literacy, especially to students preparing for college.

For this chapter I sought a set of categories that reflected the ways teachers in middle and high school use writing to engage students in knowledge construction and learning across the curriculum. Keeping that goal in mind, I decided on three learning-related categories to capture the purposes for teachers assigning writing: to assess learning, to promote learning, and to observe learning. Of course, a teacher can combine these purposes so that two or even three purposes could be combined and pursued in one assignment. Perhaps more importantly, genres of different kinds can be housed in each of the three categories proposed.

Writing to Assess Learning

Writing can have multiple purposes, but teachers tend to use it primarily to evaluate previous learning. When composing, students can't guess what answer is correct. They have to construct and organize knowledge from what they have learned and stored away. According to Applebee's (1981, 1984) studies of writing in the secondary school, teachers most frequently ask students to write for the purpose of discovering what they have learned. A quarter century after Applebee conducted his study, writing assigned to evaluate students has probably increased because of the pressure of statewide testing programs (Anagnostopoulos, 2003) and an emphasis on students learning to master a formulaic five-paragraph essay (Johnson, Smagorinsky, Thompson, & Fry, 2003) rather than allowing inquiry and discovery of content to shape the form writing might take (Hillocks, 2006).

However, always putting the teacher in the role of examiner and grader of students' writing limits the instructional purposes and potentials of writing. Applebee (1984) found that giving students opportunities to use writing to explore ideas, to promote understanding of concepts, to have a dialogue with the teacher, or to address readers other than the teacher-as-grader were limited. These alternative purposes for asking students to write enrich instruction, as we'll discover.

Applebee (1984) found that of the four uses of school writing he identified (mechanical, informational, personal, and imaginative), informational writing was the most frequently required. However, across all content areas, analytical writing was the category of informational writing in which teachers asked students to engage more than half of the time. When doing analytical writing, students draw generalizations or make classifications based on the examination of information or data. For example, in a chemistry lab report, students would be expected to analyze the results of an experiment in order to draw conclusions about it. However, Applebee found that, as students moved from observation and summary to analysis and argument, they tended to apply rigid, formulaic approaches. With these approaches, students would simply fill in slots of information. While these formulaic approaches to writing, such as the five-paragraph essay format, often help students initially to grasp the structure of a report or an essay, these same structures could limit students' analytical thinking and writing.

A couple of developments in the writing field can heighten students' essay-writing expectations and outcomes: engaging students in the writing process and using rubrics to evaluate performance. When students have opportunities to plan, draft, seek response, revise, edit, and publish, we know they are more likely to produce essays of finer quality. In addition, using a well-designed rubric or scoring guide gives students a clear picture of the criteria you will use to evaluate their work. Knowing, in advance, what standards will be applied to judgments about their writing provides students with clear targets. Many schools and districts now have generic rubrics they encourage their teachers to use. A sample of a six-level rubric for rating 8th graders' persuasive writing from the NAEP's *Writing Report Card: Writing 2002* is given in Figure 7.3. (The rubric for 12th graders' persuasive writing is nearly identical.) When NAEP readers use these rubrics for scoring, they are trained with "anchor papers" that represent student writing at each of the six levels. Although generic rubrics abound and can be useful in some assessments, I'd encourage you to develop rubrics tailored to the specific writing assignment you give and the expected learning outcomes you have.

Writing to Promote Learning

Exploratory uses of writing.   Exploratory writing can play a central and catalytic role in all the disciplines. In *Writing to Learn*, Zinsser (1988) posited two categories for writing that augment learning: explanatory ("writing that transmits existing information or ideas") and exploratory ("writing that enables us to discover what we want to say"). Because of the belief and hope that exploratory writing can help us discover

Figure 7.3 Grade 8 Persuasive Scoring Guide.

6 Excellent Response:

- Takes a clear position and develops it consistently with well-chosen reasons and/or examples across the response.
- Is well organized with strong transitions.
- Sustains variety in sentence structure and exhibits good word choice.
- Errors in grammar, spelling, and punctuation are few and do not interfere with understanding.

5 Skillful Response:

- Takes a clear position and develops it with pertinent reasons and/or examples in parts of the response.
- Is clearly organized, but may lack some transitions and/or have occasional lapses in continuity.
- Exhibits some variety in sentence structure and some good word choice.
- Errors in grammar, spelling, and punctuation do not interfere with understanding.

4 Sufficient Response:

- Takes a clear position and supports it with some reasons and/or examples.
- Is organized with ideas that are generally related, but there are few or no transitions.
- Exhibits control over sentence boundaries and sentence structure, but sentences and word choice may be simple and unvaried.
- Errors in grammar, spelling, and punctuation do not interfere with understanding.

3 Uneven Response (may be characterized by one or more of the following):

- Takes a position and offers support, but may be unclear, repetitive, list-like, or undeveloped.
- Is unevenly organized; the response may be disjointed.
- Exhibits uneven control over sentence boundaries and sentence structure; may exhibit some inaccurate word choices.
- Errors in grammar, spelling, and punctuation sometimes interfere with understanding.

2 Insufficient Response (may be characterized by one or more of the following):

- Takes a position, but response may be very unclear, very undeveloped, or very repetitive.
- Is very disorganized; thoughts are tenuously connected OR the response is too brief to detect organization.
- Minimal control over sentence boundaries and sentence structure; word choice may often be inaccurate.
- Errors in grammar or usage (such as missing words or incorrect word use or word order), spelling, and punctuation interfere with understanding in much of the response.

1 Unsatisfactory Response (may be characterized by one or more of the following):

- Attempts to take a position (addresses topic) but response is incoherent OR takes a position but provides no support; may only paraphrase the task.
- Has no apparent organization OR consists of a single statement.
- Minimal or no control over sentence boundaries and sentence structure; word choice may be inaccurate in much or all of the response.
- A multiplicity of errors in grammar or usage (such as missing words or incorrect word use or word order), spelling, and punctuation severely impedes understanding across the response.

Source: From the *The Nation's Report Card: Writing 2002* (p. 91), by H. R. Persky, M. C. Daane, and Y. Jin. Washington, DC: U.S. Department of Education, 2003.

what we want to say, I have opted to put our more adventuresome strategies in an exploratory category of their own. These strategies promote both engagement with what is to be learned and learning itself.

Exploratory writing enables students to travel through uncharted knowledge domains and (maybe) discover emerald cities of understanding. But (of course) there is a price to pay: Students are expected to be making sense of ideas, constructing new understandings, making new connections, and generating questions as they go. As a teacher, I use exploratory writing to deepen students' engagement with the course content and monitor their understanding. While I'm always hoping to discover their interests in reading assignments, I also use these exploratory writings to discover if students are doing their reading homework. When I use them, I seek these kinds of outcomes:

- connecting students to background knowledge, including other texts,
- constructing and sorting out meanings,
- discovering questions and possible answers, and
- reflecting on one's thinking or problem-solving process (metacognition).

Engaging students in one or more exploratory writing strategies is quite likely to promote learning. However, many of them still need to be studied empirically to discover how and to what degree they actually do promote learning.

I've already explained a couple of strategies in chapter 6, "Strategies to Enhance Comprehension": Know-Want to know-Learned strategy (K-W-L) and Double-Entry Journals. Both are used to activate, connect with, and extend background knowledge. However, there are many other writing strategies that engage students in the exploration and formation of knowledge. You'll find more than 30 of these in Figure 7.4. Most of these writing activities can be used in all content area courses. Although implementation methods for many of the activities described are well known, I've described a few of the lesser known ones, including Admit Slips and Exit Passes, freewrites, Question Papers, Skeletons, RAFTing, journals (or logs), and Quickwrites (such as DEAD, for Drop Everything And Draft). I've also described the potential of essays, position papers, and I-search papers to promote learning.

Admit Slips and Exit Passes. Have you ever stood in front of a class, asked your students if they have any questions, and met with a resounding stillness? When you want to get more response from them in the way of questions, try **Admit Slips**. They're none other than 3×5 cards you give to students to use for writing down questions about what you've been studying in your course. At the beginning of class, they might write questions in response to the following circumstances: a reading assignment done for homework, yesterday's lecture or discussion, a review of material to be covered on the next test, or a new topic you're about to study. When class begins, you can flip through the Admit Slips, find a few appropriate questions, and ask your students to try answering them or answer them yourself. One of my students wanted me to follow up on a concept that arose during our previous class session and asked on her Admit Slip, "What is a miscue? Could you give us more examples?" The question enabled us to review miscue analysis and explore examples.

Do you ever wonder if your students got anything out of the lecture on Reconstruction that you spent the last 45 minutes giving, or the video on mitosis and meiosis they just watched, or a team's presentation on factoring polynomials? When you want to know, try **Exit Passes**. These are 3×5 cards on which you ask your students to write a three- or four-sentence summary of what went on in class that you want them to tell you about. That summary goes on the front of the card. On the back, have students

Figure 7.4 Writing Activities Across the Curriculum.

Admit Slips	Freewrites	Question Papers
Autobiographies (Memoirs)	Interviews	Reports (Lab)
Blogs	I-Search Papers	Reviews (of movies, TV shows, parks, computers, cars, restaurants, music)
Case Studies	Journals	Research Papers
DEAD	Letters (to teachers, friends, editors, the past/future, philanthropic groups, businesses)	RAFT
Descriptions	Logs	Short Stories
Dialogues	Memos	Skeletons
Editorials	News Articles	Summaries
E-mails	Notes	Text Messages
Essays (persuasive, compare/contrast, cause-effect, process analysis, explaining concepts, evaluation, reflection)	Poems	Web Sites
Exit Passes	Position Paper	

write a question relevant to the material covered in class that day: something they want to know more about, some assumption they want to challenge, or some point they would like clarified. Math teachers use them to gather moments of understanding, questions that students have about new concepts introduced, or solutions to challenging problems. These passes are collected as students leave your class. You can review them before the next class meeting. You might even give them a quick grade and then use them to guide instructional decisions about how you'll begin tomorrow's class.

Freewrites. **Freewrites** go all the way back to the 1960s, to the time of "freeing up" in American culture. During that time, a professor from America's heartland, Ken Macrorie (1968), published the first edition of his *Writing to Be Read*. In that book, he advocated "writing freely" to get closer to a writer's "honest voice" and the "truth" of the writer's world. He began by urging teachers to encourage students to write freely without focus for 10 minutes about whatever came to mind. Let them forget spelling, punctuation, or grammar and just get all their nonstop thoughts down on paper. This was new, luscious stuff in classrooms where teachers were trying to shake off the restrictions and constrictions of the 1950s and open windows to a whiff of freshness in student writing. Macrorie's (1970, p. viii) purpose was to release "the natural urges of the writer to discover, to invent, to play with words."

Freewrites ("the 5-minute essay") live a somewhat different life in my classrooms because I assign **focused freewrites**, which can be used in any content area classroom. This more restricted form of writing, also encouraged by Macrorie (1970), provides students with time before or after a class to clarify their thoughts about a topic. While they still have the discovery element of freewrites without a focus, focused freewrites enable students to reflect on specific issues, kinds of learning, or metacognitive aspects of learning. Among their benefits, focused freewrites can

- promote students' active engagement with course content,
- get students using technical vocabulary of the discipline,
- encourage good listening because students must put knowledge into their own words,
- provide a window on students' thinking,
- set the stage for further inquiry, and
- enhance communication between teacher and student.

Andrews (1997) suggests looping freewrites to explore new concepts or topics. Following a 3- to 5-minute freewrite about a particular idea, Andrews asks her students to summarize what they've written in one sentence. Then she asks them to fold their papers so only the summarizing sentence appears and pass them along to another student, who reads that sentence and continues to write about the focus topic with the classmate's sentence as a starting point. She repeats that looping process several times. Throughout the process, students explore their understanding of a topic and respond to their peers' perspectives. At the end of the activity, students get their original paper back, share final sentences, and engage in discussion.

I like to use these freewrites after a class discussion to focus attention on what was learned, how it was learned, and what questions remain unanswered. For a focused freewrite, students could be asked to summarize what they learned and to compose questions to be asked at the beginning of the next class. Before the next class, you can review what your students have written to find out if they understood your points of instruction, to identify concepts that bear reteaching, and to select questions to which you will respond. You can also make comments on the papers, reinforce growing understandings, and answer questions that arise.

Or, you may elect not to collect the freewrites but to have students use them with each other. For example, after composing the freewrites, students could get together in pairs or teams to read and respond to each other's understandings, misunderstandings, and questions. The freewrites could then be placed in a portfolio for you to review at the end of a week or a unit to make sure students have grasped the meaning and purpose of your instruction. As Young (1997) relays, some teachers allow their students to consult their portfolio of freewrites—but not their books or lecture notes—during an open-portfolio exam. That higher stakes use of freewrites motivates students to make them accurate and lucid.

Question Papers.   When writing a **Question Paper**, students cannot write anything but questions while reading or after reading an assignment. Students can't write much that's wrong when writing a Question Paper, but they can write much that opens texts and authors to extensive questioning. Although students are limited to writing only questions, their papers still show how well they understood what they've read. The kinds of questions a student writes reveal much about the level of comprehension that student experienced and the level of doubt and curiosity engendered.

In some ways, the Question Paper is like the focused freewrite. However, rather than writing statements for a predetermined period of time, say 10 minutes, students write down all the questions they can generate in response to a reading or a lecture. The process can have a rather liberating, spontaneous, and sometimes

GREGORY

"Here's the deal, Josh—these two gentlemen want to turn that note you passed in homeroom into a movie."

humorous quality. Usually, students share the Question Papers in class on a voluntary basis; or, you could collect them, preview them, determine which papers in particular you would like to have read aloud, and ask their writers to read them in class.

Skeletons.   Pressnall (1995) originated **skeletons** in the middle of the night after a challenging day with his students' sketchy, or "skeletal," papers. He decided his students needed an exercise to show them how to "hang meat on the bones" of their papers. So the next day he gave them a skeleton:

> I walked into class late. The teacher looked at me. I sat down and opened my book. I heard footsteps approach. The teacher cleared her throat. I looked the teacher in the eye.

He explained to them that each sentence in the skeleton was a bone and that their job was to "bring the skeleton to life with muscle, blood, fur, claws, guts and a beating heart." He asked them to write from one to three sentences or phrases between each of the bones he gave them. The results were astounding. Students who had written little in the past wrote much more with skeletons.

When reviewing a unit on the civil rights movement, he gave them another skeleton to bulk up:

> In the 1960s Dr. King, Rosa Parks, Malcolm X, Thurgood Marshall and others tried to change a few things. They had many goals. They tried many tactics. They met resistance. They met success.

With expository skeletons like these, students can explore what they know about the civil rights movement, fill out the bones of history, and consolidate their learning for the test to come.

I'm sure you can see how similar skeletons could serve as a structure for your students to explore domains of knowledge in your content area before, during, or after an instructional episode. They serve some teachers as bare-bones reviews for upcoming essay tests. Given the bones by their teachers, students can review what they know, activate their knowledge, and bring the skeletons to life with key concepts and supporting details.

RAFTing.   Students, like Huck Finn floating down the wide Mississippi, can explore the environment of any content area through RAFTing. **RAFTing** (Santa, 1988) consists of four components that guide and stimulate student exploration of content knowledge: Role, Audience, Format, and Topic. When RAFTing, students are their own navigators. They decide who they want to be (Role), to whom they want to address their discourse (Audience), in what form they want to write (Format), and what topic or question they wish to pursue (Topic). RAFTing puts the rudder of choice in your students' hands for awhile, giving them time to process more abstract content knowledge in more concrete, even narrative modes. And, as the NWP recommends, you can RAFT along with your students.

Students need some instruction in RAFTing before leaving the shore. You can provide a demonstration, and they can follow your example. It's likely to save some from drowning in freedom. Although *T* (for Topics) is the last letter of the acronym, choice of topic comes first. You can show students what kinds of questions you would ask about topics your class is currently covering. If, for example, my class were reading Twain's *Huckleberry Finn*, I might become Mark Twain (Role) and write a letter (Format) to Huck (Audience) explaining why I decided to float him down the river (Topic). Or, if I were teaching about the three branches of government, I could become one of the chief justices and compose a brochure to new members of Congress explaining to them how I saw my function, especially in relation to Congress and the President. The Strategy in Practice, a matrix of RAFT examples, shows the strategy's versatility.

Strategy in Practice

RAFTING EXAMPLES

ROLE	AUDIENCE	FORMAT	TOPIC
Newspaper reporter	Readers in 1826	Obituary	Thomas Jefferson
Mitochondria	Other cell structures	Operations memo	What functions I have
Holden Caulfield	Phoebe	Letter	What happened to me during my college years
Moon	Sun	Instructions	How I move in the solar system
Pythagorian Theorem	Statue of Liberty	Love note	How I can figure out your height from your shadow

To help each other generate ideas for RAFTing, students can meet in teams. After collaborating, each student should turn in his choice of Role, Audience, Format, and Topic before beginning the written voyage so that you know where each student plans to travel. However, you ought to recognize that currents can carry students to different destinations from an initial predeparture itinerary.

Journals and Logs.   **Journals** in all content areas provide opportunities for students to heighten "low-stakes" processing and reduce apprehension over "high-stakes" products that teachers grade. Each time teachers ask students to compose in journals, they individualize instruction, forcing passive learners to become actively engaged. Fulwiler (1986) pointed out that he used journals for multiple purposes:

- to stimulate discussion,
- to start small group activities,
- to clarify hazy issues,
- to reinforce learning, and
- to stimulate imagination.

When teaching high school, I had my students bring a notebook to class at the beginning of the school year. I requested a bound notebook of at least 100 pages of $8\frac{1}{2} \times 11$-inch lined paper. They wrote in it three or four times a week as part of their in-class or homework assignment. I've asked students to use the notebook for Double-Entry Journals, dialogue journals, learning logs, and reading response logs.

The journals served as a bridge that kept me informed about what my students were learning—and not learning. They kept us connected. They enabled us to pass information back and forth and to understand each other's understandings.

I've already shown you how I would use DEJs. I designed one into the structure of each chapter in this book.

Learning logs are records of what students have learned or what they are struggling to understand. Frequently, I asked students to use their notebooks as a learning log to summarize assigned reading, whether the reading was of narrative or expository texts. I explained to them that I expected the summaries to capture the gist of what they learned from their reading. Initially, some students wrote too much detail, and some couldn't capture the essence of a reading. But, as I provided daily feedback and gave examples of logs that successfully summarized a reading, students gradually improved. Taking a few moments at the beginning of the class and as part of my checking attendance, I could walk through a classroom of 30 students to determine who did the work. If I found students who were not doing well or not doing anything, I checked their work in more detail every day. After a couple of weeks, I'd collect all the notebooks and take a few hours to read some entries more carefully. Samples of learning logs and reader response logs (presented next) can be found in chapter 3, where I document students' interpretations of Salinger's "The Laughing Man" and show how those logs became part of our negotiation over the text's meanings.

Reader response logs are closely related to learning logs. However, the response logs focus on interpreting texts and on making inferences from texts rather than on summarizing them. As a teacher committed to encouraging reader response regardless of a text's content, I wanted to make sure my students made meaning when they read and that the meaning making went beyond the literal or surface level. So, I frequently encouraged interpretation of text through a variety of strategies and activities. Frequently, I pursued subsurface meanings through probing questions that students would have to answer. These questions required students to go beneath the surface. When students read expository texts, questions required them to examine an author's assumptions, to challenge conclusions, and to weigh evidence. When students read narrative texts, questions made them analyze character and setting or to articulate and support a work's themes. Elsewhere, I've gone into more detail about how reader response can be encouraged in all the content areas (Unrau, 1997).

Dialogue journals encourage students to construct meanings for specific passages and write about those understandings. I ask students to select a passage from the text assigned and to write about their interpretation of it. I've usually accomplished this by asking students to fold a notebook page in half, transcribe the passage in the left-hand column, and provide an explanation in the right-hand column for why they selected that passage and what its meaning or significance was for them. When I read these journal entries, I get an impression of a student's engagement with a text and how much they care about understanding it.

Reading journals, as enacted in Nancy Atwell's (1998) reading workshops, consist of letters written between students and between student and teacher. These epistolary reading journals are quite different from reader response logs because they are more individually tailored to each student's personal reading. At the beginning of the school year, Atwell writes a letter to her students in which she lets them know the purposes and procedures that will govern the reading journals. The journal will be a place for each student to carry on discussions with the teacher or with friends about the "books, readings, authors, and writings. You'll think about literature in letters to me and friends; we'll write letters back to you. Our letters will become a record of the thinking, learning, and reading we did together" (p. 296).

Atwell then provides some ground rules. Letters are to be no shorter than a page and are to explore aspects of the book read, such as what the reader liked or didn't, how the author wrote, and how the reader read the book. Each student has to write at least a letter a week to Atwell or to a friend in the class. Atwell expects one letter in every 2-week period. The journal gets passed to the person to whom the letter is written. If it's to a friend in class, the writer of the letter should (usually) expect a response in 1 day. Atwell writes back to her students right after school. From Atwell's examples, a teacher can easily tell that she's having a good time learning about her students and their reading and how she can help them learn more from what they read.

A variation of Atwell's reading journal is the **two-way**, or **dialogue, journal**. With this format, student and teacher become engaged in a written conversation over not only material read but also other course content. Like the reading journal, the two-way journal is passed back and forth between student and teacher so that each gets a better idea of what the other has to say about topics being covered in class. For example, my students were doing research projects related to major issues that our society would have to face in the 21st century, such as pollution and limited energy resources. I had to keep up with what they were discovering, so I asked them to use their journals to write to me weekly. That way I would know what progress they were making and what problems they were having. I, in turn, could write back to them to encourage their successes and give suggestions to help with the problems that cropped up. The entries also served as a window through which I could observe their evolving work, and they could reflect on their project's phases.

For example, as a reader response, I might ask students to summarize and comment on coal gasification as a partial solution to our 21st-century energy crisis. A physical science or chemistry teacher might do the same by pausing in a discussion of coal gasification and asking students to summarize the process, such as that described in the text *Physical Science* (Wysession, Frank, & Yancopoulous, 2006). Students would then explain the benefits of the process and identify problems with the technology.

DEAD (Drop Everything And Draft).   I use both of these strategies spontaneously and at ANY time during class. Some teachers may call them quickwrites. If I want to know to what degree students are engaged in what I want them to learn, if I want to get students' minds reengaged, or if I want to find out what they are struggling to understand, I say, "Let's play DEAD for a few minutes." That's assuming I've already explained what I mean by playing DEAD to the class. **DEAD** stands for "drop every-thing and draft." It's a kind of time-out to reflect on what's been going on. While playing DEAD, students are to explain what they have been learning in class, how it relates to what we have already covered, what they're having trouble understanding, and/or what they'd like to hear more about so they can understand it better. Ironi-cally, playing DEAD can bring students back to life from semiconscious states.

Position Papers.   Position papers require a writer to take a stand on an issue, usu-ally a controversial one. They would be appropriate to assign before a discussion of immigration in a United States history class, genetic engineering in a biology class, or Thoreau's *Civil Disobedience* in an English class. Position papers should reflect stu-dents' opinions about a topic and include reasons that support those opinions. The position paper primes students for participation in small-group or whole-class discus-sions about issues. The writing and discussion generate perspectives and evidence that might be used in more extended written arguments. When students ask me how long these papers should be, I usually suggest 200 to 300 words—enough to get their position down along with some evidence to help it stand up.

I-Search Paper.   Ken Macrorie (1988) developed an engaging alternative to the tra-ditional research paper, namely the I-Search paper, which can be used across the con-tent areas. It's a model of exploratory writing. Students choose their own topics and learn to use primary resources, including one-on-one interviews with topic experts. While teaching the basics of research, the I-Search paper generates opportunities for deep personal connections with a topic of high interest. The research results in a first-person chronicle of discovery rather than the more distant perspective of the research paper. The I-Search paper's four sections usually include (1) a summary of what the writer already knows about the topic, (2) a description of what the writer wants to find out and why, (3) a report of the discoveries which constitute the body of the paper, and (4) a reflection on what was learned and the significance of the whole search experience to the writer.

Essays.   Our English word *essay* has its origins in the French verb *essayer*, which means to try, or to attempt. The word essay also has a very close cousin in the word *assay*, meaning to weigh. When writing an essay, we are, in a sense, trying out an idea, or weighing it. An **essay** is usually an exploration of ideas; it is a form of writing that has promoted learning for about 500 years, since Montaigne, a Frenchman, invented the personal essay and used himself as the subject of inquiry.

In many of today's middle and high schools, the dominant form of essay is the five-paragraph theme, also known as the FPT. It's been praised as a structure enabling emergent writers to organize their ideas into a coherent, readable form. But it's also been chastised as a formula for "clichés, commonplaces, and blather" (Hillocks, 2006, p. 62). There's no doubt that the FPT has been a scaffold for millions of stu-dents working their way through middle and high school writing assignments. But the FPT has also been the bane of many teachers and college instructors who have urged their students to set that Procrustean bed aside in favor of more flexible forms that open their minds to fresh perceptions and discoveries.

In comparison to writing a summary, taking notes, or answering specific ques-tions that a teacher or textbook might pose after reading a text, composing an essay involves significantly more thinking (Langer & Applebee, 1987). However, a strong relationship exists between students' topic-specific background knowledge and the quality of writing. If students' knowledge about a topic, such as the war in Vietnam or threats to the human immune system, is well organized and integrated, as compared to loosely associated, then they are more likely to write a successfully analyzed and defended thesis.

However, students can write essays of several different types to build a base of knowledge and move toward more challenging essay-writing tasks, such as the persuasive essay on a controversial issue. Students can proceed through a sequence of essay forms, such as essays that describe, explain, or compare, before they tackle the persuasive essay. As for description, students in biology can observe an insect's behavior and describe it, while students in physical education can observe a baseball or football game and depict those sporting events. When explaining, students in art can clarify how a painter has rendered a landscape, while history students can elucidate the meanings of nationalism, democracy, or diplomacy in the cold war era. In writing comparison essays, chemistry students can compare mixtures and solutions, government students can compare liberal and conservative orientations, and music students can compare rap and rock. In essays of each of these types, students can hone their skill at developing paragraphs that have effective topic sentences that promote cohesion within and between paragraphs.

For teachers developing their students' academic literacy and for students aspiring to college, writing expository prose and the persuasive essay will be ever-present challenges. Across the curriculum, students will be asked to write in response to their reading. The Pathway Project (Olsen & Land, 2007) presents teachers and their students with a method of responding to reading and writing essays that relies on explicit instruction in more than a dozen cognitive strategies. The cognitive strategies, which echo components of the writing model that began this chapter, include planning and goal setting, tapping prior knowledge, monitoring, revisiting meaning, and evaluating. Sentence starters for each of the strategies enable students to learn when and how to use them. For example, when learning about revising meaning, students complete sentences such as "At first I thought _____, but now I _____." Struggling writers and English language learners benefit from the explicit instruction because the strategies help students see what experienced writers do when they compose analytical essays and serve as stepping stones to writing sustained arguments.

Building a sustained argument stands as a significant goal, one that teachers request not only in English but also in science and social studies classes. Persuasive essays require that students formulate a thesis or central claim that will serve as a controlling idea in the development of the paper. While formulating a thesis often trumps all other troubles that students have when composing an argument, marshalling evidence to support the thesis and providing counterarguments to test the mettle of their opinions also stand as significant challenges.

Implementing Strategies

These suggested writing strategies to promote learning work best if embedded in the architecture of your classroom structure. Young (1997) makes three recommendations that serve as sensible guidelines:

1. You should integrate writing into the life of the class because it contributes to creating an interactive climate. If you do not discuss these kinds of writing activities with the class, their social and cognitive potential won't be realized. Students will view them as "tacked on."

2. You should explain to your students why you are asking them to do the writing assigned because some students may perceive it as "busywork." You are building a community in which students can explore and construct knowledge central to your discipline. Writing works well as a tool to achieve those community and knowledge-building ends.

3. You should see value in reading what you have assigned your students to write. If it's pure drudgery to you, it's unlikely to contribute to the learning community you want to create.

Writing to Observe Student Work

Few forms of student work reveal thinking and learning as transparently as writing, especially the analytic or persuasive essay. It makes thinking visible. It confirms progress in learning. It also shows breakdowns in both thinking and learning. But observing those breakdowns can provide teachers with fresh instructional challenges.

As a facilitator in seminars organized to support teachers pursuing National Board for Professional Teaching Standards Certification, I've observed how important the analysis of student work, especially student writing, has been. Through close examination of student writing, teachers strive to discover the degree to which learning goals have been achieved, to find evidence of how students are reasoning, and to discover what they could do to move students to a higher level of mastery. Content area teachers, similar to candidates for certification, can analyze their students' work to discover weaknesses in conceptual understanding and to decide what next instructional steps they can take to strengthen that understanding.

Through inquiry and reflection, teachers deepen their understanding of their students and of the impact of their instruction. Especially important is the examination of student work that reveals complex processes and problem solving, such as written documents and, better yet, portfolios of written documents, which may show the evolution of a student's writing and thinking. In general, educators and professional organizations (D. Allen, 1998) recommend an examination of individual pieces of student work, not piles of it, to describe and learn from it with colleagues—not alone. Instead of rushed discussions in hallways or lunchrooms, they encourage organized, purposeful, structured meetings set aside specifically to look at the work of their students and to converse about it.

Step-By-Step: A Protocol for Looking at Student Work

The value to participants of meeting over student work can be heightened by a couple of guidelines and a protocol to direct events (Seidel, 1998). The guidelines or rules of engagement are (a) that participants withhold judgments about the quality of the work examined and (b) that as little information as possible about the writer and the context for the writing be initially revealed. With these guidelines in place, a facilitator takes the presenter and participants through the following phases of the protocol:

Step 1. Silently, everyone reads the written text that a presenting teacher copies and brings to the session.

Step 2. Focusing first on describing the work, all participants discuss its elements.

Step 3. Participants then raise questions about the work, its author, and the context in which it was written.

Step 4. Participants next speculate on what they believe the student was working on or attempting to accomplish when the text was constructed.

Step 5. Throughout the preceding four phases, the presenter remains quiet. However, at this time, the presenter responds, adding observations about the text and answering as many of the questions raised as he can.

Step 6. As a whole group, presenter and readers weigh alternative teaching moves or instructional directions that the presenting teacher could take to support and challenge the writer of the text.

Step 7. At the end of the discussion over learning challenges to the student and instructional challenges for the teacher, the whole group reflects on the process, identifies points of satisfaction or frustration and clarification or confusion for the purpose of enhancing the next session.

Having witnessed and led teacher sessions conducted with this protocol or ones similar to it, I have learned a few things worth passing along to you.

1. Facilitators are important and require some training. If no one in your region is available to help with training facilitators, resources are available. These include a user-friendly but rigorous book, *Looking Together at Student Work* (Blythe, Allen, & Powell, 1999) designed to help teachers and teacher leaders organize student work sessions. A video of the process in action, *Looking at Student Work: A Window into the Classroom*, is also available (Annenberg Institute for School Reform, 1999). Even if seasoned teacher teams, such as those commonly formed in middle schools to serve a group of students, decide to engage in the protocol, a trained facilitator is an asset.

2. Provision of ample time for description of a student's work, discussion of instructional challenges, and review of the protocol process is essential. Too little time constricts, even frustrates, participants. I've seen teachers enter into constructive conversations, only to be stopped because time ran out or other activities were scheduled.

3. Suitable settings for the discussions contribute to the likelihood of their success. If discussions must take place in crowded, noisy facilities, teachers are less likely to concentrate and engage productively in the close reading of student work and careful analysis required by the protocol process. A relatively quiet, unperturbed room promotes the promise of these discussions over student writing.

These suggestions may help you and your colleagues engage in what I have found to be rich opportunities to gain valued insights into the work of students. Often these student work sessions clarify instructional challenges for teachers that, in turn, heighten the meaningfulness of teaching while supporting students in their growth.

Individual teachers looking at student work.   Access to student work empowers teachers. They can look closely at their students' individual performance and begin to make informed judgments about what next steps could be taken to move students closer to mastery. But what should a teacher, new or experienced, look for when looking at student work? Here are several suggested focal points for speculation, observation, and reflection:

- How has the student represented the assignment to himself or herself?
- What strategies has the student used to solve the problem(s) that the assignment presented?
- How well did the problem-solving strategies work?
- How close did the student come to meeting your learning goal or performance objective?
- What (other than failed strategies) kept students from gaining a higher level of success?
- After examining the student's work, what are all possible aspects of the work that you could pursue as teaching challenges?
- How would you rank these aspects from least to most challenging?
- Which one or two of these teaching challenges will you pursue? Why have you elected to focus on these?
- How will you pursue the most important one or two of these teaching challenges? What instructional moves will you make?
- How will you assess the degree to which your students met this new learning goal?

Teachers looking at student work to guide instructional decisions. By shifting focus from grading to observation of writing for instructional purposes, teachers begin to see what next teaching challenges make most sense for their current students. They wrestle with immediate learning problems that impede students' growth rather than plunging forward with their curricular agenda which tends to ignore the unpleasant realities of students' inability to master significant skills and knowledge.

Teacher's example of "looking at student work." I would like to share with you the work of one teacher, Maria Vega, whose findings enabled her to focus on specific teaching challenges in her ninth-grade humanities class.

Maria teaches her humanities class at Bell High School in the Los Angeles Unified School District. She described her "sheltered" class as one "designed for a wide spectrum of students." She referred to the class as "sheltered" because many of the 25 boys and 13 girls in it had recently left English Language Development (ELD) classes. Humanities traditionally covers culture, art, and literature from different periods; however, students taking the humanities course need additional help with reading and writing skills, so Maria has altered the curriculum to accommodate for their literacy needs.

The short-story writing assignment Maria gave to her class for this look at student work was part of a unit on Hispanic culture. Students had read stories from Cisneros' *The House on Mango Street* and *Woman Hollering Creek*. After they had read the latter of these, Maria asked her students to write an original folk tale that included a conflict. Part of her rationale for a series of writing assignments based on conflict came from her knowing that all ninth graders in the LAUSD would be asked to write an essay on conflict for the districtwide performance assignment. Maria explained various kinds of internal and external conflicts to her students, divided them into groups to select a conflict, and asked them to write a scenario involving the conflict they selected. Students then read these folk tales to the class, and students tried to figure out what kind of conflict the folk tale contained. This was but the first in a series of conflict exercises that led to her main assignment: a short story that turned on conflict. Students began the short story writing with a "story map worksheet" that helped students to plan their stories before beginning to write them.

When Maria got the stories back, she used a rubric to separate them into three categories. The top third consisted of "interesting, original stories." Students writing these stories recognized the centrality of conflict, had a good understanding of their task, and put in "a lot of effort." Often, writers of these stories were "gifted," or honors, students who always tried hard. The lowest third of story writers put "little or no effort into school." While understanding different conflicts, they were not excited by or interested in developing that aspect of their stories.

Maria focused on the work of one student, Hector, in the lowest category. In describing his work, she noted that he did not complete written warm-up exercises to prepare students for writing the short story, but he did participate orally. He tried to incorporate conflict, even mentioning the word as he attempted to describe a run-in between police and a group of criminals, the "Mocha Orejas," who kidnap people. After kidnapping a person, they call his family, request ransom, and, if the ransom doesn't come quickly, they cut off their victim's ear and send it home. If money doesn't come after that, other body parts arrive at the family's front door. Hector then wrote in his story that one day the police captured the leader and his band. As Maria noted, Hector did not develop his story. His writing shows that, while he struggled with sentence structure, punctuation, and spelling, he seemed most eager to be done with it "as quickly as possible." Unlike other students who asked Maria for her help, Hector turned his story in on the last day without having asked her one question.

Looking at her students' work, Maria saw many implications for her classroom practice. With regard to Hector, she would no longer take his work without his showing it to her for review before turning it in. Maria feared his shyness would prevent him from approaching her, so she thought she would pair Hector with another peer who wrote well and could work with him. She saw that in cooperative groups Hector interacted productively and contributed to the writing of the conflict scenario that each co-op team had written as another exercise.

Maria, when reflecting on the entire process of looking at her students' work, also realized that she was going to have to spend more time teaching grammar to her entire class. Because the cooperative learning activities worked well, she thought she would design grammar activities that could be done in small groups, followed by quizzes to assess how much students mastered. However, because the class included a wide spectrum of students, she worried that covering basic grammar could bore more advanced students. While Maria flirted with differentiated instruction, she was unsure of just how to make it an integral part of her diverse class. Returning to the effectiveness of small groups, she did reiterate that students may not have understood various kinds of conflict had they not been working collaboratively. Hector, in particular, "works better in groups. He seems to be more motivated." She hypothesized that, because the focus was not on him, he could blend in with the rest of the group members to get work done and ask them to clarify concepts he could not grasp.

In spite of a large, diverse class with many struggling readers and writers, Maria used her observations of student work to decide on productive instructional moves that could benefit not only the Hectors in her class but also students functioning at other levels. Rather than assigning a grade and returning the stories the students wrote, she was able to take a few additional minutes, analyze the work she witnessed, and make both short- and long-range decisions that would build essential skills and knowledge that her students will need to survive high school.

The Teacher's Dilemma: What Kind of Writing Should I Assign?

What kinds of writing assignments you give to your students will depend on several related considerations: your beliefs about what students should know and be able to do in your subject area, your state or local standards, and your commitment to knowing your students and how they learn. Once you have clarified these considerations, then you can think seriously about the role that writing will have in your classroom.

When deciding whether or not to assign writing and what kind of writing to assign, you'll need to take into consideration these benefits:

- Writing paves a pathway into a new discipline, genres specific to that discipline, its writing strategies and techniques, and the ways people think who work in those disciplines.
- Writing, including exploratory writing, should not be overlooked as a window for viewing the minds of your students, how they think, and how they process information as they create and explore new knowledge.

These alone are compelling reasons to use writing in every class.

Because every teacher in every class creates a unique teaching environment and opportunity, few generalizations about writing apply to all classrooms. However, I have some subject-specific suggestions that you may find helpful, especially if you are in your first year or two of teaching.

For English teachers, I can't emphasize enough the importance of one main message: Write, write, write. Almost all the main goals of English instruction throughout middle and high school depend on writing. If you don't write well, work on improving your writing. But don't tell your students that you either don't like to write or can't. As an English teacher, you can frequently use writing to evaluate, promote, and observe learning. And, of course, writing should be an integrated and integrating aspect of your daily instruction.

For social studies teachers, I would say almost the same thing that I've said for teachers of English. However, I know that social studies teachers also worry about covering domains of knowledge they are expected to teach and that lots of writing can impede the amount of territory they can cover in a school year. Knowing that, I still encourage you to find ways to use writing that go beyond evaluating what your students have mastered. You can use writing in the social sciences to construct knowledge, synthesize it, analyze it, and puzzle over its mysteries. All kinds of exploratory writing, such as Admit/Exit Slips or journals, will enable you to discover what your students know, how deeply they know it, and how they have made connections or seen patterns. And it can help you understand how they think and reason so that you can promote their critical reflection.

For science teachers, the potential for writing is limitless. In a practical vein, students need to learn how to compose lab reports. That is one essential skill to master on their way to understanding the scientific method and entering a scientific field. But writing can serve in several other important ways in the science classroom. Focused freewrites for the first 5 or 8 minutes in biology, for example, can open you and your students to the adventure and excitement of discovery. They can also provide you with opportunities for insights into the lives and minds of your students. That's what John Dorroh's (1993) Expressive Model (EM) notebooks did for him as his students wrote about viruses or enzymes or scores of other biology topics. Dorroh wrote with his students and sometimes read aloud his entries along with theirs. He believes that writing-based instruction enlivened his classroom and enabled him to bond with students as he never had before.

For teachers of math, writing can be a hard sell. In part, that is because new teachers of math may never have had a math teacher who used writing creatively to promote learning mathematics. However, researchers on writing in the math classroom have looked at student-generated questions, journal writing, written explanations, and other forms of expressive writing. They are, as Menon (1998) notes, "unanimous" in their support of writing to learn mathematics. The effects included increased student ownership, improved monitoring and diagnosis of learning difficulties, diminished math anxiety, and heightened motivation. Writing can also promote key ideas contained in the National Council of Teachers of Mathematics (NCTM) *Principles and Standards for School Mathematics* (NCTM, 2000). Among those principles are that students communicate mathematical concepts clearly and coherently, that they organize arguments, and that they understand their own and other's problem-solving processes. Writing serves as a means to those ends. Joseph and Nancy Martinez (2001) suggest several writing activities for middle and high school math instruction. Students keep logs in which they describe the step-by-step process they use to solve problems along with commentaries, write and solve each other's math word problems, and practice translating math terminology into everyday language. When writing process logs, students use a format Joseph and Nancy Martinez developed that includes several question prompts, such as the following:

- How many steps are involved in this problem?
- What mathematical operations are involved?
- What will you do first?
- Then what?

By completing these worksheets, students translate math concepts and procedures into ordinary language.

I've shown how writing can be productively used not only in English classes, but also in social studies, science, and math classes; it can also be used similarly in other content areas. I've known many teachers of art, music, health, vocational technology, and physical education who have designed and implemented exciting programs with writing as a tool to achieve their ends. Teachers of art have students keep journals that describe the effects of new drawing, painting, or ceramic techniques they've learned. Music teachers use writing to keep in contact with performance progress and troubles of students in bands, orchestras, and choirs. Students in health classes use writing to explore their understanding of health issues, such as diets, sexually transmitted diseases, and anger management. Teachers of woodworking, metal shop, or electronics have students describe in their own words techniques demonstrated in class. And physical education teachers ask athletes to keep records of their workout programs, their performance on teams, and their attitudes toward competition. In all these content areas, writing serves to create bonds between student and teacher while contributing to the development of knowledgeable learning communities.

Responding to Writing

One of the points of resistance among teachers when it comes to making decisions about whether or not to assign writing for any purpose (for evaluation or exploration) is the problem of responding to it. Multiple-choice and short-answer tests, while providing little information about how your students think or learn, do have an overwhelming strength: They are relatively easy to grade. Asking students to write for any reason activates a network of more complicated questions: What will I ask them to write about? How much will I ask them to write? How will I support or guide their writing? How will I respond to their papers? In effect, this last question is so overwhelming to some teachers that they completely avoid assigning any significant written work of any kind.

Helpfully, Peter Elbow (1997) suggests we look at assigning and responding to writing along a continuum from the lowest to the highest stakes. Low-stakes assignments are usually nonevaluative, such as freewrites, DEJs, journals, logs, and other forms of exploratory writing. They get students more involved in the content of the course, show us how they approach that content, and tell us about how well they understand it. Furthermore, they encourage students to keep up with their reading for the course because they usually have to read assignments in order to write about them. High-stakes writing assignments, such as essays that culminate a unit or that we use on an exam to assess mastery, are more likely to fall in the category of informational writing.

As for responding to writing, Elbow (1997) again envisions a low- to high-stakes continuum that includes the following:

- zero response (lowest stakes),
- minimal, nonverbal, noncritical response,
- supportive response—no criticism,
- descriptive or observational response,
- minimal, nonverbal critical response, and
- critical response with diagnosis and advice for improvement (highest stakes).

As you would suppose, there are links between low-stakes assignments and low-stakes response. For example, low-stakes assignments, such as freewrites that provide students with opportunities to create and explore meanings, correspond with low-stakes responses, such as simply reading the freewrite or giving it a check mark, a minimal and noncritical response. While some teachers try to set up a system whereby low-stakes writing activities are not graded, I would recommend that you devise a grading scheme for them. I used a ✓ +, ✓, ✓ −, 0 system for daily writing activities and found it amenable to my grading methods. A 4, 3, 2, 1 scoring system would work as well. You may want to explore alternative methods of evaluating and grading exploratory writing assignments.

Over the years, I discovered productive solutions to the pile of students' written papers waiting for my attention each week. Here are a few suggestions that kept my students writing and helped me maintain a sense that my time was being well used for the purpose of improving my students' writing and thinking:

- Rather than giving extensive commentary on all papers, provide a quick-grade system, such as check, check-plus, or check-minus, for selected assignments.

- If you use peer-editing procedures, provide well-structured feedback sheets so that students can fill them out in detail.

- Develop and use rubrics that you give to students before they compose papers you assign. That way they know what criteria you will apply to the evaluation of their papers. You can then assign grades from 1 to 4 or 1 to 6 based on the dimensions of the rubric you develop. Of course, grading with rubrics doesn't give students the detailed commentary they need to make specific kinds of corrections and to improve. However, rubrics work well for many assignments. You can add commentary and make specific corrections as you see fit.

- Develop minilessons and miniassignments to help students with writing problems that appear on many papers. If several students are writing fragments or comma splices, then develop a 10- or 15-minute lesson to address a specific problem. Expect, however, that one minilesson may not solve the problem.

- If you have a choice, don't assign major writing projects that come due in all classes at the same time. Schedule assignment deadlines so that you can comfortably manage the paper load.

- Explain to students that they will be writing more than you can read and grade because you want them to write as much as possible. Explain that you will read and grade only one out of two or even three lengthy, written assignments. Explain to them that you may select any of the papers they write for possible grading.

- Read selectively. Identify a limited number of elements you will address in responding to a paper. For example, if a student is having problems with topic sentences, then focus on that issue: Point out paragraphs lacking topic sentences, provide sample topic sentences, or ask a student to compose topic sentences for paragraphs needing them and to resubmit the paper before giving it a grade.

- Write your comments in pencil. It not only looks less intimidating than a red pen, it also can be erased if you want to change the way you have framed a suggestion after reading it to yourself.

- If you provide commentary for corrections and want to make sure students read and learn from your recommendations, ask students to correct their errors or submit revisions (with the previous draft) *before* you give out a grade. All too often, teachers will spend hours writing suggestions for improvement, give papers back to students, and discover that students ignore those hours of work. Students are less likely to ignore your work if they don't get a grade until they act on your corrections and commentary by submitting a revision that reflects or incorporates your recommendations.

In closing, I want to share with you a hope. I customarily ask teachers with whom I work if they use writing in their content area classes. Many say they do. However, many don't. Here are five answers I've heard from teachers when I've asked them about using writing in their classes:

1. I don't teach writing. English teachers do that.
2. I don't have time to read piles of students' writing.
3. Our state testing program is forcing us to teach to the test. It doesn't ask students to write anything about my content area.

4. If I start having students write in my class, we're going to get too far behind in the curriculum. My colleagues will wind up with students unprepared for next year's content. And you know who'll get blamed?

5. Students don't expect to do much—if any—writing in my course. They think it's weird if I assign writing in _____. (Fill in the blank: math, science, history, health, physical education, music, art, etc.)

I hope that, after reading this chapter, these will not be among the answers you would give me if I were to ask you, "Do you use writing in your classes to help students and yourself learn?"

Summary

In this chapter, we reviewed four major developments in education over the past 30 years that contributed to the expansion of writing in all subject areas:

- Research has given us a better understanding of writing processes and models that explain how writers compose texts.
- More teachers have adopted a process approach to teaching writing that encourages students to construct knowledge and develop as writers.
- The belief that writing holds considerable potential as a tool for learning across the curriculum is one research has confirmed and teachers can transform into classroom practice.
- The National Writing Project provides teacher-to-teacher instruction and support for infusing and improving writing across all grades and subject areas.

Although research has shown that writing is most frequently assigned to assess learning, teachers can use writing to help students explore and make sense of ideas. Meanwhile, teachers can transform themselves from evaluators of learning to collaborators in learning. Many writing activities, beside summary and analytical writing, promote learning. These include Admit Slips/Exit Passes, freewrites, Question Papers, Skeletons, RAFTing, and a variety of journals and logs. All these forms of writing that promote learning also provide teachers with opportunities to observe their students' learning and to use those observations to guide further instruction.

Double-Entry Journal: After Reading

After reviewing your before-reading DEJ, what additional activities might you add to your list of strategies to help your students learn? What kinds of writing would you assign in your content area? How would you use writing in your content area to assess learning?

CRITICAL READING OF PRINT AND NONPRINT TEXTS

After reading chapter 8, you should be able to answer the following questions:

1. Why do students need to read print and electronic texts more critically?

2. What conceptions of critical thinking apply productively to improve critical reading?

3. What activities foster critical reading?

4. What is critical literacy, how is it different from critical thinking, and how can it heighten students' "critical consciousness"?

5. How does media literacy contribute to the critical reading of nonprint texts?

Double-Entry Journal: Before Reading

If you "shift gears" into reading texts more critically, under what circumstances does that shift occur? What do you do differently when you read critically? How would you teach your students critical reading of print and nonprint texts in your content area?

The Need for More Critical Reading

Even though about 3 out of 4 students in 8th grade and 12th grade develop basic reading skills appropriate to their grade level (Mullis, Campbell, & Farstrup, 1993), only about 3 in 100 perform at advanced levels. At these advanced levels, readers analyze meanings and explicitly support their analysis with examples. In addition, they make connections between the texts they read and their understanding of the world. They can "synthesize and critically examine information" in texts as well as demonstrate strength in dealing "objectively and critically" with the text (p. 85).

Throughout middle and high school, students are expected to read hundreds of pages of informational texts that provide them with knowledge about history, geography, government, mathematics, biology, chemistry, health, and other fields. The majority of students reading informational texts at the basic level can identify the central purpose of straightforward texts. They can understand explicitly stated information and can connect information given at different points in a text's development. However, very few of these students can compare and contrast information within a text, draw upon knowledge from other areas, or form opinions about what they've read and use evidence from it to support their opinions. For example, only a very small percentage of students can read different accounts of a similar event, such as the battle of Lexington, decide which passage they would select as most reliable, and provide reasons for their choice based on information in the passage.

Critical reading is an essential element of academic literacy that students should acquire before they complete high school and must exhibit if they are to succeed in college. Unfortunately, a major disconnect exists between the reading expectations of most high school faculty and university faculty (American College Testing, 2006; Intersegmental Committee of the Academic Senates, 2002; Kirst, 2004; Biancarosa & Snow, 2004). For example, of nearly 40,000 first-time freshmen who entered the California State University system of 23 campuses in the 2004–2005 academic year, more than 60% (25,000 students) were required to take remedial education in English, math, or both. All these freshmen had earned a GPA of at least a B in high school, and all had completed a required college preparatory program of study. This disconnection between high school and college expectations erodes the potential of students to succeed in college, especially those students in lower income categories.

What does the academic faculty at colleges and universities expect of their entering students when they are asked to read texts? For some, academic literacy means the integrated and interactive skills of critical reading, writing, listening, and thinking that depend upon "students' abililty to postpone judgment and tolerate ambiguity as they honor the dance between passionate assertion and patient inquiry" (ICAS,

2002, p. 12). The vast majority of faculty surveyed believe that students should demonstrate the following dispositions:

- exhibit curiosity,
- experiment with new ideas,
- see others' points of view,
- challenge their own beliefs,
- ask provocative questions, and
- read with awareness of self and others.

These findings, expanded and clarified through discussion, led the committee to agree on the habits of mind students need to engage in appropriate college level discussion. While students need to define, summarize, explain, evaluate, compare/contrast, and analyze texts, they also need to identify the range of logical, emotional, and personal appeals that appear in arguments.

Members of California's intersegmental committee (ICAS, 2002) saw specific kinds of reading competencies as essential to students' success in college classes. Students should be able, first, to read for literal comprehension and retention, second, to read for depth of understanding, and third, to read for analysis and interaction with the text. Unfortunately, faculty surveyed reported that only about half of their students were prepared to provide even brief summaries of their readings. About two thirds of their students were not prepared to synthesize information from multiple texts. And two thirds were unable to analyze information or arguments following their own reading of assignments.

The reasons that students are underprepared for the critical reading expected of them upon entry into our nations' colleges and universities are not difficult to surmise (ICAS, 2002). First, reading is not an actively sought, encouraged, or supported aspect of teenagers screen-dominated world. Second, after learning to read, students' instruction in more sophisticated, higher order reading strategies are usually quite limited. Third, while secondary faculty across the curriculum should be involved in developing more sophisticated reading strategies, teaching critical reading of expository text explicitly usually occurs in English classes, if it occurs in any classroom throughout the middle and high school years.

The results of high school testing programs given by organizations such as ACT (2006) also indicate that the reading readiness of high school graduates for academic pursuits is "currently inadequate." While only about half of all ACT-tested high school graduates were ready for college-level reading, that fraction dropped precipitously in some minority and low-income groups. Among Hispanics and students from families with incomes less than $30,000, only one in three was prepared for college-level reading.

The ACT Reading Test includes texts reflecting three degrees of difficulty: uncomplicated, more challenging, and complex. While performance on complex texts differentiates most clearly between students likely to succeed and those not likely to succeed in college, students' performance on complex texts is weakest. Complex texts have several aspects that make them complex. They exhibit interaction among ideas or characters that are subtle or involved, and they convey information through literary devices or empirical data. Their text structure is more elaborate, even unconventional. Vocabulary is demanding and highly dependent on context, and their authors' purpose may be implicit or ambiguous. These characteristics of complex texts are often encountered in academic reading assignments in college and university classes.

The selection from a social science textbook in Figure 8.1 illustrates what ACT terms a complex level of text. The text is rich in concepts, terms, and names, lacks an obvious immediate thesis, has several uncommon words, and requires careful reading to discover its structure and central concern about the degree to which sociology is a science.

With regard to arguments, such as those formulated for newspaper and magazine editorials, many students have difficulty detecting patterns in their development and identifying claims made in them. Like many of her classmates, Allison, the pseudonym for an 11th grader I taught, had trouble analyzing arguments. She often struggled to identify the thesis in an argument. She also had problems sorting through, classifying, and evaluating the quality of evidence used to support a thesis after we had identified it. Like many of her classmates who tended to view text as authority, she rarely paused to reflect upon and examine the assumptions or values that were beneath the claims or the selection of evidence to support those claims. She also avoided a careful consideration of counterclaims and counterevidence. More importantly, she had rarely been encouraged to read so that she could construct different perspectives of a written argument to compare their relative merits.

Figure 8.1   Example of a "Complex" Text Used in the ACT Reading Test.

Discussions over whether or not human behavior differs from all other forms of animal behavior have been a part of sociology from its beginning. During the late 1930s, when sociology finally became accepted in the academic establishment, the question took on new importance. George A. Lundberg, the most famous and articulate spokesperson for the school that views sociology as a pure science (like physics), was roundly criticized by Robert M. MacIver, a sociologist who for many years had maintained that human life is unique and that therefore the methods of a science of society must be distinct from those of other sciences. . . .

That particular debate has never been fully resolved, nor can it be. The behavior of human beings is, no doubt, exceedingly complex when compared to that of many other forms of life. Yet even if we accept the notion that human behavior is unique, many of the assumptions of a science of society are still valid. The scientific demands for rigor and careful collection of data are very much a part of sociology. It is in this sense that almost all scholars agree sociology is a science. Practitioners of the discipline are careful to back their statements about behavior with observations. It is not enough to state that you feel or think that the middle class believes this or that. It is necessary, if you are acting as a scientist, to (1) define what you mean by "the middle class" and (2) describe the procedures you used in collecting and analyzing the data that led you to make a particular statement about the beliefs of that group.

What we are noting here is that science is, in part, a system which requires rigorous and precise definitions as well as empirical (observational) evidence. Utilizing such a system of organized facts, collected in an agreed-upon and repeatable manner, sociologists have gathered an impressive amount of information over the years. They can explain what groups tend to behave in certain ways and why. They can demonstrate that much of what is thought to be common sense and "a known fact" may really be nonsensical and factually inaccurate when examined in a scientific manner. . . .

Source: Adapted from R. W. Smith and F. W. Preston, *Sociology: An Introduction.* © 1977 by St. Martin's Press, Inc. (Sample has been reproduced with permission from ACT. Contact: Pat Farrant, Assistant Vice President, ACT Communications. E-mail address: patricia.farrant@act.org. Permission granted 5/3/06.)

The explosion of information available over the Internet and on thousands of Web sites creates a myriad of opportunities for students like Allison to be misinformed and manipulated. Exercising common sense when it comes to cyberspace messages intended to dupe readers may be the best way to exorcise electronic hoaxes and tomfoolery. But the mindful reading of more extended informative and argumentative texts requires something more: the development of skills and application of strategies for more critical responses to texts.

Although many of us would like to promote the capacity of our students to read more mindfully at advanced levels, we have known for decades that they only infrequently engage in thoughtful, critical reading (*A Nation at Risk,* 1983; Applebee, Langer, & Mullis, 1985, 1988; Boyer, 1983). In a "report card" compiled for the NAEP and entitled *Who Reads Best?,* Applebee et al. (1988, p.11) noted that, while proficient readers have a variety of "meaning-making strategies," efforts to improve students' ability "to reason more effectively about what they read" ought to be one of the schools' central goals. Students, they write, "must develop the ability to synthesize, analyze, and extend their ideas and their knowledge."

Research shows that students, such as those with basic reading strengths, could benefit from programs and strategies that empower them to read informative and argumentative texts more adequately, more thoroughly, more constructively, and with a well thought out plan.

What Is Critical Reading?

When considering what helps students read more critically, I inevitably plunge into a closely related field: critical thinking. Critical thinking has been around for a very long time. Some teachers model their critical thinking program on Socrates' methods of questioning, methods he used to pursue "truth" about 2,500 years ago. In classrooms today, the level of importance given to critical thinking depends on one central factor: how the classroom teacher's mind works. If you are disposed to thinking critically, if you pursue reasons, look at things from multiple perspectives, seek, apply, and monitor strategies, evaluate the consequences of your beliefs and decisions, and reflect on your thinking and that of others, then critical thinking will be at high water marks, and your students will flourish under thoughtful teaching.

But what is critical thinking and how does it help us develop a clearer idea of critical reading? Critical thinking has been defined in several different ways, most of which share common concepts such as analysis, reasoning, and the weighing of evidence. In *Thoughtful Teachers, Thoughtful Learners* (Unrau, 1997), I drew upon the work of Robert Ennis (1996) and defined **critical thinking** as "reasoned reflection on the meaning of claims about what to believe and what to do." For example, if a writer asserts that a state law creating a publicly funded preschool program for all 4-year-olds will help more children learn to read by third grade and reduce drop-out rates so more students will graduate from high school, a critical reader begins to comb through the argument to clarify and examine the meanings of these claims and the evidence that supports them.

In spite of universal preschool being an appealing idea, critical readers and thoughtful voters who evaluate a preschool program proposal should examine it closely to weigh its costs and benefits:

- What kind of preschool program is the writer proposing?
- What are the benefits of a preschool program to students?

- Will it really improve student performance in school as students progress through the grades?
- Will it reduce grade retention or special education designations?
- How long will the benefits persist as students proceed through their school years?
- Will it be an equalizer of opportunity for low-income families?
- Will it reduce dropouts in high school?
- How many children already attend preschool?
- What percentage of increase in preschool attendance is the program likely to bring about?
- How much would the program cost?
- How would it be funded?
- What if the method of financing proposed doesn't provide enough funding?
- What possible impact, such as a depleted teacher pool, could the program have on K–12 instruction?
- Are there better ways to improve educational achievement, perhaps by providing extended tutoring for struggling learners during the early grades or family literacy programs?
- Does the writer presenting the preschool proposal address counterarguments to the proposal?
- Is the writer biased, and do biases affect the writer's assessment of the program's value and effectiveness?

As these questions indicate, when engaged in critical thinking, readers use strategies to analyze and to evaluate, at deeper levels, the claims made in texts.

Like many other educators promoting teaching for thinking, I never believed that simply teaching skills and strategies to enable critical thinking would be sufficient for the development of thoughtful, reflective students or critical readers. The development of students' motivation and dispositions to engage in productive thinking and critical reading is essential. Students must develop a desire to think and read critically, but there seems to be no quick-fix strategy that will spark that desire. If you can start or detect a small flame burning in your students, that flame must be fed. Initiating that flame can be viewed as a teaching triumph and fanning it, a victory.

No device for igniting a skeptical spirit of critical reflection when reading books, watching evening news, or facing any of life's choices is foolproof. However, you serve as a model of thoughtful learning, as a provider of effective thinking and reading strategies, and as an encourager for engagement in critical responses to texts. When responding to texts through demonstrations, such as think-alouds, you can reveal your thinking about that text's contents and context, show students what claims should be thoughtfully examined, and demonstrate your search for valid evidence to support those claims. Besides providing models of thinking for students to emulate, you can also directly teach strategies to take arguments apart, lay out their pieces, and make judgments about each part's value to the whole. Furthermore, you can encourage signs of thoughtful response that students manifest to all kinds of texts. You can create and nourish classroom climates for questioning, analysis, and reflection that help each of your students become a more self-regulated thinker and learner.

Jason Agliolo, one of my former students, teaches trigonometry at Bell Gardens High School. I watched a video of Jason trying to teach his students, many of whom are English learners, how to use trigonometry functions (sine, cosine, tangent ratios) to solve real-world problems. As he put it, most of his students "decode quite rapidly and actually string sentences together quite cohesively, but their understanding of meaning is often lacking." That presents Jason with one of his instructional challenges. How can students read a math problem to detect essential information, transform that information into visual images to represent the problem, and then solve it?

To help his students transform text into drawings, Jason first models how he constructs meaning from the word problem, depicts the problem pictorially, and solves it. When constructing meaning, he reads and rereads the problem aloud, asks himself questions about it that the class hears, and draws a representation that reflects the language of the word problem. As he does so, he demonstrates critical reading by reasoning about the meaning of claims made in the problem, making connections between its parts, and, after creating a picture on the board, checking for evidence in the language of the word problem to confirm the accuracy of his picture.

Then he asks several students to read another similar problem aloud and showers them with questions. By doing so, he said that his students "develop a sense of ownership in the process and begin to take some stock in the meaning negotiation process." After several readings of the problem and a battery of questions about it, one of Jason's students goes to the board, follows his demonstration of pictorially representing the problem, checks its accuracy, and solves it.

As teachers, we are challenged every day during every class to observe the quality and effectiveness of our students' approaches to problems and decision making. This detective work will enable us to see what works well for our students and where improvements could be made. In a graduate course I've taught to promote teaching for thinking, I ask teachers of math, science, foreign languages, and just about every other subject to watch and record their students' thought processes and reasoning—especially when patterns of ineffective problem solving and thinking begin to appear. By reflecting on students' thinking, you can discern problems in cognition that you could then address. One math teacher, for example, saw that students in his eighth-grade honors class were so eager to get to the right answer that they usually did not show their work. Without seeing the steps they took to solve problems, he could not detect errors in their thinking. With a few adjustments, such as giving credit only for homework assignments that showed all the steps students used in their problem solving, checking homework regularly, and returning it promptly, he detected several errors in students' problem-solving performance and guided his students toward visible improvements.

Activities to Foster Critical Reading

Inquiry Questions (IQs)

"The important thing," said Albert Einstein, "is not to stop questioning." We can help students avoid this dark risk by using inquiry questions. **Inquiry Questions (IQs)** are intended to encourage readers to ask themselves questions as they read and learn. IQs are based on Bloom's (1956) *Taxonomy of Educational Objectives,* in particular those in the cognitive domain. Bloom hypothesized the existence of six cognitive domains that have gone on to influence both the development of curriculum and its assessment: knowledge, comprehension, application, analysis, synthesis, and evaluation. Frequently, thinking in the last three of these domains is referred to as *higher order* thinking. However, we can help develop more mindful readers through the asking of questions in all domains.

Educators who have written objectives for units or lessons have usually become familiar with Bloom's taxonomy of cognitive objectives. For nearly 50 years, the taxonomy has helped teachers clarify their purposes for teaching. The cognitive domains are reviewed in the Strategy in Practice, and associated stem words that you can use to develop IQs are given. You can use these stem words to explore and deepen your students' reading assignments and to demonstrate to students how they can continually question whatever they read.

Step-By-Step: Inquiry Questions (IQs)

Step 1. Identify the passage(s) that students are to read and study.

Step 2. Based on the six cognitive objects, decide what topics and concepts you want your students to be able to recall, understand, apply, take apart, put together in novel ways, and evaluate.

Step 3. Formulate questions based on different cognitive objectives that will facilitate inquiry into topics and concepts you deem essential. As you form these questions, keep in mind that you can use the stem words in the Strategy in Practice to prompt your question generation for the various objectives.

Step 4. Use your IQs to guide and strengthen your inquiry with your students.

Step 5. As a follow-up to students' learning, develop activities, projects, text prompts, and problems that will enable you to assess the degree to which your students have mastered the topics and concepts explored through your IQ-guided discussion.

Strategy in Practice

INQUIRY QUESTIONS: FOSTERING CRITICAL THINKING

COGNITIVE DOMAIN	STEM WORDS FOR QUESTIONS	EXAMPLES OF INQUIRY QUESTIONS (IQS)
Knowledge: The recall or remembering of information learned previously. Includes facts as well as generalizations.	Who, what, when, where, retell, list, define, name, state, etc.	What is the Pythagorean theorem? How would you define ecology?

Comprehension: The understanding or grasping of facts and ideas without connecting them to other concepts or seeing their implications.	Explain, which, predict, illustrate, summarize, what, conclude, rephrase.	How would you illustrate the order of operations? What would you include in a summary of the Declaration of Independence? What do you predict will happen next?
Application: Use of knowledge, including ideas or procedures, in new contexts.	Apply, solve, test, how, demonstrate.	How would you use the FOIL method to multiply polynomials?
Analysis: Taking apart or breaking down knowledge to reveal its hidden structure, as in reading between the lines.	Analyze, classify, categorize, how, explain, what, discriminate.	What are the differences between comedy and tragedy? What are the facts and opinions expressed in this argument about global warming?
Synthesis: Putting together or combining old knowledge into new forms.	Create, formulate, make up, suggest.	How would you formulate an argument supporting the view that all students should become critical readers?
Evaluation: Judging the value or worth of material used for specific purposes.	Judge, assess, defend, evaluate.	How would you evaluate Darwin's *Origin of Species?* How would you defend standards-based instruction?

Paul Perez, a high school music teacher, developed the following set of IQs to use with students who had read about jazz trumpeter Louis Armstrong and listened to several of his recordings, including those with Ella Fitzgerald and Bing Crosby:

1. What experience did Armstrong gain while playing second trumpet in Joe "King" Oliver's band? (Knowledge)

2. Why is the role of the second trumpet important in a song's harmonic structure? (Comprehension)

3. How would you demonstrate that Armstrong's use of harmony in the King Oliver band is similar to his harmonic singing with Ella Fitzgerald or Bing Crosby? (Application)

4. How would you explain the differences between a melodic line and a harmonic line? (Analysis)

5. How did Armstrong's experience as a second trumpet player in his early career benefit him in his later sessions with Bing Crosby and Ella Fitzgerald? (Synthesis)

6. How effective was Armstrong's use of harmony as a second trumpeter and singer in terms of form and aesthetics? (Evaluation)

Paul gave his last IQ to his students as a prompt for an essay in which they were to present their opinions and support them with reference to readings and recordings.

Questioning the Author (QtA)

Questioning the author (QtA), a teaching strategy developed by Beck et al. (1997), is intended to help students engage in the thoughtful construction of texts. Researchers found that using QtA brought about several changes in classroom interaction, including students talking twice as much as they had in traditional classrooms while initiating more questions, comments, and student-to-student interactions. Although the strategy can be used with both expository and narrative texts, we are going to explore QtA's use in helping students to comprehend and question more challenging expository texts.

The primary purpose for QtA is to shift your work from checking for comprehension by asking comprehension-type questions ("What . . . ?) to helping your students construct and explore meanings. Rather than encouraging a view of text as given authority in black and white, you can use QtA to present texts as some person's ideas in writing that may not always be clear and comprehensible. Authors (except this one, of course) are fallible.

I'll present the procedure for QtA in the following four sections: queries, planning, discussion, and implementation. The Strategy in Practice summarizes the QtA procedure.

Strategy in Practice

QUESTIONING THE AUTHOR

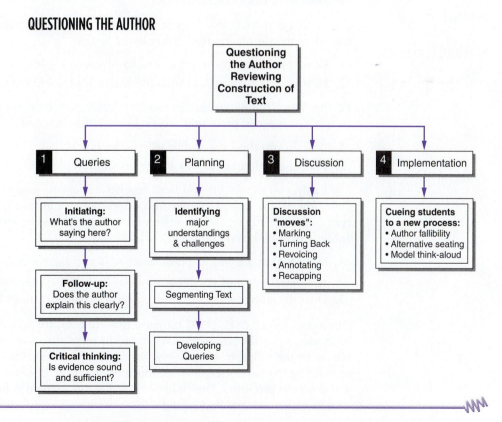

Queries.   **Queries**, unlike many teacher-made questions, are not intended to evaluate readers' understanding of a text. Rather, they are intended to help students grasp ideas presented in a text, be used while students read the text, facilitate discussion about the author's ideas, and support student-to-student dialogue. Analysis and engagement are the desired effects of queries that are designed to make students do more work on meaning construction.

For our focus on expository texts, queries are of two major kinds: Initiating and Follow-up. **Initiating queries** are intended to open the text to classwide construction of meaning, understanding, and discussion by focusing on central text ideas. Their purpose is to provide guidance for inquiry and exploration. To initiate meaning construction work on the part of students, Beck and her associates (1997) recommend three types of initiating queries:

1. What is the author trying to say here?
2. What is the author's message?
3. What is the author talking about?

Follow-up queries are intended to provide focus and guide the discussion while helping students to integrate meanings and make connections with other ideas. The questions that you ask are intended to urge readers to look more deeply into an author's language and network of ideas. Follow-up queries, such as the following two suggested by Beck et al. (1997), urge students to look beneath the surface of the author's words:

1. What does the author mean here?
2. Does the author explain this clearly?

Follow-up queries can also prompt students to make connections with stored knowledge or with information read earlier in the text:

1. Does this make sense when related to what you know about this topic?
2. How does this connect to what the author told us before?

Furthermore, follow-up queries, such as these, can help readers speculate on an author's purpose in providing certain information in a text:

1. Why do you think the author tells us this now?
2. Does the author tell us why this information is given?

Lastly, you can go beyond Beck and her associates' query types by guiding students toward the critical examination of positions an author takes, directly or indirectly, about a topic. These suggested **critical thinking queries** can probe an author's reasoning and marshalling of evidence:

1. If the author is trying to persuade us of something, what do you think that is?
2. Why has the author organized his ideas as they are presented in the text?
3. Does the author give us enough evidence to support his or her conclusions?

Planning.   Beck et al. (1997) suggest that we compare preparing to use QtA with rehearsing a play for production. When producing a play, director and actors carefully take apart the script, make decisions about actors' movements on stage, and practice responding to cues. Directors have much to anticipate in terms of audience reaction and potential problems. How a director and actors prepare radically affects what audiences experience and understand.

You will act as both director and performer when engaged in preparing and presenting a QtA lesson. As director, you "block" (or decide) what will be discussed and anticipate how a lesson will play on the classroom stage. Because teachers, like actors, cannot know in advance what will develop during the performance, you must be ready to improvise.

Planning entails three distinct phases: (a) identifying major understandings and potential problems, (b) segmenting text, and (c) developing queries.

1. *Identifying major understandings and potential problems.* Like a director and an actor, you begin working with a text by giving it a close reading. One of the purposes of the close reading is to identify the major understandings that students should gain from reading the text. The second purpose is to anticipate and solve potential problems that may arise in teaching the text, including difficult concepts or dense passages. Accomplishing these dual purposes clears the way for the author's entry into the classroom and sets the stage for a conversation that engages readers with the author. The core of that conversation is Questioning the Author.

2. *Segmenting text.* Following a close reading of the text, identifying major understandings, and anticipating problems with the text's comprehension, you next segment the text. By segmenting a text, Beck et al. (1997) mean identifying stop points at which you'll initiate questioning and discussion. Major understandings you want your students to gain drive decisions about where to segment. At times, a single sentence that has a bearing on a major understanding may signal a stop point. Much longer passages and sets of paragraphs may be summarily dealt with. Asterisks in the text can be used to identify segments.

3. *Developing queries.* Queries, as we have already learned, are of several kinds. Initiating queries launch discussions. Follow-up queries help students look beneath the text's surface, make intertextual connections, speculate on an author's purposes, and, in general, deepen discussion and the exploration of the text. Critical thinking queries guide students into an examination of an author's reasoning, organization of evidence, and conclusions based on that reasoning and evidence.

Discussion.   Beck et al. (1997) draw an analogy between solving a maze and comprehending a text. However, instead of leading your students through the maze, you'll support their own maze journey, their own meaning construction, as they work toward the goal of understanding. Discussions are where students do much of the work of making sense of the text.

During QtA discussions, students work together with each other and with you to build ideas that are discovered in the text. Discussions have two components: your role and your students' contributions. Students are active participants who develop and connect ideas encountered in the text. They share in the investigation and construction of meaning.

You will use your planning to motivate and guide students' contributions rather than to dominate the classroom discussion. You guide students in the exploration of ideas, think ideas through in relation to the text, and extend them, where possible. As you differentiate among all the students' contributions, you shepherd those contributions toward the goal of meaning construction.

Beck and her associates (1997) describe six kinds of discussion moves that you can apply to orchestrate and promote your students' comprehension and questioning of the text: marking, turning back, revoicing, modeling, annotating, and recapping.

1. *Marking.* You use marking to draw attention to particular ideas that are critical to major understandings. You may mark a student's contribution by echoing the observation or by explicitly acknowledging that someone is on to something significant, as in stating that a student is making a "very important point." Through marking you send a signal to readers that an idea is of special value.

2. *Turning back.* Turning back has a couple of meanings. On the one hand, it refers to turning responsibility back to readers for digging more deeply into ideas and clarifying their meaning. Teachers using this form of turning back often guide students toward idea elaboration and interconnection with other students' meanings. When used another way, turning back refers to turning students' attention back to the text in order to clarify their thinking. This could occur when students make statements about the meaning of a text that the text itself contradicts. In either meaning of turning back, you should avoid jumping in to explain the text's meaning. You should, however, transfer responsibility for understanding to students.

3. *Revoicing.* When you *revoice*, you interpret what students are saying about a text and echo the ideas you hear, as you do when you "listen actively." This helps students express their ideas so that they become part of the discussion.

   While marking, turning back, and revoicing are discussion interventions that nudge your students toward meaning construction, the next three moves engage you more directly in the meaning construction process.

4. *Modeling.* Through modeling, you attempt to make visible to students reading processes that are usually invisible. By revealing these reading processes, you provide opportunities for students to imitate questioning, intertextual links, and expert problem solving while grappling with text construction. When doing a comprehension think-aloud, Mrs. Silva explained her understanding of "Sea Fever" through an intertextual connection with a young adult novel about a girl who makes a life-changing voyage to America (see chapter 4). Without making her thinking visible, we could never see how her mind made meaning, and students might not realize how their intertextual links contribute to comprehension.

5. *Annotating.* When annotating, you offer information to students that an author may have left out of the text. Without that information, students would encounter grave difficulties in constructing appropriate meanings for the text. The information could include not only fleshing out assumptions but also making tricky connections in reasoning.

6. *Recapping.* When students are ready to consolidate their understanding of a text and move on to the next passages, you can use this discussion move. By summarizing major understandings and concepts, you signal students that they have grasped the essentials and are ready to progress further. You can also call on your students to recap, a move that extends responsibility to the class members for constructing and organizing text meanings.

Implementation. Because QtA varies from traditional text-oriented questioning for comprehension, you can provide cues to students that they are about to engage in a more active classroom reading process. One way to send that message is to begin by presenting to students the idea of "author fallibility" and the notion that texts are merely an author's ideas in print. Authors may not always present knowledge in easily understood language, so students will sometimes have to work very hard to construct appropriate meanings when texts seem confusing and hard to read.

Another way to cue students is to put them in a new configuration in the classroom. Beck and her associates (1997) suggest using a U-shape seating arrangement that helps students watch and interact with each other while providing easier teacher movement among students during discussion.

A third cue to prepare students for QtA is to present a model think-aloud with a text that you feel will be challenging for your students. After selecting, reading for major understandings, and segmenting the text, you can show the students how to construct meaning together through discussion. The purpose of the modeling here is to show students the kinds of thinking that an expert goes through to construct a text's meaning and to give students a clear idea of the work they will be expected to do to make sense of and to question challenging texts.

Step-By-Step: Questioning the Author (QtA)

Step 1. Read the text you will use to help students construct and examine.

Step 2. Identify the major understandings you want your students to gain and the potential problems you anticipate students may have in grasping the text's meaning.

Step 3. Segment the text by identifying stop points where you want to begin questioning and discussion. Place asterisks in the text to identify stop points.

Step 4. Develop queries for the stop points you have selected. Formulate Initiating Queries to start discussion, Follow-up Queries to probe beneath the surface and discover connections within the text as well as between students' knowledge and that the author presents, and (where appropriate) Critical Thinking Queries to examine an author's argument, evidence, and reasoning.

Step 5. Provide cues to your students that they are about to engage in something different from traditional comprehension questioning. Arrange the desks in a U-shape. Establish the notion of author fallibility.

Step 6. When engaged in discussion, use the following discussion "moves" to help students construct the text and question the author's ideas: marking, turning back, revoicing, modeling, annotating, and recapping.

Example of Questioning the Author: Questioning Emerson Excerpt from: "Self-Reliance," Ralph Waldo Emerson (1940, pp. 145–146.)

I read the other day some verses written by an eminent painter which were original and not conventional. The soul always hears an admonition in such lines, let the subject be what it may. The sentiment they instill is of more value than any thought they may contain. To believe your own thought, to believe that what is true for you in your private heart is true for all men, that is genius. Speak your latent conviction, and it shall be the universal sense; for the inmost in due time becomes the outmost, and our first thought is rendered back to us by the trumpets of the Last Judgment. Familiar as the voice of the mind is to each, the highest merit we ascribe to Moses, Plato, and Milton is, that they set at naught books and traditions, and spoke not what men but what *they* thought. A man should learn to detect and watch that gleam of light which flashes across his mind from within, more than the lustre of the firmament of bards and sages. Yet he dismisses without notice his thought, because it is his. In every work of genius we recognize our own rejected thoughts: they come back to us with a certain alienated majesty. Great works of art have no more affecting lesson for us than this. They teach us to abide by our spontaneous impression with good-humored inflexibility then most when the whole cry of voices is on the other side. Else, to-morrow a stranger will say with masterly good sense precisely what we have thought and felt all the time, and we shall be forced to take with shame our own opinion from another.

Questions for Emerson Excerpt (Suggested by Dr. Robert Land, Professor of Education, California State University, Los Angeles)

- Initiating Query: What is the gist of Emerson's essay, so far?
- Follow-up Query—reader to text: To what extent have you experienced the phenomenon Emerson describes?
- Follow-up Query—probing text/author's craft: What are some of the strategies Emerson uses to support his claim?
- Critical Thinking Query—beyond text: How might a skeptic counter Emerson's apparent argument, at this stage?
- Critical Thinking Query—within text: Can you identify potential contradictions in Emerson's logic?

Editor Interviews

As we have seen, Questioning the Author (QtA) makes the writer of a text more accessible to students. Editorials in newspapers and magazines provide opportunities to meet the editor. **Editor Interviews** permit students to assume the persona of a newspaper or magazine editor and make an appearance in the classroom so that students can talk their way into and through arguments.

Having a conversation with the writer of an argument provides students with an opportunity to raise questions in a social setting, to construct an understanding of a text, and to explore the strengths and weaknesses of an author's reasoning. Because bringing writers of arguments, like newspaper or magazine editors, to class is not usually feasible, we can ask students to immerse themselves in a writer's reasoning and then to role-play that writer. Students who role-play the writer benefit from a thorough study of a writer's argument while students who talk with the student-as-author get a chance to examine many facets of an argument in dialogue. Students can discover more about a writer's purposes, methods, likely beliefs, and thoroughness. They may also find alternative ways to view important or controversial issues.

A student asked to role-play the writer of an argument, such as a newspaper editorial, should be given time to carefully read and analyze the argument. Additional time to gather information related to the argument presented always contributes to a student's readiness. When the student-as-writer is prepared, other students can initiate the conversation in the classroom.

Before proceeding with the interview, however, students should formulate specific questions they could ask the interviewee. You can encourage generation of questions for the interview by placing students in small teams to review the argument and design questions to ask the "editor." A set of basic questions is provided here as a springboard:

- What was your purpose in writing this piece?
- Why is this argument important to you?
- Would you please summarize your argument for us?
- How did you organize the presentation of your ideas?
- How much research did you do before you finished?
- Do you make any assumptions about the ideas you present?
- What is the best counterargument that you can think of?
- Why should I agree with your argument?
- What do you consider your most persuasive premise or rationale for supporting your thesis? Why?
- How does your opinion about this topic bias your writing about it?
- What, if anything, could or would change your mind about the position you took?
- If you were to rewrite the argument today, what would you change, why would you change it, and how would you change it?

For students to see what they need to do to prepare and to perform in an Editor Interview, teacher modeling is helpful. For this, you should familiarize yourself not only with the editorial you select to demonstrate an Editor Interview but also with sufficient background knowledge germane to the argument. Ask yourself the preceding "springboard" questions, and, if you can answer them, you should be ready to dive in.

Step-By-Step: Editor Interviews

Step 1. Select an editorial from a newspaper or magazine that fits with your curriculum purposes and/or will engage the interest of your students.

Step 2. Ask all students to read and study the editorial, its position, and the argument it presents.

Step 3. Ask a student to prepare to "visit" the class as the editorial's writer. Provide time for the student to prepare by gathering background information about the editorial and its bearing on current events. (Prior to having a student role-play the editor, I encourage you to initially show how to prepare and engage in an Editor Interview with the class.)

Step 4. Ask students to formulate questions about the editorial to which the "editor" can respond. (This could be done in cooperative teams.) Students begin the question-generation process with a set of "springboard" questions such as the ones provided in this chapter. However, editorial-specific questions should also be formulated to address the specific content of the editor's argument.

Step 5. The student role-playing the editor should make a brief, general introduction to the class (perhaps putting the editorial in current context) and then request questions from the audience.

Step 6. The rest is largely dependent on the preparation and improvisational skills of both the student-as-editor and the students-as-interviewers.

ReQuest

Much like reciprocal teaching, **ReQuest** is a strategy to get students to think while they read. Originally developed by Manzo (1969) for one-on-one interaction, ReQuest can be used with a whole class. The strategy encourages student questioning while you serve as a model questioner.

In Manzo's original one-on-one guidelines for ReQuest, the teacher and a student read the text silently, one sentence at a time. They then took turns asking each other questions about what they had read. The student asked a question, and then the teacher asked a question. Like reciprocal teaching, the student was told to ask questions like those generated and delivered by the teacher. In short, the teacher served as a model for the questioning process. Both teacher and student closed their text while being asked questions. "I don't know" answers were deemed unacceptable because, Manzo believed, the student could at least try to explain why he could not answer. If questions or answers were unclear, requests for clarification were encouraged. Participants prepared to support answers with references to the text. If uncertain about an answer, students would consult the text.

My experience with the whole-class version of ReQuest has been stimulating, but students and even teachers I have trained to use ReQuest tend to ask "on-the-surface," or literal, questions. That certainly has put me on the spot from time to time because I don't always remember all the details in a passage, especially longer sections of text. But I believe there are benefits from students observing that teachers don't absorb every detail when reading and can't answer every question students ask. Among the benefits are their seeing we are not total sponges and that it's okay for them to have limited memory as well.

However, getting an avalanche of literal questions may signal that students are having trouble generating more "under-the-surface," inferential, or applied questions. And that signal means we need to design instruction so that students have more opportunities to learn how to generate questions of different kinds. Here our modeling of questions during ReQuest may help, especially if we point out what kinds of questions we are asking and why we are asking that type. You could also do some under-the-surface question training as described in the explanation of reciprocal teaching (see chapter 9). Also, you could review the Inquiry Question (IQ) chart with your students to show them the range of questions they can create. You should observe the kinds of questions your students ask during ReQuest and note the evolution in the kind and quality asked.

Step-By-Step: ReQuest

Step 1. You and your whole class of students silently read the same passages that you previously segmented. One-by-one sentence speed would be appropriate for a whole class of struggling readers. Longer passages, perhaps a paragraph or more in length, are appropriate for some classrooms.

Step 2. After closing the book, you should respond to student questions. (You have a choice at this step either to take all the questions from students or to take fewer questions, even just one, before asking students a question. I prefer the latter method.)

Step 3. Now you ask the questions of the students. (Again, you have a choice: to ask a bunch of questions at one time after receiving all the students' questions or to ask one question and then turn it over to the class for their next question in ping-pong fashion. I prefer the ping-pong method.)

Step 4. Read next passage (or sentence) silently and repeat Steps 2 and 3.

Step 5. When you sense that most of your class could make good predictions about where the text is going next, ask students to formulate a purpose-setting question for the remainder of the reading. For example, students might ask a question that they believe the remaining text will answer.

Socratic Seminars

Math textbooks have traditionally been the source of assigned problems after a teacher introduces a new concept and demonstrates its mathematical applications. Few teachers engage students with the text as a source of useful strategies or to promote reasoned mathematical discourse. When conversations occur in math, they are about answers and errors—not about the textbook.

Michael Tanner and Leah Casados (1998) explored an alternative to using math texts, an alternative that could be used with any content area text: the Socratic Seminar. The **Socratic Seminar** envisioned and implemented was to help students discover ideas through a teacher's skilled questioning and guided dialogue, as did Socrates himself. After reading a text, students participating in the Seminar would construct understandings of that text through discussion and discuss their reasons for those understandings. To a significant degree, this process parallels the meaning negotiation process described in the model of reading when teacher and students negotiate interpretations they bring into the classroom context (see chapter 3).

To prepare for a Socratic Seminar, you need to become familiar with the text students read, whether it be about math or any other subject. Familiarity entails knowing what concepts the author presents and how they are presented, including author's use of headings, vocabulary, organization, and examples. To implement a Socratic Seminar, take the following steps.

Step-By-Step: Socratic Seminars

Step 1. Select and prepare the text by focusing on key concepts and strategies presented, essential related background knowledge, and vocabulary to be taught.

Step 2. Write out questions that will facilitate students' analysis, application, and synthesis of the information presented, such as: What applications can you see for the law of sines and cosines? Are there any new ideas in this section? What steps does the author recommend? Also develop metacognitive questions that will help students focus on thinking about strategies acquired and applied, such as: How is this strategy useful? When would you use it? What was confusing in this reading? How did we resolve the confusion?

Step 3. Prior to the Seminar, assign the reading and arrange one circle of desks inside another to create a circle of observers around a "fishbowl" of those discussing the text.

Step 4. Give students a set of guidelines. The following are adapted from Tanner and Casados (1998):

- Focus on selected content.
- Listen to each other.
- Talk only if you are in the "hot seat."
- Inner-circle students talk to each other.
- Outer-circle students take notes on content and interaction.
- Time limited to 20 minutes plus 5 to 10 minutes for debriefing.
- Inner-circle students get two tokens (worth 5 points each) that must be used during the Seminar discussion.
- Each time inner-circle students speak, they place a token in a box at the center.
- Students may speak more than twice, but twice is the minimum.

Step 5. The teacher begins the discussion with a question, guides students in reconstructing the author's meanings, and helps students to construct their own meanings that are useful (in the case of math) for doing math.

Step 6. As students go to the hot seat to speak, they put a token into the box, sit down, speak, and leave the seat. (When students become comfortable participating in the Socratic Seminar, you may want to phase out the hot seat.)

Step 7. When the discussion is completed, the teacher gives or requests a summary statement.

Step 8. The teacher then conducts a debriefing of the Seminar, in which both inner- and outer-circle students participate. Sample questions about interaction include: Did all inner-circle students participate? Was the discussion clear? How did the discussion contribute to your understanding? Here the metacognitive questions formed in Step 2 can also be asked to help students look at what process or strategy was useful, why it was useful, and when to apply it.

Tanner and Casados (1998) assure us that, while the first Seminar in math was "only satisfactory," discussion about what worked and what could be done so that the Seminars worked better led to significant improvements. Initially, students were quiet and a little uncomfortable, but with some teacher encouragement and question rephrasing, they soon warmed to the process. Eventually, students articulated math strategies in their own words and made metacognitive observations about how they learned. They made connections between the text and background knowledge to construct meanings and engage in mathematical dialogue.

Challenging Texts: Close Readings

Academic reading will make demands on students, many of whom begin their freshman year of college woefully underprepared. Rigorous reading is at the core of most courses in college. However, many high school graduates are not rigorous enough to get to that core (Kirst, 2004). Development of a rhetorical lens to use when reading in different disciplines will enable students to see their way through the initial challenges of academic life. Often that reading, complex and challenging though it may be, serves as a path to entering conversations at the center of academic disciplines, be they anthropology or zoology. Without the lenses to view those texts, students may stumble and stray from that path. Without opportunities to build their academic literacy capacities, far too many undergraduates have been hobbled.

Secondary teachers can better prepare students for the challenges of rigorous reading. As Bean, Chappell, and Gillam (2004) reveal, rhetorical reading, reading "against the grain" can be enhanced with a set of five questioning strategies. These strategies help readers see deeper into a text's argument, its assumptions, and its author's methods to convey information or persuade readers. These five strategies ask readers to examine

1. a writer's credibility,
2. a writer's appeal to reason and logic,
3. a writer's means of appealing to a reader's emotions and interests,
4. a writer's language, and
5. the writer's worldview.

How are readers convinced of a writer's credibility?   Perceptive readers make many inferences about an author's perspective and personality from reading their works. What helps to determine an author's credibility is getting information about that author's background, history, political leanings, and other published work. As readers, we can ask a number of questions to asertain degrees of credibility: How sound is the writer's knowledge base? What indications of the author's values and beliefs come through the text? What tone (scholarly? light-hearted?) does the writer adopt and convey? How does the writer approach the topic? Does anything in the text make you question the author's credentials? What picture of the writer forms in your mind? (While writing this, I'm wondering, "Wow! What are you thinking of this author's credibility?")

How does a reader discover a writer's reasoning skills and rational rigor?
Some writers cover all the bases needing evidence, whereas others anticipate what readers know and believe and then limit evidence—giving only what the writer deems essential. Readers first need to identify the claims or conclusions a writer makes, maybe even the kind of claims made (fact, policy, evauative, moral, predictive, or some mix of these). Next, readers should apply the Goldilock's question to test if the claim is too broad, too narrow, or just about right. Then readers have to sift through the evidence an author gives to support claims made. As readers, we can ask ourselves a number of relevant rigor-testing questions: What is the author claiming? How does the writer use reasons and evidence to justify the claims made? What bridges does the writer make between claim, reason, and evidence?

How do readers discover a writer's appeal to emotion?   This may be both the easiest and the toughest challenge of rhetorical reading: easiest because we can detect when we are emotionally moved by a writer's narrative or argument but toughest because, while we may be aware of an emotional appeal, detaching ourselves from that appeal or gaining a modicum of distance from the appeal in order to reflect upon its power, purpose, or poignancy requires self-regulation. So the savvy writer can appeal to readers by getting them to identify with

- an issue or topic,
- specific interests, beliefs, or values,
- certain social, political, or ideological groups, or
- the writer (Bean et al., 2004).

Writers get readers to identify with each of these by using a wide range of subtle and not-so-subtle strategies. For example, to activate identification, a writer might use the first person, as in, I have an important story to tell you that will change the way you see yourself as a teacher, just as it changed me and the way I saw myself as a teacher. Okay, let's hear this self-transforming tale! On the other hand, a writer might strive to project a scholarly image, calling forth respect by avoiding "I" entirely and using only the passive voice. The author then tells the story using a more authoritative, if passive and distant, voice.

How does a reader examine a writer's language?   Watching for a writer's word choices often leads to discoveries about the writer's tone and style. A writer's careful use of slang or jargon could lead a reader to perceive a writer as hip, "with it," or an "insider" who can guide the reader to an inner circle of knowledge, light, and insight. As Bean et al. (2004) point out, writers can use words of interpretation as though they were facts. For example, is a person claiming, "I am the decider" really decisive? We know from George Lakeoff's (1980) work on metaphor that methaphors can have a profound and less than conscious impact on our thinking and decison making, including our readiness to accept arguments or to reject them. Appropriate to our discussion, Lakeoff notes that we frequently refer to argument itself in terms of war. He observes that we refer to an opponent's claims as "indefensible," that we "target" our criticism at a specific point, and that we "shoot down" our opponent's argument. In discussing rhetorical reading, we could talk about planning and using strategies to gain ground. Metaphor as a language device that enables us to experience one thing in terms of another can be demonstrated in another example. Viewing a company's management style as "glacial" conveys a multitude of impressions: cold, inhuman, slow, unrelenting, unstoppable, gigantic, mindless, and more. Some words that a writer elects to use may be "loaded"—that is, they carry much more weight and may be more explosive than they initially appear. Readers can grow antennae that are capable, like those of snails, of detecting trouble ahead and may even signal that it's time to gain distance in order to examine more closely how a writer is using language to shape or manipulate our perceptions.

How does a reader identify and examine the worldview or ideology reflected in a text?   We often find that discovering a writer's worldview and how it shapes that writer's perceptions of an issue or topic is easier than discovering our own worldviews and their effects on an issue. In fact, our personal lenses may distort our vision of the landscape that an author lays out before us. We saw in chapter 3 how a schema activated from our long-term memory can radically affect our interpretation of a text.

Furthermore, detecting a writer's worldview often entails quite a lot of background knowledge. If we're familiar with communist ideology or its neo-Marxian variants, that ideology will be more transparent in a neo-Marxian author's critique of a politician's program to reform a nation's health care, social security, or property-ownership laws.

Ideology detection requires not only acute perceptual tools, but also a broad knowledge base—often acquired only from broad reading in a field.

Bean et al. (2004) advise looking for patterns of opposites to discover which of the opposing sets of values or beliefs a writer appears to embrace. The opposites of conservative and liberal on the political spectrum present an example of such binary opposition; however, knowing what conservatives or liberals would espouse regarding a wide range of topics demands significant prior knowledge, as we've already seen. Nevertheless, looking for patterns of belief is undoubtedly a productive strategy when it comes to hunting for worldviews. Bean et al. suggest making a parallel list of valued and devalued words, concepts, and ideas that a writer embeds in his text to help in our detective work. And, after you begin to see the pattern of valued words, concepts, and ideas, that perception may lead you to the door of ideological perception.

While several of the strategies already mentioned in this chapter, along with a few to come, will help you address the five rhetorical dimensions of a text needing your close examination, playing what Peter Elbow (1971) called the "believing and doubting game" is also highly productive. If a student is to write a critique of an author's argument, the believing and doubting game can produce a harvest of ideas to both sustain and demolish (argument as war?) aspects of an arugment, even its entire structure.

Step-By-Step: The Believing and Doubting Game

Step 1. The readers read the argument carefully.

Step 2. The readers write down all the reasons they can think of for accepting or believing in the author's argument. The readers should look at the world through the writer's worldview and adopt the beliefs and values associated with that worldview and how it would support and confirm the argument. The readers may have to stretch, even strain, to fit into the writer's world, but that is part of the challenge of this game.

Step 3. The readers then write down all the reasons for doubting the argument. Now readers can take aim at each and every statement, value, or belief described and even sympathized with in the "believing" phase of this game and challenge or attack each with gusto. This process often helps readers clarify for themselves their own beliefs and the grounds upon which those beliefs are based. When engaged in the doubting phase, readers look for all the limitations and problems that arise in the text, expose them, and show why they weaken the writer's argument or point of view. Readers can use all their personal experiences, observations, reading, and research to challenge and undermine the author's position. Should readers agree with the author's argument, this doubting phase of the game may not be much fun because they are asked to confront and question their own points of view, convictions, or reasons for belief in a perspective.

TASKing in Pairs

From research I did on writing (Unrau, 1992), I discovered that the quality of students' thinking often improves if they are explicitly guided through a procedure. To help students analyze arguments, I developed a procedure called **TASK**, which stands for *Thesis Analysis and Synthesis Key* (see the Strategy in Practice). TASK guides readers through several stages as they take apart an argument. Readers first identify the topic of the argument they are reading and then state in their own words the central claim or thesis the writer has made about that topic. Once the thesis has been stated, the readers identify the argument's antithesis (or create one if the writer made no mention of any counterargument). Having articulated both the thesis and antithesis, readers next list the supports given for the thesis and the antithesis (if given). If no antithesis was provided, readers then generate evidence and reasons they believe would support the student-created antithesis and list those.

Strategy in Practice

THESIS ANALYSIS AND SYNTHESIS KEY (TASK)

Student's Name _____ Author/Title _____

1. What topic is being judged?

2. What basic claim (B) is made about that topic?

3. Antithesis (A): What would a reader most likely be for or against if he were opposed to the writer's claim about the topic?

4. What supports the basic claim and the antithetical claim?

Basic Thesis Supports	Antithesis Supports
C.	A.
C.	A.
C.	A.
C.	A.

5. Are any unclear, complex, or "loaded" words in the piece? (If so, identify and clarify them.) [Use the other side of TASK, if needed, for phases 5, 6, and 7.]

6. Evaluate supports for both thesis and antithesis. Identify any questionable inferences, irrelevant supports, fallacies, or other weaknesses in arguments.

7. If you recognize any assumptions, values, or ideological influences in the basic thesis or its supports, what are they? Do any of them shake the validity of the claim?

8. State the full thesis in the following form: "Although A (the antithesis or one of its strongest supports), B (the basic claim) because C (a major cause for belief in the basic claim)."

9. Is the full thesis debatable yet supportable beyond a reasonable doubt, unsupportable, or too complex to support?

10. If needed, revise original claim and repeat TASK.

Source: Copyright © 1997 by Pippin Publishing Corporation. Reproduced with the permission of the copyright holder. All rights reserved.

Following the analysis of the argument to identify and list supports for both the thesis and the antithesis, readers identify any unclear terms, perplexing concepts, or emotionally weighted language that appears in either the thesis or antithesis. After that, readers evaluate the soundness of the supports for the thesis and antithesis. That includes noting any fallacies discovered. Then, the readers identify any assumptions, values, or influences of ideology on the antithesis or its supports because these may strongly bias an argument. Acknowledging their presence can help readers understand the underlying principles that may be driving an argument, even though those under-the-surface principles are not explicitly stated.

Readers next put together several elements of the analysis into a sentence. That sentence takes the following form: Although A, B because C. Here A stands for some antithesis or support for the antithesis, B stands for the basic claim made in the argument, and C is one of the primary supporting reasons for believing in B. Having created this sentence, readers have the gist of the argument in a nutshell.

Step-By-Step: TASKing in Pairs

Step 1. Pair two students who are to read an argument on a controversial issue.

Step 2. Decide which student will become an expert for the argument's thesis (pro) and which will become an expert on the argument's antithesis (con).

Step 3. Pro and con students receive and complete a separate thesis analysis and synthesis key (TASK) while discussing the argument.

Step 4. Students discuss the topic being judged (less any judgment the text may make about the topic).

Step 5. The pro person states the thesis, and the con person states the antithesis or a strong counterclaim opposing the thesis. If no antithesis or counterclaim is stated, the con person creates an appropriate counterclaim to the thesis.

Step 6. The pro person identifies supports for the thesis and lists them.

Step 7. The con person identifies all the supports for the antithesis or counterclaim and lists them. If no supports for the antithesis or counterclaim are presented in the argument, the con person generates them.

Step 8. The pro person identifies any unclear, perplexing, or emotionally charged language used in the thesis. The pro person explains, expands, and tries to cleanse the argument of emotionally charged language.

Step 9. The con person identifies any unclear, perplexing, or emotionally charged language used in the antithesis or counterargument. The con person explains, expands, and tries to cleanse the argument of emotionally charged language.

Step 10. The pro person inspects and evaluates the supports for the thesis or major claim by identifying questionable logic, irrelevant supports, fallacies, and other points of weakness in the thesis.

Step 11. The con person inspects and evaluates the supports for the antithesis or counterclaim by identifying questionable logic, irrelevant supports, fallacies, and other points of weakness in the counterclaim.

Step 12. The pro person tries to identify any assumptions, values, or influences of ideology on the thesis or its supports.

Step 13. The con person tries to identify any assumptions, values, or influences of ideology on the antithesis or its supports.

Step 14. Together, the pro and con people synthesize the argument into one sentence in the following format: Although A (where A is the counterclaim or one of its strongest supports), B (where B is the thesis or basic claim) because C (where C is a major reason for belief in the basic claim).

Step 15. Pro and con experts prepare to present their sides of the argument to the class for further discussion.

Understanding Critical Literacy

While strategies like the Believing and Doubting Game or TASK contribute to readers' development of critical thinking, making more critical readers can also be achieved through the practice of critical literacy. However, "critical" takes on a somewhat different meaning in the term critical literacy from the meaning it has in the term critical thinking. In addition, the practices and outcomes of this form of critical reading are also different.

A considerable body of theory has arisen around critical literacy and its pursuit of social justice through recognizing how language shapes social interaction (Bourdieu, 1991; Freire, 1993/1970; Janks, 1993; Lankshear & McLaren, 1993; Shor, 1999). Differing from critical thinking, **critical literacy** as theory translates into ways in which reading and writing help students to understand daily social and political processes for the purpose of living more freely in a democratic society. Engaging in critical literacy practices enables readers to see their world more clearly, to understand how it works, to "rewrite" that world with their interests written in, and to take more liberating action within it. Critical literacy's intent is to emancipate, to empower those subordinated and marginalized.

In his widely read *Pedagogy of the Oppressed,* Freire (1993/1970) presents his method for developing "critical consciousness," the capacity to perceive social, political, and economic contradictions and to act against oppressive forces. He focuses on the roots of oppression and methods of unearthing them for close examination. Through reflection on the forces of oppression, the oppressed will be liberated. Liberation will come through critical dialogue with the oppressed that aims at reflection on an individual's specific situation.

According to Freire (1993/1970), there can be no true dialogue without critical thinking. Posing problems and talking about those problems turns students into critical thinkers. However, Freire's conception of critical thinking is different from the one introduced earlier in this chapter. For him, critical thinking reveals the deep, indivisible connection between people and the malleable world we inhabit. It is thinking that "perceives reality as process, as transformation, rather than as a static entity." Critical thinking for him never disengages from action. He contrasts his conception of critical thinking with naïve thinking, the intent of which is to accommodate to things as they are. For the student engaged in Freire's form of critical thinking, the aim is the continuous transformation of reality in order to humanize it.

How to transform critial literacy as theory into classroom practices across the disciplines to achieve growth in critical consciousness and social justice is a creative challenge. In pursuit of that goal, Edward Behrman (2006) found dozens of articles on electronic databases that supported critical literacy in content area classrooms. Although critical literacy can theoretically be practiced in any discipline, most of the applications he found described activities in language arts, interdisciplinary, or social science contexts. The practices Behrman discovered fell into six categories:

1. *Reading from a resistant perspective.* When reading from a resistant perspective, readers are encouraged to view a text with different identities that may be based on ethnicity, class, gender, or religion. Although similar to reading in the Believing and Doubting Game, a resistant perspective requires that the reader adopt new, perhaps unfamiliar identities. The reader thereby goes beyond "doubting" and into interpreting a text from an entirely different frame of reference. One study Behrman cites (Lien, 2003) introduces students to the concept of capital in the form of a limited supply of chocolate candies as a prelude to a critical literacy unit on Vietnam. Students then get a taste of how wealth or poverty affect interpretations of communism and the allocation of precious resources.

2. *Producing countertexts.* When producing countertexts, students create a text that addresses a topic from a nonmainstream point of view. In one example, a teacher (Hanrahan, 1999) used journal writing in a science class for students both to present their understanding of science concepts and to express their experience of learning those concepts. For many students, the dialogue that transpired over journal writing and teacher response changed the student-teacher power equation, deepened the level of student engagement, and transformed students' experience of learning in a science classroom.

3. *Taking social action.* When taking social action, students can discover and even challenge existing power structures as they try to make a difference in their surrounding world. Such a challenge to power structures occurred when students in Kentucky discovered that the highest peak in their state was scheduled for strip mining (Powell, Cantrell, & Adams, 2001). As part of the process of raising their own critical consciousness, students discovered powerful competing economic and environmental interests at work over the mountain. They heightened media

awareness, submitted a proposal with alternative solutions to a state agency, and contributed to a compromise.

4. *Conducting student-choice research projects.* An important element in building autonomy and student engagement, providing student choice in research projects also enables students to gain understandings of everyday events in their lives. Using I-Search methods developed by Ken Macrorie (1988), students can investigate issues that concern them personally. When using this approach in my junior English classes, my students choose to deepen their understanding of a range of topics, including cliques, school administration decision making, laws governing marijuana use, and dating practices among peers. As Behrman (2006, p. 495) emphasizes, however, simply investigating a topic using local resources, such as the school library and surveys, does not mean students are engaged in critical literacy. For that to occur, students need to "reflect upon the social and cultural forces that exacerbate or mitigate the problem."

5. *Reading multiple texts.* To gain multiple and critical perspectives of a topic, students can read several works related to the topic. Looking at the classroom instruction of two Australian teachers, Bronwyn Mellor and Annette Patterson (2000), we can discover how they used multiple texts to teach classical Shakespeare from a critical literacy perspective. One of their guiding principles was that students should reflect critically not only on what they are reading, but also on how they are reading it. Mellor and Patterson used multiple texts to disrupt static, traditional interpretations of Ophelia. They planned to help students see how readers construct divergent meanings for the same character by looking at interpretations of Hamlet's sometime sweetheart, Ophelia, at two ends of a continuum. At one end of the continuum was Ophelia, the virginal innocent, and at the other end was Ophelia, the sexually wise wanton. They had students read "pious" and "wanton" analyses of Ophelia. They then applied these perspectives to selected scenes and reviewed their own interpretions of Ophelia. Through critical reflection, students discovered that Shakespeare may not be historical yet eternal and that critics could overlook inconvenient details that might not sustain what they saw through their interpretive lens.

What makes this approach different? The assumptions underlying it. Now we can work under the assumptions that a text will yield multiple readings, that you can help students see what has contributed to these different readings, and that contradictions in readings can be examined through discussion and dialogue. Working under these assumptions, students are no longer expected to find the meaning the author intended to inscribe. Rather, readers are constructed by their interpretations of a text that delivers various visions of reality. Critical literacy is tied to Freire's belief that in reading we engage in an interpretation of reality—of the world in which we live.

6. *Reading supplementary texts.* When students take courses with one textbook that speaks with one voice and sees from one perspective, providing those students with opportunities to read supplementary texts, especially texts that adopt alternative points of view, contributes to the growth of critical literacy. These alternative readings need not be printed materials. Film, music, or Internet-based sources can supplement standard text treatment of course concepts. One teacher showed the film version of Mario Puzo's *The Godfather* when studying Homer's *Odyssey* to enable students to compare power struggles depicted in contemporary culture with those of ancient civilizations rendered in the Western canon (Morrell, 2000).

Step-By-Step: Critical Literacy in the Classroom

Step 1. Adopt a historical and theoretical perspective of critical literacy. Allan Luke (2000) described what he did to engage students in "redefined" critical literacy when he taught in Australia. But first, a little history: Australian educators in the 1980s faced criticism of a curriculum based on whole language, process writing, and personal-growth models that dominated instruction. That criticism led to a new focus on how texts worked. To get at how they work, educators borrowed strongly from the field of critical discourse analysis. From different theoreticians and practitioners of critical discourse analysis came the following views:

- Texts are an interplay of conflicting voices.
- Students need tools to gain access to historical and cultural positions.
- Students need to discover whose purposes and ends are fulfilled in texts.
- Discourse constructs identities for readers, defines who they are, and positions them.
- Readers construct multiple meanings for texts.
- Words are cultural coins with exchange value in communities.
- The development of a "critical consciousness" could liberate oppressed peoples by making them aware of dominant social, political, and economic forces and leading them to action.

Step 2. Applying these principles in classrooms, you could stimulate debate over what a text is trying to do, what ideologies are driving it, and how students can apply those ideologies in various domains of interest. As Luke (2000, p. 453) puts it, the purpose of critical literacy is to create classroom climates in which both you and your students collaborate to discover how texts construct your students' worlds, cultures, and identities "in powerful, often overtly ideological ways" and use the texts to reconstruct those worlds. "The *redefinition of critical literacy* (my emphasis) focuses on teaching and learning how texts work, understanding and re-mediating what texts attempt to do in the world and to people, and moving students toward active position-taking with texts to critique and reconstruct the social fields in which they live and work."

Step 3. The kinds of questions you could pose in relation to a text may be categorized into four sets of practices necessary for critical literacy. These categories and questions include the following:

- *Coding Practices.* How does the text work? How is it designed? What are its features?
- *Text-Meaning Practices.* How are ideas related to each other within the text? What cultural resources would help us make sense of this text? What cultural readings and interpretations can we construct from the text?
- *Pragmatic Practices.* What do we do, as readers, with the text? How does its function shape its form?
- *Critical Practices.* What is the text attempting to do to us individually? Whose interests are served through the agency of this text? Whose voices and interests are expressed? What positions are conveyed? Who is being left out?

Step 4. Ask your students to apply questions from the four preceding categories and write responses in their journals to a particular text you want to examine.

Step 5. Create teams of three to five students, ask students to share answers to their questions in their teams, and arrange for one member of each team to report to the whole class.

Step 6. Guide a whole-class discussion using team reports and an individual student's journal entries as springboards. Rather than asking students questions about the text that have known answers, keep in mind that teachers practicing critical literacy ask themselves questions such as these:

- How can we approach this text so that we can use it as a tool to raise critical consciousness?
- What will the text tell us about how society works and how we arrived at our current social status?
- How can we approach this work so we can understand social forces that oppress and exploit people and that lead to alienation?

In Australia, Luke (2000) writes, literacy is about social power. An education through critical literacy goes beyond skill acquisition. It engages students in the analysis and reconstruction of their worlds. Drawing upon a "social issues" curriculum used in an Australian secondary school, Luke (1995) provides an example of text analysis. One of the questions students should ask about the following passage is, What is this text trying to do to me?

> Think of your own family. You are probably aware that you belong to a separate group in society. You feel that you are in some ways "different" from the Browns or the Smiths across the road. Each member of your family plays a number of roles. You may look up to your father or mother as the "head of the family" or the "family breadwinner." Your mum or dad, for their part, will expect you to behave in certain ways—to help out with the dishes or in the garage, for example. (p. 107)

According to Luke (1995), a critical reading of this text should highlight its "monocultural social order" based on a "version of the ideal, Anglo-nuclear family" with the Browns and Smiths living across the road and expecting their children to do dishes and clean garages. Luke also sees the text as telling readers what to do when they begin reading: "Think of your own family." The author(s) constructed a role the reader is to assume when engaging with the text. For practitioners of critical literacy (Luke) critical discussion of texts laden with values and ideologies but presented as "nonfiction" begins with questions that reveal how authors "construct and position human subjects and social reality": How does this text work? What cultural interpretations can we construct from the text? What do we do with the text? What does the text do to us?

Media Literacy

Media literacy is expanding in popularity, and that expansion has its causes. First, media's influence, especially among youth, has grown more vast with the growth of the Internet and the explosion of .coms, .nets, .govs, .edus, and .orgs. Students, also known as "screenagers" (Rushkoff, 1996), hover in cyberspace reading and writing Web logs (blogs), playing computer games, and setting aside homework for "myspace.com." Second, organizations such as the National Council of Teachers of English and the International Reading Association have written curriculum standards that incorporate media literacy, giving it a more prominent role than in decades past. And third, perhaps most significantly, all 50 states have incorporated media literacy into their content standards that guide classroom instruction and guide statewide assessment programs. The Web site for Rutgers University's Center for Media Studies (www.mediastudies.rutgers.edu) describes media standards for every state. With the chance that media literacy might be assessed on high-stakes tests, interest in students taking a second look at what the media does and how it does it have skyrocketed.

However, the rise of interest in media literacy has not simplified the task of defining what media literacy should be. Its definition and scope has been made difficult because of tensions over its purposes. On one hand, a group of educators advocates the application of critical thinking to media studies. Under this umbrella, media—with its messages and methods—would be analyzed to examine the structure of the messages and their validity. What does the message convey? What evidence supports the truth of the message? On the other hand, another group of educators advocates media activism. Under this umbrella, students who analyze media and its messages are encouraged to take a stand and engage in action that could include attacks on industries promoting a product, such as cigarettes or alcohol. The ideological aim directing this approach to media literacy is reformation through information. I found a concise, practical definition on the Web site for the Center for Media Literacy:

> Media literacy provides a framework to access, analyze, evaluate and create messages in a variety of forms—from print to video to the Internet. Media literacy builds an understanding of the role of media in society as well as essential skills of inquiry and self-expression necessary for citizens of a democracy. (CML MediaLit Kit, quoted in Thoman & Jolls, 2005)

As the founder of the Center for Media Literacy, Elizabeth Thoman, and the Center's chief executive, Tessa Jolls (2005, p. 190), put it, "Media literacy is about helping students become competent, critical, and literate in all media forms so that they control the interpretation of what they see or hear, rather than letting the interpretation control them." Those media forms extend from print to video and the Internet and embrace photography, music, television, movies, radio, advertising, podcasting, and blogging.

Principles of Media Literacy

To focus media inquiry, educators (Considine & Haley, 1999: McBrien, 2005; Thoman & Jolls, 2005) have articulated core principles that include these:

1. All media and their messages are constructed.
2. Every media utilizes its own language and techniques.
3. The audience constructs its own interpretation of media messages.
4. Media, with its forms and rules of construction, transmit values and ideologies.
5. Media messages have political, economic, social, and cultural consequences.

For each of these core principles, we can propose parallel questions that would enable our students to pursue media inquiry with our guidance. These investigative questions should facilitate our unpacking all media messages.

What is the source of the message? By whom was it created?   Just as all printed texts are constructed and reconstructed when read and interpreted, media messages are constructed at least twice: once by their creator(s) and once by their viewer, listener, or reader. Discovering what was put in and left out of a message is important audience work. We should also be asking related questions about the kind of text we experience, its similarities to other messages, and the manner in which elements contribute to the message.

What techniques or strategies have gone into the construction of this message?   Every medium has its own language. Magazines, TV news programs, and Web sites are all composed of their own components. Knowing how each medium uses its language of imagery, sound, and symbols adds to our ability to appreciate the medium's message and to inoculate ourselves against its possible manipulative purposes. By asking how the creator of the message assembled it and by identifying techniques that capture our attention, we can begin to understand the moves made in the message and to free ourselves from being persuaded or manipulated to believe in or do something that, in a broader perspective, may not be in our own or our society's best interests. How is the message appealing to us and to our senses? How is its music or imagery composed to persuade us to act in some way?

What are some possible alternative ways to interpret the message?   Just as we've seen with reading printed texts, readers bring schemas of many kinds to construct their unique interpretations. Each of us sees an evening newscast or documentary somewhat differently because we bring to it schemas that shape the meanings we take away from it. How might others construct different meanings for a message or act differently once seeing it? Do their understandings have as much merit or validity as ours—or perhaps more? Which interpretations merit more measure? What kinds of evidence justify interpretations that to us seem so different that we ask ourselves if we both saw the same event or experienced the same text?

What values and perspectives are being transmitted or omitted and whose are they?   Media convey manifest and latent messages. The latent messages or subtexts transmit, without our full awareness, values and points of view even more persuasive than the overt or manifest message. What does the message say about who we are supposed to be as a recipient of it? What does the message want us to believe or do? What values or perspectives are missing? Constructing a meaning for the overt message sent should be viewed as only the beginning for us; we should heighten our perception of the less transparent material that may be part of the message's covert operation.

What does this message want me to do? What social, political, economic and/or cultural consequences could this message have?   Creators of media often earn their living by trying to bring about attitudinal change. And that can mean changes in behavior in many dimensions of our lives, including behavior at the mall or in the voting booth. Sometimes our minds are changed by heightening a need, a need often aroused so that we will purchase a publicized product— from Acuras to Xerox machines. Other consequences pursued include shaping our political positions, influencing our voting, changing our attitudes, and affecting our taste or style. It's important for us as consumers of media to always ask what the message wants us to do or to believe. If we and others believe or act in accord with the message, what are the social consequences likely to be? Would our nation go to war or pursue peace? Would we support the death penalty or gun control? Would we endorse stem-cell research or succumb to the hope of scientifically untested cancer remedies? Or, would we buy bigger SUVs to protect ourselves and our families on the freeway or purchase smaller, fuel-efficient hybrids that conserve oil and lessen pollution? In whose interest has the media been produced? Are we being served truth or persuasive manipulation that may benefit a few at the expense of many?

Media Literacy Practices Across The Content Areas

Opportunities to develop students' media literacy span the content areas (Richardson, 2006). Teachers of math and science, English and social studies, or art and physical education can design inquiry-focused instruction that draws upon multiple media sources. Teachers can design WebQuests and ask students, alone or in teams, to engage in inquiry the quest requests (Brozo, 2006). Other print sources of information can, of course, complement or serve as an anchor for a Web-centered investigation.

A WebQuest itself is an activity that engages learners in an inquiry using resources found on the Internet. Typically, teachers first introduce students to the quest by giving them background information, connections to prior or future instruction, and outcome expectations. Questions to be answered include, How does this research relate to what you've recently been learning? What elements should your completed project include? What can you expect to gain from this inquiry?

Second, teachers describe in detail the project that students are to undertake. That description could include the specific topic to be researched, such as the American Revolution, the genome project and its contribution to modern science, or baseball statistics. Specific questions can guide the inquiry: How did loyalists to the Colonists view the situation in the Colonies differently from those loyal to the British king? What has the genome project contributed to our knowledge of inherited diseases? Has the quality of pitching improved according to statistics comparing the decade of the 1960s with that of the 1990s? How would you explain any differences found?

Third, teachers describe the range of information resources available for the inquiry project. These could include print texts, such as books, magazines, and newspaper articles, and electronic resources in cyberspace. These electronic resources include search engines to identify helpful Web sites. For younger, less tech-savvy students, teachers could list relevant sites or provide a set of links taking students directly to those sites. Search engines and resources for students include www.goggle.com, www.inform.com, www.topix.net, and www.wikipedia.com

Fourth, teachers give students step-by-step guidance to conduct the inquiry. This could include procedural information about how the inquiry is to be conducted.

- Teachers decide if the quest will be a solo investigation or carried out in a team. If a team approach is deemed best, students will need information about how their teams are to be structured. (See chapter 9 on cooperative learning.)
- Directions/assignment specifications: What is to be done?
- Resources: Pro and con (three of each minimum, one in print.)
- Whether done alone or in a team, students need to know how best to approach their reading of sources both print and electronic. TASK or some alternative

procedure, such as the five core principles and their parallel questions, for the analysis of expository or argumentative texts or nonprint sources may be applied.

- Students also need to know the form of the presentation they are to create. Many variations are possible, from single-author reports to multifaceted team reports. Team reports may be an assembly of parts; one team member would be held individually accountable for each part. Teams might also give presentations or even a "performance" that demonstrates the process through which they went and their discoveries, perhaps with evidence substantiating those findings. The outcomes could be in a medium other than print, perhaps a PowerPoint presentation, a Web site, a blog, a wiki, or a podcast that reported their discoveries (Richardson, 2006). The Web site could contain the questions investigated and links to sources, so that other students could retrieve resources used in the quest and reconstruct or extend that inquiry's process. Examples of WebQuests and how to design them are available from sources like Media Literacy Clearinghouse (www.medialit.med.sc.edu) and the WebQuest Page (www.webquest.sdsu.edu).

These multimedia quests provide rich opportunities to develop media literacy in the sense of the concept adopted here. That is, students can "access, analyze, evaluate, and create messages in a variety of forms." Engaging in that process will also build students' knowledge and understanding of media in our culture. Through such building of knowledge and skills, students become more competent interpreters of media, less subject to being manipulated, and more thoughtful in forming and defending opinions not only in specific discipline domains, but also in democracy's wider discourse.

The knowledge and skills developed through these inquiry activities have the potential to both deepen engagement in content areas and to build academic literacy (Beach, 2007). They can deepen engagement because they are driven by inquiry, can provide choice in topic, resources, and outcome, encourage use of information technologies, and may be done in collaboration with others. They build academic literacy essential for future college-level work, such as the capacity to select, access, and read topic-relevant texts, to analyze and evaluate arguments, and to compose arguments from multiple sources.

Summary

In this chapter, we have examined why students in a democratic society need to expand their basic reading abilities so they can analyze texts, identify claims, search for evidence, question perspectives, and evaluate conclusions. I've provided several strategies, including inquiry questions, Questioning the Author, ReQuest, Socratic Seminars, the Believing and Doubting Game, and TASK, that promote the development of students' critical reading. I've also introduced critical literacy as a method to increase students' awareness of how texts define and shape their readers and how marginalized readers can be empowered through textual analysis. Furthermore, I've presented a framework and classroom practices that can enhance students' media literacy and enrich their critical understanding of the electronic worlds surrounding them. However, presenting strategies and methods to students does not ensure their use. Dispositions to read critically require nurturing, and as teachers, we nurture those dispositions every time we ourselves model the critical reading of texts of all kinds. Keep in mind: Questions open minds.

Double-Entry Journal: After Reading

How have you modified, if at all, your conception of critical reading now that you have read this chapter? What strategies or approaches to critical reading of print and nonprint texts in your content area could you add to those you described in your prereading DEJ? How could you integrate critical literacy and media literacy, including the treatment of bias, into your content area instruction?

Part III

DESIGNING LITERACY INTO ACADEMICALLY DIVERSE CONTENT AREA CLASSES

Knowing our students, their literacies, and how to enhance those literacies through strategic instruction lays the foundation for designing literacy into every content area classroom. Each of following three chapters presents perspectives and practices for addressing the diverse needs of literacy growth that your students bring to your classroom, whether you are teaching math, science, social studies, or any other content area.

Chapter 9, "Collaborating for Literacy and Learning: Group Strategies," offers and array of whole-class, small-group, and one-on-one practices that you can apply in diverse classrooms to guide your students' literacy development. Included are innovative whole-class reading and discussion methods, cooperative learning strategies, reciprocal teaching procedures, and a variety of tutoring formats from peer to adult-student models with guidelines for their implementation.

Chapter 10, "Struggling Readers and English Learners: Addressing Their Cognitive and Cultural Needs," offers a research-based model of reading intervention designed especially to transform struggling readers into striving readers. The model consists of 14 features that contribute to effective programs for students struggling with literacy. This chapter also includes perspectives, programs, and practices that will enable you to understand the literacy needs of your English learners and to facilitate their growth.

Chapter 11, "Designing Literacy into Academically Diverse Content Area Classes to Promote Understanding," explains and describes how standards-based instruction with integrated literacy strategies can positively impact students' engagement and learning. We examine the literacy issues that teachers of science, math, history, English, and physical education face in their specific fields and see examples of the literacy strategies these content teachers use to promote their students' learning. The chapter also presents a planning pyramid for inquiry and instruction that you can use to design units and lessons. We then see how a teacher puts the planning pyramid to use as she designs a unit on the Declaration of Independence.

Chapter 9

COLLABORATING FOR LITERACY AND LEARNING: GROUP STRATEGIES

After reading chapter 9, you should be able to answer the following questions:

1. How would you apply whole-class methods, such as oral reading and discussion techniques, to integrate literacy development with growth in content knowledge?

2. What small-group methods, including cooperative learning activities, could you apply to integrate literacy development with growth in content knowledge?

3. What principles guide acknowledged forms of cooperative learning, and what activities demonstrate these principles?

4. What is reciprocal teaching? How does it help readers improve comprehension? How would you use it in your classroom?

5. How would you integrate tutoring, including peer, cross-aged, and adult-student variations, into your content area instructional program?

What are your memories of group work in your middle and high school classes? How were they organized? How did they contribute to your learning? What kinds of whole-class, small-group, and paired activities do you plan to use in your teaching?

Building Muscle Power Cooperatively (by Cindy Thai)

I held this cooperative learning activity in the weight room so students in my health education class, where I was teaching a unit on muscular strength and endurance, would be able to explore the possibilities of different exercises. I used a Jigsaw activity while teaching the unit. Students would have to read and understand their health textbooks and supplementary reading materials I handed out. I wanted my students to identify and demonstrate several exercises for each muscle group. I divided the class into five cross-ability, cross-status teams (Home Team A to Home Team E) and asked them to come up with a team name as their first Home Team task. I explained to them that at least one member of their Home Team would become a member of an "Expert Team" and that each "expert" would return to the Home Team to teach all the team members what the expert had learned. Then I put a chart up on the wall like this one:

Expert Team Number	Muscle Group Exercised
Expert Team One	Biceps and triceps
Expert Team Two	Deltoid and pectoralis major/minor
Expert Team Three	Trapezius and latissimus dorsi
Expert Team Four	Quadriceps and hamstrings
Expert Team Five	Gastrocnemius, soleus, and abdominals

Next, I explained to my students that each Expert Team would have to identify the muscle groups they were assigned, create at least two exercises for each muscle group, and teach the exercises to their Home Team. While the Expert Teams were working on their tasks, I walked around the room monitoring and coaching the teams. After all the Expert Teams completed their task and returned to their Home Teams to teach the exercises, we had a full-class discussion to clarify any possible confusion. After completing the activity, I was convinced again that Jigsaw is an excellent way to encourage students to participate in group settings of different ethnic, cultural, and racial backgrounds.

In the cooperative learning episode that opens this chapter, Cindy Thai controlled the selection of text materials, the tasks that students were to undertake, the structure of the activities, and the means of its evaluation. Her teaching demonstrates how teachers' decisions about texts, tasks, and tactics shape classroom environments and learning. As we saw in the model of reading presented in chapter 3, our classrooms play a pivotal role in students' comprehension of texts. Meanings for what they read are negotiated every day as our students interact with texts and with each other. But other elements of meaning beyond printed texts, elements that shape learning in classrooms, also are negotiated. These other classroom elements include the assignments we give, sources of classroom authority over text interpretation, and aspects of the social and cultural setting.

We and our students bring many meanings into learning environments like those Cindy created, even before we begin to discuss our understandings of a specific text. Participants in the classroom bring their cultural heritage, their literacies, and their interpretations of the text to be discussed. As the discussion and dialogue proceed, students and teacher negotiate meanings guided by their individual backgrounds and perspectives.

During the dialogue among participants in the class, meanings are forged that the classroom community shares. These widely held interpretations form a set of expectations or assumptions on which subsequent meanings are likely to be based. All class members participate in creating this culture. However, the teacher's role is of central importance because the teacher usually brings extensive knowledge of the subject and pedagogical tools to build classroom cultures.

When organizing for instruction, some teachers begin with whole-group instruction and progress to individual applications of concepts first presented to the whole group. The gradual-release model of instruction (Pearson, 1985; Wood, 2001) demonstrates this progression (see Figure 9.1). According to the model, instruction begins with teachers explaining and demonstrating what students are to learn in whole-class settings. At the next level, small groups of students begin to take responsibility, which the teacher releases to them when he believes they sufficiently understand concepts or skills they will eventually master. These groups may be prestructured cooperative learning groups that enable students to share responsibility for each other's mastery of the material. At the next level, teachers ask students to work in pairs to practice and reinforce what they've learned. Ultimately, what students have learned can be independently applied to other subject areas or problem spaces.

A gradual-release model may not always be the best instructional model to follow. For some instructional situations, moving from individual input to small groups and then to whole-class discussion works better, especially if you want to get shy students to talk about their personal meanings or opinions first. That's the pattern I frequently followed when I wanted to encourage students to interpret texts in my

Figure 9.1 The Gradual-Release Model of Instructional Grouping.

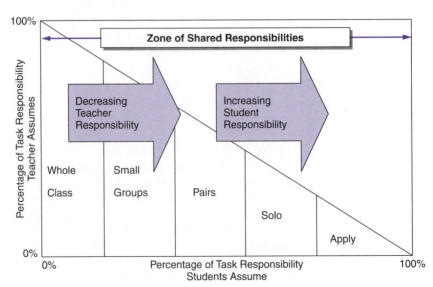

classroom, share their interpretations in small groups, and then discuss interpretations in a whole-class setting to discover what classwide meanings we could negotiate. Although the underlying structure of this chapter moves from whole-group to individual applications, I definitely want you to remain free and ready to use instructional patterns that are completely opposite. You, of course, will have to decide which models (and which variations of those models) in which situations will work best for your content area classes.

Whole Groups

Whole-class settings provide rich opportunities for teacher-student interaction of many kinds. Most typically, however, a teacher stands in front of a classroom of students, delivers information to them, instructs them to take notes, and expects them to demonstrate an understanding of what was delivered. When lecturing to students during my first months of teaching, I soon discovered that 80% of what I said went directly through them and out the window. Okay, so maybe 90%. I had few techniques to engage students, even though I believed what I had to say was of at least some significant value. I'd gone to college and listened to professors deliver lots of information that I thought was both informative and interesting. Why not do the same for my students? While lecturing works well for the delivery of some information, as it does when teachers of history weave students into an engaging narrative of events with heavy consequence, I'm going to focus primarily on whole-class reading strategies, such as oral and guided reading, and on class discussion methods. I'm adopting this focus primarily because this chapter is intended to present group strategies to acquire not only content knowledge but also literacy skills—not lecture techniques, although some of the strategies presented in this chapter, if integrated with lectures, should more deeply engage students in learning from lectures.

Whole-Class Reading Methods

Many teachers ask their students to read aloud in class. While a student reads, others follow along in their own books. One student after another reads row by row as the teacher says, "Next." It's a popular strategy to cover both narrative and expository texts. Sometimes it's called **Round Robin reading** and, though widely tried, it doesn't always fly.

Why is this traditional classroom practice so popular? Opitz and Rasinski (1998) observed that teachers often use Round Robin reading to address classroom control and management issues, not to develop reading skills or improve comprehension. M. R. Ruddell (1997) notes that teachers sometimes use it when they are so frustrated by students' not doing their reading assignments that the only way they have left to make sure everyone at least hears the text content is to read it out loud in the classroom. However, researchers have found that Round Robin reading may actually get in the way of your developing more skilled readers. Among the undesirable effects of the practice are the following:

- *It tends to arouse undue anxiety in readers who may then come to loath reading rather than pursue it.* Some students, waiting for their turn to read, spend their anticipation time trying to deal with trembling hands and upset stomachs.
- *It diminishes readers' self-monitoring and self-regulation of reading.* During Round Robin reading, other students often correct miscues and errors before the

reader has a chance to self-correct. The practice may lead away from the ideal of developing self-regulating readers.

- *It may stimulate excessive subvocalization.* We know that subvocalization can help readers comprehend texts and that skilled readers rarely subvocalize every word in a text. However, if students slow down their reading rates to repeat each word to themselves as a student reads aloud in class, that practice could transfer to silent-reading tasks, stimulate excessive subvocalization, and slow readers' rates through habituation.

- *It may reduce attention to meaning construction.* In anticipation of reading aloud to the class, students look ahead to see what they are expected to read and to rehearse their lines. However, that means they pay less attention to comprehending the whole text. Furthermore, those who've read ahead are likely to get in trouble when called upon to read but don't know the place to start.

- *It uses time that could be better spent on more meaningful and engaging activities.* Students could be developing other reading skills or building and extending their knowledge base rather than consuming time with an activity that has less educational value.

All in all, teachers should evaluate the usefulness of Round Robin reading. Although it may have a constructive place in some classrooms, more productive oral reading practices are available as strategies from which teachers can choose.

Alternatives to Round Robin Reading

Reading aloud to students. Students of all ages often enjoy having teachers read to them. Even middle and high school students are frequently delighted when their teachers read aloud. A poem, a humorous story, a passage from a book you're reading, or a newspaper editorial all provide a means to begin a class and open communication. Also, when reading aloud, you model proficient reading. The implication for students is that you would like them to read with similar fluidity and expression. For that reason, practicing the selection before reading it aloud is beneficial.

Following your reading, you should allow some time to talk with students about what you've read. You may just ask for general responses or form specific questions about the reading for students to answer. Either way, engaging students in some conversation after the reading has multiple benefits, including your discovering the quality of their listening comprehension for different kinds of texts at different levels of difficulty.

Shared reading. While reading aloud to students brings enjoyment to many, shared reading brings important added benefits. **Shared reading** combines your reading aloud plus your students following your reading in their own texts. Janet Allen (2000), in identifying its purposes, wrote that shared reading

- demonstrates fluid reading to students so they can experience the flow and charm of good writing,
- builds bridges between texts and students' lives,
- provides practice in strategies that make a text comprehensible,
- models fluent reading that students can imitate in their independent reading, and
- helps students build knowledge of texts and their world.

Even students who have trouble decoding can focus on comprehension rather than worrying about pronunciation. They can visualize the story, ask themselves questions about it, make predictions, analyze its components, and connect it with their own experiences. With practice, readers can transfer these strategies to their own independently read texts.

Think-alouds.   When discussing reading assessment in chapter 4, I explained how you can use comprehension think-alouds to discover how your students make meaning from texts, including those in the content areas. You can also use think-alouds as alternatives to Round Robin reading by asking students to share their associations to passages from a text with others in the class. You can watch for and emphasize processes that good readers engage in when they read, such as

- activating background knowledge,
- making predictions,
- forming mental images as they read,
- monitoring their comprehension progress, and
- fixing up comprehension problems as they arise.

Before students practice doing think-alouds on their own, you'll need to demonstrate the procedure for them. For guidelines to the procedure, see Table 4.8 and the following description of how to do think-alouds in class.

Step-By-Step: Think-Alouds in Class

Step 1. When you demonstrate think-alouds, select passages that are likely to reveal the cognitive processes of engaged reading. Choose passages that are likely to challenge some of your students—passages that include comprehension problems, such as unfamiliar vocabulary or concepts and complex sentence structure.

Step 2. Read the passage you intend to use for demonstration before sharing it with your class and identify several think-aloud pause points for yourself. At those points you will share with your class the associations stimulated by the content of the passage. You might want to make a few notes to focus and limit your associations.

Step 3. You should begin by reading the passage aloud to your students. At points you've identified, pause and talk out your associated thoughts, as Mrs. Silva did with "Sea Fever" (Table 4.8), so that students can hear what you do to construct meaning.

Step 4. After your demonstration, ask students to share their think-aloud thoughts and associations to parts of the same passage you used.

Step 5. After demonstrating think-alouds yourself, ask for a volunteer to do a think-aloud with a text appropriate for the class, perhaps a text that the class is currently reading. Before giving it to the volunteer, prepare the passage by identifying several think-aloud pause points. Remind the student that at those points she should share the associations stimulated by the content of the passage. As appropriate and needed, you can ask questions, such as these recommended by Gunning (2006), to get more information about the student's construction of meaning:

- What was the selection mainly about?
- How did you get the main idea of the selection?
- What were you thinking about as you read the selection?
- What do you think will happen next in the selection? Why do you think so?

Step 6. After you and the volunteer have demonstrated the technique, ask for and answer any questions about doing a think-aloud.

Step 7. Next, identify and prepare an appropriate passage with stop points for your students to use in practicing think-alouds in pairs. After pairing students, ask them to practice thinking aloud together.

Step 8. After all pairs have had an opportunity to practice, pause and talk with students about what they observed and what they learned from doing think-alouds themselves.

Encouraging imagery to enhance comprehension. You'll remember our learning about the Dual Coding Theory (DCT) in connection with our model of reading (Sadoski & Paivio, 2001). Briefly, DCT presents us with the notion that we have two processing systems, one verbal and one nonverbal. The nonverbal system includes imagery that helps us comprehend and remember texts, especially those stimulating the mental production of images, such as narratives. However, you can also encourage students to develop imagery with expository texts.

Step-By-Step: How to Induce Imagery

Step 1. To introduce this strategy to students, you should select an image-rich passage of about 200 words from your content area text. (I've included a sample from *Biology* (Miller & Levine, 2006) to serve as a promising passage for this exercise.) Such a passage is likely to demonstrate how readers form mental images when reading. Put the passage on a transparency.

Step 2. Make sure each student has a sheet of blank paper and a pencil, pen, or crayon with which to draw.

Step 3. Read the passage aloud to your students while they follow.

Step 4. Cover or remove the text and ask students to draw an image they formed in response to the text that represents its meaning.

Step 5. Ask students to form groups of two or three, share their drawings, and explain their meaning to others in the group. Ask students to explore similarities and differences between the images they created and the text from which they created the images.

Step 6. Talk with students about how imagery can enhance comprehension and recall of texts they read in the content areas.

An example of image-rich writing from a chapter on Darwin's theory of evolution in *Biology* (Miller & Levine, 2006):

> While heading home (from the Galapagos Islands), Darwin spent a great deal of time thinking about his findings. Examining different mockingbirds from the Galapagos, Darwin noticed that individual birds collected from the island of Floreana looked different from those collected on James Island. They also looked different from individuals collected on other islands. Darwin also remembered that the tortoises differed from island to island. Although Darwin did not immediately understand the reason for these patterns of diversity, he had stumbled across an important finding. Darwin observed that the characteristics of many animals and plants varied noticeably among the different islands of the Galapagos. After returning to England, Darwin began to wonder if animals living on different islands had once been members of the same species. According to this hypothesis, these separate species would have evolved from an original South American ancestor species after becoming isolated from one another. Was this possible? If so, it would turn people's view of the natural world upside down. (Miller & Levine, 2006. *Biology*. (Upper Saddle River, NJ: Pearson/Prentice Hall), p. 373).

After demonstrating this image-making strategy with passages from your content area text or another source, you can ask students to apply the strategy to the next reading assignment you give them. When they complete the reading and rendering, don't forget to take some time for students to share their imagery.

Read to discover. To encourage reading for a purpose, you can have your students silently read a text that will be used as a resource for subsequent activities (Opitz & Rasinski, 1998). Following their silent reading, students can read aloud in class sections of the text they found particularly meaningful, exciting, or informative and explain why they found them so. They can also use what they read silently as a source of information to answer questions that you'll ask. Students also discover that reading for a purpose enhances attention and aids comprehension.

Step-By-Step: How to Conduct a "Read to Discover" Session

Step 1. All students silently read a particular text (perhaps as their homework assignment).

Step 2. On 3 × 5 cards, write questions of various kinds about the text. These questions may vary from asking students to select and read a passage that they enjoyed, liked best, or found meaningful to reading a section that addresses more specific cognitive questions. For example, students might be asked to read a passage that explains the causes for an event, such as the American Revolution, in a U.S. history class or the physiological effects of a particular

Figure 9.2 Sample Questions for a Ninth-Grade Physical Science Class "Read Aloud Bag" from a Chapter Entitled "Energy" in *Physical Science: Concepts in Action.*

1. What is the relationship between work and energy?
2. What is kinetic energy?
3. Upon what does an object's gravitational potential energy depend?
4. What kind of energy is represented by a rubber band stretched between your fingers?
5. What kind of energy is released when wood burns?
6. If you saw a tree hit by lightning, what form of energy would you have seen?
7. When you heat up a can of soup on a gas stove, what kind of energy are you adding to the soup?
8. What's the difference between nuclear fission and fusion?

Source: From *Physical Science: Concepts in Action* (pp. 444–471), by M. Wyssession, D. Frank, & S. Yancopoulos. Copyright 2006 by Pearson/Prentice Hall.

drug, such as caffeine, in a health education class (see Figure 9.2). You can also ask your students to read the topic sentence in an important paragraph and two or three sentences that support it.

Step 3. Distribute the question cards to students. This could be done by having students pull questions from a "Read Aloud Bag" or by deciding which students could be optimally challenged with specific questions you write and giving those directly to specific students you think would benefit from finding and reading the answers aloud. Or, you can pull cards from the question bag yourself, read the question to the whole class, give time for students to find the answer in their texts, call upon students who raise their hands when they find the answer, and request that the student read the appropriate text aloud.

Whole-Class Discussions

Jennifer walks into one of her classes, sits down, takes out her notebook, copies the outline from the board, and then spends the better part of 40 minutes listening to her teacher, Mr. Delbanco, talk while she takes notes. The delivery is one way. Students ask few, if any, questions. In fact, when students ask questions, the teacher says he has a lot to cover and little time to cover it. He's caught in the cross fire between coverage and understanding, with little time for the latter. He believes he's doing the best instructional thing he can to "prepare these kids for college." Jennifer keeps reading sections of her textbook as assigned and taking her lecture notes, but she knows she isn't learning much that she'll retain. What she's expected to know is delivered to her, deposited for a later withdrawal. She rarely participates in thinking much about course content, and she can't recall talking with any of her classmates about it—other than confirming the time for the next multiple-choice test.

In another of her classes, Jennifer is often asked, as part of her homework assignment, to bring three questions to class that she has about the previous day's lecture-discussion, about her reading, or about her project. Her teacher, Ms. Travaille, often begins the economics class by posing one of Jennifer's questions, one of her classmate's, or one of her own to the whole class. Sometimes they have to write for a few minutes about the question while things get settled down. When Ms. Travaille is ready, she asks students to share their answers, usually with a classmate first, and then moves into a whole-class discussion about their answers.

Through negotiated construction of meanings similar to the process described in chapter 3, Ms. Travaille's students build deeper understandings of economic principles and practices. Into her economics classroom, students bring different meanings for the texts they read, the lectures they hear, and the discussion they engage in. From their discussions, common understandings of economic concepts and issues emerge. Students also construct and negotiate meanings for tasks, sources of authority, and other features of the classroom.

To guide her lecture-discussion session, Ms. Travaille often puts a set of questions on the board so students know what territory they will explore that day. Jennifer knows that the questions are like a map, telling her where they'll go and what they're expected to know. But she usually has to actively take the journey with her teacher and classmates in order to discover or construct her answers. Her teacher works as a guide, suggesting they look this way or that, sometimes giving hints but rarely giving outright answers without students getting into the venture. Earlier in the year, Ms. Travaille taught her students about the Cornell Note Taking System and reminds them about its value as a study strategy. Jennifer often thinks her way to understandings in this class by applying the Cornell method—unless she's having an "off day." Usually, she senses that she'll remember the terrain she's covered, perhaps not every square inch but certainly the landmarks, the major sites, and the important vistas.

Ms. Travaille puts into practice important principles that enable her to cover her economics course content and address the state standards while providing ample time for her students to interact, to discover, and to build understandings. What principles does she apply? She has put into practice several of them, some of which James Barton (1995) identified as those contributing to effective classroom discussions:

- Conducting a whole-class discussion is an art form, not unlike conducting an orchestra or playing in a jazz ensemble. But like conductors or musicians, teachers have to prepare and practice for class discussions. They need to know the material, discover main themes, prepare questions, and listen very carefully to the substance, texture, and tone of students' contributions.

- Talking enables students to construct new meanings, extend old ones, and make fresh connections between branches of knowledge and personal understandings. Teachers can encourage or guide students to make connections between branches of knowledge that may have been neglected or ignored and the current focus of discussion.

- Students can develop listening and speaking skills while interacting over and learning the course content. Teachers who listen effectively serve as models to their students. When needed, teachers can ask students to practice explicitly specific listening skills, such as rephrasing or summarizing what another student has said before extending the conversation.

- Students can acquire and practice thinking strategies during conversations about concepts and ideas in the course curriculum. During discussions, teachers can guide students so that they learn to differentiate opinion from supporting evidence or provide explanatory bridges between opinions and reasons supporting an opinion.

- All students should become part of the conversation. To work toward that goal, teachers need to monitor patterns of participation among students and to diagnose possible causes for nonparticipation. Some students may feel that they have little or nothing to contribute, that they can't put their thoughts into words, that they are confused, that they have been excluded from the dialogue, or that they don't want to say something dumb in front of everyone. Once a teacher has figured out what's at the root of the passivity, measures can be taken to draw in reluctant students.

Like Ms. Travaille, Barton (1995) believes that well-orchestrated discussions depend upon the teacher having a clear instructional focus. Ms. Travaille thinks through the material she needs to convey to students until she has a clear grasp of what she wants her students to understand, why she wants them to understand it, and how she is going to guide them toward that understanding. The questions she puts on the board act as landmarks or beacons that signal to students where they need to direct their attention and what they need to understand.

How to make good discussion questions.   Barton (1995) presented a system of five categories for organizing discussion questions that covers a spectrum from text-based questions to student-based questions (see Figure 9.3). Effective discussions include questions covering the entire spectrum. However, students are likely to be most comfortable with literal questions although such questions require that students have done their reading and know how to search it, if needed, for correct answers.

The other four categories of questions take students beyond the literal and into what may be less familiar territory. This is the terrain that Ms. Travaille likes to roam with her students as she explores for deeper understanding and connections. She poses *text implicit questions* when she asks her students to make inferences based upon the text they are reading. For example, she asked Jennifer's class to explain why the author of an article on obesity among teenagers mentioned that schools often encourage consumption of rich junk foods by selling them on campus but didn't say anything about why schools sold them or why they simply didn't stop providing them. When Ms. Travaille asked Jennifer's class to think of ways to apply the idea of supply and demand to our global water access, she was asking a *transfer question* that required her students to think about how the idea of supply and demand for cars could apply to a natural resource. Ms. Travaille posed an *academic question* to connect her students' understanding of information in economics to other

Figure 9.3   Continuum of Discussion Questions.

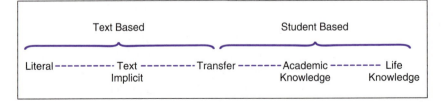

subject domains when she asked them to look for connections between their under-standing of a stock's price-earnings ratio and an athlete's workout program. And, when Ms. Travaille asked Jennifer and her classmates to discuss the connections be-tween a company merger plan and starting a new friendship, she was asking them a *life knowledge question*, in which they had to relate their academic learning about mergers to their personal life experience. Ms. Travaille explained to her students that every answer they gave didn't have to be "right on the money." She wanted them to approach these questions creatively, somewhat like writing a draft of a paper that would undoubtedly have to be rewritten. That way she provided a safe space for exploration and affirmed that searching for answers was a creative process that pro-moted learning.

The purpose of whole-class discussion is to engage students in content- or issue-focused interactions. Through these interactions between teacher and students or among students themselves, students can build understandings of key ideas and make links between what they already know and what they are learning. Although some ed-ucators believe that a teacher's role is to do as little as possible during discussions (O'Flahavan, Stein, Wiencek, & Marks, 1992), I believe that a teacher's active en-gagement in the design, development, and review of classroom conversations is opti-mum in the content areas. You are, in a sense, the lead instrumentalist in a jazz band who wants to develop a musical theme, encourage its exploration, and engage your musicians creatively. But you want your players to listen attentively to each other so they can each contribute to the performance. Accordingly, the teacher's multifaceted role is

- to decide on a discussion's purposes, including the concepts, processes, or skills students are to gain and how those purposes tie to long-range learning goals;
- to set the stage and initiate conversation;
- to guide its development by clarifying concepts or making connections between them that will deepen understanding;
- to monitor the discussion's content and the degree to which students understand it;
- to facilitate interaction that will deepen engagement among participants;
- to help students internalize skills or rigorously examine concepts;
- to offer opportunities to students for summaries, reviews, and moments of reflec-tion; and
- to analyze and reflect upon the lesson in order to learn what worked, which stu-dents need further instructional support, and what instructional steps to take next.

Without your active participation, discussions may drift off-target in too many classrooms. This is not to say that you should dominate dialogue that is important to students but not on your agenda. That would be both educationally inappropriate and psychologically oppressive. However, you will need to make judgments about the direction and value of the conversation as it evolves and, if it is too far off course, ask students to reflect on how the line of discussion contributes to learning goals or deepens understandings of the content or issues upon which the discussion is fo-cused. Perhaps most important of all, you can use each of your whole-class discussion episodes as chapters upon which to reflect for the purpose of making future decisions about how best to conduct future discussions.

Minilessons

A central feature of Nancy Atwell's (1998) teaching is the **minilesson,** a forum for sharing the teacher's knowledge and strategic skill with students. The minilesson sharing goes both ways, however, because students also share their knowledge, contributing to the growth of a classroom community. Although Atwell's minilessons used to be 5 to 10 minutes long, she extended them to 20 minutes to allow for more interaction. Topics for the minilessons arise from her analysis of students' reading, their reading logs, their letters to her about their books, and their participation in classroom conversations. Through close observation and analysis, she decides what students must learn to gain greater competence as readers and learners. The decisions she makes about what should come next form the foundation for the minilessons.

To get students to think about and internalize reading strategies that good readers use, Atwell presents minilessons about a variety of reading-related topics:

- short- and long-term memory,
- schema theory,
- reading paces,
- considerate and inconsiderate texts,
- comprehension strategies,
- various methods of monitoring comprehension while reading,
- how readers respond to unfamiliar words, and
- how to cope with standardized reading tests.

However, concentrated interaction with readers over the texts they read is at the core of Atwell's approach to teaching reading. Although she prepares her students for these interactions at the beginning of the year by explaining schema theory and other reading processes, she demonstrates how students can put that theory into daily practice while reading throughout the school year. During the yearlong reading workshops interspersed with minilessons, she learns much from students' responses and class discussions. During these discussions, she carefully notes her students' comments about their reading processes and their responses to books and texts. It's this information that, when analyzed, helps her make subsequent decisions about the content of future minilessons.

You can also grind the grains of information you gather from your students over their reading into minilessons. If you're a math teacher and discover that your students have trouble translating word problems into algebraic terms, you can design minilessons to address the specific kinds of problems your students encounter during translations. If you're a history teacher and notice that few of your students are questioning their text's assumptions or making connections between parallel ideas or events, you can offer minilessons that focus on "questioning the author" to improve your students' critical thinking. To read the cues that students present in their written work and during class discussion is the key to opening students' minds to improved reading through minilessons and content-learning workshops.

Jeff Waid, whose "student chronicles" I introduced in chapter 4, discovered early in the school year that several students in his honors ninth-grade English class needed help with subject-verb agreement. Three fourths of the students in that class were or had been students with first languages other than English contributing to their subject-verb agreement problems. To address these difficulties, Jeff designed a minilesson on subject-verb agreement that helped students understand the roots of their grammar problem and ways to reduce its prevalence in their written work.

Cooperative Learning

So what exercises best flatten tummies? This chapter began with a description of Cindy Thai, a health education teacher, using Jigsaw to help her students understand muscle groups and how to strengthen them. She got her students into home and expert teams, gave them access to their health textbooks and supplementary reading materials, assigned muscle groups to each team, and asked each team to develop a presentation, including a couple of exercises for their muscle group. While Cindy's teams successfully presented exercises that would guide her students toward flatter tummies, what principles are likely to guide you toward more successfully using cooperative learning strategies?

Principles of Cooperative Learning

Several principles of cooperative learning formulated by its inventors and innovators (Johnson & Johnson, 1999; Kagan, 1992; Slavin, 1995) typically guide its classroom applications. These principles, which are based on their creators' research and practical experience, have helped me make decisions about the design and use of cooperative learning activities in classrooms.

1. *Heterogeneous groups.* Researchers (Lou, 1996) have found that although medium-performance students learn best in homogeneous groups and high-performance students do well in either homogeneous or heterogeneous groups, low-achieving students perform best in heterogeneous groups. Furthermore, mixing students by both performance and status traits (such as ethnicity, group affiliation, or gender) is likely to yield other benefits, such as improved interethnic and interpersonal understanding. Because of these reasons, many educators prefer to create heterogeneous teams when using cooperative learning strategies.

2. *Group accountability.* Students in teams should know that their team has a specific goal or goals that each member is working to achieve. Without a clearly expected outcome in the form of a product or performance, teams drift.

3. *Positive interdependence.* Group goals, usually in the form of a group reward, and accountability are connected with team interdependence. Activities are designed so that team members must swim together or sink together as they work toward a common objective. If one person can float on the work of others, something is amiss with the activity's design.

4. *Individual accountability.* Each team member must be held accountable for his or her participation in the team's work. Individual accountability arises from specifically tailored jobs (individual task specialization) for each team member or from holding each member accountable for performance on a test of knowledge or skills learned in the team but tested independently.

These principles serve as foundational concepts to design and implement cooperative learning activities of many kinds. However, you are likely to encounter other principles that some practitioners advocate. For example, Slavin (1995) endorses activities that can be adapted to students' individual needs and provide equal opportunities for success for all team members. In adapting for the individual needs of struggling readers, for example, cooperative learning activities that involve reading would take into account those readers performance levels and provide them with skill-appropriate reading tasks and strategies. In the case of equal opportunities for all to succeed, team members would be awarded improvement points to reward the effort and growth of lower performing students.

Cooperative learning practitioners have different attitudes toward competition between teams in classrooms. Some (Slavin, 1995) advocate team competition to heighten team cohesion and suggest the use of games or tournaments that engage teams in competition for rewards. Others (Johnson & Johnson, 1999) advocate co-operatively designed activities both within and between teams and see little advantage in competition between individuals or teams.

Researchers (Antil, Jenkins, Wayne, & Vadasy, 1998) who have examined conceptions of cooperative learning and its prevalence in classrooms found that few teachers used acknowledged forms of cooperative learning. When these researchers boiled cooperative learning down to two fundamental principles—positive interdependence and individual accountability—only about 25% of teachers who said they used "cooperative learning" and who were interviewed actually applied the two fundamental principles. Only 5% of teachers met a more restrictive five-principle standard that included reflection on group process and its evaluation (Johnson & Johnson, 1999). Most teachers used their personally constructed version of cooperative learning, usually a less formal approach than that advocated by either Johnson and Johnson or Slavin (1995).

From my perspective, positive interdependence and individual accountability are essential to any small-group activity that flies the banner of cooperative learning. As Slavin (1995) reported, cooperative learning activities that include individual accountability produced significantly more gains than those group endeavors without individual accountability. Including additional principles, such as heterogeneous groups, opportunities to reflect on group process, and equal opportunities for success, into the design of cooperative learning activities may simply enhance their impact.

Informal Group Methods to Support Learning and Literacy

Before we get to more formal cooperative learning activities that may take more than a day to complete, I want to alert you to a couple of informal cooperative activities that facilitate learning and discussion. These activities can complement and enliven a more traditional lesson through guided interaction.

Numbered Heads Together.
When teaching or reviewing material that has more or less objective answers, like parts of speech in a grammar exercise, answers to math problems worked out individually, or the meaning of terms in a science class, **Numbered Heads Together** can help students learn or prepare for a quiz (Slavin, 1995). It's basically a game played between teams of four or five members, each of which is given a number and each of which provides individual accountability for learning. Once teams are formed, you present problems or questions to the whole class and give time for teams to figure out solutions or share answers so that any team member could respond successfully. Then you call out a number, say 3, and the 3s in each group who believe they can answer the question or explain the problem's solution raise their hands. You then call on one of the number 3s whose hand is in the air. If the student responds correctly, her team gets a point. Tallies can be kept on the board as the game progresses.

Think-Pair-Share.
When I'm presenting ideas to a class, seeking some interpretation of a text, or discussing various opinions about a topic, I sometimes use **Think-Pair-Share** to enrich the conversation and keep students engaged. Although Lyman (1981), who developed this activity, suggested having students sit in designated pairs,

I usually ask my students informally to find a partner in the classroom. During my lesson, I may stop and ask students to take a minute to explore, in a brief writing or journal entry, an idea I've presented. Then I ask each student to find a partner, share written work, and discuss related ideas. These Think-Pair-Share activities may last only a few minutes, and I may do more than one during a class period. If so, I usually ask students to find a new partner to share and discuss what they've written during the individual thinking phase of the activity.

After students have completed a round of Think-Pair-Share, I try to bring out what they have written and discussed by asking students to share with the whole class. That sharing gives me a pretty good idea of what's on my students' minds, what needs clarifying, and how to extend conversations begun in pairs. As I continue with my presentation of ideas, I can incorporate aspects of students' sharing of ideas. After I asked students in a teaching for thinking course to jot down the names of three individuals who have shaped our current culture of ideas, I asked them to find a partner and share who was on their lists and why. After pairing and sharing, we had an animated whole-class discussion about who was on students' lists, how they got there, and what influence they had on today's thought.

Source: CALVIN AND HOBBES © 1988 Watterson. Dist. By UNIVERSAL PRESS SYNDICATE. Reprinted with permission. All rights reserved.

Cooperative Learning Activities with Integrated Literacy Goals

Group investigation.   The roots of **Group Investigation** stretch back to John Dewey (1938/1970) and his belief that cooperation and discovery in the classroom teach students how to live in a democratic society. As in democratic communities, the growth of group investigation requires interpersonal dialogue and collaborative inquiry. Through small-group peer interaction, students pursue challenging, perhaps interdisciplinary learning goals.

Learning Goals for Group Investigation.   A major learning goal commonly sought through Group Investigation is good solutions to complex problems in a specific discipline or across disciplines. Students working in small groups can use their analytical intelligence (J. R. Sternberg & Spear-Swerling, 1996) to recognize and define a problem; formulate strategies to solve it; gather, analyze, and synthesize information relevant to the problem; allocate their time and resources to address the problem; and evaluate the success of their proposed solutions. Examples of problems across disciplines that teachers may have students address include global warming or endangered species; the investigation of trigonometry functions, their discovery, structural variety, and applications; life in France during the French revolution; the legacy of 19th-century Romantic poets in Britain; and obesity in American culture. You can present a broad problem or issue to your students, and they can then break the larger problem into smaller segments that will be the focus of each team's investigation.

Although the outcome of a Group Investigation can include a PowerPoint presentation that will engage your students' literacy skills, I would encourage you to integrate reading texts, printed and/or electronic, to gather information and writing text to demonstrate understanding of ideas or concepts contributing to each team's "product." When including reading and writing skills, you can build in opportunities to develop your students' reading and writing proficiencies, including presentation of reading or writing strategies. Using writing in the form of journal entries, essays, reports, and reflections gives you multiple opportunities to monitor and evaluate not only group progress, but also individual contributions.

Cooperative Planning in Teams.   Engaging student teams in cooperative planning to address a problem lies at the heart of Group Investigation. While you coordinate, they decide which aspect of the problem to investigate, strategies to apply, information to gather, time and personal resources to dedicate, and methods for evaluating their solutions. Positive interdependence arises from the equitable division of labor among group members.

Because interactive planning is not built into every student who walks into your classroom, you will have to test your students' group-planning skills. They will undoubtedly need some guidance and the structure that you can provide to improve the likelihood of each team's success. Whole-class discussions about the assignment help, as do structured reports from each team and continuous monitoring of progress toward learning goals. Start small and grow. Single day projects might best come before extended investigations.

Coordinating Group Investigations: The Hats Teachers Wear.   When doing Group Investigations, you will play several roles. First, you'll need to make choices about broad topics for investigation related to your long-term or standards-based instructional goals. You may also want to break the broad category down into several lesser topics. Teams may then choose from those subtopics, or, if instructionally advantageous, you can assign subtopics to teams. Second, you will need to serve as a monitor and facilitator of team planning. Students will have questions about what to do, who's to do it, and when it's to be done. Your guidance will provide solutions during their organizing episodes, and your knowledge of resources will help them realize those solutions. Schedules for work completion might also be needed for longer projects. Before teams begin to carry out their plans, I would recommend that you review their subtopic proposals so that your learning goals are aligned with their task proposals. Third, you should consider using a rubric to evaluate team products and individual contributions. (See chapter 7 on rubrics to assess writing.) A rubric will also alert teams and individual team members to the criteria that will be applied when their projects are completed. Those criteria will also enable students to see outcome expectations clearly. Fourth, when subtopic projects are completed, you will need to facilitate their presentation to the class and, perhaps, whole-class evaluation of each team's project. Lastly, all aspects of the curriculum related to the broad topic you select may not be covered through subtopic projects and presentations. In that event, you can fill in or elaborate through whole-class instructional methods and individual assignments.

Step-By-Step: How to Do a Group Investigation

When implementing a Group Investigation, you and your students will go through several stages (Sharan & Sharan, 1992; Slavin, 1995).

Step 1. *Getting Students into Teams.* After you have selected the broad topic, students can review resources related to that topic and make subtopic proposals. You can present the broad topic or problem to the class, ask them what they would like to know about it, and record their interests and questions. You might then add subtopics that students did not identify and that supplement your instructional goals. When all potential subtopics have been described, students select their subtopics and teams, depending on their interests. I suggest developing a procedure for team membership, such as giving students a list of all possible subtopics and asking them to rank the top three or four they would like to investigate. Then you put teams together, with student interests and the principle of heterogeneity guiding their team building. Before students actually meet in their teams, you may need to survey materials students can access to accomplish their team's purposes. Students in higher grades may be given more responsibility for finding resources and bringing them to class for team use.

Step 2. *Planning for Learning About the Subtopic.* Students need to meet in their teams to decide what they will study or what problem they will solve, how they will go about their work, who will do what and when, and what kinds of products or outcomes they will create. Have each team submit a worksheet (see Figure 9.4) describing their program and schedule so you can see what each team member will be individually accountable for with respect to the group outcome.

A team's subtopic can be further segmented into minitopics. After discussion and identification of minitopics whose investigation can contribute to the team's subtopic presentation, each team member selects a minitopic. Team members can share resources they uncover while pursuing their minitopics.

Step 3. *Engaging in the Investigation.* With the information they gather, students analyze their data, propose solutions, organize information, and reach conclusion. The team's work should be designed so that each member contributes and so that you can monitor each student's contribution. Usually, students interact over their resources, decide how resources will be applied to their problem, discuss their understandings of texts, clarify meanings, and pursue conclusions for their products and presentations.

If teams divide their subtopic into minitopics, each team member works independently and interacts with the team to report on problems and progress. Each team member also prepares a minitopic presentation to give to his or her own team. These individual minitopic presentations will contribute

Figure 9.4 Team Planning Worksheet.

Team name: _____

Team members: _____

Team subtopic: _____

What questions we plan to answer or problems we'll investigate and solve: _____

_____

_____

A list of our resources to accomplish the above: _____

_____

Who will do what: _____

_____

When we'll get things done: _____

_____

What we think we'll do for a presentation (not required info at this time): _____

_____

_____

to the team's presentation to the whole class later in the process. Using minitopics for which each team member is responsible makes each member's contributions more transparent and ensures individual accountability. These minitopic presentations can be in the form of written reports that could, like the team's presentation, be evaluated.

Step 4. *Designing the Final Report or Presentation.* After stating and sharing their team's central findings and their rationale, groups decide what they'll present and how they'll present it. Because the integration of literacy growth into content learning is a primary instructional aim, I recommend that reports or presentations be written. Other forms of presentation, such as debates, quiz shows, simulations, art or theatrical work, and PowerPoints or multimedia shows that draw upon the multiple intelligences of group members, can accompany the written products. You or a student committee can coordinate team presentations.

Step 5. *Presentations.* Group presentations should be made to the whole class and can actively involve all students in the class. For example, if a team is presenting what they learned about a trigonometric function, such as tangent or cosine, students in the whole class could engage in solving or creating problems that apply those functions and meet at learning stations to share their solutions. Students should also be involved in assessing the quality of a team's presentation. If you design a rubric with your class or present one to guide the evaluation of a presentation, students can apply that rubric to team presentations.

Step 6. *Assessment.* Teams should engage in self-evaluation and receive assessment feedback from other students and from you. An important aspect of cooperative learning is learning about group processes and how members contribute to team effectiveness. Students can discuss how they completed their work, how they felt about the process, and how they solved problems as a team to complete work on their subtopics. After students evaluate a team's presentation to the whole class, these evaluations can be given to each team.

In alignment with research and my own observations, I also hold students individually accountable for learning about concepts, ideas, or solutions that each team presented, including those presented by their own team. The form of that accountability is usually a test of the material covered. I have made lists of study questions to guide students' individual learning based not only upon what teams presented, but also on material related to the broad topic that I presented to the whole class. With information about how teams performed and about how individuals performed on tests covering the material presented, I can get a pretty clear picture of how well each student in the class engaged in learning and mastering key concepts and knowledge.

If teams break their subtopic into minitopics, products can be generated that enable assessment at four points: When the whole class assesses the team's subtopic presentation, when other team members assess individual minitopic contributions to the team's effort, when team members evaluate their own team's whole-class presentation, and when the teacher evaluates both individual and team learning and performance.

Group Reading Activity (GRA). Like Group Investigation, a *Group Reading Activity* (Manzo, Manzo, & Thomas, 2005) divides a complex learning task into smaller segments that each team addresses cooperatively. If you were asking a class to undertake a GRA focused on the American Civil War, you would divide the history text into roughly equal segments, as I've done in Table 9.1.

Assign students in teams of 4, determine the total number of teams composed, and then divide the text into roughly equal segments, one for each team. The Civil War reading assignment (Table 9.1) for each team arose from having 28 students in the history class. With 4 students in each team, seven assignments were needed.

Table 9.1　Group Reading Activity Team Assignment Example

SECTION	PAGES	ASSIGNED GROUP
The Roots of Civil War	pp. 225–231	
The Alignment of the States	pp. 232–238	
The Battles Begin	pp. 238–243	
Life Back Home	pp. 244–260	
Final Fighting	pp. 260–266	
The War's Consequences	pp. 266–273	
Beginning Reconstruction	pp. 274–280	

When students meet in their teams, they have several tasks to complete that lead to a class presentation. After all presentations are completed and before assessing students individually for their understanding of the text, the teacher and students decide what still needs to be covered to ensure that learning goals or standards have been met for topics included in the GRA.

Step-By-Step: How to Do a Group Reading Activity (GRA)

Step 1. Select text material that aligns with your lesson's learning goals and pertinent standards.

Step 2. After creating four-person teams, decide how many teams you'll have in a particular class. Divide the section of text material in the GRA into appropriate subsections for each team to read, as exemplified in Table 9.1.

Step 3. All students should read all team assignments, perhaps for homework the evening before beginning the GRA.

Step 4. You should assign one section to each team. For each team's reading assignment, explain to teams that they will need to identify the most important concepts or ideas in the material they will read, to decide what additional material they may need to cover relevant text topics, and to decide how to present the text's content to the rest of the class. Presentations may take a multitude of forms, including written reports, debates, simulations, round-table discussions, and audiovisuals.

Step 5. After appointing a friendly critic from each team, you should explain to the whole class that the critic is to visit another team to hear its presentation and to offer constructive suggestions for improvement.

Step 6. Let critics hear other team presentations and provide recommendations that presenting teams can use to improve their work. The visiting critic's constructive suggestions guide a team's revision before whole-class presentations begin.

Step 7. Review each team's presentation yourself, provide your own suggestions, and give teams time to digest all recommendations for improvement.

Step 8. Schedule and hear team presentations.

Step 9. Engage in a whole-class discussion to make sure key concepts are covered, misunderstandings are clarified, and questions are answered.

Jigsaw II. When concept acquisition rather than skill acquisition is your learning goal, **Jigsaw II** (Slavin, 1995) may be your instructional vehicle. Originated by Elliott Aronson and his colleagues (Aronson, Blaney, Stephen, Sikes, & Snapp, 1978), Jigsaw works like interlocking parts forming a whole picture. In Slavin's Jigsaw II, texts provide the raw material that all "home team" members read and use to teach each other. You assign chapters to read to students in a home team and give them expert sheets that identify topics to master or questions to answer while reading. Students with the same topic but from different home teams meet together in "expert teams" when they finish reading. They discuss the topics, answer their questions, and become "experts." They then return to their home teams and take turns teaching other cooperative team members the material they have mastered. Students next take a test to evaluate their command of the material, and those test scores become team scores. Slavin used an individual improvement score system to provide for individual differences and success for all. Team success motivates all members to engage in learning. Positive interdependence, with every student contributing to his or her team's success, lies at the heart of this activity. Although some teachers initially balk at complications connected with planning and organizing a Jigsaw II event in class, I have often used the activity and found it effective.

Step-By-Step: How to Do a Jigsaw II Activity

Step 1. Decide on what students are to read and study to address your learning goals and standards. On the day before you plan to begin the Jigsaw II activity, assign the reading material to be covered so that all students will have read it.

Step 2. Compose several questions for the expert sheet. Slavin advises teachers to formulate questions that are relevant to topics that appear throughout a chapter or unit. If we were to use Jigsaw II rather than a group reading activity to cover the Civil War, we would have to write expert sheets for each section that team members were to master. For example, if an expert Civil War team were to focus on "The Battles Begin" text, I would provide each student with a set of topics or questions to guide and focus their reading in preparation for expert team discussion. Those questions might look something like this:

1. What brought about the fall of Fort Sumter?
2. What general strategies for war did the Union and the Confederacy adopt?
3. What was the significance to the Confederacy of the outcome of the First Battle of Bull Run?
4. What was the outcome of the Battle of Antietam and why was it significant to the Union forces?
5. What is an ironclad and why did it change naval warfare?

Step 3. Create heterogeneous home teams so that the number of team members corresponds to the number of topic questions on the expert sheet. If you have five students in the home team, you'll need five topic questions and five expert teams. You'll also need at least 25 students in your class to have five expert teams. If you have more than 25, you can have more than one member of a team become an expert on the same topic or question.

Step 4. One question on the expert sheet should be assigned to at least one member of the home team.

Step 5. Ask all students with the same question to meet in an expert team to address that question and be ready to explain the answer to their home team. You should monitor discussion and preparation for teaching the home teams as expert teams interact.

Step 6. When ready, expert team members should return to their home teams to explain answers and concepts to their home teammates. Further discussion may arise in the home team as teaching progresses.

Step 7. After home teams have heard from all "experts," you can convene a whole-class discussion to cover any loose ends, confusion, or further questions.

Reciprocal Teaching

Although **reciprocal teaching** depends upon small-group interaction for its effectiveness, it was not originally designed as a cooperative learning activity. In its original, experimental form, reciprocal teaching engaged only a struggling reader and a researcher in a series of prescribed interactions to enhance comprehension. However, the reciprocal teaching method worked for certain students, and its original form morphed into a variety of applications, one of which engaged four students working collaboratively—if not in an acknowledged cooperative learning format. While earlier comprehension strategies in this and the previous chapter were designed to help readers' cognitive processing before, during, and after reading, reciprocal teaching was intended to foster *meta*cognitive processing. More specifically, reciprocal teaching helps readers monitor and control comprehension, important functions of metacognition that we explored in chapter 3. Following years of research and investigation, educators widely agree that metacognition while reading consists of two fundamental dimensions: monitoring and controlling comprehension.

A Brief History of Reciprocal Teaching

Charles has an IQ of about 70 and reads on a third-grade level, 4 years behind his peers in reading comprehension. In spite of his being enrolled as a special education student and receiving several forms of remedial reading instruction, he's made little progress. He can read seventh-grade texts aloud at about 90 words per minute with few errors, but he can't tell you much about what he's read. He has great difficulty answering the most basic questions you ask him about passages he reads. He can't ask you a question based on his reading of a passage. He makes only statements about the passages. You often require students to read their textbooks as part of their homework assignments, and you have learned that Charles cannot do homework assignments that require him to read the text and respond to it. He simply doesn't have enough understanding of what he's reading.

After reviewing the behaviors of good readers, Annemarie Palincsar (A. L. Brown, Palincsar, & Armbruster, 1984; Palincsar, 1982) created reciprocal teaching to address the needs of inadequately mediated learners who, like Charles, have trouble with reading comprehension. These struggling readers may lack parental modeling, such as question-answer sessions over a book read together. Disadvantaged students who can decode but not comprehend quickly may have missed important nurturing in literacy. Once at school, teachers take over the parenting role to model and promote effective reading and learning strategies. They do this by showing their curiosity about what is read, generating questions, making predictions, and searching for evidence to validate their conclusions and inferences. Good teachers become models of comprehension-fostering strategies that children internalize thorough social interaction in the classroom.

Original Reciprocal Teaching Model

If students lack reading strategies because they have not had enough interactive experience with more able readers to develop good reading tactics, couldn't these struggling readers learn strategies by interacting with teachers who modeled strategic reading? Couldn't these struggling readers, like Charles, imitate and internalize those strategies? These are the questions Palincsar, Brown, and their colleagues (A. L. Brown et al., 1984; Palincsar, 1982) asked. They identified activities underlying traditional reading education practices and theoretical treatments before selecting four particular skills for strategy instruction. These four were (a) summarizing, (b) questioning, (c) clarifying, and (d) predicting. Researchers had explored the effectiveness of these skills in isolation but had not combined them to confront the problems of readers with poor comprehension. As a package of activities, they were embedded in a training procedure called *reciprocal teaching* that mimicked parent-child interaction over books. In its earliest experimental forms, Palincsar and Brown used reciprocal teaching as a training strategy with seventh- and eighth-grade students who had adequate decoding skills but whose comprehension scores were, on average, 3 years below grade level. "Adequate decoding skills" meant that students could read grade-appropriate texts at rates of 80 words per minute with no more than two errors. In this early model of reciprocal teaching, each student worked with one of the researchers. Together both would silently read a passage, usually about one paragraph long, in an appropriately challenging book. Whoever was in the role of "teacher" first, perhaps the researcher, summarized the passage, clarified complex or misleading parts of the text, asked the student a teacherlike question based on the main idea, and made a prediction about where the text was going. While providing suggestions and encouragement, the experimenter tried to keep the dialogue informal. Then, they reversed roles, and the student became the teacher for the next passage, sometimes delighting in asking the adult a question about the text. At first, students would sometimes have difficulties putting the gist of a passage into their own words and would need some coaching from the adult, who would provide prompts, nudges, and hints along with praise for progress. After several sessions, perhaps 6 to 10, students became more adept at capturing the essence of a passage, asking a question, and making a prediction. All in all, students had about 20 reciprocal teaching sessions.

Eventually, with sufficient modeling, students were able to perform these reading strategies on their own. They had internalized the reading comprehension strategies through social interaction during several one-on-one sessions with a trained "teacher." Students' performance on experimenter-designed quizzes to determine their comprehension improved from an average of about 15% to rates of 80% to 90% after instruction in reciprocal teaching. Although performance fell off somewhat after half a year, students' performance again improved after one day of training "booster" sessions.

Through training in reciprocal teaching, Charles, who was actually a student in one of Palincsar and Brown's studies, made impressive progress in overcoming his frustrations with reading comprehension. He learned to give concise summaries, answer 80% to 90% of the comprehension questions, and formulate appropriate questions after reading passages. In addition, his comprehension score on the Gates-MacGinitie, a standardized reading test, improved by 20 months.

Step-By-Step: How to Do Basic One-On-One Reciprocal Teaching

Step 1. Determine your student's capacity to decode text by having him or her read from a text appropriate to his or her grade level. As a general guideline, if students are unable to read grade-appropriate texts at rates of 80 words per minute with no more than two errors, they would most likely benefit from instruction in decoding skills prior to or along with comprehension-fostering activities. (See chapters 5 and 10 for appropriate intervention programs.)

Step 2. Create and administer a 10- or 20-item comprehension quiz based on the text you have selected. If students who appear to be able to read the text do not perform satisfactorily on the quiz, that is, they answer less than half the questions correctly, they are likely to be candidates for reciprocal teaching.

Step 3. Arrange for a series of 20 training sessions about 30 to 45 minutes in length.

Step 4. Identify appropriately challenging instructional-level texts for the student. Books should be neither at the frustration level nor at the independent reading level for the student. Be ready to change texts if the ones selected are either too difficult or too easy.

Step 5. Prepare in advance the length of passages you and your student will read. However, maintain flexibility. You may have to change the size of passages you have planned to use as you see how your student responds to the text.

Step 6. Begin by reading the first passage silently together. (If decoding itself is a challenge, you can read the text aloud with students following.)

Step 7. Do not start by having the student summarize, question, clarify, and predict. But do begin by demonstrating these skills for the student. Initially, you may need to look at the text as you summarize, ask questions, and make predictions. However, try to work toward doing so without looking at the text. Your student may also begin by needing to consult the text, but the point is to construct a gist that can be put into the reader's own words without frequently consulting the text.

Step 8. After completing the first passage, change roles. Now the student will adopt the role of the teacher. Read the next passage silently (or aloud if decoding presents a problem) and have the student summarize, clarify, ask a question of you, and make a prediction about where the text is going. You may have to do some guiding during the first few rounds, but provide help, support, and especially praise following moments of success. Try to keep the atmosphere informal but structured.

Step 9. Continue this process until you have completed the session.

Step 10. Following each session, I'd recommend writing a log describing your student's response to reciprocal teaching. Note the appropriateness of the text you selected. Note your student's progress in response to your modeling. Watch for skills that may need more deliberate demonstration at the next session. Also, indicate your student's general response to this reading game.

Variations of Reciprocal Teaching

Early modifications.   Teachers and researchers have been prolific in creating variations on the theme of reciprocal teaching. However, Brown et al. (Brown et al., 1984) were themselves innovative. After the success of their initial studies, they replicated reciprocal teaching's key steps with classroom teachers in school settings rather than with researchers. This time they selected for their sample seventh- and eighth-grade students from the poorest reading groups in classrooms and students in reading groups that met in a resource room. While these students were about $2\frac{1}{2}$ years behind in reading comprehension, they had to meet the decoding requirement for inclusion in the training. Teachers received three training sessions in reciprocal reading, including a video of the researchers using the strategy. The researchers showed teachers how to help students who became overly detailed in summarizing and who were unable to generate appropriate teacherlike questions. Teachers also had opportunities to practice the procedure with students not taking part in the innovation. The results of this second study of reciprocal teaching in the natural setting of school classrooms was quite similar to the one-on-one study previously described. Students improved in the ability to summarize, ask questions, participate in dialogue about passages read, and answer comprehension questions. Students also transferred their newly acquired skills to other reading and learning tasks.

Later applications.   Although numerous teachers and researchers have applied reciprocal teaching in their classrooms, we are going to examine more closely its implementation in a couple of schools, a middle school and a high school.

Faced with hundreds of underprepared readers, Cindy Lenners and Kelly Smith (1999), who were teaching at Harden Middle School in Salinas, California, modified the original model of reciprocal teaching so that they and other teachers in their school could help their students become more skilled readers. In their approach to reciprocal teaching, Lenners and Smith focused on asking questions early and extensively. They begin by distinguishing between "on-the-surface" and "under-the-surface" reading. **On-the-surface reading** reveals an understanding of what was said in the text or what happened and can be demonstrated through literal retelling, simplistic paraphrasing, and summarizing. **Under-the-surface reading** gets at what the text means and includes connecting the text to the reader's life, to other texts, and to background knowledge, filling in knowledge gaps, clarifying, making predictions, questioning, evaluating, challenging, and reflecting. These differences in levels of reading are important because training in reciprocal teaching entails learning how to ask more and better questions. To teach students their variation of reciprocal teaching, Lenners and Smith encourage teachers to model all aspects of the dialogue, including reading aloud, generating both on- and under-the-surface questions, clarifying, summarizing, and predicting. They also encourage teachers to help students understand the function of different question-word categories. If the student is trying to generate on-the-surface questions, they will want to use question words such as who, where, when, what, and sometimes how. If under-the-surface questions are being generated, students should think of using question words such as these: why, how, would, should, and could.

Generating questions appears to be a critical factor in improving reading comprehension. Several researchers (Rosenshine, Meister, & Chapman, 1996) reviewed 26 intervention studies that taught students to generate questions as a way to improve comprehension and found that some procedural prompts were more successful than others in improving students' comprehension performance. The most successful prompts were the following:

1. signal words, such as those included in Lenners and Smith's (1999) intervention (e.g., who, where, how),
2. generic question stems (e.g., What are the strengths and weakness of . . . ?), and
3. story-grammar categories that helped students generate questions about a story's setting, main character, main character's purposes, and obstacles the main character confronted.

The form of question generation emphasized in training provided for teachers and students through Lenners and Smith's model is primarily that of signal words, such as who, where, and why, with some question stems, especially for under-the-surface questions, such as hypotheticals in the form of "If . . ., then would . . . ?"

In their adaptation of reciprocal teaching, Lenners and Smith (1999) have students work in pairs or groups of four who proceed in a cycle that I called a "Metacognitive Merry-Go-Round" to improve reading through self-regulation (Unrau, 1995). Let's say the group consists of Alice, Brenda, Carlos, and David (A, B, C, & D, for short). Each member of the team is initially assigned a reciprocal teaching task to either summarize, question, predict, or clarify. (Later in this chapter, I've provided a description of each of these tasks that can be put on color-coded cards for students.) So A would start as summarizer, B as questioner, C as predictor, and D as clarifier. After completing the first round of assigned responses to the passage, members of the team pass their task description card to the right. Then, after reading the next passage, B would summarize, C question, D predict, and A clarify. For clarifications sake, when the questioner poses a question, any other member of the team can answer it. As should now be clear, before each subsequent passage is read, members pass their task card to the right, merry-go-round style.

Although the original experimental model for reciprocal teaching engaged struggling readers in only a 20-day intervention program, Lenners and Smith (1999) encourage middle and secondary teachers to implement and practice reciprocal teaching activities for many months or years in their classrooms. They also believe in the importance of teachers knowing how to train their own students extensively in reciprocal teaching practices, such as asking questions of many kinds. Allowing teachers to experiment with transplanting the strategy into their own classrooms is another important principle these teachers advocate. These practices appear to be paying off in improved student reading and learning performance.

In a test of reciprocal teaching's impact on high school students in remedial reading classes, Alfassi (1998) investigated the method's impact compared with a control group that was given a traditional method of remedial reading based on skill acquisition. The study would be a test and a stretch for reciprocal teaching because, in past studies, it was applied primarily to elementary and middle school students, often in more experimenter-controlled or lab settings, which were quite different from remedial reading classrooms. Students in the study received training in reciprocal teaching for 20 days, the usual training time, and then 5 days of introduction to the four primary processes, followed by 3 weeks of activities using the method.

Reciprocal teaching met the challenges of its being taught to high school students, whose reading struggles have persisted over many years, and of its being taught in remedial reading classes that created a more authentic or natural setting for the method's implementation. The researcher found that the study supported the implementation of the method in large, intact, remedial reading high school classes. In addition, it lent credence to strategy instruction with long-struggling, high school–aged readers

Features Contributing to Reciprocal Teaching's Success

Several studies (Carter, 1997; Marks, 1993; Rosenshine & Meister, 1994) have concluded that reciprocal teaching in various forms improves the comprehension of struggling readers. However, its success may depend on its including specific elements. A review of reciprocal teaching's implementation in classrooms indicates several factors may account for its success:

1. Students should be carefully evaluated to make sure that they can decode an appropriate grade-level text at a reading rate of at least 80 words per minute with no more that two errors. If students are unable to decode at that standard, they probably need other kinds of reading interventions, such as some form of corrective reading program that emphasizes the growth of decoding skills. (To accommodate weak decoders, texts could be read aloud.)

2. During training, teachers should thoughtfully regulate the level of text difficulty. If needed, students can begin with single sentences for summarizing, asking questions, clarifying, and predicting. They can then progress to single paragraphs, to two or more paragraphs, and on to longer selections of 800 or more words. Later, students could select or be given appropriately challenging grade-level texts with which to learn and practice reciprocal teaching strategies.

3. Teachers (tutors, peers, etc.) of reciprocal teaching should be thoroughly trained in its basic activities: summarizing, questioning, clarifying, and predicting. That training should include an understanding of direct instruction, provision for ample practice, an understanding of monitoring and control over reading comprehension, and the evaluation of teachers who will be trained and who will serve as models.

    3.1. Teachers should learn to give students direct instruction in learning to summarize a passage. With the goal of enabling students to clearly explain the steps essential to quality summarizing to other students, I have used a procedure called single-sentence summaries. To create the strategy, I reviewed work on summarization (Day, 1980, 1986; Kintsch & van Dijk, 1978) and orchestrated summarizing procedures so that students work as collaborating partners (see the Strategy in Practice). A single-sentence summary sheet can be designed to fit the number of paragraphs or sections students are to summarize with a number identifying each paragraph or section.

Strategy in Practice

RECIPROCAL TEACHING FEATURE: SINGLE-SENTENCE SUMMARIES

1. Reader reads section aloud to partner. *Using own words, reader summarizes the section in one sentence.* Partner assists and records the summary.

2. Partner reads the *next* section aloud. *Using own words, partner summarizes the section in one sentence.* Reader assists and records the summary.

3. Continue to switch roles following the pattern established above.

Summarizing Hints:

1. Drop out information that is not of central importance. (Avoid trivialities.)
2. Don't repeat any information. (Avoid repetition.)
3. In place of a list of examples, use a general term that includes all the items on the list.
4. Look for the topic sentence in the paragraph. It can help you identify and state the main idea.
5. If you can't find a topic sentence in the paragraph, make one up that you think expresses the paragraph's core meaning. Try to define the paragraph's controlling idea.

Summaries

¶ 1.

¶ 2.

¶ 3.

─── ∿∿

3.2. Teachers should be trained to understand the range of questions that students can ask and the most effective means by which to teach question-generating methods to students. Studies (Rosenshine et al., 1996) suggest that best practices include initially using single-word and stem prompts to help students generate questions on the surface level and beneath the surface. As students internalize question-asking procedures, these structured prompts should be gradually withdrawn. Lenners and Smith (1999) developed a procedure to help students learn how to ask on-the-surface and under-the-surface questions. I have modified their procedure somewhat and include it as a Strategy in Practice. As was done with a single-sentence summary sheet, a question log can be designed to reflect the number of paragraphs or sections students are to base their question generation on.

Strategy in Practice
∿∿ ───

RECIPROCAL TEACHING FEATURE: ON-THE-SURFACE AND UNDER-THE-SURFACE QUESTION LOG

1. Reader reads section aloud to partner. Reader asks an on-the-surface question. Partner repeats the question and then answers. Partner records question on log.
2. Partner asks an under-the-surface question. Reader repeats the question and answers. Reader records question on log. Switch roles and go on.

ON-THE-SURFACE QUESTIONS (WHEN, WHERE, WHAT, WHO)	UNDER-THE-SURFACE QUESTIONS (WHY, HOW, WOULD, SHOULD, COULD)
¶ 1.	
¶ 2.	
¶ 3.	

3.3 Giving students cards that describe their roles when doing reciprocal teaching in a team helps everyone know what is expected of them. You can prepare color-coded cards for each of the four roles and even a fifth as visualizer; then, when teams of four or five students are assembled, give each team a set of the cards. After each passage read and following each person's carrying out his or her reciprocal teaching task, ask students to pass the cards one person to their right before beginning the next passage.

Description of Roles for Metacognitive Merry-go-round:

Summarizer Card

After reading the passage, the summarizer restates the core meaning or gist of the passage in one or two sentences.

Here are some hints:

1. Drop out information that is not of central importance.
2. Don't repeat any information.
3. In place of a list of examples, use a general term that includes all the items on the list.
4. Look for the topic sentence in a paragraph. It can often help you identify and state the main idea.
5. If you can't find a topic sentence in a paragraph, make one up that you think expresses the paragraph's core meaning. Try to define the paragraph's controlling idea.

Questioner Card

The questioner generates an on-the-surface or under-the-surface question.

On-the-surface questions (when, where, what, or who questions):

Generate a question that can be answered using the information that's right there on the page.

Under-the-surface questions (why, how, would, should, could questions):

Generate a question that makes the reader think between or beyond the lines in the text. These kinds of questions require that the reader makes inferences because the answer is not right there on the page but lies beyond it.

Predictor Card

The predictor makes a statement about where the text appears to be heading based on what has already been read. Predictions do not have to be correct. A prediction is a hypothesis or a guess. After reading further, you should be able to decide if your guess was on target or not.

Clarifier Card

The clarifier selects a word, concept, or phrase and explains its meaning, especially in relation to the context in which it appears.

Visualizer Card

The visualizer draws a quick picture representing what the text suggests to a reader and then shares that picture with others in the reading team. (These drawings are quick sketches. They should not be judged for their artistic merit.)

4. Sensitive interaction and modeling of strategies are essential. Teachers need to develop scaffolding for each student's response, regression, or progression. Through reciprocal teaching, teachers provide students with a progressively challenging scaffold that they use to gain comprehension strategies. As readers become more competent, teachers ask the readers to become increasingly responsible for more comprehension tasks while increasing the challenge in progressive, manageable degrees.

5. Teachers should evaluate students' progress toward mastery of summarizing, questioning, clarifying, and predicting. Mastery-level criteria can be established, and students can be continuously evaluated to determine whether or not they have met the criteria. Students not meeting the criteria may need further instruction.

6. Essential, too, is the frequent assessment of target students' progress with comprehension quizzes and checks on development of dialogue. Both the degree and quality of students' internalization of strategies need to be assessed.

7. The training should provide bridges and maps to show teachers and students how the strategy applies across the curriculum.

8. Teachers should be organized to observe and coach each other.

9. Teachers and administrators ought to be committed to infusing reciprocal teaching over the long haul, including the provisions of training to new teachers and students as they enter the school or district.

Many of these principles have contributed to the success of earlier reciprocal teaching efforts in several different educational settings, from elementary school to the university. Certainly, teachers need to discover how reciprocal teaching may best be adapted for their students in their classrooms. However, these guidelines, if applied, will increase the likelihood that reciprocal teaching interventions that you plan in your classroom or school will help struggling readers improve their comprehension and enjoyment when reading.

Tutoring: Working in Pairs

To promote collaborative learning and literacy in a variety of graduated forms, this chapter began with whole-group instruction techniques, moved on to small-group formats, including cooperative learning and reciprocal teaching, and now focuses on pairs, specifically tutoring pairs. Tutoring between a knowledgeable tutor and tutee has been found to be the most powerful learning context, even when two or three tutees are tutored simultaneously (Bloom, 1984). However, tutoring can take a variety of forms, including peer tutoring, cross-age tutoring, and adult-literacy tutoring in which a trained college student, adult volunteer, or teacher works one-on-one with a tutee. Although teachers can gain much diagnostic knowledge from one-on-one tutoring and give strategic instruction to students in need of special scaffolding, time limits teacher-student tutoring opportunities. We'll start our discussion of tutoring with student-to-student interaction and progress to adult-student models.

Peer Tutoring

Peer tutoring engages students of similar age and grade in helping each other master a domain of knowledge or skill. The practice has both advantages and some drawbacks. The advantages include cognitive growth through peer empathy with a learner's frustration and more supportive classroom climates arising from prosocial cooperation.

On occasion, peer tutors echo the adage "Been there; done that." Having had problems in learning they have overcome and sharing a "cognitive framework," peer tutors can help their classmates understand topics that teachers may struggle to convey (Cohen, 1986). Most teachers have had moments in class when calling on a student to explain a concept or process was just the magic needed to move beyond a sticking point. On more than one occasion while teaching an English class, I've answered a student's question about the motives behind a character's behavior with reasonable clarity, but some students found my explanation difficult to grasp. I could see perplexity written on their faces. So, I'd call on a savvy student to explain in his own words the point I was making. Just like pulling a rabbit from an empty black hat, confused students grasped the point. That magic can also occur in peer tutorials.

Competitive, tense, "Wha'd'ja get?" classrooms can become more conducive to learning with a dash of cooperation. Peer tutoring puts students in prosocial cooperative roles, helping classmates learn. Building those supportive relationships can significantly change a classroom climate. We know that school climates improve when cooperative learning programs are effectively developed (Slavin, 1995). The same cooperative dynamics that contribute to those changes work in peer-tutoring relationships within classrooms.

While peer tutoring enables students to help each other learn, every peer-tutoring relationship a teacher engineers does not always result in a well-built bridge for learning. Personalities sometimes clash when the chemistry of one learner collides with that of another. Or a tutee's self-worth may suffer from feeling stigmatized as less capable than a tutor from the same class, and so a tutee may resist help or advice. However, the likelihood of problems arising from putting peers together for tutoring drops with appropriate training, placement, assignment, and assessment. Even those few resisters may discover the benefits of tutoring and seek it rather than resist it.

Guidelines for tutoring from research.   Because I've focused this discussion of group methods on the development of reading, I want to provide you with research-based guidelines for developing and implementing reading tutorials. Martha Rekrut (1994) compiled a set of useful guidelines that her investigation of relevant research generated. These guidelines answer many questions that teachers interested in using reading tutorials ask.

1. *What elements of reading are amenable to tutorial work?* While many elements make a friendly fit, a tutor might focus on word recognition to build fluency, vocabulary development in content areas, comprehension strategies such as SQ3R and PLAN, text structure, and graphic organizers. When pairing a tutor with an English learner, a focus on oral reading, rereading, and vocabulary development would be productive.

2. *Should tutors be high-achieving students?* That's not essential. Research indicates that an achiever of any level may become a commendable tutor. What tutors of any achievement level avoid, however, is making and announcing value judgments to the tutee.

3. *What about training?* Training in interpersonal, management, and content skills is essential. Tutors should have both initial training and ongoing coaching. Debriefing of tutorial sessions helps tutors reflect on their practice and work out problems that arise during tutoring sessions.

4. *Are same-sex or opposite-sex pairs better for tutoring?* Rekrut (1994) recommends same-sex partnering because she has found that cross-gender pairing "sabotages both content and skill acquisition." She indicates from her review of research that pairing older girls with younger boys usually works well, however.

Paired reading.   Paired reading is an effective method of helping struggling and reluctant readers. Topping (1987) found that routine dyadic reading helped struggling readers improve both their word recognition and their comprehension. It's a form of one-to-one tutoring in which a proficient reader, who models and supports good reading, is paired with a struggling reader. The "proficient" reader may be a more able student reader, a teaching assistant, or a parent. Figure 9.5 provides a flowchart of the paired reading procedure (Scoble, Topping, & Wigglesworth, 1994). Steps in the strategy are given here.

Step-By-Step: How to Do Paired Reading

Step 1. Identify a struggling reader—the tutee—and a tutor who will work constructively with the tutee.

Step 2. Provide the tutor with an orientation toward dyadic reading that includes some basic, commonsense rules about working one-on-one with a student having a history of reading frustrations. Explain that the tutee needing support with reading selects books or magazines and can change texts when desired. The tutor explains the following procedure to the tutee before they begin their work.

Step 3. Tutee and tutor start by reading the same text aloud together, a kind of reading duet.

Step 4. When the tutee wants to read aloud alone, she should signal the tutor to stop vocalizing. The tutor encourages the tutee while reading progresses.

Step 5. At appropriate points, tutee and tutor should pause to talk about the text and make sure that the meaning-making process is sensibly progressing. The tutor can simply ask, "What's going on here?" or "What do you think is happening up to now?"

Step 6. If the tutee makes a mistake or miscue, the tutor should wait to see if it is corrected. If the miscue is not corrected and it could affect the meaning of the passage, the tutor can ask the tutee what the miscued word is and how it contributes to the meaning of the passage. If the tutee does not know the word, then the tutor can explain it as needed. Then the two read together again until the tutee gives the signal for reading aloud independently.

Figure 9.5 Paired Reading Procedure.

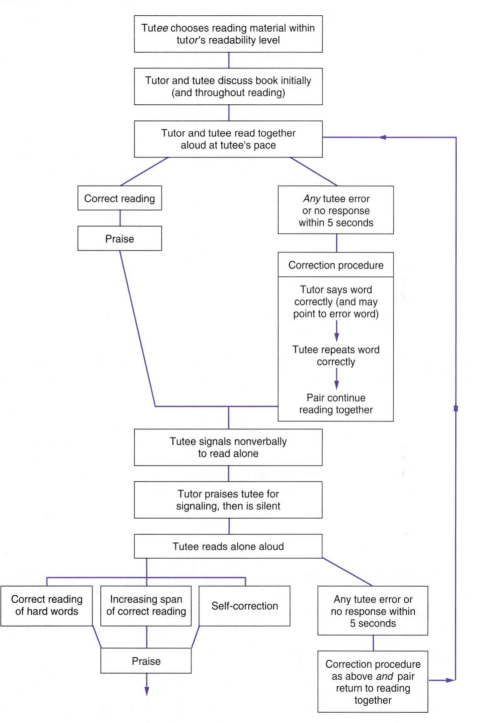

Source: Figure from John Scoble, Keith Topping, & Colin Wigglesworth, Training Family and Friends as Adult Literacy Tutors. *Journal of Reading*, 31(5) (February 1988), 410–419. Reprinted with permission of the International Reading Association.

Guided reading.   Although often used in the elementary classroom (Fountas & Pinnell, 1996), guided reading works well with struggling readers in the middle and high school (J. Allen, 2000). While it can be used in small groups and even whole classes, guided reading is a highly effective tutoring tool if properly used. Its purpose is to develop independent, proficient readers who can summarize and question the meanings they construct and who can form opinions based on the reading of a text and support those opinions with reference to the text.

Teachers and tutors use guided reading to help struggling readers learn and apply comprehension strategies so that they can move toward independent, silent reading. To use guided reading, tutors need to carefully read texts they will use with tutees and make plans to engage them in challenging dialogues. During the guided reading process, tutors model ways to make personal and critical connections with texts on multiple levels. As Allen (2000) points out in *Yellow Brick Roads,* tutors using guided readings focus on process rather than outcomes with their tutees by asking questions like these: How do we know that? What other choices did the character have? Why do you think that? What is likely to happen next? What words in the text helped us make that discovery? Furthermore, tutors make every attempt to generate questions rooted in their tutee's responses while they are making meaning rather than depending on predetermined questions, such as those at the end of a story in a school anthology.

Allen (2000) recommends the exploration of five different question categories that tutors can use during guided reading. These categories are described in Table 9.2. Tutors can also use the categories to explore think-alouds that will give their tutee ideas about how to respond to a text and construct meaning from it.

A key to success with guided readings is the choice of texts, if tutors have a choice. Allen (2000) suggests that the texts be "interesting, informative, short." However, guided readings can also be based upon the content area text that tutees are expected to read. A tutor may have to do quite a bit of scaffolding to help a tutee understand the text, but the experience will help a tutor or teacher become more deeply aware of the kinds of challenges students face when trying to read materials for a class.

Using many of the tools of one-on-one tutoring already described in these pages plus her experience of becoming a reading specialist, Stephanie Bacon (2005), a middle school teacher challenged by a humanities classroom of 30 sixth graders, trained

Table 9.2 Question Categories for Guided Readings

Personal Response Questions	How would you feel under those circumstances? How would you respond to a comment like that?
Metacognitive Response Questions	Does this passage make sense to you? When did you notice you were confused with what was going on?
Connection Response Questions	How would your best friend react to a situation like that? What was the author trying to do for you as a reader when she set up that comparison?
Critical Response Questions	How does this boyfriend compare to her other boyfriend in the story? How would you change this explanation to make it clearer to you?
Surface-Features-of-Text Questions	How does the title connect with the story? How do the chapter headings help you understand this chapter?

them to become reading coaches for each other. Many of the students in her class struggled with reading, but she didn't have 30 tutors to step in and help her out. To tackle the problem, she trained all her students to become tutors or coaches for each other. After she trained them to focus on a range of reading strategies often used with struggling or striving readers, such as word work, rereading, guided reading, and other comprehension activities, her sixth graders met in teams to read together and coach each other toward reading proficiency. Although worried about what would transpire when a group of sixth graders gathered to work together on reading, her worries were allayed when she witnessed the productive help her students gave each other as reading coaches.

Cross-Age Tutoring

Alexandra, a high school junior, got credits for enrolling in a tutoring program at her school in which she would help first and second graders learn to read. Alexandra was, herself, a struggling reader. But what made the group of tutors Alexandra joined special was that all the tutors in training were expecting to give birth to their own children in a matter of months. This cross-age tutoring program would help her prepare to teach her own child how to read.

Customarily, cross-age tutoring pairs an older student with a younger one. The more proficient reading tutor serves as a model to a less proficient tutee seeking to develop reading skills. The tutor scaffolds reading instruction while taking into account the tutee's background knowledge, reading skills, and pace. In some cross-age tutoring models, tutors make significant gains in their own reading proficiency (Jacobson et al., 2001; Paterson & Elliott, 2006).

In a tutoring program studied by Douglas Fisher (2001), middle school tutors benefited because they engaged in authentic literacy events with first and second graders, were able to emulate effective instructional models, received feedback from their tutoring efforts, and integrated writing with their tutoring assignment. In the program Fisher investigated, the middle school tutors were students significantly below average in reading competency and were enrolled in a reading class. The tutees they tutored attended a nearby elementary "feeder" school for the middle school. The reading class teacher developed reading lessons for the tutors. On the day before the tutors went to the elementary school to tutor, the teacher modeled the lesson in the reading class and gave tutors time to practice with each other. The next day they went to the elementary school to tutor. After tutoring with their first- and second-grade tutees, the tutors spent the following day back at their middle school debriefing, writing about their tutoring experiences, and preparing for the next day's tutoring episodes.

The typical lesson plan included five phases. First, tutors introduced the literature they would teach to their tutees, showed the book's pictures to the tutees, and asked them to predict from those pictures what the story would be about. Second, tutors focused on the story's challenging vocabulary by reading each unfamiliar word to the tutee, who then read the word back to the tutor. Third, tutees wrote the words down, wrote a definition, drew a picture revealing each word's meaning, and wrote a sentence using each word. Fourth, the tutors read the book to their tutee. Finally, the tutees wrote in their journals describing their feelings about the book.

Variations on the model of cross-age tutoring I've just described are plentiful. Some pair struggling or outstanding high school students with delayed readers in middle or elementary schools. For example, Connie Juel (1991) paired student athletes with at-risk children, gave the athletes authentic reasons to practice reading, and improved reading performance. Some programs train high school seniors for tutoring incoming freshmen known to be struggling readers. Programs, such as the one Alexandra entered at the beginning of this section, train pregnant adolescent girls for tutoring first graders so that, as new mothers, these one-time tutors can transfer their tutoring skills to reading time with their own children. These cross-aged tutoring programs often reveal not only improved reading performance for both tutor and tutee but also improved attitudes toward reading (Haluska & Gillen, 1995; Paterson & Elliott, 2006).

Adult-Student Tutoring

Components of effective literacy tutorials.
Reviewers (Juel, 1993; Wasik, 1998) of formal literacy tutoring programs for younger struggling readers have identified several practices contributing to their success. Lessons should have a balanced instructional design that includes reading of familiar texts to gain fluency, work on word and letter-sound correspondences, writing, and inclusion of a variety of texts to incorporate various reading strategies. Furthermore, Wasik has identified eight features contributing to tutorial success:

1. supervision by a reading specialist,
2. continuous coaching for tutors,
3. structured sessions with a balanced design, such as that described earlier,
4. consistent and intensive sessions,
5. high-quality materials,
6. periodic assessment of progress, including that of high-frequency word recognition,
7. consistent attendance, and
8. coordination between tutorial content and classroom teaching.

These features have been incorporated into many tutoring programs.

Adult tutors are valuable resources to teachers but are not easily found. Fortunately, a combination of events may help many classroom teachers find more tutor resources. First, more colleges and university are rewarding students for community services or work-study programs, including tutoring. Second, research shows that minimally trained college students can significantly contribute to young students' reading growth (J. Fitzgerald, 2004). College students were given about 30 hours of training modeled on Reading Recovery's lesson format (Invernizzi, Rosemary, Juel, & Richards, 1997). The four sections of each lesson included (a) repeated reading of a familiar text, (b) word study, (c) writing for sounds, and (d) reading a new book. The at-risk first and second graders in the study improved significantly in reading compared with a control group of children who did not receive the tutoring. Developing a tutorial training program for adolescents could be modeled on the "Guidelines for the Reading Tutorial" that appears after the next section of this chapter.

Teachers tutoring struggling readers.
To help beginning teachers learn to assess struggling readers, apply reading strategies, and foster literacy in the content areas, I ask credential candidates in my classes to engage in a literacy tutorial focused on reading development. The tutorial serves as an important fieldwork episode in which emerging teachers create and sustain a one-on-one relationship with a student who may be "at risk" and who is not "at home" with reading.

I explain to my students that the individual tutorial and the subsequent case study that they will write based on it should include at least six components:

1. *Assessment of the tutee's reading and writing abilities and attitudes.* Information about a student's reading and writing performance can be gathered from that student's current and former teachers, from formal assessment that includes standardized testing information usually available in a student's cumulative file, and from informal assessment sources, such as a Curriculum-Based Measurement (CBM), Group Reading Inventory (GRI), running records, cloze tests, and interviews (see chapter 4).

2. *Instruction designed to foster fluency and reading comprehension.* Based on the results of the assessment information, teachers design and implement a series of lessons that focus on the development of fluency, reading comprehension, and the use of writing-to-learn strategies. I ask teachers to convene no less than 10 separate sessions of about 45 minutes, gear instruction to the needs of the student, and engage in instruction within a specific content area. (The tutorial may cover more than one subject area, but it should focus on one, such as science or history).

3. *A field journal for observational and/or field notes that traces the tutorial's progress.* Tutors use a field journal to keep track of tutoring events and to record observations and impressions as the tutorial develops. I ask tutors to include their field notes as an appendix to their written case study.

4. *A 10-minute uninterrupted video of their interaction with the tutee during a tutoring session.* Tutors describe in writing their learning goal and instructional challenges during the videotaped episode, why they pursued the learning goal they pursued, how effective they believe the instructional episode was, what they would change if they could do an "instant replay," and where they will next take their tutee based on what transpired during the videotaped session.

5. *Evaluation of progress made during the tutorial.* In order to gauge the impact of the tutorial, tutors use their ongoing, benchmark, or formative evaluations as evidence upon which to measure progress. Tutors sometimes collect additional assessment information that might include (but is not restricted to) the following:

   • Readministration of a CBM, GRI, or cloze test using texts similar to the first round of testing. If the tutorial has a short run (less than 12 to 15 sessions), indications of progress on these instruments is, in my experience with them, rather unlikely. But breakthroughs happen.

   • A portfolio of the student's work (completed in the tutorial and/or in the tutee's other classes).

   • Talks with a tutee's teacher about in-class and homework performance.

   • Written measures, such as summaries or recall protocols.

6. A reflection on their tutoring experience. What did tutors discover about their tutees or themselves during the tutorial? After reflection on the tutorial, what would tutors have changed, done more of, or done less of? What did tutors learn that could be transferred to small-group or whole-class instruction?

Guidelines for the reading tutorial. When students in my credential classes asked me to help them get started on their reading tutorials, I drew up the following practical guidelines:

1. Know your tutee's background, resources, interests, motivations, and obstacles to learning. Form a positive relationship.

2. Assess the tutee's ability to read. For a quick assessment, use an oral reading test.

2.1. To evaluate reading fluency, you can give your tutee a CBM using passages from one of your tutee's content area textbooks. (See chapter 4 for procedures.)

2.2. To determine the challenges presented to your tutee by a content area textbook, you can develop and administer a GRI based on the same textbook you used for the CBM above. (See chapter 4 for procedures.)

2.3. *REMEMBER*: Some students can decode but struggle with comprehension. So ask your tutee some questions about the reading he or she is doing. A good way to find out if a tutee gets the main idea is to ask for a summary in his or her own words of a specified section of text. Then ask a few questions that require the tutee to clarify meanings or make predictions about what's to come. Your judgment on this will be critical. Does a tutee really get the meaning of what he or she is reading or is he or she just reading words?

3. Set some goals. Design a program that's responsive to your tutee's reading level, school learning situation, and interests.

4. Check to see if your tutee has a grasp of letter-sound relationships for a vocabulary of 100 basic words. (See chapter 5 on vocabulary.)

5. Include basic vocabulary (as needed) in the tutorial and build your tutee's word knowledge. (See chapter 5 on vocabulary.)

6. Help your tutee to read strategically, purposefully. Teach your tutee strategies that will help him or her become a more independent, self-regulated reader but provide scaffolding so your tutee can grow with your cognitive support. Use strategies like the following:

Paired and guided reading

VSS, keyword method, PASSION, and Word Maps (chapter 5)

Anticipation guides, DR-TA, DIA (chapter 6)

SQ3R and PLAN (chapter 6)

Text structure instruction (chapter 6)

Graphic organizers, Concept Maps (chapter 6)

Reciprocal teaching

However, a few well-mastered strategies will serve your tutee better than a glut of tactics barely understood. Select wisely.

7. Have your tutee write before, during, and after reading. Use strategies like the DEJ, freewrites, question papers, and RAFT. Have your tutee keep a log (see chapter 7).

8. Some tutees need help getting organized to learn and managing their time. As you work with your tutee, continue to evaluate his or her work habits and time allocation to see how effectively and efficiently the tutee learns. Suggest changes to improve effectiveness.

9. Keep in mind that you are the tutor. Develop an understanding of your tutee, but keep the relationship professional. Your approach and expectations can influence your tutee's productivity and learning.

Impact of reading tutorials on credential candidates.   While evidence of benefits to those tutored are prevalent (Wasik, 1998), I investigated the tutor side of the "tutor + tutee = learning" equation (Unrau, 1996). I wanted to know what teachers in training would gain from the experience of tutoring a struggling reader with strategies like those described in this book. Research and my teaching experience indicated that some credential candidates resisted the infusion of literacy strategies into their content areas and the transfer of techniques into their future classrooms (Hollingsworth & Teel, 1991; O'Brien & Stewart, 1992; Stewart & O'Brien, 1989). The reasons for this resistance to acquisition and transfer could lie in many quarters, including feelings of inadequacy, lack of training or confidence, lack of instructional time in the schools to integrate literacy strategies, and belief that such instruction should be the province of the English teacher.

My purpose for the investigation of the tutorial was simple: I wanted to know how credential candidates were affected by tutoring a struggling reader. I also wanted to know if tutorials helped these new teachers gain strategic knowledge about reading and apply that knowledge in their content area classrooms.

I had a hunch that tutorials could help satisfy new teachers' needs for independent practice and internalization of reading strategies. If tutorials were utilized as opportunities to practice and internalize knowledge, then the possibility for transfer of strategic knowledge from the university to the schools might improve. However, the usefulness of these tutorials needed to be assessed to find out which strategies got transferred to the tutorial and to discover the extent to which students found the tutorial valuable and why.

To gather information to answer my questions, I read the case studies of 178 student teachers who completed a content area literacy course, took notes from those sections of each case study that addressed relevant questions, and had all 178 student teachers complete a questionnaire.

After reviewing the information I collected from reading case studies and from the questionnaires, I was able to draw a few tentative conclusions:

1. After taking a course in content literacy, beginning teachers rarely reported no inclination to develop the reading and/or writing ability of their students. About 4% of the sample indicated that they did not think they should be expected to include the teaching of reading and/or writing in their content area. Keep in mind that the sample included teachers from all content areas normally taught in the middle and high school curriculum, including music, art, and physical education.

2. Among the most frequently used strategies in the tutorials were DR-TA, reciprocal teaching, Vocabulary Self-Collection Strategy, K-W-L, and quickwrites. Among those strategies least used were DEJs, DIAs, PreP, and other strategies that require substantial teacher preparation time because texts being taught must be read and materials prepared in advance.

3. Well over 60% of all candidates in the sample indicated that they gained confidence by applying strategies in their tutorials. Sixty-six percent agreed that the tutorial helped them to diagnose student learning problems more confidently, and 64% agreed that they felt their confidence increased as the tutorial progressed. Even a larger percentage felt a sense of satisfaction in their role as tutors.

4. About 80% of the candidates said that the tutorial gave them an understanding of how they could use reading and/or writing strategies in their classes. This suggests that, having gained an understanding of their application, teachers would actually use them.

5. A large percent of the sample (85%) agreed that the tutorial gave them a chance to learn something important about themselves as teachers. About the same

percent agreed that the tutorial helped them to find out the problems students have in reading.

6. Although the tutorial took a significant amount of time, only about one of four candidates agreed that the tutorial took too much of their time and should be eliminated as part of the course because it contributed little or nothing to their understanding of students as learners. More than half of all candidates agreed that they wished the tutorial could continue.

Many comments that candidates made on their questionnaires and in their case studies provided further indicators that beginning teachers valued the tutorials and learned from them. New teachers discovered that tutees with limited English proficiency, with learning disabilities, with low self-esteem, and with little or no parental support often had complex literacy and learning problems to overcome. One student teacher whose tutee was a 13-year-old "hard-headed, antagonistic young lady" with *cholo* (gang) affiliations in South Central Los Angeles wrote the following: "Angie was not the only one who learned how to summarize a passage and develop questions effectively. During our first sessions, I felt quite uncomfortable doing our reciprocal teaching exercises. As we went along, however, I felt much more comfortable. The same holds true for other strategies I employed. Because I actually used DR-TA, DIA, and mapping activities with Angie, I would be much more comfortable in adopting and adapting them in my curriculum." Experience with Angie strengthened this student's "resolve to incorporate reading and writing activities in my curriculum."

The vast majority of new teachers in the research I conducted said they were motivated to integrate literacy strategies into their content areas. Through the tutorial they got an opportunity to try numerous techniques to improve reading; many learned much about the literacy difficulties their tutees and future students face; and most new teachers concluded that the tutorial had considerable merit and value for them.

But what do these teacher candidates, such as yourself, really do about integrating literacy to promote learning in their content area classrooms in the years after they have received their teaching credentials and settled into their classrooms?

Summary

In this chapter, we have explored a wide range of strategies to promote literacy and learning through collaboration. We began by looking at a gradual release model that progressed from whole class instruction to individual student's applications of knowledge and skills. We surveyed whole-class reading and discussion methods and found opportunities to promote inquiry while expanding student's academic and life knowledge. Content literacy growth across the disciplines can be supported, we saw, through the principles and practices of cooperative learning. An investigation of reciprocal teaching revealed its benefits to reading comprehension, and a review of peer, cross-aged, and adult-student tutoring gave us an opportunity to see how one-on-one instruction can produce growth in literacy and learning for both tutor and tutee.

Double-Entry Journal: After Reading

Having read this chapter on group strategies, how would you modify your list of whole-class, small-group, and paired activities you would use in your instructional program to enhance literacy and learning? With reference to the model of reading in chapter 3, how do you think the collaborative methods you have included on your list promote both learning and literacy?

Chapter 10

STRUGGLING READERS AND ENGLISH LEARNERS: ADDRESSING THEIR COGNITIVE AND CULTURAL NEEDS

After reading chapter 10, you should be able to answer the following questions:

1. What contributes to struggling readers' comprehension problems?

2. What are the elements comprising the research-based model of reading intervention proposed in this chapter?

3. What kinds of resources are available to support reading intervention programs?

4. What could keep "just read more" solutions to secondary reading problems from working?

5. What five hypotheses contribute to Krashen's theory of second-language acquisition?

6. What do we know about how long it takes for an English language learner to become proficient?

7. What practices exemplify specially designed academic instruction in English (SDAIE)?

8. How can learning strategies be integrated into English language instruction?

If many of your English-speaking students were reading two or more grade levels below their assigned grade, what would you do to help them comprehend reading assignments and to catch up? If you have several English learners in your class, what accommodations would you make in your instruction to help them grasp the course content?

Addressing the Frustrations of Struggling Readers

How Serious Are Reading Problems in Our Middle and High Schools?

In spite of reports in the media that there is an adolescent literacy crisis in America, substantial evidence indicates that, for the most part, students on average are reading at least as well now as they did 30 years ago (Klenk & Kibby, 2000; Perie, Grigg, & Donahue, 2005). But that's not the end of the story. The magnitude of reading problems that middle and high school students bring with them to their content area classrooms is manifested in data collected and analyzed by the National Assessment of Educational Progress (NAEP, 1999; Perie et al., 2005) Results of NAEP studies of reading show that more than 8 million students in grades 4 through 12 read below grade level and that about two out of three 8th and 12th graders do not meet NAEP standards of reading at the "proficient" level for their grade (United States Department of Education, 2003). Large numbers of students arrive in middle and high schools unable to read grade-level texts fluently or comprehend their meaning. Although most students grasp literal meanings, they have significant difficulties with more complex reading tasks. In hundreds of urban and suburban schools, teachers work in content area classrooms with students who are reading many grade levels below their age-equivalent classmates. Although the incidence of struggling readers varies from school to school and classroom to classroom, they comprise about 25% of all middle and high school students. If you teach in classrooms with significant numbers of struggling readers, you will soon be convinced that you are in the midst of a serious literacy problem. Furthermore, urban centers are not alone in their struggles with literacy. Many students in rural schools throughout the country struggle with similar reading problems (Stephens, 1993). The discrepancy between expected reading ability and real capacity creates instructional havoc for teachers nationwide.

What's in a name?   The terms that best describe students who read several grades below their actual grade level have gotten a substantial amount of attention (Alvermann, 2001; Ivey, 1999; Smith & Wilhelm, 2002; M. R. Ruddell & Shearer, 2002; Moje, Young, Readence, & Moore, 2000). Terms used to describe these students reflect various assumptions and theoretical orientations: "struggling," "striving," "underprepared," "at-risk," "reluctant," "remedial," and "marginalized." Some literacy educators view these students through a cognitive deficiency lens ("remedial"), some through a medical model lens ("at-risk"), and others through the lens of critical theory ("marginalized"). As we all know, words can have detrimental associations and contribute to a negative identity. In this text, I use the terms "struggling," "striving," or "marginalized" because they seem to me to capture these students literacy situations in the least pejorative language.

A middle school discovers its struggling readers.   Here is a specific example of the problem content area teachers face every day in their classrooms. The data come from a Los Angeles middle school that gave about 1,550 of their students the Gates-MacGinitie reading test near the beginning of the school year. It's important to point out that the students taking the reading test included neither 267 students designated for special education classes nor about 150 students who were in English as a Second Language programs. What we found disturbed many teachers, while clarifying for them the roots of one of their major instructional frustrations: Students could not read the texts they were asked to read.

We found that among sixth graders 11% were reading at their grade level, whereas nearly 60% were reading below the fourth-grade level. Unfortunately, as these students progressed through their middle school grades, their reading levels may not have improved in accord with their age-mates nationwide. Among seventh graders, we found that 5% read at or above grade level, but 55% still read below the fourth-grade level. And among eighth graders, 2% read at their grade level or above, whereas about 45% continued to read below the fourth-grade level. In this school, the teaching problems became abundantly clear to all. Teachers in the content areas attempting to teach from texts written at or near grade level in science, history, mathematics, and English found that large numbers of students were frustrated when attempting to read the texts they were expected to read. As was reported in the *Los Angeles Times* (Sahagun, 2000), one administrator said teachers were "astounded" and "appalled" by the actual results of the reading test.

While struggling readers abounded at this Los Angeles Unified School District (LAUSD) middle school, the presence of struggling or marginalized readers—sometimes in fairly large numbers—in nearly all our middle and high schools is pretty much a given. The greater difficulty lies with teachers at the middle and secondary levels not being prepared to address the reading challenges they face.

Certainly teachers can learn strategies to heighten engagement and improve comprehension, strategies such as DR-TA, K-W-L, and reciprocal teaching. But, when faced with readers manifesting reading levels far below their grade levels, teachers face problems of a much different dimension. Few, if any, middle and high school teachers have any training in diagnosing and teaching students with profound reading limitations. Most teachers have spent years gaining mastery over their particular fields, such as math, biology, or history. Often, their greatest sense of competence and their deepest interests lie in their subject area. Most of these teachers have little motivation to drop their domain of competency to take up the teaching of reading—even though they recognize that these students will make little or no progress in the classes they are teaching because of profound literacy limitations.

Finding the roots of reading problems.   What are the specific problems behind the relatively weak reading performance of these middle school students? For the most part, we excluded students designated as needing special education intervention and many learning English as a second language. Naturally, large numbers of students are still learning academic English. Nevertheless, we suspected that weak decoding skills, few sight words (such as *and* or *ran*), deficient word attack skills, and general lack of automaticity in processing words, phrases, and clauses contributed to the frustrations these students experienced when they tried to read. Extensive fluency research supports the observations made here (Klenk & Kibby, 2000). But that's not the whole of the problem. Listening to these students read, studying their efforts to make meaning, and talking with them about strategy use, we, like C. Peterson, Caverly, Nicholson, O'Neal, and Cusenbary (2000), found that many students were limited by other important factors. Among them were limited vocabulary, background knowledge, capacity to make inferences, awareness of text structure, reading strategies, and motivation.

To gain a perspective of the kinds of choices available to teachers wanting to address these kinds of literacy challenges, a research-based model for reading intervention with striving readers is proposed. The elements making up the model will provide guidance in program design and implementation to teachers in their classrooms and to entire schools or districts contemplating broad literacy interventions. Both new and experienced teachers should be aware of steps that can be taken to address the challenges that struggling readers pose in today's classrooms.

Research-Based Model for Reading Intervention: A Constellation of Features Providing Guidance in Program Design and Implementation

During the past few years, we have gained sufficient knowledge through literacy research and practice with middle and high school students to formulate a model for reading interventions (Biancarosa & Snow, 2004; Fisher & Frey, 2004; Fisher & Ivey, 2006; Franzak, 2006; Ivey & Broaddus, 2001; J. A. Langer, 2001, 2002; Pressley, Gaskins, Solic, & Collins, 2006; Pressley, Raphael, Gallagher, & DiBella, 2004; Smith & Wilhelm, 2002; Snow & Biancarosa, 2003). That model can serve as a foundation and guide to teachers and other educators in the design and implementation of reading intervention programs.

The intervention model consists of 14 features that can be selected and implemented in a variety of patterns:

1. a broad-spectrum reading curriculum that includes decoding, word recognition, vocabulary development, fluency, comprehension strategies, writing, and study strategies as needed,
2. systematic, embedded, differentiated instruction,
3. diverse texts that cover a range of topics, reading levels, and cultural traditions,
4. technology that can be used both to investigate topics and to create texts,
5. time on task that provides students who need it with up to 4 hours per day of literacy-oriented instruction in specialized literacy, English, and content area classrooms,
6. assessment practices that are both formative and summative, that are periodic, and that enable students to be placed (and replaced) in accord with their growth,
7. a critical mass of teachers committed to the implementation of a reading intervention program and to the literacy growth of their students,
8. teacher training, on-going professional development, and organization (e.g., team meeting time) that enables teachers to extend their capacity and competence as masters of literacy in master-apprentice relationships with their students,
9. motivation that builds on students' self-determination, self-efficacy, self-regulation, and identity as they tackle increasingly challenging literacy tasks,

10. small classes of students (with a goal of 15 or fewer) that enable teachers to attend to students' individual literacy needs and motivational characteristics,

11. administrative leadership that includes participation in program design and implementation, funding resources, and school-community development,

12. parental commitment to and connections with the intervention program, including willingness to supervise homework or support students' study hall attendance,

13. tutoring provided as needed, including not only professional tutoring service but also cross-age tutoring between college and high school students or high school and middle school students, and

14. a comprehensive, integrated, ecologically sensitive literacy program that crosses subject area boundaries and out-of-school resources.

Fourteen Features of a Research-Based Literacy Intervention Model

An intensive reading/writing curriculum.
The reading curriculum for this research-based model has two major components: Literacy skills and strategies and study skills and strategies. The literacy skills and strategies include word recognition, vocabulary development, fluency development, and comprehension strategies. The study skills and strategies include note taking, background knowledge activation (such as K-W-L), organization strategies (such as graphic organizers), and reflection/monitoring strategies to promote metacognition. The design and implementation of a reading curriculum is a key feature of any intervention program. For an individual teacher developing her own intervention program, it may be the program's most vital feature. Teachers in the Benchmark School, a school known for its success with students having a history of school failure, considered word recognition and comprehension strategies two of the most important features that contribute to the impressive reading achievement of struggling readers who attend their school (Pressley et al., 2006).

Word recognition skills and their assessment and development were addressed in chapters 4 and 5. Students struggling with decoding may need significant support in the building of word recognition skills through development of sight-word knowledge, letter-sound correspondences, and word structure analysis. As marginalized readers acquire word recognition skills, they can also build fluency and vocabulary, topics also covered in chapter 5. These literacy skills need to be taught explicitly through intensive interaction, some of which could be computer enhanced.

The reading curriculum's literacy component also includes comprehension strategies, many of which were covered in chapters 6 and 8. These strategies include the Anticipation Guides, Directed Reading-Thinking Activity, Directed Inquiry Activity, SQ3R, PLAN, Inquiry Questions, and Questioning the Author. Integrated strategy systems, such as reciprocal teaching presented in chapter 9, work especially well with striving readers who need to develop their abilities to summarize, question, predict, and clarify terms in texts they read across the content areas.

Teachers should also use writing to enhance reading and concept development (Fisher & Ivey, 2006). A broad range of appropriate writing strategies to promote comprehension and learning was described and demonstrated in chapter 7. Many of those strategies, such as learning logs, letters to the teacher, and skeletons, can help teachers see how students are forming and transforming knowledge as they read and respond to content area texts.

The study skills and strategies component of the reading curriculum should include activities that help students connect with their background knowledge. Strategies such as K-W-L and Double-Entry Journals enable students to make these connections between new texts and prior knowledge. But making connections with texts or new content knowledge is just a beginning. Students also need to acquire effective note-taking strategies to organize knowledge, like outlines and the Cornell Note Taking System described in chapter 6. As teachers explicitly demonstrating note-taking strategies, we should show students how these strategies can be used to learn from lectures and reading assignments across the content areas. Methods of graphically representing new knowledge also help students progress when studying. These graphic organizers, including those that represent cause-effect, problem-solution-evaluation, or compare-contrast text structures, shown in chapter 6, help students visualize how written text is structured and organized. Finally, students learning how to use study strategies effectively need to have opportunities to monitor their learning and to reflect on it. While class discussion can help students focus on monitoring processes and reflect on them, writing about their learning processes brings additional benefits. Reflective writing in learning logs that students share with their teachers provides both students and their teachers with opportunities to think about their developing study skills and to consider what might be done to improve their learning from texts.

Systematic, embedded, and differentiated instruction.
Systematic. Teachers can deliver the curriculum described through an array of instructional methods that include modeling, scaffolding instruction, and a master-apprentice relationship (Biancarosa & Snow, 2004). One of the most efficient and productive frameworks I know of for the development of a literacy intervention program is a master-apprentice format. A master-apprentice format is at the core of the Reading Apprenticeship reading intervention program developed by WestEd (Schoenbach, Greenleaf, Cziko, & Hurwitz, 1999). Collaboration between WestEd researchers and classroom teachers resulted in a site-based literacy intervention model that engaged cross-disciplined teams of teachers in discussions and writing about literacy practices. Within a master-apprentice format, teachers become masters of literacy

skills and strategies during their training. Once teachers have acquired sufficient skills and strategies to make up the core of a site-specific intervention program, teachers become "masters" of their craft and work with their student "apprentices," whom they guide toward higher levels of expertise. The expertise of teachers as readers in their content areas forms the foundation of this approach to improving adolescent reading (Jordan, Jensen, & Greenleaf, 2001). Of course, teachers implementing the program continue to work with trainers to refine their skills and understandings. In some programs, students take their acquired mastery into another master-apprentice relationship when they engage in cross-aged tutoring, as would occur if an 11th grader were to tutor a 6th-grade struggling reader.

According to Duke and Pearson (2002), the best research-supported system for comprehension instruction connects and integrates several learning opportunities that unfold sequentially:

- an explicit description of the strategy, including when and how to use it,
- modeling of the strategy by a teacher and/or student,
- opportunities to use the strategy in collaborative/cooperative groups,
- gradual release of responsibility through guided practice, and
- strategy use on an independent basis.

While a teacher may discover that some students master strategies more quickly than others, the gradual release model (Pearson & Gallagher, 1983) describes how teachers can move from a situation in which they have full responsibility for performing or demonstrating a strategy to a point at which the student accepts full responsibility for conducting the strategy. (See chapter 9.) Students thus become more independent in stages as they demonstrate proficiency in the effective use of skills and strategies.

As Pressley et al. (2006) observed, teachers at Benchmark were consistently on-task with materials prepared and an agenda previously planned. When strategy instruction took place, teachers explained the reason for learning the strategy, explained what the strategy would accomplish or how it could be used, and explicitly modeled the strategy. You'll undoubtedly notice how this sequence follows that recommended by Duke and Pearson (2002). When teachers at Benchmark noticed a student off-task, a quick nudge to attention got the student back on-task. Tasks themselves were meaningful to students, and work completed in class or at home was monitored for quality. Students got feedback on their work and opportunities to resubmit revised work. Some items on a teacher's agenda may not have been completed on occasion; however, observers never witnessed a teacher ending a lesson before the period ended. These are qualities that emerge from Benchmark teachers' systematic and "intensive" instructional approach that literacy intervention programs could emulate.

Embedded. In schools where content area teachers see their role as teaching that content and English teachers see their role as teaching literature, who's around to teach a marginalized reader how to survive? The reading curriculum and instructional approaches just outlined benefit more students if they are embedded across the curriculum. This means that reading instruction will be manifested not only when teachers of English demonstrate strategy application to content area texts, but also when teachers of other content areas use texts in their disciplines to demonstrate use of effective reading strategies. Literacy programs of the kind envisioned here are not intended to transform math, science, and art teachers into teachers of reading. Instead, the purpose is to increase chances for teachers to know their students and to know how their literacy needs can be more productively addressed, perhaps with language arts teachers or literacy coaches offering suggestions that enrich and deepen content learning while further preparing students for the academic literacy challenges they are likely to face in college.

Differentiated.   No single reading intervention program is likely to help all our students striving to read. Providing reading instruction tailored to an individual student's strengths and needs is more likely to engage that student in productive literacy development. Individuals should get interest-specific, need-specific guidance in reading curriculum and instruction. In some instances, groups of students who have interests and literacy needs in common can be taught together effectively. When engaged in independent reading, students can join a literature circle in which everyone reads the same book, discusses the book, and writes papers or designs presentations about it. If an intervention program's assessment and placement features are operating properly, the likelihood of meeting students' literacy needs should improve. Without effective differentiation, more students will probably be less engaged in the program and its reading goals.

Diverse texts.

While a strong reading curriculum is at the heart of any successful literacy intervention program, the availability of diverse texts will keep the heart pumping and the reading muscle growing. Students who are striving to improve reading need texts that fit comfortably into their optimal zone of cognitive and motivational need. To increase the probability that texts will fit those needs, teachers require access to materials that cover a range of topics and that cover those topics with a range of reading levels. Furthermore, topics that appeal to students from diverse cultural backgrounds as well as topics appealing to both boys and girls should be included in the selections (Ivey & Broaddus, 2001). While several books about diverse reading selections are available, one of particular value is Rosalie Fink's *Why Jane and John Couldn't Read—And How They Learned: A New Look at Striving Readers* (2006). Her book, intended to promote student reading through an interest-based model, contains a wide range of recommended books for a wide range of striving readers. Many teachers have also found that programs such as Accelerated Reader (AR) enable students to discover books in their reading and interest range. Students using AR also say they enjoy taking quizzes that show they have understood the book. While AR includes hundreds of texts to recommend to students, teachers (or their schools) need to have these books available so students can use them.

Technology.

Instructional technology can augment any reading intervention program for striving readers. The technology now available can supplement instruction in decoding, fluency, spelling, vocabulary, and comprehension. Often, these programs provide practice in decoding and word recognition that builds fluency (Hasselbring & Goin, 2004). Computer-driven guided-reading programs that can monitor and correct pronunciations of extended texts have also been developed because of advances in speech recognition technology (www.soliloquylearning.com). A "reading assistant" program for middle school students allows them to read text that appears on a computer screen. Students read into a microphone that records and checks pronunciation. When errors are detected, the computer assistant corrects mispronunciations. If problems persist, the assistant repeats the word, defines it, and gives a sentence in which the word is used. Forms of computer-assisted reading, such as that described here, can provide students with guided reading activities that have substantial research support, according to the National Reading Panel (NICHD, 2000).

However, fluency is only a stepping stone to comprehension that can itself be developed with computer assisted and media-enhanced instruction. In the Peabody Literacy Lab at Vanderbilt University, Hasselbring and Goin (2004) have developed three separate reading, word, and spelling labs to take advantage of progress in technology and its potential for integration into literacy programs. These labs have been developed primarily for older struggling readers of middle and high school age.

In the reading lab, video related to texts is used to help students build background knowledge and imagery before reading texts on topics depicted in the video. With visual information already encoded, readers have an easier time envisioning and making sense of texts that activates that information. In the lab, students first view a video clip and then read a passage about that video. For example, students could view a documentary of our federal mints and then read about those mints that produce money in cities across the country. That way, students can cash in on their visual experience. When reading the computer-generated text, students can click on a word they are having trouble pronouncing and the computer will pronounce that word for them. They can even have the entire passage read word by word at varying speeds. Should they not know a word's meaning, students can click on that word and ask for its definition, which the computer will show and read simultaneously.

Students in the Peabody suite of labs can also work in a word lab that provides explicit instruction in word knowledge. The package of computer-facilitated activities includes assessment of a student's level of decoding, entry of the results of that assessment into a data base, and generation of a list of 10 words the student has difficulty decoding, as determined by the assessment activity. Instruction takes off from there. First, students see their challenging words and are asked to say each word into a microphone that records the student's voice. (The computer can even break the word down and say it for the student before the student says it.) Second, students practice reading the words in a limited time frame. After reading the words, the computer plays the correct pronunciation of the words, followed by the student's reading of the words. The students decide if they have correctly pronounced the word or not. If not, students mark words incorrectly pronounced, and those words return to the practice database. Third, students practice their "difficult" words under time constraints so that their pronunciation becomes more automatic, a process that builds fluency. A set of the difficult words appears on the screen, and the computer pronounces the words in random order one at a time. Students must click on the word that the computer pronounces as quickly as possible. Even though students may demonstrate fluency in responding to a formerly difficult word, each difficult word enters a word bank that becomes part of future reviews and quizzes.

Hasselbring and Goin (2004) designed an investigation to assess the effectiveness of an integrated intervention program for struggling middle school readers. The experimental reading intervention program included the two word and reading lab components, along with a third computer-driven spelling lab, plus daily interactions with books on tape and time every day to read low-grade-level but high-interest-level books. Although earlier efforts to find substantial benefits from computer-assisted, media-enhanced reading instruction went largely unrewarded, this integrated network of labs and literacy activities proved to have statistically significant benefits over control groups. That integrated program became the basis for READ 180, a commercially available program used in many middle and high schools to help students build their reading skills.

For students struggling with the pronunciation and/or meaning of a word encountered in a print text, such as unknown words found in a novel or content area reading assignment, there's the "Reading Pen" (www.wizcomtech.com). Students use this tool, which is about the size of a thick pen, to scan a word. The pen's internal computer reads and pronounces the word, breaks it into syllables, and provides the word's definition. The basic pen contains a dictionary of 240,000 words. Its portability is an asset.

Technology can also serve as a vehicle for the construction of texts, their editing, and their distribution. Many students use word-processing programs just like those I'm using to develop this text. Students can use word-processing programs to develop outlines or explore ideas with Inspiration. Drafts of papers can be developed through instructional technology, sent to partners through e-mail for evaluation, or shared in chat rooms. Final drafts of papers can be sent on to the teacher for assessment or gathered for electronic publication. Other ways that technology can be used to enhance writing were discussed in chapter 7.

Time on task. Based on research and expert opinion used to support this model of literacy intervention, in-school time on literacy-connected learning should be between 2 and 4 hours (Biancarosa & Snow, 2004). During that time, students should be focused on reading and writing across the content areas. Text-centered learning in science, math, social studies, or other subject areas can certainly contribute to the 2 to 4 hours of literacy development. As Biancarosa and Snow have warned, teachers in the content areas may need to reenvision instruction so that more text-centered learning occurs. But even that's not enough. After-school studies that include substantial amounts of text-centered learning should normally require about 2 additional hours. That's the norm at Benchmark school—and that doesn't include after-school tutoring and teacher-monitored homework sessions (Pressley et al., 2006). Exceptions may require significantly more time interacting with texts than these guidelines indicate.

Assessment/Placement. Nothing will poison a reading intervention program more successfully than inadequate assessment and haphazardly placing students in the program. Assessment itself should be of two kinds: formative, to observe ongoing, short-term individual literacy growth, and summative, to measure more long-term progress and program effectiveness. Formative assessments, which are usually informal and frequent, provide information about students' growth, strength, and needs. The data, which can be kept for individual students in a computer, should contribute to informed instruction that moves students toward mastery. Summative assessments, often more formal in nature, could provide data covering a students' entire academic career, or at the least literacy performance during the middle and high school years. Summative data provide a basis for program evaluation within a school and for out-of-school interest groups, such as parents or school boards, to gauge students' progress and program effectiveness. Teachers, especially those involved with planning literacy intervention, should have access to the data so their planning can reflect students' literacy development and needs.

Both formative and summative assessments can help place students into a proper literacy intervention program at appropriate levels. Their placement should be frequently reviewed to assure the best fit. Students' frustrations over literacy challenges that are too demanding or too boring must be reduced to a minimum to heighten engagement. As you can see, assessment is vital to any reading intervention endeavor.

Critical mass of teachers committed to reading intervention. Critical mass here refers to a "sufficient number" of teachers in a group or school to create a culture of literacy. For example, providers of Success for All training usually require that 80% of the teachers in an educational institution agree to support the program before they begin training (Slavin, Madden, Dolan, & Wasik, 1996). Without a critical mass of teachers on board, the successful implementation of any reading intervention is imperiled. It may not be doomed because, as time passes, more teachers may commit; however, without a critical mass actively supporting a program, it becomes more vulnerable.

In some schools, obtaining a critical mass is not a challenge because every teacher hired supports the school's stated mission to address and improve students' reading and writing. That's the case with many "small learning communities," or charter schools, that embrace literacy as a fundamental element of their reason for existence.

Teacher organization, training, and ongoing professional development.
Collaboration among teachers when it comes to reading intervention programs is essential. J. A. Langer (2001, 2002) found that collaboration was a key to student achievement in the "beating the odds" schools she studied, and it's a key to successful reading intervention. According to teachers in the Benchmark School, the professional development of teachers was considered to be by far the most important element that contributed to the impressive reading achievement of struggling readers attending that school (Pressley et al., 2006). Teams and teaming were also key elements in Biancarosa and Snow's (2004) vision of adolescent literacy programs. Coordinated planning and instruction contribute to any program's chances for effective impact on students, and, with teachers working together, more information about students can be shared within interdisciplinary teams. Finding sufficient time to meet, plan, review instruction, and provide intrateam support has been a challenge in some schools. However, time to meet is critical and must be built into a school's weekly schedule.

Training for reading interventions remains paramount. Without sufficient training, teachers and the programs they implement will be in jeopardy. We already know that a clear link exists between teacher quality and student achievement: Poor and minority children who are more likely to be among the struggling readers are too often inequitably deprived of high-quality teachers (Peske & Haycock, 2006). Even though on-the-job training has its merits, it is too detrimental to expect teachers to confidently present instructional features, such as a complex comprehension strategy, to their students when they have been rushed through limited training. Teachers need time to understand the rationale behind a strategy, to see it modeled for them, to practice the strategy, and to talk about issues related to its use with students.

A Reading Apprenticeship model for instruction fits very well with professional development. As in the original Reading Apprenticeship model (Schoenbach et al., 1999), teachers should be encouraged to develop case studies of individual students and use them as platforms to promote inquiry-based teacher development. Teachers can strongly commit to learning about their students and their practices rather than brushing up on acquired strategies that may not fit students' literacy needs. Through case study that includes student work, interview excerpts, and classroom observations, teachers can look deeper into the problems of literacy performance of students struggling to learn and discover the steps likely to encourage further literacy development of those students. One of the benefits of the master-apprenticeship format is that teachers engage in ongoing professional development that will keep intervention programs vital, vibrant, and relevant.

Motivation. It's quite remarkable that few of the widely known commercial reading intervention programs designed for struggling readers focus explicitly on the challenge of motivation. Even in the research-based model of reading intervention presented here, motivation is coming up relatively late. However, it has not been "out of mind." An entire chapter (chapter 2) of this book is devoted to literacy motivation (in a former edition, it was chapter 10), and I don't think I came close to exhausting the subject. As one of my colleagues has described the motivation issue in adolescent literacy, it's a "black hole." But we're beginning to understand how much power that black hole possesses and to understand how it works.

As I hope chapter 2 made clear, motivation is multidimensional with many dynamic, interacting factors. Students bring their own constellation of motives to the classroom, with many motivational stars in each constellation, such as a student's evolving identity, set in motion long before teachers even meet their students. Once individual students gather as a class, teachers begin to have some significant input with respect to the motivational factors they can bring to bear on a classroom and on individual students within each class. These factors include the teacher's own level of engagement and the kind of classroom climate the teacher cultivates.

An abundance of evidence reveals that students' attitudes toward and engagement with reading declines as they progress through elementary school (McKenna et al., 1995) as well as through middle school and into high school (Gottfried et al., 2001; Lepper et al., 2005; Otis et al., 2005). Of course, individual trends may vary. Nevertheless, a major objective of this model of reading intervention is to alter these general patterns of motivational deterioration, and research evidence indicates that well designed, stimulating reading intervention programs can do that (Guthrie et al., 2006; Pressley et al., 2006).

Evidence indicates that the focal point of our discussion about motivation should probably be self-determination theory and its contribution to this literacy intervention model (Deci & Ryan, 1985; Ryan & Deci, 2000). Self-determination theory, which emphasizes the central importance of each student's need for personal development and self-regulation, indicates that the development of intrinsic motivation ought to have our utmost attention no matter what feature of the model we're addressing. When we use reading to arouse curiosity, create challenges, deepen involvement, build self-efficacy, and encourage autonomy, we provide opportunities to foster intrinsic motivation. Using an instructional framework that combines motivational support and strategy instruction in various subject areas, such as Concept-Oriented Reading Instruction (CORI), not only builds intrinsic motivation, but also improves students' reading comprehension (Guthrie et al., 2004). With CORI, science inquiry can be integrated with reading and reading instruction. After arousing students' situational interests through hands-on science investigation, students can be given choices of interesting books to read related to the inquiry and can be taught explicitly about strategies to improve comprehension, such as activating background knowledge, questioning, summarizing, and graphically presenting text content. The principles of CORI can, of course, be applied to any content area.

Identity enhancing. Some intervention classes tend to embrace a "deficit" perspective and position students as "remedial" (O'Brien, Beach, & Scharber, 2007). Once placed in that framework, a student can be adversely affected, as O'Brien and his colleagues discovered in their ethnographic study of a 2-year intervention language arts program in a suburban middle school. Students who distanced themselves from the program showed little engagement with or growth in reading. However, those disengaged students enjoyed other activities that were outside the package of activities with which students were expected to engage. Many of those packaged activities, such as a computer-driven word lab, were similar to activities that Hasselbring and Goin (2004) developed and that became a commercial intervention program called READ 180. The out-of-the-package activities included creative writing, Power-Point presentations, and after-school computer games like Garage Band and Comic Life that gave students a sense of empowerment and personal worth and positioned them positively.

The risk of framing students whose reading skills and performance are below the level of their age- and classmates has gotten a substantial amount of attention (Alvermann, 2001; Franzak, 2006; Moje, Young, Readence, & Moore, 2000). To counter that danger, we can take several steps (O'Brien et al., 2007). First, when designing programs, we ought to value or legitimize academic, social, and out-of-school practices that empower students rather than devaluing those practices because of a negative perspective. Second, we can build "new literacy" practices, such as Internet and World Wide Web activities, multimedia, and video gaming, into our program design. Third, and perhaps most important, we can ourselves learn more about what adolescents discover and learn when engaged with new literacies and use those resources to build competence in both new nonprint technologies and traditional print. We saw the importance of these new literacies and a critical literacy perspective in chapter 8.

Small classes. Although one-on-one tutoring yields the most robust student learning (Bloom, 1984), tutoring usually has the most impact on a program's budget. This model includes tutoring for those needing it, but, because of its expense, we should seek alternative groupings that approximate one-on-one tutoring benefits. While Reading Recovery was effective for many emergent but delayed readers who were having trouble with literacy, schools often could not use it because of cost. However, Slavin (1989) found that student achievement increases with smaller class size, approaching maximum learning with teacher-student ratios of 1 to 4 or better. While ratios of that scale may also be prohibitive, classes for struggling readers should not exceed 15—and then only with at least one trained teaching assistant. Benchmark classes for middle school students average 12 students with two staff members assisting (Pressley et al., 2006). To tolerate classes of marginalized readers larger than 15 is likely to invite further erosion of student engagement and reading development.

Administrative leadership.   Some teachers may venture forth on their own in efforts to address the needs of struggling readers in their own classes and so have little need themselves for any significant administrative support for literacy. However, when groups of teachers or whole schools organize to attack literacy challenges, administrative leadership can be a "make-or-break" factor.

Having witnessed many degrees of program leadership, from novice principals too overwhelmed with problems and too overscheduled to show up for a 15-minute meeting to well-seasoned administrators who were ready to provide information and steady advice when designing and implementing literacy programs, I have to encourage any group of educators contemplating a reading intervention program to look closely at the hoped-for quality of leadership and how close the actual leaders come to that hope. A focused, knowledgeable, understanding, and resourceful administrator can facilitate program implementation in many ways, including funding provisions and what could be all-important school-community relationships. A politically astute administrator who can help faculty negotiate their way through lingering conflicts or sudden differences of opinion will be an invaluable asset.

Parental commitment and communication.   Although Biancarosa and Snow (2004) say little about parental involvement in their vision for school literacy development, my observations of struggling readers and their families as well as substantial research evidence supports the view that school-committed parents have a positive academic impact on students (Baker, 2003; Henderson & Mapp, 2002; Rasinski & Fawcett, 2000). At the Benchmark School (Pressley et al., 2006), parents of middle school–aged students show their commitment by supervising 1 to $1\frac{1}{2}$ hours of homework, including an assurance that their children have a study-conducive space and atmosphere to engage with the homework. Expectations of these kinds should become an integral part of a family's involvement with a teacher's or a school's literacy program. Although parents may not be able to read to their children or even to have their children read to them for 20 to 30 minutes daily, other forms of involvement and support, such as a quiet place to study, should be a minimum expectation. Should any additional weight need to be added to the importance of the family in literacy, we know from research on an international level (Postlethwaite & Ross, 1992) that the second and third most important factors associated most closely with reading achievement are reading done at home and at school.

Communication with parents of struggling readers is also important and can be accomplished through e-mail, phone contact, or periodic reports, letters, or newspapers. Teacher or student-led conferences (Austin, 1994) also facilitate communication and ought to be held at least a couple of times per year. Other opportunities to encourage parent-school communication, such as curriculum focused on the study of the family and its impact on a student's identity, should be envisioned as part of these literacy programs because the culture of the family can have profound effects on student-school connections and motivation.

Tutoring.   I've already acknowledged that tutoring can bankrupt a reading intervention program. But we must also acknowledge that tutoring may be the most promising format for a struggling reader to progress significantly (Bloom, 1984). A well-trained tutor can assess, diagnose, design individual activities, encourage, and nurture a caring relationship in forms that will rarely arise in a classroom environment. Tutors stand a far better chance of discovering a student's "zone of proximal development" and staying productive within that zone for longer periods of time than nearly any teacher dealing with an entire class, even one of only 15 students.

Tutoring can take a multitude of forms, as we saw in chapter 9. Professional, well-trained tutors who usually operate as classroom teachers or reading specialists could work daily with those students most in need. Teaching assistants who are learning to become teachers themselves could also serve as tutors. In some cases, parents who have adequate training and supervision can step in to tutor. Evidence indicates that college students (should they be available), when trained, can be quite effective tutors (J. Fitzgerald, 2004). Also worth exploring are the possibilities and benefits of developing a cross-age tutoring program, in which high school students, once trained, tutor middle or elementary school students (Paterson & Elliott, 2006).

Comprehensive, integrated, ecologically sensitive literacy program.   This feature comes last because all other features must precede its existence. To have a productive vegetable garden for summer salads, you pretty much have to first grow the elements that go into the salad: lettuce, tomatoes, radishes, cucumber, celery, and maybe onions. So now that we know much more about each feature that comprises a comprehensive literacy intervention program, we'll be in a far better position to understand how these features can best be mixed to create a nourishing program for striving readers.

When I was teaching social studies and English to 10th and 11th graders, I was frequently not sufficiently aware of what my colleagues were teaching down the hall. I knew Alex, a teaching friend of mine, had three chemistry and two physics classes that several of my students were taking, but I wasn't in on the particulars. If Alex and I had coordinated with other teachers regarding individual students' literacy needs, especially those students who were struggling, I'm convinced we could have helped more of them master concepts in their courses as well as develop reading and writing strategies. But we were far from an integrated vision of a coordinated literacy program that I'm suggesting here.

Helping striving readers who may be 2, 3, or more years behind in reading and writing is a complicated project—even more complicated than planting a summer garden that at least stays put. A literacy program requires extensive coordination between teachers and support staff. Deciding which literacy concepts and strategies will be taught is only a small, early step. Knowing how to teach those concepts and strategies so that students can internalize and apply them in different content areas is a much larger step. To coordinate a literacy program, teachers need leadership, committee structures, integrated content teams, and more.

No two vegetable gardens are alike. No two literacy programs will be either. Students' needs differ widely from school to school and from classroom to classroom. The features just described and their mix in a literacy program that you and your colleagues construct will have a unique configuration. In some schools, almost all students are years behind in their literacy development and may require massive, intensive, and extensive intervention before anything takes root. In other schools, a relatively small percentage of students may be striving readers and may be helped with a limited literacy academy they attend. I've worked in both kinds of schools. One needed a radical approach that went to the roots of students' reading development and addressed their limited knowledge of letter-sound correspondence and of vocabulary words. In another school, a large percentage of students read and wrote proficiently, a situation requiring far more modest intervention with far fewer students. Explicit reading strategy instruction to improve fluency and comprehension would have benefited almost all students in the former school but far fewer in the later school. However, some form of literacy instruction would have benefited every student in both schools. Learning to read always transforms into reading to learn, but reading to learn never stops.

Now we get to that ecologically sensitive dimension that is inherent in well-designed literacy programs. When our intent to create a comprehensive, integrated literacy program is manifested, that intent should reveal that we are creating a cognitive and social network of literacy possibilities in which students will find an optimum niche and flourish. Thus, our interest ought to be in creating an environment for engagement, interaction, and growth rather than a shopping mall climate where students pay with the currency of time to acquire information (Barab & Roth, 2006). In this ecological perspective of literacy development, we are creating literacy-promoting systems or networks that provide multiple opportunities for individual students with many different needs and motives for reading to engage in the expansion of their life-worlds.

Life-world refers to the internal life of an individual and the physical, social, and psychological surroundings in which the individual is situated. Life-worlds are interdependent and cannot be separated into their parts. In its simplest definition, a life-world is how an individual views and responds to the environment (Barab & Roth, 2006).

To some degree, each student constructs his or her own perspective of the environment. This does not mean that every student constructs a unique world independent of others. That's not possible because others play a significant role developmentally in helping a student construct his or her environment in both its material and psychosocial dimensions. Our life-worlds share similarities with those of others in our environment. Nevertheless, an individual's perceived environment may be quite different from the environment we intended to create in our classrooms and schools (Roth, Boutonne, McRobbie, & Lucas, 1999). As teachers, we may find our richest harvest of insights and understandings in observing how the inner lives of our students shape and guide the actions our students take in the outer, material world.

Our challenge is to design and implement literacy programs and instructional environments capable of gaining access to the personal life-worlds of our students. If programs we design and implement are ecologically sensitive, then that environment— or elements of it—can extend into the lives of more students. That translates into more engagement, more learning, and more life.

However, teachers may need to facilitate creative connections between environments developed and students' life-worlds (Roth, McRobbie, Lucas, & Boutonne, 1997). A walk in the garden may not suffice; students may need to discover what kinds of connections they can make with the life of that garden. What's seen in the garden must be integrated and resonate with a student's life-world so what's in the garden takes on meaning and becomes useful. The garden becomes a cognitive and social environment that promotes the dynamic evolution of each student's reality.

Program Matrix for Literacy Intervention/Evaluation

The matrix of literacy intervention features and designs of various programs, such as those designed by a teacher or for an entire district, in Figure 10.1 provides us with both a list of features and a method of seeing what features constitute certain programs. Furthermore, the matrix could be used to evaluate any school or district attempt to construct a literacy intervention program of its own. By checking off the features in the matrix that a program committee has addressed, committee members and others can quickly see what features an envisioned program has explicitly adopted and what work may remain to be done. The last column on the right can be used to assess existing literacy intervention programs to see which features have been designed into the program and which may still need to be addressed.

The first column of the matrix for an individual teacher's program identifies the features that a single teacher like the one we are about to meet might include in his attempt to address the challenges of struggling readers. The second column shows what a department-wide program might include if all the members of a social studies, English, science or other department were to commit themselves to such a project. The third column depicts what a schoolwide program might include in its literacy intervention program. But let's now return to that single teacher, in this case, a new teacher named Alex Graham.

A new teacher takes on the challenge of struggling readers.   Stepping into his first teaching assignment at Monroe High School, Alex Graham was realizing a dream while anxious about how things would go on his first day. From his credential program and several months of student teaching at a suburban high school, he thought he'd learned enough to anticipate most of the problems he'd face in early September when school began. He'd taught several sections of U.S. history, the main

Figure 10.1 Program Matrix for Literacy Intervention/Evaluation.

Features	Individual Teacher's Program	Department-wide program	School-wide program	Program Assess-ment
1. A broad-spectrum reading curriculum	✓	✓	✓	
2. Systematic, embedded, and differentiated instruction		✓	✓	
3. Diverse texts		✓	✓	
4. Technology			✓	
5. Time on task	✓	✓	✓	
6. Assessment/placement	✓	✓	✓	
7. Critical mass		✓	✓	
8. Teacher organization, training, development		✓	✓	
9. Motivation and identity enhancement	✓	✓	✓	
10. Small classes			✓	
11. Administrative leadership		✓	✓	
12. Parental commitment and communication			✓	
13. Tutoring	✓	✓	✓	
14. Comprehensive, integrated, ecologically sensitive literacy program		✓	✓	

Source: Adapted from Biancarosa, G., & Snow, C.E. (2004). Reading next—*A vision for action and research in middle and high school literacy: A report from Carnegie Corporation of New York*. Washington, D.C.: Alliance for Excellent Education.

teaching assignment he was given at Monroe. He'd spent several weeks during the late summer preparing to teach the course that would cover the major turning points in U.S. history in the 20th century. For the first few weeks, he planned to focus on a review of America's founding and the development of its democratic ideals. He was excited about digging into the enormous range of social, political, and economic problems that the nation faced in the 20th century, the legacy of history past, and the terrific challenges of the 21st century.

After a week of teaching U.S. history, he had terrific challenges himself. Many things were going well. He'd begun to learn the names of his 174 students. He made a seating chart and was taking attendance using the school's computerized system. He'd had a few good discussions with his students about how he hoped to teach history and develop their critical thinking skills. He got copies of the textbook out to all the students, and he'd given his first reading assignment with a follow-up writing task. From all of his students, 31 assignments were turned in. That was fewer than 1 out of 5 completing their homework. He was puzzled. He didn't want his dream of teaching to transform into a reading nightmare.

Alex read about teachers who had to make adjustments to their curriculum and how they taught it because of students' literacy troubles. He'd heard about teachers reading nightmares. And he knew that those who didn't learn from history were often condemned to repeat it. He did not want to be among the condemned repeaters.

So, he began to take steps. He reviewed his social studies curriculum and looked back at reading and writing strategies he learned in his credential program. He decided to give his students a CBM and took several hours over the weekend to create a Group Reading Inventory (GRI) based on his history text. He also asked one of Monroe's counselors for a copy of his students' standardized reading scores over the last 2 years.

By the end of his second week, Alex had done his diagnostic work and knew that about 20% of his students were proficient readers who could read the text without frustration. About 45% would need some significant scaffolding to manage the reading with activities that focused on vocabulary (Tier II and III) words and on comprehension. He could use DR-TAs, reciprocal teaching, Cornell Notes, and writing to learn activities to support their learning both history and reading strategies.

The remaining 35%, nearly 1 out of 3 of his students, for whom the history text was clearly at their frustration level, troubled him the most. The majority of these students had CBM rates of 80 correct words per minute (CWPM) or above but, from the GRI, he learned they had limited vocabularies. A few students, about 15 to 20 (10% of his entire array of students) read fewer than 80 cwpm. This was the group he was most concerned about because his resources for helping them were limited.

After comparing his students' standardized reading test scores with the results of his informal testing, he found that, for the most part, there was a strong relationship between students who scored about 30% or below in the standardized test and those he identified as his struggling readers. They were reading three or four grade levels lower than the average 11th grader.

Seeing the homework completion rate after his first 2 weeks and the results of his own diagnostic work, Alex knew he faced a motivational challenge as well as one rooted in literacy. He took a few steps back and began to look carefully at what motivation his students brought with them to class and at what he could do to heighten that motivation. He had a fairly wide range of options:

- develop a reward system,
- discover students' interests,
- tap technology interests,
- infuse critical and media literacy,
- dig deeper into his own enthusiasm for history, and
- build students' intrinsic motivation by feeding their interests, developing curiosity, presenting challenges, building involvement, and enhancing self-efficacy.

He began collecting information about his students so he could deepen his understanding of their interests—both short- and long-term. He watched for moments of students' situational excitement on which he might build: a student's question about Colonial religious practices, a girl's apparent curiosity about the treatment of women during the Revolutionary War, and a boy's interest in the Colonists' guerrilla tactics during the British Redcoats' retreat along Battle Road from Concord to Charlestown.

He used every moment in class to drive his instructional vehicle along the best possible route. He wasted no time. His agenda was packed. He shifted methods and activities: cooperative learning, computer demonstrations, minilectures, discussion, debates, Web searches, writing, class visits by outside "experts," I-Search papers, and student presentations based on project learning.

The steps Alex took brought him closer to his vision of an engaged classroom of students with whom he could interact as he brought them into the world of history he found so often fascinating. He could see moments when students' curiosity was aroused, moments when they were puzzled or challenged by questions, and moments when they were so involved they forgot the clock. He hadn't taken them to the history teacher's utopia, but he'd begun a journey that strengthened his belief that he was traveling in the right direction.

Resources to Support Intervention Programs

The resources for developing reading intervention programs that we are going to review in the next section have a number of features in common. Most of these programs may be implemented schoolwide or partially, depending on a school's needs and funds. Unless otherwise noted, these programs address the needs of struggling readers in grades 6 through 12. All have some system for individual student evaluation and grouping. All include comprehension strategies to develop more strategic reading approaches. However, training, implementation, and costs vary.

There are differences between the programs. While some rely on direct instruction, others are more student centered. Most of them have the capacity to help students who cannot decode text sufficiently to progress in their reading. The creators of programs that don't address decoding problems recognize that some students may need instruction in decoding to benefit from their approach to reading improvement.

It's a tad spooky and it may appear somewhat kooky, but the assumptions about reading and what promotes it that underlie some of these approaches have contributed to impressive levels of distrust and contempt among their advocates. Perhaps you've heard of the reading wars. Most of the battles have been waged in the trenches of elementary reading instruction. However, rancor over too much or too little phonics instruction of one variety or another has extended the acrimony into middle and high school reading intervention programs and instructional practices. I advocate a "what works" approach. Unfortunately, as of this writing, precise answers to questions about what program works best dwell in the future.

A brief description of each program, its base in research and theory, and an overview of its implementation are provided. The four programs reviewed (and presented alphabetically) are Corrective Reading, LANGUAGE!, READ 180, and Reading Apprenticeship.

Corrective Reading

Program description.   The primary authors of *Corrective Reading (CR)* are Siegfried Engelmann and his associates, including Susan Hanner and Gary Johnson (Englemann et al., 1998). The program is designed to assist middle and high school nonreaders or struggling readers who have weak decoding skills, weak comprehension skills, or both. Although the program has been used with students who speak English as their second language, the program's designers recommend that students should, as a minimum, speak and understand easy conversational English.

Research and theory.   CR is based on principles of Direct Instruction (Gersten, Woodward, & Darch, 1986; Kaméenui & Carnine, 1998). These principles include teaching for mastery, content presented in skill sequences, explicit and integrated strategy instruction, use of placement tests, close teacher monitoring and coaching, scripted lessons to improve communication, and common lesson formats. In the domain of decoding research, Grossen (n.d.) cites findings supporting phonemic awareness, explicit phonics, letter-sound relationships, blending, the early and consistent use of decodable texts, daily performance measures, and the correction of every oral reading error. In the domain of comprehension research, she cites findings supporting the use of interspersed questions, inclusion of expository text structures, teaching of background knowledge, direct instruction of vocabulary, and the teaching of underlying concepts and strategies.

Implementation.   Materials for the program's implementation include student books, consumable workbooks, and teacher presentation books and guides. The program is packaged at four levels of decoding and comprehension. Knowledge of letter-sound correspondence and development of comprehension are transmitted through direct instruction in a scripted presentation. Through exercises and examples, teachers present progressively complex skills and strategies to students. Each lesson takes 35 to 45 minutes of direct instruction and independent student work. Struggling readers need to be placed in levels (A, B1 or B2, and C) that are compatible with their current reading capability. According to *CR* guidelines, homogeneous grouping of students with similar diagnostic test scores will permit optimum growth in reading.

LANGUAGE!

Program description.   LANGUAGE! was developed by Jane Greene (1998), former teacher of English and reading specialist, in the early 1990s. Her goal was the development of a comprehensive literacy curriculum for delayed readers that included literature, language, and composition. The program is designed to assist middle and high school nonreaders or struggling readers who have poor decoding skills, weak comprehension skills, or both. Students should, as a minimum, speak and understand easy conversational English. LANGUAGE! serves basically the same population as that served by Corrective Reading.

Research and theory.   Greene cites evidence from research on reading that supports the central relevance of learning to decode single words rapidly, of phonemic awareness to acquire reading skills, and of abundant practice in reading decodable text at an independent reading level. She also cites research documenting the effectiveness of direct teaching of structured language (Greene, 1998).

Implementation.   The curriculum has three levels and a total of 54 units. All levels include supplementary reading integrated into the curriculum to provide practice in reading decodable, connected texts at students' independent reading levels. LANGUAGE! includes supporting materials that teachers may opt to use with the core curriculum. A student's test score on Degrees of Reading Power, a criterion-referenced reading comprehension test, can be linked with books at that student's reading level. During training, teachers implementing the program also learn to use sounds, letter cards, and a drill book. Teachers teach each unit's content directly, sequentially, and cumulatively. Each level of 18 units takes about 1 year of study to complete. Although the program is designed for individual instruction in heterogeneous classes, teachers can better serve groups of students with similar skill levels.

READ 180

Program description. Ted Hasselbring (1991) and his associates at Peabody College of Vanderbilt University developed READ 180 in the late 1980s and 1990s. In the Peabody Learning Lab, developers designed READ 180 with interactive computer technology to engage and accelerate reluctant or struggling readers. In literacy classrooms, the multimedia lab is combined with literacy workshops (J. Allen, 1995). Developers implemented, refined, and tested READ 180 as part of the Orange County (Florida) Literacy Project from 1994 through 1999.

READ 180 is tailored to address characteristics of middle and high school struggling readers, including an inability to form mental models of texts because of weak vocabulary and background knowledge and an inability to relate to and process content area texts. To address these traits of struggling readers, READ 180 includes vocabulary on topic CDs and content-related videos; software that models fluent reading and offers practice in rapid word identification to build automaticity; content to build vocabulary, fluency, and comprehension; literature and electronic interface, such as CDs, to support reluctant readers and link curricula across the content areas; and CDs that deliver and manage individualized reading and vocabulary adjusted to each student's skill level.

Research and theory. Research enabled designers of READ 180 to identify characteristics of struggling readers and discover appropriate methods and technologies to address weaknesses while building on strengths. Developers of READ 180 repeatedly refer to work conducted by Samuels (1994, 2004), who has done extensive research on word recognition and developed a theory of automatic information processing in reading that guides repeated reading practices. Developers also cite research on vocabulary instruction (Beck, Perfetti, & McKeown, 1982), the use of technology to drive literacy growth in at-risk students (Hasselbring, 1991), and the Matthew effect, which hypothesizes that those with reading skills prosper while those without fall farther and farther behind (Stanovich, 1986).

Implementation. The curriculum is organized into Stage A for elementary school, Stage B for middle school, and Stage C for high school. Materials for each stage are provided to support the program's three basic components: (1) *Instructional Reading*, which includes CD-ROMs covering several topics with videos and activities in four zones: reading, word study, spelling, and practice in comprehension skills, (2) *Modeled Reading*, which is supported by 12 audiobooks presenting a model reader and a coach for reading strategy development, and (3) *Independent Reading*, which is supported with leveled paperbacks for Stages A, B, and C. These provide independent reading practice at students' current levels.

The program is designed for groups of 20 students who are near the same reading level. However, instruction provided through software is individualized. Class sessions are designed to take 90 minutes each day. Each session includes five parts: (1) whole-class instruction; (2) small-group teaching that includes guided reading, instruction in comprehension skills, and fluency practice; (3) instructional reading with READ 180 software; (4) modeled or independent reading with READ 180 audiobooks or paperbacks; and (5) whole-class wrap-up, including journal writing, self-assessment, or discussion.

Reading Apprenticeship (RA)

Program description. The Reading Apprenticeship (RA) program is based on a partnership of expertise between teachers as content area readers and their adolescent students. RA grew out of the work of two classroom teachers and two researchers at WestEd, a nonprofit center for research and development of educational programs (Schoenbach et al., 1999). The researchers' collaboration with classroom teachers resulted in a site-based literacy intervention model that engaged cross-disciplined teams of teachers in discussions and writing about literacy practices. Reflection and professional exchange beat at the heart of the model, similar to the National Writing Project model of teacher-to-teacher interchange. The RA model can augment the reading development of all readers, including English learners.

Case methods and teacher inquiry or action research influenced the development of RA. Teachers become seriously engaged as learners about their students and their practice rather than brushing up on acquired strategies that may not fit students' literacy needs. Through the study of multimedia and print-based cases, including student work, interview excerpts, and classroom observations, teachers look deeper into the problematic literacy performance of students struggling to learn. Teachers become "masters" in their craft and work with their student "apprentices," whom they guide toward higher levels of expertise. The expertise of teachers as readers in their content areas forms the foundation of this approach to improving adolescent reading (Jordan et al., 2001).

Research and theory. The designers of this model embrace Vygotsky's beliefs that social contexts and language-based communication promote cognitive development. During "metacognitive conversations," four dimensions—social, personal, cognitive, and knowledge building—of classroom life overlap and support RA (Schoenbach et al., 1999). The social dimension entails creating a climate of safety and sharing reading problems, processes, and solutions. The personal dimension, strongly motivational at its core, promotes the development of readers' confidence, identity, and goal-setting skills. In the cognitive dimension, students are encouraged to envision the broader landscape, break it down into sectors, develop metacognition, and use strategies to build comprehension. In the fourth dimension of knowledge building, emphasis is placed on activating and building schemas, acquiring vocabulary, and developing discipline-specific content knowledge.

Implementation.

On-Site Reading Intervention Course Development. Teachers and WestEd's staff created a year-long, "mandatory elective" called Academic Literacy that was required of all freshman (Schoenbach et al., 1999). Its goal was to prepare all students to read challenging texts in various content areas with success throughout high school. The course was designed to examine reading with students as apprentices to their teachers as master readers. The learning goals reflected the four dimensions of classroom life constituting RA's framework. The curriculum consisted of four units: Reading Self and Society, Reading Media, Reading History, and Reading Science and Technology. A Sustained Silent Reading (SSR) program with required amounts of reading and responsive writing started at the beginning of the course. All four of the units included SSR and other key instructional strategies, such as reciprocal teaching and its four components (see chapter 9).

Engaging Students. Teachers worked to engage students in social and personal dimensions by forming communities of readers dedicated to investigating and improving reading. Teachers gave students a vocabulary to use when talking about reading, encouraged think-alouds while reading difficult texts, permitted confusion about reading challenging texts, built student confidence, and helped students develop an identity as readers. Meanwhile, teachers strongly supported SSR by using logs and book sharing techniques.

Teaching Students Reading Strategies for all Content Area Reading.   Teachers engage students in acquiring cognitive tools for solving the problems that reading comprehension presents. Strategies, such as reciprocal teaching, are taught in context. Teachers model reading through think-alouds (see chapters 4 and 9). Students learn that technique and then use it in pairs. As students move through the curriculum's units, they acquire more discipline-specific knowledge and strategies for reading in subject areas, such as history or science. Apprenticeship strategies, including reciprocal teaching and recognizing text structures, are integrated into the subject areas to build ways of reading into the disciplines.

Training.   Teachers attend Institutes for Reading Apprenticeship, where WestEd's staff members work with instructional leaders in an extended inquiry-based development experience designed to build capacity for site-based implementation and literacy improvement. Participants, preferably in site-based teams, return to their schools and districts to implement the RA framework and procedures. Participants become more aware of their invisible reading processes in order to make them visible to their student apprentices in various content areas. Participants also learn comprehension strategies, such as reciprocal teaching, that become part of an RA classroom. They also learn to engage students in "metacognitive conversations" about reading processes.

RA has no prepackaged program, software, or workbooks. The investment lies in teacher training and development. Specific tools likely to help, at least initially, are a guidebook entitled *Reading for Understanding* (Schoenbach et al., 1999), a collection of instructional ideas and lesson plans entitled *Building Academic Literacy: Lessons from Reading Apprenticeship Classrooms, Grades 6–12* (Fielding, Schoenbach, & Jordan, 2003), and a themed anthology for middle and high school students entitled *Building Academic Literacy: An Anthology for Reading Apprenticeship* (Fielding & Schoenbach, 2003). RA programs can be designed to focus on struggling readers or extend to an entire school's population. Building a community of committed teachers ready to reform a school's reading program is key to successful RA implementation. Elements built into RA programs increase the likelihood that teachers would learn and be moved to integrate strategic instruction in reading into their content area classes.

The "Just Read More" Program

In his review of research on reading and intervention programs for struggling readers, Allington (2001) identified an elegantly simple solution: Just read more. National Assessment of Educational Progress (1999) data in the *Reading Report Card for the Nation and the States* tell this story of correlations: The more minutes per day that students read, the higher they score on tests of reading achievement. No extensive teacher training. No one-on-one tutoring. No fancy computer programs. Just more reading. A middle school student who reads 40 minutes a day will read about 2,400,000 words a year and is likely to score in the 90th percentile.

To increase their students' volume of reading, schools could simply set aside a minimum of 90 minutes per day for *actual* in-school reading. Allington (2001) writes that schools should look closely at their daily schedules to discover how they can reduce wasted time that could be allocated to reading. Many schools, he believes, could find 30 to 50 more minutes for reading and still have plenty of time for all the other subjects.

In grades 6 through 12, teachers could select texts that increase reading opportunities. Too often an anthology in an English class, one history book, and one science book suffice as reading material for an entire year of English, social studies, and science. If teachers provided more novels, plays, and collections of stories or essays, along with several books, including biographies, to accompany the study of history and science, students could greatly expand their volume of reading.

Some states have established volume-of-reading standards. In New York State, the English Language Arts Core Curriculum calls for students in all grades to read 25 books or their equivalent across all content areas per year (New York State Education Department, 1997). In California, 8th graders are expected to read 1,000,000 words, while 11th and 12th graders should reach 2,000,000 (California Department of Education, 1998).

But to expand the volume of reading, teachers and schools need to enhance access to books. That means more books in every backpack, classroom, bookroom, home, and library. McQuillan (1998) pointed out a very high correlation (0.85) between library adequacy and NAEP reading achievement scores. However, the existence of a relationship between books on hand and the presence of better readers does not mean that books alone caused reading improvement. Other factors that contribute to good reading, such as abundant family support for reading and learning, are likely to occur in communities where books are plentiful.

English Learners

Struggling readers, most of whom speak English with at least conversational proficiency, constitute a large portion of students with exceptional language and cognitive needs. However, another large and growing number of students present classroom teachers with even more profound language, cognitive, and cultural challenges because these students have not acquired conversational or academic proficiency in English.

The number of students in classrooms who are English learners varies dramatically across America. About 15% of all public school teachers have one English learner in their classroom (August & Hakuta, 1997). In some regions, very few classrooms have any English learners at all. In other regions, classrooms with more than 80% of students identified as English learners are not unusual. In many districts, English learners are grouped together in English as a second language (or ESL) classes. In classes with even a few students who are struggling with English as their second (or third?) language, teachers must be ready to adopt strategies that will address these special language, cognitive, and cultural needs.

Looking more closely at the numbers of English learners across the United States, we discover estimates of about $3\frac{1}{2}$ to 4 million. About 40% of that total number of students attend schools in California, where one out of four students is an English learner. That comes to about $1\frac{1}{2}$ million students in California who are trying to learn English while keeping up in their content area classrooms.

From 1979 to 2003, children of ages 5 through 17 who spoke a language other than English in their homes more than doubled (National Center for Educational Statistics, 2005). Over that roughly 25-year period, the number of children in that group who spoke English with difficulty also increased "markedly."

Experts in demographics predict that more and more states and cities will have to address the needs of English learners in the years to come as increasing numbers of immigrants, especially from Central America, South America, and Asia, arrive in the United States seeking access to education. While California, Texas, and New York now have the largest numbers of English learners, many other states, such as Georgia, North Carolina, Oregon, and Kentucky, have had large percentage increases over the past 10 years (Zhao, 2002). Programs and strategies to respond to the needs of English learners are of critical importance.

Federal Law and English Learners

In accord with the Civil Rights Act and its interpretation by the U.S. Supreme Court (*Lau v. Nichols,* 1974), states and school districts are obligated to provide educational services to limited-English-proficient (LEP) students. The law requires that each educational system "take appropriate action to overcome language barriers that impede equal participation by its students in its instructional programs." "Appropriate action" does not mean that schools must provide instruction in a student's primary language, nor does the law specify any other specific methods. For the most part, appropriate action has been guided by three principles arising from another federal law decision (*Casteneda v. Pickard,* 5th cir. 1981):

1. *Use sound theory.* Some experts must view the educational theory forming the base for instruction as sound.
2. *Provide adequate support.* The school system is obligated to provide resources, procedures, and personnel to implement effectively the theory's practice in classrooms.
3. *Achieve results.* The program's implementation must result in students actually overcoming English language barriers to equal participation in a school's instructional programs. The program should not result in students revealing academic deficits.

A Glossary of Acronyms and Abbreviations

So many acronyms and abbreviations arise in discussions and descriptions of English-learner services that a glossary is essential. The glossary will also serve as an introduction to a number of concepts and programs helpful to teachers who work with English learners.

- EL stands for English learner(s). The term has been widely used in discussions about students acquiring English as their second language.
- L1 stands for an English learner's first language.
- L2 stands for the target language that a student is acquiring. In most cases in our classrooms and schools, L2 is English.
- ESL stands for English as a second language and usually refers to classes in which students learn English as a second (or perhaps third or even fourth) language. Although teachers may be fluent in their students' native language, teachers in these classes usually communicate only in English. However, students may communicate (on the side) in their L1.

- ELD stands for English language development.
- ELL stands for English language learner. At times in writing about these students, writers refer to them as ELLs.
- LEP stands for limited-English-proficient students. They have acquired some degree of oral fluency in English. However, they are not yet able to communicate comfortably in academic English or in many interpersonal situations requiring English.
- FEP stands for fluent-English-proficient students who have acquired and use English in both academic and social situations with a significant degree of ease.
- CLAD, in California, stands for cross-cultural, language, and academic development. From approved teacher credential programs in the state, teachers receive a CLAD credential after completing programs that include emphasis and curriculum on students' diverse cultures and languages. The credential authorizes them to provide instruction to limited-English-proficient students.
- BCLAD stands for bilingual, cross-cultural, language, and academic development. Students completing a bilingual program that also includes an approved program in the study of culture, language, and diversity of the classroom receive a BCLAD credential.
- SDAIE stands for specially designed academic instruction in English. When using SDAIE methods, teachers modify their teaching of the curriculum to make it more accessible to students. These methods are described in a later section of this chapter.
- SAE stands for students acquiring English and is used by some educators to emphasize the positive development in knowledge that English learners undergo rather than the implicit deficits of designations such as LEP.

Toward a Theory of How a Second Language Is Learned

Stephen Krashen (1981, 1995) has put forward five hypotheses that, when conjoined, build a valid theory for second-language acquisition. We'll review each of these five hypotheses to see how they contribute to an overall explanation of how students learn English—or how any person learns a second language.

Acquisition-learning hypothesis.   How do we gain language facility? Do we mainly absorb language through interaction with others using it to communicate or through intentional study of grammar, syntax, and vocabulary? According to Krashen, language acquisition is mainly an unconscious process that results from using a new symbol system to communicate with others. However, we clearly do learn language from its conscious, systematic study.

Natural order hypothesis.   In what order are the elements of a second language learned? The natural-order hypothesis asserts that some general order of acquisition exists; however, the particulars of that order are not clearly known for every language.

Monitor hypothesis.   Krashen hypothesizes that second-language learners must have some kind of monitoring system that will enable the new language speaker to recognize when some language form or construction is simply not right. When that recognition occurs, the L2 speaker self-corrects if the correct language forms can be adequately remembered. This process is much like metacognition, our capacity to observe mental operations, to think about mental processes, and to make appropriate adjustments in our thinking so that we can be more successful in communicating or problem solving. For this system to work, a speaker of a new language needs to know L2's linguistic rules, to focus on L2's correct expressive forms, and to have time to reflect on L2's proper use. Unfortunately, reflective conditions are often lacking when communicating in a new tongue.

Input hypothesis. As I read the Spanish newspaper in Los Angeles, *La Opinion,* listen to the radio news in Spanish, or watch a movie in Spanish, I frequently find myself striving to master a syntactic structure that is just a little beyond my current capacity to comprehend. Sometimes it's an inflected verb form used in a new sentence pattern. Sometimes it's a string of unfamiliar *palabras* that leave me searching for context cues to figure out their meaning—as you may be trying to do with the word *palabras* if you don't happen to be familiar with the word in Spanish.

This mental phenomenon of my grasping what's a little beyond me is a concrete example of Krashen's input hypothesis. It states that we acquire a new language by learning language that contains linguistic structures (or meanings) just a bit beyond what we know. We may comprehend well at Stages 3, 4, 5, or Stage i, but then we stretch for the next stage of mastery, $i + 1$, where i represents our current level of competence and $i + 1$ stands for the stage we're about to acquire. In Krashen's (1995, p. 100) words, "We acquire (not learn) language by understanding input that contains structures that are just beyond our current level of competence." By understanding the meaning of what we read or hear, we acquire language—not by explicit study of the isolated structures we are learning.

The input hypothesis helps to explain what is called the *silent period* in language acquisition. That's the period of time that the learner of a new language says nothing. Usually, lots of language is getting in. So much may be getting in that it creates a kind of mental din of words and sounds, out of which little meaning can be constructed. That is what I experience now when I hear a broadcast or conversation in Russian. Although I studied the language many years ago, I used it so infrequently over the years that almost all my knowledge of it has deteriorated. All I hear is a din of sounds, few of which I can recognize. I would surely be silent at a Russian dinner party where guests spoke only in Russian. However, that silent period is of great importance for learners of new languages. We're getting lots of incomprehensible information that will take time to sort out, digest, and understand before we're ready to produce comprehensible information ourselves in that new language.

Affective filter hypothesis. When attempting to speak Spanish, I frequently become anxious about making mistakes because I haven't become sufficiently fluent and confident in the language to always enjoy its social use. I tend to become hypercritical when I need to loosen up and let language (even with its mistakes) just flow.

Krashen identified three affective filters that may cause us to inhibit second-language acquisition and use. These three include anxiety, motivation, and self-confidence. With high anxiety accompanied by low motivation and low self-confidence, we may not easily acquire language. But, when we feel more relaxed, more motivated, and more confident, our affective filters are less active, a condition that makes acquiring and conversing in L2 much easier and more effective.

Consolidating Krashen's theory. Krashen (1995, p. 101) may have summarized his theory best when he wrote, "People acquire second languages when they obtain comprehensible input and when their affective filters are low enough to allow the input in." As teachers of students who are learning English as well as content knowledge, we need to keep in mind the importance of keeping anxiety low while keeping motivation and self-confidence high so that students receive "comprehensible input."

Having presented a theory of second-language acquisition, let's turn to an important and related pedagogical question: How long does it take English learners to become proficient?

How Long Does It Take for an English Learner to Become Proficient?

There are legal requirements for schools to provide appropriate programs for English learners, and a multitude of programs have been implemented. However, the length of time such services should be provided has been much debated and remains controversial.

Several researchers (Collier, 1987; Cummins, 1981; Hakuta, Butler, & Witt, 2000; Mitchell, Destino, & Karam, 1997) have tried to determine approximately how long it takes to learn English. Some estimated that it takes up to 10 years for a student to become fully proficient in English, that is, proficient enough to be competitive with native speakers of the same age in an academic setting.

Part of professing "proficiency" entails proclaiming some level of accomplishment. But what level of achievement or mastery of English signals proficiency? The ability to use English in academic settings would seem to signal academic English proficiency. And that level is clearly essential for success in school. Nevertheless, different standards define proficiency (Scarcella, 2003).

In his discussion of students learning English as a second language, James Cummins (1984) identified two levels of proficiency. He used the terms *basic interpersonal communication skills* (BICS) to describe proficiency in social settings and *cognitive academic language proficiency* (CALP) to identify proficiency in classroom settings. In a sense, Cummins is referring to distinct discourse communities in which students communicate. One is highly conversational and personal, while the other is more formal and abstract. In his research, Cummins found that ELLs took about 2 years to acquire age-appropriate conversational proficiency, what he called BICS and about 5 to 7 years to acquire academic proficiency (CALP). We must be careful not to assume that a student who has attained basic interpersonal communication skills (BICS) is just as proficient in cognitive academic language proficiency (CALP). Knowing how to get along on the playing field in English doesn't indicate that a student knows how to use English successfully in a math, science, or history class.

In an attempt to determine reasonable time expectations for achieving proficiency in English, Hakuta et al. (2000) examined four sets of data. The four studies included two school districts in the San Francisco Bay Area and two in Canada. The researchers came to a "clear conclusion" that oral proficiency took from 3 to 5 years to develop, whereas academic English proficiency took 5 to 7 years. The findings of the two school districts in Canada strengthened these findings. Furthermore, the findings of Hakuta and his associates more or less confirm Cummins' estimates of time to proficiency.

What factors could affect length of time needed to gain proficiency? Some educators favor bilingual education programs because of the benefits to students such programs supposedly yield. However, Hakuta et al. (2000) point out that the presence or absence of bilingual education programs had no effect on the time taken to achieve oral and academic proficiency. Only one of the four districts, one located in the San

Francisco Bay Area, offered a bilingual education program. However, Hakuta and his colleagues analyzed the data from that district's students and found no significant differences in language proficiency between students who were in its bilingual program and those in its English-only program.

One factor the Hakuta team (2000) did identify that had a significant effect on learning rate was socioeconomic status. Students attending schools with lower rates of poverty became proficient more quickly than those students from schools with higher rates of poverty. Furthermore, students who had parents with higher levels of education reached English proficiency earlier than students from families where parents had less education.

Programs for English Language Learners

We can identify and describe several programs used extensively to help English learners acquire proficiency. Even though we can label and describe these programs, we must keep in mind that wide variations exist within each of the specific program categories. Often the discrepancies arise from differences between espoused pedagogy and actual classroom practice.

Here we will define and briefly review eight different instructional approaches to address the needs of English learners: English as a second language (ESL), content-based ESL, sheltered English, structured English immersion (SEI), transitional bilingual education, paired bilingual education, two-way bilingual education, and maintenance bilingual education programs (see Figure 10.2).

- *English as a second language (ESL-only):* Using an ESL approach, teachers aim instruction at students to develop English language skills, such as grammar, vocabulary, and oral competency. Academic content areas are deemphasized.

- *Content-based ESL:* Using this approach, teachers structure ESL instruction around academic content. Generic English language skill development is not emphasized. The next two programs, sheltered English instruction and structured English immersion, are often categorized as forms of content-based ESL.

Figure 10.2 Programs for English Learners.

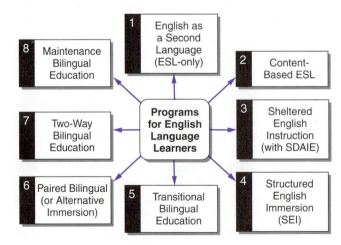

- *Sheltered English instruction:* Teachers provide EL students with subject matter instruction in English. Teachers modify instruction so that content will be accessible to students at their level of English proficiency. In these classrooms, teachers commonly apply specially designed academic instruction in English (SDAIE), the principles and practices of which we review later in this chapter. Sheltered English instruction and structured English immersion (the next program category) are so similar that the program labels are sometimes interchanged.

- *Structured English immersion (SEI):* All students learning English, regardless of their first language, are grouped together. Instruction is given only in English with little or no L1 support. However, teachers adapt instruction to fit the level of their students' English competency so that they can comprehend the content. Lessons in mathematics, for example, are carried on in English but at a level appropriate for English learners in the class. In some states, the passage of state laws mandating SEI programs (unless parents explicitly request alternatives) has caused their rapid expansion, while bilingual programs have contracted.

- *Transitional bilingual education:* Teachers provide some instruction in students' native languages until students are ready to transition to English. Bilingual teachers of transitional classes shift to English as rapidly as they can. Students are tested periodically for replacement. During the 1990s, 50% of English learners were in transitional bilingual programs (August & Hakuta, 1997).

- *Paired bilingual (aka alternating immersion):* Teachers provide reading instruction in both English and the students' L1 at different times each day or on alternating days. L1 instruction fades gradually as students acquire language skills to succeed in English.

- *Two-way bilingual programs:* Teachers using two-way programs serve in classrooms that are split roughly in half between native English speakers and English learners who share the same native language. Teachers have as their objective the development of proficiency in both languages for both groups of students they teach. Maintenance and two-way bilingual programs are relatively rare (August & Hakuta, 1997).

- *Maintenance bilingual education:* Teachers provide large amounts of instruction to students grouped according to their native language. Maintenance programs differ from transitional programs in that teachers who run maintenance bilingual programs aim to develop English fluency while developing academic proficiency in L1.

California's English Learners' Programs: An Example of the Teacher's Challenge

California's educators faced a challenging task in 1998 after citizens passed Proposition 227, an initiative directly addressing the education of English learners in the state. Similar to measures that voters passed in Arizona (Proposition 203) and Massachusetts (Question 2), the California proposition specified the kinds of instruction to be provided to English learners and the expected time frame for that instruction. "Children who are English learners shall be educated through sheltered English immersion during a temporary transition period not normally intended to exceed one year." The statute uses the terms "sheltered English immersion" and "structured English immersion" interchangeably.

Furthermore, the statute permits parents to request a waiver from the structured English immersion program so that their children can be taught English and the content curriculum through bilingual education or other recognized methods. Prior to the passage of the proposition, many administrators in California schools with English learners automatically placed most students in bilingual education classes, most of which were Spanish bilingual.

In order for students to receive structured immersion rather than submersion and possible drowning in English, the Department of Education clarified that the structured immersion program must have the following components:

- a curriculum specifically designed for English learners,
- teachers who have received training in second-language acquisition methods, and
- instructional strategies designed for language learning.

Although not an English-only program, structured English immersion makes far less use of non-English languages for instruction than bilingual methods.

Principles Guiding English Learners' Instruction

To help educators address the challenges of Proposition 227, the California Department of Education also convened a 35-member task force charged with developing recommendations that would give school systems guidance in designing programs for English learners. The task force identified several central questions that California educators would need to answer in order to serve English learners in accord with the new statute. Among those questions were the following:

- What is the responsibility of the school to English learners?
- What does it mean to know a language?
- How will English acquisition and academic progress be assessed?

These were and continue to be tough questions to answer.

However, in their report *Educating English Learners for the Twenty-First Century* (1999), the task force formulated a number of principles to guide educators in answering these questions and implementing programs for English learners. Several of these principles may help teachers address the problems of English learners in California and also in states across the country.

- *All teachers will be professionally prepared, qualified, and authorized to teach English learners.* To accomplish this, the task force recommended extensive staff development to include training in accelerated English language acquisition, training that would go beyond the foundation that CLAD-certificated teachers would already have. Greater emphasis in administrator and teacher credentialing programs on literacy development, language-acquisition strategies, assessment, and content instruction was also recommended. (Some states, such as Maryland, require twice as much course work on reading instruction as other states to obtain teaching credentials and to prepare teachers to address instructional challenges English learners present in content courses.)
- *Educators of English learners will systematically assess student performance by using valid measures and will review performance results to ensure that instruction is aligned with English language development standards and each student's needs.* To reach this goal, the task force recommended the development of statewide

performance standards for each designated level of English language proficiency. These standards should be clustered by grade spans so that teachers will have a meaningful context for levels of proficiency and will be able to focus instruction and assessment on the standards. Teachers should also have access to and training in the use of diagnostic assessment instruments so they can focus on language learning. The state should also develop a statewide instrument appropriate for the assessment of language acquisition by English learners.

- *Instruction, evaluation, and accountability of English learners will be most effective when instructional decisions are based on meaningful data related to student performance.* The task force, as should be clear from these last two principles, was intent on effective diagnostic and standards-based evaluation of English learners. Part of this continuing assessment program included the creation of criteria for the redesignation of English learners as fluent speakers of English only when they had reached grade-level standards in both English language proficiency and core academic subjects. Should English learners fail to achieve grade-level standards in a reasonable amount of time, additional services should be provided. These could include extended-day instruction, summer school, and Saturday classes.

- *All schools will provide effective, up-to-date materials, technology, and equipment for English learners.* The task force recommended that the state budget have funds specifically for instructional materials and software designed to teach English learners. The state's department of education should publish information to help practitioners select teaching materials for English learners. More specifically, these materials should directly help teachers develop students' interpersonal communication skills, comprehension of oral and written language, and academic English. Classes in the content area should include specially designed academic instruction in English (SDAIE) and English as a second language (ESL) techniques.

- *All English learners will have access to the same challenging core curriculum and receive the necessary support to achieve the high standards expected of all students.* The task force emphasizes the importance of English learners progressing in their development of content knowledge as well as English-language proficiency. With state funding, instruction outside the regular school day is recommended for English learners.

- *Rapid and effective acquisition of academic English in the structured English immersion process will be a focus and priority for all students who have less-than-reasonable proficiency in English.* The task force recommends that teachers use strategies that help English learners in three communication modes they identified: interpersonal, interpretive, and presentational. Teacher guidelines for the implementation of the structured English immersion process are also recommended. SDAIE is considered "an acceptable approach" in content areas for English learners who have progressed beyond beginning levels.

- *Instructional programs for English learners with reasonable fluency in English in mainstream classrooms or alternative courses of study will use the learner's language, literacy skills, and sociocultural experiences so that students acquire advanced reading and writing skills in English as well as content knowledge.* The task force recommends that teachers learn to use "sheltered instruction" as a method to help students master content area curriculum. Schools should also provide English learners with access to resources in their primary language to facilitate learning content in English language mainstream classrooms.

Sheltered English Instruction and Structured English Immersion

By design, English as a second language (ESL) programs help English learners gain proficiency in English as quickly as possible. Two content-based ESL programs that share many features merit our special attention because of their wide use. Sheltered English instruction and structured English immersion, as we have seen, are labels for content ESL programs that are often used interchangeably, as they are in the case of California's Proposition 227.

When teaching English learners through sheltered English instruction, teachers modify the content curriculum and its delivery to make it more accessible to students. One of the most prevalent modes of modification for English learners is specially designed academic instruction in English (SDAIE). Among the practices recommended (Chamot & O'Malley, 1994; Schifini, 1994) for SDAIE are the following:

- The level of students' English language fluency determines language objectives.
- Instruction provides access to grade-appropriate core curriculum in content areas.
- Instruction is organized around content that is appropriate for a specific grade.
- Language and content are integrated.
- Students' interests and background knowledge, including that of their culture, form the base upon which teachers build.
- Students are explicitly taught learning strategies to build content knowledge, English proficiency, and problem solving.
- Instruction allows English learners to process content in multiple forms: reading, discussing, drawing, questioning, dramatizing, and writing.
- Content becomes organized into meaningful learning sequences.
- Using total physical response, words may be acted out.
- Levels of language use are modified during classroom instruction.
- Speech rates may become slower.
- Content may be repeated.
- New words are defined in context.
- Realia in the form of concrete objects are used to represent words.
- Idiomatic speech, jargon, and slang are limited.
- Complex or sophisticated language expressions are paraphrased for understanding.
- Meaning is dramatized with actions, gestures, and facial expressions.
- Visual aids, including graphs, maps, and pictures, make content more concrete.
- Verbal expression is supported with films, videotapes, and bulletin board displays.
- All students, with appropriate sensitivity to levels of English proficiency, are drawn into participation.
- To facilitate interpersonal and academic language development, students work and learn in many grouping formats, including pairs, small groups focused on cooperative learning, and skill-building teams.
- Multiple assessment methods (performance-based, standardized, diagnostic, portfolio, self) enable students to demonstrate language and content knowledge growth and discover avenues for further development.

Cognitive Academic Language Learning Approach (CALLA)

CALLA is a content-based ESL approach for English learners (Chamot & O'Malley, 1994). However, it is quite different from sheltered instruction because it arises from a cognitive model of learning and its strategy-based instruction is integrated into both content and language learning. CALLA, its creators explain, has three components:

1. It uses content drawn from grade-level curriculum that content area teachers identify.
2. Language activities are added to the content to build vocabulary, oral skills, and reading and writing abilities designed to help students think through the concepts being learned.
3. Explicit instruction in learning strategies are seen as essential to both content and language comprehension, storage, and recall of information.

Learning strategies, as mentioned in the last of these three components, vitalize much of Anna Chamot's work on second language acquisition (Chamot, 1995; Chamot, Barnhardt, El-Dinary, & Robbins, 1999; Chamot, Keatley, & Mazur, 1999). She believes that strategies for learning or activities that enhance learning should play a pivotal role in teaching second-language learners for several reasons. First, learning strategies are dynamic processes that underlie productive learning. Second, active learners learn better. Third, students can learn strategies and transfer them to new tasks. Fourth, research shows that school-related language learning is more effective when students learn and use strategies.

Drawing on research in strategy instruction, Chamot identifies three types of learning strategies: metacognitive, cognitive, and social/affective (Brown & Palincsar, 1982). Metacognitive strategies include planning, monitoring, and evaluating. When planning, for example, students can use advanced organization to preview a text in social studies to identify its organizing principle and skim it to grasp the gist of its content. That strategy will enable learners to plan what steps they will take to accomplish the learning tasks they face. (Since this section on the French Revolution is entitled "The Reign of Terror," what does that tell me about its content? What's my purpose for reading this section?) Cognitive strategies include elaboration of prior knowledge, note taking, grouping to enhance recall, and linguistic transfer. For example, a reader approaching a social studies text in L2 could make personal connections with the text's content (What do I already know about France, especially during the period of the Revolution? What experience have I had connected to revolutions?), jot down key words and concepts in abbreviated form (How can I best organize this information about the French Revolution? Outline? Concept map? Graphic organizer?), and make connections with the native language (What terms or historical names can I recognize because of similarities to my first language?). Social/affective strategies include cooperation and self-talk. An example of this form of strategic learning lies in working cooperatively with others to solve problems in L2. (Who should I ask in class to help me understand Robespierre's role in the Revolution?) We know that such collaboration is one of the most productive paths to language learning.

CALLA includes several reading strategies that are explicitly taught and that expand students' array of strategic approaches to learning. Among these are the following:

- *English learners activate and elaborate prior knowledge.* Students work alone or in cooperative groups to jot down or illustrate what they already know about a topic about which they are going to read. (Students gather in teams to list what they know as a group about the French Revolution.)

- *English learners set a purpose and plan for reading.* After students decide why they are reading a text, they create a plan to help them see how they will approach a text to learn from it. (After reviewing what needs to be read about the French Revolution, a student sets a purpose for reading, decides what to focus upon, and selects a means for organizing knowledge gained.)
- *English learners monitor their comprehension through self-questioning.* Students ask themselves questions about texts, such as "Does this make sense to me?" As students become aware that their comprehension is breaking down, they can activate fix-up strategies. (Students reading about Robespierre's role in the French Revolution ask themselves if they understand what they've read, discover they are not sure, and decide to reread the text.)
- *English learners self-evaluate and assess their progress toward the purpose they set for reading a text.* These self-assessments can take the form of conferences with the teacher, discussions in small groups, written summaries, retellings, and journals. (After writing summaries, students reconvene in their team to discuss questions based on their reading about the French Revolution.)

None of these strategies should be taught in isolation, according to Chamot and O'Malley (1994). The strategies should be integrated and practiced with content reading. Furthermore, English learners should "experience" an entire text before trying to comprehend each individual word. To do this, Chamot and O'Malley suggest listening to the text, reading familiar words for the gist, or engaging in a form of reciprocal teaching in which students can help each other comprehend the text.

Through CALLA, English learners read "authentic" texts from different content areas, such as literature, science, history, and math. In literature, they could read stories and poems; in math, word problems. While learning to read in the content areas, students learn academic language skills through listening, talking, reading, and writing. The variety of strategies and activities included in CALLA (which, ironically, means "keep quiet" in Spanish) promotes development of both basic interpersonal communication skills and cognitive academic language proficiency.

Researchers (Chamot, Dale, O'Malley, & Spanos, 1992) compared ESL math students who received extensive instruction through CALLA with a control group. They found that students in high-implementation classrooms performed better on measures of problem solving and mentioned the use of metacognitive strategies more frequently.

How Can We Know Which Programs Serve English Learners Best?

Claiming that any one program for English learners has research-based merits that far exceed any other program would, at this point, be far from prudent. In their review of research on English language learning reported in a National Research Council study, August and Hakuta (1997, p. 23) argue that policy decisions with regard to educating English language learners have been based on a "paucity of research and a predominance of politics." Several issues have often inflamed the debate over English language instruction: the pursuit of "affirmative ethnicity" through bilingual education, the establishment of English as the official language of the United States, and national immigration policies. "When ably used by politicians who wish to define themselves to voters or by the media when they wish to create controversy," write August and Hakuta, "the educational debate over how best to teach language-minority students is overwhelmed by these controversies" (p. 14).

A review of more than 30 empirical studies (August & Hakuta, 1997) whose purpose had been to verify school and classroom practices promoting effective English language learning from elementary through high school gave little firm evidence in the form of student outcomes supporting any single instructional feature or practice. The review did suggest the importance of key attributes contributing to classrooms and schools whose English language learning instruction worked. Evidence supported a spectrum of effective school attributes, among which were the following:

- a supportive schoolwide climate;
- solid leadership in planning, coordinating, and administering programs;
- customized learning environments to reflect classroom contexts;
- use of native language and culture (but no clear answer to questions about the role that native language and culture should have in English language learning);
- a balance of both basic and higher order skill instruction;
- direct instruction in skills;
- student-directed activities;
- strategies that enhance understanding;
- opportunities for practice, discussion, and review;
- organized, purposeful, and frequent student assessment;
- staff development for all teachers; and
- parent-school involvement.

Over the past decades, increasing numbers of schools and districts have looked to research on effective schools to guide their reform efforts. About 15% of the nation's school districts use attributes of effective schools, like those just described, to design their programs, including instruction of English language learners.

Using a method called best-evidence synthesis, Slavin and Cheung (2005) reviewed 17 experimental studies comparing bilingual and English-only reading programs for English language learners that met their inclusion standards. Only 2 of the 17 were studies done at the secondary level, the others being done at the elementary level. However, the reviewers found that existing evidence favored bilingual approaches. The especially effective approaches were paired bilingual methods that taught reading in L1 and English at different times of the day.

Nevertheless, extensive research, especially that using longitudinal and randomized designs, is still needed on a wide range of critical questions and programs to help us make more informed decisions about the best practices for English learners. Fortunately, August and Hakuta (1997) compiled a comprehensive summary of work completed by a National Research Council committee charged with the development of a research agenda to improve schooling for limited-English-proficient and bilingual students. The committee identified the following research priorities of particular importance to classroom teachers:

- What programs work and under what conditions?
- What are the characteristics of effective practice with English learners?
- What role does level of proficiency in English play in content area learning?
- What, if any, modifications in language use could teachers adopt that would make complex subject matter more accessible to English learners?
- What practices are most effective for students who have had limited prior formal schooling before entering middle or secondary school?

- What factors contribute to students' continued classification as English learners even after numerous years in U.S. schools? How can we better meet their English language development needs?
- How do English language learners affect content area teachers and their classrooms?
- What English literacy instructional program or approach is best for children of different ages, for those with different native languages, for those whose native language is not written, or for those whose parents are not literate in English?
- How do teachers' attribution of status to a language affect their instructional work?

Beyond these important research questions, Hakuta et al. (2000) recognize that we need to know more about how long it takes English learners to learn basic oral English skills and how long it takes them to learn sufficient academic English to no longer be handicapped in classrooms without specially designed instruction for their language needs.

Perhaps reflecting political and policy tensions around education programs to teach English learners, the former National Clearinghouse for Bilingual Education (NCBE) has become the National Clearinghouse for English Language Acquisition & Language Instruction Educational Programs (NCELA). NCELA maintains an online resource (www.ncela.gwu.edu) for research and classroom strategies related to teaching English language learners. NCELA is funded by the U.S. Department of Education's Office of English Language Acquisition, Language Enhancement and Academic Achievement for Limited English Proficient Students (OELA) under Title III of the No Child Left Behind (NCLB) Act of 2001.

Although the problems that teachers face in classrooms with increasing numbers of English learners are often complex, we have many promising strategies to make learning the English language more efficient and effective. With insistence from educators that practices be based on careful research, we can, over time, increase the number of strategies available to teachers, our understanding of how those strategies work, and our skills in using them with English learners at different stages of proficiency. There are no easy answers to educating English learners, but we must continue to ask provocative questions that promote further inquiry and discovery.

Summary

In this chapter we addressed the challenges of struggling readers by exploring the roots of their reading problems and found that many of them struggled with word recognition, fluency, and limitations in their vocabularies, background knowledge, and strategy use. These obstacles to comprehension erode students' motivation to read. To provide teachers with perspectives and practices enabling them to understand and alleviate those obstacles, we examined a research-based model for reading intervention. That model included a constellation of 14 features, ranging from a reading curriculum for struggling readers that individual teachers could adopt in their classrooms to a comprehensive, literacy program that crossed content area boundaries and included out-of-school resources. Following the intervention model's presentation, we found that a matrix of its features can serve as a tool to evaluate the thoroughness and depth of literacy programs designed to assist struggling readers.

Reading programs, such as READ 180 and Reading Apprenticeship, that are used in the design of intervention projects for struggling readers were also described.

Students learning English as a second language also present teachers across the disciplines with literacy challenges. With the number of English learners in classrooms expanding, teachers and researchers are acquiring a deeper understanding of how a second language is learned and what teachers can do to facilitate that learning. We reviewed principles guiding English learners' instruction and strategies designed for academic instruction in English. Although knowing which specific programs work best for which students is knowledge yet to be gained through research, we have acquired significant knowledge about the effectiveness of some strategies and programs for English learners.

Double-Entry Journal: After Reading

Revisit your DEJ written before reading this chapter. How would you revise your approach to those English-speaking students who were at least a couple of grades behind in their reading? In what ways would you modify or amplify your approach to English learners in your content area class?

DESIGNING LITERACY INTO ACADEMICALLY DIVERSE CONTENT AREA CLASSES TO PROMOTE UNDERSTANDING

After reading chapter 11, you should be able to answer the following questions:

1. What is standards-based instructional planning?

2. How do the challenges and benefits of integrating literacy strategies into science, math, and physical education compare with the challenges and benefits of their integration into English and social studies?

3. What steps can teachers across the disciplines take to create a responsive standards-based instructional program that integrates literacy strategies to help their students become better readers, writers, and learners?

When putting together a unit of instruction in your content area, how would you deal with standards, literacy issues, student diversity, and assessment of student learning?

It's synthesis time. Much of what we covered in earlier chapters is put together in this one. That includes your understanding of reading processes and classroom cultures, motivation to deepen engagement, diagnosis of students, vocabulary instruction, comprehension and critical reading strategies, the uses of writing in your instructional program, and strategies for struggling readings and English learners.

However, another major purpose for this chapter is to show you how to integrate literacy strategies, such as those presented in earlier chapters, into a standards-based instructional program so that your students learn not only content but also strategies. Your students can then transfer and apply those literacy and learning strategies to other texts and contexts, enabling them to become more effective learners.

Standards-Based Instructional Planning

What Is Standards-Based Instruction?

When I began my teaching career in the mid-1960s, state standards and school accountability for achievement tied to those standards were nonexistent. What guided our secondary instructional programs then were local agreements, both schoolwide and districtwide, about what should be taught in different content areas at progressive grade levels. Now, many states have extensive and detailed standards for every grade and, beginning with the sixth grade, for every content area. But what are standards and how can they shape your teaching?

Content standards. Content, or academic, standards represent a high level of agreement among their drafters about the skills, knowledge, and abilities that all students should be able to master at each grade level. **Content standards** state the knowledge or skills that will be used as a foundation for judging learning at specific stages in students' education. A content standard for physical education could be that all students are to run the mile. Other examples of content standards for other content areas appear in Figure 11.1.

Performance standards. A **performance standard** is a level of achievement that students must attain to show they have mastered the articulated content standards. Performance standards define levels of competence at each grade level, and they indicate the degree to which a student has achieved the content standard. For example, the performance standard for running a mile is how quickly students are expected to run it. That performance standard could be expressed as a range from the maximum time allowed for "passing" the standard to Olympic records that students might strive to reach. Interim objectives or benchmarks could be set between maximum times allowed and world-class performance standards. As many educators have discovered, a standard for content is frequently much easier to articulate than deciding what makes up a level of acceptable performance for the standard.

Figure 11.1   Examples of Content Standards from Various States.

California State Content Standards: Biology/Life Sciences (Grades 9 through 12), http://www.cde.ca.gov/be/st/ss/scbiology.asp:

Cell Biology: The fundamental life processes of plants and animals depend on a variety of chemical reactions that occur in specialized areas of the organism's cells. As a basis for understanding this concept: *a) Students know* cells are enclosed within semipermeable membranes that regulate their interaction with their surroundings. *b) Students know* enzymes are proteins that catalyze biochemical reactions without altering the reaction equilibrium and the activities of enzymes depend on the temperature, ionic conditions, and the pH of the surroundings. . . . *j) Students know* how eukaryotic cells are given shape and internal organization by a cytoskeleton or cell wall or both.

Texas Essential Knowledge and Skills (TEKS) for Grade 8 History, http://www.tea.state.tx.us/rules/tac/chapter113/ch113b.html:

The student understands the foundations of representative government in the United States.

> The student is expected to: (A) explain the reasons for the growth of *representative government* and institutions during the colonial period; (B) evaluate the importance of the *Mayflower Compact,* the *Fundamental Orders of Connecticut,* and the *Virginia House of Burgesses* to the growth of representative government; and (C) describe how religion contributed to the growth of representative government in the American colonies.

California State Content Standards: English–Language Arts Standards (Ninth and Tenth Grades), http://www.ced.ca.gov/be/st/ss/enggrades9-10.asp:

2.0 Reading Comprehension (Focus on Informational Materials).

Students read and understand grade-level-appropriate material. They analyze the organizational patterns, arguments, and positions advances. . . .

> 2.1 Analyze the structure and format of functional workplace documents, including the graphics and headers, and explain how authors use the features to achieve their purposes.

Standards-based instruction.   **Standards-based instruction** is learning founded on content standards and, if available, their accompanying performance standards. The evaluation of such instruction usually goes under the name *standards-based assessment,* meaning that the assessment is based on the content standards used to guide instruction. In Texas, for example, content standards are embodied in the Texas Essential Knowledge and Skills (TEKS). TEKS identify what each student should know and be able to do at each grade level and for each content area. Aligned with TEKS are the Texas Assessment of Knowledge and Skills (TAKS), which provide information about how each child and his district are performing. The Texas Assessment of Academic Skills (TASS) measures the state's curriculum in reading, mathematics, and writing at the exit level and serves as the graduation exit requirement for students in Texas.

In some states, such as California, performances on national norm-referenced achievement tests are used to determine how well a state's students are achieving in reading and math compared with a national sample. These California Achievement Tests (CAT/6 Survey) are given to students only in grades 3 and 7. Like Texas, California also administers standards-based tests in the disciplines through high school. The California Standards Tests (CSTs) are reported using one of five categories of performance from "far below basic" to "advanced." These scores, which are weighted, are used to calculate the Academic Performance Index (API) for every school in the state.

Accountability Provisions of *No Child Left Behind (NCLB)*

The accountability provisions of NCLB have expanded the importance of standards-based instruction and assessment. Several of the law's provisions bear directly on accountability, and the results of state testing programs can radically affect schools within a district. According to NCLB (U.S. Department of Education, 2004):

- All students must be tested to measure their progress based on state standards.
- Evidence of adequate yearly progress (AYP) in closing the achievement gap of minority and disadvantaged students must be shown.
- Longitudinal measurement from grades 3–8 of individual student's performance in reading and math is required of each state.
- States can use their own existing state or local tests or a combination thereof to assess students' performance in grades 3–8.
- Disaggregated data (separating out subgroups, such as minorities) must be reported annually in a "public report card."
- All states will have 12 years (from 2002) to enable their students to attain "proficiency" in reading and math.
- Each state must raise achievement levels at least once every three years.
- If a school does not make AYP for two straight years (schoolwide or in any subgroup), that school (and its district) must allow students to select another public school, provide tutoring (or other supplemental services), and face the possible restructuring of the school.

From this list of expectations, we can see how critical each school's instructional focus on standards and its standards-based performance has become. Educators in most of our public schools do, in fact, give attention in abundance to the accountability system in their states. There are, unfortunately, some problems with NCLB's implementation. For example, states are free to develop their own standards and tests or use commercially developed, norm-referenced or criterion-referenced tests. However, that freedom has created grounds for concern about NCLB's implementation and the authenticity of state testing results.

Critics of NCLB have argued that standards-based testing programs across the states show enormous variation in scores and operational definitions of "proficiency" (Fuller et al., 2006). The discrepancies have appeared most clearly in comparisons between state test scores and those of the National Assessment of Educational Progress (NAEP). In many states, students performed much more poorly in reading on the federally conducted NAEP tests than on state-mandated performance tests in reading. In several instances, the difference between a state's NAEP scores in reading and that same state's own test scores was 50 percentage points. Even more curious are growing gaps between reading performance on federal and state tests, with that gap in some states increasing rather than diminishing over the years. Is improvement in reading really taking place in these states? Critics argue that some states' testing programs have made it relatively easy to meet AYP goals, while other states, with more rigorous testing programs or more demanding definitions of "proficiency," perform far less well. Undoubtedly, problems of this kind, which call into question the validity of state testing procedures and their methods of interpreting proficiency thresholds, will be of interest to federal legislators when NCLB comes up for reauthorization.

Standards in the content areas.   In the mid-1990s, teachers and administrators were clearly confused about which standards to use to guide their instructional programs. Teachers expressed their puzzlement over whether to follow standards from their national organizations, such as the National Council of Teachers of Mathematics, their district standards, their old department guidelines, or the newly minted state standards. Today, state standards are the ones that teachers across the country carefully review and digest. Those standards provide teachers with information about what students should know and be able to do at each grade level and for each content domain. They are the maps that guide instruction in most of today's classrooms.

In most states, departments of education initiate and guide the drafting and distribution of state standards in each content area for grades 6 through 12. Typically, teams of expert teachers, state education consultants, and university professors who are experts in their fields compile the standards. In drafting standards, committees take into account national standards developed by professional organizations such as the National Council of Teachers of English and International Reading Association or National Council of Teachers of Mathematics.

These standards are often linked to publications explaining how teachers in their classrooms can teach students so that the standards are addressed. These frameworks for the realization of standards typically contain many examples of instructional strategies that teachers can use.

Standards are usually developed, distributed, and periodically revised in the following areas:

- English/language arts
- Mathematics
- History and social studies
- Science
- Health education
- Physical education
- Visual and performing arts

Impact of standards-based instruction on learning and literacy.   What are the educational costs and benefits of standards-based instruction and accountability? From a critical perspective, much has been written to condemn standards, standardized testing, and accountability, especially with regard to their effects on the equal treatment of students in multicultural schools. A key message is that standardization damages not only teaching and learning, but also equal treatment of races and social classes (McNeil, 2000). Many of these arguments are compelling and convincing. However, individual stories expressing dismay with standards-based instruction in specific schools may not generalize to the entire practice.

Positive standards-based stories have also emerged from individual schools and entire districts where accountability and testing programs have contributed to significant improvements in students' performance and learning (Skrla, 2001). In some instances, accountability has "smoked out" and made patterns of weak performance, such as in reading, far more transparent. These patterns, once recognized on the educational playing field, could be addressed with added intensity and resources. For example, in Texas, a criterion-reference test (TAKS) sets a standard for all students. Scores are reported by school and district, and entities are held accountable for those scores. The scores, posted on a Web site (www.tea.state.tx.us), are also disaggregated and reported by racial group. All that available information clarifies the results for concerned citizens and educators.

Teachers and administrators can use knowledge of their students' performance in reading to target weaknesses and identify strengths. They can then plan literacy programs and reading instruction that address the weaknesses, implement new strategies and programs, and monitor their effects over time. Data from standards-based testing programs can promote the setting of higher performance expectations in reading and drive continuing student improvement. Many middle and high schools carefully review their performance in reading and discuss what next steps to take in order to prepare teachers to serve their students more effectively. Several studies document the positive outcome of interventions fomented by weak performance on tests and urged forward through monitoring results (Ragland, Asera, & Johnson, 1999; Reyes, Scribner, & Paredes Scribner, 1999; Schmoker, 1996, 2001).

Because results of standards-based innovations emerge with greater frequency and because new federal educational programs stimulate state accountability in reading and math, the last chapter of standards-based instruction and accountability has yet to be written. Many studies have already demonstrated that the effects of standards-based instruction and accountability vary greatly from school to school. While some effects are pernicious, as in schools whose cultures become obsessively test-oriented, other effects indicate accountability can be potent and positive. Standards can promote schoolwide clarity of purpose, focus on solutions, and stimulate collective effort.

How Can Teachers Teach to the Standards?

The main task and goal for all teachers in all content areas can be boiled down to six words: Align standards with instruction and assessment. Seasoned teachers in classrooms across the country have been faced with the challenge of adjusting their curricular and instructional program to requirements stated in their state's standards. For these seasoned teachers, I have condensed these requirements into a few steps and procedures suggested by Susan Midori of California's Institute for Teaching ("How to Cope with Standards," 1999):

1. Familiarize yourself with the standards for your content area and grade level.
2. Identify knowledge and skills for each standard you teach.
3. If there are more standards than can be taught in the school year, prioritize and select those most important.
4. Select activities from your instructional resources that will enable you to teach and reach the standards.
5. As needed, create new teaching activities that will enable you to teach and reach the standards.
6. Collaborate with other teachers in your subject area that are below and above you. Confirm that your colleagues at lower levels are going to cover the standards they are expected to cover and inform those above your level that you will be covering the standards for your grade that you are expected to cover. If there are more standards than can be covered at a particular grade level, you will need to negotiate with colleagues to confirm that all standards will eventually be covered at some level so that students do not miss out on some aspect of their educational program.

7. After taking state-mandated tests that are supposed to measure students' performance, check with students to find out if the state tests included items that had not been covered or not covered sufficiently in class. Also check to see if topics covered in class were tested and if students felt they were well prepared for those items.

Addressing Adolescent Literacy in All Content Areas

Throughout the country, new teachers—like many of you reading this book—are prepared in education programs to address the literacy challenges they will face when they begin teaching. As we found in this book's first chapter, teachers have their "reading nightmares" (Bintz, 1997) in the form of students unable to read their assignments. Regrettably, significant numbers of new teachers begin teaching to discover they were not adequately prepared to help their students acquire literacy strategies that would contribute to their students' success in school.

In response to this discovery in California, a task force of professors and instructors who teach in credential programs throughout the state university system assembled to look carefully at what could be done to improve literacy instruction for new teachers (Fleming et al., in press). Our goal was to develop curriculum guidelines for credential courses that would inform all candidates about best practices for reading and literacy development in their disciplines, including science, math, history, music, art, physical education, and English. After examining the state's content standards and current content area literacy programs throughout the state, we developed a set of six core principles to guide colleges of education within the state's university system as they reviewed and rethought their secondary reading/language arts course.

The principles and accompanying structural elements, such as key questions, activities, and expected candidate outcomes, were not intended to serve as a prescription that every professor or instructor should administer in lockstep fashion to credential candidates. The principles we articulated covered (a) reading processes, (b) comprehension and content learning, (c) adolescent literacy, (d) assessment, (e) differentiation, and (f) planning and integration. By presenting principles based on these six content literacy core concerns, our intent was to increase the likelihood that secondary reading course syllabi would gain coherence and focus and that candidates across the state university system could expect some core, research-based elements in their coursework.

Our next step focused on content-specific literacy challenges, like those of math or science teachers, that could be addressed within each discipline's methods courses. That brings us back to what we're about to undertake ourselves: examining literacy methods that subject area faculty can integrate into their instruction to foster growth in subject knowledge as well as proficiency in reading and writing. However, this is much more easily written than done. Gaining teachers' interest in integrating literacy instruction into English or even social studies is a manageable challenge. However, teachers-to-be of math, science, music, or physical education are sometimes more reluctant to adopt the approach presented in reading across the curriculum courses, and their reluctance is usually understandable.

However, many of the research-based strategies we have learned about in the preceding chapters transfer productively to each and every discipline without jeopardizing the core knowledge and skills of the discipline—whether it be history or mathematics or physical education. Among the strategies that transfer across disciplines are

1. multiple motivational methods: chapter 2;
2. informal assessments such as Curriculum-Based Measurement (CBM) and Group Reading Inventory (GRI): chapter 4;
3. vocabulary development: chapter 5;
4. comprehension strategies such as Cornell Notes and graphic representations of knowledge: chapter 6;
5. writing to promote learning: chapter 7;
6. critical reading of print and nonprint texts: chapter 8; and
7. collaborative learning strategies such as reciprocal teaching: chapter 9.

In the examples that follow of units and lessons from many disciplines, including math, science, history/social studies, and physical education, the usefulness of integrating the preceding literacy-enhancing strategies as well as others you've met in this text is demonstrated. We first discuss the concept of literacy in science, math, history, English, and physical education and show how individual teachers in those disciplines have integrated literacy strategies to enhance learning in their disciplines. Then we survey a systematic, step-by-step method of developing units and lesson plans that was designed for teachers to promote inquiry and to integrate literacy-enhancing strategies into their content area instructional objectives and plans.

Science Literacy

To many scientists "doing" science differs from reading or writing about science (Yager, 2004). The process of doing science begins with raising questions about the world around us and formulating explanations for those questions. Scientists then engage in observations, experiments, and other methods of verification to find evidence that supports or refutes the explanations they propose. Following that quest for evidence, scientists communicate with others in their communities about the evidence found. Through dialogue and discussion in those scientific communities, scientists determine if the evidence presented is convincing and supports explanations for questions that sparked scientific research. To some scientists, scientific literacy is proficiency in moving from questions to a general acceptance of the answers within the scientific community. Now here's where the challenge for literacy integration comes in. To those scientists, science literacy is not constrained to reading proficiently what has been written about science.

That difference in understanding about what constitutes science literacy is a major issue to many teachers of science—new and well seasoned. Many science teachers have been trained to be scientists and to engage in a scientific process. However, when they begin to teach, they find that their students are expected to demonstrate mastery of what has been written about science. That mastery is usually gained through memorization—not by posing questions for which students generate explanations that are supported by evidence gained from research.

What teachers of science do when confronting the tension between doing science and mastering knowledge of science depends on their beliefs about the teaching of science and what science literacy means to them. If they believe that they are in the classroom to teach students to gain science literacy in the sense of engaging in the scientific process, their students will do a lot of hands-on inquiry work. If they believe that they must teach their students concepts and knowledge about science that others have discovered, students will engage in a different learning process. That process will involve teachers transmitting knowledge to students, their reading what has been written about science, and the teacher evaluating students to determine how much they have learned. Of course, teachers need not be forced into an either-or dichotomy. Teachers of science often guide their students toward both forms of science literacy: that of productive science inquiry and that of proficient reading and learning of science.

Source: CALVIN AND HOBBES © 1995 Watterson. Dist. By UNIVERSAL PRESS SYNDICATE. Reprinted with permission. All rights reserved.

Research has shown us that literacy instruction and science instruction can interconnect and interact productively (Alvermann, 2004; Baker, 2004; Saul, 2004). Teachers of science can use literacy strategies to help students improve scientific literacy in both senses used here. Whether it's the social construction of knowledge in the science lab or the use of literacy strategies to "read" events and draw conclusions from them, literacy instruction can contribute to the improvement of learning in science.

Classrooms using literacy strategies to promote science learning.

Eva Behr, a National Board Certified teacher in Van Nuys, California, is a reflective practitioner who often reviews and remodels her curriculum and her strategies for its delivery. The immune system is one of the units she recently reconfigured to use with her ninth-grade biology students. That unit is designed to address a biology state standard (10b): "Students know the role of antibodies in the body's response to infection." That unit is also designed to meet one of her personal goals: making biology a vehicle for the improvement of critical thinking, especially reasoning and the use of evidence. She wants to see more of her biology students use evidence more rigorously, give better explanations for the reasons they do give, and provide stronger warrants for claims they make by more explicitly citing evidence from activities or experiments that would justify or support a claim.

After attending a workshop at the National Science Teachers' Association Conference about inquiry-based instruction, Eva discovered anticipation guides (see chapter 6) and began to use them as an activity intended to help her students understand the role of antibiotics in killing bacterial infections. During the activity, students toss number cubes to determine whether or not an "infected patient" remembers to take a prescribed daily dose of antibiotics. Taking or not taking the antibiotic affects take a prescribed daily dose of antibiotics. Taking or not taking the antibiotic affects the size of the patient's bacterial population. The activity is intended to drive home the lesson that it's important to remember to take doses on time and to complete the prescribed full course of antibiotics.

Eva distributes the anticipation guide before handing out the "Full Course" activity that includes an introduction and a description of the procedure for the activity. The anticipation guide includes the following items, with which students agree or disagree before reading the introductory material and carrying out the activity:

1. If you begin taking a doctor-prescribed antibiotic, you should stop taking the pills when you begin to feel better.
2. There is no such thing as harmless bacteria.
3. Our body's immune system usually keeps small populations of bacteria under control.
4. After you get an infection from a cut on your finger, bacteria can begin to move into that infection, making it worse.
5. All bacteria are quickly affected by antibiotics.
6. An antibiotic that is effective against bacteria will also be effective against viruses.
7. Antibiotics work by killing viruses that weaken your natural immunity to bacteria.

After reading the introductory material and completing the Full Course activity, students return to their anticipation guides and review their "before" responses. Then they indicate whether or not they agree or disagree with each statement once again. After completing the Full Course activity, they also explain in writing how their understanding of antibiotics and antibiotic resistance may have changed and why those understandings changed.

While Eva was generally satisfied with finding that more of her students used evidence from the Full Course activity to support their claims, she felt that she needed to give her students more opportunities to use evidence to justify the claims they made and to model this practice herself. As she states, "It is not enough in science to simply say, 'I was right.' Instead, this conclusion must be supported with evidence from multiple experiments."

After reflection on her experience with the Full Course and related efforts to help students find and use evidence to support claims, Eva decided to ask her students to write more lab reports that include analysis of an experiment. In writing lab reports, as she observed, "Critical thinking and the ability to support a conclusion with evidence, explain reasoning, and apply prior knowledge from the unit would come together." While including lab reports with more hands-on activities complicates the challenges of teaching large science classes, she saw how important the writing of lab reports could be as a bridge to her students' development of critical thinking and science literacy.

Eva prepares her students in gradual steps to write lab reports, a task that some students find intimidating. However, her graduated approach enables students to develop the skills and knowledge they need to write a coherent lab report independently. She engages her students in a simulation of scientists working together toward the common goal of discovery. She then has them conduct a couple of simple labs, such as "Drops of Water on a Penny," a lab that clearly structures all the elements that she expects her students to include in lab reports they write themselves: title, question, hypothesis, materials, procedure, results, and analysis/conclusion.

For her middle school science students, she developed an accessible guide: "How to Write a Lab Report for Ms. Behr." The directions cover the seven elements included in her more simple and structured lab activities:

I. *Title:* This is the name of the lab. It is written on the top line of the page.

II. *Purpose or Question:* This is the reason you are doing the lab.

III. *Hypothesis:* This is an educated guess of what you think will happen. A clearly written hypothesis answers the question, is brief and to the point, and uses the same word pattern as the question.

IV. *Materials:* This is a list of all the materials you need to complete the lab.

V. *Procedure:* These are the directions. They describe, in order, the steps a person needs to take to complete the experiment. They should be so clear that another person could follow them without you explaining it to them.

VI. *Results:* This is where you record your observations. You may use tables, drawings, and/or short descriptions.

VII. *Analysis/Conclusion:* A solid conclusion should always relate back to the original hypothesis, whether that hypothesis was correct or not. It should describe how the data support your conclusion.

Once Eva's students understand the expected structure and content of lab reports, she provides them with additional opportunities to have lab experiences and report them in the format she has established. With that piece of science literacy internalized and with the arrival of science fair time, students design their own experiments, present the experiments in a display, and write lab reports that follow the format she has given them and that they have practiced throughout the year.

Science literacy and English learners. Another National Board Certified teacher, Jennifer Moses, who teachers at John Muir Middle School in Burbank, California, has used KWLs with her English learners to help them gain knowledge of both science and English. Most of Jennifer's ELs known little or no English, so she must design instruction that allows her students to participate orally and that is based on lots of visual cues. Having discovered that her colleagues who teach English and history to ELs often use KWLs to activate their students' background knowledge and to discover what their students know, Jennifer decided to use them in her EL science classes. Students were not only familiar with the KWL strategy, but the strategy also provided her with information about what her students knew about a new topic: nutrition. Her purposes were to have her students examine their eating habits, compare what they ate with nutritional guidelines, and reflect on steps they could take to improve their diets. She also had critical thinking goals in mind because, like Eva Behr, Jennifer sees science as a perfect platform for teaching thinking.

Jennifer's classes are based on inquiry. For the nutrition unit, she directed inquiry at each student's eating habits and patterns. She used the KWL to stimulate discussion so that students could (a) communicate ideas with each other, (b) prioritize ideas collaboratively, (c) generate questions that would direct their inquiry, and (d) reach a consensus about key nutritional ideas. She began her inquiry by having each student complete a KWL at home. In the K column, students had to list at least five facts about nutrition and their eating habits. In the W column, they had to list five questions they had about nutrition. Before whole-class discussion, Jennifer had her students meet in small groups to share what they knew (K) or at least thought they knew about nutrition and what they wanted to learn (W). Members in their teams then selected three of the most important things their group knew about nutrition and three questions their group most wanted to answer. The teams put the three things they considered most important and their three questions on a poster. These were posted on the walls of the room, and each team's members presented their poster's information/questions to the whole class.

Jennifer knew that these students' English and history teachers also used concept maps to help their students organize ideas. Knowing that, she developed concept maps (see chapter 6) to help her students organized their ideas, to help them learn key words and concepts, and to show them how those concepts were related. She drew concept maps on the board as the whole-class discussion based on the displayed KWL posters unfolded.

Through these activities, Jennifer was able to identify what her ELs understood about nutrition and to discover some of their misconceptions. They knew, for example, that candy can be tough on the teeth, that too much coffee is "bad," and that meat has a lot of protein. Jennifer's strategies also uncovered misconceptions. One group thought that "water cleans the body" but didn't know it had other functions. The same group believed that soda was unhealthy because it had bubbles. The range of responses she got helped her to see that she would have to use not only differentiated instruction to engage her students' background knowledge, but also SDAIE techniques to help them acquire English.

The statements they made also gave her opportunities to pursue and develop their reasoning. For example, she conducted a discussion about sugar and focused on her students' apparent belief that sugar was not healthy. She was able to ask questions about that belief: "Can sugar ever be good?" She was thinking that her students might not understand that sugars come in many forms, including those from fruits. Through this discussion, she was able to help her students challenge their overgeneralization about sugar always being unhealthy and opened the door for future inquiry about sugars, their forms, and their benefits.

Math Literacy

Acknowledging that the call to help students learn to read and write in all content areas has often gone unheeded, if not unheard, an educational researcher specializing in literacy education, Roni Jo Draper, and a math educator, Daniel Siebert (2004), decided to collaborate on teaching an inquiry-based mathematics class for preservice teachers. They sought answers to two questions:

1. How do the instructional goals and practices of math and literacy educators compare?
2. Where is the common ground on which literacy and math educators can simultaneously tread in a mathematics classroom?

Each of these researchers initially had his or her model of learning that would enable students to make sense of mathematics instruction. Unfortunately, both their conceptions of teaching math had elements that got in the way of significant aspects of learning math in a standards-based classroom. After working together, however, they evolved an alternative model of learning and literacy in math that integrated both models. That alternative model represented what the two teachers discovered about the teaching of mathematics: Learning math and acquiring literacy are always and everywhere intertwined in a math classroom. The teachers came to the conclusion that in a math classroom, every occasion for learning math is also a literacy event and every occasion for literacy is a math-learning event.

Unlike most middle and high school science teachers, who combine hands-on science with reading about science, most secondary math teachers pursue doing mathematics over reading about its history. In today's mathematics classes, learning about math concepts and their discovery would not move students toward the problem-solving proficiency that students are expected to demonstrate in their courses or during high-stakes testing, such as statewide performance assessments or the SATs. The reasons for those differences may well reside in the different traditions and cultures of the two disciplines and the methods of instruction teachers have used over decades. Doing science and math has a central place in both disciplines as students acquire science or math literacy. However, many teachers have discovered that reading and writing play a key role in the development of science literacy and math literacy, especially within a framework of inquiry-oriented instruction (Borasi & Siegel, 2000; Lemke, 2004).

Students in math classes must "read" math texts and "write" math texts, but the texts they read and write are broader than a verbal text composed of words. The texts read and written in a math classroom include mathematical symbols, diagrams, tables, graphs, charts, equations, three-dimensional models, and oral explanations of problem-solving methods, all of which can be seen as symbolic forms that carry meaning. Fluency in using these symbolic forms, including natural language, are essential for students to participate in math discourse in the classroom. To learn to talk about math, students need effective math teachers focused on helping their students construct knowledge about math concepts, words, rules, procedures, and other symbolic forms that are part and parcel of math texts and math discourse.

Source: CALVIN AND HOBBES © 1990 Watterson. Dist. By UNIVERSAL PRESS SYNDICATE. Reprinted with permission. All rights reserved.

However, while focusing on math concepts and related procedural knowledge may be necessary, it may not be sufficient for every student who tries to enter the world of math discourse. Some students require something far beyond an explanation of what *slope* means and how to calculate it. Unfortunately, some math teachers have not gotten adequate training in how to help struggling math students who must strive to keep up with more-proficient students. Many math educators (Borasi & Siegel, 2000; Draper & Siebert, 2004) believe that students on the journey to math literacy can benefit from learning literacy strategies to (a) develop math vocabulary, (b) comprehend math verbal texts, (c) generate math discourse, and (d) enter math-centered conversations in classroom communities. As we saw in chapter 3 when we witnessed classroom discourse focused on the meanings of Salinger's short story "The Laughing Man," students who got strategic support in constructing and sharing interpretations of the story were better prepared to participate in meaning negotiation. Similarly, students of math may need strategic support to acquire not only math literacy in the sense of doing math, but also strategic capacities to read and write in the natural language in which math discourse is embedded.

Math vocabulary.   When reading math texts, there are many opportunities to learn vocabulary that has the potential to make talking about math much easier. Knowing what words and concepts in algebra mean—concepts such as coordinates, linear, matrix, commutative, reciprocal, rational function, radicand, and cross products—enables students to understand how to frame problems, how to proceed with their solution, and how to engage in talking about events that occur in the world of mathematics. Without knowing the meaning of key vocabulary words, math students will be unable to develop fluency or any degree of proficiency when reading math texts.

Several strategies for building math vocabulary were described in chapter 5. These include the Word Knowledge Check, whereby students can assess their own knowledge of words as they are introduced in new chapters. Students can determine if they think they are familiar enough with a word to use it properly in a sentence or if they have simply never seen it before. Students can also use the Vocabulary Self-Collection Strategy (VSS) to identify words and terms that are unfamiliar and that they want to learn. These words or terms can be placed on a students' word list, along with some that a teacher can nominate. Math teachers can then institute in their classes a student self-driven vocabulary mastery program like the one Dennis DePauw developed at Lincoln High School, described in chapter 5.

Comprehension strategies.   While math class in middle and high schools is usually not the place for learning to read, it definitely is a place for reading to learn. That reading to learn can be facilitated with appropriate comprehension strategies, many of which you met in chapter 6. Those strategies include think-alouds, double-entry journals, Anticipation Guides, Directed Reading-Thinking Activities, K-W-L, Directed Inquiry Activities, and SQ3R or PLAN. In addition, students who know text structures that commonly occur in math texts, such as problem-solution structures, are likely to find unpacking math texts more manageable because students have a clearer idea of what to expect.

Furthermore, metacognition during reading and problem solving ought to be encouraged. When students consider their thinking while reading a math problem, they will summarize, question, clarify, and predict what comes next in a text. These moments are likely to help students recognize when their problem-solving processes are revving up or breaking down, when to pause and reread, or when to seek additional help. While reading and solving math problems, think-alouds provide a window into students' minds as they construct meaning and solutions. Reciprocal teaching, which is explained in chapter 9, can also be used effectively to help students learn to summarize, ask questions, and clarify their thinking about words as they read math texts and math word problems.

Written discourse.   Both the development of math vocabulary and comprehension strategies contribute to the generation of math discourse expressed in writing and speaking. Encouraged by the National Council of Teachers of Mathematics (2000), writing about math can promote learning and deepen understanding of math concepts and their application. Two of the benefits of writing about the process of conceptualizing and solving math problems are that, when writing, more thinking about the concepts and their inter-relationship occurs and that writing provides opportunities for metacognitive growth in the domain of math. Students have occasion to observe and correct patterns in their thinking about structuring math problems and solving them.

Several writing strategies to promote learning, which were presented in chapter 7, can be productively applied to math learning. One of the most productive writing forms that math teachers use as a window into their students' minds at work in mathematics are learning logs and journals. After engaging in a close look at students' work and what students have written about their work, math teachers have frequently told me that they discovered new ways to help their students, especially those struggling with math. The students' writing facilitated the discovery of mathematical misunderstanding or of procedural breakdowns. Teachers could directly assist a student once the errors were discovered through the window of the student's writing. Admit Slips and Exit Passes (see chapter 7) also help teachers discover what students understand and where they need further instruction.

Math Discourse.   Do you recall a math class in which your teacher stood at the front of the classroom and took you through the problem-solving process for homework problems that most of your classmates had trouble solving? Your role was to listen, compare what the teacher did with what you did, ask questions, and take notes. That traditional form of direct instruction in math has benefits in that teachers know the solution process for problems has been covered. However, an alternative method of helping students construct knowledge of mathematics may be both more engaging and more effective: math discourse. For some math teachers, including several knowledgeable teachers I've had the privilege to coach in their pursuit of National Board Certification, engaging math students in math discourse either in small groups or as a whole class challenges them more than almost any other skill they must demonstrate to gain certification.

However, these National Board Certification candidates discover that methods often taught in content area literacy classes enable them to surmount this discourse challenge. Initially, math teachers get students to share what they know about a new mathematical concept by using strategies like K-W-L or Double-Entry Journals. In a form of written think-alouds, they also engage students in math discourse by asking students to write out their solution procedures in a math journal and share those procedures in small teams of three to four members. Once a team reads over its members' explanations of the problem solving process, agrees that a procedure works, and identifies common moves in solving a problem, members of the team present their solution and its possible variations to the class for further input from classmates.

Classrooms using literacy strategies to promote math learning.   David Chae, a geometry teacher who discovered the benefits of writing in math classes, created a lesson plan on proportions and ratios that demonstrates how a question map (see chapter 5) could help students develop their understanding of the concept of ratio by asking questions about it. With the constructs of ratio and proportion in the center of the map, students would surround the terms with questions: How do you use ratios? Why are ratios used? When do you use ratios? What's an example of a ratio? What are some ways of writing a ratio? What is the difference between a ratio and a proportion?

David also designed a set of Inquiry Questions (IQs) to guide his discussion of ratios (see chapter 8). These questions, as shown next, build on Bloom's taxonomy of cognitive objectives (Bloom, Englehart, Furst, Hill, & Krathwohl, 1956):

- *Knowledge:* What is a ratio?
- *Comprehension:* How can a ratio be presented as a fraction?
- *Application:* How would you use ratios in the game of baseball?
- *Analysis:* What is the difference between percentage and ratio?
- *Synthesis:* Create your own word problem that involves both ratios and proportions.
- *Evaluation:* Do you think ratios and proportions are important? Why or why not?

David can use questions like these to deepen his students' understanding of ratios and proportions while engaging them in math discourse.

Heidelyn Cortes, who teaches algebra and geometry in El Monte High School, developed a lesson plan on the Pythagorean theorem that uses Cornell Notes (see chapter 6). Heidelyn based her lesson on the following mathematics content standard: "Students use the Pythagorean theorem to determine distance and find missing lengths of sides of right triangles." She also expects all her students to be able to determine if, given the lengths of three sides of a triangle, it is a right triangle. After having her students do a few warm-up problems reviewing the coordinate system and some new problems involving right triangles, she has her students review their work on those problems and share solutions. She then introduces the distance formula and shows how students could use it to determine the distance between a pair of given coordinates in a right triangle. During the demonstration, she asks her students to take notes using the Cornell system.

For guided practice, Heidelyn asks one of her students to walk to the pencil sharpener that is on the left, front corner of the room. The student walks down the aisle to the wall, turns left, and walks, to the sharpener. Given that the coordinates of the student's seat are (0,0), students give the coordinates of the sharpener based on the number of steps to it. Heidelyn then asks another student to explain how the coordinates were found and how to find the shortest distance from the student's seat to the pencil sharpener assuming no obstacles are in the way.

For independent practice, Heidelyn uses Jigsaw II (see chapter 9) and forms "home" and "expert" teams of at least five students. She then gives each member of each home team a different set of two problems that can be solved using the Pythagorean theorem. These students assemble in their expert team to master solutions to both problems. Expert team members prepare themselves to return to their home teams to teach teammates how the two problems are solved.

In the closing phase of the lesson, Heidelyn asks her students to write in their logs what she calls a "last-minute reflection paper," in which they describe (a) what they learned in the class that day, (b) what helped them understand the new concepts, and (c) what they need to have retaught or reviewed because they don't understand it yet. What her students provide for her through their writing is that window into their learning that gives her an understanding of what's working in her classroom and what needs further work.

Before leaving our discussion of the potential benefits of integrating literacy with math instruction, I want to explain how productive think-alouds can be to you and your math students. Think-alouds were described earlier in this text to help teachers understand the kinds of strategies readers use to construct meaning from text. (See chapters 4 and 9.) In demonstrating how think-alouds worked, I used an example of a teacher explaining how she made sense of a poem. However, think-alouds can also be used in math classes to help students understand the procedures that their teachers and classmates use to think their way through to a problem's solution. Virginia Draper (2005) has used think-alouds in content area literacy courses to help her mathematics preservice teachers discover how important attending to meaning construction while reading math problems really is. But the process she uses with her teachers-to-be can also be applied to math students so that, if you're teaching math, students can begin to see what kinds of thinking goes into the solving of a problem. Using a gradual-release model (chapter 9), you can enable your students to do math think-alouds in whole-class and partner settings.

Step-By-Step: Think-Alouds in Math Class

Step 1. Gather two sets of math problems, one set of word problems in a narrative context and a second set of problems presented with only math symbols. You can use problems from your math text, original problems, or test items retired from SATs or ACTs, state accountability tests, or state high school exit exams.

Step 2. Demonstrate the think-aloud method yourself by reading the narrative problem and sharing with your students all your thoughts and procedures while working toward a solution. You can, of course, use the board or overhead projector as a "scratch pad." (Some teachers may prefer initially to tape record their think-alouds and play them to the class for demonstration purposes. Save your scratch pad and make a transparency of it so your thinking can be more visible.)

Step 3. Demonstrate the think-aloud process yourself with a problem that uses only math symbols.

Step 4. After your demonstrations (and those of your students that follow yours), engage students in a discussion to answer questions like these:
- How is reading math problems in narrative form (i.e., word problems) similar to and different from reading a newspaper article or poem?
- How was meaning for the problem constructed?
- What kinds of background knowledge and strategies enabled problem solving to proceed?
- How was information processed?
- What purposes guided the process?
- What roadblocks arose? How were they overcome?
- If the reader reread any part a problem, when and why did that happen?
- What kinds of questions arose?
- Did any words or symbols in the problem perplex the reader? What was done to overcome the perplexity?
- When (or did) the reader summarize, predict, or clarify?
- What images, if any, did the problem solver construct?

- Did the reader make any drawings to represent the problem or write anything down to represent aspects of the problem?

Step 5. Ask a couple of your students, perhaps volunteers, to do a think-aloud for a narrative and a math-symbol problem in a whole-class context. (Return to Step 4.)

Step 6. In teams of four to five with at least one more-proficient math student in each team, have each student practice doing a think-aloud with either a narrative or math-symbols-only problem. (Return to Step 4.)

Step 7. In pairs, have students practice with each other doing each of the two kinds of math problems. (Return to Step 4.)

History/English Collaborative

This unit demonstrates how to integrate literacy and history instruction while showing how teachers of English and social studies can collaborate to deepen and enrich content coverage while building academic literacy (see chapter 8). Sarah Wilkinson, an English teacher for 7 years, and Eric Frazer, a social studies teacher for 12 years, collaborated on its creation. Sarah and Eric's students were scheduled so that all those who had Sarah for third period had Eric for fifth period. However, their Timeless Bomb unit could be used in either an 11th-grade American literature course or a United States history course, usually given during the 11th grade. The focus was on John Hersey's (1985) memorable *Hiroshima*, in which the author tells what happened on August 6, 1945, through the eyes of the bombing's survivors (hibakusha). The Timeless Bomb unit serves as an example of ways to conduct inquiry and develop reasoning skills while fostering knowledge acquisition and concept attainment. The following description of the unit includes history content standards, unit objectives, materials and resources, and activities before, during, and after the book's reading. Strategies to promote the development of academic literacy have been integrated throughout the unit.

The standard for this unit came from California's 11th-grade History–Social Science Content Standards for "United States History and Geography: Continuity and Change in the Twentieth Century." The standard states, "Students analyze America's participation in World War II" (11.7). As outcomes of the study of World War II, students will be able to

- discuss the decision to drop atomic bombs and the consequences of the decision (Hiroshima and Nagasaki), and
- describe major developments in aviation, weaponry, communication, and medicine and the war's impact on the location of American industry and use of resources.

A number of other objectives that Sarah and Eric deemed important guided the development of the unit:

1. Students will enlarge their vocabularies by selecting and learning unknown words from *Hiroshima* and related readings.
2. Students will learn and apply reading comprehension strategies, such as K-W-L, to activate and augment background knowledge.

3. Students will enter and reflect upon the lives of hibakusha (bomb survivors) as depicted in *Hiroshima*.

4. Students will develop their critical reading skills by reading texts with and against the grain.

5. Students will write persuasive arguments and develop critical thinking skills by postulating opinions and challenging those opinions with counterarguments.

6. Students will explain key political and scientific stages in development of the atom bomb, such as, The Manhattan Project and the role of key scientists in its development.

7. Students will learn of the political and military factors contributing to the decision to use the atom bomb on cities in Japan and attempts to resist its use.

8. Students will understand the physical impact of the atom bomb on cities hit, their citizens, and their futures.

9. Students will learn about the historical (post-1945) arguments for and against using the atom bomb in Japan.

10. Students will learn about the controversy involving the Enola Gay exhibit at the Smithsonian Institute

11. Students will learn about the proliferation of atomic warheads and discover the politics of nuclear arms in today's world, especially in the Middle East.

Sarah and Eric marshaled an array of materials and resources to achieve these objectives. Eric's students read a chapter from their textbook on World War II, the atom bomb, and its use on Japan. Sarah focused on *Hiroshima* and editorials she found that develop positions regarding the bomb's use. The list of materials included the following:

- *America: Pathways to the Present*. A. Cayton, E. I. Perry, I. Reed, & A. M. Winkler (Boston, MA: Pearson/Prentice Hall), 2007
- *Hiroshima* by John Hersey (1985)
- A set of four editorials that take clear pro/con positions about the use of the atomic bomb on Japan (two supportive and two opposing)

The collaborating teachers also identified several Web sites that students would find useful in completing various activities and assignments the teachers designed, such as a speech about the use of the bomb and a presentation developed with a team of students:

"History Matters" at George Mason University (http://chnm.gmu.edu/us/index.html).

Encyclopedia Britannica (http://www.britannica.com).

Wikipedia: (http://www.wikipedia.org).

"The Atomic Bomb: How It Was Built, Why It Was Used, and How It Changed the World" by Charles Kappus (http://www.unm.edu/~abqteach/atomicamerica/00-01-03.htm).

Hiroshima by John Hersey in *The New Yorker* (http://www.herseyhiroshima.com/index.php).

"Hiroshima: Was It Necessary?" by Doug Long (http://www.doug-long.com).

Atomic Bombing of Hiroshima: Published in *War Times Journal* (http://www.wtj.com/archives/hiroshima.htm).

The students' use of these Web sites also requires that they apply their media literacy skills (see chapter 8) that were part of both Sarah and Eric's curriculum.

Before. The teachers designed several activities for their Timeless Bomb unit that they planned to use before, during, and after its presentation. Before the reading of *Hiroshima*, students were to complete a K-W-L (chapter 6) on the atom bombing of cities in Japan. Students were also to write a position paper (chapter 8) that addressed the following prompt: Should countries other than those that now have atomic weapons be free to develop them? Explain your position in about 300 to 500 words. Eric would use these papers as a basis for class discussion and debate. Sarah would use them to help students examine and develop their ability to compose written arguments.

During. While students read *Hiroshima*, Sarah planned to return periodically to using the reciprocal teaching (see chapter 9) that she had taught her students earlier in the school year to improve their comprehension and develop their metacognitive skills while reading. She would place her students in teams of four, explain how the Metacognitive Merry-Go-Round worked, and distribute cards describing what summarizers, questioners, clarifiers, and predictors were to do. Her plan was to engage students in reciprocal teaching for about 20 minutes several times during the reading of *Hiroshima* and to follow up the activity with discussion.

During the unit, Sarah and Eric also taught students the Believing and Doubting Game (described in chapter 8). To practice the Believing and Doubting Game, students read at least two editorials in support of the United States using the bomb on Japan and two opposed to that decision, write summaries of the editorials, and critique them. Sarah gave selected editorials to her students and let them locate editorials that were for and against the bombing of Japan using the Web or library materials.

For a major activity during the unit, Sarah and Eric worked together to coordinate the development of students' vocabulary using the Student-led Vocabulary Development method (see chapter 5). Examples of words or terms from the first chapter of *Hiroshima*, "A Noiseless Flash," that students would be expected to select as Tier II or III words included the following: affliction, compensation, estuarial, hedonistic, hullabaloo, incessant, Jesuit, notorious, prominence, prosperous, restraint, reconnaissance, repugnant, terminus, Wassermann test, and xenophobic. Words like these would become part of each student's vocabulary word bank.

Sarah and Eric also developed a set of discussion questions for *Hiroshima* (See "Whole-Class Discussions," chapter 9) that Sarah used to guide inquiry in her English classroom:

1. How does Hersey orchestrate the introduction of the hibakusha in *Hiroshima*?
2. How does Hersey bring you as the reader into the lives of these six hibakusha? With which character do you get closest and most involved? Why?
3. What is Hersey's attitude toward the six characters? To which is he most sympathetic? Why do you think so?
4. What purpose appears to have guided Hersey's writing of *Hiroshima*?
5. How do the lives of the six survivors intertwine?
6. Compare the last chapter, "Aftermath," with the original four chapters. What effect does it have on your experience of the first four sections? How does it enhance and/or detract from the original four chapters?
7. What is the most moving moment for you as reader of *Hiroshima*? Why?

The teachers also collaborated in the design of a cooperative learning activity (see chapter 9) and provided directions for its completion in Eric's history class.

Directions: Teams of four to six will be charged with investigating a specific topic and developing a PowerPoint or Podcast presentation on the topic. Students can select topics they prefer to investigate from the following list, and the teacher will constitute teams that will focus on these topics:

1. development of atomic bomb during World War II,
2. decision to use the bomb in the historical context of 1945,
3. immediate and subsequent physical impact of the bombs,
4. historical debate over use: for and against,
5. the "Enola Gay" Exhibit: the unending moral dilemma, and
6. the politics of nuclear arms in today's world.

All team members were to participate in the inquiry, the presentation's development, and its delivery. *Hiroshima*, the history textbook, Web sites, and other resources were to contribute to each team's development of its presentation.

After.   After students had read *Hiroshima*, their textbook, and selected editorials, after they had completed several discussions about their readings in both their English and U.S. history classes, and after they had completed and presented their cooperative team's inquiry and presentation, students would be asked to write a speech of 1,000 words to persuade a legislative body, such as the House of Representatives, to endorse or reject the use of the bomb on Japan in World War II. Knowing the historical context, students would have to take a position regarding the decision to use the atomic bomb, support their position with evidence, and challenge it with a counterargument that they subsequently attempt to dispel. (Students would use the Thesis Analysis and Synthesis Key (TASK) presented in chapter 8 to help themselves structure the speech.)

To determine how much each student has learned independently and to provide for individual accountability, students would also take multiple-choice, short-answer, and essay exams to determine the degree to which they achieved the standards and goals set for the Timeless Bomb unit.

The standards, goals, activities, and assessment procedures for Sarah and Eric's unit demonstrate how teachers can collaborate to further their students' growth in academic literacy. With an array of literacy strategies, including K-W-Ls, position papers, self-selected word banks, critical review of electronic media, extensive discussion of texts, cooperative learning activities, and persuasive speech writing, students have opportunities to strengthen their abilities to read, write, and think critically about a topic of timeless importance.

Literacy and Physical Education

The skill'em, drill'em, thrill'em approach to physical education has its appeals. After all the sitting students have to do in school, teachers know that for many students PE is one chance in the day to be active and to "blow off steam." However, the American Alliance for Health, Physical Education, Recreation and Dance, which includes a national association for physical education teachers, has encouraged a thorough transformation of the "roll out the ball" pedagogy that pervades perhaps too many physical education classes. And there is no question at all about the enormous potential for teachers to transform the PE class. In a nation filled with adolescents who struggle with obesity and eating disorders, opportunities for innovative teachers to promote fitness and a better understanding of body image abound. Some PE teachers have advocated a Planned Approach to Healthier Schools (PATHS) that looks more broadly at ways to make health a more central goal of schooling, including wellness programs for faculty and staff, parental awareness campaigns, and an integrated physical activity and nutrition program (Lounsbery, Gast, & Smith, 2005).

Perhaps the onus for preparing PE teachers to transform their view of physical education into a discipline that encourages the thoughtful development of body and mind lies in part with preservice teacher preparation programs. National organizations for PE teachers clearly are seeking the discipline's evolution, and their journal often runs articles about adopting new perspectives that promote the integration of literacy into the physical education curriculum (Griffin & Morgan, 1998; Hanna, 2001; Marlett & Gordon, 2004; Moen, 1996; Sanford-Smith & Hopper, 1996; Schram, 1995). Several authors have emphasized the connection between language and physical education, including the development of a sports vocabulary to comprehend the physiological aspects of sports, such as the names of muscles and a wide range of physical activities, including games and the rules that govern them. For example, Griffin & Morgan suggest that PE students collect words, phrases, and terms for a personal dictionary. Such a dictionary could be developed along the lines used for student-led vocabulary development (see chapter 5).

Other physical education educators (Behman, 2005; Doucheff, 1996; Marlett & Gordon, 2004) have advocated writing to learn (see chapter 7) in the form of journals, learning logs, or admit slips and exit passes. For example, students can learn the rules of games, such as baseball, football, and tennis, as part of classroom instruction, watch a professional game on television, and then use their journals to record connections they have made between rules applied by officials and events in the game observed, such as personal foul penalties in football. Or they could use the journal as a vehicle to record their reactions to a sport's article on a rising baseball, basketball, or tennis player from *Sports Illustrated*.

Even more ambitious and worthy of merit is to use literacy to help students develop a philosophical perspective of sports and attitudes toward participation in them (Kretchmar, 2000; Marlett & Gordon, 2004). While some students are driven to compete and to win in whatever sporting activity they undertake, others turn away from sports because they dislike pervasive, intense competition. Winning can become so important that other prosocial dimensions of sporting activities, such as building teamwork and forming the basis for good decision making, are lost in the points on the scoreboard or the rush to the finish line. A unit with the goal of developing each student's philosophy of sports participation could include the following questions: What are healthy attitudes toward athletic participation? What perspectives of athletic performance and its development can young athletes adopt? What are the physical and psychological risks of athletic participation when taken to extremes? What place do students want sports to take in their lives? These questions and others like them could be addressed in video documentaries and reading assignments by athletes, coaches, and other educators. Students' writings about issues raised in their reading assignments can be brought to class, shared during discussion, and contribute to the formulation of each student's philosophy of athletic participation. The articulation of such a philosophy could be the culminating activity for a PE class focused on the development of the whole student.

Planning Pyramid for Inquiry and Understanding

The classic pyramids of Egypt have four sides, stand as impressive monuments, and have helped to preserve their inhabitants for centuries—unless grave robbers plundered them. Creating a **Planning Pyramid** for inquiry and understanding will help you develop more effective and engaging instruction for your students—with no guarantee of monumental preservation that might cause the mighty to despair. But planning a pyramid does facilitate the transformation of instructional goals into inquiry that can deepen student engagement and understanding. Its effectiveness arises from backward planning (Wiggins & McTighe, 1998, 2006) and the pyramid's four interlocked sides:

SIDE 1: Decide what you want your students to know or be able to do (standards/goals/wanted outcomes/results).

SIDE 2: Figure out what evidence you would need to confirm that knowledge or skills have been acquired (data/evidence).

SIDE 3: Decide what instruction would generate that evidence (mode of instruction/strategies/unit & lesson design).

SIDE 4: Develop assessment tools showing to what degree students have gained the knowledge and skills you wanted them to acquire (performance measures/assessment).

Now that we know what the four sides will look like, let's clarify in more detail what building that pyramid for inquiry and understanding requires, especially in terms of the building blocks we'll have to put in place.

Side 1: What Your Students Will Know or Be Able to Do: Standards/Goals/Wanted Outcomes/Results

The first side contains the outcomes that you seek for and from your students. That side is constructed by proceeding through four building blocks.

Block 1. Review and become familiar with the standards for your grade level and content area.

Block 2. Identify the "big ideas" in your curriculum, ideas that link content-related information into networks or systems.

Block 3. Gather information about your students, especially about their literacy levels, so that you know them and their various learning needs well enough to make informed instructional decisions.

Block 4. Construct a unit trilevel triangle to help you determine the essential content that *all* your students should master, the content *some* will know, and the content that a *few* will learn; in short, plan for differentiated instruction. Several educators have developed their own approaches to accessing curriculum (Nunley, 2006; Schumm, Vaughn, & Leavell, 1994; Tomlinson, 1999). Elements from each of their models have been synthesized into a vision of how teachers can best create curriculum and decide on instruction that serves diverse students.

Side 2: Evidence That Would Be Needed to Confirm Acquisition of Knowledge or Skills

To build this evidential side of your pyramid, you plan backward by looking at where you plan to go with your students and deciding on demonstrations of students' learning that will show they got there (Wiggins & McTighe, 1998, 2006). What student behaviors

Strategy in Practice

PLANNING PYRAMID

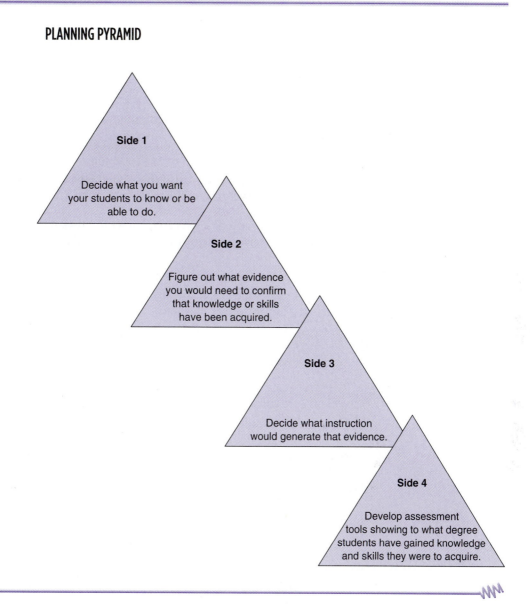

and artifacts would confirm that your students grasp standards, big ideas, and critical concepts? Once you have an understanding of your students and what they are to learn, you are in a position to decide what kinds of evidence would let your students, you, and your learning community know the degree to which the outcomes have been achieved.

Side 3: Instruction That Would Generate That Evidence: Mode of Instruction/Strategies/Unit and Lesson Design

To build this side of the pyramid, you create individual lessons with reference to your unit trilevel triangle and outcomes desired. There are five building blocks needed to construct this side of the pyramid.

Block 1: Identify learning resources (books, demonstrations, videos, Web sites, etc.) that can be used during the unit.

Block 2: Decide on instructional models most likely to deliver evidence for understanding sought.

Block 3: Select literacy strategies that enable productive comprehension and understanding.

Block 4: Create inquiry-driven lessons that weave together more than one standard or learning goal in a single task or activity.

Block 5: Integrate literacy strategies into lessons to facilitate learning and to measure progress toward desired outcomes.

Side 4: Assessment Tools Showing to What Degree Students Have Gained the Knowledge or Skills You Wanted Them to Acquire

Block 1: Develop criteria charts and rubrics for assessing learning as observed in students' performance; identify and confirm standards addressed in the criteria charts and rubrics.

Block 2: Look at student work to determine student movement toward goals.

Block 3: Enable students to identify and articulate in their own language their "next-step" goals so that they know and own their personal instructional objectives.

Block 4: Use student data from formative and summative assessments (statewide testing programs) as indicators of instructional progress.

How Sally Peterson Built a Pyramid for Inquiry and Understanding

After a first career in the film industry, Sally Peterson* discovered she wanted to work with adolescents and decided to become a teacher. At college, she had majored in history with a minor in psychology. In her sixth year of teaching, she became committed to working with middle school students. She loved her work and (usually) the kids she taught. Although she was committed to knowing her students well and to teaching them effectively, she found her fourth period a big challenge.

Sally's fourth-period history class had 30 eighth graders. Five students with mild learning disabilities had been mainstreamed into her class. Five students in the class were in the academically gifted program. Two others were consistently on the honor role. Three of her "slackers" were grossly underachieving, but she thought she could reach and engage them. Two other students were so detached and disidentified with school that she knew they would probably soon stop coming to school physically as well as mentally. She hoped the other 13 wouldn't fall through the cracks. Having gotten the grade-level-equivalent reading scores for all her students, Sally knew that, on average, they were reading at about the fourth- or fifth-grade level, about 3 or 4 years below the level at which her history text was written. She also saw that the range of reading scores spread from a grade equivalent of 3.4 to over 10.8. Sally was a diagnostic, reflective teacher who wanted to engage each of her students so that each was optimally challenged to learn and grow.

---

*Sally Peterson is a composite of several teachers I have known who confronted the challenges of standards-based teaching in urban schools.

Sally planned to put together a new unit for her American history class on the Declaration of Independence. She wanted to take into account the entire range of students she taught, including the range of students in her fourth-period class. That meant she'd have to be prepared for teaching those students who were struggling readers and discouraged students as well as those who were quite advanced in reading proficiency and highly motivated. Furthermore, she wanted to create a unit that would help all her students understand the events that led to the founding of our country and connect those events to the development of our democratic government. But she also wanted her students to gain what Grant Wiggins and Jay McTighe (1998, 2006) refer to as an "enduring understanding" of the revolutionary era that reflected big ideas students could transfer outside her classroom and that were at the core of her subject area, history. To achieve those understandings, she intended to develop an inquiry-oriented curriculum that would answer key questions about the founding of our nation and reveal deep patterns in the study of history.

In the following sections of this chapter, we follow Sally Peterson as she constructs the four sides of her pyramid to create engaging instruction.

Side 1: What your students will know and be able to do

Block 1. Reviewing the Standards.   Sally familiarized herself with the state and local standards applicable to her eighth-grade history course. She also became familiar with one other domain: that of reading, literacy, and language arts applicable to her middle school students. Her reasons for attending to the reading or language arts standards are probably quite clear already: Her students presented a fairly wide range of literacy achievements. As she created her pyramid, she could refer to the literacy standards at her students' grade level. She could then weave those standards into the standards for her history course.

In putting together a unit on the Declaration of Independence, Sally reviewed California state standards in both history and English for the eighth grade. California state history and social science "analysis skills" describe specific "intellectual skills" that students in grades 6 through 8 should learn and apply (http://www.cde.ca.gov/be/st/ss/hstgrades6through8.asp). Among the "intellectual," or thinking, skills relevant to this unit for eighth graders are the following:

- Students explain how major events are related to one another in time.
- Students frame questions that can be answered by historical study and research.
- Students distinguish relevant from irrelevant information, essential from incidental information, and verifiable from unverifiable information in historical narratives and stories.
- Students assess the credibility of primary and secondary sources and draw sound conclusions from them.
- Students understand and distinguish cause, effect, sequence, and correlations in historical events, including the long- and short-term casual relations.

The Eighth Grade Content Standards for U.S. History and Geography specify the following relevant guidelines (http://www.cde.ca.gov/be/st/ss/hstgrade8.asp):

Students understand the major events preceding the founding of the nation and relate their significance to the development of American constitutional democracy.

The content standards also specify that students will "analyze the philosophy of government expressed in the Declaration of Independence, with an emphasis on government as a means of securing individual rights."

For California teachers of eighth-grade history, the History and Social Studies Framework lays out in even greater detail how the course of study should focus on events leading up to the founding of the nation and connect them with the development of our constitutional democracy (California Department of Education, 2005). Entitled "Connecting with Past Learning: A New Nation," the unit in the framework is described as follows:

> This unit begins with an in-depth examination of the major events and ideas leading to the American War for Independence. Readings from the Declaration of Independence should be used to discuss these questions: What are "natural rights" and "natural laws"? What did Jefferson mean when he wrote that "all men are created equal" and "endowed by their Creator with certain unalienable rights"? What were the "Laws of Nature" and "Nature's God" to which Jefferson appealed?

These and additional guidelines provided Sally with directions that enabled her to address the state's content standards. While the framework need not be viewed as the sole means of addressing the standards in the state, it provides teachers, administrators, and assessment specialists with some clear expectations for what students ought to learn. The degree to which students do master the content standards and the fleshed-out conceptual material in the framework could influence a school's performance on statewide standardized testing and students' readiness to undertake subsequent study in high school history and social studies classes.

The English–Language Arts Content Standards also contained guidelines that Sally could address effectively in the unit on the Declaration of Independence. In fact, she saw that the unit provided a remarkable opportunity to help her students build vocabulary, reading comprehension, knowledge of text structure, and writing strategies.

According to the content standards, students in the eighth grade should "use word meanings within the appropriate context and show ability to verify those meanings by definition, restatement, example, comparison, or contrast." Many new and unfamiliar words with which Sally's students could become more familiar appear in the Declaration of Independence.

With respect to reading comprehension, students at the eighth-grade level are expected to "describe and connect the essential ideas, arguments, and perspectives of the text by using their knowledge of text structure, organization, and purpose." They should learn to analyze texts that use propositions and evidence to support those propositions, as does the Declaration of Independence. They are also expected to "find similarities and differences between texts in the treatment, scope, or organization of ideas," and the Declaration provided a text structure that they could analyze to discover how Jefferson put his proposal and argument together.

With respect to writing, the content standards urge teachers to have their students write compositions with a controlling idea and a coherent thesis that leads to a clear and well-supported conclusion. The Declaration served as a model of those qualities.

Block 2. Identifying the "Big Ideas" or Critical Concepts. Early in Sally's second career as a teacher of history, she discovered the tension between covering history and getting students to understand the history covered. Teaching for coverage and teaching for understanding are at war in nearly every teacher's mind in every content area. Sally learned that, as a history teacher, she would be in the middle of that battle between coverage and understanding throughout her career. Because history has produced more information than any teacher can hope to cover (and it won't stop!), she had to make decisions about what to teach and what to leave out. Besides, there were some concepts she wanted all her students to master and other information she considered less critical for all students to know.

Enter **big ideas**, the ideas that can link content-related information into networks or systems. Carnine (1994) developed the "Big Ideas Curriculum" to highlight the principles and concepts underlying content area domains. Mastery of these unifying concepts helps students overcome the problem of having bits and pieces of information, nothing but disconnected facts that fail to crystallize into any kind of holistic understanding. Without some unifying concepts, students have more trouble learning, remembering, and applying knowledge. If this reminds you of schema theory that offers an explanation of how ideas and information are organized in memory, you may be onto something. One of the merits of schemas is that they provide scaffolding that enables students to assimilate knowledge. If a student can activate a schema, it provides "slots" for incoming data, making both reading and learning more efficient and effective.

In their search for a unified social studies curriculum, Kinder and Bursuck (1991) identified some big ideas that help students understand major events in history, such as the **problem-solution-effect model**. The model makes relationships between events and concepts easier for students to comprehend and remember, just as we found that knowledge of problem-solution text structures helped students' comprehension in chapter 6. Many traditional history courses drive students nuts with dates and names that don't hang together in any meaningful way. However, individual events and historical actors make more sense to students if they fit a pattern, especially one that can be transferred to other domains of seemingly random information. An example of such a pattern is the problem-solution-effect model that students might apply when learning about the American Revolution.

The Declaration of Independence is a primary source document that Sally Peterson could teach to her students while using the big idea embodied in the problem-solution-effect model. The Declaration of Independence articulates a problem with substantial evidence, puts forth a solution, but leaves the effects rather ill defined, mainly because history had to reveal how the solution would play out. Sally decided to use the problem-solution-effect pattern in history as a schema with "slots" to be filled with information gleaned from the Declaration of Independence and its surrounding historical context. She realized that she could return to that problem-solution-effect model to help her students understand many other situations in American history, from slavery in the 19th century to terrorism in the 21st.

Block 3. Knowing Students.   Knowledge of students is essential and powerful. The first of five core propositions guiding the assessment of teachers pursuing certification by the National Board for Professional Teaching Standards is that "teachers are committed to students and their learning." Commitment to students and their learning is reflected in knowing who your students are and how they learn.

Earlier in this book, we explored the meaning of diagnostic teaching. We looked at the importance of knowing our students, their learning strengths, their interests, and their readiness to learn. And, of course, we need to discover what impedes their learning—what leaves them cold.

Diagnostic teachers, like Sally Peterson, not only watch what makes their students flourish but also search for the roots of their students' problems with learning in order to find ways to improve it. They are close observers of their students, their students' thinking, and the artifacts that represent their learning. While teaching diagnostically, these teachers are on the lookout for what works and what needs to be modified to work for specific students. They observe the fit between the texts they expect their students to comprehend and their students' resources for comprehending them. If evidence of comprehension problems does appear, they try to discover the problem's origins, or they reteach concepts that they believe their students should master. They look to see if their students' knowledge and strategies are sufficient for the tasks they give them. If tasks are beyond their students' reach, then they modify their instruction to include strategies that make texts accessible. Their constant monitoring of their students' learning and their readiness to modify instruction to improve that learning reveal their commitment to students and their students' growth.

With knowledge of her students and her students' range of reading and writing skills, Sally can make instructional decisions to move her students from a situational interest in a topic, such as the Revolutionary War, to a lifelong involvement with American history. While some students come to us fired up and ready to consume every idea we have to give, others languish in our classrooms for reasons that are not always clear to us. Part of what diagnostic teachers do is to discover the reasons for unproductive engagement and watch for small sparks that might be fanned into a guiding flame.

Block 4. Unit Triangle for Differentiated Instruction.   To know our students is to recognize the benefits that can flow from differentiated instruction. It provides opportunities for students who differ in learning style and vary in interests. It is more responsive to students who vary in English proficiency, from those learning English to highly proficient readers. It allows teachers to create more inclusive environments for students with disabilities and for students who are unusually gifted and talented. It permits teachers to plan multiple activities with multiple outcomes that demonstrate understanding of standards. It increases opportunities for self-determination and heightened intrinsic motivation. While it takes more time to plan and often requires more resources, it can transform teachers into coaches or masters of their craft. Its potential for students to experience deeper engagement with learning and schooling makes it tantalizing.

Differentiated instruction is based on a reality: Not all students can or will learn all the content presented to them, nor will they all learn it in the same way. Trileveled curriculum enables teachers to graphically see the essential content they expect *all* their students to master, the content they expect *some* of their students to gain, and the content they expect only a *few* of their students to learn (see Figure 11.2).

The base of a Sally's trileveled triangle contains essential information she believes all her students needed to understand. Those broad, more abstract concepts, or big ideas, usually encompass lots of detailed information about the specific content she plans to cover, and those concepts are ones she believes her students will encounter repeatedly in their lives. What all students would gain was likely to be broader than the level above it. Sally explains to her students that, if they expect to receive at least a C, they would need to show her that they have mastered content at the base level. The next level up, what some students would gain, includes facts and concepts about the big ideas in the level composing the triangle's base. At the second level, students might also be expected to demonstrate application of concepts. At the triangle's

Figure 11.2 Trilevel Triangle Plan for a Unit on the Declaration of Independence.

Title of unit: Declarations of Independence

What a **few**
students learn:

Influence of European
philosophers, examples
of "arbitrary government," and
elements included in a Declaration
for middle school students.

What **some** students gain:

Conditions for abolition of a government,
sources of a government's "just powers," extent to
which the Revolution broke grip of government on all citizens,
repercussions of not addressing slavery, powers Colonies
gain as "free" states.

What **all** student master:

The meaning of "natural right" and which "rights" are "self-evident,"
knowledge of several problems Colonists had with King George, understanding
of why slavery was not directly addressed, and an understanding of
problem-solution-effects model and how events of the
American Revolution fit into that pattern.

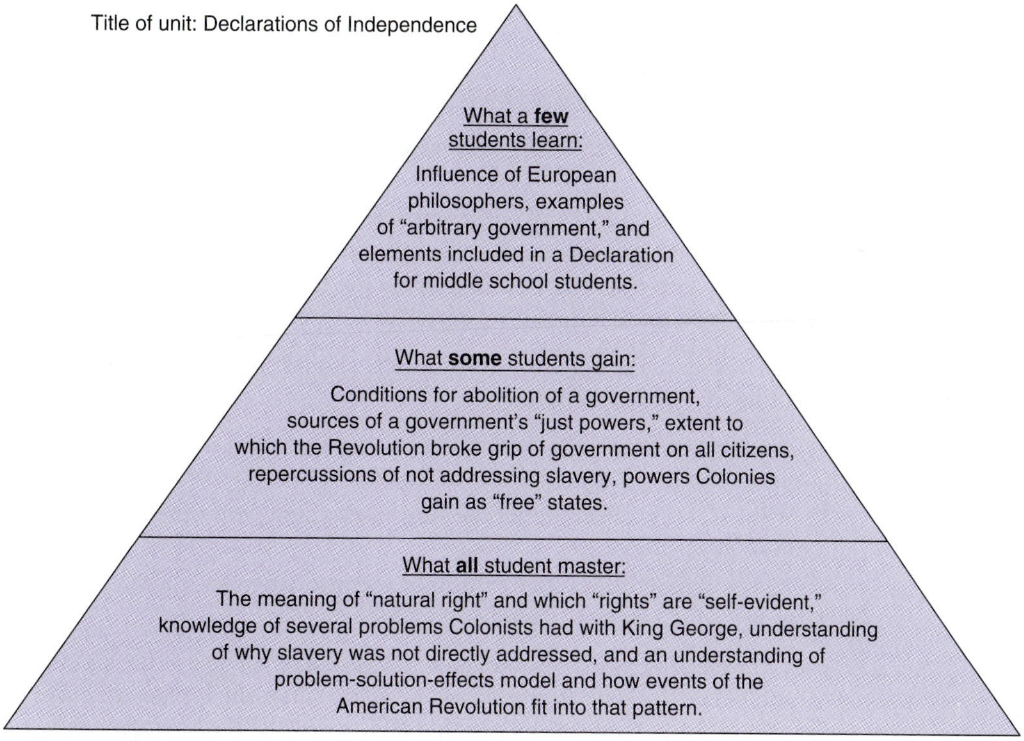

pinnacle are supplementary concepts and levels of critical thinking that a few of her students would learn. This supplementary information, which is usually more complex, often requires exceptional analytical skills and motivation on the part of students to acquire.

Resources and instruction at all three levels of the triangle should be equally available to all students, and inquiry-based activities should permeate all levels. Of course, no student should be assigned to a specific level for any reason. However, Sally Peterson has learned that sometimes only a few of her students will be more eager and interested in mastering material at the upper levels. Enticing students to pursue those trilevel challenges is an aspect of teaching that Sally often relishes.

When applying the trilevel triangle to the development of the unit on the Declaration of Independence, Sally has to make decisions about concepts and information that her diverse classroom of students will understand.

She decides that *all* her students should be able to answer the following essential questions after completing the unit:

1. What are "natural rights" and which of these is held as "self-evident" in the Declaration of Independence?
2. What are several (at least six) problems the Colonists had with King George III?
3. Why didn't the Declaration directly address the problem of slavery in America?
4. How do the Declaration of Independence and events leading up to and following it fit into the problem-solution-effects model?

She decides that *some* of her students should be able to answer the following questions after completing the unit:

1. On what grounds do people have the right to abolish a government that governs them?
2. What is the source for the just powers of governments?
3. To what extent did the American Revolution break government's grip on all its citizens?
4. What have been some of the repercussions in our history resulting from the Declaration's not addressing slavery directly?
5. What powers does the Declaration say the United Colonies will gain in their status as "free and independent states"?

She decides that a *few* of her students should be able to answer the following questions after completing the unit:

1. What ideas from European philosophers, like John Locke, influenced ideas expressed in the Declaration of Independence?
2. What are some examples of the King combining with others to establish "arbitrary government"?
3. If you were writing a Declaration of Independence for middle school students today, what elements would you include in it?

After constructing her trilevel triangle based on knowledge of her students and what she wants them to learn from their work on this unit, she is ready to move to the second side of the pyramid she is building and undertake its development.

Side 2: Evidence needed to confirm that knowledge or skills (outcomes) have been acquired.

Backward planning propels the construction of the second side of the pyramid for inquiry and understanding. Knowing what outcomes she wants her students to attain, Sally is ready to ask what evidence (in the form of behaviors and artifacts) would confirm that students attained the desired outcomes. To show her students understood the origination and impact of the Declaration of Independence, she pursues more than memorization of facts. Sally decides that several forms of evidence would confirm that her students grasped the desired outcomes.

- Vocabulary assessment through one-on-one oral quizzes.
- Journal entries: examples of problem-solution-effects from students' own learning experiences and answers to questions following class discussions.
- Cooperative team's performance on Group Investigation.
- Letter of persuasion assessed with rubric. Using a prompt related to the Declaration, students could compose a persuasive composition that includes a well-defined thesis and presents detailed evidence, examples, and reasoning to support their arguments, while acknowledging the difference between fact and opinion.
- Short essay quiz.
- Individual student scores on statewide tests in history, reading, and writing.

Sally moves toward the realization of this evidence as she creates individual lessons and a sequence of learning experiences that would show student understanding.

Side 3: Decide what instruction would generate that evidence.

To construct Side 3, teachers ask themselves, What forms of instruction maximize the likelihood of achieving the desired outcomes? To build this side of the pyramid, Sally creates individual lessons with reference to her unit triangle and the outcomes she desires. There are five building blocks needed to construct this side of the pyramid. In the following sections, we explore the relevance of learning resources (books, demonstrations, videos, Web sites, etc.), instructional models, and literacy strategies to planning for differentiated, standards-based instruction and the decisions Sally Peterson makes about each.

Block 1. Learning Resources.

When engaged in long-term planning, Sally Peterson needs to account for the learning resources that would enable her students to conduct the kind of inquiry the questions call for. These materials usually include the textbook(s) commonly used for the course, lectures or demonstrations likely to be given, videos that might be shown, Web sites, and other instructional resources. Some textbooks or anthologies provide limited access to additional information while others contain more resources than a teacher could ever use and so require thoughtful selection from them.

Block 2. Instructional Models.

Instructional models provide teachers with a framework and procedures used to teach concepts, academic content, and skills. They describe patterns of behavior that teachers apply to achieve their teaching objectives and learning goals. While an instructional model provides teachers with a broad framework that they can apply to help them achieve their aims, structured activities or plans in the form of strategies help teachers along the way. Here we learn how Sally addresses instructional models. In the next section, we discover how she worked in literacy strategies.

Teachers can choose from several instructional models, depending on their instructional purposes. While educators have grouped instructional models into many different categories, Lasley, Matczynski, and Rowley (2002) organized them into the following four:

- models that foster reasoning skills (such as inquiry),
- models that foster reorganizing skills (such as concept formation),
- models that foster remembering skills (such as direct instruction), and
- models that foster relating skills (such as cooperative learning).

On closer inspection, most of the categories "leak," by which I mean models within a category flow into or overlap with other categories. For example, while cooperative learning certainly can foster relating skills, it can also promote reasoning, reorganization, and remembering. Furthermore, some instructional models, such as lecturing, don't fit well into any of these categories. However, the categories do provide us with handy carrying cages for methods that often have a life of their own.

For this lesson on the Declaration of Independence, Sally decides that to facilitate inquiry and concept formation, her best bet is to foster reasoning and organizing skills because she wants to help students

1. organize information about the American revolution and the Declaration of Independence;
2. make connections between events, documents, and concepts; and

3. create and test hypotheses about how the data fit into a pattern, namely, the problem-solution-effects model.

To engage her students in the phases of concept formation using their knowledge of the American Revolution and the Declaration of Independence, she wanted them to

1. examine a set of data and/or documents,
2. create groupings of conceptually similar data,
3. provide concept labels for groups of data, and
4. expand categories they had created and labeled.

To achieve closure and assessment for this activity, Sally emphasizes the problem-solution-effects pattern posed in the Declaration and prepares students for that pattern's appearance throughout their study of American history.

Block 3. Literacy Strategies.   With information about the reading levels and other literacy skills her students have, Sally makes decisions about strategies that are likely to help her students gain literacy skills and strategies. When deciding which strategies to apply, she keeps these questions in mind:

- Does the reading strategy target the problems my students have?
- Am I comfortable teaching the strategy or do I need some coaching?
- How will I discover if my students have learned the strategy and can apply it?

Once she answers those questions, she is ready to decide how to teach the strategies she wants her students to know and use.

Taken as a package, those strategies prepare her students for their encounter with the Declaration of Independence, activate their background knowledge related to it, address unfamiliar vocabulary, provide opportunity for repeated exposures to the text, and include a review that reinforces all students' understanding of the problem-solution-effects model. The strategies that she thinks will enable these purposes to be achieved include the following:

1. Anticipation Guide
2. Journal writing
3. Vocabulary Self-Collection Strategy (VSS)
4. Word Cards
5. Text structure identification
6. Reciprocal teaching
7. Criteria chart and/or rubric design
8. Review questions

Most of these strategies were described earlier in this text. Criteria charts and review questions are demonstrated in this section.

Block 4: Weaving Together Language Arts and Content Standards.   With the objective of creating inquiry-driven lessons that weave language arts through her history standards, Sally notes that the English–Language Arts Content Standards include vocabulary development, reading comprehension strategy instruction (including text structure and organization), and writing documents with a coherent thesis leading to a well-supported conclusion. These language arts standards complement those of

Figure 11.3   Example of Anticipation Guide: True/False.

		True	False
1.	The Declaration of Independence was written to warn Britain that war would break out in Boston on July 4, 1776.		
2.	According to the Declaration, no truths are self-evident because evidence must be provided to prove a truth.		
3.	According to the Declaration, the holding of slaves directly contradicts the claim that "all men are created equal."		
4.	The Declaration includes a list of facts said to prove that the King of Great Britain pursued an absolute tyranny over the colonies.		
5.	Among the facts listed is the claim that the King kept a standing army in the colonies without the consent of their legislatures.		

history and social studies, especially the ones calling for students to explain how historical events are connected to each other, to distinguish relevant from irrelevant information, to assess the credibility of sources, and to understand sequence and causal relations in historical events. Noting how these strands from the language arts and social studies support each other, Sally sees several opportunities to weave them together in her lessons on the Declaration of Independence. She can integrate literacy strategies into lessons to facilitate learning and to measure progress toward desired outcomes.

Block 5: Daily Lesson Plans.   Sally's daily lesson plans that she developed with reference to her unit goals are presented next in summary form, with an explanation of some of the strategies she selected.

Day 1:   *Activities: Anticipation Guide, Vocabulary Self-Collection Strategy, Journal Entry to Introduce Problem-Solution-Effects Model, Homework.*

The first day's lesson began with an Anticipation Guide (see Figure 11.3). After students completed the guide, Sally led them in a discussion based on their answers. As she talked with her students, she tried to discover their understandings, misconceptions, and attitudes about the Declaration of Independence. Sally looked for possible conflicts between their beliefs and the content of the text that students would rectify as they became more familiar with the document.

After completing a Vocabulary Self-Collection Strategy (VSS), Sally asked her students to take out their journals and describe a problem that they had experienced personally, read about, or studied in school. She asked them to select a problem that had some solutions and effects attached to it and gave as an example a conflict she had with her daughter, several solutions she and her daughter developed, and the effects of those solutions. Sally then gave her students 15 minutes to write the entry, suggesting they give about 5 minutes to each section: problem, solution, and effect. After completing the entries, she asked her students to pair up and share their entries. She later asked for volunteers to share their entries with the whole class and worked toward showing students how the examples fit a problem-solution-effects pattern.

Day 2:   *Activities: Distribute Vocabulary List for Word Cards, Reciprocal Teaching, Text Structure, Homework.*

Sally compiled a list of vocabulary words based on the Vocabulary Self-Collection Strategy she conducted and made a couple of additions. Preferring vocabulary and concepts important to understanding the Declaration of Independence, Sally selected the following 15 terms, almost all coming from her students' lists: natural right, despotism, tyranny, formidable, appropriation, arbitrary, abdicate, perfidy, insurrection, petition for redress, unwarrantable jurisdiction, magnanimity, consanguinity, acquiesce, and rectitude. After distributing the list, she explained to her students that they should construct 3 × 5 word cards for each of these terms and five more words of their own choice (see the Strategy in Practice). She showed students what the word card should contain: the term, its meaning, its part of speech, the original sentence where it occurred, a synonym, a keyword (if appropriate) to help them remember the word's meaning, and a situation in which they might use or apply the term. As an example, she put the term *rectitude* on the board and provided all the information about the word that she requested. Students copied her sample from the board on the 3 × 5 cards she distributed. Then, after distributing dictionaries, she let her students practice with the word *acquiesce*. While they filled in required information on 3 × 5 cards, she walked around the room, giving help as needed. After students completed a word card, she explained that their homework for the next day would be to complete cards for the remaining terms.

Strategy in Practice

VOCABULARY WORD CARD AND COMPLETED EXAMPLE

Vocabulary Word Card

Term: rectitude

Meaning: moral integrity; being correct in judgment or procedure

Part of Speech: noun

Original Sentence from Text: "We, therefore, the Representatives of the United States of America, . . . , appealing to the Supreme Judge of the World for the *rectitude* of our intentions, do, . . . , solemnly publish and declare, That these United Colonies are, and of Right ought to be Free and Independent States. . . ."

Synonym: rightness

Key Word (if appropriate): Those who do not show themselves to be honest people are a wreck and make up a *Wreck*-titude, the very opposite of rectitude.

A situation in which you might use this term: A judge in a court might show *rectitude* during the prosecution of a defendant charged with treason and terrorist activity.

Sally had already taught her students the procedures for reciprocal teaching. Students knew that the strategies included summarizing, questioning, predicting, and clarifying. However, she knew that they would need a brief review before moving ahead, so she asked one of her cooperative learning teams to demonstrate reciprocal teaching using the first paragraph from the Declaration. She asked the team of four students to practice all four strategies that make up reciprocal teaching: summarizing, questioning, predicting, and clarifying. She reminded the teams that, as they go through each section or sentence of the Declaration, they should rotate roles as summarizer, questioner, predictor, and clarifier. She then asked her class to move into their cooperative learning teams to apply reciprocal teaching to passages from the Declaration of Independence. Knowing that students might find large passages in the Declaration frustrating, she provided each student with a copy of the document marked with stop points at shorter sections, even down to some difficult individual sentences, for the reciprocal teaching activity. While students engaged in the activity, she moved from team to team, listening, monitoring, and assisting as needed.

Day 3:   *Cooperative Learning/Group Investigation, Homework.*

To conduct a Group Investigation (see chapter 9) focused on the Declaration, Sally took several steps. Rather than letting each team decide on a Declaration-related topic to investigate, she decided on a set of topics for student inquiry. She limited the topics for this investigation because she had gathered resources in the form of books, articles, and electronic media for each of those specific topics. However, she let students indicate their preferences by ranking their interests and taking those preferences into consideration when forming teams.

The topics focused on the questions, such as the following: (1) How did everyday citizens in the Colonies, from farmers to plantation owners, view the coming of revolution from Britain? (2) What is the evidence from primary and secondary historical sources for the grievances reported in the Declaration? (3) How was the Declaration of Independence drafted from beginning to end? (4) What is the meaning of "natural rights" and "self-evident" truth? (5) What role did slaves and slavery play in the development of the Declaration and the Revolutionary War? (6) How did women view the revolutionary movement and their place in it?

Once students were teamed up, Sally provided each team with a list of resources and a team planning worksheet (see chapter 9) to describe the questions the team planned to answer (including the primary question they were given), the resources they would use, who would do what in the team, and what kind of presentation the team would give. The presentations could take multiple forms: simulations, quiz shows, newspapers, speeches, debates, posters, or even podcasts or Power-Points. Each team member had to contribute to the team's project so that Sally could monitor and evaluate each member's participation. Sally also structured the Group Investigation assessment so that each team would self-evaluate its work and receive feedback from the class and from her for its class presentation.

Homework for the third day was a journal entry in response to the following prompt: Many colonists were also "loyalists," meaning they did not want to separate from Britain. Taking the position of a loyalist, write a 100- to 150-word position paper in which you defend your point of view toward independence.

Day 4–5:   *Group Investigation Team Work: Preparing for Presentations.*

Day 6:   *Introduction of Writing Assignment, Development of Criteria Chart, Work in Class on Letter, Vocabulary Review and Quiz, Homework (Complete Letter to Newspaper).*

At the beginning of class, Sally had several students read their "loyalist" position statements. As students provided reasons and evidence for taking the loyalist position, Sally jotted them on the board as a set of reminders to students. Sally then introduced a writing assignment that would weave together several of the standards from both history and English: a letter of persuasion to a Revolutionary-period newspaper in America or Britain explaining in their own words why they were convinced that the Colonies must separate from Great Britain.

Wanting to assess her students' learning with more than factual questions, Sally introduced a writing assignment on day four of her unit that would weave together several standards from both history and English. The assignment was as follows:

Write a letter of persuasion to a Revolutionary-period newspaper in America or Britain explaining in your own words why you are convinced that the Colonies must separate from Great Britain. Your letter must include the following concepts and information: natural right, consent of the governed, exposition of several problems the Colonists had with the British, and benefits of the solution. One paragraph of the letter must contain an explanation of your understanding of the loyalist position and why you reject that position. The letter should be about 600 words.

Day 7:   *Peer Response with Criteria Check Sheet, "Next Steps" to Improve Letter in Student's Own Words, Prepare for Quiz on Concepts.*

Day 8:   *Group Investigation Presentations; Revision of Persuasive Letter Submitted.*

Day 9–10:   *Discussion (to promote inquiry through questions), Review, Letter Returned with Teacher Assessment and Recommendation for Further Development; Short-essay Test.*

Side 4: Develop assessment tools showing to what degree students have gained the knowledge and skills (outcomes) you wanted them to acquire.   The completion of Side 4 requires four building blocks.

Block 1: Criteria Charts and Rubrics.   Although Sally could have developed criteria for her own assignments, allowing her students to participate in creating criteria had several distinct advantages. First, all students got a clearer picture of what she expected them to do for an assignment. By going over each criterion that would be used to evaluate their performance, they knew more clearly how to perform. Second, if all her students participated in establishing criteria, they could not blame anyone else for judging their work by standards they knew nothing about. They "owned" the criteria applied to their work. Third, with all her students involved in setting criteria, the opportunities for each to succeed was enlarged, in part, because she gave each student more responsibility to contribute to the criteria that would be used to evaluate their work. Fourth, her students were more likely to focus on their learning than on their grades. However, she knew a price was to be paid for student participation in setting criteria. The process took time, even though she thought the time was well invested.

Developing Criteria T-Charts. Gregory, Cameron, and Davies (1997) suggest introducing the process of developing criteria by using students' personal experiences, something all Sally's students knew and could draw upon. Sally had her students begin by exploring what makes a good friend. After brainstorming on paper for 5 minutes, her students met in small teams, shared their features, and agreed to a team list. Each team then contributed that list to a master list of features that a recorder wrote on the board. At that point, Sally and the class began to see what features fit into categories that she could help them label. After completing the friendship exercise, students were ready to create criteria for the persuasive essay.

Step-By-Step: Creating Criteria with Students (Gregory et al., 1997)

Step 1. *Brainstorming.* Because her assignment was to write a persuasive letter, she began criteria collection by distributing copies of a couple of model letters of persuasion from newspapers and asking her students to discuss what elements made these persuasive letters successful or effective. As they made observations, she recorded elements on the board. She contributed some of her own criteria to those that students identified because her students did not identify characteristics she knew were essential to excellent letters of persuasion, such as a clear statement of the writer's position and supporting evidence. She wanted to ensure that state content standards that were guiding her instruction were addressed in the criteria if students did not explicitly include them in their brainstorming. Furthermore, she wanted to include assessment criteria for key concepts, such as natural right, that were included in the prompt she gave them for the letter.

Step 2. *Sort and Categorize.* With student participation, she reviewed the list of elements developed through brainstorming and grouped related elements together into categories. For example, while she was working on criteria for persuasive letters, all the elements related to the writer's position (or thesis) were grouped together, as were elements related to clear written communication.

Step 3. *Make and Post a Chart.* Making and posting a chart that included criteria for a persuasive letter and specific details of each category would remind her students of their goals. The categories used to evaluate the work went in the left-hand column, while the more specific elements that made up each category went in the right-hand column (see the Strategy in Practice).

Step 4. *Add, Revise, and Refine.* Sally assumed that criteria for persuasive writing assignments would continuously be reviewed and evolve. After an assignment had been completed and she returned it to her students with her evaluation based on the criteria, students could look at their own work and compare it with the criteria posted. New criteria might need to be added. Irrelevant criteria might need to be dropped. Criteria need to be reviewed and revised continually, especially for documents in other disciplines, such as lab reports for science classes.

Strategy in Practice

CRITERIA T-CHART FOR LETTER OF PERSUASION

CRITERIA	DETAILS/SPECIFICS
States a position.	Develops position consistently; doesn't contradict position stated; writer's voice reveals conviction.
Examples of problems with British.	Gives about 5 or 6 different examples.
Includes "natural right."	Defines concept in own words; provides examples; shows how it's related to Colonists' concerns.
Includes "consent of governed."	Explains in writers' own words; explains why consent was critical to Colonists.
Includes "loyalist" position.	Explains loyalist stance; gives reasons for rejecting.
Paragraphs have topic sentences.	No sentences that aren't relevant to topic of paragraph.
Well organized with transitions.	Ideas flow from paragraph to paragraph.
Variety of sentence structure.	No choppy, stiff sections.
Mechanics don't interfere with message.	Few spelling, grammar, or punctuation errors.

From Criteria T-Charts to Rubrics.   Once Sally's students generated features for a criteria chart, she had but a short trip to rubrics. Papers would be scored from 4 (highest) to 1 (lowest) as follows:

4. The letter clearly addresses all parts of the writing task. It makes a clear, sustained claim that the Colonies should break with Great Britain and seek independence. It contains evidence in the form of at least five problems, or "complaints," contained in the Declaration. It presents a consistent, solidly convincing argument for Colonists seeking independence from the homeland. It makes clear the meanings of "natural right" and "consent of the governed" and shows how those

concepts were important to the Colonists. It develops and refutes the "loyalist" counterargument. Organization, paragraph structure, sentence structure, grammar, punctuation, and spelling all contribute to a letter that clearly and convincingly communicates the writer's intent to seek independence from Britain.

3. The letter addresses most parts of the writing task. It claims that the Colonies should break with Great Britain and seek independence. It contains evidence in the form of at least three problems, or complaints, contained in the Declaration. It presents an argument for Colonists seeking independence from the homeland. It explains the meanings of "natural right" and "consent of the governed" and explains the importance of these concepts to the Colonists. It presents and refutes the "loyalist" counterargument. Organization, paragraph structure, sentence structure, grammar, punctuation, and spelling all contribute to a letter that communicates the writer's intent to seek independence from Britain.

2. The letter addresses only some parts of the writing task. It claims that the Colonies should break with Great Britain and seek independence. It defends that position with at least one problem, or complaint, contained in the Declaration. It presents a weak argument for Colonists seeking independence from the homeland. It may not explain the meanings of "natural right" and "consent of the governed" or may not explain the importance of these concepts to the Colonists. It may not present or refute the "loyalist" counterargument. Problems appear in the letter's organization, paragraph structure, sentence structure, grammar, punctuation, and/or spelling to an extent that they detract from the letter's intent.

1. The letter addresses only a few parts of the writing task. The letter makes no central claim about the Colonies breaking from Great Britain and seeking independence. The letter contains little or no evidence supporting the facts or complaints contained in the Declaration. The letter does not clarify the meanings of "natural right" and "consent of the governed" or show how those concepts were important to the Colonists. The letter does not develop or refute the "loyalist" counterargument. The letter fails to develop a coherent or convincing argument for Colonists seeking independence from England. Organization, paragraph structure, sentence structure, grammar, punctuation, and spelling (singularly or in combination) detract significantly from the letter's message.

Block 2: Look at Student Work to Determine Student Movement Toward Goals.   Sally used student writing to observe progress toward standards and learning goals, a process described in chapter 7 on writing across the curriculum. She often examined her students' written work to generate next-step improvements. Following an analysis of her students' work, she could use her observations to guide her students' development in writing. Having a clear idea of what next steps would be beneficial to her students, a teacher like Sally could then help her students formulate in their own words what targets they should focus upon to move closer to mastery of articulated standards or learning goals.

Prior to class on day 5, Sally identified students she planned to pair for peer response. For this day's peer-response activity, she decided to pair what she considered a stronger writer with a weaker one. She recognized that some students were likely to get more guidance from the first round of response than others. However, by using a peer-response format, she could give students an opportunity to become more familiar with the concepts she wanted them to learn and with criteria for successfully writing persuasive letters. Meanwhile, they could acquire tutoring skills.

Figure 11.4 Criteria Feedback for Letter of Persuasion.

Criteria	Met	Not Yet	What's Needed Next
States a position			
Examples of problems with British			
Includes "natural right"			
Includes "consent of governed"			
Includes "loyalist" position			
Paragraphs have topic sentences			
Well organized with transitions			
Variety of sentence structure			
Mechanics don't interfere with message			

However, without suggesting to students that she'd placed a stronger with a weaker writer, she simply paired them as she had planned and gave each student a sheet labeled "Criteria Feedback for Letter of Persuasion" (see Figure 11.4). That assessment sheet, a modification of one suggested by Gregory, Cameron, and Davies (1997), included all the criteria the class and she agreed should be applied to the letters, along with three columns for evaluation and comments: Met, Not Yet, and What's Needed Next. After students read over their partner's paper, they checked off the appropriate category and, as they saw it, what steps in the paper's development should come next. Sally was finding that these structured responses during peer evaluation provided more students with more productive information to develop their papers further. As students read over their partner's papers, they could look up to see the criteria T-chart with the detail they had filled in a day or two ago. The additional detail helped students communicate to their partners what needed to be improved to come closer to meeting the standards established.

Block 3: Enable Students to Identify and Articulate in Their Own Language Their "Next-Step" Goals So That They Know and Own Their Personal Instructional Objectives.   Sally believed her students needed to know clearly what had to be done next to improve the quality of their work. For Sally to be sure that they knew what should come next, she wanted her students to be able to put into their own words what they would have to do to improve their performance. She knew that with clear "next steps," both direction and desire for improvement would benefit.

After students completed assessment sheets for each other, Sally explained to the class that they should use these peer assessments and their own self-assessment to write out what next steps they would take to revise their letters. She asked each student to write these next-step goals in their own words on the bottom of the "Criteria Feedback for Letter of Persuasion."

The range of next-step goals was extensive. A few students had omitted concepts, such as "natural right," and needed to include those concepts in their papers along with examples. A couple of students had introduced the concept but hadn't explained it clearly or provided an illustration of it. Two or three students had left out the counter argument to independence that a "loyalist" would make, and some that included it forgot to rebut it. While individuals would work on their own next-step goals, Sally also recognized that she could schedule some minilessons on topics, such as paragraph and sentence structure, with which many students struggled.

Sally noticed that a couple of students were struggling to organize their entire letter and appeared to be confused about how to handle the concepts she wanted them to address. She held brief conferences with these struggling writers as they formulated and wrote down their next-step goals.

Block 4: Use Student Data from Formative and Summative Assessments (Statewide Testing Programs) as Indicators of Instructional Progress. Results that Sally's students produced in the form of homework, Group Investigation presentations, discussion, persuasive letters, and unit test scores should contribute to Sally's determination of understandings that students gained. If annual state assessment programs, especially those in history, reading, and writing, are well aligned with state standards, then Sally should be able to use them to quantify her students' progress toward the mastery of standards, goals, and "big ideas" she identified early in her planning.

Summary

In this chapter we described standards-based instruction and its impact on content area learning and literacy. We focused especially on addressing literacy across the disciplines and saw how teachers integrate literacy strategies into instruction to deepen students' engagement and learning. We looked closely at literacy issues, productive literacy strategies, and ways teachers use them in science, math, history, English, and physical education. We then walked through step-by-step a planning pyramid for inquiry and instruction created to design units and lessons. Its four sides include (1) desired outcomes, (2) evidence needed to confirm that students mastered the outcomes, (3) instruction that would generate that evidence, and (4) assessment tools to reveal students' mastery of outcomes initially desired. We then saw how a teacher, Sally Peterson, used the planning pyramid to construct her Declaration of Independence unit. The process revealed how she integrated literacy strategies to help her students acquire vocabulary, key concepts, and a deeper understanding of the Declaration of Independence while building their own capacity to become independent, self-regulated learners.

Double-Entry Journal: After Reading

Review your response to the DEJ you wrote before reading this chapter. Having now read the chapter, how would you modify your approach to managing standards, literacy issues, student diversity, and assessment of student learning when planning instruction? What elements in your planning could you alter that you think might benefit your students' engagement and learning?

Glossary

Achievement goals are motive-driven end states that learners pursue as they achieve. Learners select, structure, and make sense of their attainments in terms of their achievement goals. According to theorists and researchers, achievement goals may be either mastery oriented or performance oriented. *See* mastery goal and performance goal.

Admit Slips are 3 × 5 cards on which students write down questions about what they have been studying in class. Questions might be about a reading assignment, a lecture or discussion, a review of material for a test, or a new topic about to be introduced.

Aesthetic stance, as described by Louise Rosenblatt, is a perspective and orientation that readers adopt when interacting with a text. With an aesthetic reading, the reader becomes absorbed in the imaginative world of character, plot, and setting evoked by the text. *See* efferent stance.

Analytical writing describes a form of writing that engages writers in taking apart, reformulating, and extending a text, for example, in comparing two views of a historical event. *See* summary and restrictive writing.

Anticipation guide is a list of statements a teacher generates about a subject that students react to before they read about that subject.

Approach performance goals describe motives that would move students to perform in class to show others their skills, perhaps to show them off in order to impress classmates with their accomplishments. *See* avoidance performance goals.

Automaticity is the cognitive processing of information without need for significant amounts of attention, thought, decision making, or working memory. Efficiency in reading depends upon automatic or nearly automatic word recognition.

Autonomy is the capacity to make independent decisions, have our actions arise from within ourselves, and feel that those actions are our own rather than arising from some external source.

Autonomy support is a motivational condition that occurs when a teacher nurtures a student's internally centered, freely chosen actions.

Authentic work, in contrast to "busy work," has been defined as "tasks that are considered meaningful, valuable, significant, and worthy of one's effort" (Newmann, Wehlage, & Lamborn, 1992). Authentic work is more likely to engage students and promote achievement because it leads to "socially valued outcomes."

Autotelic experiences, which are self-contained and self-rewarding, are not pursued for any future purpose or goal but for their intrinsic worth and their sheer enjoyment.

Avoidance performance goals describe motives that would move a student to attempt to avoid appearing incompetent, ignorant, or foolish. That avoidance orientation would most likely result in students avoiding opportunities to demonstrate knowledge or skills because they would fear their classmates' disapproval or disdain. *See* approach performance goals.

Big ideas are those that link content-related information into networks or systems in content area domains. Mastery of these unifying concepts helps students overcome the problem of having bits and pieces of information. Without unifying concepts, students have more trouble learning, remembering, and applying knowledge. (For examples, see chapter 11.)

Cause-effect organizers are designed to graphically represent an array of causes that contributed to some specific event. They can be used to display causation text structures.

Characteristic organizers are used to depict features or traits that characterize a concept. In the graphic organizer, features are displayed around a target term, such as polynomial, with elements characterizing polynomials arrayed around that term.

Clusters are all-purpose visual arrangements of terms, events, people, or ideas. They serve as an alternative to linear outlining, a strategy for studying, and a method of brainstorming. They help us envision how things relate or connect.

Cognitive processes describe a series of mental events, thoughts, or cognitions that are directed toward a particular mental outcome, such as understanding a printed sentence. In reading, these cognitive processes include word recognition, fluency, comprehension, and the construction of an internal text representation. *See* metacognition.

Community literacies include out-of-school cultures and literacies, such as that of a student fluent in Spanish who speaks the language with his newly immigrated family. These out-of-school literacies may or may not be accommodated in school. *See* school and personal literacies.

Compare/contrast organizers enable readers to summarize visually similar features of two concepts and their unique characteristics. The similarities and differences between two concepts, such as comedy and tragedy, can be represented in these organizers.

Comprehension can be viewed as the interaction of many cognitive elements and processes, such as word recognition, schema activation, imagery, and mental models, until those elements form a stable and interacting relationship in the mind of the reader. That stable relationship constitutes comprehension. The RAND Study Group (2002) defined comprehension as "the process of simultaneously extracting and constructing meaning through interaction and involvement with written language."

Comprehension strategies are techniques or activities that facilitate a reader's understanding of a text. Readers apply these strategies to promote meaning construction and learning from texts under certain conditions, for example, when faced with an unfamiliar text structure, when comprehension breaks down, or when engaged in critical reading.

Concept map is a method of showing key concepts and their relationships in graphic form. Concept words and propositions can be configured into a constellation to represent the knowledge that a learner has constructed. Given a set of concepts, students arrange them to show how they relate to the students' current knowledge structure and how connections between the concepts can be described.

Concept mastery maps graphically present information about a word or concept, how it interrelates with other knowledge, and how it might be integrated with memory enhancing features.

Conditional knowledge refers to the "when and why" of using information, such as when and why to apply a known classroom management procedure like assertive discipline. *See* declarative and procedural knowledge.

Construct validity refers to the degree to which some theory (or construct) is reflected in a test. Thus, if students were able to rapidly identify the meaning of words on a test

of vocabulary, they would, in theory, have enough automaticity and semantic knowledge to read well. Hence, a test measuring a student's memory for the meaning of a list of vocabulary words would have construct validity as a test of reading.

Content standards are skills, knowledge, and abilities that all students should be able to master at each grade level. They state the knowledge or skills that will be used as a foundation for judging learning at specific stages in students' education. *See* performance standards.

Content validity refers to the match between the content of a test and the reading or tasks that are taught in the curriculum. A valid test of reading strategy instruction would need to reflect the strategies taught as part of the curriculum. If students learned how to activate background knowledge related to a topic about which they were to read and were gave a test to see if they used that approach when reading, the test would have content validity.

Cornell Note Taking System, which is useful for taking lecture notes, adapts readily to taking notes while reading to gather main and supporting concepts for study. When used for taking lecture notes, students draw a 2-inch-wide left margin on ruled paper and take notes only to the right of that margin. After class, students reorganize and rephrase their notes for clarity and accuracy. In the left margin, they insert questions, headings, and cues to facilitate learning and mastery of content.

Critical literacy translates into ways in which reading and writing help students to understand daily social and political processes for the purpose of living more freely in a democratic society. Engaging in critical literacy practices enables readers to see their world more clearly, to understand how it works, to "rewrite" that world with their interests written in, and to take more liberating action within it.

Critical thinking, which may be defined in many ways, is usefully understood to be reasoned reflection on the meaning of claims about what to believe and what to do.

Critical thinking queries, an extension of queries normally used in Questioning the Author, probe an author's reasoning and marshalling of evidence to discover if the author is trying to persuade us of something, if the author has organized his or her ideas as presented in the text, and if the author provides enough evidence to support conclusions drawn.

Curriculum-Based Measurement (CBM) is a quick procedure to evaluate the oral reading fluency of students and their improvement. Fluency can be measured by counting the number of words a student reads correctly in one minute. (For step-by-step directions, see chapter 4.)

DEAD stands for "Drop Everything And Draft." It provides a time-out for students to reflect on classroom instruction. While playing DEAD, students explain what they have been learning in class, how it relates to what has been covered, what they are having trouble understanding, and/or what they would like to hear more about so they can understand it better.

Declarative knowledge is knowledge of facts, objects, events, language, concepts, and theories which contributes to our personal construction and understanding of "reality." *See* procedural and conditional knowledge.

Dialogue journals come in different forms. One form of dialogue journal engages students in constructing meanings for specific passages and writing about those understandings. With a second form of dialogue journal, also known as a two-way journal, student and teacher become engaged in a written conversation over not only material read but also other course content.

Directed Inquiry Activity (DIA) activates students' topic knowledge while providing both purposes for reading and some degree of teacher control over concepts students must master. DIAs enable teachers to guide their students' inquiry and discovery through inquiry questions based on a text to be read. (For step-by-step directions, see chapter 6.)

Directed Reading-Thinking Activity (DR-TA) engages students in making predictions about a text, reading the text, and discovering the accuracy of those predictions. (For step-by-step directions, see chapter 6.)

Direction of a goal refers to its location in an instructional setting and the sequence of actions that need to take place to reach that goal.

Double-entry journal (DEJ) is a form of written response to a text in which readers answer questions before the reading to activate background knowledge and after the reading to integrate new learning. (For step-by-step directions, see chapter 6.)

Editor interviews permit students to assume the persona of a newspaper or magazine editor and make an appearance in the classroom so that students can talk their way into and through arguments presumed to be composed by that editor. (For step-by-step directions, see chapter 8.)

Efferent stance, as described by Louise Rosenblatt, is a perspective and orientation that readers adopt when interacting with a text. With efferent reading, the reader focuses on information to be taken from the text. *See* aesthetic stance.

Ego-oriented, or performance, goals drive students toward opportunities to demonstrate their skills or knowledge in a competitive, public arena. *See* mastery goals.

Exit Passes are cards on which students write a three- or four-sentence summary of what went on in class, perhaps with a teacher-selected focus. The summary goes on the front of the card, and on its back students write a question relevant to the material covered in class that day. *See* Admit Slips.

Exploratory writing is writing that enables students to construct or discover knowledge in response to reading, inquiry, or classroom instruction.

Extrinsic motivation describes performance that is externally regulated through rewards or punishments. *See* intrinsic motivation.

Fluency refers to automatic (or nearly so) word recognition that allows readers to construct the meaning of text, that manifests itself in accurate expressive oral reading, and that makes silent reading comprehension possible.

Focused freewrites are a more restricted form of freewrites that provide students with time before or after a class to clarify their thoughts about a topic. They enable students to reflect on specific issues, kinds of learning, or metacognitive aspects of learning. (*See* freewrites.)

Follow-up queries, as used in Questioning the Author, are questions intended to provide focus and guide the discussion beneath the surface of the author's words. They are intended to urge readers to look more deeply into an author's language and network of ideas.

Freewrites are a form of writing in which students write freely without focus for 10 minutes or so about whatever comes to mind without regard to spelling, punctuation, or grammar. Students are urged to get all their nonstop thoughts down on paper. *See* focused freewrites.

Goal intensity refers to the energy a learner allocates to achieve a specific goal. Goal intensity varies and is affected by many variables, including the value placed on the goal, the difficulty of reaching the goal, and the resources that can be activated to achieve the goal.

Grade-equivalent scores (GEs) rank students' reading performance within groups that include students from all grades. They characterize performance in terms equal to that of other readers in a particular grade.

Graphic organizers enable students to organize knowledge and see more clearly how elements in a text are related. They help students to represent visually a variety of text structures.

Group investigation is a cooperative learning activity that helps students recognize and define problems; formulate strategies to solve them; gather, analyze, and synthesize information relevant to the problem; allocate time and resources to address the problem; and evaluate the success of their proposed solutions. (For step-by-step directions, see chapter 9.)

Group Reading Inventory is an informal assessment instrument that content area teachers use to determine students' reading rates and comprehension with a set of questions assessing vocabulary and various forms of comprehension. (For step-by-step directions, see chapter 4.)

Guided reading allows tutors to model ways to make personal and critical connections with texts on multiple levels.

Tutors need to carefully read texts used with tutees and make plans to engage them in a challenging dialogue through a variety of questions. (See chapter 9 for question categories.) *See* paired and shared reading.

Hermeneutic circle represents how meanings we evoke as readers can perpetually reemerge in modified or new forms. As we voice our views about a text's meaning, a cycle of hypothesis and confirmation or disconfirmation spins. Meanings we evoke as readers can perpetually reemerge in modified or new forms.

High-frequency words are vocabulary words, such as girl, fun, and run, that appear relatively more often than other words found in texts. *See* low-frequency words.

Identity is a sense of self that includes remembered and imagined images of the self and stories about the self that tell us who we are, who we were, and who we hope to become.

Informal Reading Inventory (IRI) yields estimates for a student's independent, instructional, and frustration levels of reading and information about performance on different kinds of comprehension and aspects of word recognition.

Initiating queries, as used in Questioning the Author, open a text to classwide construction of meaning, understanding, and discussion by focusing on central text ideas. Their purpose is to provide guidance for inquiry and exploration.

Inquiry Questions (IQs), based on Bloom's cognitive objectives, are intended to encourage readers to ask themselves questions as they read and learn. (For step-by-step directions, see chapter 8.)

Intertextuality is the process of connecting currently developing internal text representations with past texts to construct meanings.

Intrinsic motivation describes internal tendencies to seek challenges, explore interests, satisfy curiosity, expand personal capacities, and enjoy the process of learning. *See* extrinsic motivation.

Involuntary minorities, as defined by John Ogbu, are minority groups that have been enslaved, colonized, or conquered. They became part of American society unwillingly and usually view their being in America as a condition forced upon them. *See* voluntary minorities.

Jigsaw II, a cooperative learning activity, consists of home and expert teams working together to help all team members master texts and concepts in a cooperative context. (For step-by-step directions, see chapter 9.)

Journals provide opportunities for students to increase opportunities for "low-stakes" processing and reduce apprehension over "high-stakes" products, such as tests. Journals individualize instruction, forcing passive learners to become actively engaged.

Keyword method is a means of learning vocabulary words that entails recoding, relating, and retrieving. (For step-by-step directions, see chapter 5.)

K-W-L strategy is a method of discovering what students already know about a topic and what more they would like to learn. To gather that information and more, teachers can find out what their students already know (K), what they would like to learn (W), and (following reading and instruction) what they learned (L). (For step-by-step directions, see chapter 6.)

Learning goal, also known as mastery goal, describes learners' intrinsically motivated objective to acquire knowledge and skills that lead to learners becoming more competent.

Learning logs are records of what students are learning or struggling to understand. *See* reader response logs.

Lexical knowledge, also known as semantic memory, refers to knowledge of words and their meanings.

Living word vocabulary (LWV) is a comprehensive assessment of 44,000 word meanings known by children through high school and into adulthood.

Locus of control refers to an individual's perception of who or what has command or regulatory power over his or her actions. Usually identified as internal or external locus of control.

Long-term memory (LTM) holds abundant information for long periods of time, such as schemas activated when reading. Information stored in LTM helps us construct meanings for texts and address issues or problems that are currently alive in working memory. *See* working memory.

Low-frequency words are vocabulary words, such as obdurate, mercurial, and enigmatic, that appear relatively less often than other words found in texts. *See* high-frequency words.

Mastery goals, also known as learning goals, describe learners' intrinsically motivated objectives to acquire knowledge and skills that lead to learners becoming more competent. *See* performance goals.

Metacognitive processes entail both the monitoring and controlling of cognition while reading. Metacognition itself describes cognition that has as its object cognitive processes, which, in colloquial terms, is what we know about what we know. *See* cognitive processes.

Minilesson is a forum for sharing knowledge and strategic skills. With the minilesson, sharing goes both ways because teachers impart information and students contribute their knowledge. Minilessons may range from 5 to 20 minutes.

Miscue is an oral reading response that varies from that expected. (See chapter 4 for a description of miscue types.)

Mnemonic is a systematic procedure designed to improve memory use, such as the keyword method to acquire word meanings.

Morpheme is a distinct unit of meaning in a word. Morphemes can be added to a root word to create inflected or compound words based on that root, such as when adding un- to the front or -ed to the back of *lock*.

Normal curve equivalents (NCEs) present a student's reading level relative to other students at the same grade level. NCEs are based on percentile ranks, but those percentiles have been changed into a scale of equal reading achievement units. Because each NCE unit is equal throughout the scale, they can be used for computing averages and making comparisons between scores.

Numbered Heads Together is a group learning game played between teams of four or five members, each of which is given a number and each of which provides individual accountability for learning. (See chapter 9 for directions.)

Orthographic knowledge is declarative knowledge of letter patterns and word spellings in long-term memory. *See* phonological knowledge.

Orthographic processing refers to a series of mental actions using the visual representations of letters and words. *See* phonological processing.

Paired reading is a form of one-to-one tutoring in which a proficient reader, who models and supports good reading, is paired with a struggling reader. (For step-by-step directions, see chapter 6.) *See* guided and shared reading.

PASSION is an acronym for a series of steps designed to help readers figure out the meaning of unfamiliar or unknown words encountered when reading. (See chapter 5 for description of its use.)

Percentile rank tells where, in percentage categories from 0% to 99%, a student's raw score lies within a range of scores.

Performance goal. *See* ego-oriented goal.

Performance standard is a level of achievement that students must attain to demonstrate their mastery of articulated content standards. Performance standards define levels of competence at each grade level, and they indicate the degree to which a student has achieved the content standard. *See* content standard.

Personal literacies reflect students' self-knowledge and critical awareness of themselves that arises from their examination of their backgrounds and histories in their schools and communities. Personal literacies influence the ways readers responds to and understands texts. (See school and community literacies)

Phonological knowledge is knowledge of the sound of letters and letter patterns that enables readers to identify words that conform to English phonology in contrast to sound clusters that make no sense. *See* orthographic knowledge.

Phonological processing occurs as letters, associated patterns of letters, or words activate their corresponding sounds. *See* orthographic processing.

PLAN is an acronym for four separate tactics (Predict, Locate, Add, and Note) that are integrated to facilitate comprehension before, during, and after independent reading. (For directions, see chapter 6.)

Planning Pyramid is a structure that represents backward planning a teacher can use to design instruction for the purpose of achieving specified goals. Completing the pyramid's four interlocked sides facilitates the transformation of instructional goals into inquiry that can deepen student engagement and understanding. (For step-by-step directions, see chapter 11.)

Portfolio is a collection of student work that can be selected, organized, analyzed, and reviewed to provide a kaleidoscopic as well as microscopic view of each student's engagement in content area learning. It reveals how much work students have done, how well they are doing it, what kinds of help they need to progress, and how they view their own progress.

Prereading Plan (PreP) was developed to encourage students to think about ideas soon to be encountered in a reading assignment. Students recollect prior knowledge and reflect on the sources of that knowledge. After class discussion, they think about the effects the discussion had on their thinking about the topic and articulate any changes in their knowledge and understanding. Then they read the assigned text. (For step-by-step directions, see chapter 6.)

Problem-solution-evaluation model is a "big idea" that makes relationships between events and concepts easier for students to comprehend and remember. The pattern of problem, solution, and evaluation often occurs in the study of history and can be transferred to other domains of seemingly random information. (See chapter 11 for an example of the model's application.)

Problem-solution-evaluation organizers provide a visual method to represent texts that are problem oriented, as is the case with problem-solution text structures.

Procedural knowledge consists of strategies and skills for using and applying knowledge, from knowing how to replace an electrical wall outlet to starting a barbecue. *See* declarative and conditional knowledge.

Process organizers offer a means of visually presenting a series of events or actions that result in a particular outcome that may be depicted in a process text structure.

Queries, as occur in Questioning the Author, are intended to help students grasp ideas presented in a text, be used while students read the text, facilitate discussion about the author's ideas, and support student-to-student dialogue.

Question maps, as a tool to facilitate word learning, help students generate questions about important words and concepts. Students list any and all questions they have about an unknown or unfamiliar word or concept.

Question papers limit students to writing only questions while reading or after reading an assignment. The strategy opens texts and authors to extensive questioning. The questions students write reveal much about the level of comprehension and the level of doubt and curiosity engendered.

Questioning the Author (QtA) is a reading strategy whose main purpose is to shift a teacher's work from checking for comprehension to helping students construct, explore, and challenge meanings. Used with both expository and narrative texts, QtA helps students to question both texts and their authors. (For step-by-step directions, see chapter 8.)

RAFTing is a writing/comprehension strategy that consists of four components to guide and stimulate students' exploration of content knowledge: Role, Audience, Format, and Topic. (For directions, see chapter 7.)

Raw score is the total number of items a test taker got correct on a test or on one of its subparts.

Reader response groups are mixed-ability groups in which members share responsibilities for learning, get a group grade, and are individually accountable for their learning and contributions.

Reader response logs are closely related to Learning Logs. However, the response logs focus on interpreting and making inferences from texts rather than on summarizing them. *See* learning logs.

Reading journals consist of letters written between students and between student and teacher. These epistolary reading journals differ from reader response logs by being more individually tailored to each student's personal reading.

Reciprocal teaching is a comprehension fostering strategy that engages readers in summarizing, questioning, predicting, and clarifying texts to develop metacognition while reading. (For step-by-step directions, see chapter 9.)

Reliable test is one that consistently measures what it is designed to measure. *See* valid test.

Restricted writing is a form of writing that usually engages students in a basic search and transcription process and is exemplified by answering study questions focused on comprehension of a text. *See* analytical and summary writing.

Retelling is an informal reading assessment strategy in which, after reading a text, students tell a teacher what meanings they have constructed. Rather than mere recognition, as in multiple choice questions, retellings require recalling knowledge.

ReQuest is a strategy to get students to think while they read. Originally developed for one-on-one interaction, it can be used one-on-one or with a whole class. While a teacher serves as a model questioner, students are encouraged to question the teacher. (For step-by-step directions, see chapter 8.)

Round Robin reading is a read-aloud classroom strategy. While a student reads, others follow along in their own books. Students, one after another, read row by row as the teacher calls on them. (See chapter 9 for creative alternatives.)

Running record is an informal oral reading assessment used to discover if material presented to students is at a manageable reading level and what strategies students use to decode difficult words. As students read, teachers record the students' performance using predetermined miscue guidelines.

Saccade is a jump that takes about 20 milliseconds between fixations on words or a small group of them as a reader reads.

Schema is a knowledge network that guides human behavior. A schema can be compared to files of knowledge with associated "slots" that readers fill with related information gained from a text. Schemas are often activated when reading and influence meaning construction.

School literacies encompass not only cognitive processes, such as reading, but also social, cultural, and political processes acquired in school contexts. Standard English is usually the prime literacy, but students also acquire content area literacies in math, science, and history. They also acquire whole bodies of culture-based knowledge. *See* community and personal literacies.

Self-determination theory (SDT) provides a research-based perspective of motivation, especially motivation related to school and literacy growth. SDT emphasizes the central importance of each person's need for personal development and self-regulation.

Self-efficacy is a psychological construct that describes an individual's sense of what he or she believes he or she is capable of doing or learning.

Self-expectations are what students expect of their own behavior but can be shaped by the expectations of others, especially friends, parents, and teachers.

Semantic feature analysis is a strategy that facilitates word learning. It enables students to externalize conceptual networks and so reveal how their minds organize knowledge about their world into categories. Through semantic feature analysis, students activate and compare some of their existing categories with new or unfamiliar words and concepts they encounter. (For step-by-step directions, see chapter 5.)

Semantic maps, which are used to develop vocabulary, present a theme or concept at the map's heart, important ideas or terms highlighted with boxes or circles, and lines connecting related ideas or concepts that are not hierarchically organized. (For step-by-step directions, see chapter 5.)

Sentence outline is a linear approach to organizing knowledge sequentially. Main points and supporting details are built into the outline and reflect the author's knowledge structure as depicted in the text. Readers state key and subordinate concepts in complete sentence form. *See* topic outline.

Shared reading combines your reading aloud plus your students following your reading in their own texts. *See* paired and guided reading.

Situated learning is knowledge and skill acquisition that is embedded in and affected by a particular social context or environment, such as the effect of multicultural urban classrooms on students' writing development.

Skeleton is a bare-bones sentence or network of sentences to which students add the flesh of more specific sentences. As a writing strategy, skeletons provide students with a framework that helps them organize knowledge and develop writing skills.

Socratic Seminar is an interactive classroom session that helps students discover ideas through a teacher's skilled questioning and guided dialogue. (For step-by-step directions, see chapter 8.)

Stance is, within the framework of Louise Rosenblatt's transactional theory of reading, a perspective and orientation toward the text that readers adopt when transacting with a text. *See* aesthetic and efferent stance.

Standards-based instruction is teaching in a particular subject that adheres to and is guided by content and performance standards usually articulated by state departments of education. The evaluation of that instruction usually goes under the name standards-based assessment, meaning that the assessment will be based on the content standards used to guide instruction. *See* content standards and performance standards.

Standards of evaluation are criteria that good readers use to enhance their comprehension of a text. Researchers have identified several comprehension-monitoring standards that influence the quality of comprehension. (For a list of standards, see chapter 3.)

Stanines divide the spectrum of reading achievement scores into nine relative broad bands or categories.

Strategy instruction, which includes direct instruction, scaffolding, and guided practice to improve comprehension and vocabulary acquisition, has been found to positively influence students' motivation when integrated with content area reading.

Structured overview is a method of graphically organizing concepts to show their subordinate and superordinate relationships.

Student-led conference is a meeting at school between a student and parent or other adult to review course work kept in a portfolio.

SQ3R is a reading and study strategy to help students set purposes for reading and engage them in reading for answers to significant questions. SQ3R stands for Survey, Question, Read, Recite, and Review. (For directions, see chapter 6.)

Summary writing focuses on ideas at a deeper level than a mental review but at a more superficial level than analytic writing. *See* analytical and restricted writing.

Synonym webs limit the exploration of semantic relationships only to words similar in meaning in comparison to semantic maps that include all types of concepts related to the target word. (For step-by-step directions, see chapter 5.)

Syntactical knowledge refers to knowledge about the order and relationship among words and other grammatical structures in phrases and sentences. The basic ability to understand and generate syntactic structures is inborn but requires a social environment that encourages language acquisition.

TASK is a procedure designed to facilitate the analysis and construction of arguments. TASK stands for Thesis Analysis and Synthesis Key. (For step-by-step directions, see chapter 8.)

Task environment, a component of the individual-environmental writing model, consists of both social and physical dimensions. The social dimensions include the audience for whom the writer is writing and any cowriters with whom a writer collaborates. The physical dimensions include the text as written so far, including the space in which it is being written and the medium through which it is composed.

Task-oriented goal. *See* mastery or learning goal.

Think-Pair-Share is an informal group method in which students take a few minutes to write about their interpretation or opinion of a text (Think), find someone with whom they can talk about their writing (Pair), and then discuss their thoughts and ideas for a few minutes (Share).

Think-aloud is a strategy that opens a window to cognitive processes that readers use to make sense of what they are reading. During a think-aloud, readers describe their thoughts as they form meanings through interaction with the text. (For step-by-step directions, see chapter 4.)

Topic outlines use a linear format to present information by key concepts or key words. Readers constructing them must have the capacity to capture the gist or essence of passages and paragraphs as well as subordinate ideas and the ability to state those gists and subordinate ideas in the readers' own concise words. *See* sentence outline.

Two-way (or dialogue) journals engage student and teacher in a written conversation over not only material read but also other course content. The two-way journal is passed back and forth between student and teacher, so that each gains a better idea of what the other thinks about topics being covered in class.

Valid test is one that measures what its designers claim it will measure. *See* reliable test.

Vocabulary Self-Collection Strategy (VSS) is a word-learning method in which students identify and select words they want to know because those words are important for understanding a passage or because of their curiosity. Through VSS, students integrate new content words into their vocabularies. (For step-by-step directions, see chapter 5.)

Voluntary minorities immigrated to America willingly, usually to improve their opportunities and those of their children. *See* involuntary minorities.

Work Knowledge Check is a technique to determine how well students know certain words. (For directions, see chapter 5.)

Word recognition, the foundation of the reading process, is the perception by a reader that a word's pronounciation and perhaps even its meaning are known.

Working memory is the form of memory used to represent the immediate world, actively compute solutions, such as constructing meaning for a text, and remember the results for rather short periods of time. *See* long-term memory.

Zone of Proximal Development (ZPD), which emphasizes the importance of the interactive, socially based nature of learning, is the difference between what one can achieve alone and what one can achieve with the help of a more knowledgeable or capable person.

References

Ackerman, J. M. (1993). The promise of writing to learn. *Written Communication, 10,* 334–370.

Adams, M. (1990). *Beginning to read: Thinking and learning about print.* Cambridge, MA: Bradford Books/MIT Press.

Adams, M. (2004). Modeling the connections between word recognition and reading. In R. B. Ruddell & N. J. Unrau (Eds.), *Theoretical models and processes of reading* (5th ed., pp. 1219–1243). Newark, DE: International Reading Association.

Alderman, M. K. (1999). *Motivation for achievement: Possibilities for teaching and learning.* Mahwah, NJ: Erlbaum.

Alexander, P. (2003). The path to competence: A lifespan developmental perspective on reading. Paper commissioned by the National Reading Conference. Retrieved January 8, 2006, from National Reading Conference Web site: http://www.nrconline.org

Alfassi, M. (1998). Reading for meaning: The efficacy of reciprocal teaching in fostering reading comprehension in high school students in remedial reading classes. *American Educational Research Journal, 35*(2), 309–332.

Allen, D. (1998). *Assessing student learning: From grading to understanding.* New York: Teachers College Press.

Allen, J. (1995). *It's never too late: Leading adolescents to lifelong literacy.* Portsmouth, NH: Heinemann.

Allen, J. (1999). *Words, words, words: Teaching vocabulary in grades 4–12.* York, ME: Stenhouse Publishers.

Allen, J. (2000). *Yellow brick roads: Shared and guided paths to independent reading 4–12.* Portland, ME: Stenhouse Publishers.

Allington, R. L. (2001). *What really matters for struggling readers: Designing research-based programs.* New York: Longman.

Alvermann, D. E. (2001). Reading adolescents' reading identities: Looking back to see ahead. *Journal of Adolescent and Adult Literacy, 44,* 676–690.

Alvermann, D. E. (2004). Multiliteracies and self-questioning in the service of science learning. In E. W. Saul (Ed.), *Crossing borders in literacy and science instruction* (pp. 226–238). Newark, DE. International Reading Association.

Alvermann, D. E., Smith, L., & Readence, J. (1985). Prior knowledge activation and the comprehension of compatible and incompatible text. *Reading Research Quarterly, 20,* 420–436.

American College Testing (ACT). (2006). Reading between the lines: What the ACT reveals about college readiness in reading. Retrieved April 11, 2006, from http://www.act.org/path/policy/pdf/reading_report

Ames, C. (1992). Classrooms: Goals, structures, and student motivation. *Journal of Educational Psychology, 84*(3), 261–271.

Ames, C., & Archer, J. (1987). Mothers' beliefs about the role of ability and effort in school learning. *Journal of Educational Psychology, 79,* 409–414.

Ames, R., & Ames, C. (1996). Motivation and effective teaching. In J. L. Idol & B. F. Jones (Eds.), *Educational values and cognitive instruction: Implications for reformation* (pp. 247–261). Hillsdale, NJ: Erlbaum.

Anagnostopoulos, D. (2003). Testing and student engagement in urban classrooms: A multilayered approach. *Research in the Teaching of English, 38*(2), 177–212.

Anaya, R. (1972). *Bless me, Ultima.* New York: Warner.

Anderson, R. C. (2004). Role of the reader's schema in comprehension, learning, and memory. In R. B. Ruddell & N. J. Unrau (Eds.), *Theoretical models and processes of reading* (5th ed., pp. 594–606). Newark, DE: International Reading Association.

Anderson, R. C., & Nagy, W. E. (1992, Winter). The vocabulary conundrum. *American Educator, 15,* 14–18, 44–47.

Anderson, R. C., Reynolds, R. E., Schallert, D. L., & Goetz, E. T. (1977). Frameworks for comprehending discourse. *American Educational Research Journal, 14,* 367–382.

Andrews, S. E. (1997). Writing to learn in content area reading class. *Journal of Adolescent & Adult Literacy, 41*(2), 141.

Annenberg Institute for School Reform. (1999). *Looking at student work: A window into the classroom* [Video]. New York: Teacher College Press.

Annis, L. F., & Annis, D. B. (1982). A normative study of students' reported preferred study techniques. *Reading World, 21*, 201–207.

Antil, L., Jenkins, J., Wayne, S., & Vadasy, P. F. (1998). Cooperative learning: Prevalence, conceptualizations, and the relation between research and practice. *American Educational Research Journal, 35*(3), 419–454.

Applebee, A. N. (1981). *Writing in the secondary school*. Urbana, IL: National Council of Teachers of English.

Applebee, A. N. (1984). *Contexts for learning to write: Studies of secondary school instruction*. Norwood, NJ: Ablex.

Applebee, A. N., Langer, J. A., & Mullis, I. V. S. (1985). *The reading report card, progress toward excellence in our schools: Trends in reading over four national assessments, 1971–1984*. Princeton, NJ: Educational Testing Service.

Applebee, A. N., Langer, J. A., & Mullis, I. V. S. (1988). *Who reads best?* Princeton, NJ: Educational Testing Service.

Armbruster, B. (2000). Taking notes from lectures. In R. Flippo & D. Caverly (Eds.), *Handbook of college reading and study strategy research* (pp. 175–199). Mahwah, NJ: Erlbaum.

Aronson, E., Blaney, N., Stephan, C., Sikes, J., & Snapp, M. (1978). *The Jigsaw classroom*. Beverly Hills, CA: Sage Publications, Inc.

Arzubiaga, A., Rueda, R., & Monzo, L. (2002). Family matters related to the reading engagement of Latino children. *Journal of Latinos and Education, 1*(4), 231–243.

Atkinson, R. C. (1975). Mnemotechnics in second-language learning. *American Psychologist, 30*, 821–828.

Atwell, N. (1998). *In the middle: New understandings about writing, reading, and learning* (2nd ed.). Portsmouth, NH: Boynton/Cook Publishers.

August, D., & Hakuta, K. (1997). *Improving schooling for language-minority children: A research agenda*. Washington, DC: National Academy Press.

Austin, T. (1994). *Changing the view: Student-led parent conferences*. Portsmouth, NH: Heinemann.

Ausubel, D. P. (1968). *Educational psychology: A cognitive view*. New York: Holt, Rinehart & Winston.

Axelrod, R. B., & Cooper, C. R. (2006). *Reading critically, writing well: A reader and guide (7th ed.)*. New York: Bedford/St. Martin's Press.

Bacon, S. (2005). Reading coaches: Adapting an intervention model for upper elementary and middle school readers. *Journal of Adolescent and Adult Literacy, 48*, 416–427.

Baines, L. (1996). From page to screen: When a novel is interpreted for film, what gets lost in translation? *Journal of Adolescent and Adult Literacy, 39*, 612–622.

Baker, L. (1985). Differences in the standards used by college students to evaluate their comprehension of expository prose. *Reading Research Quarterly, 20*(3), 297–313.

Baker, L. (2003). The role of parents in motivating struggling readers. *Reading Writing Quarterly: Overcoming Learning Difficulties, 19*, 87–106.

Baker, L. (2004). Reading comprehension and science inquiry: Metacognitive connections. In E. W. Saul (Ed.), *Crossing borders in literacy and science instruction* (pp. 239–257). Newark, DE: International Reading Association.

Baker, L. (2005). Developmental differences in metacogniton: Implications for metacognitively oriented reading instruction. In S. E. Israel, C. Block, K. L. Bauserman, & K. Kinnucan-Welch (Eds.), *Metacognition in literacy education: Theory, assessment, instruction, and professional development* (pp. 61–79). Mahwah, NJ: Erlbaum Publishers.

Baker, L., & Wigfield, A. (1999). Dimensions of children's motivation for reading and their relations to reading activity and reading achievement. *Reading Research Quarterly, 34*, 452–477.

Baker, L., Scher, D., & Mackler, K. (1997). Home and family influences on motivations for literacy. *Educational Psychologist, 32*, 69–82.

Bandura, A. (1986). *Social foundations of thought and action*. Englewood Cliffs, NJ: Prentice Hall.

Banks, J. A. (2000). *Ancient world: Adventures in time and place*. New York: McGraw-Hill/National Geographic.

Barab, S. A., & Roth, W. (2006). Curriculum-based ecosystems: Supporting knowing from an ecological perspective. *Educational Researcher, 35*(5), 3–13.

Bartlett, B. (1978). *Top-level structure as an organizational strategy for recall of classroom text*. Unpublished doctoral dissertation, Arizona State University.

Barton, J. (1995). Conducting effective classroom conversations. *Journal of Reading, 38*(5), 346–350.

Battin-Pearson, S., Newcomb, M. D., Abbott, R., Hill, K., Catalano, R. F., & Hawkins, J. D. (2000). Predictors of early high school dropout: A test of five theories. *Journal of Educational Psychology, 92*(3), 568–582.

Bauer, J. (1994). *Schools for thought*. Cambridge, MA: MIT Press.

Baumann, J. F., & Kaméenui, E. J. (1991). Research on vocabulary instruction: Ode to Voltaire. In J. Flood, J. M. Jensen, D. Lapp, & J. R. Squire (Eds.), *Handbook of research on teaching the English language arts* (pp. 604–632). New York: Macmillan.

Baumann, J., Edwards, E. C., Font, G., Tereshinski, C., Kaméenui, E. J., & Olejnik, S. (2002). Teaching morphemic and contextual analysis to fifth-grade students. *Reading Research Quarterly, 37*(2), 150–173.

Beach, R. (1993). *A teacher's introduction to reader-response theories.* Urbana, IL: National Council of Teachers of English.

Beach, R. (2007). *Teachingmedialiteracy.com: A Web-linked guide to resources and activities.* New York: Teachers College Press.

Bean, J. C., Chappell, V. A., & Gillam, A. M. (2004). *Reading rhetorically* (brief edition). New York: Pearson/ Longman.

Beck, I. L. (1989). Improving practice through understanding reading. In L. B. Resnick & L. E. Klopfer (Eds.), *Toward the thinking curriculum: Current cognitive research. Yearbook of the Association for Supervision and Curriculum Development* (pp. 40–58). Alexandria, VA/Hillsdale, NJ: ASCD/Erlbaum.

Beck, I. L., & McKeown, M. G. (1991). Conditions of vocabulary acquisition. In R. Barr, M. L. Kamil, P. B. Mosenthal, & P. D. Pearson (Eds.), *Handbook of reading research* (Vol. II, pp. 789–814). Mahwah, NJ: Erlbaum.

Beck, I. L., McKeown, M. G., Hamilton, R. L., & Kucan, L. (1997). *Questioning the author: An approach for enhancing student engagement with text.* Newark, DE: International Reading Association.

Beck, I. L., McKeown, M. G., and Kucan, L. (2002). *Bringing words to life: Robust vocabulary instruction.* New York: Guilford Press.

Beck, I. L., McKeown, M. G., & Omanson, R. C. (1987). The effects and uses of diverse vocabulary instructional techniques. In M. G. McKeown & M. E. Curtis (Eds.), *The nature of vocabulary acquisition* (pp. 147–163). Hillsdale, NJ: Erlbaum.

Beck, I. L., Perfetti, C. A., & McKeown, M. G. (1982). Effects of long-term vocabulary instruction on lexical access and reading comprehension. *Journal of Educational Psychology, 74,* 506–521.

Becker, W. C. (1977). Teaching reading and the language arts to the disadvantaged—What we have learned from field research. *Harvard Educational Review, 47,* 518–543.

Beers, B. F. (1993). *World History: Pattern of Civilization.* Englewood Cliffs, NJ: Prentice Hall.

Beers, K. (1998). Choosing not to read: Understanding why some middle schoolers just say no. In K. Beers & B. G. Samuels (Eds.), *Into focus: Understanding and creating middle school readers* (pp. 37–63). Norwood, MA: Christopher-Gordon Publishers.

Beers, K. (2003). *When kids can't read: What teachers can do: A guide for teachers 6–12.* Portsmouth, NH: Heinemann.

Behman, E. (2005). Writing in the physical education class. *Journal of Physical Education, Recreation and Dance, 75*(8), 22–28.

Behrman, E. (2006). Teaching about language, power, and text: A review of classroom practices that support critical literacy. *Journal of Adolescent and Adult Literacy, 49*(8), 490–498.

Bereiter, C., & Scardamalia, M. (1980). From conversation to composition. In R. Glaser (Ed.), *Advances in instructional psychology, Vol. 2.* Hillsdale, NJ: Erlbaum.

Biancarosa, G., & Snow, C. (2004). *Reading next—A vision for action and research in middle school and high school literacy: A report to Carnegie Corporation of New York.* Washington, DC: Alliance for Excellent Education.

Biemiller, A., & Slonim, N. (2001). Estimating root word vocabulary growth in normative and advantaged populations: Evidence for a common sequence of vocabulary acquisition. *Journal of Educational Psychology, 93*(3), 498–530.

Bintz, W. P. (1997). Exploring reading nightmares of middle and secondary school teachers. *Journal of Adolescent and Adult Literacy, 41*(1), 12–24.

Blachowicz, C., & Fisher, P. (1996). *Teaching vocabulary in all classrooms.* Columbus, OH: Merrill.

Blachowicz, C., & Fisher, P. (2000). Vocabulary instruction. In M. L. Kamil, P. B. Mosenthal, P. D. Pearson, & R. Barr (Eds.), *Handbook of reading research* (Vol. III, pp. 503–523). Mahwah, NJ: Erlbaum.

Bleich, D. (1980). Epistemological assumptions in the study of response. In J. P. Tompkins (Ed.), *Reader-response criticism: From formalism to post-structuralism* (pp. 134–163). Baltimore, MD: Johns Hopkins University Press.

Bloom, B. S. (Ed.). (1956). *Taxonomy of educational objectives: Handbook I: Cognitive domain.* New York: David McKay.

Bloom, B. S. (1984). The 2 sigma problem: The search for methods of group instruction as effective as one-on-one tutoring. *Educational Researcher, 13*(6), 4–16.

Bloom, B. S., Englehart, M., Furst, E., Hill, W., & Krathwohl, D. (1956). *Taxonomy of educational objectives: The classification of educational goals. Handbook I: Cognitive domain.* New York: Longmans Green.

Bloome, D., & Bailey, F. (1992). Studying language and literacy through events, particularities, and intertextuality. In R. Beach, J. Green, M. Kamil, & T. Shanahan (Eds.), *Multidisciplinary perspectives on literacy research* (pp. 181–210). Urbana, IL: National Council of Teachers of English.

Blythe, T., Allen, D., & Powell, B. (1999). *Looking together at student work: A companion guide to assessing student learning.* New York: Teachers College Press.

Boone, R., & Higgins, K. (2003). Reading, writing, and publishing digital text. *Remedial and Special Education, 24*(3), 132–140.

Borasi, R., & Siegel, M. (2000). *Reading counts: Expanding the role of reading in mathematics classrooms*. New York: Teachers College Press.

Bormuth, J. R. (1968). The cloze readability procedure. In J. R. Bormuth (Ed.), *Readability in 1968*. Champaign, IL: National Council of Teachers of English.

Bourdieu, P. (1991). *Language and symbolic power*. Cambridge, MA: Harvard University Press.

Bower, G., Black, J., & Turner, T. (1994). Scripts in memory for text. In R. B. Ruddell, M. R. Ruddell, & H. Singer (Eds.), *Theoretical models and processes of reading* (4th ed., pp. 538–581). Newark, DE: International Reading Association.

Boyer, E. (1983). *High school: A report on secondary education in America*. New York: Harper and Row.

Bransford, J. D., Brown, A. L., & Cocking, R. R. (Eds.), (1999). *How people learn: Brain, mind, experience, and school*. Washington, DC: National Academy Press.

Breznitz, Z. (1997). Effects of accelerated reading rate on memory for text among dyslexic readers. *Journal of Educational Psychology, 89*, 289–297.

Breznitz, Z. (2006). *Fluency in reading: Synchronization of processes*. Mahwah, NJ: Erlbaum Publishers.

Britton, J. (1970). *Language and learning*. Middlesex, England: Penguin Books.

Broadbent, D.E. (1975). The magic number seven after fifteen years. In A. Kennedy & A. Wilkes (Eds.), *Studies in long-term memory* (pp. 3–18). London: Wiley.

Brown, A. L., & Palincsar, A. S. (1982). Inducing strategic learning from texts by means of informed, self-control training. *Topics in Learning and Learning Disabilities, 2*(1), 1–17.

Brown, A. L., Palincsar, A. S., & Armbruster, B. B. (1984). Instructing comprehension-fostering activities in interactive learning situations. In H. Mandl, N. Stein, & T. Trabasso (Eds.), *Learning and comprehension of text* (pp. 255–285). Hillsdale, NJ: Erlbaum.

Brown, B. B. (1993). School culture, social politics, and the academic motivation of U.S. students. In T. M. Tomlinson (Ed.), *Motivating students to learn* (pp. 63–98). Berkeley, CA: McCutchan.

Brown, O. M. (1996). *Tips at your fingertips: Teaching strategies for adult literacy tutors*. Newark, DE: International Reading Association.

Brozo, W., Valerio, P., & Salazar, M. (1996). A walk through Gracie's garden: Literacy and cultural explorations in a Mexican American junior high school. *Journal of Adolescent and Adult Literacy, 40*(3), 164–170.

Brozo, W.G. (2006). WebQuests: Supporting inquiry with primary sources. *Thinking Classroom, 7*(1), 47–48.

Bruner, J. (1986). *Actual minds, possible worlds*. Cambridge, MA: Harvard University Press.

Bullough, R., Jr., & Gitlin, A. (1995). *Becoming a student of teaching: Methodologies for exploring self and school context*. New York: Garland Publishing.

Burns, P. C., & Roe, B. D. (1999). *Informal reading inventory: Preprimer to twelfth grade*. Boston, MA: Houghton Mifflin.

California Department of Education (1998). *English–Language Arts content standards for California public schools, K–12*. Sacramento, CA: California Department of Education.

California Department of Education (2005). *History social science framework for California public schools: Kindergarten through grade twelve*. Sacramento, CA: California Department of Education.

California State University (2005). More California 11th-graders volunteer to get "Early Signal" of their readiness for college. Retrieved April 15, 2006, from http://www.calstate.edu/PA/news/2005/EAP05.shtml

Calkins, L., Montgomery, K., & Santman, D. (1998). *A teacher's guide to standardized reading tests*. Portsmouth, NH: Heinemann.

Cameron, J., & Pierce, W. D. (1994). Reinforcement, reward, and intrinsic motivation: A meta-analysis. *Review of Educational Research, 64*, 363–423.

Carey, L., Flower, L., Hayes, J. R., Schriver, K. A., & Haas, C. (1989). *Differences in writers' initial task representations* (Tech. Rep. No. 35). Berkeley, CA: Center for the Study of Writing at UC, Berkeley and Carnegie Mellon University.

Carnine, D. (1994). The BIG Accommodations Program. *Educational Leadership, 51*, 87–88.

Carrington, V., & Luke, A. (1997). Literacy and Bourdieu's sociological theory: A reframing. *Language and Education, 11*(2), 96–112.

Carroll, J. B., Davies, P., & Richman, B. (1971). *The American Heritage word frequency book*. Boston: Houghton Mifflin.

Carter, C. J. (1997, March). Why reciprocal teaching? *Educational Leadership, 54*(6), 64–68.

Casteneda v. Pickard, 648 F.2D 989 (5th cir., 1981).

Caverly, D., Mandeville, T., & Nicholson, S. A. (1995). PLAN: A study-reading strategy for informational text. *Journal of Adolescent & Adult Literacy, 39*(3), 190–199.

Caverly, D., Orlando, V., & Mullen, J. (2000). Textbook study reading. From R. Flippo & D. Caverly (Eds.), *Handbook of college reading and study strategy research* (pp. 105–147). Mahwah, NJ: Erlbaum.

Cayton, A., Perry, E. I., Reed, L., & Winkler, A. M. (2007). *America: Pathways to the present*. Boston, MA: Pearson/Prentice Hall.

Chall, J. S. (1987). Two vocabularies for reading: Recognition and meaning. In M. G. McKeown & M. E. Curtis (Eds.), *The nature of vocabulary acquisition* (pp. 7–17). Hillsdale, NJ: Erlbaum.

Chall, J. S., Jacobs, V., & Baldwin, L. (1990). *The reading crisis*. Cambridge, MA: Harvard University Press.

Chamot, A. U. (1995). Learning strategies in listening comprehension: Theory and research. In D. Mendelsohn & J. Rubin (Eds.), *The theory and practice of listening comprehension for the second language learner* (pp. 13–26). San Diego, CA: Dominie Press.

Chamot, A. U., & O'Malley, J. M. (1994). Instructional approaches and teaching procedures. In K. Spangenberg-Urbschat & R. Pritchard (Eds.), *Kids come in all languages: Reading instruction for ESL students* (pp. 82–107). Newark, DE: International Reading Association.

Chamot, A. U., Barnhardt, S., El-Dinary, P. B., & Robbins, J. (1999). *The learning strategies handbook*. White Plains, NY: Addison Wesley Longman.

Chamot, A. U., Dale, M., O'Malley, J. M., & Spanos, G. (1992). Learning and problem solving strategies of ESL students. *Bilingual Research Journal, 16*(3–4), 1–33.

Chamot, A. U., Keatley, C., & Mazur, A. (1999). Literacy development in adolescent English language learners: Project Accelerated Literacy (PAL). Paper presented at the 1999 Annual Meeting of the American Educational Research Association, Montreal, Canada.

Chmielewski, T. L., & Dansereau, D. F. (1998). Enhancing the recall of text: Knowledge mapping training promotes implicit transfer. *Journal of Educational Psychology, 90*(3), 407–413.

Chomsky, N. (1959). A review of B. F. Skinner's Verbal Behavior. *Language, 35*(1), 26–58.

Chomsky, N. (1965). *Aspects of the theory of syntax*. Cambridge, MA: MIT Press.

Cohen, J. (1986). Theoretical considerations of peer tutoring. *Psychology in the Schools, 23*(2), 175–186.

Collier, V. (1987). Age and rate of acquisition of second language for academic purposes. *TESOL Quarterly, 21,* 617–641.

Collins, B. (2001). *Sailing alone around the room*. New York: Random House.

Considine, D. M., & Haley, G. E. (1999). *Visual messages: Integrating imagery into instruction* (2nd ed.). Englewood, CO: Teachers Ideas Press.

Corkill, A. J. (1992). Advance organizers: Facilitators of recall. *Educational Psychology Review, 4,* 33–67.

Cottle, T. J. (2001). *Mind fields: Adolescent consciousness in a culture of distraction*. New York: Peter Lang.

Covington, M. (1992). *Making the grade: A self-worth perspective on motivation and school reform*. Cambridge: Cambridge University Press.

Crystal, D. (2001). *Language and the Internet*. Cambridge: Cambridge University Press.

Csikszentmihalyi, M. (1990a). *Flow: The psychology of optimal experience*. New York: Harper & Row.

Csikszentmihalyi, M. (1990b). Literacy and intrinsic motivation. *Daedalus, 119*(2), 115–140.

Culler, J. (1980). Literary competence. In J. P. Tompkins (Ed.), *Reader-response criticism: From formalism to post-structuralism* (pp. 101–117). Baltimore, MD: Johns Hopkins University Press.

Cummins, J. (1981). Immigrant second language learning. *Applied Linguistics, 11,* 132–149.

Cummins, J. (1984). *Bilingualism and special education: Issues in assessment and pedagogy*. Clevedon, UK: Multilingual Matters.

Curriculum Associates. (2003). *Milestones in reading*. North Billerica, MA: Curriculum Associates, Inc.

Cziko, G. A. (1983). Another response to Shanahan, Kamil, and Tobin: Further reasons to keep the cloze case open. *Reading Research Quarterly, 18,* 361–365.

Dale, E. (1965). Vocabulary measurement: Techniques and major findings. *Elementary English, 42,* 82–88.

Dale, E., & O'Rourke, J. (1981). *The living word vocabulary: The words we know*. Boston: Houghton Mifflin.

Davey, B. (1983). Think-aloud–modeling the cognitive processes of reading comprehension. *Journal of Reading, 27,* 44–47.

Davidson, J. E., & Sternberg, R. J. (1998). Smart problem solving: How metacognition helps. In D. J. Hacker, J. Dunlosky, & A. C. Graesser (Eds.), *Metacognition in educational theory and practice* (pp. 47–68). Mahwah, NJ: Erlbaum.

Day, J. (1980). *Training summarization skills: A comparison of teaching methods*. Unpublished doctoral dissertation, University of Illinois, Champaign-Urbana.

Day, J. (1986). Teaching summarization skills: Influences of student ability level and strategy difficulty. *Cognition and Instruction, 3*(3), 193–210.

Deci, E. L. (1971). Effects of externally mediated rewards on intrinsic motivation. *Journal of Personality and Social Psychology, 18,* 105–115.

Deci, E. L., & Ryan, R. M. (1985). *Intrinsic motivation and self-determination in human behavior*. New York: Plenum.

Deci, E. L., Vallerand, R. M., Pelletier, L. G., & Ryan, R. M. (1991). Motivation and education: The self-determination perspective. *Educational Psychologist, 26,* 325–346.

Delpit, L. (1986). Skills and other dilemmas of a progressive black educator. *Harvard Educational Review, 56,* 379–385.

Delpit, L. (1988). The silenced dialogue: Power and pedagogy in educating other people's children. *Harvard Educational Review, 58,* 280–298.

Dewey, J. (1970). *Experience and education*. New York: Collier. (Original work published 1938.)

Dilthey, W. (1976). The development of hermeneutics. In H. Rickman (Ed. & Trans.). *Selected writings*. Cambridge: Cambridge University Press. (Original work published in 1900).

Dorroh, J. (1993). Reflections on expressive writing in the science class. *Quarterly of the National Writing Project and the Center for the Study of Writing and Literacy, 15*(3), 28–30.

Doucheff, D. (1996). Homework . . . in physical education. *Runner, 34*(3), 18–20.

Draper, R. J., & Siebert, D. (2004). Different goals, similar practices: Making sense of the mathematics and literacy instruction in a standards-based mathematics classroom. *American Educational Research Journal, 41*(4), 927–962.

Draper, V. (2005). Appendix B: Reading in mathematics: Inquiry with preservice teachers. In J. Braunger, D. M. Donahue, K. Evans, & T. Galguera. *Rethinking preparation for content area teaching* (pp. 269–281). San Francisco: Jossey-Bass.

Duke, N., & Pearson, P. D. (2002). Effective practices for developing reading comprehension. In S. J. Samuels & A. E. Farstrup (Eds.), *What research says about reading instruction* (3rd ed., pp. 205–242). Newark, DE: International Reading Association.

Durst, R. K. (1987). Cognitive and linguistic demands of analytic writing. *Research in the Teaching of English, 21,* 347–376.

Dweck, C. S., & Leggett, E. L. (1988). A social-cognitive approach to motivation and personality. *Psychological Review, 95,* 256–273.

Educating English learners for the twenty-first century (1999). Sacramento, CA: California Department of Education.

Ehri, L. C. (1991). Development of the ability to read words. In R. Barr, M. L. Kamil, P. Mosenthal, & P. D. Pearson (Eds.), *Handbook of reading research* (Vol. II, pp. 383–417). White Plains, NY: Longman.

Ehri, L. C. (1994). Development of the ability to read words: Update. In R. B. Ruddell, M. R. Ruddell, & H. Singer (Eds.), *Theoretical models and processes of reading* (4th ed., pp. 323–358). Newark, DE: International Reading Association.

Eichinger, J. (1997). Successful students' perceptions of secondary school science. *School Science and Mathematics, 97*(3), 122–131.

Eisner, E. W. (1988). The ecology of school improvement. *Educational Leadership, 45*(5), 24–29.

Elbow, P. (1971). *Writing without teachers.* New York: Oxford University Press.

Elbow, P. (1997). High stakes and low stakes in assigning and responding to writing. In M. Sorcinelli & P. Elbow (Eds.), *Writing to learn: Strategies for assigning and responding to writing across the disciplines* (pp. 5–13). San Francisco: Jossey-Bass Publishers.

Eldridge, J. L. (2005). Foundations of fluency: An exploration. *Reading Psychology, 26*(2), 161–181.

Elliot, A. J. (1997). Integrating the "classic" and "contemporary" approaches to achievement motivation: A hierarchical model of approach and avoidance achievement motivation. In M. L. Maehr & P. R. Pintrich (Eds.), *Advances in motivation and achievement* (Vol. 10, pp. 143–179). Greenwich, CT: JAI Press.

Elbow, P. (1971). *Writing without teachers.* New York: Oxford University Press.

Emerson, R. W. (1940). *The selected writings of Emerson.* New York: Random House.

Emig, J. (1971). *The composing process of twelfth graders* (Research report no. 13). Urbana, IL: National Council of Teachers of English.

Englemann, S., Carnine, L., Johnson, G., Hanner, S., Osborn, S., & Haddox, P. (1998). *Corrective reading: Decoding and corrective reading: Comprehension.* Columbus, OH: SRA/McGraw.

Englert, C. (1990). Unraveling the mysteries of writing through strategy instruction. In T. Sruggs & B. Y. L. Wong (Eds.), *Intervention research in learning disabilities* (pp. 186–223). New York: Springer-Verlag.

Ennis, R. H. (1996). *Critical thinking.* Upper Saddle River, NJ: Prentice Hall.

Ericsson, K. A., & Kintsch, W. (1995). *Long-term working memory. Psychological Review, 102,* 211–245.

Erikson, E. (1968). *Identity: Youth and crisis.* New York: Norton.

Everson, B. J. (1991). Vygotsky and the teaching of writing. *Quarterly of the National Writing Project and the Center for the Study of Writing and Literacy, 13*(3), 8–11.

Fecho, B. (1999). Crossing boundaries of race in a critical literacy classroom. In D. E. Alvermann, K. A. Hinchman, S. F. Moore, S. F. Phelps, & D. R. Waff (Eds.), *Reconceptualizing the literacies in adolescents' lives* (pp. 75–101). Mahwah, NJ: Erlbaum.

Fielding, A., & Schoenbach, R. (2003). *Building Academic Literacy: An Anthology for Reading Apprenticeship.* San Francisco: Jossey-Bass/WestEd.

Fielding, A., Schoenbach, R., & Jordan, M. (2003). *Building Academic Literacy: Lessons from Reading Apprenticeship classrooms, grades 6–12.* San Francisco: Jossey-Bass/WestEd.

Fink, R. (2006). *Why Jane and John couldn't read—and how they learned: a new look at striving readers.* Newark, DE: International Reading Association.

Fish, S. (1980). *Is there a text in this class? The authority of interpretive communities.* Cambridge, MA: Harvard University Press.

Fisher, D. (2001). Cross age tutoring: Alternatives to the reading resource room for struggling adolescent readers. *Journal of Instructional Psychology, 28*(4), 234–241.

Fisher, D., & Frey, N. (2004). *Improving adolescent literacy: Strategies at work.* Upper Saddle River, NJ: Pearson/Merrill/Prentice Hall.

Fisher, D., & Ivey, G. (2006). Evaluating the interventions for struggling adolescent readers. *Journal of Adolescent and Adult Literacy, 50*(3), 180–189.

Fitzgerald, F. S. (1925). *The Great Gatsby.* New York: Charles Scribner's Sons.

Fitzgerald, J. (2004). Can minimally trained college student volunteers help young at-risk children learn to read? In R. B. Ruddell & N. J. Unrau (Eds.), *Theoretical models and processes of reading* (5th ed., pp. 1083–1113). Newark, DE: International Reading Association.

Fleming, D., Unrau, N., Cooks, J., Davis, J., Farnan, N., & Grisham, D. (in press). A California State University initiative to improve adolescent reading in all content areas. *Teacher Education Quarterly.*

Flower, L. (1979). Writer-based prose: A cognitive basis for problems in writing. *College English, 41,* 19–37.

Flower, L. (1987). *The role of task representation in reading to write* (Technique Rep. No. 6). Berkeley, CA: Center for the Study of Writing.

Flower, L., & Hayes, J. R. (1977). Problem-solving strategies and the writing process. *College English, 39,* 449–461.

Flower, L., & Hayes, J. R. (1980). The dynamics of composing: Making plans and juggling constraints. In L. Gregg & E. Steinberg (Eds.), *Cognitive process in writing: An interdisciplinary approach* (pp. 31–50). Hillsdale, NJ: Erlbaum.

Flower, L., & Hayes, J. R. (1981). A cognitive process theory of writing. *College Composition and Communication, 32,* 365–387.

Flower, L., Schriver, K. A., Carey, L., Haas, C., & Hayes, J. R. (1989). *Planning in writing: The cognition of a constructive process* (Tech. Rep. No. 34). Berkeley, CA: Center for the Study of Writing at UC, Berkeley and Carnegie Mellon University.

Flower, L., Stein, V., Ackerman, J., Katz, M. J., McCormick, K., & Peck, W. C. (1990). *Reading-to-write: Exploring a cognitive and social process.* New York: Oxford.

Fountas, I., & Pinnell, G. S. (1996). *Guided reading: Good first teaching for all children.* Portsmouth, NH: Heinemann.

Franzak, J. K. (2006). Zoom: A review of the literature on marginalized adolescent readers, literacy theory, and policy implications. *Review of Educational Research, 76*(2), 209–248.

Freedman, S. W., Dyson, A. H., Flower, L., & Chafe, W. (1987). *Research in writing: Past, present, and future* (Tech. Rep. No. 1). Berkeley, CA: Center for the Study of Writing at UC, Berkeley and Carnegie Mellon University.

Freedman, S. W., Flower, L., Hull, G., & Hayes, J. R. (1995). *Ten years of research: Achievements of the National Center for the Study of Writing and Literacy* (Tech. Rep. No. 1C). Berkeley, CA: Center for the Study of Writing at UC, Berkeley and Carnegie Mellon University.

Freedman, S. W., Simons, E. R., Kalnin, J. S., Casareno, A., & The M-CLASS teams. (1999). *Inside city schools: Investigating literacy in multicultural classrooms.* New York: Teachers College Press.

Freire, P. (1970/1993). *Pedagogy of the oppressed* (M. B. Ramos, Trans.). New York: Continuum.

Fry, E. (1977). Fry's readability graph: Clarifications, validity, and extension to level 17. *Journal of Reading, 21,* 242–252.

Fry, E., Kress, J., & Fountoukidis, D. (2000). *The reading teacher's book of lists* (4th ed.). Paramus, NJ: Prentice Hall.

Fuchs, L., Fuchs, D., Hosp, M. K., & Jenkins, J. R. (2001). Oral reading fluency as an indicator of reading competence: A theoretical, empirical, and historical analysis. *Scientific Studies of Reading, 5*(3), 239–256.

Fuchs, L. S., Fuchs, D., & Maxwell, L. (1988). The validity of informal reading comprehension measures. *RASE: Remedial and Special Education, 9*(2), 20–28.

Fuller, B., Gesicki, K., Kang, E., & Wright, J. (2006). Is the *No Child Left Behind Act* working? Berkeley, CA: Policy Analysis for California Education.

Fulwiler, T. (1986). Journals across the disciplines. In T. Newkirk (Ed.), *To compose: Teaching writing in the high school* (pp. 186–197). Portsmouth, NH: Heinemann.

Gallego, M., & Hollingsworth, S. (2000). Introduction: The idea of multiple literacies. In M. Gallego & S. Hollingsworth (Eds.), *What counts as literacy: Challenging the school standard* (pp. 1–23). New York: Teachers College Press.

Gambrell, L. B. (1996). Creating classroom cultures that foster reading motivation. *The Reading Teacher, 50,* 14–25.

Gambrell, L. B., & Marinak, B. A. (1997). Incentives and intrinsic motivation to read. In J. Guthrie & A. Wigfield (Eds.), *Reading engagement: Motivating readers through integrated instruction* (pp. 205–217). Newark, DE: International Reading Association.

Gamoran, A., & Nystrand, M. (1992). Taking students seriously. In F. M. Newmann (Ed.), *Student engagement and achievement in American secondary schools* (pp. 40–62). New York: Teachers College Press.

Garcia, T., & Pintrich, P. R. (1994). Regulating motivation and cognition in the classroom: The role of self-schemas and self-regulatory strategies. In D. H. Schunk & B. J. Zimmerman (Eds.), *Self-regulation of learning and performance: Issues and educational applications* (pp. 127–153). Hillsdale, NJ: Erlbaum.

Garner, R. (1992). Metacognition and self-monitoring strategies. In S. J. Samuels & A. E. Farstrup (Eds.), *What research has to say about reading instruction* (2nd ed., pp. 236–252). Newark, DE: International Reading Association.

Gee, J. (2006). Self-fashioning and shape-shifting: Language, identity, and social class. In D. E. Alvermann, K. Hinchman, D. W. Moore, S. Phelps, & D. R. Waff (Eds.), *Reconceptualizing the literacies of adolescents' lives* (2nd ed., pp. 165–185). Mahwah, NJ: Erlbaum Publishers.

Gee, J. P. (1996). *Social linguistics and literacies: Ideology in Discourses* (2nd ed.). London: Taylor & Francis.

Gee, J. P. (2000). Teenagers in new times: A new literacy studies perspective. *Journal of Adolescent & Adult Literacy, 43*, 412–420.

Gee, J. P. (2001). Reading as situated language: A sociocognitive perspective. *Journal of Adolescent & Adult Literacy, 44*, 714–725.

Geertz, C. (1973). *Interpretation of cultures.* New York: Basic Books.

Gersten, R., Fuchs, L., Williams, J., & Baker, S. (2001). Teaching reading comprehension strategies to students with learning disabilities: A review of research. *Review of Educational Research, 71*(2), 279–320.

Gersten, R., Woodward, J., & Darch, C. (1986). Direct instruction: A research-based approach to curriculum design and teaching. *Exceptional Children, 53*, 17–31.

Gibson, E. J., & Levin, H. (1985). *The psychology of reading.* Cambridge, MA: MIT Press.

Ginsberg, M. B., & Wlodkowski, R. J. (2000). *Creating highly motivating classrooms for all students: A school-wide approach to powerful teaching with diverse learners.* San Francisco: Jossey-Bass.

Good, T. L., & Brophy, J. E. (2003). *Looking in classrooms* (9th ed.). Boston, MA: Allyn and Bacon.

Goodlad, J. I. (1984). *A place called school: Prospects for the future.* New York: McGraw-Hill.

Goodman, K. (1969). Analysis of reading miscues: Applied psycholinguistics. *Reading Research Quarterly, 5*(1), 9–13.

Goodman, K. (1994). Reading, writing, and written texts: A transactional sociopsycholinguistic view. In R. B. Ruddell, M. R. Ruddell, & H. Singer (Eds.), *Theoretical models and processes of reading* (4th ed., pp. 1093–1130). Newark, DE: International Reading Association.

Goswami, U. (2000). Phonological and lexical processes. In M. Kamil, P. Mosenthal, P. D. Pearson, & R. Barr (Eds.), *Handbook of reading research* (Vol. III, pp. 251–267). Mahwah, NJ: Erlbaum.

Gottfried, A. E., Fleming, J. S., & Gottfried, A. W. (2001). Continuity of academic intrinsic motivation from childhood through late adolescence: A longitudinal study. *Journal of Educational Psychology, 93*, 3–13.

Graves, M. F., & Watts-Taffe, S. M. (2002). The place of word consciousness in a research-based vocabulary program. In A. Farstrup & S. J. Samuels (Eds.), *What research has to say about reading instruction* (3rd ed., pp. 140–165). Newark, DE: International Reading Association.

Gray, J. (2000). *Teachers at the center: A memoir of the early years of the National Writing Project.* Berkeley, CA: National Writing Project.

Gray, W. S. (1946). *On their own in reading.* Chicago: Scott-Foresman.

Greaney, V., & Hegarty, M. (1987). Correlates of leisure-time reading. *Journal of Research in Reading, 10*, 3–27.

Greene, J. F. (1998, Spring/Summer). Another chance: Help for older students with limited literacy. *American Educator, 22*, 74–79.

Greenwald, E. A., Persky, H. R., Campbell, J. R., & Mazzeo, J. (1999). *The NAEP 1998 writing report card for the nation and the states,* 144. Washington, DC: U.S. Department of Education.

Gregory, K., Cameron, O., & Davies, A. (1997). *Setting and using criteria.* Mervilli, British Columbia: Connections Publishing.

Griffin, J., & Morgan, L. (1998). Physical education—WRITE ON! *Strategies, 11*(4), 34–37.

Grimm, J., & Grimm, W. (1823/1971). *Grimms' Fairy Tales.* Middlesex, England: Penguin Books.

Grossen, B. (n.d.). *The research base for Corrective Reading, SRA.* Columbus, OH: SRA/McGraw-Hill.

Gruenert, S. (2000). Shaping a new school culture. *Contemporary Education, 71*(2), 14–18.

Gunning, T. G. (2006). *Assessing and correcting reading and writing difficulties* (3rd ed.). Boston: Allyn & Bacon.

Guthrie, J. T., Van Meter, P., McCann, A. D., Anderson, E., & Alao, S. (1998). Does Concept-Oriented Reading Instruction increase strategy-use and conceptual learning from text? *Journal of Educational Psychology, 90*(2), 261–278.

Guthrie, J. T., & Wigfield, A. (2000). Engagement and motivation in reading. In M. L. Kamil, P. B. Mosenthal, P. D. Pearson, & R. Barr (Eds.), *Handbook of reading research* (Vol. III, pp. 403–422). Mahwah, NJ: Erlbaum.

Guthrie, J., Wigfield, A., Barbosa, P., Perencevich, K. C., Taboada, A., Davis, M. H., Scafiddi, N. T., & Tonks, S. (2004). Increasing reading comprehension and engagement through Concept-Oriented Reading Instruction. *Journal of Educational Psychology, 96*(3), 403–423.

Guthrie, J., Wigfield, A., Humenick, N., Perencevich, K., Taboada, A., Barbosa, P. (2006). Influences of stimulating tasks on reading motivation and comprehension. *Journal of Educational Research, 99*(4), 232–245.

Guthrie, J. T., Wigfield, A., & VonSecker, C. (2000). Effects of integrated instruction on motivation and strategy use in reading. *Journal of Educational Psychology, 92*(2), 331–340.

Hacker, D. J. (1998a). Definitions and empirical foundations. In D. J. Hacker, J. Dunlosky, & A. C. Graesser (Eds.), *Metacognition in educational theory and practice* (pp. 1–24). Mahwah, NJ: Erlbaum.

Hacker, D. J. (1998b). Self-regulated comprehension during normal reading. In D. J. Hacker, J. Dunlosky, & A. C. Graesser (Eds.), *Metacognition in educational theory and practice* (pp. 165–191). Mahwah, NJ: Erlbaum.

Hagen, A. S., & Weinstein, C. E. (1995). Achievement goals, self-regulated learning, and the role of classroom context. In P. R. Pintrich (Ed.), *Understanding self-regulated learning* (pp. 43–55). San Francisco: Jossey-Bass.

Haggard, M. R. (1982). The Vocabulary Self-Collection Strategy: An active approach to word learning. *Journal of Reading, 27,* 203–207.

Haggard, M. R. (1986). The Vocabulary Self-Collection Strategy: Using student interest and world knowledge to enhance vocabulary growth. *Journal of Reading, 29,* 634–642.

Hakuta, K. Butler, Y. G., & Witt, D. (2000). *How long does it take English learners to attain proficiency?* University of California Linguistic Minority Research Institute Policy Report 2000-1. Santa Barbara, CA: UC Linguistic Minority Research Institute.

Haluska, R., & Gillen, D. (1995). Kids teaching kids: Pairing up with cross-grades pals. *Learning, 24*(3), 54–56.

Hanna, J. (2001). The language of dance. *Journal of Physical Education, Recreation and Dance, 72*(4), 40–45.

Hanrahan, M. (1999). Rethinking science literacy: Enhancing communication and participation in school science through affirmational dialogue journal writing. *Journal of Research in Science Teaching, 36,* 699–717.

Harmon, J. M. (2000). Assessing and supporting independent word learning strategies of middle school students. *Journal of Adolescent & Adult Literacy, 43*(6), 18–27.

Harris, T. L., & Hodges, R. E. (1995). *The literacy dictionary.* Newark, DE: International Reading Association.

Hart, B, & Risley, T. R. (1995). *Meaningful differences in the everyday experiences of young American children.* Baltimore: Brookes.

Hart, B, & Risley, T. R. (2003). The early catastrophe: The 30 million word gap. *American Educator, 27*(1), 4–9.

Harter, S. (1981). A new self-report scale of intrinsic versus extrinsic orientation in the classroom: Motivational and informational components. *Developmental Psychology, 17,* 300–312.

Hartman, D. K. (1991). *8 readers reading: The intertextual links of able readers using multiple passages.* Unpublished doctoral dissertation, University of Illinois, Urbana, IL.

Hartman, D. K. (1994). The intertextual links of readers using multiple passages: A postmodern/semiotic/cognitive view of meaning making. In R. B. Ruddell, M. R. Ruddell, & H. Singer (Eds.), *Theoretical models and processes of reading* (4th ed., pp. 616–636). Newark, DE: International Reading Association.

Hasselbring, T. S. (1991). Improving education through technology: Barriers and recommendations. *Preventing School Failure, 35,* 33–37.

Hasselbring, T. S., & Goin, L. I. (2004). Literacy instruction for older struggling readers: What is the role of technology? *Reading & Writing Quarterly, 20,* 123–144.

Hattie, J., Biggs, J., & Purdie, N. (1996). Effects of learning skills interventions on student learning: A meta-analysis. *Review of Educational Research, 66*(2), 99–136.

Hayes, D. P. (1988). Speaking and writing: Distinct patterns of word choice. *Journal of Memory and Language, 27,* 572–585.

Hayes, D. P., & Grether, J. (1983). The school year and vacations: When do students learn? *Cornell Journal of Social Relations, 17*(1), 56–71.

Hayes, J. R. (1996/2004). A new framework for understanding cognition and affect in writing. In R. B. Ruddell, & N. J. Unrau (Eds.), *Theoretical models and processes of reading* (5th ed., pp. 1399–1430). Newark, DE: International Reading Association.

Hayes, J. R., & Flower, L. S. (1980). Identifying the organization of writing processes. In L. Gregg & E. Steinberg (Eds.), *Cognitive process in writing: An interdisciplinary approach* (pp. 3–30). Hillsdale, NJ: Erlbaum.

Heath, S. B. (1983). *Ways with words: Language, life, and work in communities and classrooms.* Cambridge, UK: Cambridge University Press.

Heath, S. B., & McLaughlin, M. W. (1993). Building identities for inner-city youth. In S. B. Heath & M. W. McLaughlin (Eds.), *Identity and inner-city youth* (pp. 1–12). New York: Teachers College Press.

Helmus, T. M., Toppin, E. A., Pounds, N., & Arnsdorf, V. (1988). *The United States yesterday and today.* Lexington, MA: Silver Burdett & Ginn.

Henderson, A. T., & Mapp, K. L. (2002). *A new wave of evidence: The impact of school, family, and community connections on student achievement.* Austin, TX: Southwest Educational development Laboratory.

Herrington, A., & Moran, C. (2005). The idea of genre in theory and practice: An overview of the work in genre in the fields of composition and rhetoric and new genre studies. In A. Herrington & C. Moran (Eds.), *Genre across the curriculum.* Logan, UT: Utah State University Press.

Hersey, J. (1985). *Hiroshima.* New York: A.A. Knopf.

Hidi, S. (1990). Interest and its contribution as a mental resource for learning. *Review of Educational Research, 60*(4), 540–571.

Hidi, S., & Harackiewicz, J. M. (2000). Motivating the academically unmotivated: A critical issue for the 21st century. *Review of Educational Research, 70*(2), 151–179.

Hiebert, E. H. (2002). Standards, assessments, and text difficulty. In A. Farstrup & S. J. Samuels (Eds.), *What* research has to say about reading instruction (3rd ed., pp. 337–369). Newark, DE: International Reading Association.

Higgins, E. L., & Raskind, M. H. (2005). The compensatory effectiveness of the Quicktionary Reading Pen II on the reading comprehension of students with learning disabilities. *Journal of Special Education Technology, 20,* 29–38.

Hillocks, G. (2002). *The testing trap: How state assessments of writing control learning.* New York: Teachers College Press.

Hillocks, G. (2006). Middle and high school composition. In P. Smagorinsky (Ed.), *Research on composition: Multiple perspectives on two decades of change* (pp. 48–77). New York: Teachers College Press.

Hirsch, E. D. (1987). *Cultural literacy: What every American needs to know.* Boston, MA: Houghton Mifflin.

Hollingsworth, S., & Teel, K. (1991). Learning to teach reading in secondary math and science. *Journal of Reading, 35,* 190–194.

Hootstein, H. (1995). Motivational strategies of middle school social studies teachers. *Social Education, 59,* 23–26.

How to cope with standards. (1999). *California Educator, 4*(3), 14–15.

Hyerle, D. (1996). *Visual tools for constructing knowledge.* Alexandria, VA: Association for Supervision and Development.

Intersegmental Committee of the Academic Senates (ICAS) (2002). Academic literacy: A statement of competencies expected of students entering California's public colleges and universities. Retrieved April 11, 2006, from http://www.academic senate.cc.ca.us/icas.html

Invernizzi, M., Rosemary, C., Juel, C., & Richards, H. C. (1997). At-risk readers and community volunteers: A 3-year perspective. *Scientific Studies of Reading, 1,* 277–300.

Irvin, J. L. (1990). *Vocabulary knowledge: Guidelines for instruction.* Washington, DC: National Education Association.

Ivey, G. (1999). Reflections on teaching struggling middle school readers. *Journal of Adolescent and Adult Literacy, 42,* 372–381.

Ivey, G., & Broaddus, K. (2001). "Just plain reading": A survey of what makes students want to read in middle school classrooms. *Reading Research Quarterly, 36*(4), 350–377.

Jacobson, J., Thrope, L., Fisher, D., Lapp, D., Frey, N., & Flood, J. (2001). Cross-age tutoring: A literacy improvement approach for struggling adolescent readers. *Journal of Adolescent and Adult Literacy, 44*(6), 528–536.

Jago, C. (2000, Spring). Editor's column. *California English, 5,* 4.

Janks, H. (1993). *Language and power.* Johannesburg, South Africa: Hodder & Stoughton.

Jastak, S., & Wilkinson, G. S. (1984). *Wide Range Achievement Test—Revised (WRAT-R) for word recognition.* Wilmington, DE: Jastak Associates.

Johns, J. L., & Berglund, R. I. (2002). *Fluency: Answers, questions, evidence-based strategies.* Dubuque, IA: Kendall/Hunt.

Johnson, D. D., Toms-Bronowski, S., & Pittelman, S. D. (1981). *A review of trends in vocabulary research and the effects of prior knowledge on instructional strategies for vocabulary acquisition.* Madison, WI: Wisconsin Center for Educational Research.

Johnson, D. W., & Johnson, R. T. (1999). *Learning together and alone: Cooperative, competitive, and individualistic learning.* Boston, MA: Allyn & Bacon.

Johnson, G. B. (1998). *Biology: Visualizing life.* Austin, TX: Holt, Rinehart and Winston.

Johnson, T. S., Smagorinsky, P., Thompson, L., & Fry, P. (2003). Learning to teach the five-paragraph theme. *Research in the Teaching of English, 38*(2), 136–176.

Jordan, M., Jensen, R., & Greenleaf, C. (2001). "Amidst Familial Gatherings": Reading Apprenticeship in the middle school classroom. *Voices from the Middle, 4*(8), 15–24.

Juel, C. (1991). Cross-age tutoring between student athletes and at-risk children. *The Reading Teacher, 45,* 178–186.

Juel, C. (1993). What makes literacy tutoring effective? *Reading Research Quarterly, 31,* 268–289.

Just, A. J., & Carpenter, P. A. (1987). *The psychology of reading and language comprehension.* Boston, MA: Allyn & Bacon.

Kagan, S. (1992). *Cooperative learning resources for teachers.* San Juan, CA: Kagan Cooperative Learning.

Kaméenui, E. J., & Carnine, D. W. (1998). *Effective teaching strategies that accommodate diverse learners.* Upper Saddle River, NJ: Merrill.

Kamil, M. L., & Hiebert, E. H. (2005). Teaching and learning vocabulary: Perspectives and persistent issues. In M. L. Kamile & E. H. Hiebert (Eds.), *Teaching and learning vocabulary: Bringing research to practice* (pp. 1–23). Hillsdale, NJ: Erlbaum.

Kibby, M. W. (1995). *Practical steps for informing literacy instruction: A diagnostic decision-making model.* Newark, DE: International Reading Association.

Kinder, D., & Bursuck, W. (1991). The search for a unified social studies curriculum: Does history really repeat itself? *Journal of Learning Disabilities, 24*(5), 270–284.

Kintsch, W. (1994). The role of knowledge in discourse comprehension: A construction-integration model. In R. B. Ruddell, M. R. Ruddell, & H. Singer (Eds.),

Theoretical models and processes of reading (4th ed., pp. 951–995). Newark, DE: International Reading Association.

Kintsch, W. (1998). *Comprehension: A paradigm for cognition*. Cambridge: Cambridge University Press.

Kintsch, W. (2004). The construction-integration model of text comprehension and its implications for instruciton. In R. B. Ruddell & N. J. Unrau (Eds.), *Theoretical models and processes of reading* (5th ed., pp. 1270–1328). Newark, DE: International Reading Association.

Kintsch, W., & van Dijk, T. (1978). Toward a model of text comprehension and production. *Psychological Review, 85*(5), 363–394.

Kirst, M. W. (2004). The high school/college disconnect. *Educational Leadership, 62*(3), 51–55.

Klenk, L., & Kibby, M. W. (2000). Re-mediating reading difficulties: Appraising the past, reconciling the present, constructing the future. In M. Kamil, P. Mosenthal, P. D. Pearson, & R. Barr (Eds.), *Handbook of reading research* (Vol. III, pp. 667–690). Mahwah, NJ: Erlbaum.

Knowles, K. T. (1999). The effect of teacher engagement on student achievement and motivation. Dissertation Abstracts International, 60, 4A. (University Microfilms No. 0419-4209).

Kohn, A. (1993). *Punished by rewards: The trouble with gold stars, incentive plans, A's, praise, and other bribes*. Boston, MA: Houghton Mifflin.

Koponen, M., & Riggenbach, H. (2003). Overview: Varying perspectives on fluency. In H. Riggenbach (Ed.), *Perspectives on fluency* (pp. 5–24). Ann Arbor, MI: University of Michigan Press.

Krashen, S. (1981). *Second language acquisition and second language learning*. London: Pergamon Press.

Krashen, S. (1995). Bilingual education and second language acquisition theory. In D. B. Durkin (Ed.), *Language issues: Reading for teachers* (pp. 90–115). White Plains, NY: Longman.

Kretchmar, R. (2000). Movement subcultures: Sites for meaning. *Journal of Physical Education, Recreation & Dance, 71*(5), 19–24.

Kucer, S. B. (1985). The making of meaning: Reading and writing as parallel processes. *Written Communication, 2,* 317–336.

Kucer, S. B. (2001). *Dimensions of literacy: A conceptual base for teaching reading and writing in school settings*. Mahwah, NJ: Erlbaum Publishers.

Kucera, H., & Francis, W. N. (1967). *Computational analysis of present-day American English*. Providence, RI: Brown University Press.

Kuhn, M. R., & Stahl, S. A. (2004). Fluency: A review of developmental and remedial practices. In R. B. Ruddell & N. J. Unrau (Eds.), *Theoretical models and processes of reading* (5th ed., pp. 412–453). Newark, DE: International Reading Association.

Kuhn, T. S. (1962). *The structure of scientific revolutions*. Chicago, IL: University of Chicago Press.

Lakeoff, G. (1980). *Metaphors we live by*. Chicago, IL: University of Chicago Press.

Lambert, B. (2000, July 24). 40 percent in NY are foreign born, study finds. *The New York Times*, p. A10.

Langer, E. (1989). *Mindfulness*. Reading, MA: Perseus Books.

Langer, E. (1997). *The power of mindful learning*. Reading, MA: Addison-Wesley.

Langer, J. A. (1981). From theory to practice: A prereading plan. *Journal of Reading, 25,* 152–156.

Langer, J. A. (1982). Facilitating text processing: The elaboration of prior knowledge. In J. A. Langer & M. T. Smith-Burke (Eds.), *Reader meets author/bridging the gap* (pp. 149–162). Newark, DE: International Reading Association.

Langer, J. A. (1987). A sociocognitive perspective on literacy. In J. A. Langer (Ed.), *Language, literacy, and culture: Issues of society and schooling* (pp. 1–20). Norwood, NJ: Ablex.

Langer, J. A. (2000). Excellence in English in middle and high school: How teachers' professional lives support student achievement. *American Educational Research Journal, 37*(2), 397–439.

Langer, J. A. (2001). Beating the odds: Teaching middle and high school students to read and write well. *American Educational Research Journal, 38*(4), 837–880.

Langer, J. A. (2002). *Effective literacy instruction: Building successful reading and writing programs*. Urbana, IL: National Council of Teachers of English.

Langer, J. A., & Applebee, A. N. (1987). *How writing shapes thinking*. Urbana, IL: National Council of Teachers of English.

Langer, S. (1942). *Philosophy in a new key*. New York: Mentor Books.

Lankshear, C., & McLaren, P. L. (Eds.) (1993). *Critical literacy: Politics, praxis, and the postmodern*. Albany: State University Press of New York.

Lasley, T. J., Matczynski, T. J., & Rowley, J. B. (2002). *Instructional models: Strategies for teaching in a diverse society*. Belmont, CA: Wadsworth.

Lau v. Nichols, 414 US 563 (1974).

Lemke, J. L. (2004). The literacies of science. In E. W. Saul (Ed.), *Crossing borders in literacy and science instruction* (pp. 33–47). Newark, DE: International Reading Association.

Lenners, C., & Smith, K. (1999, September). *Explicit Instruction of Comprehension Skills*. Workshop presented at Burbank Middle School, Burbank, CA.

Lepper, M. R., Greene, D., & Nisbett, R. E. (1973). Undermining children's intrinsic interest with extrinsic reward. *Journal of Personality and Social Psychology, 28,* 124–137.

Lepper, M. R., Corpus, J. H., & Iyengar, S. S. (2005). Intrinsic and extrinsic motivational orientations in the classroom: Age differences and academic correlates. *Journal of Educational Psychology, 97*(2), 184–196.

Lepper, M. R., & Henderlong, J. (2000). Turning "play" into "work" and "work" into "play": 25 years of research on intrinsic and extrinsic motivation. In C. Sansone & J. M. Harackiewicz (Eds.), *Intrinsic and extrinsic motivation: The search for optimal motivation and performance* (pp. 257–307), San Diego, CA: Academic Press.

Leu, D. J., Kinzer, C. K., Coiro, J. L., & Cammack, D. W. (2004). Toward a theory of new literacies emerging from the Internet and other information and communication technologies. In R. B. Ruddell & N. J. Unrau (Eds.), *Theoretical models and processes of reading* (5th ed., pp. 1570–1613). Newark, DE: International Reading Association.

Levy, B. A. (2001). Moving the bottom: Improving reading fluency. In M. Wolf (Ed.), *Dyslexia, fluency, and the brain* (pp. 357–382). Timonium, MD: York Press.

Lieberman, M., & Langer, E. (1995). Mindfulness and the process of learning. In P. Antonacci (Ed.), *Learning and context.* Cresskill, NJ: Hampton Press.

Lien, A. (2003, April). *Urban classrooms as sites of reading the world: Negotiating critical literacy in a test-driven era.* Paper presented at the annual meeting of the American Educational Research Association, Chicago. (ERIC Document Reproduction Service No. ED 479196)

Lippmann, W. (1913/1962). *A preface to politics.* Ann Arbor. MI: University of Michigan Press.

Loera, G. (2006). *Latino parental aspirations and literacy practices related to children's reading engagement.* Unpublished doctoral dissertation, University of Southern California, Los Angeles.

Long, D. L., Seely, M. R., Oppy, B. J., & Golding, J. M (1996). The role of inferential processing in reading ability. In B. K. Britton & A. C. Graesser (Eds.), *Models of understanding text* (pp. 189–214). Mahway, NJ: Erlbaum.

Lou, Y. (1996). Within-class grouping: A meta-analysis. *Review of Educational Research, 66*(4), 423–458.

Louis, K. S., & Smith, B. (1992). Cultivating teacher engagement: Breaking the iron law of social class. In F. M. Newmann (Ed.), *Student engagement and achievement in American secondary schools* (pp. 119–152). New York: Teachers College Press.

Lounsbery, M., Gast, J., & Smith, N. (2005). The integrated curriculum of "Planned Approach to Healthier Schools." *Journal of Physical Education, Recreation and Dance, 76*(3), 34–38.

Lubliner, S., & Smetana, L. (2004). The effects of comprehensive vocabulary instruction on Title I students' metacognitive word-learning skills and reading comprehension. *Journal of Literacy Research, 37,* 163–200.

Luke, A. (1995). When basic skills and information processing just aren't enough: Rethinking reading in New Times. *Teachers College Record, 97*(1), 95–116.

Luke, A. (2000). Critical literacy in Australia: A matter of context and standpoint. *Journal of Adolescent and Adult Literacy, 43*(5), 448–461.

Lyman, F. (1981). The responsive classroom discussion. In A. S. Anderson (Ed.), *Mainstreaming Digest.* College Park: University of Maryland, College of Education.

Mac Iver, D. J. (1993). Effects of improvement-focused student recognition on young adolescents' performance in the classroom. In M. L. Maehr & P. R. Pintrich (Eds.), *Advances in motivation and achievement* (pp. 191–216). Greenwich, CT: JAI Press.

Macrorie, K. (1968). *Writing to be read.* Rochelle Park, NJ: Hayden Book Co.

Macrorie, K. (1970). *Telling writing.* New York: Hayden Book Co.

Macrorie, K. (1988). *The I-search paper.* Portsmouth, NH: Boynton/Cook Heinemann.

Malinowski, B. (1944). *A scientific theory of culture and other essays.* New York: Oxford University Press.

Manzo, A. V. (1969). The ReQuest procedure. *Journal of Reading, 13,* 123–126.

Manzo, A., Manzo, U., & Thomas, M. M. (2005). *Content area literacy: Strategic teaching for strategic learning* (4th ed.). Hoboken, NJ: John Wiley.

Marks, H. M. (2000). Student engagement in instructional activity: Patterns in the elementary, middle, and high school years. *American Educational Research Journal, 37*(1), 153–184.

Marks, M. (1993). Three teachers' adaptations of reciprocal teaching in comparison to traditional reciprocal teaching. *Elementary School Journal, 94*(2), 267–283.

Markus, H., & Nurius, P. (1986). Possible selves. *American Psychologist, 41*(9), 954–969.

Marlett, P. B., & Gordon, C. J. (2004). The use of alternative texts in physical education. *Journal of Adolescent and Adult Literacy, 48*(3), 226–237.

Marshall, H. (1992). Associate editor's introduction to centennial articles on classroom learning and motivation. *Journal of Educational Psychology, 84*(3), 259–260.

Martinez, J. G., & Martinez, N. C. (2001). *Reading and writing to learn mathematics: A guide and a resource book.* Boston: Allyn & Bacon.

Marxen, D. E. (1996). Why reading and underlining a passage is a less effective study strategy than simply rereading the passage. *Reading Improvement, 33,* 88–96.

Mayer, R. E. (1984). Twenty-five years of research on advance organizers. *Instructional Science, 8,* 133–169.

McAndrew, D. A. (1983). Underlining and notetaking: Some suggestions from research. *Journal of Reading, 27,* 103–108.

McBrien, J. L. (2005). Uninformed in the information age: Why media necessitate critical thinking education. In G. Schwarz & P. U. Brown (Eds.), *Media literacy: Transforming curriculum and teaching* (pp. 18–34). Chicago, IL: National Society for the Study of Education.

McConkie, G. W., & Zola, D. (1981). Language constraints and the functional stimulus in reading. In A. M. Lesgold & C. A. Perfetti (Eds.), *Interactive processes in reading* (pp. 155–175). Hillsdale, NJ: Erlbaum.

McCormick, S. (2007). *Instructing students who have literacy problems* (5th ed.). Columbus, OH: Merrill.

McKenna, M. C., Kear, D. J., & Ellsworth, R. A., (1995). Children's attitudes toward reading: A national survey. *Reading Research Quarterly, 30,* 934–956.

McLuhan, M. (1964). *Understanding media: The extensions of man.* New York: McGraw-Hill.

McNeil, L. M. (1988). *Contradictions of control: School structure and school knowledge.* New York: Routledge.

McNeil, L. M. (2000). *Contradictions of school reform: Educational costs of standardized testing.* New York: Routledge.

McQuillan, J. (1998). *The literacy crisis: False claims, real solutions.* Portsmouth, NH: Heinemann.

McVee, M. B., Dunsmore, K., & Gavelek, J. R. (2005). Schema theory revisited. *Review of Educational Research, 75*(4), 531–566.

Meece, J. L. (1994). The role of motivation in self-regulated learning. In D. H. Schunk & B. J. Zimmerman (Eds.), *Self-regulation of learning and performance: Issues and educational applications* (pp. 25–44). Hillsdale, NJ: Erlbaum.

Meece, J. L., Wigfield, A., & Eccles, J. S. (1990). Predictors of math anxiety and its consequences for young adolescents' course enrollment intentions and performances in mathematics. *Journal of Educational Psychology, 82,* 60–70.

Mellor, B., & Patterson, A. (2000). Critical practice: Teaching "Shakespeare." *Journal of Adolescent and Adult Literacy, 43*(6), 508–517.

Menon, R. (1998). Mathematics and language. In A. McIntosh & N. Ellerton (Eds.), *Research in mathematics education: A contemporary perspective.* Perth, Australia: MASTEC, Edith Cowan University.

Meyer, B. J. F. (1984). Text dimensions and cognitive processing. In H. Mandl, N. Stein, & T. Trabasso (Eds.), *Learning from texts* (pp. 3–52). Hillsdale, NJ: Erlbaum.

Meyer, B. J. F., Brandt, D., & Bluth, G. (1980). Use of the top-level structure in text: Key for reading comprehension of ninth-grade students. *Reading Research Quarterly, 16,* 72–103.

Meyer, B. J. F., & Freedle, R. (1984). The effects of different discourse types on recall. *American Educational Research Journal, 21,* 121–143.

Meyer, B. J. F., & Poon, L. (2001). Effects of the structure strategy and signaling on recall of text. *Journal of Educational Psychology, 93,* 141–159.

Meyer, B. J. F., Young, C. J., & Bartlett, B. J. (1989). *Memory improved: Reading and memory enhancement across the life span through strategic text structures.* Hillsdale, N.J.: Erlbaum.

Michigan State Board of Education. (1994). *Assessment frameworks for the Michigan high school proficiency test in communication arts, Part I: Writing.* Lansing, MI: Michigan Department of Education.

Midgley, C., Feldlaufer, H., and Eccles, J. (1989). Change in teacher efficacy and student self- and task-related beliefs in mathematics during the transition to junior high school. *Journal of Educational Psychology, 49,* 529–538.

Miller, G. A. (1956). The magical number seven, plus or minus two: Some limits of our capacity for processing information. *Psychological Review, 63,* 81–97.

Miller, K. R., & Levine, J. (2006). *Biology.* Upper Saddle River, NJ: Pearson/Prentice Hall.

Mitchell, D., Destino, T., & Karam, R. (1997). *Evaluation of English language development programs in the Santa Ana Unified School District: A report on data system reliability and statistical modeling of program impacts.* University of California, Riverside: California Educational Research Cooperative. Available on http://cerc.ucr.edu/publications

Moats, L. C. (2001). When older students can't read. *Educational Leadership, 58,* 36–40.

Moen, S. (1996). Circuit training through the muscular system. *Journal of Physical Education, Recreation and Dance, 67*(2), 10–23.

Moffett, J. (1989). *Bridges: From personal writing to the formal essay* (Occasional Paper No. 9). Berkeley, CA: Center for the Study of Writing.

Moje, B. M., & Dillon, D. R. (2006). Adolescent identities as demanded by science classroom discourse communities. In D. E. Alvermann, K. Hinchman, D. W. Moore, S. Phelps, & D. R. Waff (Eds.), *Reconceptualizing the literacies of adolescents' lives* (2nd ed., pp. 85–106). Mahwah, NJ: Erlbaum Publishers.

Moje, E. B., Young, J. P., Readence, J. E., & Moore, D. W. (2000). Reinventing adolescent literacy for new times: Perennial and millennial issues. *Journal of Adolescent and Adult Literacy, 43,* 400–410.

Mokhtari, K., & Reichard, C. A. (2002). Assessing students' metacognitive awareness of reading strategies. *Journal of Educational Psychology, 94*(2), 249–259.

Moline, S. (1995). *I see what you mean.* Portland, ME: Stenhouse Publishers.

Moore, D. W., Bean, T. W., Birdyshaw, D., & Rycik, J. A. (1999). Adolescent literacy: A position statement. *Journal of Adolescent & Adult Literacy, 43,* 97–112.

Moore, D. W., & Stefanich, G. P. (1990). Middle school reading: A historical perspective. In G. G. Duffy (Ed.), *Reading in the middle school* (2nd ed., pp. 3–15). Newark, DE: International Reading Association.

Moore, M. (1975). *Paragraph development.* Boston, MA: Houghton Mifflin Company.

Morehead, D. M. (1971). Processing of phonological sequences by young children and adults. *Child Development, 42,* 279–289.

Morrell, E. (2000, April). *Curriculum and popular culture: Building bridges and making waves.* Paper presented at the annual meeting of the American Educatinal Research Association, New Orleans, LA. (ERIC Document Reproduction Service No. ED 442720)

Morse, S. (Ed.). (1998). *Separated by sex: A critical look at single-sex education for girls.* Washington, DC: American Association of University Women Educational Foundation.

Moustafa, M. (1997). *Beyond traditional phonics: Research discoveries and reading instruction.* Portsmouth, NH: Heinemann.

Moyer, B. (1995). *The language of life.* New York: Doubleday.

Mullis, I. V. S., Campbell, J. R., & Farstrup, A. E. (1993). *NAEP 1992 reading report card for the nation and the states.* Princeton, NJ: Educational Testing Service.

Nagy, W. B., & Anderson, R. C. (1984). How many words are there in printed school English? *Reading Research Quarterly, 19,* 304–330.

Nagy, W. E., & Scott, J. A. (2000). Vocabulary processes. In M. L. Kamil, P. B. Mosenthal, P. D. Pearson, & R. Barr (Eds.), *Handbook of reading research* (Vol. III, pp. 269–284). Mahwah, NJ: Erlbaum.

A nation at risk: The imperative for educational reform (1983). Washington, DC: Government Printing Office.

National Assessment of Educational Progress (1999). *Reading report card for the nation and the states.* Washington, DC: U.S. Department of Education.

National Assessment of Educational Progress (2003). *The nation's report card: Writing 2002.* Washington, DC: National Center for Educational Statistics.

National Board for Professional Teaching Standards (2007). Standards. Retrieved March 5, 2007, from NBPTS: http://nbpts.org/help_and_faqs/standards#1902

National Center for Education Statistics (NCES). (2005). *The Condition of Education 2005* (NCES 2005-094). Washington, DC: U.S. Government Printing Office.

National Council of Teachers of Mathematics (NCTM). (2000). *Principles and standards for school mathematics.* Reston, VA: NCTM.

National Council of Teachers of Mathematics (NCTM). (2006). *Curriculum focal points for prekindergarten through grade 8 mathematics: A quest for coherence.* Reston, VA: NCTM.

National Reading Panel (2000). *Report of the National Reading Panel: Teaching children to read.* Bethesda, MD: National Institute of Child Health and Human Development.

National Research Council & Institute of Medicine (2004). *Engaging schools: Fostering high school students' motivation to learn.* Washington, DC: National Academy Press.

National Writing Project (2001). NWP assumptions. Retrieved July 20, 2001, from http://www.writing project.org/About/assumptions.html

New London Group (1996). A pedagogy of multiliteracies: Designing social futures. *Harvard Educational Review, 66*(1), 60–92.

New York State Education Department (1997). *English Language Arts resource guide.* Retrieved September 1, 2002, from http://www.nysed.gov

Newell, G. E. (1998). "How much are we the wiser?": Continuity and change in writing and learning in the content areas. In N. N. Nelson & R. C. Calfee (Eds.), *The reading-writing connection: The yearbook of the National Society for the Study of Education* (pp. 178–202). Chicago, IL: University of Chicago Press.

Newell, G. E., & Winograd, P. (1995). Writing about and learning from history texts: The effects of task and academic ability. *Research in the Teaching of English, 29,* 133–163.

Newmann, F. M. (1992a). Conclusion. In F. Newmann (Ed.), *Student engagement and achievement in American secondary schools* (pp. 182–217). New York: Teachers College Press.

Newmann, F. M. (1992b). *Student engagement and achievement in American secondary schools.* New York: Teachers College Press.

Newmann, F. M., Wehlage, G. G., & Lamborn, S. D. (1992). The significance of sources of student engagement. In F. M. Newmann (Ed.), *Student engagement and achievement in American secondary schools* (pp. 11–39). New York: Teachers College Press.

Nicholls, J. G. (1984). Achievement motivation: Conception of ability, subjective experience, task choice, and performance. *Psychological Review, 91,* 328–346.

Nist, S. L., & Olejnik, S. (1995). The role of context and dictionary definitions on varying levels of word knowledge. *Reading Research Quarterly, 30,* 172–193.

Novak, J. D. (1991). Clarify with concept maps. *The Science Teacher, 58*(7), 45–49.

Novak, J. D. (1998). *Learning, creating, and using knowledge: Concept maps as facilitative tools in schools and corporations.* Mahwah, NJ: Erlbaum.

Nunley, K. A. (2006). *Differentiating the high school classroom: Solution strategies for 18 common obstacles.* Thousand Oaks, CA: Corwin Press.

O'Brien, D., Beach, R., & Scharber, C. (2007). "Struggling" middle schoolers: Engagement and literate competence in a reading writing intervention class. *Reading Psychology, 29*(1), 51–73.

O'Brien, D., & Stewart, R. (1992). Resistance to content area reading: Dimensions and solutions. In E. D. Dishner, T. W. Bean, J. E. Readence, & D. W. Moore (Eds.), *Reading in the content areas: Improving classroom instruction* (3rd ed.). Dubuque, IA: Kendall/Hunt.

O'Flahavan, J. F., Stein, C., Wiencek, J., & Marks, T. (1992). *Interpretive development in peer discussion about literature: An exploration of the teacher's role.* Paper presented at the 42nd annual meeting of the National Reading Conference, San Antonio, TX.

Ochs, E., & Schieffelin, B. (1984). Language acquisition and socialization: Three developmental stories and their implications. In R. A. Shweder & R. A. Levine (Eds.), *Culture theory: Essays on mind, self, and emotion* (pp. 276–320). Cambridge: Cambridge University Press.

Official voter information guide. (2006). Accessed 2006 May 9, 2006, from http://www.ss.ca.gov/elections/elections_viguide05.htm

Ogbu, J. (1983). Minority status and schooling in plural societies. *Comparative Education Review, 27*(2), 168–190.

Ogbu, J. (1991). Immigrant and involuntary minorities in comparative perspective. In M. A. Gibson & J. Ogbu (Eds.), *Minority status and schooling: A comparative study of immigrant and involuntary minorities* (pp. 3–33). New York: Garland.

Ogbu, J., & Simons, H. (1998). Voluntary and involuntary minorities: A cultural-ecological theory of school performance with some implications for education. *Anthropology & Education Quarterly, 29*(2), 155–188.

Ogle, D. (1986). K-W-L: A teaching model that develops active reading of expository text. *The Reading Teacher, 39,* 564–570.

Olsen, C. B., & Land, R. (2007). A cognitive strategies approach to reading and writing instruction for English language learners in secondary school. *Research and the Teaching of English, 41*(3), 269–303.

Opitz, M. F., & Rasinski, T. V. (1998). *Good-bye Round Robin: 25 effective oral reading strategies.* Portsmouth, NH: Heinemann.

Otis, N., Grouzet, F., & Pelletier, L. G. (2005). Latent motivational change in an academic setting: A 3-year longitudinal study. *Journal of Educational Psychology, 97*(2), 170–183.

Palincsar, A. (1982). *Improving the reading comprehension of junior high students through reciprocal teaching of comprehension-monitoring strategies.* Unpublished doctoral dissertation, University of Illinois at Urbana-Champaign.

Paribakht, T. S., & Wesche, M. B., (1997). Vocabulary enhancement activities and reading for meaning in second language vocabulary instruction. In J. Coady & T. Huckins (Eds.), *Second language vocabulary acquisition* (pp. 174–200). Cambridge, UK: Cambridge University Press.

Paris, S. G., & Flukes, J. (2005). Assessing children's metacognition about strategic reading. In S. E. Israel, C. Block, K. L. Bauserman, & K. Kinnucan-Welch (Eds.), *Metacognition in literacy learning: Theory, assessment, instruction, and professional development* (pp. 121–139). Mahwah, NJ: Erlbaum.

Paris, S. G., Lipson, M., & Wixson, K. (1983). Becoming a strategic reader. *Contemporary Educational Psychology, 8,* 293–316.

Paris, S. G., Wasik, B. A., & Turner, J. (1991). The development of strategic readers. In R. Barr, M. L. Kamil, P. B. Mosenthal, & P. D. Pearson (Eds.), *Handbook of reading research* (Vol. II). Mahwah, NJ: Erlbaum.

Paterson, P. O., & Elliott, L. N. (2006). Struggling reader to struggling reader: High school students' responses to a cross-age tutoring program. *Journal of Adolescent and Adult Literacy, 49*(5), 378–389.

Pauk, W. (1989). *How to study in college* (4th ed.). Boston: Houghton Mifflin.

Pearson, P. D. (1985). Changing the face of reading comprehension instruction. *The Reading Teacher, 38,* 724–738.

Pearson, P. D., & Gallagher, M. C. (1983). The instruction of reading comprehension. *Contemporary Educational Psychology, 8,* 317–344.

Pearson, P. D., Roehler, L. R., Dole, J. A., & Duffy, G. G. (1992). Developing expertise in reading comprehension. In S. J. Samuels & A. E. Farstrup (Eds.), *What research has to say about reading instruction* (2nd ed.). Newark, DE: International Reading Association.

Penrose, A. M. (1989). *Strategic differences in composing: Consequences for learning through writing* (Tech. Rep. No. 31). Berkeley, CA: Center for the Study of Writing at UC, Berkeley and Carnegie Mellon University.

Penrose, A. M. (1992). To write or not to write: Effects of task and task interpretation on learning through writing. *Written Communication, 9*(4), 465–500.

Perie, M., Grigg, W., & Donahue, P. (2005). *The nation's report card: Reading 2005* (NCES 2006–451). Washington, DC: U.S. Department of Education.

Perie, M., Moran, R., & Lutkus, A. D. (2005). *NAEP 2004 trends in academic progress: Three decades of student performance in reading and mathematics* (NCES 2005-464). U.S. Department of Education, Institute of Education Sciences, National Center for Education Statistics. Washington, DC: Government Printing Office.

Perl, S. (1979). The composing processes of unskilled college writers. *Research in the Teaching of English, 13,* 317–336.

Peske, H. G., & K. Haycock (2006). *Teaching inequality: How poor and minority students are shortchanged on teacher quality.* Washington, DC: Education Trust.

Peterson, C., Caverly, D., Nicholson, S., O'Neal, S., & Cusenbary, S. (2000). *Building reading proficiency at the secondary level: A guide to resources.* Austin, TX: Southwest Educational Development Laboratory.

Peterson, S. E. (1992). The cognitive function of underlining as a study technique. *Reading Research and Information, 31,* 49–56.

Philips, S. (1983). *The invisible culture: Communication in classroom and community on the Warm Springs Indian Reservation.* New York: Longman.

Pikulski, J. J., & Chard, D. J. (2005). Fluency: Bridge between decoding and reading comprehension. *The Reading Teacher, 59*(6), 510–519.

Pilgreen, J. L. (2000). *SSR handbook: How to organize and manage a sustained silent reading program.* Portsmouth, NH: Heinemann.

Pintrich, P. R. (2000a). Multiple goals, multiple pathways: The role of goal orientation in learning and achievement. *Journal of Educational Psychology, 92,* 544–555.

Pintrich, P. R. (2000b). The role of goal orientation in self-regulated learning. In M. Boekaerts, P. R. Pintrich, & M. Zeidner (Eds.), *The handbook of self-regulation* (pp. 451–502). San Diego, CA: Academic Press.

Pope, D. (2002). *Doing school: How we are creating a generation of stressed-out, materialistic, and miseducated students.* New Haven, CT: Yale University Press.

Postlethwaite, T. N., & Ross, K. N. (1992). *Effective schools in reading.* The Hague, Netherlands: International Association for the Evaluation of Educational Achievement.

Powell, R., Cantrell, S. C., & Adams, S. (2001). Saving Black Mountain: The promise of critical literacy in a multicultural democracy. *The Reading Teacher, 54,* 772–781.

Prescott-Griffin, M. L., & Witherell, N. L. (2004). *Fluency in focus: Comprehension strategies for all young readers.* Portsmouth, NH: Heinemann.

Pressley, M. (2000). What should comprehension instruction be the instruction of? In M. L. Kamil, P. B. Mosenthal, P. D. Pearson, & R. Barr (Eds.), *Handbook of reading research* (Vol. III, pp. 545–561). Mahwah, NJ: Erlbaum.

Pressley, M., El-Kinary, P. B., & Brown, R. (1992). Skilled and not-so-skilled reading: Good information processing and not-so-good information processing. In M. Pressley, K. R. Harris, & J. T. Guthrie (Eds.), *Promoting academic competence and literacy in school* (pp. 91–127). San Diego: Academic.

Pressley, M., Gaskins, I., Solic, K., & Collins, S. (2006). A portrait of Benchmark School: How a school produces high achievement in students who previously failed. *Journal of Educational Psychology, 98*(2), 282–306.

Pressley, M., Levin, J. R., & Delaney, H. D. (1983). The mnemonic keyword method. *Review of Educational Research, 2,* 6–91.

Pressley, M., Levin, J. R., & McDaniel, M. A. (1987). Remembering versus inferring what a word means: Mnemonic and contextual approaches. In M. G. McKeown & M. E. Curtis (Eds.), *The nature of vocabulary acquisition* (pp. 107–127). Hillsdale, NJ: Erlbaum.

Pressley, M., Raphael, L., Gallagher, J. D., & DiBell, J. (2004). Providence-St. Mel School: How a school that works for African-American students works. *Journal of Educational Psychology, 96,* 216–235.

Pressley, M., Woloshyn, V., Lysynchuk, L. M., Martin, V., Wood, E., & Willoughby, T. (1990). A primer of research on cognitive strategy instruction: The important issues and how to address them. *Educational Psychology Review, 2,* 1–58.

Pressley, M., Wood, E., Woloshyn, V. E., Martin, V., King, A., & Menke, D. (1992). Encouraging mindful use of prior knowledge: Attempting to construct explanatory answers facilitates learning. *Educational Psychologist, 27,* 91–110.

Pressnall, B. (1995). Skeletons out of the closet: The case of the missing 162%. *Quarterly of the National Writing Project and the Center for the Study of Writing and Literacy, 17*(3), 20–25.

Radsinski, T. (1990, November). *Predicting reading rates that correspond to independent, instructional, and frustration reading levels for third and fifth grade students.* Paper presented at the Annual Meeting of the National Reading Conference, Miami, FL.

Ragland, M. A., Asera, R., & Johnson, J. F. (1999). *Urgency, responsibility, efficacy: Preliminary findings of a study of high performing Texas school districts.* Austin, TX: Charles A. Dana Center.

Rakes, T. A., & Smith, T. L. (1992). Assessing reading skills in the content areas. In E. K. Dishner, T. W. Bean, J. E. Readence, & D. W. Moore (Eds.), *Reading in the content areas: Improving classroom instruction* (3rd ed., pp. 399–426). Dubuque, IA: Kendall/Hunt.

RAND Reading/Study Group (2002). *Reading for understanding: Toward an R & D program in reading comprehension.* Santa Monica, CA: RAND

Rasinski, T. V., & Fawcett, G. (2000). Encouraging family involvement in the intermediate and middle grades. In K. Wood & T. Dickinson (Eds.), *Promoting literacy in grades 4–9: A handbook for teachers and administrators* (pp. 63–76). Needham Heights, MA: Allyn & Bacon.

Rasinski, T. V., Padak, N. D., McKeon, C. A., Wilfong, L. G., Friedauer, J. A., & Heim, P. (2005). Is reading fluency a key for successful high school reading? *Journal of Adolescent and Adult Literacy, 49*(1), 22–27.

Reeve, J., & Jang, H. (2006). What teachers say and do to support students' autonomy during a learning activity. *Journal of Educational Psychology, 98,* 209–218.

Reeve, J., Jang, H., Carrell, D., Jeon, S., & Barch, J. (2004). Enhancing students' engagement by increasing teachers' autonomy support. *Motivation and Emotion, 28,* 147–169.

Reeves, A. R. (2004). *Adolescents talk about reading: Exploring resistance to and engagement with text.* Newark, DE: International Reading Association.

Rekrut, M. D. (1994). Peer and cross-age tutoring: The lessons of research. *Journal of Reading, 37*(5), 356–362.

Reutzel, D. R., & Hollingsworth, P. M. (1993). Effects of fluency training on second graders' reading comprehension. *Journal of Educational Research, 86*(6), 325–331.

Rex, L. A. (2001). The remaking of a high school reader. *Reading Research Quarterly, 36*(3), 288–313.

Reyes, P., Scribner, J. D., & Paredes Scribner, A. (1999). *Lessons from high performing Hispanic schools: Creating learning communities.* New York: Teachers College Press.

Richards, J., & Gipe, J. (1995). What's the structure? A game to help middle school students recognize common writing patterns. *Journal of Reading, 38*(8), 667–669.

Richardson, W. (2006). *Blogs, wikis, podcasts, and other powerful Web tools for classrooms.* Thousand Oaks, CA: Corwin Press.

Robinson, F. P. (1946). *Effective study* (2nd ed.). New York: Harper & Row.

Rosenblatt, L. M. (1978). *The reader, the text, the poem: The transactional theory of the literary work.* Carbondale, IL: Southern Illinois University Press.

Rosenblatt, L. M. (1985). The transactional theory of the literary work: Implications for research. In C. R. Cooper (Ed.), *Researching response to literature and the teaching of literature* (pp. 33–53). Norwood, NJ: Ablex.

Rosenblatt, L. M. (2004). The transactional theory of reading and writing. In R. B. Ruddell & N. J. Unrau (Eds.), *Theoretical models and processes of reading* (5th ed., pp. 1363–1398). Newark, DE: International Reading Association.

Rosenshine, B., & Meister, C. (1994). Reciprocal teaching: A review of the research. *Review of Educational Research, 64*(4), 479–530.

Rosenshine, B., Meister, C., & Chapman, S. (1996). Teaching students to generate questions: A review of the intervention studies. *Review of Educational Research, 66*(2), 181–221.

Roth, W. M., Boutonne, S., McRobbie, C., & Lucas, K. B. (1999). One class, many worlds. *International Journal of Science Education, 21,* 59–75.

Roth, W. M., McRobbie, C., Lucas, K. B., & Boutonne, S. (1997). Why do students fail to learn from demonstrations? A social practice perspective on learning in physics. *Journal of Research in Science Teaching, 34,* 509–533.

Ruddell, M. R. (1994). Vocabulary knowledge and comprehension: A comprehension-process view of complex literacy relationships. In R. Ruddell, M. Ruddell, & H. Singer (Eds.), *Theoretical models and processes of reading* (4th ed., pp. 414–447). Newark, DE: International Reading Association.

Ruddell, M. R. (1997). *Teaching content reading and writing* (2nd ed.). Boston, MA: Allyn & Bacon.

Ruddell, M. R. (2004). *Teaching content reading and writing* (4th ed.). New York: John Wiley & Sons.

Ruddell, M. R., & Shearer, B.A. (2002). "Extraordinary," "tremendous," "exhilarating," "magnificent": Middle school at-risk students become avid word learners with the Vocabulary Self-Collection Strategy (VSS). *Journal of Adolescent and Adult Literacy, 45,* 352–366.

Ruddell, R. B. (1994). The development of children's comprehension and motivation during storybook discussion. In R. B. Ruddell, M. R. Ruddell, & H. Singer (Eds.), *Theoretical models and processes of reading* (4th ed., pp. 281–296). Newark, DE: International Reading Association.

Ruddell, R. B. (1995). Those influential literacy teachers: Meaning negotiators and motivation builders. *The Reading Teacher, 48,* 454–463.

Ruddell, R. B., Draheim, M., & Barnes, J. (1990). A comparative study of the teaching effectiveness of influential and non-influential teachers and reading comprehension development. In J. Zutell & S. McCormick (Eds.), *Literacy theory and research: Analyses from multiple paradigms* (pp. 153–162). Chicago, IL: National Reading Conference.

Ruddell, R. B., & Haggard, M. R. (1982). Influential teachers: Characteristics and classroom performance. In J. A. Niles & L. A. Harris (Eds.), *New inquiries in reading research and instruction,* 31st Yearbook of the National Reading Conference (pp. 227–231). Rochester, NY: National Reading Conference.

Ruddell, R. B., & Unrau, N. J. (1997). The role of responsive teaching in focusing reader intention and developing reader motivation. In J. T. Guthrie & A. Wigfield (Eds.), *Reading engagement: Motivating readers through integrated instruction* (pp. 102–125). Newark, DE: International Reading Association.

Ruddell, R. B., & Unrau, N. J. (2004). Reading as a meaning-construction process: The reader, the text, and the teacher. In R. B. Ruddell & N. J. Unrau (Eds.), *Theoretical models and processes of reading* (5th ed., pp. 1462–1521). Newark, DE: International Reading Association.

Rumelhart, D. E. (1980). *An introduction to human information processing*. New York: Wiley.

Rushkoff, D. (1996). *Playing the future*. New York: Riverhead Books.

Ryan, R. M., & Deci, E. L. (2000). Self-determination theory and the facilitation of intrinsic motivation, social development, and well-being. *American Psychologist, 55*, 68–78.

Sadoski, M., & Paivio, A. (2001). *Imagery and text: A dual coding theory of reading and writing*. Mahwah, NJ: Erlbaum.

Sahagun, L. (2000, March 27). School strains under effort to end social promotion. *Los Angeles Times*, p. A1.

Salinger, J. D. (1981). The laughing man. In J. D. Salinger (Ed.), *Nine stories* (pp. 56–73). Boston, MA: Little, Brown and Company.

Samuels, S. J. (1994). Word recognition. In R. B. Ruddell, M. R. Ruddell, & H. Singer (Eds.), *Theoretical models and processes of reading* (4th ed., pp. 359–380). Newark, DE: International Reading Association.

Samuels, S. J. (2002). Reading fluency: Its development and assessment. In S. J. Samuels & A. E. Farstrup (Eds.), *What research says about reading instruction* (3rd ed., pp. 166–183). Newark, DE: International Reading Association.

Samuels, S. J. (2004). Toward a theory of automatic information processing in reading revisited. In R. B. Ruddell & N. J. Unrau (Eds.), *Theoretical models and processes of reading* (5th ed., pp. 1127–1148). Newark, DE: International Reading Association.

Samuels, S.J. (2006). Toward a model of reading fluency. In S. J. Samuels & F. Farstrup (Eds.), *What research has to say about fluency instruction* (pp. 24–46). Newark, DE: International Reading Association.

Sanford-Smith, K., & Hopper, T. (1996). Teaching the mind and body: Connecting physical education and language arts. *Runner, 34*(1), 12–13.

Santa, C. (1988). *Content reading including study systems*. Dubuque, IA: Kendall/Hunt.

Saul, W. (2004). What's next? A view from the editor's perch. In E. W. Saul (Ed.), *Crossing borders in literacy and science instruction* (pp. 447–453). Newark, DE: International Reading Association.

Scarcella, R. C. (2003). *Accelerating academic English: A focus on the English learner*. Oakland, CA: Regents of the University of California.

Schank, R. C., & Abelson, R. P. (1977). *Scripts, plans, goals, and understanding*. Hillsdale, NJ: Erlbaum.

Schiefele, U. (1996). Topic interest, text representation, and quality of experience. *Contemporary Educational Psychology, 21*, 3–18.

Schifini, A. (1994). Language, literacy, and content instruction: Strategies for teachers. In K. Spangenberg-Urbschat & R. Pritchard (Eds.), *Kids come in all languages: Reading instruction for ESL students* (pp. 158–179). Newark, DE: International Reading Association.

Schmoker, M. (1996). *Results: The key to continuous school improvement*. Alexandria, VA: Association for Supervision and Curriculum Development.

Schmoker, M. (2001). *The results fieldbook: Practical strategies from dramatically improved schools*. Alexandria, VA: Association for Supervision and Curriculum Development.

Schoenbach, R., Greenleaf, C., Cziko, C., & Hurwitz, L. (1999). *Reading for understanding: A guide to improving reading in middle and high school classrooms*. San Francisco: Jossey-Bass.

Schram, J. (1995). Physical education and language. *Runner, 33*(1), 9–10.

Schumm, J. S., Vaughn, S., & Leavell, A. (1994). Planning pyramid: A framework for planning for diverse student needs during content area instruction. *The Reading Teacher, 47*(8), 608–615.

Schunk, D. H. (1994). Self-regulation of self-efficacy and attributions in academic settings. In D. H. Schunk & B. J. Zimmerman (Eds.), *Self-regulation of learning and performance: Issues and educational applications* (pp. 75–99). Hillsdale, NJ: Erlbaum.

Schunk, D. H., & Zimmermann, B. J. (1997). Developing self-efficacious readers and writers: The role of social and self-regulatory processes. In J. T. Guthrie & A. Wigfield (Eds.), *Reading engagement: Motivating readers through integrated instruction* (pp. 34–50). Newark, DE: International Reading Association.

Scoble, J., Topping, K., & Wigglesworth, C. (1994). Training family and friends as literacy tutors. In M. C. Radencich (Ed.), *Adult literacy: A compendium of articles from the Journal of Reading* (pp. 219–226). Newark, DE: International Reading Association.

Seidel, S. (1998). Wondering to be done: The collaborative assessment conference. In D. Allen (Ed.), *Assessing student learning: From grading to understanding* (pp. 21–39). New York: Teachers College Press.

Sfard, A., & Prusak, A. (2005). Telling identities: In search of an analytic tool for investigating learning as a culturally shaped activity. *Educational Researcher, 34*(4), 14–22.

Shanahan, T., & Kamil, M. L. (1984). The relationship of three concurrent and construct validities of cloze. In J. A. Niles & L. A. Harris (Eds.), *Changing perspectives on research in reading/language processing and instruction* (pp. 334–338). Rochester: National Reading Conference.

Shapiro, J., & Whitney, P. (1997). Factors involved in the leisure reading of upper elementary school students. *Reading Psychology, 18,* 343–370.

Sharan, Y., & Sharan, S. (1992). *Group investigation: A strategy for expanding cooperative learning.* New York: Teacher's College Press.

Shor, I. (1999). What is critical literacy? In I. Shor & C. Pari (Eds.), *Critical literacy in action* (pp. 1–30). Portsmouth, NH: Boynton/Cook.

Shuell, T. J. (1996). Teaching and learning in a classroom context. In D. C. Berliner & R. C. Calfee (Eds.), *Handbook of educational psychology* (pp. 726–764). New York: Simon & Schuster Macmillan.

Simpson, M., & Nist, S. (2002). Encouraging active reading at the college level. In C. C. Block & M. Pressley (Eds.), *Comprehension Instruction: Research-based best practices* (pp. 365–379). New York: Guilford Press.

Singer, H. (1992). Friendly texts: Description and criteria. In E. K. Dishner, T. W. Bean, J. E. Readence, & D. W. Moore (Eds.), *Reading in the content areas* (3rd ed., pp. 155–168). Dubuque, IA: Kendall/Hunt.

Sizer, T. (1992). *Horace's school: Redesigning the American high school.* Boston: Houghton Mifflin.

Skinner, E. A., & Belmont, M. J. (1993). Motivation in the classroom: Reciprocal effects of teacher behavior and student engagement across the school year. *Journal of Educational Psychology, 85,* 571–581.

Skrla, L. (2001). Accountability, equity, complexity. *Educational Researcher, 30*(4), 15–21.

Slavin, R. E. (1980). Effects of Individual Learning Expectations on student achievement. *Journal of Educational Psychology, 72,* 520–524.

Slavin, R. E. (1989). Cooperative learning and student achievement. In R. E. Slavin (Ed.), *School and classroom organization.* Hillsdale, NJ: Erlbaum.

Slavin, R. E. (1995). *Cooperative learning* (2nd ed.). Boston, MA: Allyn & Bacon.

Slavin, R. E., & and Cheung, A. (2005). A synthesis of research on language of reading instruction for English language learners. *Review of Educational Research, 75*(2), 247–284.

Slavin, R. E., Madden, N. A., Dolan, L. J., & Wasik, B. A. (1996). *Every child, every school: Success for All.* Newbury Park, CA: Corwin.

Slavin, R. E., Madden, N. A., Karweit, N. L., Dolan, L. J., & Wasik, B. A. (1994). Success for all: Getting reading right the first time. In E. H. Hiebert & B. M. Taylor (Eds.), *Getting reading right from the start,* pp. 125–147. Boston, MA: Allyn & Bacon.

Smith, M. K. (1941). Measurement of the size of general English vocabulary through the elementary grades and high school. *Genetic Psychological Monographs, 24,* 311–345.

Smith, M. W., & Wilhelm, J. D. (2002). *"Reading don't fix no Chevys": Literacy in the lives of young men.* Portsmouth, NH: Heinemann.

Snow, C. E., & Biancarosa, G. (2003). *Adolescent literacy and the achievement gap: What do we know and where do we go from here?* New York: Carnegie Corporation of New York.

Solomon, M. Z., & Morocco, C. C. (1999). The diagnostic teacher. In M. Z. Solomon (Ed.), *The diagnostic teacher: Constructing new approaches to professional development* (pp. 231–246). New York: Teachers College Press.

Spear-Swerling, L., & Sternberg, R. J. (1996). *Off track: When poor readers become "learning disabled."* Boulder, CO: Westview Press.

Spiro, R. J., Coulson, R. L., Feltovich, P. J., & Anderson, D.K. (1988/2004). "Cognitive flexibility theory: Advanced knowledge acquisition in ill-structured domains." In R. Ruddell & N. J. Unrau (Eds.), *Theoretical models and processes of reading* (5th ed., pp. 640–653). Newark, DE: International Reading Association.

Spiro, R. J. (2000/2004). Principled pluralism for adaptive flexibility in teaching and learning to read. In R. B. Ruddell & N. J. Unrau (Eds.), *Theoretical models and processes of reading* (5th ed., pp. 653–659). Newark, DE: International Reading Association.

Stanovich, K. E. (1986). Matthew effects in reading: Some consequences of individual differences in the acquisition of literacy. *Reading Research Quarterly, 21*(4), 360–406.

Stanovich, K. E. (1990). Explaining the differences between the dyslexic and the garden-variety poor reader: The phonological-core variable-difference model. In J. K. Torgesen (Ed.), *Cognitive and behavioral characteristics of children with learning disabilities* (pp. 7–40). Austin, TX: Pro-Ed.

Stanovich, K. E. (1991). Word recognition: Changing perspectives. In R. Barr, M. Kamil, P. Rosenthal, & P. D. Pearson (Eds.), *Handbook of reading research* (Vol. 2, pp. 418–452). New York: Longman.

Stanovich, K. E. (1993). Does reading make you smarter?: Literacy and the development of verbal intelligence. In H. Reese (Ed.), *Advances in Child Development and Behavior* (Vol. 24, pp. 133–180). San Diego, CA: Academic Press.

Stanovich, K. E. (2000). *Progress in understanding reading: Scientific foundations and new frontiers.* New York: Guilford.

Stanovich, K. E., Cunningham, A. E., & West, R. F. (1998). Literacy experiences and the shaping of cognition. In S. Paris & H. Wellman (Eds.), *Global prospects for education: Development, culture, and schooling* (pp. 253–288). Washington, DC: American Psychological Association.

Stanovich, K. E., & Siegel, L. S. (1994). Phenotypic performance profile of children with reading disabilities: A regression-based test of the phonological-core variable-difference model. *Journal of Educational Psychology, 86,* 24–53.

Stauffer, R. (1969). *Teaching reading as a thinking process.* New York: Harper & Row.

Stefanou, C. R., Perenceivich, K. C., DiCintio, M., & Turner, J. C. (2004). Supporting autonomy in the classroom: Ways teachers encourage student decision making and ownership. *Educational Psychologist, 39*(2), 97–110.

Stein, N. L., & Glenn, C. (1979). An analysis of story comprehension in elementary school children. In R. O. Freedle (Ed.), *New directions in discourse processing* (pp. 53–120). Norwood, NJ: Ablex.

Steinberg, L. (1996). *Beyond the classroom: Why school reform has failed and what parents need to do.* New York: Simon & Schuster.

Stephens, M. A. (1993). *Developing and implementing a curriculum and instructional program to improve reading achievement of middle-grade students with learning disabilities in a rural school district.* Unpublished doctoral dissertation, Nova University, Ft. Lauderdale, Florida.

Sternberg, R. J. (1985). *Beyond I. Q.: A triarchic theory of human intelligence.* Cambridge, UK: Cambridge University Press.

Sternberg, R. J. (1987). Most vocabulary is learned from context. In M. G. McKeown & M. E. Curtis (Eds.), *The nature of vocabulary acquisition* (pp. 89–105). Hillsdale, NJ: Erlbaum.

Sternberg, R. J. (1988). *The triarchic mind: A new theory of human intelligence.* New York: Viking.

Sternberg, R. J., & Powell, J. S. (1983). Comprehending verbal comprehension. *American Psychologist, 38*(8), 878–893.

Sternberg, R. J., & Spear-Swerling, L. (1996). *Teaching for thinking.* Washington, DC: American Psychological Association.

Stevens, W. (1999, February 22). Everglades restoration plan does too little, experts say. *The New York Times,* p. A1.

Stewart, R., & O'Brien, D. (1989). Resistance to content area reading: A focus on preservice teachers. *Journal of Reading, 33,* 395–401.

Stipek, D. J. (2002). *Motivation to learn: From theory to practice* (4th ed.). Boston, MA: Allyn & Bacon.

Street, B. (1995). *Social literacies: Critical approaches to literacy in development, ethnography, and education.* New York: Longman.

Stuckey, S., & Salvucci, L. K. (2000). *Call to freedom: Beginnings to 1914.* Austin, TX: Holt, Rinehart and Winston.

Symcox, L. (2002). *Whose history?: The struggle for national standards in American classrooms.* New York: Teachers College Press.

Tan, A., & Nicholson, T. (1997). Flashcards revisited: Training poor readers to read words faster improves their comprehension of text. *Journal of Educational Psychology, 89,* 276–288.

Tanner, M. L., & Casados, L. (1998). Promoting and studying discussions in math classes. *Journal of Adolescent and Adult Literacy, 41*(5), 342–350.

Taylor, W. (1953). Cloze procedure: A new tool for measuring readability. *Journalism Quarterly, 30,* 415–433.

Thoman, E., & Jolls, T. (2005). Media literacy education: Lessons from the Center for Media Literacy. In G. Schwarz & P. U. Brown (Eds.), *Media literacy: Transforming curriculum and teaching* (pp. 180–205). Chicago, IL: National Society for the Study of Education.

Thomas, K. J. (1986). The Directed Inquiry Activity: An instructional procedure for content reading. In E. K. Dishner, T. W. Bean, J. E. Readence, & D. W. Moore (Eds.), *Reading in the content areas* (2nd ed., pp. 278–281). Dubuque, IA: Kendall/Hunt.

Thompson, E. (1958). The "master word" approach to vocabulary training. *Journal of Developmental Reading, 2,* 62–66.

Tierney, R. J. (1994). Dissension, tensions, and the models of literacy. In R. B. Ruddell, M. R. Ruddell, & H. Singer (Eds.), *Theoretical models and processes of reading* (4th ed., pp. 1162–1182). Newark, DE: International Reading Association.

Tishman, S., Perkins, D. N., & Jay, E. (1995). *The thinking classroom: Learning and teaching in a culture of thinking.* Boston, MA: Allyn & Bacon.

Tomlinson, C.A. (1999). *The differentiated classroom: Responding to the needs of all learners.* Alexandria, VA: Association for Supervision and Curriculum Development.

Topping, K. (1987). Paired reading: A powerful technique for parent use. *The Reading Teacher, 40,* 608–614.

Torgesen, J., & Hudson, R. F. (2006). Reading fluency: Critical issues for struggling readers. In S. J. Samuels & A. Farstrup (Eds.), *What research has to say about fluency instruction* (pp. 130–158). Newark, DE: International Reading Association.

Trabasso, T., & Stein, N. L. (1997). Narrating, representing, and remembering event sequences. In P. W. vanden Broek, P. J. Bauer, & T. Bourg (Eds.), *Developmental spans in even comprehension and representation* (pp. 237–270). Hillsdale, NJ: Erlbaum.

United States Department of Education (2003). *Nation's report card: Reading 2002.* Washington, DC: National Center for Educational Statistics.

United States Department of Education (2004). *No Child Left Behind: A Toolkit for Teachers.* Washington,D.C.: U.S. Department of Education.

Unrau, N. J. (1992). The TASK of reading (and writing) arguments: A guide to building critical literacy. *Journal of Reading, 35*(6), 436–442.

Unrau, N. J. (1995, May). *Tactics to engage readers in reflection and self-regulation: Paths to critical literacy across the curriculum.* Paper presented at the Annual Convention of the International Reading Association, Anaheim, California.

Unrau, N. J. (1996, April). *Using tutorials to teach literacy strategies across the content areas: Do they work for pre-service teachers?* Paper presented at the annual meeting of the American Educational Research Association in New York City.

Unrau, N. J. (1997). *Thoughtful teachers, thoughtful learners: A guide to helping adolescents think critically.* Scarborough, Ontario: Pippin Press.

Unrau, N. J., & Ruddell, R. (1995). Interpreting texts in classroom contexts. *Journal of Adolescent and Adult Literacy, 39*(1), 16–27.

Unrau, N. J., & Schlackman, J. (2005, April). *Dimensions and change in motivation for reading and its relationship to achievement among middle school students.* Paper presented at the annual meeting of the American Educational Research Association in Montreal, Canada.

Unrau, N. J., & Schlackman, J. (2006, November/December). Motivation and its relationship with reading achievement in an urban middle school. *Journal of Educational Research, 100*(1), pp. 81–101.

van den Broek, P., Young, M., Tzeng, Y., & Linderholm, T. (2004). The landscape model of reading: Inferences and the oline construction of a memory representation. In R. Ruddell & N. Unrau (Eds.), *Theoretical models and processes of reading* (5th ed., pp. 1244–1269). Newark, DE: International Reading Association.

Van der Bogert, R., Donaldson, M., & Poon, B. (1999). *Reflections of first-year teachers on school culture: Questions, hopes, and challenges.* San Francisco: Jossey-Bass.

van Dijk, T. A., & Kintsch, W. (1983). *Strategies of discourse comprehension.* New York: Academic.

Vaughan, C. L. (1990). Knitting writing: The double-entry journal. In N. Atwell (Ed.), *Coming to know: Writing to learn in the intermediate grades* (pp. 69–75). Portsmouth, NH: Heinemann.

Vigil, J. D. (1993). Gangs, social control, and ethnicity: Ways to redirect. In S. B. Heath & M. W. McLaughlin (Eds.), *Identity and inner-city youth* (pp. 94–119). New York: Teachers College Press.

Volk, P. (1999, September 2). Can you spare 7 minutes of life to read this? *The New York Times,* p. B7.

Vygotsky, L. S. (1978). *Mind in society: The development of higher psychological processes.* Cambridge, MA: Harvard.

Vygotsky, L. S. (1986). *Thought and language.* Cambridge, MA: MIT Press.

Wagner, T. (1994). *How schools change: Lessons from three communities.* Boston: Beacon Press.

Waid, J. (2002). Through the looking glass and back: The pursuit of National Board for Professional Teaching Standards certification. Unpublished master's thesis, California State University, Los Angeles.

Wasik, B. A. (1998). Volunteer tutoring programs in reading: A review. *Reading Research Quarterly, 33,* 266–292.

Waters, G., Caplan, D., & Hildebrandt, N. (1987). Working memory and written sentence comprehension. In M. Coltheart (Ed.), *Attention and performance XII: The psychology of reading,* 531–555. Hillsdale, NJ: Erlbaum.

Weaver, P. (1979). Improving reading instruction: Effects of sentence organization instruction. *Reading Research Quarterly, 15,* 127–146.

Wehlage, G. G., Rutter, R. A., Smith, G. A., Lesko, N., & Fernandez, R. R. (1989). *Reducing the risk: Schools as communities of support.* Philadelphia: Falmer.

Wells, M. C. (1996). *Literacies lost: When students move from a progressive middle school to a traditional high school.* New York: Teacher College Press.

Whimbey, A., & Lochhead, J. (1999). *Problem solving and comprehension* (6th ed.). Mahwah, NJ: Erlbaum.

White, S. (1995). Listening to children read aloud: Oral fluency. *NAEPFacts.* National Center for Education Statistics, U.S. Department of Education.

Wigfield, A. (1994). The role of children's achievement values in the self-regulation of their learning outcomes. In D. H. Schunk & B. J. Zimmerman (Eds.), *Self-regulation of learning and performance: Issues and educational applications* (101–124). Hillsdale, NJ: Erlbaum.

Wigfield, A., & Eccles, J. S. (1992). The development of achievement task values: A theoretical analysis. *Developmental Review, 12,* 265–310.

Wiggins, G., & McTighe, J. (1998). *Understanding by design.* Alexandria, VA: Association for Supervision and Development.

Wiggins, G., & McTighe, J. (2006). *Understanding by design* (2nd ed.). Upper Saddle River, NJ: Prentice Hall.

Wilbraham, A., Staley, D., Matta, M., & Waterman, E. (2000). *Chemistry.* Menlo Park, CA: Prentice Hall.

Wilde, S. (2000). *Miscue analysis made easy: Building on student strengths.* Portsmouth, NH: Heinemann.

Wilkinson, L. C., & Silliman, E. R. (2000). Classroom language and literacy learning. In M. L. Kamil, P. B. Mosenthal, P. D. Pearson, & R. Barr (Eds.), *Handbook of reading research* (Vol. III, pp. 337–360). Mahwah, NJ: Erlbaum.

Williams, B. T. (Ed.) (2006). *Identity papers: Literacy and power in higher education.* Logan: Utah State University Press.

Wood, K. (2001). *Literacy strategies across the subject areas.* Boston: Allyn & Bacon.

Wysession, M., Frank, D., & Yancopoulos, S. (2006). *Physical science: Concepts in action.* Needham, MA: Pearson/Prentice Hall.

Yager, R. E. (2004). Science is not written, but it can be written about. In E. W. Saul (Ed.), *Crossing borders in literacy and science instruction* (pp. 95–107). Newark, DE: International Reading Association.

Young, A. (1997). Mentoring, modeling, monitoring, motivating: Response to students' ungraded writing as academic conversation. *New Directions for Teaching and Learning, 69,* 27–39.

Zeno, S. M., Ivens, S. H., Millard, R. T., & Duvvuri, R. (1995). *The educator's word frequency guide.* Brewster, NY: Touchstone Applied Science Associates.

Zhao, Y. (2002, August 5). Waves of pupils lacking English strain schools. *The New York Times,* pp. A1, A11.

Zinsser, W. (1988). *Writing to learn.* NY: Harper & Row.

Name Index

Pilgreen, J. L., 47
Pinnell, G. S., 312
Pintrich, P. R., 38, 44
Pittelman, S. D., 80
Poon, Brian, 8, 9
Poon, L., 194
Pope, D., 19
Postlewaite, T. N., 333
Pounds, N., 191
Powell, B., 234
Powell, J. S., 175
Powell, R., 267
Prescott-Griffin, M. L., 119
Pressley, M., 68, 160, 163, 180, 323, 324, 326, 329, 332, 333
Pressnall, B., 228
Preston, F. W., 245
Prusak, A., 38
Purdie, N., 180

R

Radsinski, Timothy, 75
Ragland, M. A., 363
Rakes, T. A., 114
Ransdell, S., 212
Raphael, L., 323
Rasinski, T. V., 119, 281, 285, 333
Raskind, M. H., 176
Readence, J. E., 114, 145, 321, 332
Reed, I., 376
Reed, L., 196
Reeve, J., 56
Reeves, Anna, 47
Reichard, C. A., 88, 131, 132, 134
Rekrut, Martha, 309, 310
Reutzel, D. R., 76
Rex, L. A., 38
Reyes, P., 363
Reynolds, R. E., 63
Richards, H. C., 314
Richards, Janet Clarke, 198, 199
Richardson, W., 273, 274
Richman, B., 154
Riggenbach, H., 75
Risley, T. R., 38, 153
Robbins, J., 353
Roberts, Julian, 161
Robinson, F. P., 190
Roe, B. D., 117
Roehler, L. R., 68
Rosemary, C., 314
Rosenblatt, L. M., 48, 49, 70, 88
Rosenshine, B., 303, 305, 306

Ross, K. N., 333
Roth, W. M., 334, 335
Rowley, J. B., 389
Rowling, J. K., 85
Ruddell, M. R., 161, 168, 281, 321
Ruddell, R. B., 50, 52, 85, 88, 100, 212
Rumelart, D. E., 77
Rushkoff, D., 270
Rutter, R. A., 41
Ryan, R. M., 34, 35, 36, 56, 58, 331
Rycik, J. A., 23

S

Sadoski, M., 84, 284
Sahagun, L., 322
Salazar, Minerva, 21
Salinger, J. D., 63, 65, 92
Samuels, S. J., 7, 70, 72, 81, 149, 154, 340
Sanford-Smith, K., 379
Santa, C., 228
Santman, D., 112
Saul, W., 366
Scardamalia, M., 214
Schallert, D. L., 63
Schank, R. C., 78
Scharber, C., 331, 340
Scher, D., 38
Schiefele, U., 47
Schieffelin, Bambi, 7
Schifini, A., 352
Schmoker, M., 363
Schoenbach, R., 325, 330, 341, 342
Schram, J., 379
Schriver, K. A., 214
Schumm, J. S., 380
Schunk, D. H., 42
Scoble, John, 310, 311
Scott, J. A., 151, 154, 165, 174
Scribner, J. D., 363
Seely, M. R., 85
Seidel, S., 233
Sfard, A., 38
Shakespeare, William, 66, 86
Shanahan, T., 143
Shapiro, J., 39
Sharan, S., 295
Sharan, Y., 295
Shearer, B. A., 321
Shor, I., 266
Shuell, T. J., 52
Siebert, Daniel, 369, 370
Siegel, L. S., 137
Siegel, M., 370

Subject Index